# *Introduction to Sociology*

SECOND EDITION

Edited by
Kevin Sullivan

*Sociology: A Down-to-Earth Approach*, Second Edition, by James M. Henslin

A Division of Simon & Schuster
Needham Heights, MA 02194

*Sociology*, Third Edition, by John E. Farley

A Division of Simon & Schuster
Upper Saddle River, NJ 07458

*Sociology*, Fourth Edition, by John J. Macionis


*Breaking the Ice: A Guide to Understanding People from Other Cultures*,
by Daisy Kabagarama


*Sociology: Experiencing Changing Societies*, Sixth Edition, by
Kenneth C.W. Kammeyer, George Ritzer, and Norman R. Yetman


This special edition published in cooperation with
Simon & Schuster Custom Publishing.



Printed in the United States of America

10 9 8 7 6 5

*Please visit our web site at www.pearsoncustom.com*

ISBN 0-536-59521-6

BA 98684

PEARSON CUSTOM PUBLISHING
75 Arlington Street, Boston, MA 02116
A Pearson Education Company

# Copyright Acknowledgments

Grateful acknowledgment is made to the following sources for permission to reprint material copyrighted or controlled by them:

Excerpt from *Invitation to Sociology*, by Peter L. Berger, 1963, reprinted by permission of Doubleday.

"Knowing About Things," by Jonathan Turner, 1985, reprinted by permission from *Sociology: A Student Handbook*, McGraw Hill.

"The Uses of Poverty: The Poor Pay All," by Herbert J. Gans, reprinted by permission of the author from *American Journal of Sociology*, Vol. 78, September 1972. Dr. Gans is Robert S. Lynd Professor of Sociology at Columbia University and he is the author of, most recently, *War Against the Poor: The Underclass and Antipoverty Policy.*

"Manifest & Latent Functions," by Robert K. Merton, 1968, reprinted by permission from *Social Theory and Social Structure*, revised and enlarged edition, Free Press.

"Alienated Labor," by Karl Marx, reprinted from *Karl Marx: Early Writings*, translated and edited by T.B. Bottomore, copyright © 1963, McGraw-Hill. Reproduced by permission of the McGraw-Hill Companies.

"The Presentation of Self," by Erving Goffman, 1959, reprinted by permission from *The Presentation of Self in Everyday Life*, Doubleday.

"How Cultures Collide," by Edward Hall, reprinted by permission from *Psychology Today*, July 1976. Copyright © 1976, Sussex Publishers.

"Primary Groups," by Charles Horton Cooley, 1909, reprinted from *Social Organization: A Study of the Larger Mind*, Schocken Books, 1962.

"Corner Boys: A Study of Clique Behavior," by William Foote White, reprinted by permission from *American Journal of Sociology*, Vol. 46, March 1941.

"The Functions of Crime," by Emile Durkheim," 1966, reprinted by permission from *The Rules of Sociological Method*, translated by Sarah A. Solovay and John A. Mueller, edited by George E.G. Catlin, Free Press.

Excerpts from *The Bohemian Grove and Other Retreats*, by G. William Domhoff, Harper & Row, 1974. Reprinted by permission of HarperCollins Publishers.

# INTRODUCTION TO SOCIOLOGY

SO–101 Sociology is an examination of the culture and structure of human societies. The course focuses on social groups and institutions, their norms and controls, and how and why they change. Topics of discussion include the family, education, deviance, race and ethnicity, gender roles, social change, and social inequalities.

## ACKNOWLEDGMENTS

I would like to express my thanks to Jacqueline Behn and John Patierno who have reviewed and support this project.


To the students of Bergen Community College.

# Table of Contents

# Chapter 1

## Introduction

***Even from the dim glow*** of the faded red-and-white exit sign, its light barely reaching the upper bunk, I could see that the sheet was filthy. Resigned to another night of fitful sleep, I reluctantly crawled into bed—tucking my clothes firmly around my body, like a protective cocoon.

*The next morning, I joined the long line of disheveled men leaning against the chain-link fence. Their faces were as downcast as their clothes were dirty. Not a glimmer of hope among them.*

*No one spoke as the line slowly inched forward. When my turn came, I was handed a styrofoam cup of coffee, some utensils, and a bowl of semiliquid that I couldn't identify. It didn't look like any food I had seen before. Nor did it taste like anything I had ever eaten.*

*My stomach fought the foul taste, every spoonful a battle. But I was determined. "I will experience what they experience," I kept telling myself. My stomach reluctantly gave in and accepted its morning nourishment.*

*The room was eerily silent. Hundreds of men were eating, but each was sunk deeply into his own private hell, his head aswim with disappointment, remorse, bitterness.*

*As I stared at the styrofoam cup holding my solitary postbreakfast pleasure, I noticed what looked like teeth marks. I shrugged off the thought, telling myself that my long weeks as a sociological observer of the homeless were finally getting to me. "That must be some sort of crease from handling," I concluded.*

*I joined the silent ranks of men turning in their bowls and cups. When I saw the man behind the counter swishing out styrofoam cups in a washtub of water, I began to feel sick at my stomach. I knew then that the jagged marks on my cup really had come from a previous mouth.*

*How much longer did this research have to last? I felt a deep longing to return to my family—to a welcome world of clean sheets, healthy food, and "normal" conversations.*

## THE SOCIOLOGICAL PERSPECTIVE

Why were these men so silent? Why did they receive such despicable treatment? What was I doing in that homeless shelter? (After all, I hold a respectable, secure professional position, and I have a home and family.)

Sociology offers a perspective, a view of the world. The **sociological perspective** (or imagination) opens a window onto unfamiliar worlds, and offers a fresh look at familiar worlds. In this text you will find yourself in the midst of Nazis in Germany, chimpanzees in Africa, and warriors in South America. But you will also find yourself looking at your own world in a different light. As you look at other worlds, or your own, the sociological perspective casts a light that enables you to gain a new vision of social life. In fact, this is what many find appealing about sociology.

The sociological perspective has been a motivating force in my own life. Ever since I took my first introductory course in sociology, I have been enchanted by the perspective that sociology offers. I have thoroughly enjoyed both observing other groups and questioning my own assumptions about life. I sincerely hope that the same happens to you.

### Seeing the Broader Social Context

The sociological perspective stresses the broader context of life in society. To find out why people do what they do, sociologists look at **social location,** where people are located in history and in a particular society. Sociologists focus on such characteristics of people as their jobs, income, education, gender, and race. At the center of the sociological perspective is the question of how people are influenced by **society—**

a group of people who share a culture and a territory. Take, for example, how growing up identified with a group called females or a group called males affects people's ideas of what they should attain in life.

Sociologist C. Wright Mills (1959b) said that the sociological perspective enables us to grasp the connection between history and biography. Because of its history, a society has certain broad characteristics—such as its commonly accepted ideas of the proper roles of men and women. By biography, Mills meant the individual's specific experiences in society. This intersection of history and biography results in people having particular values, goals, aspirations, and even self-concept. In short, in the sociological view people don't do what they do because of some sort of inherited internal mechanism, such as instincts. Rather, external influences—people's experiences—become internalized, become part of an individual's thinking and motivations.

An example will make this point obvious. If we were to take a newborn baby away from its U.S. parents today and place that infant with a Yanomamo Indian tribe in the jungles of South America, you know that when the child begins to speak, his or her sounds will not be in English. You also know that the child will not think like an American. He or she will not grow up wanting credit cards, for example, or designer jeans, a new car, and the latest video game. Equally, the child will unquestioningly take his or her place in Yanomamo society—perhaps as a food gatherer, a hunter, or a warrior—and will not even know about the world left behind at birth. And, whether male or female, that child will grow up, not debating whether to have one, two, or three children, but assuming that it is natural to want many children.

People around the globe take their particular world for granted. Something inside us Americans tells us that hamburgers are delicious, small families attractive, and designer clothing desirable. Yet something inside some of the Sinai Desert Arab tribes used to tell them that warm, fresh camel's blood makes a fine drink and that everyone should have a large family and wear flowing robes (Murray 1935; McCabe and Ellis 1990). And that something certainly isn't an instinct. As sociologist Peter Berger (1963) phrased it, that "something" is "society within us."

Although obvious, this point frequently eludes us. We often think and talk about people's behavior as though it is caused by their sex, their race, or some other factor transmitted by their genes. The sociological perspective helps us to escape from this cramped personal view by exposing the broader social context that underlies human behavior. It helps us to see the links between what people do and the social settings that shape their behavior.

## SOCIOLOGY AND THE OTHER SCIENCES

Just as humans today have an intense desire to unravel the mysteries around them, people in ancient times also attempted to understand their world. Their explanations, however, were not based only on observations, but were mixed with magic and superstition as well.

To satisfy their basic curiosities about the world around them, humans gradually developed **science**, systematic methods used to study the social and natural worlds, as well as the knowledge obtained by those methods. **Sociology**, the scientific study of society and human behavior, is one of the sciences that modern civilization has developed.

A useful way of comparing these sciences—and of gaining a better understanding of sociology's place—is to first divide them into the natural and the social sciences.

### The Natural Sciences

The **natural sciences** are the intellectual and academic disciplines designed to comprehend, explain, and predict the events in our natural environment. The natural sciences are divided into specialized fields of research according to subject matter, such as biology, geology, chemistry, and physics. These are further subdivided into even more highly specialized areas, with a further narrowing of content. Biology is divided into botany and zoology, geology into mineralogy and geomorphology, chemistry into its inorganic and organic branches, and physics into biophysics and quantum mechanics. Each area of investigation examines a particular "slice" of nature (Henslin 1993).

## The Social Sciences

People have not limited themselves to investigating nature. In the pursuit of a more adequate understanding of life, people have also developed fields of science that focus on the social world. These, the **social sciences,** examine human relationships. Just as the natural sciences attempt to objectively understand the world of nature, the social sciences attempt to objectively understand the social world. Just as the world of nature contains ordered (or lawful) relationships that are not obvious but must be discovered through controlled observation, so the ordered relationships of the human or social world are not obvious, and must be revealed by means of controlled and repeated observations.

Like the natural sciences, the social sciences are divided into specialized fields based on their subject matter. These divisions are anthropology, economics, political science, psychology, and sociology. And the social sciences, too, are subdivided into further specialized fields. Thus, anthropology is divided into cultural and physical anthropology; economics has macro (large-scale) and micro (small-scale) specialties; political science has theoretical and applied branches; psychology may be clinical or experimental; and sociology has its quantitative and qualitative branches. Since our focus is sociology, let us contrast sociology with each of the other social sciences.

**Political Science** *Political science* focuses on politics and government. Political scientists study how people govern themselves; the various forms of government, their structures, and their relationships to other institutions of society. Political scientists are especially interested in how people attain ruling positions in their society, how they then maintain those positions, and the consequences of their activities for those who are governed. In studying a system of government with a constitutional electorate, such as that of the United States, political scientists also focus on voting behavior.

**Economics** *Economics* also concentrates on a single social institution. Economists study the production and distribution of the material goods and services of a society. They want to know what goods are being produced at what rate and at what cost, and how those goods are distributed. They are also interested in the choices that determine production and consumption, for example, the factors that lead a society to produce a certain item instead of another.

**Anthropology** *Anthropology,* in which the primary focus has been preliterate or tribal peoples, is the sister discipline of sociology. The chief concern of anthropologists is to understand *culture,* a people's total way of lief. Culture includes (1) the group's artifacts such as its tools, art, and weapons; (2) the group's structure, that is, the hierarchy and other patterns that determine its members' relationships to one another; (3) a group's ideas and values, especially how its belief system affects people's lives; and (4) the group's forms of communication, especially language. The anthropologists' traditional focus on tribal groups is now giving way to the study of groups in industrialized settings.

**Psychology** The focus of *psychology* is on processes that occur *within* the individual, within the "skin-bound organism." Psychologists are primarily concerned with mental processes: intelligence, emotions, perception, and memory. Some concentrate on attitudes and values; others focus on personality, mental aberration (psychopathology, or mental illness), and how individuals cope with the problems they face.

**Sociology** *Sociology* has many similarities to the other social sciences. Like political scientists, sociologists study how people govern one another, especially the impact of various forms of government on people's lives. Like economists, sociologists are concerned with what happens to the goods and services of a society—but sociologists place their focus on the social consequences of production and distribution. Like anthropologists, sociologists study culture; they have a particular interest in the social consequences

## DOWN-TO-EARTH SOCIOLOGY

### AN UPDATED VERSION OF THE OLD ELEPHANT STORY

It is said that in the recent past five wise men and women, all blindfolded, were led to an elephant and asked to explain what they "saw." The first, a psychologist, feeling the top of the head, said, "This is the only thing that counts. All feeling and thinking takes place inside here. To understand this beast, we need study only this."

The second, an anthropologist, tenderly touching the trunk and the tusks, said, "This is really primitive. I feel very comfortable here. Concentrate on these."

The third, a political scientist, feeling the gigantic ears, said, "This is the power center. What goes in here control the entire beast. Concentrate your studies here."

The fourth, an economist, feeling the mouth, said, "This is what counts. What goes in here is distributed through the body. Concentrate your studies on this."

Then came the sociologist (of course!), who, after feeling the entire body, said, "You can't understand the beast by concentrating on only one part. Each is but part of the whole. The head, the trunk and tusks, the ears, the mouth—all are important. But so are the parts of the beast you haven't even mentioned. We must remove our blindfolds so we can see the larger picture. We have to see how everything works together to form the entire animal."

Pausing for emphasis, the sociologist added, "And we also need to understand how this creature interacts with similar creatures. How does their life in groups influence their behaviors?"

I wish I could conclude this fable by saying that the psychologist, the anthropologist, the political scientist, and the economist, dazzled upon hearing the wisdom of the sociologist, amidst gasps of wonderment threw away their blindfolds and, joining together, began to examine the larger picture. But, alas and alack! Upon hearing this sage advice, each stubbornly bound their blindfolds even tighter to concentrate all the more on the single part. And if you listened very, very carefully you could even hear them saying, "The top of the head is mine—stay away from it." "Don't touch the tusks." "Take your hands off the ears." "Stay away from the mouth—that's my area."

of material goods, group structure, and belief systems, as well as in how people communicate with one another. Like psychologists, sociologists are also concerned with how people adjust to the difficulties of life.

Given these overall similarities, then, what distinguishes sociology from the other social sciences? Unlike political scientists and economists, sociologists do not concentrate on a single social institution. Unlike anthropologists, sociologists focus primarily on industrialized societies. And unlike psychologists, sociologists stress factors *external* to the individual to determine what influences people. In succeeding chapters, these distinctions will become clearer. The Down-to-Earth Sociology box above revisits an old fable about how members of different disciplines perceive the same subject matter.

## The Goals of Science

The first goal of each science is to *explain* why something happens. The second goal is to make **generalizations,** that is, to go beyond the individual case and make statements that apply to a broader group or situation. For example, a sociologist wants to explain not only why Mary went to college or became an armed robber but also why people with her characteristics are more likely than others to go to college or to become armed robbers. To achieve generalizations, sociologists and other scientists look for **patterns,** recurring characteristics or events. The third scientific goal is to *predict,* to specify what will happen in the future in the light of current knowledge.

To attain these goals, scientists must rely not on magic, superstition, or common beliefs but on conclusions based on systematic studies. They need to examine evidence with an open mind, in such a way that it can be checked by others. Secrecy, prejudice, and other biases, with their inherent closures, go against the grain of science.

Sociologists and other scientists also move beyond **common sense,** those ideas that prevail in a society that "everyone knows" are true. Just because "everyone" knows something is true does not make it so. "Everyone" can be mistaken, today just as easily as when common sense dictated that the world was flat or that no human could ever walk on the moon. As sociologists examine people's assumptions about the world, their findings may contradict commonsense notions about social life.

Sometimes the explorations of sociologists take them into nooks and crannies that people would prefer remain unexplored. For example, a sociologist might study how people make decisions to commit a crime or to cheat on their spouses. Because sociologists want above all to understand social life, they cannot cease their studies because people feel uncomfortable. With all realms of human life considered legitimate avenues of exploration by sociologists, their findings sometimes challenge even cherished ideas.

As they examine how groups operate, sociologists often confront prejudice and attempts to keep things secret. It seems that every organization, every group, nourishes a pet image that it presents to the public. Sociologists are interested in knowing what is really going on behind the scenes, however, so they peer beneath the surface to get past that sugarcoated image of suppressed facts (Berger 1963). This approach sometimes brings sociologists into conflict with people who feel threatened by that information—which is all part of the adventure, and risk, of being a sociologist.

## DOWN-TO-EARTH SOCIOLOGY

### ENJOYING A SOCIOLOGY QUIZ—SOCIOLOGICAL FINDINGS VERSUS COMMON SENSE

Some findings of sociology support commonsense understandings of social life, while others contradict them. Can you tell the difference? If you want to enjoy this quiz fully, before turning the page to check your answers complete *all* the questions.

1. True/False The earnings of U. S. women have just about caught up with those of U. S. men.
2. True/False When faced with natural disasters such as floods and earthquakes, people panic and social organization disintegrates.
3. True/False Revolutions are more likely to occur when conditions are consistently bad than when they are improving.
4. True/False Most people on welfare are lazy and looking for a handout. They could work if they wanted to.
5. True/False Most U. S. Roman Catholics oppose birth control.
6. True/False Compared with men, women touch each other more while they are conversing.
7. True/False Compared with women, men maintain more eye contact while they are conversing.
8. True/False Because of the rapid rise in the divorce rate in the United States, U. S. children are much more likely to live in single-parent households now than they were a century ago.
9. True/False The more available alcohol is (as measured by the number of places to purchase alcohol per one hundred people), the more alcohol-related injuries and fatalities occur on U. S. highways.
10. True/False Couples who live together before marriage usually report higher satisfaction with their marriages than couples who do not live together before marriage.

## THE DEVELOPMENT OF SOCIOLOGY

Just how did sociology begin? Has it always been around? Or is it relatively new?

In some ways it is difficult to answer these questions. By the time Jesus Christ was born, the Greeks and Romans had already developed intricate systems of philosophy about human behavior. Even preliterate peoples made observations about their tribal lives and were likely aware, for example, which classes of people were more privileged and powerful. They also analyzed *why* life was as it was, but in doing so they often depended on magic and superstition, such as explanations based on the positions of the stars.

Simple assertions of truth—or observations mixed with magic or superstition or the stars—are not adequate. *All science requires the development of theories that can be proved or disproved by systematic research.*

This standard simplifies the question of the origin of sociology. Measured by this standard sociology is clearly a recent discipline. It emerged about the middle of the nineteenth century when European social observers began to use scientific methods to test their ideas. Three factors combined to lead to the development of sociology.

### DOWN-TO-EARTH SOCIOLOGY

#### SOCIOLOGICAL FINDINGS VERSUS COMMON SENSE—ANSWERS TO THE SOCIOLOGY QUIZ

1. False. Over the years, the income gap has narrowed, but only slightly. On average, full-time working women earn only about 65 percent of what full-time working men earn; this low figure is actually an improvement, for in the 1970s women's incomes averaged about 60 percent of men's.
2. False. Following such disasters, people develop *greater* cohesion, cooperation, and social organization to deal with the catastrophe.
3. False. Just the opposite is true. When conditions are constantly bad people are more likely to be resigned to their fate, while rapid improvement causes their aspirations to outreach their circumstances, which can increase frustrations and foment revolution.
4. False. Most people on welfare are children, the old, the sick, the mentally and physically handicapped, or young mothers with few skills. Less than 2 percent meet the common stereotype of an able-bodied male—and many of these are actively looking for jobs.
5. False. About 80 percent of U. S. Roman Catholics favor birth control.
6. False. It is men who touch each other more during conversations (Henley et al. 1985; Whyte 1989).
7. False. Female speakers maintain considerably more eye contact (Henley and Hamilton 1985).
8. False. Strange as it may sound, the proportion of children who live with one parent is roughly the same today as it was one hundred years ago. A century back, many parents died at an early age, leaving only one parent to rear the children. With today's advances in public health and medicine, few people die young. Although death as a source of one-parent families is now lower, our much higher divorce rate has made up the difference.
9. False. In California, researchers compared the number of alcohol outlets per population with the alcohol-related highway injuries and fatalities. They found that counties in which alcohol is more readily available do not have more alcohol-related injuries and fatalities (Kohfeld and Leip 1991).
10. False. The opposite is true. The reasons are unknown, but researchers suggest that many couples who marry after cohabiting are less committed to marriage in the first place—and a key to marital success is firm commitment to one another (Larson 1988).

The first was social upheaval in Europe. By the middle of the nineteenth century, Europe found itself in the midst of the Industrial Revolution. This change from agriculture to factory production brought violent changes to people's lives. Masses of people were forced off the land. They moved to the cities in search of work where they were met with anonymity, crowding, filth, and poverty. Their ties to the land, to the generations that had lived there before them, and to their way of life were abruptly broken. The city greeted them with horrible working conditions: low pay; long, exhausting hours; dangerous work; bad ventilation; and much noise. To survive, families had to permit their children to work in these same conditions, some of them even chained to factory machines to make certain they did not run away.

With the successes of the American and French revolutions, in which the idea that individuals possess inalienable rights caught fire, the political systems in Western countries slowly began to give way to more democratic forms. As the traditional order was challenged, religion lost much of its force as the unfailing source of answers to life's perplexing questions. Each fundamental social change further undermined traditional explanations of human existence.

When tradition reigns supreme, it provides a ready answer: "We do this because it has always been done this way." Such societies offer minimal encouragement for original thinking. Since the answers are already provided, there is little impetus to search for explanations. Sweeping change, however, does the opposite: by upsetting the existing order, it encourages questioning and demands answers.

The second factor that encouraged the development of sociology was the development of imperialism. The Europeans had been successful in conquering many parts of the world. Their new colonial empires, stretching from Asia through Africa to North America, exposed them to radically different cultures. Startled by these contrasting ways of life, they began to ask why cultures differed.

The third impetus for the development of sociology was the success of the natural sciences. Just at the time when the Industrial Revolution and imperialism moved people to question fundamental aspects of their social worlds, **the scientific method**—objective, systematic observations to test theories—used in chemistry and physics had begun to transform the world. Given these successes, it seemed logical to apply this method to the questions now being raised about the social world.

## Auguste Comte

This idea of applying the scientific method to the social world, known as **positivism**, was apparently first proposed by Auguste Comte (1798–1857). With the French Revolution still fresh in his mind, Comte left the small, conservative town in which he had grown up and moved to Paris. The changes he himself experienced, combined with those France underwent in the revolution, led Comte to become interested in the twin problems of social order and social change (which he called "social statics" and "social dynamics"). What holds society together? he wondered. Why is there social order instead of anarchy or chaos? And once society becomes set on a particular course, what causes it to change? Why doesn't it always continue in the direction it began?

As he pondered these questions, Comte concluded that the right way to answer them was to apply the scientific method to social life. Just as it had revealed the law of gravity, so, too, it would uncover the laws that underlie society. This new science, based on positivism, not only would discover social principles but it would also apply them to social reform. Comte called this new science *sociology*— "the study of society" (from the Greek *logos,* "study of," and the Latin *socius,* companion, "being with others").

Comte had some ideas that today's sociologists find humorous. For example, as Comte saw matters, there were only six sciences—mathematics, physics, chemistry, biology, astronomy, and sociology—with sociology far superior to the others (Bogardus 1929). To Comte, applying the scientific method to social life apparently referred to "armchair philosophy"—drawing conclusions from informal observations of social life. He did not do what today's sociologists would call research, and his conclusions have been abandoned.

Nevertheless, Comte's insistence that we cannot be dogmatic about social life, but that we must observe and classify human activities in order to uncover society's fundamental laws, is well taken. Because he developed this idea and coined the term *sociology*, Comte is often credited with being the founder of sociology.

## Herbert Spencer

Herbert Spencer (1820–1903), who grew up in England, is sometimes called the second founder of sociology. He, too, believed that society operates according to fixed laws. Spencer became convinced that societies evolve from lower ("barbarian") to higher ("civilized") forms. As generations pass, he said, the most capable and intelligent ("the fittest") members of a society survive, while the less capable die out. Thus, over time, societies steadily improve.

Spencer called this principle "the survival of the fittest." Although Spencer coined this phrase, it is usually attributed to his contemporary, Charles Darwin, who proposed that living organisms evolve over time as they survive the conditions of their environment. Because of their similarities, Spencer's views of the evolution of societies became known as *social Darwinism.*

Unlike Comte, Spencer did not think sociology should guide social reform. In fact, he was convinced that no one should intervene in the evolution of society. The fittest members didn't need any help. They would always survive on their own and produce a more advanced society unless misguided do-gooders got in the way and helped the less fit survive. Consequently, Spencer's ideas—that charity and helping the poor were wrong, whether carried out by individuals or by the government—appalled many. Not surprisingly, wealthy industrialists, who saw themselves as "the fittest" (superior), found Spencer's ideas attractive. And not coincidentally, his views also helped them avoid feelings of guilt for living like royalty while people around them starved.

Like Comte, Spencer was more of a social philosopher than a sociologist. Also like Comte, Spencer did not conduct scientific studies, but simply developed ideas about society. Eventually, after gaining a wide following in England and the United States, Spencer's ideas about social Darwinism were discredited.

## Karl Marx

Karl Marx (1818–1883), a third individual who influenced sociology, also left his mark on world history. Marx's influence has been so great that even that staunch advocate of capitalism, the *Wall Street Journal,* has called him one of the three greatest modern thinkers (the other two being Sigmund Freud and Albert Einstein).

Like Comte, Marx thought that people should take active steps to change society. Marx, who came to England after being exiled from his native Germany for proposing revolution, believed that the key to human history was **class conflict**. He said that the *bourgeoisie* (the controlling class of *capitalists,* those who own the means to produce wealth—capital, land, factories, and machines) are locked in inevitable conflict with the *proletariat* (the exploited class, the mass of workers who do not own the means of production). This bitter struggle can end only when members of the working class unite in revolution and throw off their chains of bondage. The result will be a classless society, one free of exploitation in which all individuals will work according to their abilities and receive according to their needs (Marx and Engles 1848/1967).

Marxism is not the same as communism. Although Marx stood firmly behind revolution as the only way for the proletariat to gain control of society, he did not develop the political system called *communism,* which was a later application of his ideas (and rapidly changing ones at that). Indeed, Marx himself felt disgusted when he heard debates about his insights into social life. After listening to some of the positions attributed to him, he even declared, "I am not a Marxist" (Dobriner 1969:222).

Unlike Comte and Spencer, Marx did not think of himself as a sociologist. He spent years studying in the library of the British Museum in London, where he wrote widely on history, philosophy, and, of course, economics and political science. Because of his insights into the relationship between the social classes, especially the class struggle between the "haves" and the "have-nots," many sociologists today claim Marx as a significant early sociologist. He also introduced one of the major perspectives in sociology, conflict theory, which is discussed on pages 25–26.

## Harriet Martineau

At this time in history, it was difficult for women to obtain an education as the man who ran society felt that formal education for females was unnecessary and dangerous: unnecessary as they did not need it to run a household, and dangerous for it might make them discontent with their subservient role to men. A handful of women from wealthy families, however, managed to get an education. One of these was Harriet Martineau (1802–1876), a native of England, who studied social life in both the United States and Great Britain. In 1837, she published *Society in America,* in which she reported on this new nation's family customs, race relations, gender relations, politics, and religion. She also helped to popularize Comte's ideas by translating them into English.

## Emile Durkheim

Emile Durkheim (1858–1917), who was born and reared in eastern France, was educated in both Germany and France. Durkheim received the first academic appointment in sociology in a French university, teaching first at the University of Bordeaux in 1887, and moving to the more prestigious Sorbonne in 1906 (Coser 1977).

Durkheim insisted on rigorous research. In a study still quoted today, he compared the suicide rates of several European countries. He (1897/1966) found that each country's suicide rate was different and that it remained remarkably stable year after year. He also found that different groups within a country had different suicide rates. For example, Protestants, the wealthy, males, and the unmarried killed themselves at a higher rate than did Catholics, Jews, the poor, females, and the married. From this, Durkheim drew the highly insightful conclusion that suicide is not simply a matter of individuals here and there deciding to take their lives for personal reasons. Rather, *social factors underlie suicide,* and this is what keeps those rates fairly constant year after year.

Durkheim identified **social integration,** the degree to which people are tied to their social group, as a key social factor in suicide. He found that people with weak social ties were more likely to commit suicide. This factor explained the higher suicide rate of Protestants, males, the wealthy, and the unmarried. Protestantism, Durkheim argued, encourages greater freedom of thought and action; males are more independent than females; wealthy people have greater choices in life; and the unmarried are less socially integrated than those bound by the ties and responsibilities of marriage. In other words, because their social integration is weaker, people in these groups have fewer social ties that keep them from committing suicide.

Although strong social bonds help to protect people from suicide, Durkheim noted that in some instances strong bonds can encourage suicide. To illustrate this type of suicide, which he termed *altruistic suicide,* Durkheim used the example of grieving people who kill themselves following the death of a dearly loved spouse. Their own feelings are so integrated with those of their spouse that they prefer death rather than life without the one who gave meaning to life. Another example of altruistic suicide is the Japanese kamikaze pilots in World War II, whose missions were to ram their bomb-laden planes into enemy ships.

Almost one hundred years later, Durkheim's work is still quoted because of its scientific rigor and excellent theoretical interpretations. Durkheim's research was so thorough that its principles still apply to contemporary life: People who are less socially integrated continue to have a higher rate of suicide. Those same categories of people that Durkheim identified—Protestants, males, the wealthy, and the unmarried—are still more likely to kill themselves than are others.

Durkheim was concerned about the tendency of modern society to produce what he called anomie, and thereby suicide. By **anomie,** Durkheim referred to a breaking down of the controlling influences of society, which leaves people without the moral guidance that societies usually offer. People become detached from society, they lack social-support, and their desires are no longer regulated by clear norms (Coser 1977). Durkheim's analysis of suicide provides a good example of the sociological perspective we reviewed earlier—the idea that human behavior (even suicide) cannot be understood simply in individualistic terms, that it must be understood within its larger social context.

Like Comte, Durkheim (1893/1933) also proposed that sociologists actively intervene in society. To overcome anomie, he suggested that new social groups be created. Standing somewhere between the state and the family, those groups would help meet the need for a sense of belonging that the impersonality of industrial society was eroding.

### Max Weber

Max Weber (1864–1920) (Mahx Váy-ber), a German sociologist and a contemporary of Durkheim's, also held professorships in the new academic discipline of sociology. He was a renowned scholar who, like Marx, wrote in several academic fields. He agreed with much of what Marx wrote, but he strongly disagreed that economics is the central force in social change. That role, he said, belongs to religion. Weber (1904/1958) theorized that the belief system provided by Roman Catholicism encouraged Roman Catholics to hold onto traditional ways of life, while the belief system of Protestantism encouraged its members to embrace change. To test his theory, Weber compared the economic development of several countries with the dominance of Protestantism or Catholicism within those countries. His conclusion—that Protestantism, specifically Calvinism, encouraged people to work hard, to save money, and to invest it, and thus was the central factor in the rise of capitalism in those countries—was controversial when he developed it and is still debated by scholars today (Dickson and McLachlan 1989). Weber's analysis of the significance of religion in economic development is discussed in more detail on pages 164–166.

## THE ROLE OF VALUES IN SOCIAL RESEARCH

Weber also raised another issue that remains controversial among sociologists when he declared that sociology should be **value free.** By this, he meant that a sociologist's **values,** personal beliefs about what is good or worthwhile in life and the way the world ought to be, should not affect his or her social research. Weber wanted **objectivity,** total neutrality, to be the hallmark of sociological research. If values influence research, he said, sociological findings will be biased.

Objectivity as an ideal is not a matter of debate in sociology. On the one hand, all sociologists agree that objectivity is a proper goal, in the sense that sociologists should not distort data to make them fit preconceived ideas or personal values, and that research reports must accurately reflect actual, not desired findings. On the other hand, it is equally clear that no sociologist can escape values entirely. Like everyone else, sociologists are members of a particular society at a given point in history and are therefore infused with values of all sorts, and these inevitably play a role in their research. For example, values are part of the reason that one sociologist chooses to do research on the Mafia, while another turns a sociological eye on kindergarten students. To overcome the distortions that values can cause, sociologists stress **replication,** that is, the repetition of a study by other researchers to see how the results compare. If values have unwittingly influenced research findings, replication by other sociologists should uncover this problem and correct it.

**FIGURE 1.1: The Debate over Values.**

In spite of the consensus, however, the proper role of values in sociology is still hotly debated (Seubert 1991). The problem especially concerns ideas about the proper purposes and uses of sociological research. Regarding the *purpose* of sociology, some sociologists take the position that sociology's proper role is to advance understanding. Sociologists should gather data on any aspect of social life in which they are interested and then use the best theory available to interpret their findings. Others are convinced that it is the responsibility of sociologists to explore harmful social arrangements of society—to investigate what causes poverty, crime, war, and other forms of human exploitation.

Regarding the *uses* of sociology, those who say that understanding is sociology's proper goal take the position that the knowledge gained by social research belongs to the scientific community and to the world. Accordingly, it can be used by anyone for any purpose. In contrast, those who say that sociology should explore harmful social arrangements take the position that sociological knowledge should be used to reform society. They say that sociologists should use their studies to alleviate human suffering and make society a better place to live. (See Figure 1.1.)

Although the debate about the proper role of values in social research is infinitely more complicated than the argument presented here—few sociologists take such one-sided views—the preceding sketch does identify its major issues. Perhaps sociologist John Galliher (1991) best expresses the majority position:

> Some argue that social scientists, unlike politicians and religious leaders, should merely attempt to describe and explain the events of the world but should never make value judgments based on those observations. Yet a value-free and nonjudgmental social science has no place in a world that has experienced the Holocaust, in a world having had slavery, in a world with the ever-present threat of rape and other sexual assault, in a world with frequent, unpunished crimes in high places, including the production of products known by their manufacturers to cause death and injury as had been true of asbestos products and continues to be true of the cigarette industry, and in a world dying from environmental pollution by these same large multinational corporations.

## *VERSTEHEN* AND SOCIAL FACTORS

### Weber and Verstehen

Weber also stressed that one cannot understand human behavior simply by looking at statistics. Those cold numbers may represent people's activities, he said, but they must be interpreted. To do so, he said that we should use **Verstehen** (a German word meaning "to understand"). Perhaps the best translation of this term is "to grasp by insight." By emphasizing *Verstehen,* Weber meant that the best interpreter of human action is someone who "has been there," someone who can understand the feelings and motivations of the people they are studying. In short, we must pay attention to what are called **subjective meanings**, the ways in which people interpret their own behavior. We can't understand what people do, Weber insisted, unless we look at how people themselves view and explain their own behavior.

To better understand this term, let's return to the homeless in the opening vignette. Why were the men so silent? Why were they so unlike the noisy, sometimes boisterous college students in their dorms and cafeterias?

*Verstehen* can help examine this. When I interviewed men in the shelters (and in other settings, homeless women), they talked about their despair. As someone who knows—at least on some level—what the human emotion of despair is, you are immediately able to apply it to their situation. You know that people in despair feel a sense of hopelessness. The future looks bleak, hardly worth plodding toward. Consequently, what is there worth talking about anyway? Who wants to hear another hard-luck story?

By applying *Verstehen*—your own understanding of what it means to be human and to face various situations in life—you gain an understanding of people's behavior, in this case the silence, the lack of communication, among the homeless.

## Durkheim and Social Facts

In contrast to Weber's use of *Verstehen,* or subjective meanings, Durkheim stressed what he called **social facts.** By this term, he meant the patterns of behavior that characterize a social group. (Note however that Weber did not disagree about the significance of social facts, for they are the basis of his conclusions about Protestantism and capitalism.) Examples of social facts in the United States include June being the most popular month for weddings, suicide being higher among people 65 and over, and more births occurring on Tuesday than any other day of the week.

Durkheim said that we must use social factors to interpret social facts. In other words, each pattern reflects some underlying condition of society. People all over the country don't just coincidentally decide to do similar things, whether getting married or committing suicide. If that were the case, in some years middle-aged people would be the most likely to kill themselves, in other years, young people, and so on. Patterns that hold true year after year, however, indicate that as thousands and even millions of people make individual decisions, they are responding to conditions in their society. It is the job of the sociologist, then, to uncover social facts and then to explain them through other social facts. In the following section, we shall see how these particular social facts are explained by the school year, conditions of the aged, and the social organization of medicine, respectively.

## How Social Facts and *Verstehen* Fit Together

Social facts and *Verstehen* go hand in hand. As a member of U.S. society, you know how June weddings are related to the end of the school year and how this month, now locked in tradition, common sentiment, and advertising, carries its own momentum. As for suicide among the elderly (see chapter 13), you probably already have a sense of the greater despair that many Americans of this age feel.

But do you know why more Americans are born on Tuesday than any other day of the week? One would expect Tuesday to be no more common than any other day, and that is how it used to be. But no longer. To understand this change, we need a combination of social facts and *Verstehen.* Four social facts are relevant: First, technological developments have made the hospital a dominating force in the U. S. medical system. Second, current technology has made delivery by cesarean section safer. Third, as discussed in chapter 19, males took over the delivery of babies. Fourth, profit is a top goal of medicine in the United States. As a result, an operation that used to be reserved for emergencies has become so routine that one-fourth of all U. S. babies are now delivered in this manner (*Statistical Abstract* 1992:86), the highest rate of such births in the world (Wolff et al. 1992). To these social facts, then, we add *Verstehen.* In this instance, it is understanding the preferences of mothers-to-be to give birth in a hospital, and their perceived lack of alternatives. Consequently, physicians schedule large numbers of deliveries for their own convenience, with most finding that Tuesdays fit their week best.

## SOCIOLOGY IN NORTH AMERICA

Transplanted to U. S. soil in the late nineteenth century, sociology first took root at the University of Chicago and at Atlanta University, then an all-black school. From there, academic specialties in sociology spread throughout U. S. higher education. The growth was gradual, however. Although the first departments of sociology in North America opened in 1889 at the University of Kansas and in 1892 at the University of Chicago, it was not until 1922 that McGill University gave Canada its first department of sociology. Harvard University did not open its department of sociology until 1930, and the University of California at Berkeley did not follow until the 1950s.

At first, sociology in the United States was dominated by the department at the University of Chicago, founded by Albion Small (1854–1926), who also founded the *American Journal of Sociology* and was its editor from 1895 to 1925. Members of this first sociology department whose ideas continue to influence today's sociologists include Robert E. Park (1864–1944), Ernest Burgess (1886–1966), and George Herbert Mead (1863–1931), who developed the symbolic interactionist perspective examined below.

In the late 1800s, the dominant sentiment was that a woman's place was in the home. Women who became sociologists during this period were not welcome as professors, and many turned to doing practical work with the poor. The outstanding example is Jane Addams (1860–1935), the founder of Hull-House in Chicago in 1889. She came from a privileged background and attended The Women's Medical College of Philadelphia, dropping out due to illness. On one of her many trips to Europe, she was impressed with work being done on behalf of London's poor. From then on, she tirelessly worked for social justice, concentrating on housing, education, and the working conditions of the poor, especially immigrants. Hull-House, located in the midst of Chicago's slums, was open to people who needed refuge—to the sick, the aged, the poor. Sociologists from nearby University of Chicago were frequent visitors at Hull-House. With her piercing insights into the social classes, the adjustment of peasant immigrants to industrializing cities, and the exploitation of workers, Addams constantly strived to bridge the gap between the powerful and the powerless. Her efforts at social reform were so outstanding, and so effective, that in 1931 she was a co-winner of the Nobel Peace Prize (Addams 1910/1981).

W. E. B. Du Bois (1868–1963), an African American who completed his education at the University of Berlin, created a sociological laboratory at Atlanta University in 1897. His lifetime research interest was relations between whites and African Americans in the United States, and he published a book on this subject every year between 1896 and 1914. At first, Du Bois was content simply to collect and interpret objective data. Later, frustrated at the continuing exploitation of blacks, Du Bois turned to social action and helped found the National Association for the Advancement of Colored People (NAACP). Continuing to battle racism both as a sociologist and as a journalist, he embraced revolutionary Marxism. Dismayed that so little improvement had been made in race relations, when he was 93 he moved to Ghana, where he is buried (Stark 1989).

Like Du Bois, and following the advice of Comte, many of the early North American sociologists combined the role of sociologist with that of social reformer. They saw society, or parts of it, as corrupt and in need of serious reform. During the 1920s and 1930s, Park and Burgess not only studied prostitution, crime, drug addiction, and juvenile delinquency, but they also offered suggestions for how to alleviate these social problems.

During the 1940s, the sociology departments at Harvard, Michigan, Wisconsin, and Columbia universities challenged the preeminent position of the University of Chicago. At the same time, the academic emphasis shifted from social reform to social theory. Talcott Parsons (1902–1979), for example, developed abstract models of society that exerted great influence on sociology. These models of how the parts of society harmoniously work together did nothing to stimulate social activism.

Robert K. Merton (b. 1910) stressed the need for sociologists to develop **middle-range theories**, explanations that tie together many research findings but avoid sweeping generalizations that attempt to account for everything. Such theories, he claimed, are preferable because they can be tested. Grand theories, in contrast, while attractive because they seem to account for so much of social life, are of little value because they cannot be tested. Merton (1968) developed a middle-range theory of crime and deviant behavior that explains how U. S. society's emphasis on attaining material wealth encourages crime.

C. Wright Mills (1916–1962) deplored the theoretical abstractions of this period, which he said were accompanied by empty research methods. Mills (1956) urged sociologists to get back to social reform, seeing imminent danger to freedom in the coalescing of interests of the power elite—the wealthy, the politicians, and the military. After his death, the turbulence in U. S. society in the 1960s and 1970s, fueled by the Vietnam War, also disturbed U. S. sociology. As interest in social activism revived, Mills's ideas became popular among a new generation of sociologists.

**The Present** Since the 1970s, U. S. sociology has not been dominated by any one theoretical orientation or by any single concern. Three theoretical frameworks are most commonly used, as we shall see later, and social activism remains an option for sociologists. Some sociologists are content to study various aspects of social life, interpret their findings, and publish these findings in sociology journals. Others direct their research and publications toward social change and actively participate in community affairs to help bring about their vision of a more just society.

During the past two decades, the activities of sociologists have broadened. Once just about the only occupation open to a graduate in sociology was teaching. Although most sociologists still enter teaching, the government has now become their second-largest source of employment. Many other sociologists work for private firms in management and planning positions. Still others work in criminology and demography, in social work, and as counselors. Sociologists put their training to use in such diverse efforts as tracking the spread of AIDS and helping teenage prostitutes escape from pimps. This book later looks more closely at some of these applications of sociology.

At this point, however, let's concentrate on a better understanding of sociological theory.

# Chapter 2

# Perspectives on Society and Interaction

*Consider the following three statements:*

*"The system is stacked against us. The rich people make the rules, and they make rules that let them keep their money while we have to pay. Ordinary working people don't have a chance; the rich just get richer and the poor get poorer."*

*"The system certainly isn't perfect, but most of the time it works well foremost people. People have been mistreated in the past, but our system allows them to act to change that; look at all the once-poor immigrant groups that are now solidly middle class. If you start messing with what works, a lot of people could suffer."*

*"The problem is that poor people have such low expectations. They believe that they will never have a chance to amount to anything, so they don't even try. They give up, drop out of school, and raise their children with the same sense of hopelessness. Change those perceptions and you begin to change society."*

Clearly, these three statements represent very different viewpoints. The third differs from the other two in that it sees a societal characteristic—the distribution of poverty—as reflecting the thoughts and perceptions of individuals. Change those thoughts and perceptions, it suggests, and the income distribution might well change as a result. The other two look at things the opposite way: They see society as a force acting on the individual. However, they see the nature of the force quite differently. The first quote sees us as largely programmed by society for wealth or poverty, depending on the group into which we were born. The second sees society as functioning effectively—though imperfect, it nonetheless offers us opportunities and its effectiveness could be diminished were the structures of society changed.

## PERSPECTIVES IN SOCIOLOGY

The opinion of each of the people quoted above reflects one of the three main *perspectives* that have been influential in sociology. A **perspective** can be defined as an overall approach or viewpoint toward a subject, including (1) a set of *questions* to be asked about the subject, (2) a general *theory* or theoretical approach to explaining the nature of the subject, and often (3) a set of *values* relating to the subject.

Sociologists propose dozens of important theories and ask thousands of questions, but to a large extent these theories and questions can be linked to one or more of the three major perspectives in the field. These perspectives are the *functionalist perspective* (represented by the second quote above), the *conflict perspective* (represented by the first quote ), and the *symbolic-interactionist perspective* (represented by the third quote). Each of these perspectives offers a distinct theory concerning the key social forces that shape human behavior and society. In other words, they offer different explanations for why people behave as they do. For this reason, each of them asks and attempts to answer somewhat different kinds of questions. A sociologist's preference for one or the other of these perspectives may also reflect his or her values to some extent. Here I am referring to two kinds of values: views about what society should be like, and preferences concerning the kinds of questions the sociologist asks.

## MACROSOCIOLOGY I: THE FUNCTIONALIST PERSPECTIVE

Two of the three perspectives we shall be considering, the functionalist perspective and the conflict perspective, fall under the category of **macrosociology**. In other words, they are mainly concerned with explaining large-scale social patterns. Often the unit of analysis is an entire society, and these perspectives may compare different societies or the same society in different historical periods. The third perspective, the symbolic-interactionist perspective, is *microsociological*, largely concerned with the subfield of sociology known as *social psychology*. In other words, it is more concerned with processes that operate at the

## SOCIOLOGICAL INSIGHTS

### FUNCTIONALIST THEORY

#### EMILE DURKHEIM (1858–1917)

Much of functionalist thinking about the importance of interdependency as a force for cohesion in society can be traced to the writings of Emile Durkheim. In his first major work, *De la Division du Travail Social (The Division of Labor in Society)* (Durkheim, 1947 [orig. 1893]), he argued that in preindustrial societies, tradition, unquestioned belief, and forced conformity are the main forces holding society together. He referred to this as *mechanical solidarity.* In modern societies, these forces are replaced by interdependency. Durkheim called this new pattern *organic solidarity* because he saw the interdependency in society as being similar to the interdependency of the organs of a living being.

Durkheim's recognition of the importance of consensus can be seen in another major concept he developed, *anomie* or the state of normlessness (Durkheim, 1964 [orig. 1897]). By this Durkheim meant that in certain situations norms—rules of behavior—break down and become inoperative. This may occur during periods of rapid social change or intense conflict, and when it does, people are more likely to engage in behavior that is destructive to them or their society. Durkheim (1964 [orig. 1897]) illustrated this point in his pioneering study of suicide.

#### TALCOTT PARSONS (1902–1979)

Functionalist theory became especially influential in the United States, where its leading proponent was Talcott Parsons. One of Parsons's major contributions to sociology was the notion that each piece of the social structure represents some underlying function. According to his theory of *structural-functionalism* there are four particularly crucial functions, necessary in any society, that in turn are met by particular *systems of action* within society (Parsons, 1966, 1971): *integration,* holding the society together and forming a basis for cooperation, which is attained through the social system: *pattern maintenance,* the development and maintenance of common values, which is attained through the cultural system; *goal attainment,* a motivational force that creates the incentive to work and cooperate, which is attained through the personality system; and *adaptation* to the environment, which is attained through the behavioral organism, which Parsons took to include the economic system.

#### ROBERT MERTON (1910– )

Although Robert Merton studied under Parsons and is generally identified with the functionalist perspective, certain elements of his thinking have been influenced by the conflict perspective as well. Unlike Durkheim and Parsons, who attempted to develop grand theories to explain the basic nature of society, Merton has often sought to develop *middle-range theories* that seek to describe and explain a narrower range of behaviors with a greater degree of precision. Merton (1967) has argued that such theories better lend themselves to testing through research than do larger-scale theories.

In keeping with his notion of middle-range theories, Merton has written on a number of specialty areas within sociology, including the sociology of science and race and ethnic relations and especially deviant behavior (Merton, 1938, 1968).

individual level and with the interaction between individuals and the larger society. We shall turn our attention first to the functionalist perspective.

## The Functionalist Perspective Defined

The **functionalist perspective** is known by a number of different names, including *order perspective* and *structural-functionalism,* all of which refer to the same general theoretical viewpoint. The basic social theory underlying this perspective is sometimes referred to as *systems theory.* The early sociologist who probably had the greatest influence over the development of this theory was Emile Durkheim. Among the most influential modern functionalist theorists have been the American sociologists Talcott Parsons and Robert Merton. These individuals are examined in the box entitled "Functionalist Theory."

The functionalist perspective is primarily concerned with why a society assumes a particular form. This perspective assumes that *any society takes its particular form because that form works well for the society given its particular situation.* Societies exist under a wide range of environmental situations. Some, for example, exist in harsh Arctic, desert, or mountain climates, whereas others exist in temperate climates and fertile environments. Levels of technology also vary widely. Some societies have highly advanced industrial technologies, whereas others engage in subsistence farming. Societies also differ in terms of their interaction with other societies. Some have hostile neighbors; other have friendly neighbors. All of these elements make up the total environment within which a society must exist, and each combination of these elements force a society to adapt in a particular set of ways. Thus, what works for one society cannot be expected to work for another.

In any society, however, the functionalist theoretical perspective makes one basic argument. Whatever the characteristics of the society, *those characteristics developed because they met the needs of that society* in its particular situation. Having now provided a general statement describing the functionalist perspective, let us look at several of its key principles in greater detail. These principles include *interdependency, functions of social structure and culture, consensus and cooperation,* and *equilibrium.*

## Key Principles of the Functionalist Perspective

**Interdependency** One of the most important principles of functionalist theory is that *society is made up of interdependent parts.* This means that every part of society is dependent to some extent on other parts of society, so that what happens at one place in society has important effects elsewhere. Early social thinkers in this tradition often likened the operation of society to that of a living organism. Auguste Comte, Herbert Spencer, and Emile Durkheim all used this analogy. Think of your own body. Your entire body depends upon your heart, brain, lungs, stomach, and liver for its survival. Each of these organs provides a vital function. A malfunction in any one of them can affect the health of your entire body. These early sociologists saw society as operating in much the same way.

If this was true a century ago when Comte and Spencer were developing their social theories, it is even more true today. Society has become more complex and more interdependent, not less so. Just think for a moment of all the people upon whom your participation in your introductory sociology course depends. Obviously, the class requires a faculty member to teach it and students to take it. However, it also depends on many other people and organizations. Someone has to provide the electricity to light the room, and in order for that electricity to be provided, someone had to build a dam or mine some coal, oil, or uranium and get that fuel to the power plant. Someone also had to decide when the class would be held and in what room, communicate that information to you, and enroll you in the class. Someone had to write the book, with the assistance of many other people: printers, editors, proofreaders, salespeople, and bookstore employees. Thus, a class that seems to involve just you, your fellow students, and your professor is in fact the product of the efforts of hundreds of people. Consider also that a failure on the part of any element of this complicated system could affect your participation in this class. Your name could be left off the instructor's class list; the book could arrive late or in insufficient numbers at the bookstore; there could be a power failure; the class could be scheduled in the same room as another class.

**Functions of Social Structure and Culture** Closely related to interdependency is the data that each part of the social system exists because it serves some **function.** This notion is applied by functionalists to both social structure and culture. *Social structure* refers to the organization of society, including its institutions, its social positions, and its distribution of resources. *Culture* refers to a set of beliefs, language, rules, values, and knowledge held in common by the members of society. (These concepts are discussed in more detail in Chapter 4.) According to the functionalist perspective, each of the various elements of social structure performs a function for society. In other words, it meets some need in the society or somehow contributes to the effective operation of the society. Here again, the analogy to a living organism is apparent: Just as each organ has its function to perform, so does each part of society.

Much the same is true of culture. If a society has a rule or belief, the theory argues, that rule or belief likely exists because it is in some way useful for society. Consider, for example, the *postpartum sex taboo,* a common rule in many preindustrial societies. This rule specifies that a woman may not have sex for some set period after the birth of a child. The length of time covered by the postpartum taboo has ranged from a few weeks to several years. Although few people realized it, this rule was very useful. When the mother is breast-feeding her baby and her own diet is barely adequate, becoming pregnant could so deplete the nutrients in her breast milk that her baby could become seriously malnourished. Thus, in such societies, the health of babies—and consequently, the perpetuation of the society itself—depends on the mother's not becoming pregnant again too soon after giving birth. The postpartum sex taboo prevented this. Therefore, whatever religious or mystical beliefs may have served as the basis for this rule, it turns out that the rule performed an important function for society.

Societal functions that are obvious and openly stated are referred to as **manifest functions.** A manifest function of education, for example, is to teach children about such subjects as reading, writing, and arithmetic. Sometimes, however, functions are not obvious or openly acknowledged. These are called **latent functions.** A latent function of education is baby-sitting: School relieves parents of the responsibility of taking care of their children. Thus, the parents are free to pursue other efforts or simply to take a break from child care. Latent functions are often unintentional: The school system was not set up for the purpose of baby-sitting, but it does serve that purpose. Although latent functions are less obvious than manifest functions, they can be just as important to society. For this reason, sociologists operating out of the functionalist perspective have devoted much effort to identifying the latent functions of social structure and culture.

**Consensus and Cooperation** Another key principle in functionalist theory is that societies have a tendency toward *consensus;* that is, to have certain basic values that nearly everyone in the society agrees upon. Americans, for example, nearly all agree that they believe in freedom and democracy. They may not agree on exactly what they mean by either freedom or democracy, and they also may disagree on the extent to which the United States has attained these ideals. However, as ideals or principles that a society ought to strive for, the overwhelming majority of Americans express support for freedom and democracy.

According to functionalists, societies tend toward consensus in order to achieve *cooperation.* As we have already seen, the interdependency in society requires that people cooperate. If people in even one part of such an interdependent system fail to cooperate with people elsewhere the system, the effects will be felt throughout the entire system. People are more likely to cooperate when they share similar values and goals. According to Durkheim (1947 [orig. 1893]; 1953 [orig. 1898]), they are especially likely to cooperate when they feel that they share things in common with one another; he referred to such unity as *solidarity.*

What happens when a society lacks consensus? According to functionalists, inability to cooperate will paralyze the society, and people will devote more and more effort to fighting one another rather than getting anything done. This process can be seen in former Yugoslavia and parts of the former Soviet Union as well as in Lebanon. When the fall of communism brought an end to forced conformity in the former Soviet Union and eastern Europe, lack of consensus led to social breakdown in several areas. Civil war erupted between Armenians and Azerbaijanis in the former Soviet republic of Azerbaijan, and between Bosnians and Serbians in the former Yugoslav republic of Bosnia-Herzegovina, leading to thousands of deaths and state of virtual anarchy. In 1992 and 1993, Serbian residents of the Bosnian capital, Sarajevo, laid siege to the city and bombarded their own neighbors, schools, and businesses. The reason for this self-destruction was the lack of consensus between the Christian Serbs and the Bosnian Muslims who controlled the city. Lebanon has similarly been paralyzed by the inability of the Sunni Muslims, Shi'ite Muslims and Christians (as well as several other religious groups) to cooperate.

While they are extreme cases, all of these examples illustrate a key point: a society that lacks any consensus whatsoever will have a very hard time surviving as a society.

**Equilibrium** A final principle of functionalist theorists is that of *equilibrium.* This view holds that, once a society has achieved the form that is best adapted to its situation it has reached a state of balance or equilibrium, and it will remain in that condition until it is forced to change by some new condition. New technology, a change in climate, or contact with an outside society are all conditions to which a society might have to adapt. When such conditions occur, *social change* will take place: Society will change just enough to adapt to the new situation. However, once that adaptation has been made, the society has attained a new state of balance with its environment, and it will not change again until some new situation requires further adaptation. The picture that emerges from the functionalist perspective, then, is that of a basically stable, well-functioning system that changes only when it has to, and then only enough to adapt to changes in its situation. In short, the natural tendency of society is to be stable, because society is a smoothly operating, interdependent system.

## Functions and Dysfunctions

An important refinement of the functionalist perspective has been made by Robert Merton (1968). Merton has argued that even social arrangements that are useful to society can have **dysfunctions** or consequences that are harmful to society. No matter how useful something is, it can still have negative side effects. In general, functionalist theory argues that when the functions outweigh the dysfunctions, a social arrangement will likely continue to exist because, on balance, it is useful to society. However, because situations change, a condition that is functional today can become dysfunctional in the future. Thus, when studying any element of social structure or culture, sociologists typically raise questions about its possible functions and dysfunctions.

# MACROSOCIOLOGY II: THE CONFLICT PERSPECTIVE

Although the **conflict perspective** can trace its intellectual roots to ancient Chinese, Greek, and Arabian philosophers, modern conflict theory is largely an outgrowth of the theories of Karl Marx. There are many kinds of conflict theories today, a number of which disagree in important ways with Marx's analysis. Nonetheless, the basic Marxian notion of different groups in society having conflicting self-interests remains influential in most modern conflict theories. Modern conflict theory has been refined by the German theorist Ralf Dahrendorf (1959) and by American sociologists C. Wright Mills (1956) and Randall Collins (1979, 1975).

## The Conflict Perspective Defined

Like the functionalist perspective, the conflict perspective is a macrosociological perspective that addresses the question "Why does society take the form that it does?" However, conflict theory gives a very different answer to this question. Its answer is that *different groups in society have conflicting self-interests, and the nature of the society is determined by the outcome of the conflict among these groups.* To conflict theorists, the most important force shaping society is conflicting self-interests among different groups within society. The conflict perspective is examined in the "Conflict Theory" box.

# SOCIOLOGICAL INSIGHTS

## CONFLICT THEORY

### KARL MARX (1818–1883)

Karl Marx has probably had more influence over conflict theory than any other sociologist. Marx's theories concerning ownership of the means of production and concerning the bourgeoisie and the proletariat were discussed in Chapter 1. He argued that in industrial societies, the bourgeoisie uses its power to ensure that all elements of the social structure and ideology support its continued ownership of the means of production. The proletariat, in contrast, has an interest in change.

*Much of Marx's social thinking can be found in Capital (1967), originally published in three volumes between 1867 and 1894.*

### RALF DAHRENDORF (1929– )

The German sociologist Ralf Dahrendorf is credited with making important modifications in conflict theory to make it more applicable to twentieth-century industrial societies. One way his theories differ from those of Marx is that he gives *power* a more central role than Marx did. Marx saw power as purely an outgrowth of owning the means of production, whereas Dahrendorf has identified other bases of power, including legal authority. Thus, conflicts of interest exist between those who have power and those who lack it, just as they exist between those who own wealth and those who do not. Like Marx, Dahrendorf does not believe that people are always aware of what their self-interests are. When a group of people share a common social position (such as being employed in similar types of work around the country by the same employer), they have common self-interests. When they are unaware of these self-interests, they have what Dahrendorf (1959) calls *latent interests.* At some point, however, they may become aware of their common self-interests and try to advance them. At this stage, they have developed an articulated *manifest interests.*

This step represents an intermediate step between the existence of conflicting interests (always present in society) and the actual emergence of social conflict (only sometimes present).

### C. WRIGHT MILLS (1916–1962)

Probably the most influential conflict theorist in American sociology has been C. Wright Mills. Like Dahrendorf, Mills sought to apply conflict theory to modern industrial capitalism. He felt that one consequence of the massive scale of corporations and government in modern society is to make the elite less visible and more removed from the people. As a result, the elite have greater power, and the masses feel powerless and, therefore, increasingly cynical and apathetic about politics (Mills, 1956).

Mills (1956) believed that in the United States major political decisions are made by a power elite consisting of top corporate executives, high military commanders, and the executive branch of the federal government. Mills's ideas set the stage for an important tradition of research in sociology and there are some who say that they offer a good explanation of such events as the Vietnam War, Watergate, and the Iran-contra scandal.

Mills also spoke and wrote often of "the sociological imagination"; in fact, he published a book with that title in 1961. By this term, Mills meant that we should seek to distinguish personal troubles—problems affecting particular individuals as a result of something they did or didn't do—from social problems—conditions affecting many people, which, although they may think of them in personal terms, are in reality a product of larger societal processes or conditions.

**Conflicting Self-Interests** Why, according to conflict theorists, do different groups in society have conflicting self-interests? The reason is that every society experiences competition over **scarce resources.** A scarce resource is anything that does not exist in sufficient amounts for everyone to have all that he or she wants. The most important scarce resource in society, those which produce the greatest competition, are money (and the things it can buy) and power. Whenever a resource is scarce, one person's gain is potentially another's loss. If you have more money or power, the result may very well be that I have less, because there is only so much to go around. It is this feature that produces conflict: Groups struggle with one another to increase their share of money and power, often by reducing the money and power of others. In this struggle, the interests of those who have a good deal of money and power conflict with the interests of those who do not. The self-interest of those who have money and power is to keep things as they are so that they can continue to enjoy an advantaged position. This group will attempt to preserve the **status quo**—the existing set of arrangements. The self-interest of those who lack money and power is just the opposite. They want to create *change* so that they can get a bigger share of wealth and power.

This point of view differs significantly from the functionalist perspective. Whereas the functionalist perspective sees the various elements of society as being interdependent, conflict theorists believe that the various human elements of society are in conflict with one another because one group's gain is potentially another group's loss.

**Bias in Social Structure and Culture** As noted above, the distribution of scarce resources such as money and power is usually unequal. Those who have money often have power, and vice versa. There are many debates among conflict theorists about the precise relationship between money and power, but there is one key point on which most conflict theorists agree: Those who have disproportionate amounts of money and power can use their power to maintain their privileged position. In other words, they have the power to shape society to their own advantage. The result of this is that a society tends to take on characteristics that work to the further advantage of the dominant groups within that society.

Here, too, there is an important parallel to functionalist theory. As we saw, functionalists argue that societies assume the characteristics they do because those characteristics are functional—useful to the society. Conflict theorists agreed up to a point—but they ask the question, "Functional for *whom?*" In other words, they believe that social arrangements exist because they are useful—but *not* to the whole society. Rather, they are useful to the *dominant group* in society—whatever advantaged group has the power to shape society according to its own interests. This power can be exercised in a variety of ways. The wealthy are frequently in positions to influence public opinion. Dominant groups in many societies try (often successfully) to gain control of the media, which is why freedom of the press is repressed in much of the world. Even where it is not, those with money have a better chance than others of being able to communicate through the media. The wealthy may be overrepresented in governments or may even control them directly. Other key institutions such as education and religion are often disproportionately influenced by dominant groups, or if not, they may be unwilling to challenge such groups. Finally, there is always the possibility of a dominant group using force to shape a society to its own interests.

**Conflicting Values and Ideologies** Because different groups in society have conflicting self-interests, it is virtually certain, according to conflict theory, that they will have different views about social issues. In short, their values and *ideologies*—systems of belief about reality—will be based in large part on what serves their self-interests. Those in the dominant group use their considerable power to promote belief in the values and ideologies that support the existing order (Mannheim, 1936 [orig. 1929]; Marx, 1964). When they succeed, as they often do, subordinate groups accept the dominant group's ideology and believe things that are not in their own interest to believe, a condition Marx called *false consciousness.* Sooner or later, however, subordinate groups come to see that their interests conflict with those of the dominant group, and when this happens, they develop their own values and beliefs, which naturally conflict with those advocated by the dominant group. Thus, the inherent tendency of society is toward conflict, not consensus. Conflict comes from within society because different groups have conflicting self-interests and thus try to shape society and its values in different and conflicting ways.

**CONFLICT VERSUS VIOLENCE** It is very important to stress here that *conflict does not mean the same thing as violence.* Certainly conflict can be violent, as in the case of riots and revolutions. However, nonviolent conflict is more common. Conflict occurs in legislatures, as opposing interest groups seek to pass laws and policies from which they can benefit. It occurs in the courts, as different groups pursue legal strategies to get the law interpreted in their interests. Collective bargaining and civil rights panels are other mechanisms for dealing with conflict. All of these processes reflect the **institutionalization** of conflict. They reflect the fact that society has recognized that conflict will occur and has developed ways of dealing with it. You can argue, as many conflict theorists do, that dominant groups develop institutions for dealing with conflict that favor their own interests. Even so, the fact remains that conflict does often occur in peaceful, institutional settings. It also sometimes occurs peacefully outside such institutional settings, as in the case of mass demonstrations and nonviolent civil disobedience. In general, when institutional means of resolving conflict exist, *and* when disadvantaged groups perceive that such institutional settings offer a fair opportunity for resolving conflict, these groups will use them. If such means do not exist however, or if disadvantaged groups believe that these means favor the advantaged groups, conflict will occur outside institutional settings (Coser, 1956). In this situation, violence becomes more likely.

**THE ROLES OF CONFLICT** Conflict theorists see conflict not only as natural and normal, but also as useful to society. Conflict, they argue, brings social change, which makes two things possible. First, it offers disadvantaged groups an opportunity to improve their position in society through a more equitable distribution of scarce resources. Second, it offers society an opportunity to function better, because conflict creates the possibility of eliminating social arrangements that are harmful to the society as a whole but serve the interests of the dominant group.

Consider environmental pollution as an example of this principle. At one time in the United States and other countries, there was very little regulation of industrial activities that pollute the air or water or of the dumping of hazardous wastes. Because it was cheaper to discharge hazardous materials into the environment than to dispose of them properly, many industries did so. These industries opposed any attempt to stop them from such dumping by appealing to distrust of government and invoking the evils of government regulation. However, heightened public awareness of the risks to health, quality of life, and long-term survival led to strong environmental movements in the 1960s and early 1970s, and again in the late 1980s and early 1990s. In both time periods, conflicts arose between environmentalists and industrial polluters. These conflicts led to passage of environmental regulations, such as the banning of new cars using leaded gasoline in the 1970s, and the 1990 Clean Air Act. They also led to heightened public consciousness of environmental issues that forced even the industrial polluters to profess concern for the environment by the late 1980s—in contrast to Earth Day 1970, Earth Day 1990 received millions of dollars in corporate support. The new regulations and the heightened public awareness led in turn to considerable reductions in some kinds of pollution. Lead pollution, for example, decreased sharply in both the air and water as use of leaded gasoline declined during the 1980s (Alexander and Smith, 1988; Smith, Alexander, and Wolman, 1987; U.S. Environmental Protection Agency, 1990). Similarly, the 1990 Clean Air Act was passed with the express purpose of reducing emission of pollutants that deplete the ozone layer and that cause acid rain.

Of course, the decreases in air and water pollution mentioned above do not mean that the problem of the environment has been solved. As gains are made in some areas, we continue to discover new ways in which human activity is threatening the environment. A growing current threat is the risk of global warming resulting from both air pollution and massive cutting of rain forests. A related problem is the extinction of growing numbers of life forms because of elimination of habitat resulting from logging, farming, and urbanization. At the environmental summit in Rio de Janeiro in 1992, the U.S. government resisted taking strong action on these issues because of the threat such action would pose to American corporate interests. At the same time, the environmental movement in the United States and elsewhere exerted strong pressure to adopt different policies. Again, conflict is playing a central role in the formation of environmental policy, and the outcome of that conflict will likely have important effects on global warming and endangered species.

**CONFLICT AND SOCIAL CHANGE** The environment is a good example of how conflict can result in social change. However, functionalist and conflict theorists disagree about the role played in social change by conflicts within society. Functionalists see social change as coming largely from outside society. They see it as a response to some new technology, some change in the environment, or some interaction with another society. Conflict theorists, however, see change as coming from within society. Different groups have opposing interests and thus engage in conflict; that conflict produces change. Therefore, to conflict theorists, it was not simply the presence of air pollution that brought about regulations to control it. Rather, change arose from people's reaction to the fact that they were threatened by pollution. They developed a social movement, engaged in conflict with those who had an economic self-interest in continuing to pollute, and helped bring about a new policy and a cleaner environment.

## MACROSOCIOLOGICAL PERSPECTIVES: IS SYNTHESIS POSSIBLE?

The differences between the functionalist and conflict schools have led sociologists to ask an important question: Are the two theories incompatible, or are societies sufficiently complex so that both theories could be right at the same time?

This question has not been answered to the satisfaction of all sociologists, and debate continues concerning the compatibility or incompatibility of the two perspectives. However, I believe—and I think most sociologists believe—that although they disagree on key points, the functionalists and conflict perspectives are not totally incompatible. In the first place, certain social arrangements might be useful to society in some ways and useful to the dominant group in others. Society might also contain forces for both consensus and conflict; under different conditions, one or the other can predominate. Let us examine each of these ideas a bit further.

### Can Social Structure Be Simultaneously Biased and Functional?

Can social structure serve the interests of the dominant group and society as a whole at the same time? Let us illustrate this question with an example. Functionalists and conflict sociologists have been debating the causes of social inequality for decades. In short, functionalists have argued that inequality exists because it creates incentives that make society more productive, whereas conflict theorists have argued that inequality exists because it benefits the rich and powerful. They argue that the level of inequality in the United States cannot be explained by a need for productivity, partly because much of the inequality is inherited and thus cannot operate as an incentive. To this, the functionalists reply, "Show me a society without inequality. Inequality exists in all societies that produce a surplus because it serves a useful purpose in those societies." I shall explore this debate much further in later and have no intention of trying to resolve it here. However, I would like to point out that *both* theories could be partly correct. Perhaps inequality does produce incentives that societies need, and perhaps that is why it exists in essentially every society, as functionalists point out. It may also be true, however, that *more* social inequality exists in the United States than is needed to create incentives for productivity, and the reason for this could be the use of power by the wealthy to keep and expand their wealth. Assuming that each theory is partly right, the key sociological question becomes this: What is the relative importance of the two causes of social inequality? That is a challenging research question. Suppose for a moment that each reason—society's productivity needs and the desire of the powerful to maintain their wealth—offers part of the answer. If this were the case—and it is very possible that it is (see Lenski, 1966)—we would have to consider both the functionalists and conflict theories in order to ask the right research questions and to understand the causes of social inequality in the United States.

## Simultaneous Forces for Conflict and Cooperation

As was noted in Chapter 1, Talcott Parsons and his structural-functionalist theories heavily dominated American sociology from the end of World War II into the early 1960s. Since that time, however, conflict theories have become much more influential in American society, and since the late 1960s, Marx has been taken far more seriously as a sociologist theorist than he was in the 1950s. Today, no single theoretical paradigm dominates American society the way functionalism did in the 1950s. Why? Although there are undoubtedly many reasons, one likely reason is that society changed.

In the United States in the 1950s, the economy was growing, we had recently been victorious in two wars that had enjoyed popular support, and, to all outward appearances, we enjoyed consensus on basic values. By 1970, things had changed dramatically. The country was bitterly divided over the war in Vietnam, and the civil rights movement had brought dramatic changes in race relations (legally, at least). Hundreds of cities had experienced racial violence. John and Robert Kennedy and Martin Luther King and Malcolm X had been assassinated, demonstrators had been beaten outside the Democratic Convention in Chicago, and students had been shot by National Guardsmen on college campuses. Old rules no longer seemed to operate, as young people smoked marijuana, preached "free love," and dressed and wore their hair in ways that shocked many in the older generation. In short, conflict seemed to have become the rule overnight.

Sociologists responded to these developments by re-thinking their theories. Those theories that emphasized change and conflict became far more popular than they had been a decade earlier. From the hindsight of another two decades, though, many sociologists have come to believe that forces for both conflict and change exist in American society, and that the different conditions of the 1950s and 1960s brought different forces to the surface. From this viewpoint, society always had a need to cooperate, but it also always had certain conditions that divided it.

In the 1950s, consensus was easy to attain. Most people's lives were getting better (the economy was growing dramatically), and the world seemed simple (most world conflict was seen as a struggle between communism and freedom). Hence, the forces for cooperation predominated, and conflict, though present, was low-key. Still, certain underlying conflicts simmered. Black Americans remained disadvantaged, even if the promise of civil rights seemed to offer a better future. Women were becoming more educated, yet they were still expected to remain in the home if they could afford to do so, a situation that was to bring about great conflict and change in the future.

By the late 1960s, though, things had changed. America was in a war it did not understand and seemed unable to win. Many African Americans, their hopes buoyed by the prosperity of the 1950s and the idealism of the early 1960s, realized that their economic situation was not getting better. The antiwar and Black Power movements ended the appearance of consensus, and the conflict spread to other areas as well—as it usually does during periods of social change and upheaval. In particular, American women began to demand a more equal role in American society. None of this meant that the forces of cooperation were no longer operative. Despite the deep divisions, society did not collapse, the economy continued to produce, and many of the old rules that had been rejected were eventually replaced by new ones—different, indeed, but still rules. Thus, just as the forces for conflict were present but subdued in the 1950s, the forces of cooperation remained present but were less evident in the 1960s.

From the mid-1970s through the 1980s, there was a more even balance between the forces of conflict and cooperation in American society than in either the 1950s or the 1960s. Social conflict, as represented in such events as riots and mass demonstrations, was less common during this period, but it did occasionally occur, as in the case of racial violence in Miami in 1980 and 1989. A conservative who extolled traditional societal values was twice elected president by big majorities—but massive opposition forced him to abandon certain policies, such as aid to the Nicaraguan contras. The excesses of the "free love" mentality of the 1960s had been soundly rejected by the end of the 1980s, but even AIDS could not bring about a return to the restrictive sexual values of the 1950s. Not surprisingly, U.S. sociology became theoretically balanced during this time. Functionalists reasserted the validity of their viewpoint, and a

## SOCIOLOGICAL INSIGHTS

## ECLECTIC MACROSOCIOLOGY

### MAX WEBER (1864–1920)

No sociologist has had a greater influence on the field than the social theorist Max Weber (pronounced vā-ber). Weber's thinking drew on a variety of ideas, some associated with conflict theory, some with what we now call the functionalist perspective, and some with neither. Thus, he cannot be clearly linked to any particular perspective.

Like other sociologists of his time, Weber was greatly interested in the process of modernization associated with urbanization and the Industrial Revolution. A key element of modernization, according to Weber (1962), is rationalization—a process whereby decisions are made on the basis of what is effective in helping people attain their goals rather than on the basis of tradition. This notion is similar to functionalist theory in the sense that it focuses on what *works.* However, Weber was aware of conflicts and competing interests in society, and rationalization included the notion of what is effective for one group in its competition or conflict with another, a concept that borrows heavily from the conflict perspective.

### GERHARD LENSKI (1924– )

The American sociologist Gerhard Lenski (1966) has drawn upon the functionalist and conflict theories to explain social inequality. He agrees with the functionalists—but only up to a point—that inequality creates incentives and rewards people in accordance with their skills. However, he also argues that much inequality exists beyond what can be accounted for on this basis, and that the power arising from wealth allows the advantaged to hang on to their wealth long after their advantage serves any use to society. Lenski also notes that the degree of inequality in any society is linked to its system of production. As societies advance from the hunting-and-gathering stage to agriculture (and, usually, some form of feudalism), the degree of social inequality increases dramatically. Once society industrializes, however, this trend is reversed. Although modern industrial societies have considerable inequality, they have less than preindustrial societies. The reasons for this include the complexity of the division of labor and the presence of a large skilled and educated segment that pushes society in the direction of democratization.

### LEWIS COSER (1913– )

The American sociologist Lewis Coser has been interested in group dynamics, although he defines a group as everything from a small gathering to an entire social system. Much of his work has focused on ways that conflict—both within groups and between groups—can improve the functioning of these groups (Coser, 1956). Thus, it could be said that Coser has conducted a functional analysis of conflict. He argues that conflict within groups can benefit the group as long as it does not challenge the group's purpose for existence. He sees the normal state as a combination of consensus on core values and conflict over specifics. Conflict offers groups ways to adapt to changing needs and can also increase long-run group cohesion by offering a way to address dissatisfactions. Conflict in general is more likely to produce breakdown in small, close-knit groups, and adaptation in large, diverse ones. Conflict over many unrelated issues is also less disruptive than sustained conflict over one issue. Conflict between groups (external conflict) can perform the functions of defining group boundaries and promoting cohesion within groups.

view that came to be known as *neofunctionalism* gained significant support among sociologists (Alexander, 1985, 1988). At the same time, however, a Section on Marxist Society was formed within the American Sociological Association, and its sessions were among the best attended at the annual meetings.

By the early 1990s, conflict seemed to be increasing again in American society. 1992 brought the bloodiest urban riot of the twentieth century, "alternative" styles of dress and music were enjoying a resurgence in popularity, and there were signs of renewed social activism among college students and other young people. It is not yet clear what course these trends will take or how sociology will respond to them. But they do remind us that the forces for both conflict and stability are always present in society, a point well recognized by sociology's most important theorists. These theorists have sought to understand the conditions under which each of these forces predominates. In fact, this tradition of balanced consideration of both kinds of forces can be traced at least to Max Weber, though some of Weber's theories are not easily classified as either functionalist or conflict. The views and contributions of Weber and two contemporary theorists—Gerhard Lenski and Lewis Coser—are further explored in the box entitled "Eclectic Macrosociology."

## Macrosociological Perspectives: A Final Note

As we finish our discussion of macrosociological perspectives, we have seen important areas of consistency and overlap between functionalist and conflict thinking. We have seen, too, that social arrangements can be useful to society in some ways, but—at the same time—useful to special interests and perhaps even dysfunctional to society in other ways. Forces for conflict and forces for cooperation are both present in society, and each may dominate under different conditions. Moreover, as Coser notes, even conflict can in some ways be useful for the larger society. Finally, society is in part shaped by relationships of exchange that involve elements of both cooperation and domination. All of these things suggest that the most useful macrosociology may be one that incorporates ideas from both theoretical perspectives.

Even so, the debate goes on between functionalist and conflict sociologists. This is not just a debate about theories; it is also a debate about values. Functionalism, because it notes society's tendencies toward stability and balance, appeals to conservatives and cautious liberals. It stresses the advantages of the status quo, which appeals to those who oppose major change. Its emphasis on conformity has a similar appeal, warning of the dangers of a divided society and opposing suggestions to do things in any radically different way.

Similarly, conflict theory appeals to radicals and strong liberals who favor fundamental changes in social institutions. It stresses society's inequalities, which liberals and radicals see as society's unfairness. It is favorable to new ideas and to social change, which appeals to those who think society needs to change.

Although political views may well influence sociologists' preferences for one perspective or the other, it is important to distinguish such views, which represent *values*, from what the two perspectives say about social reality, which is a matter of *theory*. One can never prove that a conservative, moderate, liberal, or radical political view is "right" or "wrong," because that is a matter of values. However, society has gone a long way toward understanding the forces that shape society, and the evidence here suggests that both the functionalist and the conflict perspectives have important insights to offer in this regard. Thus, it would be highly incorrect to say that these perspectives are "just a matter of opinion."

# MICROSOCIOLOGY: THE SYMBOLIC-INTERACTIONIST PERSPECTIVE

Almost from the time sociology emerged as an academic discipline, some people within the field felt that, to understand even large-scale patterns of human behavior, it was not enough to study only the characteristics of society. Rather, these social theorists argued that you must study the *processes by which human interaction occurs*. These processes of interaction involve social psychology or **microsociology**, in that they

## SOCIOLOGICAL INSIGHTS

### SYMBOLIC-INTERACTIONIST THEORY

#### CHARLES HORTON COOLEY (1864–1929)

Much of what later came to be known as the symbolic-interactionist perspective is based on the ideas of Charles Horton Cooley. Cooley is best known for his theories concerning self-image and the looking-glass self, which are discussed in this chapter. Cooley also proposed that the formation of self-image occurs mainly through communication with a fairly limited number of individuals, called *significant others,* with whom a person interacts on a regular basis. In childhood, parents, peers, teachers, relatives, neighbors, and religious leaders are most likely to be the significant others. In later life, co-workers, supervisors, spouses or lovers, and children are the most important significant others.

#### GEORGE HERBERT MEAD (1863–1931)

George Herbert Mead's thinking was similar in many ways to that of Cooley, but he added two important elements to Cooley's theories. First, he clarified the means by which the communication processes of interest to Cooley occurred. Mead (1934) pointed out that one of the features that distinguishes human beings from animals is their ability to use *symbols.* A symbol can be defined as anything that stands for or represents something else. This includes words, gestures, signs, and images. Most human communication uses symbols, and it is through symbols that the processes of interest to symbolic-interactionist occur. Symbols are used to communicate the expectations associated with roles, and, in response, they are used to present the image to others that an individual is attempting to fulfill the expectations of those roles. Finally, symbols are used by others to let the individual know how well or poorly he or she is doing in meeting those role expectations.

Mead's other important addition to Cooley's thinking was the concept of the *generalized other.*

#### HERBERT BLUMER (1900–1987)

Herbert Blumer was one of Mead's many students in his famous social psychology course, which formed the basis of *Mind, Self, and Society* (Mead, 1934). Blumer went on to become the most influential symbolic-interactionist theorist of recent years, although he also made important contributions to macrosociological analysis, particularly in the area of race relations (for example, Blumer, 1965).

It was Blumer who first used the term *symbolic-interactionism* in a 1937 article. According to Blumer (1969), symbolic-interactionism is based on three key premises. The first is that human beings behave toward things on the basis of the meaning that those things have for them. The second is that the meanings of things for each individual are derived from social interaction with other people. This premise challenged two dominant views in the social sciences: the belief that the meaning of things is a matter of objective reality and the conviction that the meaning of things a person observes is a product of the person's psychological makeup. Blumer's third key premise is that meanings are shaped through an interpretive process used by the individual in dealing with the things he or she encounters. Thus, the actions of others are interpreted, and this interpretation is part of what defines meaning. Moreover, because of this process of interpretation, meanings of things can change as the interpretation changes.

often include interaction *between individuals and the larger society.* Societies do present situations, send messages, and give rules to individuals, but it is on the individual level that these situations, messages, and rules are interpreted. Moreover, how these situations, messages, and rules are interpreted is a key factor in determining how people behave. These realizations have given rise to the third major perspective in sociology, the **symbolic-interactionist perspective.** Because of its concern with the interaction between the individual and the larger society, it is also sometimes called the *microinteractionist perspective* (Collins, 1985c), or simply the *interactionist perspective.*

## The Interactionist Perspective Defined

If the interactionist perspective could be summarized in one general statement, that statement might begin with the notion that the *interpretation* of reality can often be an important factor in *determining* the ultimate reality. As previously noted, society continually presents individuals with situations, messages, and rules. Taken together, these elements, and the *meaning* given to them by the individual, define the individual's experience of social reality. Sometimes the meaning of these situations, messages, and rules is clear, and to the extent that this is the case, the individual's social reality is obvious to him or her. Usually, however, the meaning of the situations, messages, and rules is not completely clear to the individual, and the individual must *interpret* them as best he or she can (Blumer, 1969a). This interpretation occurs, of course, in the context of past messages the individual has received from society. Nonetheless, it *is* interpretation, and individuals with different sets of past experiences frequently interpret the same message or situation differently. Hence, the individual's understanding of social reality depends in part on the content of the messages and situations he or she encounters and in part on how he or she interprets those messages and situations. How the individual understands reality, of course, will have an important effect on how he or she will behave, which can further alter the situation. For these reasons, *the interactionist perspective focuses first on how messages are sent and received and on how social situations are encountered by individuals, then upon how people interpret the meanings of these messages and situations, and finally on how these processes shape human behavior and society.*

## Interpreting Situations and Messages

As noted above, one key concern of the interactionist perspective is how people interpret the messages they receive and the situation they encounter. Interactionists believe these issues are important because people's interpretations of reality are an important factor in determining how they will behave. Consider an example. You are waiting at the bus stop, and the person next to you says, "Hello, Isn't this a nice day?" Your behavior in response to this message will depend on your interpretation of the message, which in turn will be a product of past messages and experiences. If, for example, your experience has been that people at the bus stop like to chat to pass the time while waiting for the bus, you will probably respond in a friendly way and carry on a conversation with the person until the bus arrives. If, however, your experience has been different, you will probably respond differently. Suppose your experience has been that people at the bus stop usually don't talk to one another, but keep to themselves. On the few occasions when people did try to strike up a conversation with you, it turns out they were trying to sell you something, begging for money, or seeking to convert you to their religious beliefs. In this case, you would interpret the situation differently, assume the person wanted something from you, and likely try to avoid further interaction.

## The Social Construction of Reality

What is significant about the above example is that *the real intentions of the person speaking to you were not important.* Even the person's behavior does not give us the entire explanation of why you experienced the reality of the situation as you did. Rather, it was your understanding of the meaning of the person's behavior, including your interpretation of his or her intentions, that determined the reality that you experienced (Charon, 1989). Sociologists refer to this process as the **social construction of reality** (Berger and Luckmann, 1966). By this, they mean that the reality that you experience is not simply determined by what goes on in an objective sense; rather, it is determined by your understanding of the meaning of what happens. Thus, depending on that understanding, the reality you experienced could have been either "This person is friendly" or "This person is trying to hit me up for something."

There are two additional important points concerning this process. First, the meaning you attribute to the person's behavior is largely a product of your past experiences in similar social situations. Thus, there is a clear social influence on your interpretation of situations you encounter. Second, how you interpret the meaning of the situation you encounter will influence how you respond to it. This principle was recognized as early as the 1920s by W. I. Thomas, in a statement today known as the **Thomas theorem**: "If men (sic) define situations as real, they are real in their consequences" (Thomas, 1966). In other words, whatever the objective reality, people behave on the basis of their *understanding* of reality, and that behavior in turn shapes subsequent realities, including objective realities of human behavior. As Collins (1985a, p. 199) put it, "If the definition of reality can be shifted, the behavior it elicits will switch, sometimes drastically."

**Ethnomethodology** Symbolic-interactionist theory, then, argues that your interpretations of reality are in part socially determined, and that these interpretations in turn partly determine how you will behave. To put this a bit more broadly, human behavior is in part a product of the structure of society and in part a product of how individuals interpret that social structure. Attempting to understand the forces that influence how individuals interpret the situations and messages they encounter has developed into a major subfield within the interactionist perspective known as **ethnomethodology.** It was given this name by Harold Garfinkel, who has written extensively about it (ee Garfinkel, 1967; and Handel, 1982). Ethnomethodology has been applied to a variety of topics in sociology. It has been suggested, for example, that one factor influencing people's scores on intelligence tests is their interpretation of the meaning and importance of the test and what it will be used for (Ogbu, 1978).

**The Looking-Glass Self** Another important concept that has long been used by symbolic-interactionists is the **looking-glass self.** This concept was developed by the early symbolic-interactionist theorist Charles Horton Cooley, who is discussed further in the box entitled "Symbolic-Interactionist Theory." The basic notion of the looking-glass self could be summed up as "We see ourselves as others see us." In other words, we come to develop a self-image on the basis of the messages we get from others, as we understand them. If your teachers and fellow students give you the message, in various ways, that you are "smart", you will come to think of yourself as an intelligent person. If others tell you that you are attractive, you will likely think of yourself as attractive. Conversely, if people repeatedly laugh at you and tease you about being clumsy, you will probably come to decide that you are clumsy. Over the years, you gradually develop a complex set of ideas about what kind of person you are, and to a large extent, these ideas are based on the messages you get from others (Matsueda, 1992). In Cooley's terms, you use other people as a mirror into which you look to see what you are like.

Of course, the message we get from others about ourselves is partly a product of the intended content of the message and partly a product of how we *perceive* the message. To Cooley, an important part of the looking-glass self was how we understand the messages we get from others. In Cooley's terms, we *imagine* what others think of us on the basis of our understanding of the messages we get from them. Thus, if we misunderstand the messages of others, we may form our self-image on the basis of a different message than what was intended. For this reason, processes of communication—the sending and receiving of messages about our personal characteristics—play a key role in the formation of self-image.

The kind of self-image this process produces, moreover, will influence many aspects of your life. Self-esteem, clearly part of this process, has been shown to be linked to success in business life and in personal life, and the lack of it has been linked to substance abuse, unemployment, suicide, and a host of other personal and social problems.

**The Self-Fulfilling Prophecy** A concept closely related to the looking-glass self, but applicable to an even broader range of human behavior, is the **self-fulfilling prophecy.** The self-fulfilling prophecy is a situation in which people *expect* something to happen, and because they expect it to happen, they behave in such a way that they cause it to happen. Sociologists have discovered numerous examples of self-fulfilling prophecies. The best known concerns teacher expectations and student achievement (Brophy, 1983; Rosenthal and Jacobson, 1968). Generally speaking, students will outperform others of equal ability when teachers have higher expectations of them. Similarly, countries sometimes engage in military build-ups because they expect to be attacked, which their potential enemies interpret as an aggressive move that requires a response. A cycle of this type between two polarized alliances in Europe was one of the causes of World War I (Farrar, 1978). Another example concerns the often poor relations between inner-city black and Hispanic youths and the police. The police view the youths as troublemakers who must be shown the "force of the law." The youths see the police as brutal and often racist, and they frequently respond with behavior to show them that "Nobody's going to push us around." In other words, both the police and the youth "act tough" toward each other because each expects trouble from the other. These responses virtually ensure conflict between the two groups (Kuykendall, 1970).

## Social Roles

An important concept in symbolic-interactionist sociology is the notion of **social roles:** sets of expectations about how people are supposed to behave, which are attached to positions within the social system. Human interaction is defined by the relationships among various roles, such as student, teacher, parent, and school bus driver. Each day, everyone fills a variety of roles such as these, and each role carries a set of expectations about how people are supposed to behave in various situations. The exact content of these roles depends on the nature of the particular social system. Moreover, knowledge of how to behave in roles is learned through contact with others and through the messages we receive from others about (1) what expectations are attached to a particular role and (2) how well we are meeting the expectations associated with the roles we fill. The latter process, of course, is part of what Cooley meant by the looking-glass self.

A related concern of symbolic-interactionists has been with how people learn the relationships among various roles in the social system, such as that of teachers and students. As with learning the content of roles, this occurs largely through the messages people receive from others, as well as through observation. These learning processes have a large impact on how people behave: People usually try to behave in ways that fulfill the expectations of their roles as they understand them, and that interact in the expected way with other roles. As discussed in the box entitled "Symbolic-Interactionist Theory," the contributions of George Herbert Mead have been particularly important in this area. Symbolic-interactionists have been particularly interested in the childhood socialization process, because the learning of social roles is such a critical part of that process.

## Sending Messages: The Presentation of Self

Just as the symbolic-interactionist perspective is concerned with how people get and interpret social messages, it is also concerned with how messages are sent. In particular, people want to convince others that they are succeeding in meeting the expectations of the roles they are attempting to fill. Thus, just as people respond to the expectations and messages they get from others, they also attempt to send messages regarding their own behavior and characteristics. To any given individual, the importance of different roles will vary. In addition, people exercise some choice in the roles they fill. Most of us, for example, must fill the role of "employee" in some way or other. However, the particular jobs we hold—and thus the particular characteristics of our employment role—vary widely. Moreover, roles are typically something over which people have some choice. In part, people manage the self-image that they project to others by choosing what roles to fill and emphasize in their lives (see Backman and Secord, 1968; Kemper and Collins, 1990). They also manage their self-image by presenting to other people the image that they feel is appropriate to the particular role that they are in at any particular time. The early Chicago School sociologist Robert Park (1927) put it this way: "One thing that distinguishes men from the lower animals is the fact that he has a conception of himself, and once he has defined his role, he tries to live up to it. He not only acts, but he dresses the part, assumes quite spontaneously all the manners and attitudes he conceives as proper to it." Sociologists refer to this process as the *presentation of self,* or *impression management.*

**The Dramaturgical Perspective** The analogy of human behavior to acting is made most explicitly by a particular interactionist theory known as the **dramaturgical perspective.** This theory, generally identified with Erving Goffman (1959, 1967, 1971), argues that in each role we fill, we try to convince people that we are filling it in a particular way, generally the way to which we think they will respond positively. Thus, the self-image a person attempts to project at work will be different, for example, from the impression he or she would likely try to project on a weekend "singles" ski excursion. In Goffman's terms, people give different performances on different occasions. These performances, however, are always shaped by what people think others expect and will respond to positively. Thus, it is only through messages from others that we develop our ideas of what is a proper image to project at work or on a ski trip.

**FRONT-STAGE AND BACK-STAGE BEHAVIOR** An important distinction in the dramaturgical approach is that of "front-stage" and "back-stage" behavior (Goffman, 1959). "Front-stage" behavior—the performances aimed at impression management—takes place in settings where others can see us. However, there are also private settings in which we "let our guard down" and behave in ways that we would not want others to see. Goffman called this "back-stage" behavior. Collins (1985c, p. 157) illustrated the distinction this way:

> [Front stage] is the storefront where the salesperson hustles the customer, [back stage] is the backroom where the employees divide up their sales territories, establish their sales line, and let their hair down after the manipulation they have gone through. In another sphere, there is an analogous distinction between the cleaned-up living room and a carefully laid table where the ritual of a dinner party is to reaffirm status membership with one's guests, and the backstage of bathroom, kitchen, and bedroom before and afterwards, where emotional as well as physical garbage is disposed of.

A fascinating aspect of the process of impression management is that we generally assist one another with our performances (Goffman, 1959). Most of us are sufficiently insecure about our own performances that we do not make others aware of the flaws in theirs. Imagine, for example, that your professor or classmate enters your classroom with his zipper open or her blouse unbuttoned. There may be a bit of snickering, but most people will try to spare the person involved embarrassment by pretending nothing is wrong. In fact, some people will experience discomfort or embarrassment over the situation, even though it is someone else whose performance is flawed. This embarrassment or discomfort will probably increase if anyone says anything about it in front of the class. Many people will think "That could just as easily be me." Therefore, people usually engage in what Goffman called "studied nonobservance": They go out of their way to ignore flaws in others' performances. To create or even acknowledge awareness of flaws in performances is to "create a scene": It leads to embarrassment, not only for the person whose performance is flawed, but for others as well.

The dramaturgical perspective has sometimes been criticized for attempting to reduce human behavior to a continuous process of impression management. To do this would clearly be an oversimplification, for two reasons. First, as macrosociology tells us, a person's position in the larger social structure clearly is an important force in shaping behavior. By position in the social structure, I am referring to the functions a person's roles must fill (as stressed by the functionalist perspective) and the resources attached to those roles (as stressed by the conflict perspective). Second, whatever self-image we try to project to theirs, we are likely to influence our own self-image in the attempt. In other words, if we "act" to impress others, we will often come to believe our own act. This will be particularly true if *others* respond positively to the act. In other words, the messages from others are once again affecting our own self-images.

## MICRO- AND MACROSOCIOLOGY: IS SYNTHESIS POSSIBLE?

### Simultaneous Effects of Function, Conflict, and Interaction

As we saw earlier, there has been considerable effort among sociologists to combine the insights of the functionalist and conflict perspectives in order to understand social situations more fully. Is it similarly possible to combine the microsociological interactionist perspective with the two macrosociological perspectives? Increasingly, sociologists like George Homans and Randall Collins (see box) have been

#### SOCIOLOGICAL INSIGHTS

#### MICRO-MACRO LINKS

##### GEORGE C. HOMANS (1910–1989)

The American sociologist George Homans (1961) has been one of the leading advocates in sociology of *exchange theory,* discussed in the text. He argues that in any human exchange, the objective is to maximize profit, which he defines broadly as reward minus cost. Because people bring unequal resources into such exchanges, they often expect and receive unequal profits.

Homans (1950) has also devoted a good deal of effort to studying group dynamics. He believes that human interaction within groups is shaped by an *external system* and an *internal system.* The external system refers to the interaction of the group with its larger environment, including other groups: an environment to which the group must adapt if it is to survive. The internal system refers to the interaction of individuals and coalitions within the group, which define group sentiment and lead to the development of a group culture. These processes involve elements of both cooperation and conflict.

##### RANDALL COLLINS (1941– )

Randall Collins has been one of the most prolific writers among sociological theorists in the 1970s and 1980s. His early work centered around the conflict perspective, addressing a wide range of issues relating to that perspective. In *Conflict Sociology* (1975), he discusses ways in which the propositions arising from conflict theory (and other sociological theories as well) can be scientifically tested, and he assesses the contribution of the conflict perspective to the understanding of several areas of social life. He has applied the conflict perspective to religion (1975), marriage (1985b), gender inequality (1971a), and education (1971b).

Recently, however, Collins has sought to combine insights from the conflict perspective with those from microsociology. Like other sociologists in recent years, he stresses the idea that individual actions shape social structures. His interaction ritual chain theory, discussed in the text, is one example of this thrust. He has also devoted some effort to understanding the intellectual roots of the three main sociological perspectives, noting, among other things, that several philosophical viewpoints that were prominent in the early days of sociology have influenced all three perspectives (Collins, 1985a). Thus, from the very start, the three sociological traditions have had at least something in common.

attempting to do exactly this. It is my view that most social situations can be more fully understood by using all three perspectives (or theories that combine them) rather than by using just one or two. I shall briefly outline the reasons why I think this is so, discuss some examples of theories combining the perspectives, and then give a concrete example of a common social situation that is best understood by all three perspectives.

Although most sociologists operate primarily as either macrosociologists or microsociologists, I believe that there is one sense in which few would dispute the usefulness of both types of approach. To put it simply, the different approaches may be useful for understanding different aspects of the social situation. Any social arrangement may exist in part because it is useful to the society—as argued by the functionalist perspective. At the same time, it may also exist partly because it meets the needs of some particular interest group within the society—as argued by the conflict perspective. It may, in fact, even be harmful to other interest groups or, in some way, to the larger society. Despite these larger societal influences, though, the exact form of the social arrangement is likely to be shaped by the understandings of reality held by those participating in it, and by their consequent behavior—which is what the symbolic-interactionist view argues. These understandings are partly a product of the objective reality of the larger social structure, but they are also partly a product of people's response to that reality (Handel, 1979, pp. 863-867).

**Attempts at Synthesis** Sociology has witnessed many recent attempts to establish links between micro and macro social influences. One example is Giddens's (1978, 1984, 1985) *structuration theory.* Giddens criticizes both functionalism and conflict theory for viewing social structure as an unchanging force that shapes the individual. Though structure does influence the individual, Giddens points out that individuals can do and do shape structures. Structures provide people with knowledge and capabilities, which they use to either change or reproduce the structure. If individuals act in innovative ways, their actions can change the social structure (Sewell, 1992). Such actions might include invention of a new technology, or the organization or leadership of a social movement. Similar ideas can be seen in Randall Collins's (1981, 1988) *interaction ritual chain theory.* Interaction rituals are encounters in which individuals exchange performances of the type described in Goffman's dramaturgical perspective, discussed on pp. 66-67. Each of these interaction rituals defines a relationship, the nature of which is determined by the knowledge, skills, ideas, and ways of thinking of the people involved. In each such ritual, there is an exchange of these cultural resources between the participants. These exchanges may increase or decrease the cultural resources of each participant. Ultimately, they may either perpetuate or break down social inequality, depending on who gains and who loses resources in these exchanges.

Most recently, Kemper and Collins (1990) have argued that both macro, society-level interactions (for example, between interest groups, organizations, or countries) and individual, one-to-one relationships are shaped by the same two dimensions. One is a power dimension, characterized by being able to make others behave as you want them to; the other is what Kemper and Collins call a status dimension, characterized by voluntarily conferring status, as though expressions of friendship and warmth; gifts; social recognition; and liking, love, or trust. Further, they argue that the outcomes of processes involving these dimensions at the societal level affect people's interaction at the individual level, and vice versa.

Both micro and macro perspectives study the mechanisms by which social inequality is maintained or broken down. Conflict theorists, for example, argue that social inequality largely reflects unequal access to education and to the kinds of cultural resources of interest to Collins. They contend that the educational system makes it difficult or impossible for people of lower socioeconomic status to gain educational credentials, knowledge, or cultural capital. When sociologists ask *how* the educational system may perpetuate such inequalities, however, they usually focus on microsociological processes, such as the effect of teacher expectations on student achievement. Thus, the *outcome* may be structured inequality, as argued by conflict theory, but to understand the *process* that leads to that outcome, we must use interactionist theory.

## Exchange Theory

One important theory that represents a linkage between macro- and microsociology is **exchange theory** (Blau, 1964; Homans, 1961, 1984; for examples of recent work in this tradition, see Clark, 1987; Mortensen, 1988; Molm, 1991; Uhara, 1990; Yamagishi, Gilmore, and Cook, 1988). Exchange theory, like conflict theory, begins with the assumption that people seek to advance their self-interests. These interests sometimes conflict and sometimes coincide with those of other people. According to this theory, people enter into relationships with one another when each participant has something to offer that the other desires. Thus, each person has something to give and something to gain. Exchange theory has been applied to a wide range of relationships, from pure business relationships such as that between buyer and seller to intimate personal relationships such as that between husband and wife. In the latter case, for example, consider the personal needs of two individuals who get married. One partner may primarily have a need for companionship, whereas the other seeks status through the marriage relationship. According to Blau, people assess their needs and pick their partners accordingly, and, as long as these needs stay the same and each partner meets the other's need, the relationship is likely to remain stable. Of course, should either partner's need change, or should one partner stop meeting the other's needs, the marriage could be in trouble.

Exchange relationships also can operate between groups and individuals. Consider the case of an individual joining a club. The club gains increased membership, dues money, and possibly someone new to work on its projects. The individual gains the personal interaction the club provides, as well as whatever activities and programs it offers members. However, if the relationship does not prove to be mutually beneficial, it will likely end.

**Exchanges and Power** Ideally, social changes are equal. Each partner in the exchange gets a fair "return" for what he or she puts in. Many business and personal relationships in our society are governed by a norm of *reciprocity*—the view that a fair exchange is one in which there is a more-or-less even trade. Similarly, studies of attractiveness show that, in the majority of cases, partners in love relationships rate fairly similarly to one another on attractiveness (Berscheid et al., 1971; Penrod, 1986, pp. 189-190; Walster and Walster, 1969). Thus, attractiveness operates as a resource for which partners in courtship make an "even" trade. Sometimes, however, people accept a lower level of attractiveness in their mate in order to get more of something else, such as money or prestige.

Exchange theorists also note that many exchange relationships are characterized by *unequal power*, in which one partner sometimes brings greater resources to exchange than the other, as in the case of the relationship between employer and employee. When this happens, the more powerful partner usually expects and gets more (Molm, 1990). Those who lack resources—the poor, the sick, the unattractive—may have little choice but to enter relationships of unequal exchange. This concept also explains one reason why women have traditionally been more concerned about appearance then men: In a sexist society, they have had fewer alternative resources like wealth and power to offer to a potential mate. Thus, although exchange theory resembles functionalism in the sense that each partner often benefits from the exchange, it resembles conflict theory in the sense that one partner can benefit much more than the other. Although it resembles the macro theories in some regards, its focus is on the actions of individuals (Alexander, 1988, p. 87), which arise largely from their perceptions about what they have to gain or lose in a relationship.

Although exchange theory has been influential in both macrosociology and social psychology and acts as something of a bridge between the two, it has its critics. The strongest criticism is that it reduces all human interaction to calculated, rational exchanges. The critics argue that in reality people enter into social relationships for all kinds of reasons—some rational, some based heavily on emotion. A more balanced view, then, might be that people enter into relationships with one another partly for reasons of exchange and partly for other reasons.

We have seen, then, that there are some cases in which ideas arising from two or all three of the sociological perspectives are combined, as in exchange theory, and other cases in which different perspectives make competing claims. Through the cycle of theory and research, claims arising from each perspective are put to the test: Some are supported by research findings; others are not. Let us now consider an everyday example where the three perspectives combined can give us insights that go beyond those of any perspective by itself.

## Using All Three Perspectives: An Example

Every Saturday morning from late spring through early fall, hundreds of thousands, perhaps even millions, of Americans participate in an event that takes place in big cities and small towns, in rural areas and suburbans, in all 50 states. I am speaking of the garage sale. This is an ordinary event, not the stuff of which headline news or path-breaking sociological students are made. Nonetheless, it is important to millions of Americans. Moreover, I would argue that it is precisely for the ordinary, everyday event like the yard sale that society is useful for giving us special insights. Hence, I choose the yard sale, not only as an event about which sociology offers interesting insights, but also as one that illustrates the usefulness of each of the three perspectives for letting us see a part of the social reality that is occurring.

Consider how a yard sale might be analyzed from the functionalist perspective. A yard sale performs the important function of allowing things that would otherwise go to waste to be used and, for the seller, to be turned into a little extra cash. These are the functions of a yard sale that readily come to mind—in other words, its *manifest functions.* Consider, though, some *latent functions* of yard sales. For one, they offer people an enjoyable outing, an opportunity to get out of the house. In addition, they may perform the important social function of enabling people to see one another on a regular basis.

Yard sales also can be analyzed from a conflict perspective. In fact, I first became aware of this when I saw an article about yard sales in an "underground newsletter" published by a group of politically radical students on the campus where I teach. The article touted yard sales as "striking a blow at capitalism through people's recycling." In a sense, it was right: Those who attend yard sales can be seen as an interest group; specifically, people with limited incomes who have a particular interest in getting things inexpensively rather than purchasing "flashy and new" merchandise. Surely this interest runs contrary to that of another set of interest groups: the manufacturers, advertisers, and department stores, whose interests lie in persuading people to buy the "newest and best," even if something older and less flashy would work equally well. Thus, shopping at yard sales could be seen as being in the interest of those with limited incomes, and there is evidence suggesting that this is happening. In the past decade or two, as people's purchasing power has failed to grow as it did in the past, the popularity of yard sales has soared. Some evidence does indicate that the established business interests have come to see yard sales as a threat. In my town, for example, several city council members have called for a crackdown on the posting of signs advertising yard sales, proclaiming them to be an unsightly nuisance. (Interestingly, no similar argument had been made by the city council a few months earlier when the town was flooded with political campaign signs!)

Finally, yard sales can be analyzed from a symbolic-interactionist perspective. They are often characterized by considerable bargaining between buyer and seller, and the course of this bargaining is certainly shaped by the perceptions the buyer and seller have of each other. If the seller is perceived as "wanting too much," the entire interaction can come to a quick end. Evidence of "wanting too much" can only include not only prices that are too high, but also an unwillingness to bargain. As symbolic-interactionists point out, it is the person's perception of the meaning of the other's behavior that is critical. In other words, the reality that each of us experiences is socially constructed. It may be that the seller is having his or her first yard sale and doesn't' know what prices to charge or that one is supposed to bargain. That doesn't really matter to the buyer, though, because it is the buyer's *perception* that determines his or her behavior. If they buyer misinterprets the seller's lack of experience as greed, the buyer experiences the seller as "wanting too much" rather than not knowing you're supposed to bargain. With this understanding of reality, the buyer will likely end the interaction.

Of course, the seller's behavior is also influenced by the process of interaction. A novice seller may realize, after a few such interaction, that something is wrong. If the disgruntled buyers give the seller the right set of messages, the seller may learn from them that buyers expect the prices to be lower and to be subject to bargaining. Once the seller lowers his or her prices and begins to bargain, the entire interaction may be different. In short, the communication that occurs between buyer and seller, as well as how each interprets the other's messages, has a crucial impact on the outcomes of the yard sale. To put in Blumer's terminology, behavior has been influenced by the meanings of the yard sale situation to the participants, which in turn is largely a product of their communication with one another.

We have seen, then, that each perspective—functionalist, conflict, and interactionist—has added something to our understanding of the yard sale. Each has helped us understand a somewhat different part of its reality. In this particular case, none of the three perspectives is in any sense "wrong," even though proponents of the three perspectives can and do debate their relative usefulness for understanding reality. Rather, as noted, each helps us understand a slightly different aspect of what is taking place. Most important, our understanding of the social meaning and significance of the yard sale is greater when we use all three perspectives than when we use any one, because each offers us part of the "big picture."

## The Three Perspectives and This Book

I have provided an extensive introduction to the three sociological perspectives in this chapter because I believe that they give greater meaning to the more specific theorizing and research that will be discussed in the remainder of this book. The rest of the book will concern a number of major topics that make up the key subject matter of sociology. Each of these topics has a number of specific theories and lines of research pertaining to it. Many of these theories and lines of research, though specific to the topic of interest, arise in large part from one of the three perspectives introduced here. Some go further and attempt to combine insights from two or all three of the perspectives and to apply them to a particular topic. I believe that your understanding of sociology will be enhanced if you see how a theory about, for example, race relations, may relate to theories about aging, or drug use, or formal organizations. The best way to do this is to try throughout the book to link specific theories to the larger sociological perspectives from which they arise. Thus, in virtually every chapter in this book that linkage will be made. As you read this text, I hope you will see that at least one of the major perspectives, and often all three, can be used to gain important insights about every major topic discussed in the rest of this book.

## SUMMARY

In this chapter, we have examined the three theoretical perspectives that have had the greatest influence in sociology. Two of them, the functionalist and conflict perspectives, are macrosociological, focusing mainly on large-scale societal processes. The functionalist perspective holds that social arrangements exist because they meet needs in society, and it stresses interdependency, the functions of social structure and culture, consensus, cooperation, and equilibrium. The conflict perspective holds that society is made up of competing interest groups with unequal power and that social structure exists because it meets the needs of interest groups, usually those with power. It stresses conflicting interests, the relationship of culture and social structure to group interests, and the inevitably of conflict and change.

In part, these perspectives reflect competing values that cannot be judged scientifically. In larger part, though, they reflect different theories about human behavior and society, which are subject to scientific evaluation. Although the two macrosociological perspectives disagree on some key points, many sociologists believe that the two schools are not incompatible. Social structure, for example, may meet society's needs in some ways and the needs of dominant groups in other ways. Similarly, it is reasonable to argue that forces for both stability and change are always present in society, but that under different social conditions, different forces predominate.

The microsociological symbolic-interactionist perspective gives greater attention to processes involving individuals. It holds that people's understanding of reality is determined by the messages they get from others and by how they interpret these messages. This, in turn, is an important influence over how people behave. Among key concepts stressed by interactionists are social roles, the looking-glass, self, the self-fulfilling prophecy, and the social construction of reality.

Attempts have been made to build links between micro- and macrosociology. As illustrated by the example of the yard sale, each perspective—the functionalist, conflict, and interactionist—can add to our understanding of a social situation. In large part, this is true because each addresses a different piece of the reality of that situation.

## GLOSSARY

**perspective** A general approach to a subject, including a set of questions to be addressed, a theoretical framework, and, often, a set of values.

**macrosociology** Those areas of sociology that are concerned with large-scale patterns operating at the level of the group or society.

**functionalist perspective** A macrosociological perspective stressing the basic notion that society is made up of interdependent parts that function together to produce consensus and stability.

**function** A consequence of a social arrangement that is in some way useful for the social system.

**manifest function** A function of a social arrangement that is not evident and is often unintended.

**dysfunction** A consequence of a social arrangement that is in some way damaging or problematic to the social system.

**conflict perspective** A macrosociological perspective based on the key premise that society is made up of groups that compete, usually with unequal power, for scarce resources; conflict and change are seen as the natural order of things.

**scarce resources** Material goods, statuses, and other things that people want, but that do not exist in sufficient quantities to satisfy everybody's needs or desires.

**status quo** The existing set of arrangements within a society.

**institutionalization** A process whereby a condition or social arrangement becomes accepted as a normal and necessary part of a society.

**microsociology** An area of sociology that is concerned with the interaction of the individual with larger societal influences.

**symbolic-interactionist perspective** A major microsociological perspective stressing the importance of messages from others and from society, how people understand and interpret these messages, and how this process affects people's behaviors.

**social construction of reality** A process in which people's experience of reality is largely determined by the meanings they attach to that reality.

**Thomas theorem** A sociological principle that states that situations defined by people as real are real in their consequences.

**ethnomethodology** A theory arising from the symbolic-interactionist perspective that argues that human behavior is a product of how people understand the situations they encounter.

**looking-glass self** A self-image based on an individual's understanding of messages from others about what kind of person that individual is.

**self-fulfilling prophecy** A process in which people's belief that a certain event will occur leads them to behave in such a way that they cause the event to happen.

**social role** A set of behavioral expectations that are attached to a social position or status.

**dramaturgical perspective** A theory arising from the symbolic-interactionist perspective that holds that human behavior is often an attempt to present a particular self-image to others.

**exchange theory** A theory holding that people enter a relationship because each participant expects to gain something from it.

## FURTHER READING

CHARON, JOEL. 1989. *Symbolic Interactionism: An Introduction, an Interpretation, an Integration,* 3rd ed. Englewood Cliffs, NJ: Prentice-Hall. A highly readable introduction to the symbolic-interactionist perspective. It also includes a useful discussion of what is meant by a perspective.

COLLINS, RANDALL. 1985. *Three Sociological Traditions.* New York: Oxford University Press. An excellent discussion of major sociological theoreticians, which locates each major theorist in terms of the three major perspectives, explores the intellectual origins of each perspective, and examines the possibilities of combining ideas arising from each perspective for a better understanding of human society.

COLLINS, RANDALL. 1975. *Conflict Sociology: Toward an Explanatory Science.* New York: Academic Press. A bit more technical than Collins's 1985 book described above, this book offers a thorough assessment of the contribution of the conflict perspective to our understanding of human society. It also includes some valuable insight about the nature of scientific inquiry in sociology.

GIDDENS, ANTHONY. 1986. *Sociology: A Brief but Critical Introduction.* New York: Harcourt, Brace, Jovanovich. An examination of the role sociology has to play in society—and of some major theoretical viewpoints in sociology—by a theorist who has taken a leading role in attempts to combine insights from microsociology and macrosociology.

MERTON, ROBERT. 1968. *Social Theory and Social Structure,* 2nd ed. New York: Free Press. Discusses Merton's midlevel variety of functionalist theory, applied to a wide variety of issues of interest to sociologists.

WALLACE, RUTH A., and Alison Wolfe. 1991. *Contemporary Sociological Theory: Continuing the Classical Tradition.* Englewood Cliffs, NJ: Prentice Hall. A comprehensive source that discusses the major perspectives of modern sociological theory: functionalism, conflict theory, theories of rational choice, symbolic-interactionism and phenomenology. Also provided is an overview of recent theoretical developments.

# Chapter 3

# How Sociology Is Done

*The city was aflame. Anyone within miles could see and smell the acrid pall of smoke from fires set by the rioters. People were dragged from vehicles and beaten by the angry mobs. A news reporter described seeing men stoned as they begged for mercy and women beaten by attackers who laughed and joked. In what seemed like no time, over 300 businesses and homes had been burned, some with people still in them. Exit routes were jammed with people fleeing the violence. By now, your mind's eye probably sees the news video you watched of Los Angeles aflame in the spring of 1992 after the Rodney King verdict. But I am not writing about Los Angeles in 1992. The scene described above occurred in East St. Louis, Illinois, in 1917. Until the Los Angeles violence 75 years later, the East St. Louis riot, which took 48 lives, was the deadliest American riot in the twentieth century. But unlike those in Los Angeles, the mobs in East St. Louis were all white, and nearly all of the people who were beaten and had their homes and businesses attacked were black.*

The East St. Louis and Los Angeles riots illustrate many of the questions sociologists try to answer through their research . Why do we have mob violence in our cities at some times in our history, and relative calm in others? From 1917 to 1992, the United States experienced four periods of serious urban violence—with about two decades of relative calm interspersed between each period of violence. What determines whether we have relative calm or widespread violence? The racial composition of the rioting groups and their pattern of rioting have been different in different periods. In the 1910s and 1940s, the riots were mainly initiated by whites and involved widespread attacks on black individuals. In the 1960s, riots were initiated by blacks and involved attacks on property. In 1992, blacks, Hispanics, and a sizable number of whites rioted side by side, sometimes looting and fighting police in racially mixed crowds. Yet, the old pattern of attacks on individuals was also more evident, as a number of people were dragged from vehicles and beaten. Why did the racial composition of the rioters change, and why did they sometimes attack mainly individuals and other times mainly property? Finally, all four periods of rioting came during or within about one year after a major U.S. war—World War I, World War II, Vietnam, and Desert Storm (Farley, 1992). Does war somehow act as a trigger that precipitates violence at home? Can questions like these be answered? If so, how?

Sociologists try to explain how and why society changes over time, and how and why one society differs from another. They try, too, to explain why different groups of people respond differently to similar situations. After the event in Los Angeles, for example, some people were outraged mainly by the beating of Rodney King, the acquittal of his attackers, and by the worsening condition of the inner cities, while others were outraged mainly by the riot itself, viewing it as simple lawlessness. In asking such questions sociologists make the important assumption that people think and behave as they do for identifiable reasons. Thus, if we measure the right things, we can answer such questions as why society experiences relative calm during some periods of history and widespread upheaval during other periods.

## SOCIAL THEORY AND RESEARCH

The opening vignette illustrates the point, noted briefly in Chapter 1, that sociology is largely concerned with *cause and effect.* Sometimes it seeks to *explain:* Why were American cities wracked with mass violence in the 1910s, 1940s, 1960s, and 1990s, but relatively calm during the periods between? Sometimes, too, it seeks to *predict:* Under what conditions are cities in the future likely to be calm or violent? Of course, there are also times when sociology merely seeks to *describe:* How many people actually participate in outbreaks of urban violence, and how are people who participate different from people who don't? Most of the time, though, description is a step toward either explanation or prediction, both of which involve the notion of cause and effect.

## Cause and Effect

By **cause and effect**, social scientists mean that the presence of one condition ( the *cause)* makes the occurrence of some other condition (the *effect)* more likely than it would otherwise have been. This is a somewhat broader definition than the popular notion of cause and effect. To social scientists, the cause does not *always* have to be followed by the effect, but the effect does occur more often when the cause is present than when it is absent. Consider the example of unemployment and divorce. Social research has indicated that unemployment is a cause of divorce. By this, I mean that when one of the breadwinners in a family becomes unemployed, the family is more likely to experience a divorce than it would have done had that unemployment not occurred. It does *not* mean that a divorce will *always* follow the loss of a job, nor does it mean that the absence of unemployment guarantees that a couple will not get divorced. It simply means that, all other things being equal, divorce is more likely in the presence of unemployment than in its absence.

## Theory and Values

A *theory* can be defined as a set of interrelated statements about reality, usually involving one or more cause-effect relationships. Ideally, these statements can be tested through *research*—the process of systematic observation. This is what distinguishes theories from other kinds of arguments: Theories are made up of verifiable statements about reality that, with the right information, can be tested (Lenski, 1988).

In contrast to theories are **values**: personal judgments or preferences about what is considered good or bad, or about what is liked or disliked. Unlike theories, values can never be proved or disproved because they reflect personal preference or judgments. Such judgments, of course, are largely products of culture, and people from different cultures have different values. Still, no culture's values are "right" or "wrong," "true" or "false."

Consider the following statement: "Poverty causes conflict in society." This is a statement about reality that—given the right information—could be shown to be either true or false. Thus, this statement could stand as a part of a theory. In contrast, consider the following statement: "Conflict in society is undesirable." This statement is a *value judgment.* It cannot be proved true or false because it is simply a matter of what people consider good or bad. Some people regard conflict as bad per se because it often leads to anger, violence, and hatred. Others consider at least some conflict to be good because it can help to change society for the better. Which group of people is "right"? That question cannot be answered. The two groups simply have different desires and priorities. In other words, they have different *values.*

**Distinguishing Theories from Values** Why this discussion of theories and values? These concepts are important because our thinking about society and human behavior is bound to be influenced by both values and factual questions. This is true for sociologists as well as for "ordinary people." Therefore, you must be able to look at an argument and distinguish what part of the argument involves testable theories and what part involves values, which cannot be tested. This principle is illustrated by the example above. When we speak about social conflict, we are likely to ask and debate questions about what causes it. These are factual questions concerning cause and effect, which is exactly what theories address. Questions of this type can be answered by research. However, when we speak about social conflict, we are also likely to debate whether it is good or bad, and the answer, at least in part, involves values. Science, through theory and research, might be able to identify some consequences of conflict (for example, how likely it is to bring about a certain kind of change), but it *cannot* prove that conflict and its consequences are either good or bad. Judgments of this type are a matter of values and cannot be answered scientifically, even though scientists, like everyone else, have their values.

You will often encounter arguments such as the following: "Conflict is bad because it usually leads to violence, and it rarely changes anything away." This argument is a mix of values and theories, and to evaluate it you have to be able to determine which is which. The part asserting that "conflict is bad" is a value judgment because it reflects a personal preference. In fact, even if the rest of the statement were true, you could still reasonably disagree with the "conflict is bad" part. (Perhaps conflict also challenges people and leads them to work harder and be more creative, so it could be seen as good for that reason.) However, the parts of the statement concerning the effects of conflict on violence and social change concern faculty reality. Those parts of the statement could be thought of as a rudimentary social theory, and, given the right information, could be proved either true or false. Thus, when you encounter statements or arguments about society, you should ask yourself the following questions:

1. What parts of the statement or argument reflect people's values and therefore are a matter of personal attitude or preference that cannot be judged true or false through observation?

2. What parts of the statement concern reality and therefore could be demonstrated to be true or false if you could get the right information?

**Values and the Social Sciences** The above discussion holds true whether you are studying the works of social scientists, reading a newspaper, watching a television program, or having a discussion with your friends. Although social scientists place a primary emphasis on theory and research—that is, on addressing factual questions about the realities of human behavior—they, too, are human, and their work is often influenced by their values. Inevitably, the topics that social (or, for that matter, natural) scientists choose to study will be influenced by their values. In addition, scientists are not value-free concerning their theories. Science today is very competitive, and every scientist wants to gain recognition (and grant money and publications) by developing a theory that works better than anything else's. Consequently, scientists sometimes try to interpret their results to fit their theories. Finally, because social scientists study human beings, they frequently bring strong values to their research that can influence their interpretations of their findings. Both social scientists and natural scientists often have a strong interest in applying their research for some useful purpose, and they frequently make policy recommendations. These recommendations can be influenced by both their research findings and their values. All of this is fine, as long as the principle of *sharing* is followed. The scientific community can thus debate the interpretations, the policy recommendations, and even the appropriateness of the topic for study. Such debate strengthens rather than weakens science, and for this reason few people today argue that science can or should be totally value-free.

## The Relationship between Theory and Research

Science consists of a cycle that includes observation (research), generalization, explanation, and prediction. This leads to a new round of the cycle, which may begin with new research to test the predictions generated from the previous round. This cycle is illustrated in Figure 2–1. This diagram illustrates the reciprocal relationship between research and theory. Research findings are most meaningful when considered in the context of a theory, which *explains* the findings by proposing cause-effect relationships that can account for them. Similarly, theory is of little use unless it can be shown by research to be correct, at least under some specified set of conditions (Lieberson, 1992, p. 4).

**Explanation versus Prediction** Consider the top half of Figure 3–1, which shows research being used to *generate* theory. Here a research finding is obtained and is found to be generally true, and a theory is then developed to *explain* it. Jiobu (1988) used this method of reasoning to develop a theory to explain the relatively high income of Japanese Americans. Compared with most other racial minority groups in the United States—even compared with much of the white majority group—Japanese Americans on the average have high levels of income and education. How did the Japanese succeed where others could not? Jiobu developed a theory that their success was based in part on their ability to gain control of certain segments of the California vegetable industry—including tomatoes, asparagus, and spinach—that required high levels of labor but little land to produce, and had wide market demand that extended far beyond the Japanese-American market.

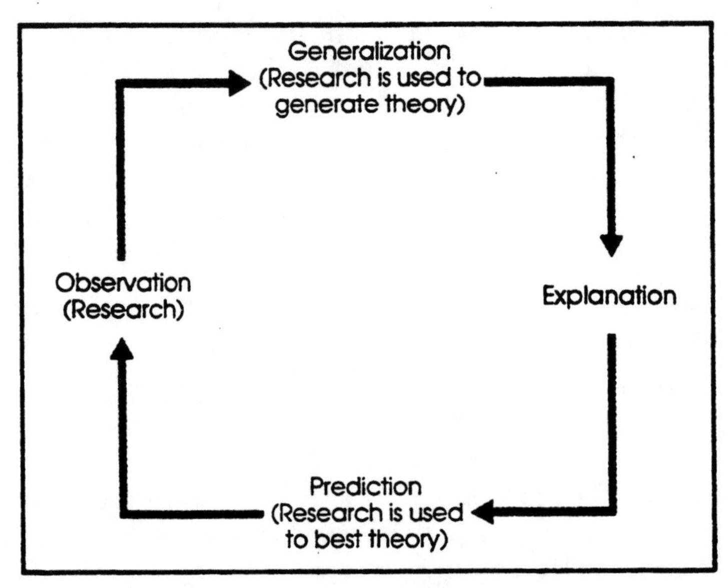


**FIGURE 3–1 The Cycle of Scientific Inquiry**

Now, consider the bottom half of the figure. Here, research is being used to *test* theory. The theory predicts a particular result, and the scientist does the research to see if the predicted result can be obtained. Again, the ethnic group success example can be used to illustrate this procedure. Jiobu's theory predicts that *any* ethnic group that gains control of an industry that produces a product for which there is a wide market should experience success to a greater extent than other ethnic groups. An obvious way to test this theory is to examine the economic history of a wide variety of ethnic groups. If we were to do such a study and find that, consistently, ethnic groups that at some point in history gained control of such an industry today have higher incomes than comparable groups that did not gain control of such an industry, we would have an important piece of evidence in support of Jiobu's theory. If, however, we found no difference in the average incomes of ethnic groups that did and did not gain control of such an industry at some time in the past, we would probably conclude that Jiobu's theory was wrong.

As shown in Figure 3.1, the relationship between theory and research works two ways. Sometimes, as in the top half of the figure, scientists do research in order to develop theories, or develop theories in order to explain a research finding. In this case, the scientists are engaging in a process of *explanation,* or *theory generation.* Other times, as in the bottom half of the figure, scientists do research in order to test a theory. In this case, the scientists do research in order to test a theory. In this case, the scientists are engaging in a process of *prediction,* or *theory testing.*

**Research and Theory Testing** When social scientists use research for theory testing, they usually make use of a **hypothesis,** a single testable statement about reality that is developed for the purpose of testing a piece of a theory. A hypothesis always takes the form of a statement, not a question. It usually involves some kind of cause-effect relationship between two or more variables. (Some examples of hypotheses, as well as related examples that are not hypotheses, are shown in the box entitled "Which Ones Are Hypotheses?") The reason a hypothesis is used is that a theory is usually too large and complex to test at one time. Hence, scientists test one part of the theory at a time and develop a hypothesis. A hypothesis, then, may be thought of as an educated guess, based on a theory, of what finding a research project will obtain. When research is done for the purpose of theory testing, the scientist develops a hypothesis from a theory, then conducts research to see whether the actual evidence obtained is consistent with the hypothesis.

## SOCIOLOGICAL INSIGHTS

### WHICH ONES ARE HYPOTHESES?

Now that you've been introduced to the concept of a hypothesis and have seen an example of one, consider the following examples and decide whether each is or is not a hypothesis.

1. Are older people more conservative than younger people?
2. The membership will have greater influence in organizations that regularly change their leadership than in organizations that do not.
3. People should always strive to please others.
4. There is no difference in the innate intellectual ability of men and women.
5. As people's level of education increases, their level of prejudice tends to decrease.

Now turn to the next page to see the answers.

**A CASE STUDY: DURKHEIM ON SUICIDE** This process can be illustrated by the first sociological study conducted according to the scientific model, Emile Durkheim's *Suicide* (1964 [orig. 1897]). Durkheim sought to explain why some people commit suicide while others don't. He developed the theory that suicide was often the result of isolation or lack of social integration. This theory suggests several hypotheses. If we can identify groups of people who are more individualistic and less integrated into some type of group life, we would expect such people to have a higher rate of suicide. Durkheim identified three such groups of people: Protestants, men, and unmarried people. Protestant religions emphasize an individual relationship with God rather than the community orientation stressed by Catholics and Jews. Men are expected to be "strong" and do things on their own, whereas the traditional females role emphasizes family and community relationship. Unmarried people may be alone much of the time and often do not have the kinds of relationships that married people have with their spouse and (usually) children.

Thus, Durkheim developed three hypotheses: Suicide rates would be higher among Protestants than among Catholics and Jews, higher among men than among women, and higher among unmarried than among married people. He then tested the hypotheses by examining data archives on suicide cases and computing suicide rates for different categories of the population in several European countries. As he expected, he found higher suicide rates among Protestants, men, and unmarried people than among Catholics and Jews, women, and married people. These findings supported his hypotheses. Moreover, they offered an important piece of evidence in support of his larger theory.

Usually no single study suffices to accept or reject a theory. At best, it will support or refute a few hypotheses that are derived from, or consistent with, a theory. Still, each confirmed hypothesis adds support to a theory (as in the case of Durkheim's theory about the causes of suicide), and if enough hypotheses relating to a theory are confirmed on a consistent basis, the theory will come to be widely supported. In the case of Durkheim's theory, the notion of isolation and disconnection from others as a cause of suicide has become widely accepted among sociologists. This is because (1) Durkheim and others have confirmed a number of hypotheses, all of which are consistent with the theory; and (2) many of the hypothesized relationships have held up consistently over time and in a number of different societies. Although Durkheim conducted his research in a number of European nations during the nineteenth century, similar patterns can be found in the United States today. American males today, for example, remain much more likely than American females to commit suicide. Also, church members in

## SOCIOLOGICAL INSIGHTS

### WHICH ONES ARE HYPOTHESES? THE ANSWERS

Here are the answers to the quiz on the preceding page:

1. This is not a hypothesis. A hypothesis must always be a statement, and this is a question. A question can never be a hypothesis.
2. This is a hypothesis. Assuming that we could develop a reasonable measure of membership influence, we could compare organizations that do and do not regularly change their leadership to determine whether this statement is true.
3. This statement is a value judgment. To some people, pleasing others is important; to others, it is not. What is *good,* or what *should be,* cannot be determined scientifically. Hypotheses deal only with what *is.*
4. This is a hypothesis. This hypothesis proposes that there is *no* relationship between sex and intellectual ability, which is just as acceptable in a hypothesis as to propose that there is a relationship. Sometimes a hypothesis that there is *no* relationship between two things is called a *null hypothesis.* The hypothesis in this example could be tested by comparing the scores of males and females on various tests of intellectual ability—preferably at a young age when social factors have had the least possible influence.
5. This is a hypothesis. It could be tested by applying some measure of prejudice to people of various educational levels.

the United States have lower suicide rates than do nonmembers, and married people are less likely to commit suicide than are divorced people (Breault, 1986, 1988).

**Research and Theory Generation** Researchers who are interested in topics about which there is no well-developed theory are likely to engage in research for the purpose of *theory generation.* The main purpose of such research is to develop some theory to explain some pattern of behavior. Rather than use a hypothesis to predict the research result, the researcher conducts research as a way of *generating* or developing hypotheses that can then be used to build a theory.

**Fascism: A Case Study** An example of this can be seen in the research of Theodor Adorno, Else Frenkel-Brunswick, and others (1950) concerning *fascism.* Adorno, who fled Germany to escape the Nazis, was interested in why people would support a movement like Nazism. Because Nazism and fascism were very recent developments at the time, no sizable body of theory on these subjects existed. Thus, researchers had to either develop their own theory or adopt theories about related topics that might be relevant to fascism. They reasoned that some clues to the thinking of people who supported fascism might be found in the speeches and writings of Nazi leaders. Thus, they analyzed these speeches and writings for common themes. Assuming that personality need might be relevant to support for the Nazis, they particularly looked for themes that appeared regularly even though they were not directly related to fascism's political message. They found a number of such themes, including superstition, stereotyped thinking, simplistic good/bad categorization, aggression against non-conformers, and cynicism. These same themes appeared repeatedly in the speeches and writings of Nazis, fascists, Ku Klux Klan members, and other right-wing extremists. This led researchers to hypothesize that a personality test could be developed to predict intolerance of the type practiced by such extremists. They developed such a test and found that people with the personality traits measured by the test were indeed more prejudiced against racial and religious minority groups. The purpose of their initial analysis of the speeches and writings of extremists, however, was simply to generate the hypothesis, not to test it.

# STEPS IN A SOCIAL RESEARCH PROJECT

In any social-science research project, a certain sequence of steps must be followed. These steps vary somewhat depending upon whether the objective of the research is to generate hypotheses or to test hypotheses. These steps are outlined in a general form in Figure 3–2 and are discussed in greater detail in the following pages.

## Defining the Research Problem

Regardless of whether a social scientist is interested in theory testing or theory generation, the first (and perhaps most important) step in any research project is to define clearly the problem the researcher wishes to study. Thus scientists usually begin by stating a question that the research is intended to answer. In our first example, Durkheim asked whether sex, religion, and marital status—all of which he thought were linked to isolation or individualism—were correlated to suicide rates. This was a form of theory testing. In our second example, the researchers asked if there were common themes in the writings of fascists which might point to a personality pattern associated with fascism. In this instance research was used for theory generation. In both types of research it is important to clearly identify the research problem or question. Doing so helps the researcher limit his or her inquiries to things that are relevant to answering the question. In other words, the research problem gives definition or focus to the entire research project. Although a good, clear definition of the problem does not guarantee a successful research project, the absence of a clear definition often results in a bad one.

In order to define a problem researched, the researcher must be thoroughly familiar with theory and past research concerning the chosen topic. A good research question will usually accomplish one of two things. If the mode of research is theory testing, the question will suggest some hypothesis to be tested, which will help to confirm or disconfirm some part of a theory. If the purpose is to generate theory, the objective will be to look for some pattern or regularity that might serve as the basis for a theory or hypothesis. Neither objective can be accomplished, however, without a thorough knowledge of what is already known, what is plausible but unconfirmed, what is already disproved, and what is uncharted territory.

## Identifying and Defining Variables

As previously stated, social scientists are interested in cause and effect. To measure cause and effect they use *variables.* A **variable** is any concept that can take on different values or that has two or more categories. In other words, the concept can *vary* among the different values or categories. Temperature is a variable, as are age and income. All of them vary from time to time in the same people and places, as well as between people or places. These variables can be expressed as numbers—75 degrees, $50,000, or 18 years old. Other variables cannot be expressed as numbers. Religion and ethnicity are examples of this type of variable. Religion, for example, can be classified as Protestant, Catholic, Jewish, Muslim, or "all other." However, none of these categories is "more" or "greater" than another in the sense that $50,000 is more than $25,000. They are simply different categories. Beginning students sometimes confuse categories of variables with the variables themselves. Protestant, Catholic, Jewish, Muslim, and "all other" are *not* variables. They are simply *categories* of the same variable, religion.

**Independent Variables** Social-science research typically involves cause-effect relationships among variables. Similarly, most hypotheses concern such relationships. Some variables in the social sciences represent causes, others represent effects. In a hypothesis or a research project, a variable that the researcher thinks is a *cause* is called an **independent variable** (or sometimes, a *predictor variable).* In a study involving a relationship between two variables, then, the independent variable is the variable that the researcher thinks influences the other variable or precedes it in time.

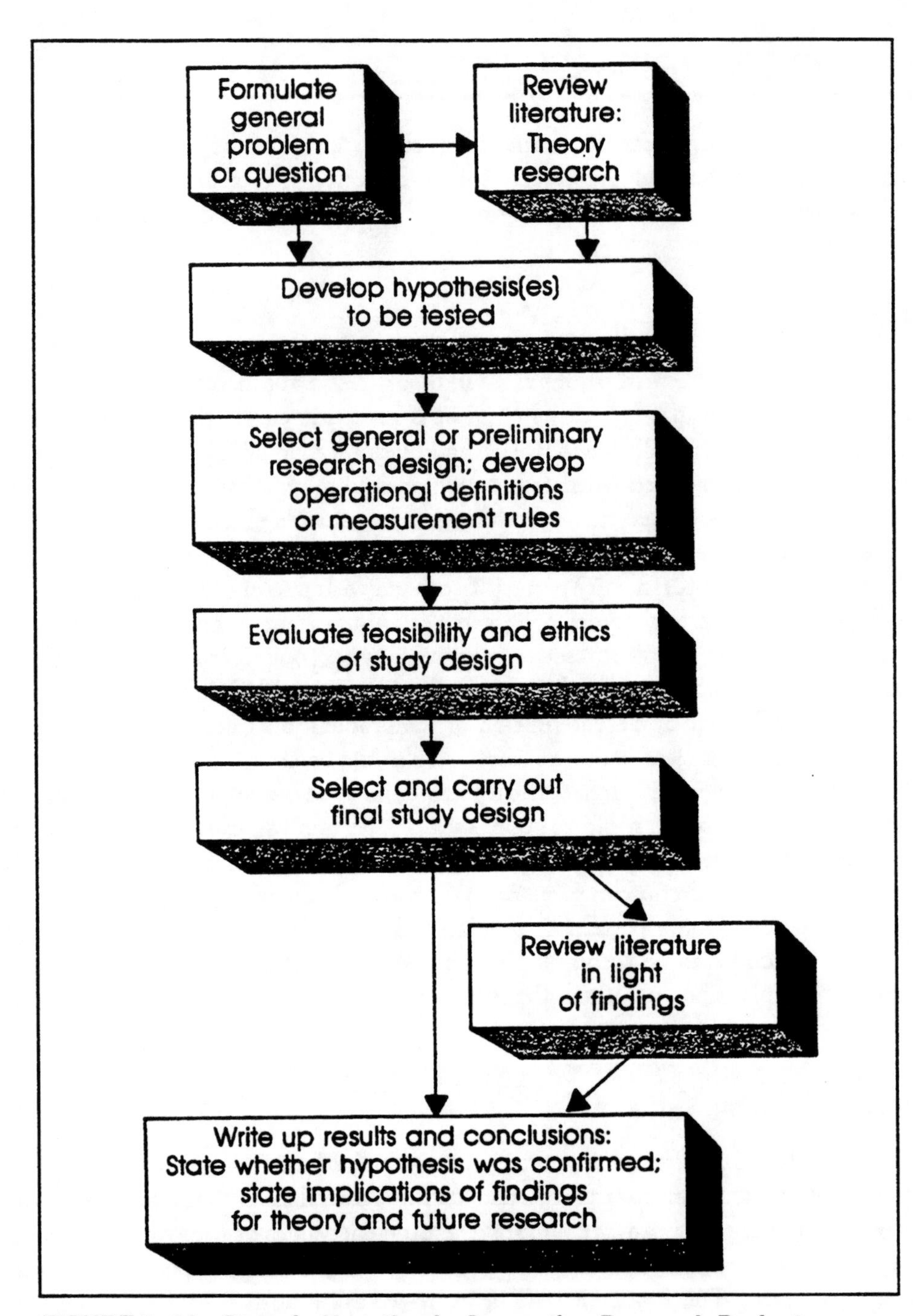


**FIGURE 3–2A Steps in Hypothesis-Generation Research Projects**

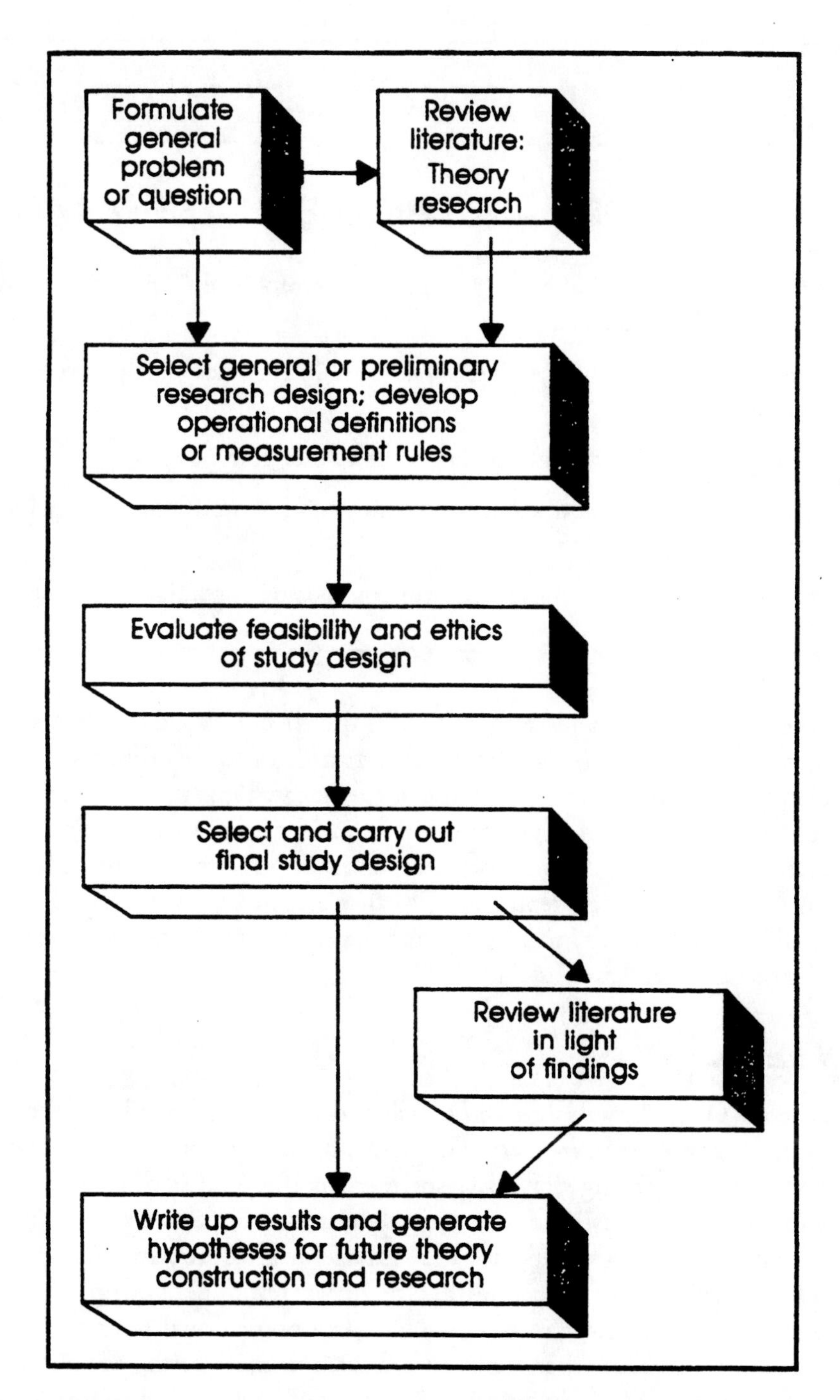


**FIGURE 3–2B Steps in Hypothesis-Testing Research Projects**

## SOCIOLOGICAL INSIGHTS

### IDENTIFYING INDEPENDENT AND DEPENDENT VARIABLES

Listed below are three examples of hypotheses or research problems. What are the independent and dependent variables in each example?

1. A researcher wishes to test the hypothesis that Catholics are more likely to vote Democratic than Protestants.
2. A criminologist wants to find out whether crime results from poverty.
3. A group of students debates whether it does any good to study for the Graduate Record Examination (GRE).

Now turn to page 55 to discover the independent and dependent variables in each example.

**Dependent Variables** A variable that a researcher thinks is the effect is called the **dependent variable.** This variable is thought to follow the independent variable in time or to be influenced by the independent variable. It is called the dependent variable because, if the researcher is right, its value in part *depends on* the value of the independent variable. If education is the independent variable and income is the dependent variable, for example, then a person's income depends, in part, on the amount of education that he or she has. In this example, education represents the cause and income the effect. For more examples—and to see how well you can identify independent and dependent variables—see the box entitled "Identifying Independent and Dependent Variables."

## Measuring Variables

**Operational Definitions** Once the variables to be included in a study have been decided upon, the researcher must decide on how to *measure* them. The precise means by which the variables will be measured depends on the type of study being done. Measurement is the process of determining the value of a variable. This is accomplished by using an **operational definition,** a precise statement of the meaning of a variable or of the categories of a variable for the purpose of measurement. An operational definition of income could be "the adjusted gross income that the survey respondent claims to have reported on his or her income tax form for the most recent tax year." In observational research, the racial categories white, black, Asian, Hispanic, and other might be defined according to the observer's judgment: A person is white if the observer in the study judges him or her to be white, and so forth.

There is no "right" or "wrong" way to define a variable operationally. Take, for example, the operational definition of a Jewish person. If a researcher were interested in the effects of religious identity, anyone who considers himself or herself to be Jewish might be defined as Jewish. If the researcher were interested in the effect of religious participation, a Jewish person might be operationally defined as someone who has attended temple on the Sabbath at least once within the past month. Neither operational definition is "right" or "wrong"; they just capture different aspects of what it means to be Jewish.

Although any variable can be operationally defined in several ways, all operational definitions *must* be clear and unambiguous. We would not, for example, want to define as Jewish "anyone who believes in the Jewish faith." That definition is too ambiguous because it does not tell us how to decide who believes in the Jewish faith and who doesn't.

## SOCIOLOGICAL INSIGHTS

### IDENTIFYING INDEPENDENT AND DEPENDENT VARIABLES: ANSWERS

Here are the answers to the quiz on identifying independent and dependent variables that appeared on page 54.

1. The independent variable is religion (whether one is Protestant or Catholic), and the dependent variable is voting preference. Because people are usually born into a religious affiliation and develop their political preferences later, religion would be the independent variable because it normally comes first in time.
2. Because the question clearly specified crime as the result, the incidence or amount of crime is the dependent variable; poverty or lack thereof is the independent variable.
3. Presumably, what the students are debating is whether studying raises one's GRE score. Therefore, the independent variable is whether one studies (or how much one studies), where as the dependent variable is the source on the GRE.

**Validity and Reliability** However we measure our variables, two conditions must be met for successful measurement: validity and reliability. Reliability is the easier of the two to assess. **Reliability** refers to consistency in measurement. When a given variable is measured several times, do we get the same result? If we ask the same person his or her race several times and get different answers each time, we clearly have a reliability problem. Similarly, if we have five questions in a survey intended to measure social class, and every question produces different results in the same individuals, the reliability of our instrument is poor: Questions that are supposed to be measuring the same thing are in fact measuring different things.

Even if we have good reliability, we may have a problem of poor validity. **Validity** refers to measuring correctly the concept we intend to measure. Consider an example. You are using a yardstick to measure the width of a desk. You see that the width of the desk is exactly two times the length with the yardstick. You can measure the desk 20 times, and you will get the same result each time. However, you didn't notice that your "yardstick" is really a meter stick. Your measurement is therefore *not valid.* The desk is wider than you thought, because it is really 2 meters wide, not 2 yards wide.

As a practical matter, validity is much harder to assess than reliability. Social scientists look for clues that support the validity of their measures, but in some instances they can never be sure. This is particularly true when they are attempting to measure some abstract concept, such as intelligence, happiness, or power. Sociologists refer to such concepts as **constructs** because, to some extent, their precise meaning must be constructed by the researcher. They are too abstract to measure directly. Take the case of intelligence tests. Are they valid measures of intelligence? Well, just what is intelligence? We could define it as the ability to learn. That is a reasonable definition, but there is no way to measure this ability directly. It is a truism among educators that some people don't work up to their ability. Yet, all we can measure directly is what people know or can do at some point in time—and in one way or another, that is what all intelligence tests measure.

We cannot directly judge the validity of intelligence tests because we have no way to measure intelligence precisely and directly. We can get some hints about the validity of such tests, though. If a new intelligence test produced similar results to several existing tests of intelligence, we would have more faith in its validity than if it did not. Similarly, we would have more faith in the test of those who score high on it get better grades in school than those who score low. Even in these cases, however, questions of validity would remain. Perhaps all the tests are measuring social class, not intelligence, and children from higher social classes do better in school. If this were the case, our test could give similar results to other tests and predict school grades, but still not be measuring intelligence.

## Identifying Cause-Effect Relationships

Consider a situation in which a scientist is trying to find out whether a cause-effect relationship exists between two variables. Let us call the independent variable the *presumed cause* and the dependent variable the *presumed effect.* How does the scientist decide whether or not such a cause-effect relationship exists? In other words, how do we determine whether the independent variable causes the dependent variable? Basically, the scientist must ask three questions. The first is: "Is there *correlation* between the two variables?" The second is: "Is the *time order* correct?" If the answers to these questions are both "yes," the scientist then asks: "Are there any *alternative explanations* for the observed correlation?" Let us consider each question in more detail.

**Correlation** The term **correlation** means that when the independent variable changes, the dependent variable also has a tendency to change. Consider again the first two examples from the box on independent and dependent variables. In the first example, the hypothesis was that Catholics are more likely to vote Democratic than Protestants. Suppose you conducted an exit poll at a presidential election and found that a higher percentage of Catholics than Protestants reported voting for the Democratic candidate. Such a finding would be an example of correlation: There was a difference in the voting patterns of Catholics and Protestants. Similarly, in the second example, crime statistics showed a higher incident of crime in poor neighborhoods. You would again have evidence of correlation: Crime rates do correlate with poverty. Conversely, if you found no difference between the voting patterns of Catholics and Protestants or no difference in crime statistics between middle-class and poor neighborhoods, you would have an absence of correlation. In such situations you would usually conclude that there is no cause-effect relationship between the variables. Some reports of scientific studies use the terms *covariation* or *statistical relationship*. These terms mean the same thing as correlation.

**Positive and Negative Correlation** Correlation can be *positive* (direct) or *negative* (inverse). Consider the example in the box concerning the relationship between studying and GRE scores. In this example, the hypothesis assumes that the more you study, the higher your score. If research showed this to be true, there would be a *positive* relationship between the amount of studying and the score. In other words, as one variable increases, the other also increases. In contrast, a researcher investigating the example of poverty and crime might find that as people's incomes rise, the likelihood of their committing certain crimes decreases. In this case, where one variable (income) increases, the other (crime rate) decreases. This is a *negative* relationship.

Correlation alone is never enough to prove a cause-effect relationship between the independent variable and the dependent variable. Consider the following example. The more hospital beds a city has, the more deaths it will have each year. If you compare all American cities, you will find that this correlation is true. However, it does *not* mean that having more hospital beds will cause more people to die. Rather, larger cities have more hospital beds because they have more people, and for the same reason, they also have more deaths. This is why we must answer the other two questions: Is the time order between the variables correct, and are there any alternative explanations for the correlation between the two variables?

**Time Order** If correlation between two variables is established, the next step in trying to determine whether the independent variable causes the dependent variable is to determine whether the variables occurred in the correct time order. This step is very simple: *The cause must happen before the effect.* Something taking place today cannot cause something that happened yesterday. As we previously pointed out, religious affiliations generally is acquired before political preference. Hence, it is reasonable to argue that religious affiliation could cause or influence political preference; it is not plausible to argue the contrary. Sometimes in social research it is very clear which variable came first, but in other cases the social scientist must make a judgment. In general, when correlation exists between two variables, the researcher must

## SOCIOLOGICAL INSIGHTS

### SORTING OUT CAUSE-EFFECT RELATIONSHIPS: SINGLE-PARENT HOMES AND TEENAGE PARENTHOOD

How sociologists sort out cause-effect relationships using control variables can be illustrated by the findings of a study of the effect of parental absence resulting from separation or divorce (the independent variable) on teenage parenthood (the dependent variable) (McLanahan and Bumpass, 1988). We know that teenage girls from single-parent homes are more likely than other girls to have babies. But is it because they are from *single-parent families,* or is it because of other aspects of their *social background?* People from low-income families, for example, have above-average divorce and separation rates, and therefore their children frequently grow up in single-parent families. At the same time, growing up poor may by itself put a person at a high risk of teenage parenthood. Thus, to determine whether growing up in a one-parent family "causes" a higher rate of teenage parenthood, we must introduce one or more *control variables.* (We shall slightly simplify the McLanahan and Bumpass study by combining their social background and education variables into one control variable.)

The diagrams below illustrate two possibilities. In Example 1, the relationship is spurious: There is no cause-effect relationship between growing up in a single-parent home and teenage parenthood. There is a statistical relationship between the two variables *only* because people of certain social backgrounds are more likely to grow up in single-parent homes *and* to have babies as teenagers. This spurious relationship is represented by a dotted line, while the true cause-effect relationship are represented by solid arrows. In this example, there is no relationship between growing up in a single-parent home and teenage parenthood *among people whose social background is otherwise similar.*

In Example 2, there is a real cause-effect relationship between growing up in a single-parent home and teenage parenthood. In this example, the relationship between growing up in a single-parent home and teen parenthood remains present even among people with similar backgrounds. Introducing a control variable does not eliminate the covariation between the independent variable (single-parent home) and the dependent variable (teenage parenthood). Thus, there is a solid arrow between single-parent home and teenage parenthood. The arrow between social background and teenage parenthood has a question mark because in this case a cause-effect relationship might or might not exist.

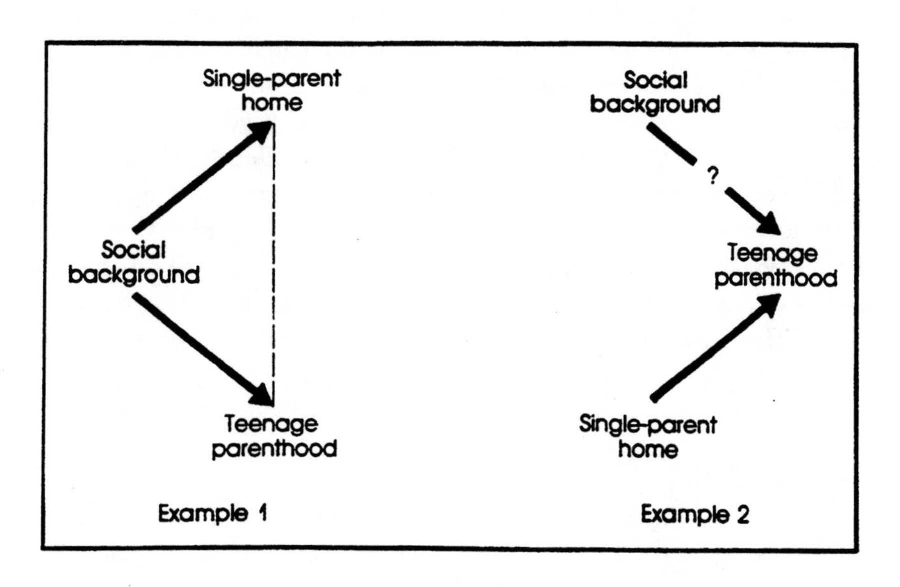

What did the study actually find? It found that even among people with similar backgrounds, those who grew up in single-parent families were more likely to have babies as teenagers. In the population as a whole, white teenagers who grew up in one-parent families were 111 percent more likely than other white teenagers to give birth as teens. Among those whose social background and education were similar, those from one-parent homes were 58 percent more likely to give birth. Among black teenagers, the difference was 50 percent in the whole population and 36 percent for those with similar education and background. Thus, for both races, the control variables of education and background explained away only part of the relationship between growing up in a one-parent home and having a baby as a teenager. In this case, Example 2 was the correct choice.

determine the time order of the two variables. If evidence indicates that the presumed cause came before the presumed effect, the scientist can move on to address the question of alternative explanations. If there is no such plausible evidence, the scientist will probably conclude that the independent variable is *not* causing or influencing the dependent variable.

**Eliminating Alternative Explanations** Once a social scientist has established correlation and correct time order between two variables, the remaining task is to ask whether anything else—some third variable or combination of variables—could be causing the correlation without the independent variable actually causing or influencing the dependent variable. Consider again the example of religion and voting preference. As the example has been stated, we have correlation (the exit poll showed that Catholics were more likely to vote Democratic than Protestants), and we have correct time order (religious affiliation is usually acquired before political preference). We still cannot conclude that being Catholic by itself has any effect on voting, however. We must consider *alternative explanations* for the relationship we have observed. Consider, for example, the possibility that Catholics as a group have lower incomes than Protestants. If this were true, it could be income, not religion, that is influencing voting preference. In general, people of lower incomes *are* more likely to vote Democratic, and people of higher incomes *are* more likely to vote Republican. If Catholics did have lower average incomes than Protestants, they would than be more likely to vote Democratic, even if religion by itself had no effect on voting.

How would we know whether religion made any difference in voting if Protestants had higher incomes than Catholics? We would have to compare Catholics and Protestants *with the same income.* If, among Catholics and Protestants with the same income, the Catholics were still more likely to vote Democratic, we would be more likely to conclude that religion has a cause-effect relationship with voting. If, however, Catholics and Protestants of the same income were equally likely to vote Democratic, we would conclude that religion has no effect on income and that the original correlation was *spurious;* that is, it was a product of a third variable. In other words, an alternative explanation—income differences between Catholics and Protestants—accounted for the relationship.

**Control Variables** In the example above, income was introduced as a **control variable.** A control variable is a third variable that is introduced to determine whether the relationship between the independent variable and the dependent variable can be accounted for by an alternative explanation. In this example, we wanted to know whether the correlation between religion and voting preference represented a true cause-effect relationship or whether it was merely a product of income differences between Catholics and Protestants. We answered this question by introducing income as a *control variable.* In the box "Sorting Out Cause-Effect Relationships," you can see how a control variable was used in a real sociological study.

## Interpretation and Dissemination

The final stage in a research project is to interpret and disseminate the findings. This process involves writing up the results and making them available to others. Professional sociologists do this by publishing books, reports, and journal articles, and by presenting research papers at professional meetings. You might do it by submitting a paper to your instructor. In addition to describing the results, this process involves interpreting them: *Why* did the researcher get the results she or he obtained? Sometimes—particularly when the purpose of the research was to test a hypothesis, all of the appropriate control variables were included, and the hypothesis was confirmed—the meaning of the findings seems quite clear. If the hypothesis was not supported by the data, of course, the question becomes "Why not?" In other cases, the objective is to generate hypotheses, and this, by its very nature, requires interpretation of the findings. Interpretation takes the researcher full circle, because once again he or she must use theory and past research to make a judgment about what interpretations are plausible. Once an interpretation has been offered, an addition has been made to existing theory. A new cycle of theory and research can now begin, as the same researcher or other researchers develop and test hypotheses arising from the interpretation.

For a real-life example of this, see "Personal Journey into Sociology: Joan McCord."

## KEY RESEARCH METHODS IN SOCIOLOGY

The principles discussed thus far in this chapter are applicable to all of the social sciences, and often to the natural sciences as well. Now we shall narrow our focus somewhat to consider the particular research methods that are used in sociology. Once a sociologist has selected a research problem and reviewed the sociological literature to identify theories and past research that relate to the topic, the next task is to design and carry out the research. Sociologists use four major approaches to research: *experiments, surveys, field observation,* and *analysis of existing data.*

## EXPERIMENTS

An **experiment** is research that is carried out in a situation, such as a laboratory or classroom, that is under the control of the researcher. In an experiment, the researcher changes or manipulates the independent variable, tries to keep everything else constant, and measures the dependent variable before and after the change in the independent variable. Suppose, for example, that a researcher wanted to find out if seeing a movie advocating tolerance would reduce people's levels of racial prejudice. The researcher could give a group of people a questionnaire measuring prejudice, show them the movie, then give them the scale again to see if their attitudes had changed. If they had, there would be evidence both of correlation between seeing the movie and prejudice score and of correct time order.

### Experimental and Control Groups

To be really confident of their results, however, researchers must use not one, but two groups of people in their experiments. One group, called the **experimental group,** goes through an experience like that described above. They are given a "before" measure of the dependent variable (called the *pretest),* the independent variable is changed or manipulated (as in the showing of the movie), and the dependent variable is measured again (the *posttest).* The other group, the **control group,** goes through the pretest and posttest, but there is no manipulation of the independent variable. In the example above, the *control group* would be given the "before" and "after" prejudice questionnaire but would *not* be shown the movie. Why is this necessary? Without the control group, the scientist would have no way of knowing whether people's attitudes changed because of seeing the movie or for some other reason. It could be, for example, that their attitudes changed because answering the questionnaire made them think in ways that changed their minds. Using the control group eliminates this alternative explanation because that group also took the questionnaire twice. If the experimental group (the group that saw the movie) changed more than the

## PERSONAL JOURNEY INTO SOCIOLOGY

### CHANGING TIMES / JOAN McCORD, Ph.D.

The year 1956 was a beginning of sorts, for me. That was the year H. L. A. Hart was teaching a seminar on Causation and the Law. One day, several of us spent hours arguing that it was impossible to know more than that events were or were not "conjoined." Hart suddenly reached for a heavy glass ashtray and slid it across the table against the stomach of Henry Aiken, a human. "I caused that!" he announced. Heart's shove ensued the challenge that drove my interest in longitudinal research.

How can we learn that one thing causes another? Despite the appeal of radical skepticism, it was impossible to reject the idea that at least sometimes, people cause things to happen. And, as Hart's gesture indicated, detection of causal relations cannot be entirely dependent on perceiving constancy of conjunction. Hart had not previously shoved anything across the conference table—much less an ashtray. Yet it seemed clear that Hart had been the cause of his colleague's pain. We had seen Hart touching the ashtray; the touching had preceded the ashtray's movement; and we could follow the trail as the ashtray crossed the table en route to Aikin's stomach. Temporal priority seemed to be central to the causal relationship.

Also in 1956, I became a Research Assistant at Palfrey House, the study center for Child Psychology at Harvard. My first assignment introduced me to the Human Relations Area Files then being created. I was asked to code for the child-rearing section of these cross-cultural resources. Fascinating anecdotes. We were supposed to classify societies on the basis of reports for which, often, only one or two cases had been described. I could not overcome my doubts about generalizing from what might well be atypical families or erroneous reports. We were to rate cultures on such things as maternal warmth, use of physical punishment, and permissiveness of aggression. After classifying a culture on a particular dimension, we recorded our confidence in the rating as representing a picture of the society. My constant rating of "doubtful" led to a reassignment! I became Eleanor Maccoby's research assistant.

Data for the classic Sears, Mccoby, and Levin study had been collected by asking parents to describe their children and to respond to questions about their own child-rearing techniques. The source of information both for the child's behavior and for the home environment had been the mother. Alternative explanations for the relationships were equally plausible. Although mothers might be accurately reporting their own and their children's behavior, for example, their reports might merely reflect justifications of their behavior. Alternatively, the reports of both sets of data could be reflections of different biases about idealized parent-child relationships. At least partly to overcome these problems, we were coding children's behavior from an independent source: the children's "doll play." Doll play had been developed as a technique for understanding how children perceived the world. The children in the Sears, Maccoby, and Levin study had told stories using dolls to represent their families. The measure assumed that a child identified with a doll assigned the same sex as the child. We were measuring conscience by counting punishing events for which the cause was unknown.

A few months earlier, Gordon Allport had asked William and me to reevaluate The Cambridge-Somerville Youth Study, a program designed to prevent delinquency. The Cambridge-Somerville Youth Study had included random assignment of high-risk children to treatment and control groups. Almost a decade earlier, Edwin Powers and Helen Witmer had evaluated the program and concluded that no beneficial effect had been demonstrated. Hoping to understand the development of conscience, we extended our work beyond comparing the randomly assigned treated and control groups.

On December 10, 1956, I put the finishing touches on our book *Origins of Crime*. Then I went to the hospital to deliver the first of our two sons.

Although 1956 marks an important beginning for me, my interest in studying society began, of course, much earlier. As a child, I had to cope with understanding why people threw snowballs with rocks inside—calling "Jew, Jew"—as I walked home from first grade. We moved from Scarsdale to New York City to Tucson, Arizona. I was perpetually an "outsider."

My high school boyfriend and I were married as Stanford undergraduates and went to Harvard together. I taught elementary school while my husband earned his Ph.D. Just as my turn came to complete graduate school, my husband was invited to become Assistant Dean of Humanities and Sciences at Stanford.

Upon our return from a year in France in 1961 I resumed studies aiming toward a Ph.D. in Philosophy. At about that time, our marriage broke down. I struggled to keep food on the table. Without a Ph.D., I could not get the positions for which my experience and training had qualified me; yet employers will unwilling to hire me in assistant positions because, they said, "You will be bored." Finally in 1965, the National Institute of Mental Health funded my return to graduate school I earned a Ph.D. in Sociology, from Stanford, in 1968.

During these years the boys from the Cambridge-Somerville Youth Study had become middle-aged. During the 1950s, I had directed coding of the records describing family interactions. These records included detailed information about how fathers, mother, and siblings interacted. The lure of discovering delayed benefits of treatment—which I fully expected—in combination with the possibility of a more adequate study of the influence of child rearing on adult behavior drove me and a small cadre of assistants to retrace the group although 30 years had passed without contact. We learned that self-reports of benefits from treatment were untrustworthy. Despite their descriptions of how the treatment had been beneficial, men in the treatment group actually turned out worse than those in the matched control group. The early records have proved their value in showing that child-rearing differences predict many features of adult behavior. I am still working with the mountains of data produced from this retracing.

control group, it was clearly influenced by something more than just taking the test—most likely by the movie.

Of course, other possibilities exist. Perhaps the people in the experimental group were more easily persuaded than the people in the control group and thus were more likely to change their minds. Fortunately, there is also a way of dealing with problems like this, which involve preexisting differences between the people in the two groups. It is important in experiments that people in the experimental group be as similar as possible in all respects to people in the control group. The safest way to ensure this is to have large experimental and control groups (100 or more) and to assign people *randomly* between the groups. This will ensure that the groups are similar in all respects. If this cannot be done, the next best thing is to see that people in the two groups are similar with respect to any social characteristics that the researcher considers important, such as age, sex, race, and education level.

## Reactivity in Experimental Research

The experimental research design described here, sometimes called the "classic experimental design," is outlined in Table 3.1. This design eliminates possible effects of preexisting differences between the groups, of taking the pretest and posttest. Thus, it narrows considerably the number of explanations for any differences between the two groups in the degree to which the dependent variable changes between the pretest and the posttest. When such differences are found in this experimental design, there is strong reason to suppose that the cause of the change is the independent variable—though this cannot be proved conclusively in most cases. Why not? Because there is still the potential problem of *reactivity*. It is possible, for example, that nobody's attitudes really changed, but that subjects wanted to please the researcher, and that those who saw the movie advocating tolerance were tipped off to what the researcher "wanted." Hence, they could have reported greater tolerance on the posttest, not because they had really changed their minds, but rather because they thought that was what the researcher wanted them to do. This behavior is an example of what is known as the **Hawthorne effect.** Researchers usually cannot be completely sure when their results are being influenced by the Hawthorne effect or by other types of reactivity. By being alert to the possibility, however, they can often detect it and interpret their findings accordingly.

**TABLE 3.1 The Classic Experimental Design**

| Step | Experimental Group | Control Group |
|---|---|---|
| 1. Random assignment of subjects between groups | Yes | Yes |
| 2. Pretest (measurement of dependent variable) | Yes | Yes |
| 3. Change or manipulation of independent variable | Yes | No |
| 4. Posttest (measurement of dependent variable) | Yes | Yes |

## Field Experiments

Although true experiments are conducted in situations where the researcher can control all the elements, the experimental technique is sometimes taken into situations not fully under the control of researchers, in an approach called *field experiments.*

**Natural Experiments** Two common types of field experiments are natural experiments and social experiments. *Natural experiments* use pretests and posttests with naturally occurring events to assess the effects of such events on some dependent variable. My own Ph.D. dissertation can serve as an example of a natural experiment. I was interested in the effect of different types of housing on children's day-to-day activities. I was permitted to use data from a survey conducted at the University of Toronto (Michelson, 1977), which had asked questions of both children and their parents about their daily activities before and after they moved into either single-family houses or high-rise apartments. By so doing, I was able to compare the activities of children both before (pretest) and after (posttest) they moved into one type of housing or the other. In this example, the naturally occurring event of the family's move substituted for the manipulation of the independent variable that would have taken place in a true experiment.

**Social Experiments** In *social experiments,* some type of social policy is tried out in a real-life setting, and a pretest, posttest, and control group are used to assess its effects. An example of this can be seen in the federal government's Housing Allowance Experiment of the mid-1970s (U.S. Department of Housing and Urban Development, 1979). In this study, low-income families in the experimental group were given housing allowances—money to be used for the purpose of helping them pay for their housing. In pretests and posttests, the amount of money spent on housing by the experimental and control groups was measured to see if the people in the experimental group used their housing allowances to increase what they spent on housing and thereby increase the quality of their housing. For the most part, the experiment found that they did not. Instead, by paying for their housing with the housing allowance, they freed up personal funds to cover other expenses.

## SOCIOLOGICAL INSIGHTS

### CAN YOU FIND THE LOADED QUESTIONS?

Consider the following questions that might be used in survey research. Do some of these questions bias the results by leading the respondent to answer in a particular way? Are some of the questions here better survey questions than others?

1. Indicate below your opinion about the current level of spending by the federal government on social services
   a. Much too high
   b. Too high
   c. About right
   d. Too low
2. Do you agree that the death penalty should be abolished?
3. Should the law protect freedom of choice in the matter of abortion?
4. Should the law protect unborn children by forbidding abortion?
5. Would you favor or oppose a law that would forbid the distribution of contraceptives at any clinic located on school property in this state?

Now turn the page to see what's wrong or right with these questions.

## SURVEY RESEARCH

Actually, both of the housing examples above (like most field experiments) did not strictly use the experimental method of research. Rather, they combined that method with *survey research,* which is the most widely used type of research design in sociology. **Survey research** is any research in which a population or a sample of a population is asked a set of questions that are worked out in advance by the researcher. In survey research, the variables are constructed from people's responses to the survey questions. Researchers attempt to measure all of the independent and control variables that might be relevant to whatever dependent variable they are interested in. Survey research is conducted in three common ways: the questionnaire, the telephone interview, and the personal interview.

## QUESTIONNAIRES

In the *questionnaire,* the people answering the survey read the questions and mark or write their answers on the survey form or an answer sheet. Questionnaires are simple and inexpensive to administer. However, the researcher might not always know when people have a problem understanding questions. Also, depending on how the survey is administered, the response rate can be low. Mail-out/mail-back questionnaires frequently have low response rates, often well under 50 percent and sometimes as low as 10 percent. The response rate can be improved if the survey is handed out to a group and people fill it out on the spot. As we shall see later, however, both of these methods present problems in terms of obtaining a sample that is representative of the population of interest to the researcher.

## SOCIOLOGICAL INSIGHTS

### WHAT'S WRONG WITH THE QUESTIONS? SOME ANSWERS

1. This question will tend to produce an excessive number of "too high" responses because respondents are given two choices on the "too high" side—"too high" and "much too high"—but only one choice on the "too low" side. On fixed-response items, there should always be an equal number of choices on both sides of the issues. Politicians and advocacy groups often deliberately violate this principle in order to make their surveys come out in favor of their views.

2. This question leads respondents in the direction of agreeing by starting out "do you agree" without mentioning disagreement. More neutral wording would be "Should the death penalty be abolished?" or "Do you agree or disagree with the view that the death penalty should be abolished."

3 and 4. These items, on another controversial topic, show opposite biases. Item 3 contains the phrase "protect freedom of choice," which calls to mind the primary argument of people who favor keeping abortion legal. This viewpoint generally sees abortion as a private matter about which people should be free to choose. Item 4 contains the phrase "protect unborn children," which calls to mind the primary argument of people who favor passing laws against abortion. This view generally sees abortion as taking a life. Whether one views abortion as private, personal choice or as a matter of taking a life is at the heart of one's opinions on this issue, so a question that calls to mind the key argument of one side in the debate will be very leading. A more neutral wording would be "Do you feel that abortion should be legal or illegal?"

5. This probably the most neutral of the questions listed. It used both "favor" and "oppose," thus avoiding the tendency to lead people either way. It is also relatively free of any words or phrases that would evoke an emotional response in one direction or the other.

## Telephone Interviews

A second way of doing survey research is the *telephone interview.* this method is particularly advantageous if quick results are needed, because answers can be entered immediately into the computer by the interviewer and analyzed quickly. Telephone interviews produce a better response rate than questionnaires, though answering machines have presented an increasing problem in this regard. Biases can occur because of people not owning phones or having unlisted numbers, but these problems have decreased. Random-dialing computer programs can reach unlisted numbers, and only about 3 percent of households today lack phones. For these reasons, use of telephone surveys has increased sharply (Babble, 1992, p. 275).

During the 1930s and 1940s (when more households lacked telephones than today), telephone polls occasionally made incorrect predictions of election outcomes because Democrats, with lower average incomes, were less likely to have telephones. Consequently, the polls predicted Republican victories in elections that were won by the Democrats. A classic case is the famous *Literary Digest* presidential poll of 1936. Although it was not a telephone poll, it got into trouble by drawing much of its sample from telephone directories. Because the poll greatly overrepresented Republicans, it predicted that Alf Landon would defeat Franklin D. Roosevelt by about 15 percentage points. Roosevelt subsequently won in a landslide, carrying every state but two.

## SOCIOLOGICAL INSIGHTS

### SAMPLING: A NATIONAL NEWS STORY

Most major medical research studies in the United States—those receiving federal funds—are coordinated through a central agency, the National Institutes of Health (N.I.H). Large research projects using taxpayers' money are thus expected to be well-designed and to have wide applicability for public health.

In 1986 the news broke that many of the major N.I.H. studies on aging, heart disease, and AIDS had a serious problem in their research design: Women had been routinely excluded from research samples. In one study financed by the N.I.H. to determine the effects of aspirin in reducing heart attacks, the sample consisted of over 22,000 people—all men.

Since it is well accepted in science that the sample should be representative of the larger population to which the research and the results apply, serious questions were raised. The research results could not be applied to women's health if women had been excluded from the samples. It was thus unknown, for example, whether the strategy of taking aspirin to prevent heart attacks (proven effective for men) would help, harm, or have no effect on women, over half the population.

How had the exclusion come about? Some reasons given to investigators were: reluctance to include women in drug studies because of possible birth defects that might result; difficulty in finding appropriate women subjects; added cos in including women.

In answer to the public outcry that women's health had been put at risk because of technical and ethical obstacles that could be overcome, in 1986 the N.I.H. officially stated a policy encouraging its researchers to include women. But in 1990, congressional hearings showed there had been little change. Renewed attention to the issue of sampling inclusion prompted the N.I.H. to start an Office of Research on Women's Health. The issue of who is "in" a sample (or not in, and why) thus affected public health in the United States and led to the creation of a national office for women's health.

SOURCE: Gina Kolata, "N.I.H. Neglects Women, Study Says," *The New York Times*, June 19, 1990. p. C6; Philip J. Hilts, "N.I.H. Starts Women's Health Office," *The New York Times*, Sept. 9, 1990, p. C4.

## Personal Interviews

The third way of doing survey research is the *personal interview.* Unless results are needed very quickly, the personal interview is usually the most thorough and reliable method of survey research. If done properly, most of the intended sample can be reached, interviewers can recognize ambiguous questions, and visual aids can be used. The main drawback of this method of research is its expense. Each interview can take an hour, and another hour or more may be spent traveling. The researcher must pay trained interviewers for this work. Someone else must then code the results and enter them into the computer for analysis. Thus, one of the biggest factors researchers must take into consideration when they decide what kind of survey research to do is what they can afford.

## Survey Questions

Two general types of question are commonly used in survey research: fixed-response and open-ended. *Fixed-response* questions are like multiple-choice exam questions: The respondent (the person answering the survey) is asked a question and then chooses one of several possible answers listed on the questionnaire or by the interviewer. Advantages of this approach are that the results are easy to process and the respondent picks the category that his or her answer will be placed in, rather than having that done by the researcher. The disadvantage, of course, is that none of the categories may represent the respondent's true feelings about the question. The other kind of question is the *open-ended* question. This type of question has no fixed choices; rather, the respondent states or writes an answer to the question in his or her own words. This offers the advantage of enabling respondents to say what they really think without limiting them to a preconceived set of categories. However, in order to analyze large numbers of such responses, researcher must usually code each response according to its meaning, so that similar responses from different people can be grouped together. This process involves a great deal of work, and there is always the risk that the coder will interpret the response differently than the respondent intended. Thus, open-ended and fixed-response questions both have their advantages and disadvantages.

**How to Phrase Survey Questions** Regardless of the types of questions they use, researchers must be careful not to word their questions in a way that will bias their results. As is illustrated in the box (page 63) on loaded questions, such elements as the particular words used in the question, leading phrases, and the number of response choices offered on each side of the issue can all affect questionnaire results. Sometimes, though, the bias in question wording is not as obvious as it is in the examples given in the box. Some sociologists argue that *any* wording of a question contains some bias, because different question wordings call to mind different aspects of an issue. In addition, the nature of such biases may vary from one survey respondent to another, because the same word often calls to mind different meanings, or evokes different emotions, for different people (Denzin, 1989, pp. 148-150).

The problems associated with the wording of questions are especially critical when people are confused and uncertain in the first place. Research has shown, for example, that question wording has an especially strong effect in research on attitudes toward abortion (Cohut, 1982). Despite strong opinions at the extremes on this issue, most Americans are not firmly committed to one side or the other and have somewhat ambiguous feelings about abortion (Farley, 1987a, p. 218). Thus, different question wordings get difficult results. Another example can be seen in polls rating the president. Different pollsters have different ideas about which characteristics people value in a president. For this reason, they word their poll questions somewhat differently and thus obtain somewhat different ratings of the same president. For these reasons, you should always pay attention to the wording of the questions when considering the results of survey research, and the researcher should always make this information available to the reader.

## Sampling

Although some surveys include everyone in the population the researcher is interested in, most surveys are based on *samples*. A **sample** is a subset of a population that is used to represent the entire population. If a sample is properly drawn, it can produce a result that is almost as trustworthy as if the entire population had been surveyed—and at a tremendously lower cost. A poorly drawn sample can render a research project useless. In order to be trustworthy, a sample must have two key characteristics. First, and most important, it must be *representative* of the population. Second, it must be *large* enough to give reliable results.

**Representative Samples** In order for a sample to be representative of a population, every individual in the population must have the same chance of getting in the sample. This ensures that no one segment of the population, such as males, Lutherans, college students, or poor people, will be overrepresented or underrepresented in the sample. Were this the case, such a group would influence the results of the sample more or less than its numbers in the population warrant. The basic way to obtain a representative sample is by a random draw from everyone in the population in question. In a very large population, such as the United States, this may be done in a complicated process involving several steps. However, such procedures follow two important principles that are the same as in a simple random sample. First, everyone in the population of interest to the researcher must have the same chance of getting into the sample. Second, individuals to be included are drawn on a random basis.

Probably you have heard of, or even participated in, certain types of surveys that violate these principles. "Person on the street" interviews violate it, because who is on a given street at a given time is far from random. If the survey is conducted downtown at lunch time, for example, clerical workers will probably be overrepresented relative to their numbers in a city's population. Also violating this principle are "phone-in" surveys conducted by television stations in which people call one number if they agree and another if they disagree with a certain position, and the mail-in surveys that are sometimes included in magazines. In both cases, the respondent has to initiate the response to the survey—a process that is hardly random. People who choose to respond are almost certainly different in important ways from those who do not. Moreover, there is no way to tell who saw the television show or read the magazine where the survey appeared, and thus no way to tell which population the sample was drawn from. That is why people who conduct such surveys often note that they are "not scientific." They most certainly are not, and their results cannot be assumed to generalize to any population.

**Sample Size** Surveys where the sample is representative can very accurately represent the responses that would have been obtained by surveying the entire population, if one additional condition is met. The sample must be of adequate size for the population in question. What matters most is the number of people in the sample, not the percentage of the population that is sampled. Even for a very small local population, a sample size of a few hundred will usually be needed to get reliable results. At the same time, a representative national sample of 2,000 or 3,000 people is adequate for a population as large as that of the U. S.

Social researchers have developed elaborate methods to measure the reliability of survey results based on the size of their samples. An estimate, such as the proportion of people who favor capital punishment, can be placed in a *confidence interval*. In other words, based on a given sample size, a researcher can be 95 percent certain that the true percentage favoring capital punishment is within, say, two percentage points of the figure obtained in the survey. When researchers obtain a statistical relationship between an independent and a dependent variable in their sample, they can use a measure called *statistical significance* to judge the likelihood that the relationship exists in the population the sample represents. If the result comes out to be statistically significant, the researchers can be confident that the result did not occur by chance and that it holds for the population they are interested in. In general, the stronger the correlation and the larger the sample, the more likely that any given relationship between two variables will be statistically significant.

## Multivariate Analysis

A great advantage of survey research is its ability to measure an analyze the effects of large numbers of variables at once. The ability to conduct such *multivariate analysis* has been greatly enhanced by computer technology. Multivariate analysis can accomplish two important things. First, a researcher can hold a large number of control variables constant and sort out the effect of one independent variable. Thus, in one of the examples used earlier, a researcher could assess the effect of religion on voting behavior while holding constant not only income but other variables such as sex, race, education level, and membership in a labor union. To put it differently, computerized multivariate analysis could compare Catholics and Protestants who are identical on all of these other variables to determine whether Catholics are more likely to vote for Democrats.

Multivariate analysis can also assess the relative influence of a number of independent variables all at once. Suppose, for example, that we were *not* merely interested in the effect of religion on voting behavior, but were trying to learn as much as possible about voting behavior, using any independent variable that might be relevant. With multivariate analysis, we could look at the effects of religion, age, sex, race, educational level, income, and union membership on voting all at once. Through multivariate analysis, we could find out which of these independent variables influences voting the most, which the least, and how influential each variable is relative to each of the others. We would also get information on the direction of the effect of each variable. Moreover, with modern high-speed computers, any of this information could be obtained from a data archive in a matter of seconds or minutes.

Multivariate analysis of survey data is a very powerful tool for sorting out alternative explanations for correlation. Still, it must be used with caution for several reasons. First, a researcher conducting a multivariate analysis must specify which variables are to be treated as independent, control, and dependent variables. This must be done in a manner consistent with the time order in which the variables occurred. If the researcher specifies as an independent variable a variable that actually is an effect, not a cause, he or she will get results back from the computer, but they will be wrong. Second, the question must be worded so that it accurately measures what it is intended to measure. Third, the survey must be conducted either on the population of interest to the researcher or on a proper sample of that population. In the following sections, we shall consider question wording and sampling a bit further.

# FIELD OBSERVATION

**Field observation** is a method of research in which human behavior is observed by researchers as it occurs in ordinary, "real-life" situations. It is the only method of research that permits social scientists to see directly how people actually behave in ordinary situations not under the control of the researcher. In experiments, the behavior is ordinarily observed in artificial settings such as classrooms or laboratories, so the researcher cannot assume that people will behave the same way in real-life situations. In survey research, researchers must depend upon what respondents tell them. We know that when it comes to behavior, people do not always know how they would behave in some situations, so the answers they give survey takes are not always accurate. Even accounts of what people have actually done in the past frequently contain considerable inaccuracies. Field observation gets around these problems by observing carefully and systematically how people actually behave in ordinary situations.

## Field Observation and Theory Generation

Field observation is especially useful for theory generation. Often, if a researcher does not have a clear theory or a body of past research findings to work with, field observation can disclose patterns that can be used to generate hypotheses. Field observation is similar in some ways to the ordinary observations of the behavior of others that we all make. The difference is that field observations are most systematic. Field observers take care to make prompt and detailed notes about their observations and to distinguish *observations* ("the woman was smiling") from *interpretations* ("the woman was happy").

Although field observation has an important advantage over other research methods in that the social scientist sees real behavior in uncontrived situations, this method also has some limitations. Most important is that the observer is never sure whether the behavior observed is representative of anyone beyond the people actually observed. In field observations there is no way to draw a random sample of the population. The observer must, rather, observe the behavior of those with whom he or she comes into contact in the situation in which the observation is being done.

## Participant Observation

The two main types of field observation are *participant observation* and *unobtrusive observation.* In **participant observation,** the researcher participates in some way in the behavior being observed. This can be accomplished by attending a meeting, participating in a group activity, or perhaps living for a time with the people being studied. A critical question here is whether the researcher should reveal his or her identity. There are arguments both for and against doing this. The main argument against it is that when people realize that they are being studied, they behave differently. Those in favor of revealing their identity argue that people may alter their behavior even more if they suspect they are secretly being studied.

There is also an ethical argument in support of researchers' revealing their identities: Some social scientists feel that people have a right to know when they are being studied and a right not to be studied if they don't want to be. Others, however, argue that when people are in a public place, social scientists have the same right to observe them that anyone else has.

In most cases, participant observation is less quantitative and more *qualitative* than other methods of research. Whereas surveys and experiments produce numbers that can be used to test hypotheses and clarify relationships between variables, participant observation is often more subjective in nature. It offers less-precise numbers, but it allows far greater depth of knowledge. No matter what group of people a sociologist is trying to study, there are some things that he or she will not find out simply by asking questions as an "outsider." Every group of people has its informal norms and "inside information." It is not likely that the answers given to a survey taker will reveal much about this aspect of group life. To get this information, a sociologist must literally become a part of the group and have moved into neighborhoods, or even lived with families, for periods ranging from one year to four or five years.

Many social scientists feel that no other method can gain the degree of insight that is possible through ongoing, intimate contact. Many of the sociology's most important studies have been based on participant observation, and they have often produced results that have contradicted conventional wisdom—even sometimes the conventional wisdom of sociologists. Sociologists William F. Whyte (1981 [originally published in 1943]) and Herbert Gans (1962) conducted long-term participant observation studies in Boston's low-income Italian neighborhoods. They found that the neighborhoods, which were generally regarded as disorganized, vice-ridden slums, were actually stable, well-organized neighborhoods where the residents worked hard and took care of one another. The residents had low incomes and were uninvolved in the city's political life, but these neighborhoods were nothing like the dens of social pathology that they were widely believe to be. Some of the things Whyte learned were surprising even to him. In his words: "As I sat and listened, I learned the answers to questions that I would not even have had the sense to ask."

In spite of these advantages, participant observation, like other problems of research, is subject to problems of reactivity. The mere presence of an observer may, for example, alter people's behavior. To lessen this problem, a researcher may try to remain as uninvolved as possible. Another strategy is to try to act like most of the people being observed. There is, however, one method of field observation that entirely avoids reactivity problems—*unobstrusive observation.*

## Unobtrusive Observation

**Unobtrusive observation** can be defined as field observation in which the researcher does not in any way become involved in the behavior being observed. One type of unobtrusive observation is observing human behavior from a position out of sight—through a window, across the street, and so forth. Another type is observation of *physical traces*—evidence that people leave behind them. A sociologist might, for example, get an idea of how safe people feel in a neighborhood by examining the proportion of cars that are locked. Frequently, such methods lead to the development of *unobtrusive measures,* which are quantifiable measures, such as the percentage of males and females entering a grocery story at a certain time of day, that result from unobtrusive observation.

The great advantage of unobtrusive observation over all the methods of research discussed thus far is that, if done properly, it avoids problems of reactivity. The disadvantage is that it tends to be somewhat lacking in depth. One can obtain only so much information without any direct interaction with other people. Still, unobtrusive observation is an important social research tool, particularly in urban sociology, where researchers are interested in the characteristics of people living in and using different kinds of city neighborhoods.

# USE OF EXISTING DATA SOURCES

A final type of research that is of great importance in sociology is the use of existing data sources. Very often a social scientist need not collect original data to study an issue or a problem because the necessary data have already been collected by someone else and are available. There are three main sources of existing data: various public and private data archives, the U. S. Census and related sources, and published or broadcast media suitable for content analysis. Let us consider each further.

## Data Archives

As you are probably aware, thousands of surveys have been taken in recent decades by college- and university-based researchers, private organizations and corporations, and various government agencies. Most of these surveys have resulted in computerized data archives, many of which are available to researchers. Many college professors conducting research are willing to share their data with others who research interests are slightly different from their own. In fact, some do this on a regular basis through organizations like the Inter-University Consortium for Political and Social Research (ICPSR), a national organization in which most major universities participate. Professional organizations often conduct surveys of participants in their professions and sometimes make such data available to researchers with related interests. Many government agencies conduct surveys and other forms of research and then sell computer archives of the data at cost. The U.S. government also has a registration system that records births, deaths, marriages, and divorces as they occur, which is an important source for researchers interested in these topics.

## The U. S. Census

A second major source of data, available to anyone with access to a good library, is the U.S Census. The Census, conducted every 10 years, includes comprehensive data on a wide range of population and housing characteristics for areas as small as a city block and as big as the entire country. A glance through any major sociological journal will reveal that the Census is one of the most important sources of data for sociological research. In addition to population and housing, regular census are also conducted on manufacturing, wholesale trade, retail trade, service industries, agriculture, mineral industries, and government. The results of all of these census can be looked up at any major library or purchased on computer tape or CD ROM from the Census Bureau or any number of universities and private firms.

The population Census is only conducted every 10 years, however, and there is a need for more current data. This need is met by the Census Bureau's *Current Population Survey.* This survey, conducted on an ongoing basis, provides annual updates on such things as population size, age structure, racial composition, income, household and family characteristics, education, and employment and unemployment. If you need up-to-date data on any of these issues, the *Current Population survey* is the place to look.

## Content Analysis

A slightly different approach to using existing data sources is *content analysis.* We have already seen one example of this—Adorno's research on the speeches and writings of Nazis and similar extremists. **Content analysis** involves some type of systematic examination of the content of books, articles, speeches, movies, television programs, or other similar communications. Such analysis can look for regular patterns, as Adorno's research did, or it can examine the handling of some area of subject matter. One might, for example, compare the number and types of roles filled by male and female characters in a set of television programs. Is there any difference, for example, in the proportion of males and females who are portrayed as people in a position to make important decisions? Such portrayals can tell a good deal about

## SOCIOLOGICAL INSIGHTS

### FIVE OLD PROSPECTORS

Imagine an old western mining town with a population of six people. In this town lived five old prospectors, none of whom, unfortunately, has found any gold this year. Each of them therefore has an income of $0. Also in this town lives one old mine owner who had an income of $1,200,000 last year. What is the mean income in the town?

The *mean* income in this town is $200,000. This is the total income of everyone in the town, $1,200,000, divided by the number of people in the town, 6. Obviously, this is not representative of typical income in the town: Most of the people in this town had no income. Although this is an extreme example, it illustrates an important point: The mean is disproportionately affected by even a small number of scores or numbers that fall far above or below what is typical of the population being studied. Thus, for any variable—such as income—where a few people score far higher (or lower) than the majority, the mean can be a misleading statistic. For such distributions, it is preferable to use the median discussed in Appendix 2. In this example, the median income is $0, which is much more representative of the "typical" miner than $200,000.

how the writers of television programs feel about the roles of men and women in society. They also say a lot about what television is teaching youngsters about men and women in society.

## EXPRESSING SOCIAL RESEARCH RESULTS AS NUMBERS

The results of social research methods ranging from experiments to surveys to unobtrusive observation to analysis of census data are commonly expressed as numbers. Such a system allows a more precise measurement than simply saying "some," "many," or "most." One common numerical concept used in social research is **central tendency**—what we commonly think of as an average. Measures of central tendency tell us where the middle or typical people fall on some distributions of scores, age, incomes, or other numerical variables. The three common measures of central tendency are the *mean, median,* and *mode.*

Although measures of central tendency are widely used in the social sciences, it is also important to consider whether most people score near the average or whether scores are very spread out.

### Reading Tables

In reports of sociological research, results are often presented in *tables,* like Table 3.2. Thus, being able to read tables is an essential skill for anyone who wishes to make sense of sociological research. It is also a skill of some broader usefulness, because many other kinds of information also appear in tables. In fact, in many sociological research reports, most of the actual research findings appear in the tables rather than in the text. As one of my professors in graduate school put it, "If you don't have time to read both the tables and the verbiage, skip the verbiage and read the tables." Using Table 2.2 as an example, we shall go through the things you need to know as you read tables.

**The Table Title** The title of the table should give you a clear description of the information that appears in the table. It should tell you specifically what the two variables in the table are. In this example, one variable is education, and the other is the number of people who have heard the AIDS virus called HIV.

**TABLE 3.2 Number and Percentage of Persons 18 Years of Age and Over Who Have Heard the AIDS Virus Called HIV, by Education, 1991**

| | EDUCATION | | | |
|---|---|---|---|---|
| | Less Than 12 Years | 12 Years | More Than 12 Years | Total |
| Yes | 6,084 (67%) | 13,889 (88%) | 16,777 (94%) | 36,750 (86%) |
| No | 2,546 (28%) | 1,619 (10%) | 892 (5%) | 5,054 (12%) |
| Don't know | 454 (5%) | 204 (1%) | 179 (1%) | 837 (2%) |
| Total | 9,081 | 15,712 | 17,848 | 42,641 |

SOURCE: National Center for Health Statistics. Advance Data, No. 225, January 6, 1993. AIDS Knowledge and Attitudes for 1991.

**Headings** Every table will also contain headings that describe the variables or categories of variables that appear in the table. In this case, the headings reveal that the education variable has three categories—"less than 12 years," "12 years," and "more than 12 years"—and that the responses to the statement were classified as "yes" or "no."

**Unit of Analysis** The title or the headings should indicate the *unit of analysis* of the table; that is, what the numbers represent. In this case, the title tells you that the numbers in the table represent the number of people and the percentage of people who say yes to the statement. Thus, for example, the results show that 6,084 of the people with less than 12 years of education surveyed said "yes" (upper left number in the table). In other tables, the unit of analysis might be cities. In such a case, each number would tell you how many cities fell into a particular category of the table. Other possible units of analysis are countries, organizations, companies, and, perhaps, thousands of people. The title or headings should always contain this information as well as whether you are being given *raw frequencies*—the number of people, places, and so forth— or *percentages*. Some tables, like Table 2.2, give you both. Some tables, rather than classifying people, places, or groups of people, show some statistical measures of correlation.

**Marginals** Many tables, like Table 2.2, have a column at the right and a row at the bottom labeled "Total." This row and column, called the *marginals,* give you important information about the breakdown of each variable. In Table 2.2, for example, the marginal column at the right tells you that, of the total of 42,641 people who answered the item, 36,750, or 86 percent, said "yes," and 5,054, or 12 percent, said "no." From the marginal row at the bottom, you can see that of the same 42,641, 9,081 had less than 12 years of education, 15,712 had 12 years, and 17,848 had more than 12 years. A little further computation based on these numbers would tell you that of the 42,641, 21% had less than 12 years, 37% had 12 years, and 42% had more than 12 years of education.

**Table Cells** The data for people with each possible combination of these variables are shown in the *cells* of the table. Again, look at the upper left number in Table 3.2; 6084. This cell represents the number of people in the sample who had less than 12 years *and* said "yes." The number in the cell to the right, 13,889, represents the number who had 12 years and said "yes," and the number in the cell below, 2,453, represents the number who had less than 12 years and said "no." To determine the meaning of the number in any cell, read down from the column heading and across from the row heading. These headings will identify the particular combination of categories represented by any given cell. In this particular table, each cell also contains a percentage, which we shall explore next.

**Percentages** As noted above, some tables will give you percentages. If this is the case, you need to know how to interpret them. For example, the upper left cell gives a percentage, 67 percent. To interpret the percentages properly, you must know which way they total. In this case, they total down: 67 percent plus 28 percent plus 5 percent = 100 percent. Whether they total down or across is arbitrary, but an important rule is at work here. Ordinarily, *the dependent variable will be broken down into percentages within each category of the independent variable.* Thus, you must know—from the text or from your own knowledge of which variable would come first in time—which variable in the table is the independent variable and which is the dependent variable. In this case, the independent variable is clearly education because we can reasonably assume that educational level will influence AIDS knowledge, rather than vice versa. Thus, we look at each category of the independent variable—under 12 years, 12 years, and more than 12 years—and within each category we convert the dependent variable (saying "yes" or "no" to the question about HIV) to percentages. Thus, we see that among people with less than 12 years, 67% said yes and 28% said no; among people with 12 years, 88% said yes and 10% said no; and so forth.

Why are tables read this way? Because this system best illustrates how the independent variable correlates with the dependent variable. In this case, for example, we can immediately see that the percentage of people with 12 years of school who said yes was 21 points higher than that of people with less than 12 years. Thus, we can see that people with more education are more likely to have heard the AIDS virus called HIV.

Sometimes you will encounter tables that only show raw frequencies and not percentages. If this happens, you can always convert the table to percentages yourself. Just remember the principle stated above: Within each category of the independent variable, convert the dependent variable to percentages

**Source of Data** Finally, any table should tell you the source of the data (occasionally you will be told this in the text). In the case of Table 3.2, the data came from the National center for Health Statistics conducted in 1991 and published in 1993.

## SUMMARY

In this chapter, we have elaborated upon the scientific method and explored the relationship between theory and research. Research generates theory, as theorists seek to explain research findings. These theories then stimulate new research by predicting what such research may be expected to find. When researchers operate in the mode of prediction and theory testing, they often use hypotheses. Hypotheses are specific statements about reality, derived from theories as a way of testing parts of those theories. A hypothesis usually contains one or more independent variables (presumed causes) and a dependent variable (presumed effect). Scientists test for such cause-effect relationships by looking for correlation between independent and dependent variables, by checking the time order (cause must precede effect), and by eliminating alternative explanations, often through the use of control variables.

In sociology, the major methods of research are experiments, survey research, field observation, and use of existing data sources. Which of these methods a sociologist will use depends in part on that sociologist's purpose in research (for example, theory testing versus theory generation), and in part on the sociologist's judgment concerning the strengths and weaknesses of each method.

Results derived from any method of research are commonly expressed as numbers. Comparison of different groups or populations often involves use of measures of central tendency, such as the mean, median, and mode. Such results frequently are presented in tables; being able to read tables correctly is an essential skill for anyone trying to make sense of sociological research.

# Chapter 4

## Culture

*A small aluminum motorboat chugged steadily along the muddy Orinoco River, deep within South America's vast tropical rain forest. Anthropologist Napoleon Chagnon was nearing the end of a three-day journey to the home territory of the Yanomamö, one of the most technologically primitive societies remaining on earth.*

*Some twelve thousand Yanomamö live in villages scattered along the border of Venezuela and Brazil. Their way of life could hardly be more different from our own. The Yanomamö wear little clothing and live without electricity, automobiles, or other conveniences that most people in the United States take for granted. Their traditional weapons, used for both hunting and warfare, are the bow and arrow. Many of the Yanomamö have experienced little contact with the outside world. Thus Chagnon would be as strange to them as they would be to him.*

*By 2:00 in the afternoon, Chagnon had almost reached his destination. The hot sun made the humid air almost unbearable. The anthropologist's clothes were soaked with perspiration, and his face and hands swelled from the bites of innumerable gnats swarming around him. But he scarcely noticed, so preoccupied was he with the fact that in just a few moments he would be face to face with people unlike any he had ever known.*

*Chagnon's heart pounded rapidly as the boat glided onto the riverbank near a Yanomamö village. Sounds of activity came from nearby. Chagnon and his guide climbed from the boat and walked toward the village, stooping as they pushed their way through the dense undergrowth. Chagnon describes what happened next.*

*I looked up and gasped when I saw a dozen burly, naked, sweaty, hideous men staring at us down the shafts of their drawn arrows! Immense wads of green tobacco were stuck between their lower teeth and lips making them look even more hideous, and strands of dark green slime dripped or hung from their nostrils—strands so long that they hung to their [chests] or drizzled down their chins.*

*My next discovery was that there were a dozen or so vicious, underfed dogs snapping at my legs, circling me as if I were to be their next meal. I just stood there holding my notebook, helpless and pathetic. Then the stench of the decaying vegetation and filth hit me and I almost got sick. I was horrified. What kind of welcome was this for the person who came here to live with you and learn your way of life, to become friends with you? (1983:10)*

*Fortunately for Chagnon, the Yanomamö villagers recognized his guide and lowered their weapons. Reassured that he would survive at least the afternoon, Chagnon was still shaken by his inability to make any sense of the people surrounding him. And this was to be his home for a year and a half! He wondered why he had forsaken physics to study human culture in the first place.*

The 5.5 billion people living on the earth are members of a single biological species: *Homo sapiens.* Even so, the differences among people the world over can easily overwhelm us. Entering the world of the Yanomamö, Chagnon experienced a severe case of **culture shock,** *personal disorientation that accompanies exposure to an unfamiliar way of life.* Like most of us, Chagnon had been raised to keep his clothes on, even in hot weather, and to use a handkerchief when his nose was running—especially in front of others. The Yanomamö clearly had other ideas about how to live. The nudity that embarrassed Chagnon was customary to them. They recognized the green slime hanging from their nostrils as the result of inhaling a hallucinogenic drug, a practice common among friends. The "stench" that made Chagnon recoil in disgust no doubt smelled like "Home Sweet Home" to the inhabitants of that Yanomamö village.

In short, despite being the same creatures biologically, human beings have very different ideas about what is pleasant and repulsive, polite and rude, beautiful and ugly, right and wrong. This capacity for startling difference is a wonder of our species: the expression of human culture.

# WHAT IS CULTURE?

Sociologists define **culture** as *the beliefs, values, behavior, and material objects that define a people's way of life.* Culture includes what we think, how we act, and what we own. But culture is also a bridge linking the past, the present, and the future. In short, culture is nothing less than an ongoing social heritage (Soyinka, 1991).

To begin to understand all that culture entails, it is helpful to distinguish between ideas and objects. What sociologists call **nonmaterial culture** is *the intangible creations of human society,* including ideas ranging from altruism to zen. **Material culture,** on the other hand, is *the tangible products of human society,* involving objects ranging from armaments to zippers.

Taken together, cultural patterns form a broad plan for living: The way we dress, when and what we eat, where we work, and how we spend our free time are all grounded in culture. Chemists tell us that only ninety-two elements occur naturally on earth, but sociologists know that the world is home to countless variations of human culture. Our own culture leads us to sleep in houses of wood or brick, but people of other cultures live in huts fashioned from brush, igloos of ice, or tepees made of animal skins. Culture also provides us with standards of success, beauty, and goodness, as well as reverence for a superhuman power, be it a deity, the forces of nature, or long-dead ancestors.

Culture also shapes our personalities—what we commonly (yet inaccurately) describe as "human nature." The warlike Yanomamö look on aggression as natural in their children, just as the Semai of Malaysia expect their young to be peaceful and cooperative. The cultures of the United States and Japan both stress achievement and hard work, but members of our society value individualism more than do the Japanese, who embrace tradition more strongly.

No cultural trait is inherently "natural" to humanity, although most people around the world view their own way of life that way. What is natural to our species is the capacity to create culture, and we realize this potential as members of a particular society. Every other form of life—from ants to zebras—behaves in uniform, species-specific ways. To a world traveler, the enormous diversity of human life stands out in contrast to the behavior of, say, cats, which is much the same everywhere. This uniformity follows from the fact that most living creatures are guided by *instincts,* biological programming over which animals have no control. A few animals—notably chimpanzees and related primates—have the capacity for basic elements of culture, as researchers have noted by observing them use tools and teach simple skills to their offspring. But the creative power of humans far exceeds that of any other form of life; *only humans rely on culture rather than instinct to ensure the survival of their kind* (Harris, 1987).

To understand how this came to be, we must briefly review the history of our species on the earth.

## Culture and Human Intelligence

In a universe perhaps 15 billion years old, our planet is a relatively young 4.5 billion years of age, and the human species is a wide-eyed infant of only 250,000. Not for a billion years after the earth was formed did life appear on our planet. Far later—some 65 million years ago—our history took a crucial turn with the appearance of the mammals we call primates.

What sets primates apart is their intelligence, based on the largest brains (relative to body size) of all living creatures. As primates evolved, the human line diverged from that of our closest relatives, the great apes, about 12 million years ago. But our common lineage shows through in the traits humans share with today's chimpanzees, gorillas, and orangutans: great sociability, affectionate and long-lasting bonds for child rearing and mutual protection, the ability to walk upright (normal in humans, less common among other primates), and hands that manipulate objects with great precision.

Studying fossil records, scientists conclude that, about 2 million years ago, our distant ancestors grasped cultural fundamentals such as the use of fire, tools, and weapons, created simple shelters, and fashioned basic clothing. Although these Stone Age achievements may seem modest, they mark the point at which our ancestors embarked on a distinct evolutionary course, making culture the primary strategy for human survival.

To comprehend what newcomers to the earth humans are, Carl Sagan (1977) suggests superimposing the 15-billion-year history of our universe on a single calendar year. The life-giving atmosphere of the earth did not develop until the autumn, and the earliest humanlike beings did not appear until December 31—the last day of the year—at 10:30 at night! Yet not until 250,000 years ago, which is mere minutes before the end of Sagan's "year," did our own species finally emerge. These *Homo sapiens* (derived from Latin meaning "thinking person") have continued to evolve so that, about 40,000 years ago, humans who looked more or less like ourselves roamed the earth. With larger brains, these "modern" *Homo sapiens* produced culture at a rapid pace, as the wide range of tools and cave art from this period suggests. Still, what we call "civilization," based on permanent settlements and specialized occupations, began in the Middle East (especially in what is today Iraq and Egypt) only about 12,000 years ago (Hamblin, 1973; Wenke, 1980). In terms of Sagan's "year," this cultural flowering occurred during the final *seconds* before midnight on New Year's Eve. And what of our modern, industrial way of life? Begun only 300 years ago, it amounts to a mere millisecond flash in Sagan's scheme.

Human culture, then, was a long time in the making. As culture became a strategy for survival, our ancestors descended from the trees into the tall grasses of central Africa. There, walking upright and hunting in groups had clear advantages. From this point on, the human capacity to create a way of life—as opposed to simply acting out biological imperatives—steadily increased along with the size of the human brain. Gradually, culture pushed aside the biological forces we call instincts so that humans gained the mental power to *fashion the natural environment for our benefit.* Ever since, people have made and remade their worlds in countless ways, which explains today's fascinating (and, as Napoleon Chagnon's experiences show, sometimes disturbing) cultural diversity.

## Culture, Nation, and Society

At this point, clarification of the proper use of several terms will be helpful. We often use the concepts "culture," "nation," and "society" interchangeably. But, to sociologists, each word has a precise meaning. *Culture* refers to a shared way of life. A *nation* is a political entity, that is, a place within designated borders such as the United States, Canada, or Zimbabwe. *Society,* the topic of the next chapter, is the organized interaction of people in a nation or within some other boundary.

We correctly describe the United States, then as both a nation and as a society. But many societies—including the United States—are *multicultural,* meaning that they include various ways of life that blend (and sometimes collide) in our everyday lives.

In the world as a whole, how many cultures are there? The number of cultures contained in the human record is a matter of speculation. Based on the number of human languages that are known, we can estimate that between five and six thousand distinctive cultures have existed on earth (Durning, 1993). As Chapter 22 ("The Natural Environment") and Chapter 24 ("Social Change and Modernity") explain, the cultural diversity of the world recently has been decreasing. Even so, at least one thousand different cultures continue to flourish, and hundreds of them, some with greater presence than others, are found in the United States.

The tally of world nations has risen and fallen throughout history as a result of political events. The dissolution of the former Soviet Union added fourteen nations to the count; the ongoing strife in the former Yugoslavia will add several more. At present, there are 190 politically independent nations in the world.

# THE COMPONENTS OF CULTURE

Although the cultures found in all the world's nations differ in many ways, they all are built on five major components: symbols, language, values, norms, and material objects. We begin with the most important: symbols.

## Symbols

Reality for human beings is not objects or actions but meaning. In other words, we are human to the extent that we create an environment that is *symbolic*. A **symbol**, then, *is anything that carries a particular meaning recognized by people who share culture.* A whistle, a wall of graffiti, a flashing red light, and a fist raised in the air all serve as symbols. We can see the human capacity to create and manipulate symbols reflected in the very different meanings associated with the simple act of winking the eye. In some settings this action conveys interest; in others, understanding; in still others, insult.

We are so dependent on our culture's symbols that we take them for granted. Occasionally, however, we become keenly aware of a symbol when someone uses it in an unconventional way, as when a person in a political demonstration burns a U.S. flag. Entering an unfamiliar society also reminds us of the power of symbols; culture shock is really the inability to "read" meaning in one's surroundings. Like Napoleon Chagnon confronting the Yanomamö, we feel lost, unsure of how to act, and sometimes frightened—a consequence of being outside the symbolic web of culture that joins individuals in a meaningful social life.

Because cultures vary, an action or object with a specific meaning in one time or place may have a very different significance in another. To people in North America, a baseball bat symbolizes sport and recreation, but the Yanomamö would probably view this well-carved club as an implement of hunting or war. A dog is a beloved household pet to people in North America but a prized wintertime meal to residents of northern China. Likewise, cows revered as sacred by India's Hindus are routinely consumed as "quarter-pounders" by hungry people in the United States. Thus symbols both bind together individuals of one society and separate people living in different societies of the world.

In global perspective, we need to remember that behavior that seems normal to us may offend people elsewhere. Women serving in the 1991 Gulf War discovered that simply wearing shorts in an Islamic society like Saudi Arabia was widely condemned as inappropriate. An innocent gesture for members of one society may provoke an angry response from people in another who "read" according to a different symbolic system.

Then, too, symbolic meanings vary even within a single society. A fur coat, prized by one person as a symbol of success, may represent to another the inhumane treatment of animals. Similarly, a Confederate flag that for one individual embodies regional pride may symbolize to someone else recall oppression.

Cultural symbols also change over time. Blue jeans were created more than a century ago as sturdy and inexpensive clothing for people engaged in physical labor. In the liberal political climate of the 1960s, this working-class aura made jeans popular among affluent students—many of whom wore them to look "different" or sometimes to identify with working people. A decade later, "designer jeans" emerged as fashionable "status symbols," signifying big clothing budgets, the opposite of their working-class roots. In recent years, everyday jeans remain as popular as ever, simply as comfortable apparel.

In sum, symbols allow people to make sense of their lives, and without them human existence would be meaningless. Manipulating symbols correctly allows us to operate and be understood by others within our own culture. In a world of cultural diversity, however, the use of symbols may cause embarrassment and even conflict.

## Language

Helen Keller (1880-1968) became a national celebrity because she overcame a daunting disability: being blind and deaf from infancy. As a young girl, she was cut off from the symbolic world around her. Only when her teacher, Anne Mansfield Sullivan, broke through Keller's isolation with the concept of language did Helen Keller begin to realize her human potential. This remarkable woman, who later became a renowned educator herself, recalls the moment she acquired language.

> We walked down the path to the well-house, attracted by the smell of honeysuckle with which it was covered. Someone was drawing water, and my teacher placed my hand under the spout.

> As the cool stream gushed over one hand, she spelled into the other the word water, first slowly, then rapidly. I stood still, my whole attention fixed upon the motions of her fingers. Suddenly I felt a misty consciousness as of something forgotten—a thrill of returning thought; and somehow the mystery of language was revealed to me. I knew then that "w-a-t-e-r" meant the wonderful cool something that was flowing over my hand. That living word awakened my soul; gave it light, hope, joy, set it free! (1903:21-24)

**Language**, the key to the world of culture, is a system of symbols that allows members of a society to communicate with one another. All cultures have a spoken language, although some, including the Yanomamö, have no system of writing. Written symbols themselves are culturally variable, and various alphabets are used around the world. Moreover, members of societies in the Western world write from left to right, people of North Africa and West Asia write right to left, and people in East Asia write from top to bottom.

Global Map 3.1 shows regional use of the world's three most widely spoken languages. Chinese is the official language of one-fifth of humanity (more than 1 billion people). English is the mother tongue of about 10 percent (500 million) of the world's people and Spanish the official language of 6 percent (300 million). Notice, too, that English is close to becoming a global language, since it is given preference as a second language in most of the world.

For people everywhere, cultural heritage is rooted in language. Language is, in fact, the major means of **cultural transmission**, the process by which one generation passes culture to the next. Just as our bodies contain the genes of our ancestors, so we think and act every day using the symbolic system those who came before us. The power of language lies in gaining access to centuries of accumulated wisdom.

For most of human history, people have transmitted culture through speech, which sociologists term the *oral cultural tradition.* Not until five thousand years ago did humans devise writing, and, even then, only a relatively few people ever learned to read and write. When the United States was founded just over two centuries ago, only a small elite was literate. Today, perhaps 25 million adults (about one in seven) in this country cannot read and write—an almost insurmountable barrier to opportunity in a society that increasingly demands symbolic skills. In the poorest societies of the world, moreover, four out of five people cannot use written language.

Language skills not only put us in touch with the past, they also free the human imagination. Connecting symbols in new ways, we can conceive of life other than as it is. Language—both spoken and written—distinguishes human beings as the only creatures who are self-conscious, mindful of our limitations and aware of our ultimate mortality. Yet our symbolic power also enables us to dream and hope for a future better than the present.

### *Is Language Uniquely Human?*

Creatures great and small direct sounds and other physical cues to one another, and these are certainly forms of communication. Although in most cases, such signals are instinctive, research has shown that some animals have at least a rudimentary ability to use symbols to communicate with one another and with humans.

Perhaps the most significant achievement of this kind is the capacity of a twelve-year-old chimp named Kanzi. Chimpanzees lack the physical ability to speak words as humans do. But researcher E. Sue Savage-Rumbaugh noticed that Kanzi was able to learn language the same way a human child does—by listening and observing adults. Savage-Rumbaugh has raised Kanzi to have a vocabulary of several hundred words, which he "speaks" by pointing to pictures or pushing keys on a special keyboard. Kanzi's learning is more than simple rote; he spontaneously replies to spoken English he has not heard before. For example, Kanzi has correctly responded to questions like "Will you get a diaper for your sister?" or "Put the melon in the potty." In short, Kanzi has the language ability of a human child of two-and-one-half years (Eckholm, 1985; Linden, 1993).

## Window on the World

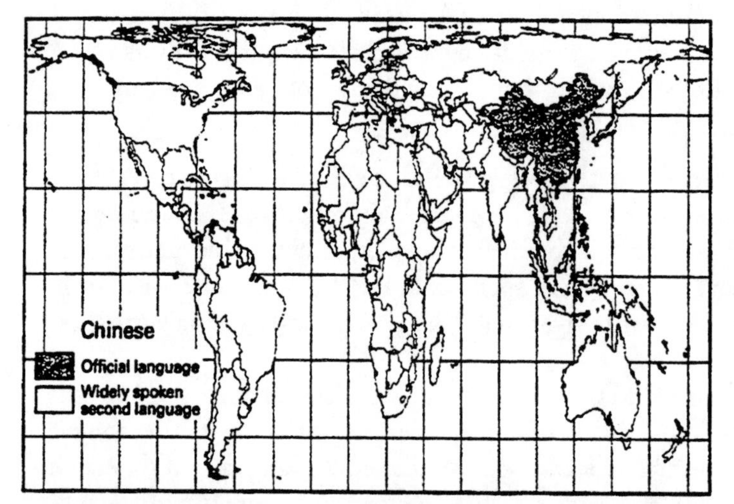


### GLOBAL MAP 3–1
### Language in Global Perspective

Chinese (including Mandarin, Cantonese, and dozens of other dialects) is the native tongue of one-fifth of the world's people, almost all of whom live in Asia. More precisely, although all Chinese people read and write with the same characters, they employ any of several dozen dialects. The "official" dialect, taught in schools throughout the People's Republic of China and the Republic of Taiwan, is Mandarin (the dialect of Beijing, China's historic capital city). Cantonese (the language of Canton, which differs in sound from Mandarin roughly the way French does from Spanish) is the second most common Chinese dialect.

English
Official language
Widely spoken second language

English is the native tongue or official language in several world regions and has become the preferred second language in most of the world.

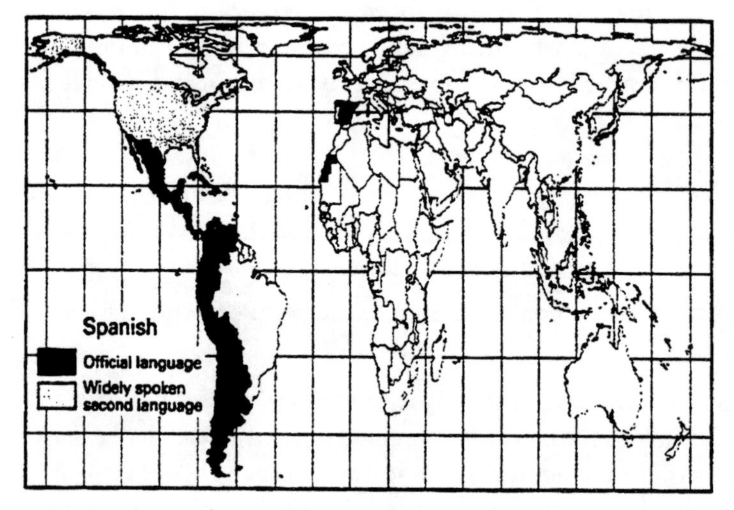


The largest concentration of Spanish speakers is in Latin America and, of course, in Spain. Spanish is also the preferred second language of the United States.

From *Peters Atlas of the World* (1990).

By human standards, the language skill of chimps such as Kanzi (as well as dolphins and a few other animals) are limited. Further, research confirms that even specially trained animals cannot, on their own, pass on language skills to others of their kind. But animals' demonstrated language warns us against assuming that humans alone can lay claim to culture.

### *Does Language Shape Reality?*

Because the Yanomamö have many different words for warfare and fighting, do they actually experience the world differently from people whose language lacks these symbols? The answer is yes, since language provides the building-blocks of reality.

Edward Sapir (1929, 1949) and Benjamin Whorf (1956), two anthropologists who specialized in linguistic studies, argued that languages are not just different sets of labels for the same reality. Rather, symbolic systems differ in various ways, since every language has words or expressions with no precise counterparts in other tongues. Further, each language fuses symbols with distinctive emotions. Thus, as multilingual people can attest, a single idea often "feels" different if spoken in, say, Spanish rather than in English or Chinese (Falk, 1987).

Formally, then, what we now call the **Sapir-Whorf hypothesis** states *that people perceive the world through the cultural lens of language.* Using different symbolic systems, a Turk, a Brazilian, and a Filipino actually experience "distinct worlds, not merely the same world with different labels attached" (Sapir, 1949:162).

Of course, with the capacity to manipulate and create language, humans everywhere can shape for themselves how they experience the world. Consider how an invention like the computer has introduced new symbols including "bytes," "interface," and "E-mail" to our language. In addition, people deliberately change language. The pursuit of social equality in a predominantly white society led African Americans to replace the word "Negro" first with the term "black" and then with "African American" or "person of color." A generation later, such symbolic changes have helped improve white people's perceptions of African Americans. Similarly, although adult males in English-speaking societies have long been called "men," adult females often have been condescendingly referred to as "girls." The recent emphasis on calling women "women" is both cause and effect of a heightened awareness of sexual equality. In short, a system of language guides how we understand the world but does not limit how we do so.

## Values and Beliefs

What accounts for the popularity of film characters such as James Bond, Dirty Harry, Rambo, and Thelma and Louise? The answer tells us as much about ourselves as about them. Each is ruggedly individualistic, suspicious of "the system," and relies primarily on personal skill and effort. The fact that we applaud such people suggest that we celebrate sturdy individualism, traditionally for men but increasingly for women, too.

Sociologists call such patterns ***values,*** *culturally defined standards by which people judge desirability, goodness, and beauty, and which serve as broad guidelines for social living.* Values are judgments, from the standpoint of a culture, of what ought to be.

Values are broad principles that support ***beliefs,*** *specific statements that people who share culture hold to be true.* While values are abstract standards, in other words, beliefs are particular matters that individuals consider to be valid.

Cultural values and beliefs shape our personalities and affect how we perceive our surroundings. We learn from families, schools, and religious organizations to think and act according to approved principles, to pursue worthy goals, and to believe a host of cultural truths while rejecting alternatives as false.

In a nation as large and diverse as the United States, of course, few cultural values and beliefs are shared by everyone. Over the centuries, people from around the world have entered this country, producing a cultural mosaic. Relatively speaking, then, our society is more culturally diverse than a historically isolated nation such as Japan. Even so, there is a broad shape to our national life that most people recognize and that persists over time.

*Key Values of U.S. Culture*

According to sociologist Robin Williams (1970), the following ten values are among the most central to our way of life.

1. **Equal opportunity** Our sense of fairness dictates that everyone should have the opportunity to get ahead, although, due to varying talents and efforts, we expect that some people will end up being more successful than others. In other words, while people in the United States do not endorse equality of *condition*, we do believe in equal *opportunity*, that everyone should have a chance to obtain the good things in life.
2. **Achievement and success** Our way of life encourages competition. In principle, we believe, each individual's rewards should reflect personal merit. Moreover, the greater success one garners, the more he or she is seen as a worthy person—a "winner."
3. **Material comfort** Success, in the United States, generally means making money and enjoying what it will buy. People in the United States may quip that "money won't buy happiness," but most diligently pursue wealth all the same.
4. **Activity and work** U.S. heroes, from Olympic figure skating star Kristi Yamaguchi to film's famed archeologist Indiana Jones, are "doers," people who get the job done. Members of our society prefer *action* to *reflection;* through hard work, we try to control events rather than passively accepting our fate. For this reason, many of us take a dim view of cultures that appear more easygoing or philosophical.
5. **Practicality and efficiency** Just as people in the United States value activity (especially that which earns money), so we praise the ability to solve problems with minimal effort. "Building a better mousetrap" is a cultural goal, especially when it's done in the most cost-effective way.
6. **Progress** Despite occasional waves of nostalgia, members of our society historically have believed that the present is better than the past. Compared to the Japanese, moreover, we are far more optimistic about the future. This embrace of progress is evident in widespread advertising that what is the "very latest" is necessarily the "very best."
7. **Science** We often turn to scientists to solve problems, convinced that the work of scientific experts will improve our lives. We believe we are rational people, which probably explains our cultural tendency (especially among men) to devalue emotions and intuition as sources of knowledge.
8. **Democracy and free enterprise** Members of our society recognize numerous individual rights that cannot be overridden by government. Our political system has come to be based on the ideal of free elections in which all adults freely select their own leaders. In the same way, we believe that the U.S. economy responds to the needs and choices of selective, individual consumers.
9. **Freedom** our cultural value of freedom means that we favor individual initiative over collective conformity. Although we acknowledge that everyone has responsibilities to others, we believe that individuals should be free to pursue personal goals without unreasonable interference from anyone else.
10. **Racism and group superiority** Despite our ideas about equality and freedom, most people in the United States evaluate individuals according to their sex, race, ethnicity, and social class. Our society values males over females, whites over people of color, people with northwestern European backgrounds over those whose ancestors came from other lands, and more privileged people over those who are disadvantaged. Although we like to describe ourselves as a nation of equals, there is little doubt that some of us are "more equal" than others.

## SOCIOLOGY OF EVERYDAY LIFE

### DON'T BLAME ME! THE NEW "CULTURE OF VICTIMIZATION"

A New York man recently survived his leap in front of a subway train; he then successfully sued the city for $650,000, claiming the train failed to stop in time to prevent his serious injuries. In Washington, D.C., after realizing that he had been videotaped smoking crack cocaine in a hotel room, the city's mayor blamed his woman companion for "setting him up" and suggested that his arrest by police was racially motivated. After ten women accused Oregon Senator Bob Packwood of sexual harassment, he tried to defuse the scandal by checking into an alcohol treatment center. In the most celebrated case of its kind, Dan White gunned down the mayor of San Francisco and a city council member only to tell the jury that eating "junk food" (the so-called Twinkie defense) had driven him temporarily insane.

Each of these cases involves a claim of victimization. Rather than taking the blame for our mishaps and misdeeds. In other words, more and more members of our society are pointing the finger elsewhere and painting themselves as victims. Sociologist Irving Horowitz claims we are developing a new "culture of victimization" in which "everyone is a victim" and "no one accepts responsibility for anything."

One indication of this cultural trend is the proliferation of "addictions," a term that once was associated exclusively with the uncontrollable use of drugs. We now hear about gambling addicts, compulsive overeaters, sex addicts, and even people who excuse mounting credit card debts as a shopping addiction. Bookstores overflow with manuals to help people come to terms with numerous new medical or psychological conditions ranging from the "Cinderella Complex" to the "Casanova Complex" and even "Soap Opera Syndrome." And the U.S. courts are ever more clogged by lawsuits driven by the need to blame someone—and often to collect big money—for the kind of misfortune that we use to accept as part of life.

What's going on here? Is U.S. culture changing? Historically, our way of life has been based on a cultural idea of "rugged individualism," the notion that—for better or worse—people are responsible for whatever triumph or tragedy befalls them. But this value has been eroded by a number of factors. First, we have become more aware (partly through the work of sociologists) of how society shapes our lives. This knowledge has expanded the categories of people claiming to be victims well beyond those who have suffered historical disadvantages (such as African Americans and woman) to include even well-off people. In a 1991 issue, for example, Newsweek touted the emerging movement among affluent white men seeking help in overcoming the alleged pressures of privilege.

Second, there has been a small revolution in the legal system by which many lawyers—especially since gaining the right to advertise their services in 1977—now encourage a sense of injustice among clients they hope to shepherd into court. The number of million-dollar lawsuit awards has risen more than twenty-five-fold in the last twenty-five years.

Third, there has been a proliferation of "rights groups" that promote what Amitai Etzioni calls "right inflation." Beyond the traditional constitutional liberties are many newly claimed rights, including those of hunters (as well as those of animals), the rights of smokers (and nonsmokers), the right of women to control their bodies (and the rights of the unborn), the right to own a gun (and the right to be safe from violence). Expanding the competing claims for unmet rights, then, generate victims on all sides.

Does this shift signal a fundamental realignment in our culture? Perhaps, but the new popularity of being a victim also springs from some established cultural forces. For example, the claim to victimization depends on a long-standing belief that everyone has the right to life, liberty, and the pursuit of happiness. What is new, however, is that the explosion of "rights" now does more than alert us to clear cases of injustice; it threatens to erode our sense of responsibility as members of a larger society.

### *Values: Inconsistency and Conflict*

As the listing above suggests, cultural values can be inconsistent and even outright contradictory (Lynd, 1967; Bellah et al., 1985). Living in the United States, we sometimes find ourselves torn between the "me first" attitude of an individualistic, success-at-all-costs way of life and the opposing need to belong to some larger community. Similarly, we affirm our belief in equality of opportunity only to turn around and promote or degrade others because of their race or sex.

Some value inconsistency is the product of change. New trends sometimes are at odds with older cultural orientations. For example, what some observers have tagged a new "culture of victimization" now challenges our society's longtime belief in individual responsibility. The box on page 85 takes a closer look.

Value inconsistency also occurs because cultural patterns vary according to people's age, sex ethnicity, religion, race, and social class. Individuals who are favored in one sense while disadvantaged in another—a situation sociologists term status inconsistency—are especially prone to contradictory values. Clarence Thomas, an African American appointed to the Supreme Court in 1991, began his climb to prominence in a poor Georgia family. His changing fortunes left him with both an appreciation for the plight of poor minorities and a strong belief in the ability of each individual to rise above circumstance.

In sum, value inconsistency and conflict lead to strained and awkward balancing acts in how we view the world. Sometimes we may pursue one value at the expense of another, believing in the idea of equal opportunity, say, while opposing the acceptance of gays by the U.S. military. At other times, we try to ignore such contradictions. National surveys, for example, show that while most U.S. adults acknowledge that some people are born to great fortunes while others confront abject poverty, they also maintain that the United States offers equal opportunity for all (NORC, 1993). Clearly, both views cannot be completely true. But we seem to have learned to live with significant cultural contradictions.

### *Values in Action: The Games People Play*

Cultural values affect every aspect of our lives. Children's games, for example, may seem like lighthearted fun, but they are also an important way we teach young people what our culture deems important.

Using the sociological perspective, James Spates (1976a) sees in the familiar game King of the Mountain our cultural emphasis on achievement and success.[1]

> In this game, the King (winner) is the one who scrambles to the top of some designated area and holds it against all challengers (losers). This is a very gratifying game from the winner's point of view, for one learns what is it like (however brief is the tenure at the top before being thrown off) to be an unequivocal success, to be unquestionably better than the entire competition. (1976a:286)

Each player endeavors to become number one at the expense of all other players. But success has its price, and King of the Mountain teaches that as well.

> The King can never relax in such a pressurized position and constant vigilance is very difficult to endure, psychologically, for long. Additionally, the sole victor is likely to feel a certain alienation from others: Whom can he trust? Truly, "it is lonely at the top." (1976a:286)

Just as King of the Mountain conveys our cultural emphasis on winning, Tag, Keep Away, and Monkey in the Middle teach the lessons of being a loser. Spates observes that the loser in Tag, designated as "It," is singled out as unworthy of joining the group. This experience of being excluded can be so difficult to bear that other players may allow themselves to be tagged just to end "It's" ordeal. All players thus learn the importance of competing successfully, as well as the trials of not fitting in. Drawing on these sociological observations, we can appreciate better the prominence of competitive teams sports in U.S. culture and why star athletes are often celebrated as cultural heroes.

[1]The excerpt presented here has been slightly modified on the basis of unpublished versions of the study, with the permission of the author.

## Norms

For most of our history, women and men in the United States held to the idea that sexual intercourse should occur only within the bounds of marriage. By the late 1960s, however, beliefs had changed so that sexual activity became viewed as a form of recreation, sometimes involving people who hardly knew each other. By the mid-1980s, the rules changed again. Amid growing fears of sexually transmitted diseases, especially the deadly acquired immune deficiency syndrome (AIDS), people began rethinking the wisdom of the "sexual revolution," and more men and women were limiting their sexual activity to a single partner (McKusick et al., 1985; Smilgas, 1987).

Such patterns illustrate the operation of **norms**, rules and expectations by which a society guides the behavior of its members. Norms may be *proscriptive,* mandating what we should not do, as when health officials warn us to avoid casual sex. **Prescriptive** norms, on the other hand, state what we should do. Following practices of "safe sex," for example, has become such a norm in recent years.

Some norms apply virtually anywhere and at any time. For example, parents expect obedience from children regardless of the setting. Other norms, however, are situation-specific. We expect an audience to applaud at the completion of a musical performance; applause at the end of a classroom lecture if acceptable (if rare); applause at the completion of a sermon by a priest or rabbi, however, would be considered rude.

### *Mores and Folkways*

Norms have varying importance. William Graham Sumner (1959; orig. 1906), an early U.S. sociologist, used the term **mores** (pronounced More-ays; the rarely used singular form is mos) to refer to *norms* that *have great moral significance.* Proscriptive mores, often called *taboos,* include our society's prohibition against adults having sexual relations with children. Prescriptives mores include "standards of decency" that require people in public places to wear a certain minimal amount of clothing.

Because they are deemed vital to social life, mores usually apply to everyone, everywhere, all the time. For the same reason, violation of mores typically bring a swift and strong reaction from others. From early childhood, for example, we learn that stealing is a serious wrong that provokes a stern response.

Sumner used the term **folkways** to designate *norms* that have less *moral significance than mores.* Folkways include countless norms that guide our everyday lives, including how we dress and interact with others. In short, while mores distinguish between right and wrong, folkways draw a line between right and rude. Because they are less important than mores, societies afford individuals more personal discretion in matters involving folkways and punish infractions leniently. For example, a man who does not wear a tie to a formal dinner party is violating a part of folkways we call "etiquette." Although perhaps the subject of derisive comment, his action is likely to be tolerated. But imagine if the man were to arrive at the dinner party wearing only a tie. Violating cultural mores, he would be inviting more serious sanction.

Cultural norms, then, steer behavior by defining what is right and wrong, proper and improper. Although we sometimes bristle when others pressure us to conform, we generally embrace norms as part of the symbolic road map of culture because they make our encounters with others predictable and trustworthy.

### *Social Control*

Generally, students remain quiet in class, listening attentively to the teacher while occasionally taking notes. The enthusiastic student who looks for every chance to speak up is therefore courting criticism as a "nerd."

As members of cultural systems, we respond to each other with *sanctions,* which take the form of either reward or punishment. Sanctions can be powerful even when they are informal, as when a student who talks too much provokes groans of irritation from others. Some sanctions are formal, ranging from grades in school to prosecution by the criminal justice system. Taken together, all kinds of sanctions form the heart of a culture's system of **social control,** *various means by which members of society encourage conformity to norms.*

As we learn cultural norms, we develop the capacity to respond critically to our own behavior. Doing wrong—for instance, stealing from another—provokes us to experience guilt, the discomfort of judging our actions as wrong. Both guilt and *shame*—the painful acknowledgment of the disapproval of others—stem from internalizing cultural norms; that is, building them into our own personalities. Only cultural creatures can experience guilt and shame: This is probably what Mark Twain had in mind when he quipped that human beings "are the only animals that blush . . . or need to."

## "Ideal" and "Real" Culture

Societies employ values and norms as moral guidelines for their members. Such as, these cultural elements do not capture actual behavior as much as they state how we should behave. We must remember, then, that **ideal culture,** *social patterns mandated by cultural values and norms,* is not the same as **real culture,** *actual social patterns that only approximate cultural expectations.*

To illustrate, most women and men acknowledge the importance of sexual fidelity in marriage. Even so, at least one-third of married people are sexually unfaithful to their spouses at some point in the marriage. Such discrepancies are common to all societies, since no one lives up to ideal standards all the time. But a culture's moral prodding is crucial to shaping the lives of individuals all the same, calling to mind the old saying "Do as I say, not as I do."

## Material Culture and Technology

In addition to intangible elements such as values and norms, every culture encompasses a wide range of tangible (from Latin meaning "touchable") human creations that sociologists term *artifacts.* The Yanomamö gather forest materials to construct huts and hammocks. They craft bows and arrows to hunt and defend themselves, fashion tools for farming, and beautify their bodies with colored paints. An unfamiliar people's material culture may seem as strange to us as their language, values, and norms.

Although distinct, material and nonmaterial elements of culture are related. The material creations of a particular society typically express its cultural values. The fact that the Yanomamö spend much of their time making weapons, for instance, reflects the importance they place on warfare and militaristic skills. A Yanomamö male's poison-tipped arrows, for example, are among his most prized possessions.

Artifacts also provide clues to our own cultural values. Surely, our cherished values of individuality and independence have driven us to have a high regard for privately owned automobiles (and just as much scorn for mass transportation). We have constructed some 4 million miles of freeways in the United States, and our own nation's people own 150 million cars, about one car for every licensed driver!

In addition to reflecting values, material culture also reveals a society's **technology,** *knowledge that a society applies to the task of living in a physical environment.* In short, technology ties the world of nature to the world of culture. With their relatively simple technology, the Yanomamö interfere little with the natural environment. They are forced to remain keenly aware of the cycles of rainfall and the movement of animals they hunt for food. By contrast, technologically complex societies (such as those of North America) have an enormous impact on the natural world, reshaping the environment (for better or ill) according to their own interests and priorities.

Because we give science such great importance and praise the sophisticated technology it has produced, members of our society tend to judge cultures with simpler technology as less advanced. Some facts would support such an assessment. Life expectancy is one good measure of a society's level of well-being. Females born in the United States in 1990 can expect to live almost to the age of eighty, males to about seventy-two. Napoleon Chagnon estimated the life expectancy of the Yanomamö at only about forty years.

However, we must be careful not to make self-serving judgments about cultures that differ from our own. Although many Yanomamö are eager to gain modern technology (such as steel tools and shotguns), it may surprise you to learn that they are generally well fed by world standards and most are quite satisfied with their lives (Chagnon, 1992). Remember, too, that while our powerful and complex technology has produced work-reducing devices and seemingly miraculous forms of medical treatment, it has also contributed to unhealthy levels of stress, eroded the quality of the natural environment, and created weapons capable of destroying in a flash everything that humankind has managed to achieve throughout history.

Finally, technology is another cultural element that varies substantially within the United States. Although many of us cannot imagine life without CD players, televisions, and microwave ovens, some members of our society cannot afford such items, and others reject them on principle. The Amish, for example, live in small farming communities across Pennsylvania, Ohio, and Indiana. They shun most modern conveniences as a matter of religious conviction. With their traditional black garb and horse-drawn buggies, the Amish may seem like a curious relic of the past. Yet their communities thrive, grounded in strong families and individuals who enjoy a sense of identity and purpose. And many of the thousands of outsiders who observe them each year come away with the suspicion that Amish communities may be "islands of sanity in a culture gripped by commercialism and technology run wild" (Hostetler, 1980:4).

## High Culture and Popular Culture

In everyday conversation, we usually reserve the term "culture" for sophisticated art forms such as classical literature, music, dance, and painting. We praise college professors, film directors, or dance choreographers as "cultured," because they presumably appreciate the "finer things in life." The term "culture" itself has the same Latin root as the word "cultivate," suggesting that the "cultured" individual has cultivated or refined tastes.

By contrast, we speak less generously of ordinary people, assuming that they are less cultivated and their cultural patterns are somehow less worthy. In more concrete terms, we are tempted to judge the music of Mozart as "more cultured" than Motown, fine cuisine as better than fish sticks, and polo as more polished than ping pong.

When we make judgments, we are recognizing that all cultural patterns are not equally accessible to all members of a society (Hall & Neitz, 1993). Sociologists use the shorthand term **high culture**[2] to refer to *cultural patterns that distinguish a society's elite;* **popular culture**, then, designates *cultural patterns that are widespread among a society's population.*

Common sense may suggest that high culture is superior to popular culture. It is the lives of elites, after all, and not those of ordinary women and men, that make up most of documented history. But sociologists are uneasy with such a sweeping evaluation (Gans, 1974). When sociologists use the term "culture," they refer to all elements of a society's way of life, even while recognizing that cultural patterns vary throughout a population.

One reason to resist quick judgments about the merits of high culture versus popular culture is, first, that neither elites nor ordinary people have uniform tastes and interests; people in both categories differ in numerous ways. Second, do we praise high culture because it is inherently better than popular culture, or simply because its supporters have more prestige and power to begin with? For example, there is no difference between a violin and a fiddle; however, we name the instrument one way when it is used to produce a type of music typically enjoyed by a person of higher position, and the other way when producing music appreciated by an individual with lower social standing.

One additional point: Given their technological know-how, modern, industrial societies like our own create and disperse many cultural elements on an unprecedented scale. In other words, as John Hall

[2] The term "high culture" is derived from the more popular term "highbrow." Influenced by phrenology, the bogus nineteenth-century theory that personality was affected by the shape of the human skull, people a century ago contrasted the praiseworthy tastes of those they termed "highbrows" with the contemptible appetites of others they derided as "lowbrows."

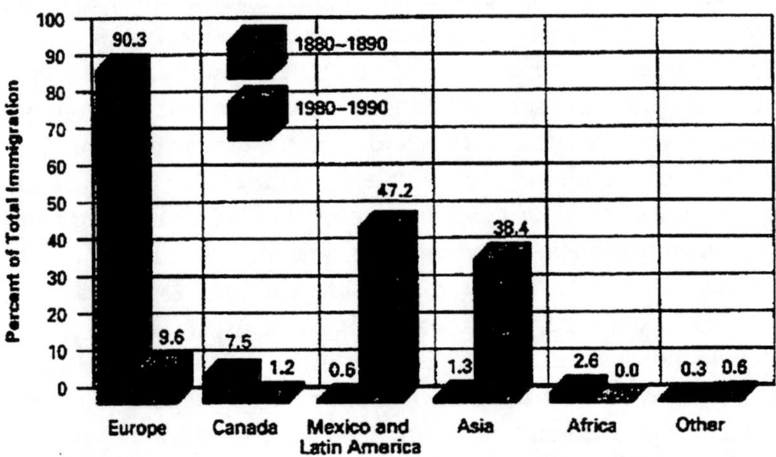


**FIGURE 4–1**
**Recorded Immigration to the United States, by Region of Birth, 1880–1890 and 1980–1990**

and Mary Jo Neitz (1993:6) point out, culture in the United States is now a process of mass production, mass distribution, and mass consumption. This mass scale means that the production of material things (clothing, for example) as well as the shaping of public attitudes (say, about fashion) are under the control of large organizations that utilize vast marketing systems and the mass media. Again, the popularity of such cultural patterns does not mean that they are good or bad, but it does imply that industrial societies are very efficient in generating many, changing cultural elements.

## CULTURAL DIVERSITY: MANY WAYS OF LIFE IN ONE WORLD

The United States has never been characterized by a single way of life, a fact that follows from this nation's history of immigration. Between 1820 (when the government began keeping track of immigration) and 1990, more than 55 million people came to these shores from other countries. A century ago, as shown in Figure 4-1, most immigrants hailed from Europe. By the 1980s, however, a large minority of newcomers were arriving from Latin America and Asia. This massive immigration has made the United States—far more than most nations of the world—a land of cultural diversity.

Cultural variety has always been with us, evident in the distinctive accents of, say, New Englanders or southerners. Ours has also been a nation of religious pluralism, a land of many ethnic traditions, and a home to countless people who try to be like no one else.

Given this diversity, what sociologists sometimes describe as our "cloth of culture" might more accurately be called a "patchwork quilt." To understand the reality of life in the United States, then, we must move beyond widespread cultural patterns, such as the key values identified by Robin Williams (1970), to consider cultural diversity.

### Subculture

The term **subculture** refers to *cultural patterns that distinguish some segment of a society's population.* Inner-city teens, elderly Polish Americans, "Yankee" New Englanders, homeless people, and very rich families all display subcultural patterns. Occupations, too, foster distinctive subcultures, involving unusual ways of acting, speaking, and dressing, as anyone who has ever spent time with surfers, cowboys, race-car drivers, jazz musicians, or even sociologists can attest. Rural people sometimes poke fun at the ways of "city slickers," who, in turn, jeer back at their "country cousins." Sexual orientation generates yet another subculture in our society, especially in cities like San Francisco, Los Angeles, and New York, where large numbers of gay men and women live.

Although categories of people may differ among themselves in some respects, we should be careful not to assume that any particular individuals are defined by one or another subculture. We all participate simultaneously in numerous subcultures without necessarily becoming very committed to any of them.

In some cases, however, important cultural traits such as ethnicity or religion do set off people from one another—sometimes with tragic results. Consider the former nation of Yugoslavia in southeastern Europe. The recent turmoil there has been fueled by astounding cultural diversity. This *one* small country (which before its breakup was no bigger than the state of Wyoming, with a population of 25 million) made use of *two* alphabets, *three* religions, and *four* languages; it was home to *five* major nationalities, was divided into *six* separate republics, and absorbed the cultural influences of *seven* other nations with which it shared borders. The cultural conflict that threw this nation into civil war shows that subcultures are a source not only of pleasing variety but also of tensions and outright violence.

We in the United States have historically taught our children to view this country as a "melting pot" in which many nationalities blend into a single "American" culture. But, given the extent of our cultural diversity, we might well question the truth of this notion. People of different ways of life have mixed and melded to some extent in the United States, but cultural divisions in our society remain powerful and persistent.

The problem here is that cultural diversity involves not just *variety* but also *hierarchy*. Too often, what we view as "dominant" cultural patterns characterize powerful segments of the U.S. population, while those we term "subcultures" are traits of disadvantaged people. This dilemma has led some researchers to focus on the less powerful members of our society in a new approach called multiculturalism.

## Multiculturalism

In recent years, the United States has been facing up to the challenge of **multiculturalism**, *an educational program recognizing past and present cultural diversity in U.S. society and promoting the equality of all cultural traditions*. This movement represents a sharp turn from the past, when our society downplayed cultural diversity and defined itself primarily in terms familiar to European (and especially English) immigrants. At this point, a spirited debate continues over whether we should stress the common elements in our national experience, or highlight the diversity that characterizes a nation of immigrants.

*E Pluribus Unum*, the familiar Latin words that appear on each U.S. coin, means "out of many, one." This motto symbolizes not only our national political confederation, but it also describes the cultural goal of forging a new and distinctive way of life from the varied experiences of immigrants from around the world. The notion of the United States as a cultural "melting pot" is as old as the nation itself. George Washington, the first U.S. president, confidently predicted that future immigrants would learn the new nation's ways to become "one people" (Gray, 1991).

But, from the outset, reality differed from this ideal. Instead of melting together into a single heritage, cultures in the United States hardened into a hierarchy. Dominating the public life of this nation were English social patterns and institutions (including language, economy, legal system, and religion). Members of the non-English minority were advised to model themselves after "their betters." "Melting," in effect, turned out to be a process of Anglicizing. As multiculturalists see it, early in our history, this society set up the English way of life as an ideal to which all should aspire and by which all should be judged.

For more than two centuries, historians in the United States have highlighted the role of descendants of the English and other Europeans and described events from their point of view, in the process pushing to the side the perspectives and accomplishment of Native Americans, people of African descent, and immigrants from Asia. Multiculturalists condemn this singular pattern as **Eurocentrism**, *the dominance of European (particularly English) cultural patterns*. Molefi Kete Asante, a leading advocate of multiculturalism, suggests that like "the fifteenth-century Europeans who could not cease believing that the earth was the center of the universe, many today find it difficult to cease viewing European culture as the center of the social universe" (1988:7).

## Seeing Ourselves

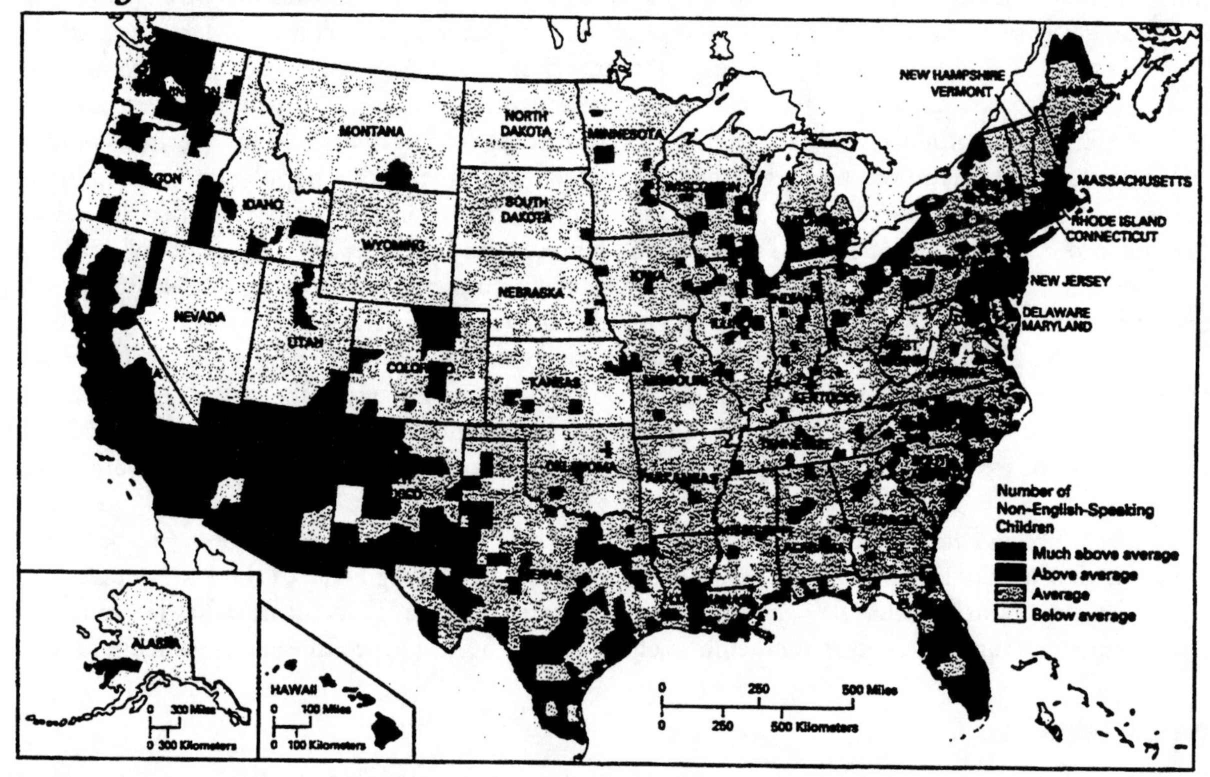


**NATIONAL MAP 4–1 Language Diversity Across the United States**
According to the 1990 Census, 6.3 million children (14 percent of all children aged five through seventeen) speak a language other than English at home. Most of these children are of Hispanic ancestry. These boys and girls are not spread equally throughout the country, however. Children in California, for example, speak more than one hundred languages at home and at school. How would you describe the geographical distribution of these children? What do you think accounts for this pattern?

Adapted from *American Demographics* magazine, April 1993, p. 40. Reprinted with permission. © 1993. *American Demographics* magazine, Ithaca, New York. Data from the 1990 decennial census.

Few deny that our culture has wide-ranging roots. But multiculturalism is controversial at the very least because it asks us to rethink the norms and values at the core of our society. Not surprisingly, battles over how to describe our nation's culture are now raging on many fronts.

A first contested issue centers on language. For a decade, Congress has debated a proposal to designate English as the official language of the United States. It has yet to decide the matter, although, by 1991, legislatures in sixteen states had enacted such a directive. To some, "official English" may seem unnecessary, since for centuries this language has been central to U.S. culture. Yet, by 1990, some 30 million men and women—at least one in ten—spoke a language other than English in their homes. And their ranks will swell to an estimated 40 million by the beginning of the next century. Spanish is our second national language, and other U.S. tongues include Italian, German, French, Filipino, Japanese, Korean, Vietnamese and a host of Native-American languages—several hundred languages in all. National Map 4-1 takes a look at where in the United States there are large numbers of children whose first language is not English.

A second controversy involves how our nation's schools—from the early grades through college—should teach about culture. It is among educators that the clash over multiculturalism has been most intense. Two basic positions have emerged from this discussion.

Proponents defend multiculturalism, first, as a strategy to present a more accurate picture of our country's *past.* Proposed educational reforms seek, for example, to temper the simplistic praise directed at

Christopher Columbus and other European explorers by recognizing, first, that the so-called "New World" had been inhabited for tens of thousands of years before Europeans arrived here and, second, by assessing the tragic impact of the European conquest on the native peoples of this hemisphere. From the point of view of Native Americans, contact with Europeans unleashed five centuries of domination and death from war and disease. In short, a multicultural approach would recover the history and achievements of many women and men whose cultural backgrounds up to now have kept them on the sidelines of history.

Second, proponents claim, multiculturalism is a means to come to terms with our country's even more diverse *present*. During the 1980s, the Hispanic population of the United States increased by more than 50 percent, and the number of Asian Americans doubled. According to some projections, children born in the 1990s will live to see people of African, Asian, and Hispanic ancestry become a *majority* of this country's population.

Third, proponents assert that multiculturalism is a way to strengthen the academic achievement of African-American children and others who may feel left out of traditional educational programs. To counter pervasive Eurocentrism, some multiculturalists are calling for **Afrocentrism,** *the dominance of African cultural patterns in people's lives,* which they see as a corrective for centuries of minimizing or altogether ignoring the cultural achievements of African societies and African Americans.

Fourth and finally, proponents see multiculturalism as worthwhile preparation for all people in the United States to live in a world that is increasingly interdependent. As various chapters of this book explain, social patterns in this country are becoming more closely linked to issues and events elsewhere in the world. Multiculturalism undermines nationalistic prejudices by pointing out global connectedness.

Although multiculturalism has found widespread favor in the last several years, it has provoked its share of criticism as well. What most troubles opponents of multiculturalism is that it encourages divisiveness rather than unity by urging individuals to identify with their own category rather than with the nation as a whole.

A second criticism is that multiculturalism erodes any claim to common truth by maintaining that we should evaluate all ideas according to the race (and sex) of those who present them. Is there no common humanity, critics ask, but only an "African experience," a "European experience," and so on?

A third problem, say the critics, is that multiculturalism may not end up helping minorities as proponents say it does. Critics argue that multiculturalist initiatives (from African-American studies to all-black dorms) seem to demand precisely the kind of racial segregation that our nation has struggled for decades to end. Then, too, an Afrocentric curriculum may well deny children a wide range of important knowledge and skills by forcing them to study only certain topics from a single point of view. Historian Arthur Schlesinger, Jr. (1991:21) puts the matter bluntly: "If a Kleagle of the Ku Klux Klan wanted to use the schools to handicap black Americans, he could hardly come up with anything more effective than the 'Afrocentric' curriculum."

Is there any common ground in this debate? Although sharp differences exist, the answer is yes. Virtually everyone agrees that we all need to gain greater appreciation of our cultural diversity. Further, because racial and ethnic minorities may constitute a majority of the U.S. population during the next century, efforts in this direction are needed now. But precisely where the balance is to be stuck—between the pluribus and the unum—will likely remain a divisive issue for some time to come.

## Counterculture

Cultural diversity sometimes takes the form of active rejection of some widely shared ideas or objects. **Counterculture** *refers to cultural patterns that strongly oppose those widely accepted within a society.* People who embrace a counterculture may well challenge widely held notions about morality, perhaps provoking efforts by others to repress them.

In many societies, countercultures spring from adolescence (Spates, 1976b, 1983; Spates & Perkins, 1982). More of us are familiar with the youth-oriented counterculture of the 1960s that attracted considerable media coverage. Hippies criticized the cultural mainstream as overly competitive, self-centered, and materialistic. Instead, they favored a cooperative lifestyle in which "being" took precedence over "doing" and the capacity for personal growth—or "expanded consciousness"—was prized over material possessions like homes and cars. Such differences led many hippies at that time to "drop out" of the larger society. Note, however, the growing popularity of the idea of personal growth over the last several decades. This trend reminds us that what is countercultural at one point in time may become much more popular later on.

Counterculture may involve not only distinctive values, but unconventional behavior (including dress and forms of greeting) as well as music. Many members of the 1960s counterculture, for instance, drew personal identify from long hair, headbands, and blue jeans, from displaying a peace sign rather than offering a handshake, and from enjoying ever-present rock and roll music, a music form that had far less of the mainstream respectability it enjoys today.

Countercultures still exist, of course. In the United States, the Ku Klux Klan and other white supremacist groups promote violence and racial hatred in order to protect what they see as "real American values." In Europe, young "punks" express contempt for others by shaving their heads or multicolored hairstyles, black leather, and chains—all intended to offend more conventional members of their societies.

## Cultural Change

All societies throughout history have recognized the basic human truth that "All things shall pass." Even the dinosaurs, who thrived on this planet for some 160 million years, remain only as fossils. And what of the human species, which, at 250,000 years of age, is far too young to have left fossils? Whether humanity will survive for millions of years to come is a hotly debated question. All we can say with certainty is that, given our reliance on culture, for as long as we survive our record will be one of rapid and dramatic change.

Cultural change is continuous, even though we may perceive it only over a period of years. Consider, for example, recent trends in family life. As more women have joined the labor force, many have delayed marriage and having children, or remained single and had children all the same. With both women and men now enjoying greater financial independence, the divorce rate has risen to twice what it was fifty years ago. And over one generation, the number of single-parent households more than doubled, so that a majority of our nation's children now live with only one parent before they reach the age of eighteen.

Table 4.1 presents another dimension of change, comparing the attitudes of first-year college students in 1968 with those of men and women matriculating in 1992. Some things have changed only slightly: About the same proportion of students look forward to raising a family. But the students of the 1990s are much more interested in being well off financially, while their counterparts in the late 1960s were concerned with developing a philosophy of life. (Worth noting is an emerging countertrend during the last five years, suggesting young people are moving away from the materialism of the 1980s). Note, too, that changes in attitude have generally been greater among women than among men. This differential, no doubt, reflect the fact that the women's movement, concerned with social equality for the two sexes, intensified after 1968.

Change in one dimension of a culture usually sparks other transformations as well. As noted earlier, for instance, women's rising participation in the labor force involves changing patterns of marriage. Such connections illustrate the principle of **cultural integration,** *the close relationship among various elements of a cultural system.* Some elements of a cultural system, however, typically change more rapidly than others. William Ogburn (1964) observed that technology moves quickly, generating new elements of material culture (like "test-tube babies") faster than nonmaterial culture (such as ideas about parenthood) can keep up with them. Ogburn called this inconsistency **cultural lag,** *the fact that cultural elements change at different rates, which may disrupt a cultural system.* In a culture with the technical ability to allow one woman to give birth to a child by using another woman's egg, which has been fertilized in a laboratory

**TABLE 4.1 Attitudes Among Students Entering U.S. Colleges, 1968 and 1992**

| Life Objectives (Essential or Very Important | | 1968 | 1992 | Change |
|---|---|---|---|---|
| Develop a philosophy of life | Male | 79 | 44 | –35 |
| | Female | 87 | 47 | –40 |
| Keep up with political affairs | Male | 52 | 41 | –11 |
| | Female | 52 | 37 | –15 |
| Help others in difficulty | Male | 50 | 52 | + 2 |
| | Female | 71 | 72 | + 1 |
| Raise a family | Male | 64 | 69 | + 5 |
| | Female | 72 | 72 | 0 |
| Be successful in my own business | Male | 55 | 48 | – 7 |
| | Female | 32 | 37 | + 5 |
| Be well off financially | Male | 51 | 76 | +25 |
| | Female | 27 | 71 | +44 |

NOTE: To allow comparisons, data from the early 1970s rather than 1968 are used for some items.

SOURCES: Richard G. Braungart and Margaret M. Braungart, "From Yippies to Yuppies: Twenty Years of Freshmen Attitudes, "*Puplic Opinion*, vol. 11, no. 3 (September–October 1988): 53–56; Eric L. Dey, Alexander W. Astin, William S. Korn, and Ellyne R. Riggs, *The American Freshman: National Norms for Fall 1992* (Los Angeles: UCLA Higher Education Research Institute, 1992).

with the sperm of a total stranger, how are we to apply the traditional notions of motherhood and fatherhood?

Cultural changes are set in motion in three ways. The first is *invention,* the process of creating new cultural elements. Invention has given us the telephone (1876), the airplane (1903), and the aerosol spray can (1941), all of which have had a tremendous impact on our way of life. The process of invention goes on constantly, as indicated by the thousands of applications submitted annually to the United States Patent Office.

*Discovery,* a second cause of cultural change, involves recognizing and understanding something not fully understood before—from a distant star, to the foods of another culture, to the muscle power of U.S. women. Discovery often results from scientific research; many medical breakthroughs occur this way. Yet discovery can also happen quite by accident, as when Marie Curie left a rock on a piece of photographic paper in 1898 and thus discovered radium.

The third cause of cultural change is *diffusion,* the spread of cultural traits from one society to another. Missionaries and anthropologists like Napoleon Chagnon have introduced new cultural elements to many Yanomamö villages. Cultural traits have likewise spread from the United States throughout the world: jazz music, with its roots deep in the culture of African Americans; computers, first constructed in the mid-1940s in a Philadelphia laboratory; and even the United States Constitution, used by several other countries to construct their own political system.

Diffusion works the other way as well, so that much of what we assume is inherently "American" actually comes from other cultures. Ralph Linton (1937) explained that many commonplace elements of our way of life—most clothing and furniture, clocks, newspapers, money, and even the English Language—are all derived from other cultures. As the technology of travel and communication makes the world smaller, the rate of cultural diffusion increases as well.

## Ethnocentrism and Cultural Relativity

A question in the well-known game Trivial Pursuit asks which beverage is most popular in the United States. Milk? Soft drinks? Coffee? The answer is soft drinks, but all of the beverages mentioned are favored by members of our society. But if members of the Masai of eastern Africa were to join the game, their answer might well be, "goat blood." To most of us, of course, the idea of drinking blood is downright unnatural, if not revolting. But we should keep in mind that drinking cow's milk (which we all "know" is healthier than soft drinks or coffee) is intolerable to billions of people in the world, including most Chinese (Harris, 1985).

People everywhere consider their own values, norms, and beliefs to be natural and right. For example, the tradition in Japan is to name intersections, rather than streets; to North Americans, whose practice is to do the opposite, this cultural pattern is irritating, at best. Most North Americans are particular about keeping several feet of "personal space" between them and others; most Arabs, who routinely stand much closer to one another while engaging in conversation, thus view North Americans as rude and stand-offish (Hall, 1966).

Favoring what is familiar in this way, we often respond with suspicion or hostility to others who offend our own ideas of what is proper. Even Napoleon Chagnon, trained as an anthropologist to have an open mind, recoiled with disgust at the "naked, sweaty, and hideous" Yanomamö. Later, Chagnon encountered several cultural practices that, from his point of view, seemed outrageous. For example, Yanomamö men offer to share their wives sexually with younger brothers or friends. From the men's point of view, this practice symbolizes friendship and generosity. By our cultural standards, however, this behavior smacks of moral perversity and gross unfairness to women. Would we be right in condemning the Yanomamö for their actions?

At first glance, the answer would seem to be yes. After all, our culture provides us with standards to judge right and wrong. People everywhere exhibit **ethnocentrism,** *the practice of judging another culture by the standards of one's own culture.* Although some amount of ethnocentrism is universal, it is also troubling. Why should we expect others to endorse our ethical principles rather than their own? Should we assume our norms are in some sense superior to those of others?

Ethnocentrism is deeper in our way of life than we may initially think. Take the seemingly trivial matter of people in north America referring to the region of the world dominated by China as the "Far East." Such a term, which has little meaning to the Chinese, is an ethnocentric expression for an area that is far east of *us.* For their part, the Chinese use a character to designate their nation that is translated as "Middle Kingdom," suggesting that they, too, see their society as the center of the world.

Ethnocentrism functions to enhance morale and solidarity among members of a society. But it can be dysfunctional as well, since judging practices of others as an outsider yields not only a self-serving but a distorted view of our culturally diverse world. Note how odd Figure 4-2, on page 97, appears to us, since we are accustomed to placing the United States at the top and center of a map of the Western Hemisphere.

An alternative to ethnocentrism is to try to imagine unfamiliar cultural traits from the point of view of others rather than ourselves. The casual observer who puzzles at an Amish farmer tilling hundreds of acres with a team of horses rather than a tractor might initially dismiss such a farming strategy as hopelessly backward and inefficient. But, from the Amish point of view, hard work is a foundation of religious discipline. The Amish are well aware of farm tractors; they simply realize that using such machinery would be their undoing.

This alternative approach is **cultural relativism,** *the practice of judging a culture by its own standards.* Cultural relativism is a difficult attitude to assume because it requires not only understanding the values and norms of another society but also suspending cultural standards we have known all our lives. But, as people of the world come into increasing contact with one another, the need to more fully understand other cultures grows steadily.

**FIGURE 4–2 The View from "Down Under"**
North America should be "up" and South America "down," or so we think. But, because we live on a globe, such notions are conventions rather than absolutes. The reason that this map of the Western Hemisphere looks wrong to us is not that it is geographically inaccurate; it simply violates our ethnocentric assumption that the United States should be "above" the rest of the Americas.

In the ever-expanding global economy, for example, U.S. business is learning that success depends on cultural sophistication and sensitivity. Consider the troubles several corporations had when they carelessly translated their advertising slogans into Spanish. General Motors soon learned that sales of its Nova were hampered by a product name that in Spanish means "Doesn't Go." The phrase "Turn It Loose," used in a promotion of Coors beer, startled customers who read words meaning "Suffer from Diarrhea." Braniff airlines turned "Fly in Leather" into clumsy Spanish reading "Fly Naked." Eastern Airlines transformed its slogan "We Earn Our Wings Daily" into words consumers read as "We Fly Daily to Heaven." And even Frank Perdue fell victim to poor marketing when his pitch "It Takes a Tough Man to Make a Tender Chicken" ended up as Spanish for "It Takes a Sexually Excited Man to Make a Chicken Affectionate" (Helin, 1992).

Cultural understanding is the key to successful business ventures. It may also turn out to be crucial to a peaceful world as well. But cultural relativity has problems of its own. One can find virtually any kind of behavior somewhere in the world; does that mean that anything and everything has equal claim to being morally right? What about Yanomamö men who routinely offer their wives to others or violently punish a woman who displeases them? Even in the unlikely event that Yanomamö women accept this sort of treatment, should we pronounce such practices morally right simply because the Yanomamö themselves accept them?

Since we all are members of a single species, we might assume there must be universal standards of conduct for everyone. But what are they? In trying to discern what is truly good, how can we avoid imposing our own standards of fair play on everyone else? There are no simple answers. But here are several guidelines to keep in mind when encountering other cultures.

First, realize that, while cultural differences may be fascinating, they can also be deeply disturbing; be prepared for an emotional dimension in encountering them. Second, try to observe unfamiliar cultural surroundings with an open mind. At best, resist making quick judgments of others. Third, try to imagine what you see from *their* point of view rather than yours. Fourth, after careful and critical thought, try to evaluate what you find in another culture. After all, there is no moral virtue in passively accepting everything one encounters. But, in reaching that judgment, bear in mind that—despite sensitivity and imagination—you can never really experience the world as others do. Fifth, and finally, turn the argument around and try to evaluate your own way of life as others might see it. After all, in studying others, ultimately we learn about ourselves.

## A Global Culture?

Today, more than ever before, we can observe many of the same cultural patterns the world over. Walking the streets of Seoul (South Korea), Kuala Lumpur (Malaysia), Madras (India), Cairo (Egypt), and Casablanca (Morocco), we find familiar forms of dress, hear well-known pop music, and see advertising for many of the same products we use at home. Just as important, as suggested earlier by Global Map 4-1, English is rapidly emerging as the preferred second language of most of the world. Are we witnessing the birth of a global culture?

The world is still broken up into about 190 nation-states and thousands of different societies based on common language, cultural heritage, and kinship ties. Further, as the recent violence in Germany, the former Yugoslavia, the Middle East, India, and elsewhere attests, many people are intolerant of others who differ culturally from themselves. Yet, on a broader level, the societies of the world now have more contact with one another, and enjoy more cooperation, than ever before. Global connections involve the flow of goods, information, and people.

1. **The global economy: the flow of goods.** Throughout history, societies have traded with each other. The extent of international trade, however, has never been greater. Since products are an important dimension of culture, the emerging global economy has introduced many of the same consumer goods (from T-shirts to rock music to automobiles) the world over.

2. **Global communications: the flow of information.** Satellite-based communications now enable people throughout the world to experience—often as they happen—the sights and sounds of events taking place thousands of miles away. Even a century ago, communication links in most of the world were based on written messages delivered by boat, train, horse and wagon, or occasionally by telegraph wire. Today, there are few regions where a person cannot locate a telephone, radio, television, computer and modem, or a facsimile (fax) machine that transmits information almost instantly.
3. **Global migration: the flow of people.** As people learn more about the rest of the world, they are increasingly likely to relocate to a place where they imagine life will be better. War and other strife also force people to move. Whatever the reason, new transportation technology—especially air travel—now makes relocating easier than ever before. As a result, most societies contain significant numbers of people born in another country (22 million people, about 9 percent of the U.S. population, were born abroad).

These global links have made the cultures of the world more similar in at least superficial respects. But there are three important limitations to the global culture thesis. First, the flow of goods, information, and people has been uneven throughout the world. Generally speaking, urban areas (that are centers of commerce, communication, and people) are more closely linked to one another, while rural villages remain isolated. Chagnon (1992) reports, for example, that there are still a few Yanomamö settlements in Venezuela that have had little or no contact with outsiders. Then, too, the greater economic and military power of North America and Western Europe means that nations in these regions influence the rest of the world more than the other way around.

A second problem with the global culture thesis is that it assumes that people everywhere want and are able to *afford* various goods and services. The grinding poverty in much of the world deprives people of even the basic necessities of a safe and secure life.

Third, although any number of cultural traits are now found throughout much of the world, we should not conclude that people everywhere attach the same meanings to them. When we in the United States eagerly embrace, say, a "new" form of African music, we do so on our own terms with little understanding of the music's meaning to its creators. Similarly, when people in other parts of the world begin playing basketball or reading the U.S. press, they will always view these things through their own cultural "lenses" (Featherstone, 1990; Hall & Neitz, 1993).

## THEORETICAL ANALYSIS OF CULTURE

Culture provides us with the means to understand ourselves and the surrounding world. Sociologists and anthropologists, however, have the special task of comprehending culture. Analyzing such a complex concept requires employing several theoretical approaches.

### Structural-Functional Analysis

The structural-functional analysis presents society as a relatively stable system of integrated parts functioning to meet human needs. From this point of view, then, various cultural traits each work to maintain the overall operation of society.

The reason for the stability of a cultural system, as functionalists see it, is that core values, like the U.S. values noted earlier, anchor its way of life (Parsons, 1964; Williams, 1970). This assertion that ideas (rather than, say, the system of material production) are the basis of human reality aligns structural-functionalism with the philosophical doctrine of *idealism.* Core values are evident in most everyday activities, serving both to direct and bind together members of a society. New arrivals, of course, will not necessarily share a society's core values. But, according to the functionalist melting-pot idea, immigrants gradually embrace such values over time.

The structural-functional approach helps make sense of an unfamiliar cultural setting. Recall, for example, the Amish farmer plowing hundreds of acres with a team of horses. Within the Amish cultural system, relying on horses while rejecting tractors and automobiles makes sense because it ensures that there is plenty of hard work. Continuous labor—usually outside the home for men and inside for women—functions to maintain the Amish value of discipline, which shapes Amish religious life. Long days of teamwork, along with family meals and recreation at home, not only make the Amish self-sufficient but unify families and local communities (Hostetler, 1980).

Of course, Amish practices have dysfunctions as well. Their trait of "shunning," by which a community ends social contact with anyone judged to have violated Amish mores, may ensure conformity but at the cost of generating tensions and, from time to time, lasting divisions in a community.

Because cultures are strategies to meet human needs, we would expect that cultures the world over would have some elements in common. The term **cultural universals** refers *to traits that are part of every known culture.* Comparing hundreds of cultures, George Murdock (1945) found dozens of traits common to them all. One cultural university is the family, which functions everywhere to control sexual reproduction and to care for children. Funeral rites, too, are found everywhere, because all human communities cope with the reality of death. Jokes are also a cultural universal, acting as a relatively safe means of releasing social tensions.

**Critical evaluation** A strength of the structural-functional paradigm is showing how culture operates as an integrated system for meeting human needs. One limitation of this approach, however, is its tendency to paint cultural values as embraced by everyone in a society. As we have explained, the cultural patterns favored by powerful people often dominate a society, while the ways of life of others are pushed to the margins. Put another way, societies typically have more culture-based conflict than structural-functional analysis suggest. Similarly, by emphasizing cultural stability, this paradigm downplays the extent of change.

## Social-Conflict Analysis

The social-conflict paradigm presents culture in a very different light. To conflict theorists, social inequality transforms a cultural system into a dynamic arena of controversy. Conflict analysis draws attention to the ways in which any particular aspect of culture benefits some members of society at the expense of others.

Social-conflict analysis critically questions why certain values dominate in a society. What forces generate one set of values rather than another? Who benefits from these social arrangements? Sociologists using this paradigm, especially those influenced by Karl Marx, argued that values are shaped by a society's system of economic production. "It is not the consciousness of men that determines their existence," Marx proclaimed. "It is their social existence that determines their consciousness" (1977:4; orig. 1859). Social-conflict theory, then, is rooted in the philosophical doctrine of *materialism,* the assertion that how people fashion their material world (for example, the capitalist economy in the United States) has a powerful effect on other dimensions of their culture. Such a materialist approach contracts with the idealist learnings of structural-functionalism.

Social-conflict analysis suggests that the competitive and individualistic values of U.S. society reflect our capitalist economy and thus serve the interests of people who own factories and other businesses. The culture of capitalism further teaches us to believe that the rich and powerful have more talent and discipline than others and therefore deserve their wealth and privileges. Viewing capitalism as somehow "natural," then, leads people to distrust efforts to decrease the economic disparity found in the United States.

Eventually, however, the strains fostered by social inequality push a society toward transformation. The civil rights movement and the women's movement exemplify the drive for change supported by disadvantaged segments of the U.S. population. Both, too, have encountered opposition from defenders of the status quo.

**Critical evaluation** The strength of the social-conflict paradigm lies in showing that, if cultural systems address human needs, they do so unequally. Put otherwise, this orientation holds that a key function of cultural elements is to maintain the dominance of some people over others. This inequity, in turn, generates pressure toward change. A limitation of the social-conflict paradigm is that, stressing the divisiveness of culture, it understates the ways in which cultural patterns integrate members of society. Thus we should consider both social-conflict and structural-functional insights to gain a fuller understanding of culture.

## Cultural Ecology

A third theoretical paradigm is derived from ecology, the natural science that explores the relationship between a living organism and its environment. **Cultural ecology**, *then, is a theoretical paradigm that explores the relationship between human culture and the physical environment.* This paradigm leads us to ask, for instance, how climate or the availability of natural resources shape cultural patterns.

Consider the case of India, a nation that contends with widespread hunger and malnutrition, yet has cultural norms that prohibit the killing of cows. According to Hindu belief, cows are sacred animals. To North Americans who enjoy so much beef, this is puzzling. Why should Indians not consume beef to supplement their diet?

Investigating rural India's ecology, Marvin Harris (1975) concluded that the Hindu veneration of the cow makes sense because the importance of these animals extends well beyond their value as a food source. Harris points out that cows cost little to raise, since they consume grasses of no interest to humans. And cows produce two valuable resources: oxen (their neutered offspring) and manure. Unable to afford expensive farm machinery, Indian farmers rely on oxen to power their plows. For Indians, killing cows would be as clever as farmers in the United States destroying factories that build tractors. Furthermore, each year millions of tons of cow manure are processed into building material and burned as fuel (India has little oil, coal, or wood). To kill cows, then, would deprive Indians of homes and a major source of heat. In sum, there are sound ecological reasons for Indian culture to protect the cow.

**Critical evaluation** Cultural ecology expands our understanding of culture by highlighting its interplay with the environment. This approach reveals how societies devise cultural patterns in response to particular natural conditions. However, this paradigm has two limitations. First, only rarely can we draw simple or direct connections between the environment and culture because cultural and physical forces interact in complex ways. Second, it is easier to discern the effect of environment on culture in technologically simple settings like rural India. A far more difficult task is investigating cases of technologically sophisticated societies that extensively manipulate the natural world.

## Sociobiology

Sociology has maintained a rather uneasy relationship with biology. In part, this uneasiness stems from a rivalry between two disciplines that study human life. But it also runs deeper because early biological assertions about human behavior—for example that some categories of people are inherently "better" than others—were expressions of historical racism and ethnocentrism rather than legitimate science. Early sociologists provided evidence to refute such thinking.

By the middle of this century, sociologists had demonstrated that culture rather than biology is the major force shaping human behavior. But this does not mean that biology has nothing to do with how we live. Exploring the connections between our biological existence and the culture we create is the task of **sociobiology**, *a theoretical paradigm that explores ways in which biological forces affect human culture.*

Sociobiology rests upon the logic of evolution. In *On the Origin of Species,* Charles Darwin (1859) asserted that living organisms change over long periods of time as a result of natural selection, a matter of four simple principles. First, all living things live and reproduce within a natural setting. Second, genes—

the basic units of life that carry traits of one generation into the next—vary randomly in each species. Genetic variation allows any species to "try out" new life patterns in a particular environment. Third, due to this variation, some organisms are more likely to survive than others and to pass on their advantageous genes to their offspring. Fourth and finally, over thousands of generations, genetic patterns that promote survival and reproduction become dominant. In this way, as biologists say, a species *adapts* to its environment, and dominate traits represent the "nature" of the organism.

Sociobiologists suggest that the large number of cultural universals reflects the fact that we are all members of a single biological species. One example of special interest to sociobiologists is the universal pattern we commonly call the "double standard" by which men engage in sexual activity more freely than women do. As sex researcher Alfred Kinsey put it, "Among all people everywhere in the world, the male is more likely than the female to desire sex with a variety of partners" (quoted in Barash, 1981:49).

We all know that children result from joining a woman's egg with a man's sperm. But the biological significance of a single sperm and a single egg are dramatically different. For healthy men, sperm represents a "renewable resource" produced by the testes throughout most of life. A man releases hundreds of millions of sperm in a single ejaculation—technically, enough to fertilize every woman in North America (Barash, 1981:47). A newborn female's ovaries, however, contain her entire lifetime allotment of follicles or immature eggs. A woman commonly releases a single mature egg cell from her ovaries each month. So, while a man is biologically capable of fathering thousands of offspring, a woman is able to bear only a relatively small number of children.

Given this difference, each sex is well served by a distinctive reproductive strategy. Biologically, a man reproduces his genes most efficiently through a strategy of sexual promiscuity. This scheme, however, opposes the reproductive interests of a woman. Each of her relatively few pregnancies demand that she carry the child for nine months, give birth, and provide care for some time afterward. Thus, efficient reproduction on the part of the woman depends on carefully selecting a mate whose qualities will contribute to their child's survival and successful reproduction (Remoff, 1984).

The "double standard" certainly involves more than biology; it is also a product of the historical domination of woman by men (Barry, 1983). But sociobiology suggests that this cultural pattern, like many others, has an underlying biologic. Simply put, it has developed around the world because women and men everywhere tend toward distinctive reproductive strategies.

**Critical evaluation** Sociobiology has succeeded in generating insights about the biological roots of some cultural patterns, especially those that are universal. But sociobiology remains controversial for several reasons.

First, some critics fear that sociobiology may revive older biological arguments that supported the oppression of one race or sex. Defenders respond, however, that sociobiology has no connection to any past pseudoscience of racial superiority. On the contrary, sociobiology serves to unite rather than divide humanity by asserting that we all share a single evolutionary history. The notion that men are inherently superior to women is also inconsistent with sociobiological thinking. Sociobiology does rest on the assumption that men and women differ biologically in some ways that culture will not overcome—if, in fact, any society intended to. But, far from asserting that males are somehow more important than females, sociobiology emphasizes how both sexes are vital to human reproduction.

Second, say the critics, sociobiologists have as yet amassed little evidence to support their theories. Edward O. Wilson (1975, 1978), generally credited as the founder of this field, optimistically claimed that sociobiology would reveal the biological roots of human culture. But a generation of work shows that biological forces do not shape human behavior in any rigid sense. Rather, abundant evidence supports the conclusion that human behavior is *learned* within a cultural system. The contribution of sociobiology, then, lies in its explanation of why some cultural patterns are more common than others.

# CULTURE AND HUMAN FREEDOM

We have introduced the elements of human culture, examined cultural diversity and change, and drawn insights about culture from various theoretical paradigms. Our final question is how culture affects us as individuals. Does it bind us to the past, constraining our human imagination? Or does it enhance our capacity to think critically and to make choices?

## Culture as Constraint

Over the long course of human evolution, culture became our strategy for survival. But though we cannot live without it, culture does have some negative consequences. Cultural beings experience the world through symbols and meaning; just as we are the only species that names itself, so we are the only animal that can experience alienation. Further, with its roots deep in the past, culture becomes mostly a matter of habit, limiting our choices and perhaps driving us to repeat troubling patterns. Racial prejudice, for example, manages to find its way into the lives of each new generation. Similar, women of all colors have often felt powerless in the face of cultural patterns that reflect the dominance of men.

No cultural pattern is entirely positive. Our society's insistence on competitive achievement urges us toward excellence, yet this same pattern also isolates us from one another. Material comforts improve our lives in many ways, yet our preoccupation with objects diverts us from the security and satisfaction of close relationships or strong religious faith. Our emphasis on personal freedom affords us privacy and autonomy, yet our culture often denies us the support of a human community in which to share life's problems (Slater, 1976; Bellah et al., 1985). In short, culture is as vital to humans as biological instinct is to other forms of life. But, all the same, it poses special problems for us.

## Culture as Freedom

Human beings may appear to be prisoners of culture, just as other animals are prisoners of biology. But careful thought about the ideas presented in this chapter suggests a crucial difference. Over millions of years of human evolution, the unfolding of culture gradually took our species from a world shaped largely by biology to a world we highly intelligent creatures shape for ourselves.

Therefore, although culture seems at times to circumscribe our lives, it embodies the human capacity for hope and creative choice. The evidence that supports this conclusion lies all around us. Fascinating cultural diversity exists in our own society, and even greater variety is found around the world. Furthermore, far from being static, culture is ever-changing, and it presents us with a continuous source of human opportunity. The more we discover about the operation of our culture, the greater our ability to use the freedom it offers us.

# SUMMARY

1. Culture refers to a way of life shared by members of a society. Several species have limited forms of culture, but only human beings rely on culture for survival.
2. As the brain grew larger over the long course of human evolution, culture steadily replaced biological instincts. The first elements of culture appeared some 2 million years ago; the complex culture that we call civilization emerged during the last 10,000 years.
3. The term "culture" refers to a way of life; the concept "nation" means a political entity; the term "society" designates the organized interaction of people in a nation or within some other boundary.

4. Culture is built on symbols, which come into being as we attach meaning to objects and actions. Language is the symbolic system by which we transmit culture from generation to generation.
5. Values represent general orientations to the world around us; beliefs are statements people who share a culture hold to be true.
6. Cultural norms guide human behavior. Mores consist of norms of great moral significance; folkways, norms that guide everyday life, permit greater individual discretion.
7. Values and norms are expressions of ideal culture; in practice, real culture varies considerably from these standards.
8. Material creations reflect cultural values as well as a society's technology.
9. High culture refers to patterns that distinguish a society's elites; popular culture includes patterns widespread in a society.
10. All societies contain some cultural diversity; our own contains a great deal. Subculture refers to distinctive cultural forms that characterize a segment of society; counterculture means patterns strongly at odds with a wide accepted way of life. Multiculturalism represents efforts to enhance awareness and appreciation of cultural diversity.
11. Culture is never static: Invention, discovery, and diffusion all generate cultural change. Not all parts of a cultural system change at the same rate, however; this differential produces cultural lag.
12. Having learned the standards of one culture, we often evaluate other cultures ethnocentrically. One alternative to ethnocentrism, called cultural relativism, means judging different cultures according to their own standards.
13. The structural-functional paradigm views culture as a relatively stable system built on core values. Specific cultural traits function to help maintain the overall social system.
14. The social-conflict paradigm envisions cultural systems as dynamic arenas of inequality and conflict. Cultural patterns typically benefit some categories of people more than others.
15. The cultural-ecology paradigm explores ways in which human culture is shaped by the natural environment.
16. Sociobiology studies the influence of humanity's evolutionary past on present patterns of culture.
17. Culture can constrain human needs and ambitions; yet as cultural creatures we have the capacity to shape and reshape the world to meet our needs and pursue our dreams.

## THE TRANSFORMATION OF SOCIETIES

When societies modernize, the types and nature of their groups are transformed. For instance, in hunting and gathering societies, age and gender provide virtually the only bases for group membership other than the tribe itself. As a result, the simplest societies contain few distinct groups. Contrast this with industrialized societies, which are fragmented into countless groups. Here, in addition to groups based on age and sex, we also find groups based on religion, ethnicity, neighborhoods, politics, sports, recreation, hobbies, and even opinions—for instance prochoice and prolife groups. Enveloping these many smaller groups, however, is the larger group known as society—which, by its particular characteristics and conditions, gives shape to these smaller groups.

To better understand this envelope that surrounds us and sets the stage on which we grow up, let us trace the development of societies from their earliest beginnings. As we examine the evolution of societies

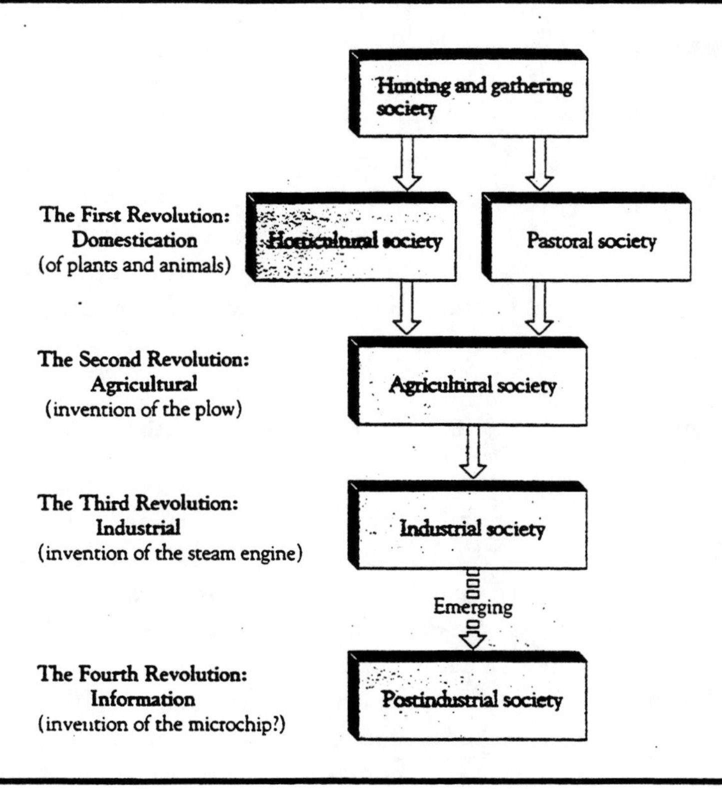


portrayed in Figure 4-3, we will not only see how our own society emerged, but we will also see how each type of society is marked by fundamentally different characteristics. These patterns are significant because they determine our basic orientations to life.

## Hunting and Gathering Societies

The simplest societies are called **hunting and gathering societies.** As the name implies, these groups depend on hunting and gathering for their survival. The men do the hunting (of animals), the females the gathering (of plants). Beyond this basic division of labor by sex, there are few social divisions. The groups usually have a **shaman,** or priest, but they, too, must help procure food. Although these groups give greater prestige to the male hunters, the women gatherers contribute much more food to the group, perhaps even four-fifths of their total food (Bernard 1992).

In addition to gender, the major unit of organization is the family. Most members are related by ancestry or marriage. Because the family is the only distinct social institution in these societies, it fulfills functions that are divided among many specialized institutions in modern societies. The family distributes food to its members, educates its children (especially in food skills), nurses the sick, and so on.

Because an area cannot support a large number of people who hunt animals and gather plants (they do not plant, only gather what is already there), hunting and gathering societies are small, usually consisting of only twenty-five to forty members. They are also nomadic, moving from one place to another as the food supply of an area gives out. These groups are usually peaceful and place high value on sharing food, which is essential to their survival. The high risk of destruction of the food supply, however—by disease, drought, famine, and pestilence—makes their death rate very high. Members of hunting and gathering groups have only about a fifty-fifty chance of surviving childhood (Lenski and Lenski 1987).

Of all societies, hunters and gatherers are most egalitarian. Because what the people hunt and gather are perishable, they can't accumulate possessions. Consequently, no one becomes wealthier than anyone else. There are no rulers, and most decisions are arrived through discussion. Because their needs are simple and they do not accumulate material possessions, hunters and gatherers also have the most leisure of all human groups (Lee 1979; Sahlins 1972).

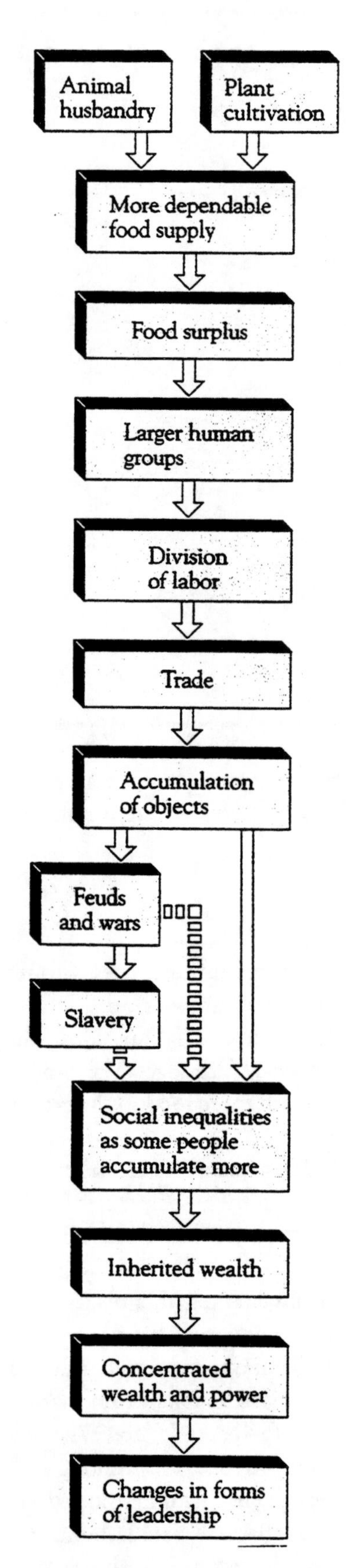


**FIGURE 4-4 Fundamental Consequences of Animal Husbandry and Plant Cultivation**

All human groups were once hunters and gatherers, and until several hundred years ago such societies were still fairly common. Now, however, only a few remain, such as the pygmies of central Africa, the San of the Namibian desert, and the aborigines of Australia. Sociologist Gerhard and Jean Lenski (1987) pointed out that modern societies have increasingly taken over the areas on which such groups depend for their food. They suggested that the few remaining hunting and gathering societies will soon disappear from the human scene.

## Pastoral and Horticultural Societies

About ten thousand to twelve thousand years ago, hunting and gathering societies branched in one of two directions. Very gradually, over thousands of years, some groups found that they could tame and breed some of the animals they hunted—primarily goats, sheep, cattle, and camels—others that they could cultivate plants.

The key to understanding the first branching is the word *pasture;* **pastoral societies** are based on the *pasturing of animals.* Pastoral societies developed in arid regions, where lack of rainfall made it impractical to build life around crops. Groups that took this turn remained nomadic, for they followed their animals to fresh pasture. The key to understanding the second branching is horticulture, or plant cultivation. **Horticultural societies** are based on the *cultivation of plants by the use of hand tools.* No longer having to abandon an area as the food supply gave out, these groups developed permanent settlements.

We can call the domestication of animals and plants the *first social revolution.* Although the **domestication revolution** was extremely gradual, it represents a fundamental break with the past and changed human history.

Horticulture apparently first began in the fertile areas of the Middle East. Primitive agricultural technology—hoes and digging sticks (to punch holes in the ground for seeds)—gradually spread to Europe and China. Apparently these techniques were independently inverted in Central and South America, although they may have arrived there through *cultural diffusion* (the spreading of items from one culture to another) due to contacts yet unknown to us.

These discoveries of animal husbandry and plant cultivation transformed human society. By creating a more dependable food supply, they ushered in a series of interrelated changes that altered almost every aspect of human life. Because a more dependable food supply could support more people, human groups became larger. There also was more food than was necessary for survival. This food surplus allowed groups to develop a specialized division of labor: not everyone had to produce food, and some became full-time priests, other the makers of jewelry, tools, weapons, and so on. This production of objects, in turn, stimulated trade. As groups that had lived largely in isolation traded with one another, people began to accumulate objects they considered valuable, such as gold, jewelry, utensils, and a greater variety of food.

These changes set the stage for social inequality, for now some families (or clans) accumulated more surplus goods or wealth than others. Feuds and wars then erupted, for groups now possessed animals, pastures, croplands, jewelry, and other material goods to fight about. War, in turn, let slavery enter the human picture, for people found it convenient to let captives from their battles do their drudge work. Social stratification remained limited, however, for the surplus itself was limited. As individuals passed on their possessions to their descendants, wealth grew more concentrated and power more centralized. Forms of leadership then changed as chiefs emerged. These changes are depicted in Figure 4-5.

Note that the primary pattern that runs through this fundamental transformation of group life is the change *from greater to lesser equality.* The essential significance of this change was that where people were located *within* a society came to be vital in determining what happened to them in life.

## Agricultural Societies

About five to six thousand years ago came the *second social revolution,* much more sudden and dramatic than the first. The **agricultural revolution** was brought about by the invention of the plow, an invention with such far-reaching effects that it produced a new type of society. This new **agricultural society** was based on large-scale agriculture, which depended on plows drawn by animals. Compared with hoes and digging sticks, the use of animals to pull plows was immensely efficient. More nutrients were returned to the soil as the ground was turned up, and much more land could be farmed by a smaller number of people. The result was a huge agricultural surplus, which allowed more people to engage in activities other than farming—to develop the things popularly known as "culture," such as philosophy, art, literature, and architecture. The changes during this period in history were so profound that they are sometimes referred to as "the dawn of civilization." Not only the plow but also the wheel, writing, and numbers were invented. The developments just outlined, some of which were only tendencies during the earlier period, grew more pronounced.

One of the most significant changes was the growth of social inequality. When the agricultural surplus allowed the population to increase beyond anything previously known, cities developed. As groups began to be distinguished by their possessions, what earlier had been only a tendency now became a pronounced feature of social life. As conflict theorists point out, an elite gained control of the surplus resources and wielded them to reinforce their own power. This concentration of resources and power was the precursor of the state, or the political institution, for to protect their privileged positions, the elite surrounded themselves with armed men to maintain their position. After taking control, the elite levied tax on groups who had now become their "subjects," a fundamental step in oppression.

No one knows exactly how it happened, but sometime during this period females also became subjugated to males. Sociologist Elise Boulding (1976) theorizes that this change occurred because men were in charge of plowing and the cows. She suggests that when metals were developed, men took on the new job of attaching the metals as tips to the wooden plows and doing the plowing. As a result,

> the shift of the status of the woman farmer may have happened quite rapidly, once there were two male specializations relating to agriculture: plowing and the care of cattle. This situation left women with all the subsidiary tasks, including weeding and carrying water to the fields. The new fields were larger, so women had to work just as many hours as they did before, but now they worked at more secondary tasks. . . . This would contribute further to the erosion of the status of women.

Although Boulding's theory hasn't been proven, it matches the available evidence. As new evidence comes to light, we must expect to modify the theory.

## Industrial Societies

Just as the agricultural revolution was based on a single invention, so was the much later *third social revolution.* Just like the second revolution, it, too, turned society upside down. The **Industrial Revolution** began in Britain, where in 1765 the steam engine was first used to run machinery. Before this time some machines had harnessed nature (such as wind and water mills), but most had depended on human and animal power. This new source of energy led to the development of what is called **industrial society,** defined by sociologist Herbert Blumer (1990) as a society in which goods are produced by machines powered by fuels instead of by the brute force of humans or animals.

A group's technology is an essential part of its culture, and any change in technology requires that the group make some sort of adjustment. Sociologist William Ogburn (1922, 1961) concluded that a certain amount of time is required before people change their patterns of living in response to a change in technology. He called this time gap **cultural lag.** In other words, industrial societies are always playing catch-up: Nonmaterial cultures (values, beliefs, folkways, and how we relate to one another) always trails the more rapidly changing material culture (technology). Critics of this view point out that the process is not always so one-sided and that changes in the nonmaterial culture, such as values, also stimulate change in the material culture (Barber 1959).

Let us look at some of the social changes that followed industrialization. This new form of production was far more efficient than anything the world had seen. Just as its surplus was greater, so were its effects on the human group. Highly significant was a growth in social inequality, especially during the first stage of industrialization. The individuals who first used the new technology accumulated great wealth, their riches in many instances outrunning the imagination of kings. Gaining an early position in the markets, they were able not only to control the means of production (factories, machinery, tools), but also to dictate the conditions under which people could work. A huge surplus of labor had already developed at this time, for feudal society was breaking up and masses of people were thrown off the lands that they and their ancestors had farmed as tenants for centuries. Moving to the cities, these landless peasants faced the choice of stealing, starving, or working for starvation wages (Chambliss 1964; Michalowski 1985).

At that time, workers had no legal rights to safe, or even humane, working conditions; nor had they the right to unionize to improve them. The law considered employment to be a private contract between the employer and the individual worker. If workers banded together to ask for higher wages or to improve some condition for their work, they were fired. If they returned to the factory, they were arrested for trespassing. In the United States—where striking was illegal—strikers were beaten or shot by private police, and even by the National Guard.

As workers gradually won their demands for better working conditions, however, wealth spread to even larger segments of society. Eventually, home ownership became common, as did the ownership of automobiles and an incredible variety of consumer goods. Beyond the imagination of social reformers, in the later stages of industrial societies the typical worker enjoys a high standard of living in such terms as material conditions, health care, longevity, and access to libraries and education.

The progression of industrialization to some extent reversed the earlier pattern of growing inequality. Indicators of greater equality include better housing and a vast increase in consumer goods; the abolition of slavery; the shift from monarchies to more representative political systems; the right to be tried by a jury of one's peers and to cross examine witnesses; the right to vote; and greater rights for women and minorities.

It is difficult to overstate the sociological principle that the type of society we live in is the fundamental reason that we become who we are. To see how industrial society affects your life, note that you would not be taking this course if it were not for industrialization. Clearly you could not have a car, or your type of clothing or home, a telephone, stereo, television, computer, or even electric lights. On a deeper level, you would not feel the same about life or have your particular aspirations for the future. Actually, probably no aspect of your life would be the same, for you would be locked into an agricultural

## PERSPECTIVES

### CULTURAL DIVERSITY IN U.S. SOCIETY

#### *A Tribal Mountain People Meets Postindustrial Society*

What happens when a proud, tribal people from the agricultural society is suddenly transplanted to a postindustrial society?

When U.S. forces withdrew from Vietnam and the North Vietnamese took over Laos in 1975, about 100,000 Hmong emigrated to the United States, mainly to California, Minnesota, and Wisconsin. The Hmong had fought loyally on the side of the United States against the North Vietnamese, sustaining a casualty rate five times that of U.S. forces. Part of a huge wave of immigration of some 850,000 postwar Southeast Asian refugees, this little-known people had distinctive needs that often went unmet by overwhelmed resettlement officials.

In Laos, the Hmong were tribal mountain dwellers whose agricultural life was light-years removed from the world they encountered in the United States. They had no knowledge of cars, telephones, television, not even plumbing or electricity. They did not even have a written language until American and French missionaries invented one in the mid-1950s.

Resettled to U.S. cities, the Hmong abruptly confronted a totally bewildering way of life for which their agricultural society had left them quite unprepared. Many did not understand what locks were for, or the purpose of light switches. They had never seen a stove, and refugee workers would find them huddled around open fires in their living rooms. Some tried to make inside gardens by bringing in soil from the outside and spreading it around the living room floor. The Hmong used the toilet to wash rice—a local adaptation of "water bowl" from their culture—but were perplexed when the rice disappeared if the toilet were accidentally flushed.

Perhaps the most poignant story of all is told by Sgt. Marvin Reyes of the Fresno city police: One night he pulled over a driver who was jerking his way through an intersection. The driver would stop, suddenly dart a few feet, then stop again. Figuring that the man was drunk, the officer was astonished when the Hmong driver said that he had been told to stop at every red light. It was late; the stoplight was blinking.

The resettlement of the Hmong in cities across the United States proved a failure, for by isolating families, it undermined the clan and tribal bond on which Hmong identify is based. The youth, knowing more English, began to take on greater authority, while Hmong women began to assert new, culturally unfamiliar independence.

As they make their perilous adjustment—holding on to what they can of their old way of life while changing what they must to survive in their new land—the Hmong are attempting to maintain their tribal closeness. So far, they have succeeded to an amazing degree; Hmong who travel to a strange town can look in the telephone book for a Hmong name and be welcomed into that home even if they do not know the family. "This keeps us alive as a people, as a clan," say the Hmong.

Yang Dao, the first Hmong to earn a Ph.D., says that the Hmong must shake off their refugee status. "We must start thinking like Hmong Americans," he says, "Take the best of Laos and the best of America and live like that."

Certainly the new identify destined to arise from this mixing of cultures will be sociologically interesting, another part of the cultural diversity that makes up the American folkscape.

SOURCES: Based on Meredith 1984; Jones and Strand 1986; Spencer 1988; Mitchell et al. 1989; Cerhan 1990; Snider 1990; Trueba et al. 1990; Lopez-Romano 1992.

or horticultural way of life. The Perspectives box on page 109 reports on how the Hmong, a group from an agricultural society in Southeast Asia, are adapting to their sudden immersion in the postindustrial society of the United States.

## Postindustrial Societies

Sociologists have identified the emergence of an entirely new type of society. The basic trend in advanced industrial societies is away from production and manufacturing to service industries. The United States was the first country to have more than 50 percent of its work force employed in service industries—health, education, research, the government, counseling, banking and investments, sales, law, and the mass media. Australia, New Zealand, western Europe, and Japan soon followed. The term **postindustrial society** refers to this emerging society—one *based on information, services, and high technology* rather than on raw materials and manufacturing (Bell 1973; Lipset 1979; Toffler 1980; Beck 1993).

*The basic component of the postindustrial society is information.* People who offer services either provide or apply information of one sort or another. Teachers pass on knowledge to students, repair technicians use knowledge to service technological gadgets, while lawyers, physicians, bankers, pilots, and interior decorators sell their specialized knowledge of law, the body, money, aerodynamics, and color schemes to clients. Unlike factory workers in an industrial society, they don't *produce* anything. Rather, they transmit or use knowledge to provide services that others are willing to pay for.

As reviewed, early technological developments brought wrenching changes to past cultures. What will happen to ours? It may be that social analysts in years to come will speak of the current changes as the *fourth revolution.* Often called the **information revolution,** it is based on technology that processes information. Specifically, the computer chip is the primary technological change that is transforming society and with it, our social relationships. This tiny device, with its miniaturized circuitry, allows some people to work at home, others to talk to people in distant cities and even other countries while they drive their automobiles. Because of it, we can peer farther into space than ever before. And because of it, millions of children spend countless hours struggling against video enemies, at home and in the arcades. The list of changes ushered in by this one technological advance is practically endless.

Although the full implications of the information explosion are still unknown, of this we can be certain: Just as the larger group called society has historically exerted a fundamental force on people's thinking and behavior, so it will in its new form. As society is transformed, then we too shall be swept along with it. As history is our guide, the change will be so extensive that even our attitudes about the self and life will be transformed.

# COMMUNICATION: THE HEARTBEAT OF HUMAN INTERACTION

Miller and Steinberg have defined *communication* as a process whereby one person deliberately attempts to convey meaning to another.[1] They imply that we communicate with the intention of attempting to modify behavior. Words are selected and organized in such a way as to have maximum impact on the individual whose behavior we are trying to modify.

However, Ruesch and Bateson[2] have argued that communication is not always aimed at modifying behavior. They stress the unintended messages that very often get communicated and greatly impact behavior. Scholars of this view define communication as a process that takes place whenever meaning is attached to messages. This can take place even when the sender did not intend the message to be part of the process. A group of people could be at a long meeting, for example, where one of the members yawns unintentionally. This very act may be interpreted as a signal to end the meeting. It could also suggest that the group leader is boring or that the person who is yawning did not get enough sleep the previous night.

Samovar and Porter[3] suggest that communication occurs whenever meaning is attributed to behavior or its residue. On entering an elevator, for example, someone may smell the perfume of a person who previously rode on this same elevator. A conclusion could be reached that the person who wore the perfume is very rich. On the other hand, another conclusion might be that the person who wore the perfume is going on a date. When such conclusions are made, communication has taken place. Residue takes into account consequences of past experiences, which are very often culture-related.

Whatever approach is used to define communication, it is important to note that this process is critical to human existence. It is through communication that human beings have accomplished seemingly simple tasks like fire lighting or complicated ones like going to the moon. It is important to recognize that people from different cultures communicate differently. In recognizing this fact, we come to understand each other better as we patiently listen to one another.

Hall,[4] in an attempt to provide a theoretical framework for understanding cross-cultural communication, classifies world cultures into two categories: *low* and *high context.* Although simple and sometimes limited in generalizability, the model offers a starting point into the study of this intricate subject.

According to Hall, in low-context cultures, examples of which include the United States and northern Europe, meaning is derived from the message itself, which might be in the form of a spoken word, a memo, or a computer program. Among high-context cultures, such as East Asian, Arab, Southern European, Native American, and Latin American, meanings are derived from the context in which the communication takes place. To this list can be added the Africans, the majority of whom share the proverb, "Words which are left unsaid leave the paths clean." Bennett[5] summarizes Hall's scheme in Table 4.2 on page 112.

There are remarkable differences between communication patterns of people from low- and high-context cultures. Stewart[6] notes, for example, that because U.S. people emphasize rationality, they assume that events can be explained and reasons for their occurrence determined. They see the world as composed of facts from which ideas can be generated, thus the emphasis on explicit meaning. Arabs and Asians, on the other hand, look for the implicit level and metaphoric association in messages. In Arab culture, poetry, plays, and story-telling are regarded as inspired language because they portray an image of a well-educated speaker, capable of rendering judgment and advice. There is a high value placed on the persuasive power, rhythm, and sound of words because these heighten the impact of the message.[7] This is unlike the dominant U.S. style of speech in which communication is individualistic, whereby each communicator is a separate individual, engaging in diverse communicative activities to maximize self-interest, usually by persuasion.[8]

Differences in communication patterns can be noted even among the various subcultures in the United States. As Kochman[9] points out, for example, African-American speech patterns have been ignored for a long time based on the assumption that they need to operate according to speech patterns established by the dominant Caucasians. During the mid-1960s, schools were committed to eradicating the African-American language patterns for they were regarded as "improper." More recently, educators have begun to sense that the African-American language is functional, particularly when the people are communicating with those from their communities.

According to Kochman, African-American and Caucasian speech patterns are different. On observing a meeting between African-American community leaders and faculty representatives in Chicago, he observed that the two groups hardly understood one another's speech patterns. While the faculty thought the behavior of the community leaders did not meet requirements for rational discussion and called it a "Baptist revival meeting" or "pep rally," the faculty were considered lacking in sincerity, honest conviction and sometimes "devious."[10]

Debates between students from the two cultural backgrounds produced similar results. The African-American speech patterns were high-keyed, animated, interpersonal, confrontational, and affect-generating. The Caucasians were low-keyed, dispassionate, impersonal, nonchallenging and without affect. The author suggests that because the two groups have different perceptions about certain aspect of reality, their speech patterns are bound to differ. The African Americans often use argument as a way to

**TABLE 4.2 Summary of Hall's Conception of Culture According to Context**

| | High Context | Low Context |
|---|---|---|
| Time | *Polychronic*<br>Loose schedules, flux, multiple simultaneous activities.<br>Last minute changes of important plans.<br>Time is less tangible. | *Monochronic*<br>Tight schedules, one event at a time, linear.<br>Importance of being on time.<br>Time is more tangible (e.g., is spent, wasted, is "money"). |
| Space and Tempo | *High-Sync.*<br>Synchrony, moving in harmony with others and with nature, is consciously valued.<br>Social rhythm has meaning. | *Low-Sync.*<br>Synchrony is less noticeable.<br>Social rhythm is underdeveloped. |
| Reasoning | *Comprehensive Logic*<br>Knowledge is gained through intuition, spiral logic, and contemplation.<br>Importance of feelings. | *Linear Logic*<br>Knowledge is gained through analytical reasoning (e.g., the Socratic method).<br>Importance of words. |
| Verbals Messages | *Restricted Codes*<br>"Shorthand speech," reliance on nonverbal and contextual cues. Overall emotional quality more important than meaning of particular words. Economical, fast, efficient communication that is satisfying; slow to change; fosters interpersonal cohesiveness and provides for human need for social stability.<br>Stress on social integration and harmony; being polite. | *Elaborate Codes*<br>Verbal amplification through extended talk or writing,<br>Little reliance on nonverbal or contextual cues.<br>Doesn't foster cohesiveness but can change rapidly.<br>Provides for human need to adapt and change.<br>Stress on argument and persuasion; being direct. |
| Social Roles | *Tight Social Structure*<br>Individual's behavior is predictable; conformity to role expectations. | *Loose Social structure*<br>Behavior is unpredictable; role behavior expectations are less clear. |
| Interpersonal Relations | *Group Is Paramount*<br>Clear status distinctions (e.g., age, rank, position), strong distinctions between insiders and outsiders.<br>Human interactions are emotionally based, person oriented. | *Individual Is Paramount*<br>Status is more subtle, distinctions between insiders and outsiders less important.<br>Human interactions are functionally based, approach is specialized. |

**TABLE 4.2 Continued**

| | High Context | Low Context |
|---|---|---|
| | Stronger personal bonds, bending of individual interests for sake of relationships.<br>Cohesive, highly interrelated human relationships, completed action chains.<br>Members of group are first and foremost. | Fragile, interpersonal bonds due to geographic mobility.<br>Fragmented, short-term human relationships, broken action chains when relationship is not satisfying<br>Individuals are first, groups come second. |
| Social Organization | *Personalized Law and Authority*<br>Customary procedures and who one knows are important. Oral agreements are binding.<br>In face of unresponsive bureaucracies, must be an insider or have a "friend" to make things happen (e.g., going through the "back door").<br>People in authority are personally and truly responsible for actions of every subordinate. | *Procedural Law and Authority*<br>Procedures, laws and policies are more important than who one knows.<br>Written contracts are binding.<br>Policy rules, unresponsive bureaucracy.<br>People in authority try to pass the buck.<br>Impersonal<br>Legal procedures |

test their own views. This is deeply rooted in their oral tradition whereby a scholar acts as an advocate for the material presented. Struggle for a particular position is viewed as a positive thing because it shows that one cares very much about that idea. There is also an assumption that ideas become authoritative by being tested through argument. In debates, therefore, reference is constantly made to the initiator of the idea, and there is concern for the argument as well as the art through which it is expressed; thus the use of body language. Caucasians, on the other hand, equate confrontation with conflict and try to avoid it as much as possible. Because this culture separates the material from the presenter, how a person feels about the idea is not fundamental to its value—"The truth of the matter is in the matter."[11] Ideas derive authority through publication or they are certified by experts in the field. This assumption limits the role of the presenter, often making such an individual appear overly impersonal. While African Americans may view the Caucasian style as an avoidance of responsibility or evasive, their style may be viewed by the latter as "too emotional." To sum up the African American communication style, Harrison[12] notes that there is usually a high spiritual intensity based on the assumption that internal forces are controlled by the structure and mode through which they are released—"An emotion is never out of control when it fits the modality it is released in."[13]

## INGREDIENTS OF COMMUNICATION

A model presented by Shannon and Weaver[14] includes the following communication components: the *sender*, the *message*, and the *receiver* of the message. The sender engages in the process of *encoding*, that is, converting an idea into a set of symbols to be communicated. Such symbols are transmitted through a *medium*. The message is comprised of symbols which have to be *decoded* by the receiver. The decoding process involves an interpretation of the message's semantic content. In addition, Shannon and Weaver suggest that usually the message is interrupted by "noise."

They add that whatever is communicated is merely a sign that stands for some meaning that we read into it. The signs in the message have meaning that we give them as a result of our experiences. Distortions may occur if the sender's encoding and the receiver's decoding do not converge. This happens if their shared frame of reference is minimal, causing the message to mean different things to each.

Hopman[15] suggests that the greater the gap between the shared experiences of individual senders and receivers of messages, the greater the differences in their interpretations of the same messages and hence, the greater the distortion in the process of communication. He also stipulates that the greater the noise or random disturbance in a communication channel, the greater the distortion in the communication process. Individual traits and geocultural factors also play a big role in influencing communication. These are usually very difficult to interpret, particularly if the communicating parties come from different cultural backgrounds.

## INDIVIDUAL TRAITS

When people communicate with one another, they bring to the situation their whole state of being, comprised of sentiments, values, emotions, attitudes, and physical dispositions. It is therefore important that we know as much as we can about the person we are interacting with in order to avoid misinterpretation of the information received. Research has found age, race, and gender to be key variables in influencing communication across cultures. A number of studies have, for instance, observed differences between various categories of people in their use of space while communicating with one another. Dean[16] observed that adults tend to react more favorably to an invasion of their space by children than fellow adults. Curt and Nine's[17] research concluded that in Puerto Rico, people of the same age and gender touch more and stand closer to each other during conversation than those who differ in the two characteristics. When relationships between males and females are close, females do touch males but males rarely reciprocate. Shunter's[18] study, which includes Costa Ricans, Colombians, and Panamanians, observed that directness of interactions diminishes as one travels from Central to South America. The mean distances between the communicating parties in Costa Rica were much smaller. The same study observed that more Costa Ricans touched each other than the others did. However, for all three, there was more contact between female/female dyads, followed by female/male, and lastly, male/male dyads.

A study of the differences in personal space needs among Hispanic, Caucasian, and African Americans conducted by Baxter[19] arrived at interesting conclusions. Overall, mixed-race dyads exhibited greater distance than any single-race pair. Bauer,[20] in an attempt to assess use of personal space among African Americans and Caucasians, observed significant differences between the two groups. When instructed to approach same race, same gender confederates to the highest level of comfort in personal space, Caucasian males stood farthest, followed by Caucasian females, then African-American males, and finally African-American females who stood closest. It is important to note that theories of contact versus noncontact hold in same-culture interactions, speaking the native language. Sussman and Rosenfeld[21] observed that Japanese, Venezuelan, and U.S. student dyads all maintained farther distances when speaking a foreign language. His conclusion was that both culture and language influence conversational distance.

## GEOCULTURAL FACTORS

Geocultural factors include such things as the location where interaction is taking place, climate, time of the conversation, and the discussion topic. If, for example, one of the parties is from a cold climate and the other from a warm one, their conversation will be affected by these climatic differences. While someone from a cold climate may spend a great deal of time talking about the beautiful spring flowers, the one from the warm climate where flowers are seen all year round might find such conversation boring. The same may be true with regard to other types of nature. I remember an English girl with whom I shared a house while both of us taught at a high school in Western Uganda. The girl often talked about butterflies and asked me to accompany her to the woods to catch some. Although I found this conversation extremely boring, I decided to go with her out of courtesy. I had a very difficult time convincing my relatives that catching butterflies was a worthwhile exercise.

Time is important because it puts a certain routine in people's lives. In one culture, evenings may be times to be with one's family whereas in another, it is time to get out to be with friends. While supper time may be around six o'clock for one group of people, it may be nine o'clock for another. When people with different body clocks are interacting, they may not understand each other's behavior. I remember struggling with the idea that I had to eat dinner around six o'clock in the United States, whereas the same activity took place between eight and nine o'clock in the culture where I grew up.

Events such as birth, death, graduation from college, and marriage are interpreted differently by various cultures. While, for example, among the Igbo of Nigeria, the bride-to-be dances before the potential in-laws, this is not the case among traditional Batoro of Western Uganda. The young lady is expected to show sorrow because she is about to leave her family. In some cases, brides are pinched by their aunts in order to evoke tears or to at least show a sorrowful face. Although this no longer goes on among more educated groups, it is still common among traditional families.

## THE ROLE OF VERBAL COMMUNICATION

Sapir[22] observes that human beings do not let in the objective world alone. They are very much at the mercy of the particular language which has become the medium of expression for their society. It is through language that people conceptualize the world around them. Languages differ so much in grammar and structure that no two languages can be considered as representing the same social reality.

Hoijer,[23] in his study among the Navajo of Arizona and New Mexico, observed that their grammar emphasizes movement, specifying the nature, direction and status of such movement because they perceived the universe to be in motion. While the English speakers would say, "One dresses," "One is young," "He is carrying a round object," the Navajo counterpart would say, "One moves into clothing," "One moves about newly," "He moves along handling a round object." This motion is deeply rooted in Navajo mythology whereby the gods and culture heroes move restlessly from place to place, seeking to perfect the universe.[24]

Verbal communication plays a very significant role in human communication. All languages use a limited number of sounds to refer to many objects and experiences, thus making human language very efficient. Another quality that makes human language unique is its productivity. The same set of words can be used to convey different meanings if arranged differently. The example below illustrates this point.

*I went there to watch the only game.*
*I went there only to watch the game.*
*Only I went there to watch the game.*

Samovar and Porter[25] add that human language has the ability to communicate something or some idea that is not in the immediate environment. Things that took place in the past are described and so are those that are to happen in the future. In addition, the displacement nature of human language creates room for hypothetical thinking. The ability to think in abstract terms that is characteristic of human beings is influenced by culture. Important images like that of God are culture specific and so are expressions of various emotions such as anger, pain, joy, love, and sorrow.

## NONVERBAL COMMUNICATION

Samovar and Porter[26] suggest that nonverbal communication has several uses. It helps us learn about the *affective* or *emotional* states of others. Someone saying "I am fine," with a frown is in a different emotional state from someone who says it with a smile. We also get first *impressions* of others from nonverbal communication. This type of communication also helps in *repeating* messages. After offering a seat to someone, for example, pointing to the actual chair confirms the offer and assures the receiver that the speaker is serious about it.

Nonverbal communication also *complements* verbal messages. Food offered with a smile, for example, is much better received. Messages can also be contradicted by nonverbal communication. Many African languages use parables and poetic forms of expression. Upon arrival at someone's residence for example, the host may say, "I am not greeting you. Where have you been all these months?" These words may sound frightening to someone who does not understand the culture. From the nonverbal expressions, this same person may be expressing joy and a lot of affection. Alternatively, the host may welcome the visitor by dancing or singing without necessarily saying any words of welcome.

Another use of nonverbal communication is *substituting* gestures for words. While members of a U.S. football team may make the "thumbs up" sign after a victory, this same gesture is a curse among the Batoro because the "master" finger is being pointed at someone. Nonverbal communication can also be used to *regulate* conversation. While at a meeting, one person could signal another to start speaking by a certain look. The same is true for a choir director who uses gestures as a way of telling the group to perform in a certain way.

In addition to the uses outlined by Samovar and Porter, nonverbal communication can also play the role of *correcting, shielding, excluding,* and *positioning*. There are times when we want to correct an error that was made during a certain conversation and may feel embarrassed or afraid to apologize in words. This mistake can be corrected by using nonverbal messages. Lovers who have just had a fight, for example, may embrace each other after a while as a sign of reconciliation. The person who started the fight may initiate the embrace as a sign of admitting to a mistake that was made. Reconciliatory behavior is interpreted differently by various cultures. While flowers may please a U.S. woman and convince her that her lover is sorry, the African woman may interpret this act as merely playing games. Flowers are a less valued commodity by the latter because they are seen all year round, whereas in the former culture, they are seasonal.

Languages have taboo words that are not spoken very often or are excluded from certain company. In such cases, nonverbal communication protects people from saying words that might be embarrassing. Instead of saying "shut up" or "keep quiet" to someone, a certain look or "shh" said softly prevents ill feelings that could result from harsh words.

When people do not want to include others in their conversation, they usually do not tell them directly, especially if they are adults. By observing the nonverbal communication, the person who is not wanted as part of the conversation knows and can leave. While in some cultures the exclusion is done primarily by manipulating space and altering body posture, other groups may stop conversation or the intruders may be looked at in such a way as to suggest that this conversation is not meant for them.

In every culture, status is conferred on people in different ways. From nonverbal cues, we can rank ourselves in society. This view agrees with Charles Horton Cooley's[27] idea of the "looking-glass self." He suggests that our image is a function of what other members of society confer on us. Concepts such as "beauty," "charm," "power," and "failure" are in and of themselves meaningless until other members of society use them either directly or indirectly in reference to us.

## THE ROLE OF SILENCE IN COMMUNICATION

A great deal can be learned about a culture from the way it treats silence. Bruneau[28] points out that silences are not only based in the very comprehensibility of each world language but they are also the stuff out of which social acts, social actions, social presence, and social events are created and articulated. Customs, traditions, social mannerisms, social stability, and normative actions can all be viewed as they relate to habitual silences. There is an interdependent relationship between speech and silence.

The role of silence in the communication process is interpreted differently in every culture. Whereas the Western tradition views silence and ambiguity negatively, in Far Eastern cultures there is a bias toward silence. Bruneau[29] observes that there is a general misconception in the West regarding silence. The U.S. culture, for example, interprets it to mean sorrow, critique, obligation, regret, or embarrassment. The Japanese, on the other hand, have a mistrust for verbal skills, thinking that these tend to show superficiality in contrast to inner, less articulate innuendo.[30] In this culture, anticipatory communication is common, whereby the listener has to guess and accommodate the speaker's needs. Sensitivity and "catching on" quickly to the unsaid meaning are very valuable skills, showing intelligence.[31]

## AN ASSESSMENT

This chapter has highlighted the importance of communication in human interaction. While different languages use specific words to convey certain meanings, many messages are transmitted nonverbally. It is therefore not enough to learn other languages in order to understand how other people live. It is equally necessary to place particular words in their proper contexts and to recognize the importance of nonverbal cues in fostering human understanding.

## DISCUSSION TOPICS

1. Show ways in which your first language has influenced your outlook on life.
2. With other members of your group, discuss various ways in which your language takes people from other cultures for granted.
3. How is learning a foreign language beneficial to an individual?
4. What sounds can't you make because you are limited by your first language?
5. With examples, discuss various ways in which nonverbal communication is used to convey messages in your culture.

## EXERCISES

1. Write ten words in your native language.
   a. List as many alternative ways of saying the same ten words as you can think of (using the same language).
   b. Look up the same ten words in at least two other languages.
2. Look for someone from another country who lives in your community. Interview that person with regard to what shocked him/her about your culture. Write a summary of your findings from the interview and share these with your group or class. Pay particular attention to differences brought about by language.
3. Visit a popular shopping place on a busy day and observe the people for one or two hours.
   a. Make a note of how people communicate both verbally and nonverbally.
   b. Write a brief report of your experience, paying particular attention to the similarities and differences between the behavior of the people you observed and your own.
   c. Divide into two groups of equal size. Each group member should use a nonverbal cue. Members of the same group should try to guess what the cue stands for. Each correct guess is worth a point. After three attempts without success, the other group is given a chance and if they guess it, they get the point. The game ends when either group scores up to 20 points, after which another round can begin.
4. List as many taboo words in your language as possible. Why are these words considered taboo?

## ENDNOTES


1. Gerald R. Miller and Mark Steinberg, *Between People: A New Analysis of Interpersonal Communication* (Chicago: Science Research Associates, 1975).
2. Jurgen Reusch, "Values, Communication, and Culture," *Communication: The Social Matrix of Psychiatry,* ed. Jurgen Ruesch and Gregory Bateson (New York: W.W. Norton, 1951), 5-6.
3. Lary A. Samovar and Richard E. Porter, *Intercultural Communication: A Reader* (Belmont: Wadsworth Publishing Company, 1991), 28.
4. E.T. Hall, *The Hidden Dimension* (New York: Doubleday, 1966); *Beyond Culture* (New York: Doubleday, 1976).
5. Christine I. Bennett, *Comprehensive Multicultural Education* (Boston: Allyn and Bacon, 1990), 55-56.
6. Edward Stewart, *American Cultural Patterns: A Cross-Cultural Perspective* (Yarmouth: Intercultural Press, 1985).
7. Samuel H. Hammod, "Arab and Moslem Rhetorical Theory," *Central States Speech Journal* (1963), 97-102.
8. R. Bellah, R. Madsen, W. Sullivan, A. Swidler and S. Tipton, *Habits of the Heart: Individualism and Commitment in American Life* (New York: Harper & Row, 1985).
9. Thomas Kochman, *Black and White Styles in Conflict* (Chicago: The University of Chicago Press, 1981).
10. Ibid., 14.

11. Ibid., 21.

12. Paul C. Harrison, *The Drama of Nommo* (New York: Grove, 1972), xv.

13. Ibid., 157.

14. Claude E. Shannon and Warren Weaver, *The Mathematical Theory of Communication* (Urbana: University of Illinois Press, 1949).

15. Terrence P. Hopmann, "Communication and Bargaining in International Diplomacy," *Intercultural and International Communication,* ed. Fred Casmir (Washington, D.C.: University of America Press, 1978), 579-613.

16. L.M. Dean, F.N. Willis and J.N. LaRocco, "Invasion of Personal Space as a Function of Age, Sex and Race" (*Psychological Reports,* 1976), 959-965.

17. C. Curt and J. Nine, "Hispanic-Anglo Conflicts in Non-Verbal Communication," *Perspectives Pedagogicas,* ed. Isidora Albino (San Juan, Puerto Rico: Universidad de Puerto Rico, 1983).

18. Robert Shuter, "Non-Verbal Communication: Proxemics and Tactility in Latin America," *Journal of Communication 26* (1976), 46-52.

19. J. Baxter, "Interpersonal Spacing in Natural Settings," *Sociometry 33* (1970), 444-456.

20. E.A. Bauer "Personal Space: A Study of Blacks and Whites," *Sociometry 36* (1973), 402-408.

21. N. Sussman and H.M. Rosenfeld, "Influence of Culture, Language and Sex on Conversational Distances," *Journal of Personality and Social Psychology 42* (1982), 66-74.

22. Edward Sapir, "The Status of Linguistics as a Science," *The Selected Writings of Edward Sapir in Language, Culture and Personality,* ed. David Mandelbaum (Berkeley: University of California Press, 1949), 160-166.

23. Harry Hoijer, "Cultural Implications of Some Navajo Linguistic Categories," *Language in Culture and Society,* ed. D. Hymes (New York: Harper & Row), 142-160.

24. Ibid.

25. Larry A. Samovar and Richard E. Porter (ibid.), 180-182.

26. Ibid.

27. Charles H. Cooley, *Human Nature and the Social Order* (New York: Scribner's, 1902-1904).

28. T.J. Bruneau, "Communicative Silences: Forms and Functions," *Journal of Communication 56* (1973), 17-46.

29. Ibid.

30. E. Reischauer, *The Japanese* (Cambridge, Mass.: Harvard University Press, 1977).

31. T.S. Lebra, *Japanese Patterns of Behavior* (Honolulu: The University Press of Hawaii, 1976).

# Chapter 5

## Socialization

*Human history is replete with legends of lost or deserted children who were raised by wild animals. Legend has it, for example, that Rome was founded by Romulus and Remus, who had been raised in the wild by a wolf. More recently, Walter Cronkite reported on the evening news that a child in Africa had been raised by monkeys. Legend and reality are quite different, however. No such case has ever been authenticated. Cronkite, for example, was obliged to report the next night that news reporters had been unable to verify the story about the child raised by monkeys.*

*There are known cases of children raised in isolation who are sometimes called "feral children" (wolf children) because, like legendary Romulus and Remus, they were raised essentially without human contact. However, unlike Romulus and Remus, such children usually are unable to participate in human society in a normal way. Two well-known and authenticated cases of isolated children are "Anna" and "Genie" (not their real names). "Anna" was locked in an attic in a Pennsylvania farmhouse for six years, her existence denied because she had been born out of wedlock. She had received some physical care but no social interaction. When discovered, tied to a chair, she was unable to walk, talk, or feed herself (Davis, 1940, 1948). She was taken to the University of Chicago, where efforts were made to socialize her with other socially isolated children. In one year, a staff member there required medical treatment more than a dozen times as a result of being bitten by Anna (Bettelheim, 1959). Although Anna learned to walk, say some words, and wash her hands and brush her teeth, she never learned to speak in sentences. By the time she died at the age of 11, four years after being taken to the university, she was functioning only on the level of a 2- or 3-year old.*

*A more recent case is that of "Genie" (Curtiss, 1977; Pines, 1981). She had been kept harnessed to a potty seat until the age of 13 in a small room in a California house, hidden away to avoid the wrath of her father, who hated children. She was fed only milk and baby food, and was never spoken to by anyone. Occasionally, in fits of rage, her father beat her, usually when she tried to speak or made noise. She was discovered after her mother fled with her following a fight with her father, and she was placed in a children's hospital. At that time, Genie could not stand straight, chew, or see beyond 10 feet. She blew her nose into the air and urinated and masturbated in the presence of others. Like Anna, she was later able to learn a few words and phrases, but not to ask questions or speak sentences. She did, however, use gestures well, and was able to learn sign language. She was inquisitive, and after seven years in the hospital, her IQ score had increased from 38 to 74. When her mother eventually removed her from the hospital, she still had not come close to normality in many aspects of her behavior and development.*

The cases described in the opening vignette show that, while a newborn baby has the *capacity* to become a member of human society, this capacity can be realized only through interaction with other human beings. In the first few years of life, a baby is completely dependent upon other human beings for survival. In the first few months, he or she literally can survive for only a matter of hours without assistance from other people. In addition to assistance with physical needs, a newborn baby requires consistent social interaction with other human beings. This need is so great that if a baby is deprived of it for an extended period, he or she may never be capable of becoming "normal." As illustrated by "Anna" and "Genie," the total absence of interaction with other human beings produces personalities that cannot participate in human society or even display what would be regarded as normal behavior. Even a partial absence of interaction can be quite harmful: Babies whose parents do not isolate them but who largely ignore them over an extended time typically show poor intellectual development and high rates of personality difficulties, as do institutionalized children who have sometimes been deprived of interaction because their harried caretakers simply don't have time to provide it (Goldfarb, 1945; Spitz, 1945). Such children typically experience ongoing developmental and emotional problems, even if they receive all the necessary *physical* care.

## BECOMING "HUMAN" THROUGH SOCIALIZATION

These effects of social isolation dramatically illustrate the human need for **socialization.** Socialization is the process whereby people learn, through interaction with others, that which they must know in order to survive and function within their society. In other words, it is the means by which people learn the roles, knowledge, beliefs, and values of their culture.

Even among animals, studies have shown the need for interaction. The best-known example is a series of studies of monkeys by Harry Harlow and his colleagues (Harlow, 1958; Harlow and Harlow, 1970, 1962; Harlow and Zimmerman, 1959). Two key findings of these studies illustrate the importance of interaction for normal development.

First, monkeys raised in isolation from other monkeys did not develop normal behavior. Rather, they were withdrawn, responded to other monkeys with fear or aggression, and did not engage in sex. If the females were artificially impregnated, they usually neglected or abused their offspring. Among the behaviors observed were sitting on the baby monkeys, holding them upside down, and attacking them. Significantly, the effects of such isolation became harder to reverse the longer the monkeys were kept in isolation.

Second, consistent patterns were observed when monkeys in isolation were given a choice between a cloth "dummy mother" and a wire "dummy mother." Even when the wire "mother" had a feeding bottle and the cloth "mother" did not, the monkeys preferred the soft cloth "mother."

### Learning about Norms and Social Roles

Studies like the ones discussed above show that primates, including human beings, have an innate need for interaction with others of their kind. Thus, we have seen that babies are dependent on others for (1) meeting basic physical needs, without which they cannot survive; and (2) meeting the need for social interaction, without which their learning capacity is lost and normal behavior is impossible. Two key functions of the socialization process, then, are to provide needed care and needed interaction. The third key function of socialization is to teach people the basic information they need in order to survive in their society. Everyone must learn the social roles that exist in his or her society and how to play them. Furthermore, everyone must learn the norms of his or her society. As social animals, people must know how to participate in the society into which they are born.

## THEORIES OF SOCIALIZATION AND DEVELOPMENT

Social scientists have developed a number of theories about how this process of learning norms and roles takes place. Although these theories disagree on some key points, many of the differences arise because different theories emphasize different aspects of the socialization and development processes. Among the most important and influential theories of socialization and development are *interactionist theories, Freudian theories*, and *cognitive-developmental theories.*

### Nature versus Nurture

In psychology and, to a lesser extent, sociology, there has been considerable debate about the relative importance of nature versus nurture in shaping human behavior. The term *nature* refers to natural or biological influences over human behavior. Those who argue on behalf of nature as the more significant force shaping human behavior believe that human behavior is in substantial part a product of:

the individual's genetic or hormonal makeup (Pines, 1982;
natural instincts or drives that act as influences on the behavior of all human beings (Freud, 1970 [orig. 1920) 1962 [orig. 1930]; Lorenz, 1966; E. Wilson, 1978); and
physiological processes of development that place limits on the range of thought and behavior of which a person is capable at any given age (Piaget, 1952, 1926; Piaget and Inhelder, 1969).

Although these theories do not all argue that human behavior is *entirely* a product of nature, they do argue that nature has extensive influence over human behavior.

The term *nurture* refers to the influence of *social forces* in shaping human behavior. Those who emphasize nurture as the major influence over human behavior argue that behavior is a product of interactions with other people (emphasized by symbolic-interactionists such as Mead, 1934, and Cooley, 1964) and the situations in which people find themselves, including their share of limited resources such as wealth, status, and power, and the relationship of their situations to larger societal needs.

In no area of human behavior has this debate been more intense than in childhood socialization. All schools of thought agree that what happens in childhood has important influences throughout a person's life, because it is in childhood that people first develop their patterns of thought and behavior. Although sociologists generally give greater attention to nurture than to nature, the theories we will be considering do disagree about the relative importance of nature versus nurture. We shall consider first interactionist theories of socialization, which weigh in heavily on the side of nurture.

## Interactionist Theories of Socialization

Of all the substantive areas of sociology, socialization is the one in which theories arising from the symbolic-interactionist perspective have had their greatest influence. Interactionists see human behavior as the result of how people understand their situations, which in turn is the result of messages they get from others and how they interpret those messages. Because a child is born without *any* understanding of his or her situation, it is clear that these processes are especially important in childhood socialization. Thus, interactionist theories of socialization focus on the ways that messages from others do the following things: (1) provide the child with an understanding of his or her situation; (2) teach the child about the roles that he or she will be expected to play; (3) teach the child the norms that will govern his or her behavior and the ways that some of these norms differ from role to role; (4) provide the child with messages concerning how well the child is doing at playing his or her roles. These messages, in turn, lead to the development of the child's self-image.

**Mead on Socialization** One of the first sociologists to examine the socialization process from the interactionist perspective was George Herbert Mead, whose ideas were introduced briefly in Chapter 3. They continue to rank among the most influential theories about socialization. As we saw in our examples of feral children, normal human development is impossible without human interaction. Mead believed, in fact, that human behavior is almost totally a product of interaction with others. As he put it:

> The self, as that which can be an object to itself, is essentially a social structure, and it arises in social experience . . . it is impossible to conceive of a self arising outside of social experience. (Mead, 1934, p. 13)

Thus, to Mead, social, not biological, forces are the primary source of human behavior. To a large extent, he accepted the notion that a newborn baby is *tabula rasa*, or a "blank slate," without predispositions to develop any particular type of personality. The personality that develops is thus a product of that person's interactions with others. Mead referred to the spontaneous, unsocialized, unpredictable self as the *I*. In the process of socialization, others interact with the individual, developing in him or her the attitudes, behaviors, and beliefs needed to fit in to society. Mead referred to the socialized self that emerges from this process, reflecting the attitudes of others, as the *me* (Mead, 1934, pp. 175–178). Although the *me* becomes predominant with socialization, the *I* still exists, and is the source of the spontaneous and seemingly unpredictable side of a person's behavior (Mead, 1934).

**THE PLAY STAGE** Social interactions begin in early childhood—a period Mead referred to as the **play stage**—with contacts with **significant others**. These are particular individuals with whom a child interacts on a regular basis early in life, including parents, teachers, and schoolmates. In the play stage, which begins with the acquisition of language, typically around the age of one, children learn several important things through interaction with significant others. First, they learn that they exist as a separate object. Sociologists refer to the awareness of that separate identity as the **self**.

Children also learn at this stage that others, too, have separate identities, separate selves. They learn that different people behave differently, and that different people also *expect* children to behave in different ways. This leads to the third key role of significant others at this point: They teach children social norms, Children learn norms both through concrete messages given by significant others ("Do this, but don't do that") and by using significant others as **role models**—persons from whom children learn how to play roles. In other words, children learn what is appropriate behavior in part by observing the behavior of significant others and then trying out that behavior themselves.

Why does Mead call this the "play stage"? Essentially, the reason is that the child at this stage is capable only of play and cannot yet engage in the organized activity necessary, for example, to participate in a game such as baseball. To put it a bit differently, at the play stage children are interacting with particular *individuals* (Mommy, Daddy, Kelly, Christopher) and not *roles* (mother, father, big sister, outfielder). They do not yet really understand that, to a large extent, how they are expected to behave toward people is determined by those people's roles. Rather, they just know that different people act differently and expect them to act differently.

**THE GAME STAGE** As they get older and interact with a wider range of significant others, children move beyond thinking merely in terms of particular individuals. They begin, in effect, to learn the concept of social roles. They learn that certain positions are occupied by a variety of people, such as mothers, fathers, salespeople, and teachers. They also learn that people in similar social positions frequently behave alike, and that they, in turn, are expected to behave in particular ways toward people with particular social positions. To a large extent, this is true regardless of who fills these social positions. When a child has learned this, he or she has moved beyond interacting with particular individuals and has begun to interact with roles. In Mead's terms, the child has gone from interacting with significant others to a new and higher stage of interacting with the *generalized other*. At this stage, the child has generalized from the behavior and expectations of particular individuals to those of anyone playing various roles that relate to whatever role the child is playing at the time. He or she has, in effect, learned to respond to the expectations of his or her society.

When the child has learned to do this, he or she has reached the **game stage**—the ability to play roles and to interact with other roles which makes organized activity, such as games, possible. Take, for example, the game of baseball. Each position in the game, such as shortstop or outfielder, has a set of expectations—a role—attached to it. If you play shortstop, you must know not only that you are expected to stop the ball if it is hit to you, but also what base you should throw to. Anybody playing shortstop needs to know this; the expectations are the same regardless of who plays the position. The same is true of any other organized activity.

A person attains this game stage through repeated messages from others. It is also through communication with others that the specific expectations of each role, such as shortstop, are learned. Through social interaction, the child learns to play different roles attached to positions that he or she occupies at various times, and to respond appropriately to the behavior of others playing various roles. People's ability to play and respond to various roles is essential in order for them to participate in society. As is shown in the box on page 127, it also turns out that playing a wide variety of roles is good for your health.

## SOCIOLOGICAL INSIGHTS

### MULTIPLE SOCIAL ROLES: GOOD FOR YOUR HEALTH?

At the beginning of this chapter, it was stressed that human beings have an innate need for interaction with other human beings. One of the main ways we meet this need is by learning and playing a variety of roles. Recently, a study by Phyllis Moen, Donna Dempster-McClain, and Robin Williams (1992) showed that this need is both psychological and physiological. In 1986, Moen, Dempster-McClain, and Williams sought out and interviewed a group of women who had participated in a study of their involvement in various social roles 30 years earlier, in 1956. They found and re-interviewed more than 90 percent of the women who had participated in the 1956 study and were still alive in 1986—no small feat in itself! What they wanted to find out was whether women who had been actively involved in a greater variety of roles in 1956—such as friend, worker, church member, neighbor, relative, and club member—were healthier in 1986 than those with fewer active role involvements. The answer, it turns out, is a clear yes: The more roles in which a woman was actively involved in 1956, the healthier she turned out to be 30 years later.

This was true even after adjusting for age, education and other measures of socioeconomic status, earlier health, and current family status. (All of the women were married with children in 1956, but about a third of them were divorced or widowed by 1986.)

One type of role involvement turned out to be particularly beneficial for the women's health. Women who belonged to clubs or organizations in 1956 were a good deal healthier 30 years later than women who did not. Again, this was true after adjusting for other factors that might influence health. It may be true that healthier, more affluent people are more likely to get involved in clubs, but at any given level of socioeconomic status or previous health, a person involved with clubs or organizations in 1956 turned out to be healthier in 1986. Why did a woman's involvement in a club or organization turn out to be particularly beneficial, even compared with other kinds of role involvement? Moen, Dempster-McClain, and Williams speculate that the reason may have to do with the fact that our roles are most beneficial to us when we find them rewarding. We *choose* club or organization involvement more voluntarily than other role involvements, and we can more freely end them and shift to other clubs or organizations if our roles are not rewarding. Thus, because of its voluntary nature, club and organizational involvement may be among the most rewarding kind of role involvement there is. Supporting this interpretation is the fact that unpaid volunteer work was also found to be quite strongly correlated with women's health. Thus, socialization into roles—particularly ones you have some choice about taking on—is not only good for you socially; it also seems to be good for you physically.

SOURCE: Phyllis Moen, Donna Dempster-McClain, and Robin M. Williams, Jr. 1992. "Successful Aging: A Life-Course Perspective on Women's Multiple Roles and Health." American Journal of Sociology 97:1612-1638, University of Chicago Press.

**Socialization and the Looking-Glass Self** Interactionists believe that in addition to teaching us to play our own social roles and to respond appropriately to the roles of others, the socialization process helps us develop a *self-image*—a sense of what kind of person we are. This self-image relates closely to the various roles that we play. We normally come to think of ourselves as being very good at playing some roles and not so good at playing others. This self-image is developed through the process of the *looking-glass self* (Cooley, 1964 [orig. 1902]), which was introduced in Chapter 2. As children try out playing new roles, they try to imagine how they appear to others, and they pay attention to others in order to get messages about how well they are doing in these roles.

Children, then, try to imagine what other people think about how they are doing in their various roles and look for explicit and implicit messages from others to find out. Once they get such messages, they develop ideas about what kind of person they are based on their interpretation of these messages. This process, in turn, affects how they think of themselves. Two elements are critical to this process: the *content* of the messages a child gets from others, and the child's *interpretation* of these messages.

**Self-Esteem and Significant Others** As we have indicated, a child will normally come to think of himself or herself as being good at playing some roles and not as good at playing others. In most cases, this process leads to the gradual development of a balanced self-image. Sometimes, though, children are intentionally or unintentionally given messages that are harmful to their overall self-image. Excessive criticism, for example, can lead a child to think of himself or herself as not very good at anything, which produces low *self-esteem*. Self-esteem refers to one's judgment of oneself: Do you look upon yourself positively or negatively? This can refer to your *overall* judgment of yourself—called *global self-esteem*—or to your judgment of your performance in a particular role. How well we perform in a role affects our self-esteem, at least as it relates to that role. At the same time, however, self-esteem also affects how well we perform in a role (Rosenberg, Scheeler, and Schoenbach, 1989). This suggests that if children are given negative messages that harm their self-esteem, their achievement will suffer. Poor achievement can lead to further erosion of their self-esteem.

Overly busy parents who consistently fail to take time to do things with their children and to respond to their children's concerns can unintentionally give their children such messages. To a young child, "I'm too busy" can easily sound like "I don't want anything to do with you" or "You're a pest." A child who comes to think of himself or herself in these terms might never develop good self-esteem. Young children develop images of themselves that, to a substantial degree, will influence how they think of themselves throughout life. Thus, poor global self-esteem at this stage can be a source of lifelong difficulties (see Clausen, 1991). This does not mean that children need to be told they are good at everything. A balanced self-image is much healthier than one that cannot accept any shortcomings. However, it is important for children to get sufficient attention and emotional support from their parents to know that they are loved and wanted, be given credit and praise when they do things well, and be reassured that it is not necessary to be good at everything.

## Freudian Theories of Socialization

Whereas symbolic-interactionists such as Mead and Cooley see human behavior and personality as almost totally the product of social interaction, their contemporary Sigmund Freud (1856–1939) saw behavior and personality as being the product of the interaction between nature and nurture.

Freud believed that human beings are born with certain innate *natural drives*, or behavioral needs, including a tendency toward aggression and the desire for physical (particularly sexual) pleasure (Freud, 1962 [orig. 1930]). Freud called these natural drives, which he believed to be present in some form from infancy on, the **id**. Opposing the id are the requirements of society that we control our aggression and our pleasure-seeking. Society's norms restricting these natural drives were referred to by Freud as the **superego**, which he saw as a socially learned *conscience* arising from messages we get from others about acceptable and unacceptable behaviors. According to Freud, everyone experiences an *inner conflict* between the id, which says "I want to do that," and the superego, which says "You can't do that." The dynamics of this conflict and the way an individual resolves them form the basis of one's personality.

Depending on the strictness of his or her home environment, and to a lesser extent the restrictiveness of other childhood environments, each person develops a somewhat different balance between the id and the superego. This balance is managed by the **ego**, the ultimate expression of the personality each person develops. The more restrictive the childhood environment is, the stronger the influence of the superego will tend to be. When the environment is too restrictive, Freud believed, natural drives are repressed but do not go away. Rather, they build up pressures that lead to increased frustration until they

**TABLE 5.1** Summary of Key Theorists on Socialization and Development

| | Mead | Freud | Erikson | Piaget | Kohlbert |
|---|---|---|---|---|---|
| Socialization viewed as process of: | Learning roles and self-concept through interaction with others. | Struggle between natural drives and societal expectations. | Series of dilemmas to be resolved, relating to social expectations and self-identity. | Development of increasingly sophisticated interpretations of physical and social environment. | Development of increasingly sophisticated moral reasoning, through cognitive development and interaction with others. |
| Views on nature (natural/biological influences) versus nurture (social influences) | Emphasized nurture; little if any consideration of nature. | Socialization seen as struggle between nature and nurture. | Emphasized nurture, in context of natural development. | Emphasized natural development of reasoning ability, which allows understanding of social environment. | Reasoning seen as joint outcome of natural development and social interaction. |
| Stages of socialization and development, with typical age range | 1 Play Stage:* interaction with specific persons, "I" predominates.<br>2. Game Stage: interaction with roles, "me" predominates. | 1. Oral (0–1)<br>2. Anal (1–3)<br>3. Phallic (3–4)<br>4. Oedipal (4–6)<br>5. Latency (6–11)<br>6. Genital (11 and up) | 1. Trust vs. mistrust (0–1)<br>2. Autonomy vs. doubt, shame (1–2)<br>3. Initiative vs. guilt (3–5)<br>4. Industry vs. inferiority (6–11)<br>5. Identify vs. role confusion (12–18)<br>6. Intimacy vs. isolation (young adult)<br>7. Generativity vs. self-absorption (middle adult)<br>8. Integrity vs. despair (old age) | 1. Sensorimotor `(0–2)<br>2. Preoperational (2–7)<br>3. Concrete operations (7–11)<br>4. Formal operations (12 & up) | Preconventional Level*<br>Stage 1: punishment avoidance<br>Stage 2: need satisfaction<br>Conventional Level<br>Stage 3: nice person<br>Stage 4: law and order<br>Postconventional Level<br>Stage 5: social contracts<br>Stage 6: universal ethical principles |

• Stages are not strongly linked to age; they depend on social interaction.

may eventually surface in a destructive way. Depressed people, Freud believed, felt that way because they had taken the anger and frustration they felt about having to repress too much of their aggressive and sexual selves and turned it against themselves. Less commonly, too little restriction of the natural drives may lead a person to behave amorally—exhibiting no sense of right or wrong and no sense of guilt or remorse for anything he or she does.

Today, most social scientists would agree that how conflicts between individual drives or desires and societal expectations are resolved in childhood does have some effect on behavior later in life. At the same time, most sociologists argue that the situations people encounter in later life are important social forces in their own right, and they reject the notion that *all* behavior in adulthood is a product of childhood experiences. Recent research supports the notion that both sociological *and* biological influences are at work in shaping human behavior (Udry, 1988; Udry and Billy, 1987).

**Erikson's Eight Stages of Life** Like Freud, Erik Erikson felt that children face dilemmas involving choices between two opposites. However, Erikson argued in *Childhood and Society* (1950) that the dilemmas people face at different stages of their lives are related more to social expectations and self-identity than to natural drives. Erikson argued that people experience a series of *psychosocial stages*, each of which contains opposing positive and negative components. At each stage, people face a dilemma or crisis as they make choices between the two components. As Mead and Cooley suggested, the choices that are made are largely a product of the social environment and messages that children receive from significant others. In the first several stages, children who receive encouragement and positive messages about themselves tend to achieve healthy modes of adaptation; children who are ignored or who get excessively negative messages tend to adapt poorly.

Erikson's eight stages are summarized in Table 5.1, which also compares Erikson's theories of socialization with other theories. We can use Erikson's second stage, autonomy vs. shame, to illustrate the type of dilemma children encounter. At this stage, which occurs between the ages of one and two or three, children are trying out their physical skills through walking, climbing, manipulating objects, and toilet training. If they master these skills—and are given the message that they have done so—they become more autonomous and self-confident. If they do not, they face shame and self-doubt. A sense of inferiority often results, and the child may either become compulsive about following fixed routines or reject all controls. Note that Erikson's approach shares an important commonality with interactionist theories such as those of Mead and Cooley: Successful or unsuccessful resolution of Erikson's dilemmas is based in large part on the messages a child gets from his or her significant others.

Although Erikson's stages effectively outline some of the major dilemmas that must be addressed in socialization, they should not be seen as exact descriptions of the process of development. Discrete stages have not for the most part been scientifically validated, and to the extent that they occur in a sequence, they overlap considerably. While an unresolved issue at one stage often has effects at later stages, there always remains some possibility that it can be addressed successfully later in life.

## Cognitive Development Theories of Socialization

**Cognitive-developmental theories** resemble the theories of Freud and Erikson in two important ways. First, they rely on the idea that people move through a series of stages as they develop and experience the socialization process. Second, they include a place for the forces of nature as well as those of nurture. However, they also differ in two important ways. First, rather than dilemmas or choices, cognitive-developmental theories focus on **cognitive processes**: learning, reasoning, and the actions by which knowledge is obtained and processed. Second, they relate the role of nature to physiological development in that they acknowledge that the development of the body and brain places an upper limit on the child's capacity to learn, reason, and process knowledge at any given age.

However, although the limits on human potential may be physiologically defined, the actual level and process of learning and reasoning in any individual is mostly a function of social influences. For most of us, learning modes of reasoning and information processing are very much influenced by the social environment. To see how this occurs, let us begin with the cognitive theories of the Swiss psychologist Jean Piaget.

**Piaget: Stages of Cognitive Development** Central to Piaget's theory of development was the concept of a *schema*—a behavior sequence involving recognition of a stimulus (sight, sound, object, person, or message) in the environment and a motor (behavioral) response to that stimulus based on our understanding of its meaning. As new information becomes available, it is assimilated into existing schemas, and these schemas may be modified to accommodate new information that does not fit the existing schemas. Thus, cognitive reasoning becomes a process of assimilation and accommodation of new information into existing schemas, which become increasingly complex as new information becomes available. According to Piaget (1926), this process of cognitive reasoning develops through the following four stages:

1. *Sensorimotor stage (until age 2).* This stage involves the development of a physical understanding of the environment by touching, seeing, hearing, and moving around. At this stage, schemas involve

purely physical objects and properties. Children learn *object permanence*—if you show a child something and then hide it, the child will learn that it is still there and look for it.

2. *Preoperational stage (ages 2 - 7).* Children learn to represent schemas in their minds. They engage in symbolic play, using one object as a symbol to represent another. They may, for example, pretend that a block is a car and move it around the way a car would move. At this stage, children also develop *language*—not merely saying words, but putting them together in sentences that express increasingly complex ideas. This clearly demonstrates that they are using mental, not purely physical, schemas. They still, however, look at things from their own viewpoint, not that of someone else, and they have trouble with any task that requires them to look at themselves or their environment from someone else's viewpoint. A boy at this stage, for example, may report having two brothers, Henry and Paul. If asked how many brothers Henry has, however, the child will mention only Paul—not himself (Foss, 1973).

3. *Stage of concrete operations (ages 7-11).* At this stage, children gain several new capabilities. Although they still think mainly in terms of concrete, readily visible objects rather than abstract concepts, they are able to think in terms of cause and effect. They can draw conclusions about the likely physical consequences of an action without always having to try it out. They also learn that quantities can remain constant even if they take different shapes and forms. They understand, for example, that if a given amount of milk is poured from a tall thin glass into a short wide one, or from a large glass into two small ones, it is still the same amount of milk. Finally, as stressed earlier in our discussion of George Herbert Mead, children at this stage can respond to the roles of others, consider things from the viewpoint of others, and play different roles themselves. Thus it is now possible for them to play games.

4. *Stage of formal operations (ages 12 and up).* When they reach this stage, children can reason not only in terms of the physical world, but also in terms of abstract concepts, such as love, happiness, wealth, intelligence, and remorse. They can think in terms of future consequences and evaluate the probable outcomes of several alternative courses of action. They can also evaluate their own thoughts and self-image. Finally, they can begin to think about major philosophical issues, such as why pain and suffering exist.

**Social and Cultural Influences on Cognitive Development** As was indicated earlier, cognitive theorists believe that the *capacity* to attain these stages is defined by physiological development, but that the actual extent to which people attain them, and the ages at which they attain them, are socially determined. The ability to do these things is learned from others, and if a child is not exposed to others engaging in the type of reasoning that normally occurs at a given stage, the child may have difficulty developing that reasoning ability on his or her own. Both the larger culture in which a child grows up and the child's immediate social environment influence this process. If a culture places little value on abstract reasoning—for example, a culture in which reality is determined by tradition and not by scientific discovery—a child is much less likely to develop abstract reasoning skills. At the more immediate level, if a child's parents do not think in terms of abstract concepts, and this skill is not emphasized in school, the child has little or no way of learning it. For this reason, a sizable part of the population—even in countries like the United States where scientific knowledge is valued—never reaches the cognitive stage of formal operations. The four stages of cognitive reasoning do appear to occur in sequence, but how far people get through that sequence seems to vary.

**Piaget on Moral Reasoning** Cognitive reasoning enables people to make moral judgments—that is, to distinguish between right and wrong. Piaget (1932) offered the important insight that how children (and adults) distinguish right from wrong is greatly influenced by their process of cognitive reasoning. A child at the preoperational stage, for example, cannot and will not make judgments about right and wrong in the same way as a child at the stage of formal operations.

**THE MORALITY OF CONSTRAINT** According to Piaget, children at young ages act on the basis of reward and punishment: They avoid behaviors that bring punishment and repeat ones that are rewarded. They see rules as existing for their own sake (not some larger social purpose), and they do not realize that rules are subject to change. Because it is the punishment or consequence that makes something bad, the rightness or wrongness of an act is judged purely on the basis of its consequences, not its intent. In one experiment, for example, Piaget (1932) found that children thought it was worse to break 15 cups left behind a door where they could not be seen than to break one cup climbing to get some jam that had been placed out of reach. In other words, the *consequences* were greater in the first case. Significantly, the younger children typically paid little attention to the fact that in the second case the child's *intentions* had been worse—to get at something his mother had intended him not to have. Piaget referred to this stage of moral behavior as the *morality of constraint.*

**THE MORALITY OF COOPERATION** Piaget argued that, given the appropriate social environment, children will move from the morality of constraint to a *morality of cooperation.* As Piaget's theory suggests, young children will often admit doing the right thing only because it brings a reward or prevents a punishment. Among older children, *intention* becomes a more important factor in determining right and wrong. In Piaget's experiments, for example, older children were more likely to say that the child climbing up to get the jam had behaved worse, because he was doing something he knew his mother didn't want him to do.

Most sociologists agree that for the majority of people moral behavior is more than a matter of reward and punishment. Most crimes—particularly, but not only, minor ones like petty theft—are not solved, and the offenders are never punished. Even so, most people most of the time do not steal, According to Piaget, the reason they don't is that they realize that stealing is wrong. If everyone stole, nobody would be secure in his or her property, and the world would be a miserable place. Thus, the recognition that stealing prevents cooperation and hurts everyone's quality of life keeps most people from stealing. This is what is meant by the morality of cooperation.

Unfortunately, many people never fully develop the morality of cooperation. Even among some adults, consequence and punishment are the main factors influencing moral behavior. At the same time, some very young children have been shown to understand intention and take it into consideration (Shultz et al., 1980). Morality of constraint always appears to precede morality of cooperation, but the age at which morality of cooperation develops, if it develops at all, is quite variable. Thus, moral reasoning, like other aspects of cognitive development, is heavily influenced by social interaction. This is clearly shown in the work of Lawrence Kohlberg, who has elaborated on Piaget's theories of moral reasoning.

**Kohlberg's Stages of Moral Development** Lawrence Kohlberg (1974, 1969) expanded on Piaget's ideas by conducting research in which people were presented with moral dilemmas and asked what they would do and why they would do it. In one such dilemma, a man's wife was dying, and the druggist who had invented the only medicine that could save her was charging ten times what the medicine cost to produce-far more than the man could afford. As a result, the man stole the drug. Subjects in Kohlberg's experiments were then asked questions such as whether the man was right to steal the drug, and why. It was the "why" part that was of greatest interest to Kohlberg. He found, based on the *reasons* they gave for their responses to his moral dilemmas, his subjects could be classified into three general levels of moral reasoning, each of which could be subdivided into two more specific stages of moral reasoning. Kohlberg argues that these six stages generally occur in a set sequence: One must pass through Stage 1 before going on to Stage 2, and so forth. However, many people never develop beyond Stage 3 or 4, and some do not even get that far.

**THE PRECONVENTIONAL LEVEL** Subjects at the preconventional level, consisting of Stages 1 and 2, are self-centered. They view the world in terms of their own interests, needs, and desires, without giving much consideration to the views of others. In Stage 1, *punishment avoidance*, people are concerned with avoiding that which brings punishments or bad consequences. It is very much like Piaget's morality of constraint. In the sample story, a Stage 1 subject might say "Steal the drug if you can get away with it; don't if it looks like you'll get caught." At Stage 2, *need satisfaction*, moral reasoning is a little more developed but remains very self-centered. At this stage, behavior is acceptable if it satisfies your wants or desires. A Stage 2 subject might say the man should steal the drug because his wife needs it, without addressing the druggist's behavior at all.

**THE CONVENTIONAL LEVEL** At the *conventional level*, which Kohlberg believes characterizes most adult behavior in industrialized countries, behavior is considered right if it is approved by others. Thus, a Stage 3 subject might say stealing is acceptable behavior because the druggist is a bad man, or not acceptable because stealing "isn't nice." A bit more developed is Stage 4, *law and order*. At this stage of moral reasoning, right and wrong are defined on the basis of rules and laws. By and large, such rules and laws are not thought of as changeable, and to violate any of them is nearly always seen as wrong. This group would be more likely than others to say that stealing the drug is wrong because stealing is against the law. It appears that Stage 4 is the most prevalent in the adult U.S. population (Colby et al., 1983).

**THE POSTCONVENTIONAL LEVEL** People at the *postconventional level* of morality realize that laws and the approval of others do not simply happen; rather, they often have some basis in people's needs and the general welfare. The stages in this level are harder to define because relatively few people—only about one in five Americans—reach this level (Kohlberg, 1975; see also Colby et al., 1983; Kohlberg, 1986, 1984). In Stage 5, people are governed by *social contracts*— agreements, implicit or explicit, that they enter into for their mutual benefit. People have an obligation, out of fairness, to live up to their end of the bargain. Stage 5 people recognize that laws exist for a reason and that there are bad laws that—even if one obeys them—can and should be changed. In Stage 6, *universal ethical principles*, people live by principles based on human rights that transcend government and laws. Stage 6 people believe that sometimes these ethical or moral principles obligate them to violate laws that work against basic human rights. Dr. Martin Luther King, Jr., is often cited as an example of a person with Stage 6 moral reasoning (Penrod, 1986, P. 74).

Like most of the other theories we have considered, Kohlberg's theory sees social interaction as highly important. Although the sequence always begins with Stage 1 and develops in order, when and how far it develops depends on the messages and examples a child gets from others. In general, urban and well-educated children attain higher levels in Kohlberg's classification system than rural and poorly educated children. Overall, people in modern industrial societies outscore those in rural and less economically developed ones.

Kohlberg's work has been criticized as containing both social class and sex biases. In fact, a general problem with all developmental theories is that the stages may vary among different groups and societies (Danneter, 1984). Middle-class people score higher on Kohlberg's scale than those of lower socioeconomic status, a difference that no doubt reflects both real differences in reasoning and social class differences in self-expression. Men also score higher than women. This may reflect Kohlberg's system of classification. Men tend to emphasize "justice," which is closely linked to Kohlberg's Stages 5 and 6. Women, however, emphasize "caring," which also reflects a concern with the welfare of others, but is not as highly rated by Kohlberg's coding system (Gilligan, 1982). Thus, both people's actual mode of moral reasoning and the way they express or conceptualize their reasoning are socially influenced.

**Moral Reasoning and Moral Behavior** Does moral reasoning affect human behavior? In other words, do people who display different levels of moral reasoning respond differently when confronted with a real-life moral dilemma? Evidence that they do is supplied by a study of student participation in the Free

Speech Movement (FSM) at the University of California at Berkeley in 1964, the first of the major student demonstrations of the 1960s.

The Free Speech Movement began when the university announced that it would no longer permit students and student organizations to set up tables in a specified area of the campus. By the time the university capitulated and permitted the tables, its administration building, Sproul Hall, had been taken over by student demonstrators, and a police car had been surrounded by a crowd of several thousand students and abandoned by the officers.

Haan, Smith, and Block (1968) interviewed a large sample of students on the campus, administering moral-reasoning tests developed by Kohlberg and asking the students what they thought of the FSM. In this college population, virtually everyone had reached at least Stage 2, and the sample included people from Stages 2 through 6. Students who supported or participated in the protest were more likely to have achieved certain stages of moral reasoning than other students. Although the majority of students at every stage expressed support of the movement, the percentage who did so was much higher among those at Stages 2, 5, and 6 than among those at Stages 3 or 4. It is not surprising that those at Stage 3 (be nice) or Stage 4 (follow rules) would be less likely to participate.

Of particular interest were the reasons for support or participation given by those at various stages of moral reasoning. The Stage 2 people participated out of self-centered motivation, as Kohlberg's theory predicts: "No university administrator is going to tell me what I can and can't do." Protestors in Stage 3 or 4 who supported the movement emphasized bad university administrators who violated the university's own rules or those of the U.S. Constitution concerning free speech. The Stage 5 and 6 students emphasized the basic human right to free speech. Thus, the probability of supporting the FSM and the reasoning of those who did support it were greatly influenced by where students fell in Kohlberg's six-stage model.

These findings suggest that although moral reasoning is related to behavior, it is more closely related to the process by which people decide *how* to behave when confronted with a moral dilemma such as fellow students requesting their support for the FSM. In fact, a review of the literature on moral development and behavior by Blasi (1980) indicates that the relationship between moral development, as defined by Kohlberg, and moral behavior is far from consistent. Although the majority of studies have found such a link, others have not (see also Kutnick, 1986). Certainly, other factors, such as peer pressures and the particular characteristics of a situation, also have important effects on behavior. However, even if people at different stages of moral development do not always *behave* differently, they do appear to *reason* differently—in real life as well as the laboratory.

### Overview of Theories of Socialization

As is evident from the material above, theorists such as Mead, Freud, Erikson, Piaget, and Kohlberg emphasized different aspects of the socialization process, and had different ideas about the roles of nature and nurture and their relative importance in the socialization process. The ideas of these theorists are summarized in Table 5.1. Although they do offer us very different views of the socialization process, these theories cannot be classified as "right" or "wrong." In an important sense, they are all at least partially "right," in that they emphasize different aspects of socialization and development, and seek to understand different processes that contribute to the overall course of socialization and development.

## AGENTS OF SOCIALIZATION

All the theories that we have discussed agree that significant others play a prominent role in the socialization process. What we have not yet addressed is the fact that *social institutions* also play an important role. In fact, both people and institutions can act as **agents of socialization**. Agents of socialization influence the development of people's attitudes, beliefs, self-images, and behavior. In a sense, it could be said that they carry out the process of socialization, interacting with the individual in a way that permits him or her to become a participating member of human society. Agents of socialization may or may not have the primary purpose of carrying out the socialization process, but they always have that effect.

The most important agents of socialization are the family (particularly parents), the school, religion, peers, and the media. Some of these—the family, religion, the school—are institutions whose manifest function is, at least in part, to be agents of socialization. They exist at least partly to provide children with knowledge, values, or—most often—both. These are not the only influential agents of socialization, however. Peers and the mass media also play an important role. Neither peers nor the media exist for the *purpose* of socialization; that is, socialization is not their manifest function. However, they do have the *effect* of shaping knowledge, beliefs, and attitudes—in some cases, just as much as the family, religion, or school. Thus, socialization can be described as an important latent function of peers and the media.

## The Family

In the early years, the family is the most important agent of socialization. This is especially true of parents, but it is also true to a lesser extent of older siblings who are present. More than anyone else, the parents define the attitudes and beliefs of a young child. To a large extent, truth to preschool children is what their parents tell them. Parents remain important as agents of socialization throughout childhood and adolescence, although as children age, parents increasingly share their role with other agents of socialization.

The effects of socialization in the family are often lifelong. The family's religion usually becomes the child's, and the child's political attitudes, world view, and lifestyle are substantially influenced by those of the family. Children who experience undesirable behaviors or attitudes in the home are more likely than other children to exhibit them in adulthood. Child and spouse abuse, alcoholism and drug abuse, and racial prejudice are all passed on through the family.

Even within the same family, however, not all children are treated the same way. Boys and girls usually undergo a different socialization experience, as we shall see in a later chapter. First-born and only children receive greater attention and often grow up to be greater achievers. A child who is highly active from infancy on is usually treated differently than one who is less active. The child's size and health status also influence parental behavior. Thus, although certain common patterns appear in every family, even brothers or sisters in the same family do not have exactly the same socialization experience.

## Schools

The school is an institution with a profound effect not only on children's knowledge, but also on their self-image, their understanding of reality, and their mode of reasoning. The school also plays an important role in teaching students the beliefs and values of their society. The role of the school in the socialization process has become more important in modern industrial societies, as the amount of specialized technical and scientific knowledge has expanded beyond what parents could possibly teach in the home. Some of the teaching of both knowledge and values that used to occur in the home today takes place in the school. Even more recently, as the two-career family and single-parent family have become more commonplace, school influences children at an early age in the form of day care.

## Religion

The influence of religion as an agent of socialization varies widely. Although most Americans identify with some organized religion, fewer than half typically attend religious services at some time during the week. Of those who do, however, many bring their children to religion classes, and some children attend religious rather than public schools. Among people who are religious, religion is a powerful agent of socialization because it specifies what is right and what is wrong. Moreover, in religious families, religion and the family frequently (though not always) give similar messages. Religion is an important influence on the values and beliefs of the parents, who join with it to pass those values on to their children.

## Peers

Peers begin to be an influence at a very young age, as children form friendships with other children (Corsaro and Rizzo, 1988, 1990). However, it is in the junior-high- and high-school years that peer influence is the greatest, as young people seek to establish their independence by turning to influences other than the home and the school. Although peer subcultures are often at odds with those of the parents and the school, peers in another sense demand a tremendous amount of conformity. Often, little deviation from the peer-group norm in dress, speech, attitude, and behavior is tolerated. The price the peer group exacts for nonconformity is high: ridicule or ostracism precisely at a time when a young person must gain acceptance from a group outside the family in order to establish independence from it. Because of this need and because of the strong pressure for conformity, the influence of the peer group on attitudes and behaviors is, for a time during adolescence, very high—perhaps greater than that of any other agent of socialization. This effect is greatest in the areas of dress, speech, entertainment preferences, and leisure activity. Often it can extend to attitudes and behaviors in the areas of sexuality and drug and alcohol use. However, it is somewhat weaker (though often still significant) in such areas as religious and political beliefs.

## The Media

In recent decades, the media, particularly television, have become very influential as agents of socialization. The average American child spends well over three hours per day watching television—in many cases, more time than he or she spends talking with parents or siblings. The spread of cable television and VCRs has probably enhanced the influence of the media by encouraging people to watch more television.

One of the more fundamental effects of the mass media on the socialization process has been to provide everyone—regardless of their social status or where they live—with the same entertainment, information, and imagery. As a result, *place*, either geographic or social, has come to be less important (Meyerowitz, 1985). Whether you are a teenager on an Iowa farm, a New York stockbroker, or an assembly line worker in Detroit, you can watch the same television programs, see the same movies, and use the same computer programs. You can communicate with people far away and different from yourselves by telephone, fax, or computer link. According to Meyerowitz, this has broken down boundaries and traditional status distinctions, made us in many ways more similar to one another, and weakened local influences such as family, neighborhood, and religious congregation on the socialization process. Another effect of the visual media, particularly television is that we have come to expect entertaining messages and attractive personal images in everything—just like TV and the movies (Postman, 1985). Thus an unattractive politician has a more difficult time getting elected regardless of his or her message or abilities, and a teacher must be entertaining in order to keep students' attention.

**THE MEDIA AND SEXUAL AND VIOLENT BEHAVIOR** Although there is great debate over precisely how television influences attitudes and behavior, there is no doubt that television has become an important means by which young people come to understand their world. As children grow into adolescence, rock music and motion pictures also play some role in the socialization process.

One area of particular concern has been media portrayals of sexuality and violence. Most Americans have seen thousands of people killed in television dramas, and there is some evidence that this desensitizes people to violence and, at least in the short term, increases aggressive behavior (National

Institute of Mental Health, 1982). Whether or to what degree the media increase the overall level of violence in American society remains unclear.

American children, like children in many other societies where television is widespread, also view a great deal of actual or implied sexual activity. However, in contrast to most European countries, in the United States television provides little information concerning how to avoid the undesired consequences of sexual activity, such as unwanted pregnancy or sexually transmitted diseases (Jones et at., 1986). Also, in contrast to practice in most European countries, the advertising of condoms was forbidden on American television until 1987. Even now the great majority of stations refuse to accept such advertising. This gives American youngsters a mixed message—sex is glamorized but its consequences are not discussed frankly.

**ONE-WAY COMMUNICATION** A significant difference between the media and all other agents of socialization is that the media usually communicate one way. Unlike all other agents of socialization, the people we experience through television, movies, radio, and music videos are *not* personal acquaintances, and we cannot really exchange ideas with them. All of the communication is in one direction—from the media to the viewer or listener.

## How Socialization Works

How do agents of socialization shape the thinking and behavior of those being socialized? Social scientists have focused on these main processes: *selective exposure and modeling, reward and punishment*, and *nurturance and identification*. Let us consider each.

**Selective Exposure** One of the ways that agents of socialization influence attitudes and behaviors is through selective exposure. Children are exposed to those behaviors and attitudes considered desirable and sheltered from those regarded as undesirable. Parents do this by the ways they speak and behave in front of their children and by the reading material and television shows to which they expose their children. Parents try to maximize exposure to "good influenced and protect their children from "bad influences." It is not only parents who do this. Peer cultures, for example, expose children to certain modes of dress, speech, and behavior, and not to others. Schools attempt—through the content of classroom materials, for example—to expose children to sets of ideas and role models that are supportive of core cultural values. In the United States, such values include individual rights, hard work, and private ownership. Even the media, in the content of their entertainment, largely reinforce such values, although there may be other areas—most notably sex and violence—where their content differs from what children experience in the home.

**Modeling** We know that children often exhibit behavior to which they are repeatedly and systematically exposed, through a process called **modeling** (Bandura, 1977). Modeling begins with observing the behavior of significant others and with retention of the images of such behavior in a person's memory. The next stage is imitation, or reproduction, of that behavior. Eventually, however, this goes beyond mere imitation: The behavior is repeated until it becomes a matter of habit, and it is repeated in situations beyond that in which it was originally observed (Bandura, 1977). Moreover, the child comes to develop attitudes and beliefs that are supportive of the behavior. Obviously, you cannot model behaviors to which you are not exposed, which is what makes selective exposure such a powerful tool of socialization. Of course, what agents of socialization *say* and what they *do* are not always the same, and when there is a discrepancy between the two, what they do seems to have a greater effect than what they say (Bryan and Walbek, 1970a, 1970b; Rushton, 1975). If, for example, a parent preaches patience but shows a child impatience, the child will likely learn impatience to a greater extent than patience.

**Reward and Punishment** When children imitate and repeat behaviors they learned from significant others, these significant others respond with approval. Approval can be verbal or nonverbal, sometimes taking the form of a concrete reward, such as a cookie or a trip to the beach. Thus, the processes of reward and punishment reinforce what is already being learned through selective exposure and modeling (Sears et al., 1957; Skinner, 1938, 1968). Both behavior and the expression of attitudes can be rewarded or punished by agents of socialization. Because merely expressing an attitude increases the probability that we will come to believe that attitude (see Festinger and Carlsmith, 1959), the process of reward and punishment acts to shape not only behavior, but attitudes and beliefs as well (Insko and Melson, 1969).

Reward and punishment are not always as obvious as giving or denying a child a cookie. Peer groups, for example, have a variety of ways to reward conformity and punish nonconformity. A friendly slap on the back or an invitation to join a group activity may be a reward for an approved action or viewpoint. Conversely, peer groups can be very harsh in their punishment of nonconformity, through ridicule, collective expressions of anger, or—worst of all—ostracism. In fact, with the exception of the mass media, which can only communicate one way, all agents of socialization use some form of reward and punishment to shape attitudes and behavior.

**Nurturance and Identification** Both of the processes discussed above—selective exposure and modeling, and reward and punishment—are more effective if the child *identifies* with the person who is acting as an agent of socialization. By **identification,** we mean positive feelings toward that individual that lead the child to want to be like that person. These feelings are built in large part by the agent of socialization's nurturant behavior toward the child. These agents love and care about the child, and, in the case of parents, are the child's main source of support. When they help the child, he or she has an obligation to cooperate. All of this leads the child to love, admire, and want to please these agents.

Besides teaching and reinforcing desired behavior and beliefs, agents of socialization also give children important messages about how well they are playing their roles, as well as about what kind of person they are overall. Several of the theories of socialization we considered earlier, such as those of Mead, Cooley, and Erikson, hold that developing a healthy self-image and making normal process through the steps and stages of life depend upon the messages given by agents of socialization. Thus, what kind of person a child grows up to become is shaped in no small part by such messages about self and role performance from agents of socialization.

## Conflicting Messages

Agents of socialization do not always give a person the same message, either about what kind of person you *are* or what kind of person you *should be.* The kind of person your parents want you to be is not always the same kind of person your teachers, your clergy, or your peers want you to be. The media, too, present you with images of the ideal person, which may vary widely depending on what you read or watch. Handling these conflicting messages and expectations is a very important part of the socialization process. How do you respond when your parents want you to go to a family gathering, your athletic coach wants you to work out, your teacher expects you to do homework, and your friends want you to party with them, *all at the same time*? More fundamentally, how do you respond when different agents of socialization want you to be a different kind of person? What happens when you have to decide whether you want to be fun-loving and carefree or serious and achievement-oriented? These choices present both opportunities and difficulties.

**Conflicting Agents and Stress** Clearly, these conflicting pressures from significant others can be a real source of stress in life. For many, they are the first experience with the condition of role conflict. In some cases, it is simply impossible to do what all the agents of socialization are demanding. When this happens, there are two possible responses. One is to try to do part of what each agent of socialization wants: Go to the family event this week, party with your friends next week, work out at some other available time, and stay up late to finish your homework. If the demands are too many, you can wind up exhausted or burned out, but most people seem to manage without reaching these extremes.

## SOCIOLOGICAL INSIGHTS

### SCHOOL AND LIBRARY BOOK CONTROVERSIES: AGENTS OF SOCIALIZATION IN CONFLICT

*Question*: What do *Huckleberry Finn; Our Bodies, Ourselves; The Grapes of Wrath; Black Boy; The Canterbury Tales;* and a host of history, science, and family-life textbooks have in common?

*Answer*: Somewhere in the United States, somebody has tried to ban them, either from the classroom or from library shelves. Controversies have erupted over school or library books in hundreds of communities throughout the United States in the past few decades. In a few cases, the conflict has even become violent. During the 1974-75 school year, some coal miners in West Virginia were so angry about the books being used in their children's schools that they went on strike and shut down the mines for an extended time. Children were withdrawn from school, and a number of school buildings were vandalized. This case was unusual only for the severity of the conflict. In fact, not only rural areas but big cities and "sophisticated" college towns as well have experienced attempts to ban certain books from the school curriculum or the library. A national survey of high-school librarians in 1982 showed that about one-third had experienced some attempt to get books out of the library; such efforts were most common in the Northeast. About half of the attempts to remove books from school libraries were successful (*The New York Times*, 1982). The 12 most frequently censored books as of 1988 were the following (Mitgang, 1988):

*Go Ask Alice,* by parents of an anonymous teenage girl; *Catcher in the Rye,* by J. D. Salinger *Our Bodies, Ourselves*; by Boston Women's Health Collective; *Forever*, by Judy Blume; *Of Mice and Men*, by John Steinbeck; *My Darling, My Hamburger*, by Paul Zindel; *The Grapes of Wrath*, by John Steinbeck; *Huckleberry Finn*, by Mark Twain; The *Learning Tree*, by Gordon Parks; *1984*, by George Orwell; *Black Boy*, by Richard Wright; *The Canterbury Tales*, by Geoffrey Chaucer.

Why do school and library books generate such intense and widespread controversy? The answer lies in disagreement among different agents of socialization concerning what children should be exposed to. Some of the disagreement is between teachers and parents. Often teachers want to expose children to the ideas contained in great literary works, while parents regard the ideas, language, or behavior depicted in the books as setting a bad example.

Some critics, for example, object to *Huckleberry Finn* because it contains language that is considered racist. Their opponents argue that the book presents a certain historical context, and in fact makes an important statement against racism. What is more important—the risk that children may imitate the language, or the possibility that they will benefit from the message? Even more controversial are books like *Our Bodies, Ourselves*, where some parents and teachers cannot agree on the desirability of the message itself. Many people want children to be exposed only to material consistent with their own viewpoint, which is impossible in a community with divergent views.

The fight is not just between parents and teachers. Even parents do not agree on what they want their children exposed to because their values differ. What some parents regard as a "bad influence," others regard as a "broadened perspective." Thus, school boards have been placed in a position whereby they will anger teachers and some parents if they do ban a book and other parents if they do not. The mere fact that such controversies are so common and can become so intense is powerful evidence of the extent to which agents of socialization engage in selective exposure.

One strategy people use is to cite the demands of one agent of socialization as the reason for not complying with those of another: "My parents say I can't go with you because we have to go to my family reunion," or "If I don't go to this dance when all my friends are going, people will think there's something wrong with me!" The alternative is to block out or withdraw from some agents of socialization. To please your parents, you may stop seeing your friends and classmates socially. Or, to please your friends, you may skip your homework or even drop out of school. To use this mode of adaptation with the most important agents of socialization, such as family, school, and peers, is more risky. Often it results in a poorly developed personality.

Sometimes, the messages of different agents of socialization are so different that, in addition to creating stress and conflict within the individual being socialized, the agents of socialization come into direct conflict with one another. One example, discussed in the box, "School and Library Book Controversies," is the sometimes intense conflict between educators and librarians seeking to broaden students' viewpoints and parents who seek to protect their children from what they see as harmful influences.

Conflicting demands among agents of socialization may give children different messages about themselves. Parents value children for who they *are* and love them unconditionally, while teachers and peers in different ways value them for what they *do*; approval and liking are not automatic. This can make going to school a difficult transition for some children. In addition, one agent of socialization may give a child a positive message at the same time that another is giving that child a negative message—sometimes in relation to the same behavior. Finally, peer socialization is different from other kinds of socialization in that it is the child's first experience of interacting with equals. To be integrated successfully into peer cultures, in both childhood and later life, children must discover how to team from equals as well as from authority figures.

**Conflicting Agents and Choice** While these conflicts among agents of socialization can be stressful, they also make choices possible, and indeed help teach us how to make choices. Suppose, for example, that you find that tuition, rent, and other expenses are exceeding your limited income as a college student, so you decide to save money by buying your clothes at a secondhand store. The next time your parents see you, they ask "What's the matter with you? Are you trying to look like some kind of bum?" In the meantime, however, a friend tells you, "I like the way you're dressing lately. It's so much less pretentious than the way you used to dress." While you are in the process of changing your appearance, your parents and friends have offered you some new ideas to consider about the meaning of how you dress.

These different messages also help us develop beliefs, values, and skills in many areas of life. Political, religious, and goal-related attitudes are largely learned in the home, while aspects of lifestyle relating to entertainment and leisure, and skills related to cooperation, intimacy, and interpersonal relations, are more likely to be learned from peers (Davies and Kandel, 1981; Youniss, 1980). Work habits and how to participate in organizations are largely learned in school (Bowles and Gintis, 1976; Jackson, 1968).

**Conflicting Agents and Social Change** In addition to offering choices at the individual level, the messages of different agents of socialization perform an important function at the societal level: They can act as a source of social change. The college student peer group, for example, functioned as a source of opposition to the Vietnam War, offering young college students in the 1960s a contrasting viewpoint about the war from what most were getting from authority figures. During the 1950s and 1960s the black churches in the United States offered African Americans an alternative to the dominant view of race relations, as well as a forum for social change (Morris, 1984). In both cases, the media took these messages and presented them to a larger audience. The broadcast media reported and televised the brutalization of black civil rights marchers in the South, and Hollywood began to produce anti-war movies and music. Eventually, these other agents of socialization spread the values associated with the peace movement and the civil rights movement through much of American society (Yankelovich, 1974, 1981). Thus, the new messages from an agent of socialization that conflicted with messages from mainstream society eventually became part of the mainstream.

An important side lesson of this experience is that what appears to be nonconformity often is not. While the college student participating in a peace march or the African-American marching for racial equality may be seen as violating the expectation of some agents of socialization (their parents, school authorities, or police, for example), they are in most cases conforming to the expectations of other agents of socialization (a college student peer group or an African-American church group, for example).

## SOCIALIZATION IN ADULTHOOD

Thus far, we have spoken of the socialization process primarily with reference to how it works in childhood and adolescence. It is in childhood that we encounter the most new roles and new situations, and thus it is in childhood that the socialization process is experienced most intensely. For this reason, childhood socialization is sometimes referred to as *primary socialization.* Socialization, however, does not end when one becomes an adult. Although many attitudes, beliefs, and behavior patterns have become fairly well established by this time, the process of socialization continues throughout life. Every time we enter a new situation or learn to play a new role, we go through a socialization process.

One example of adult socialization can be seen in the parenting process. While parents are socializing their children concerning how to take care of themselves and participate in society, their children are also socializing *them.* The adults are, in effect, learning the role of parent. In part, parents learn this role from their children, as they find out what "works" and what doesn't in the rearing of their children.

### Life-Cycle Roles

The adult life cycle presents us with numerous new situations that require the learning of new roles. In each of these, a socialization process occurs. Among these situations are leaving home to live on your own, entering college, beginning a career, changing jobs, getting married or cohabiting, becoming a parent, getting divorced or "breaking up," adjusting when your children grow up and leave home, retiring, and losing parents or a spouse through death. Not everyone experiences all of these things, and others experience some of them more than once. Thus, these changes should not be thought of as a clearly defined cycle through which everyone passes. In fact, the life cycle has become less uniform today than it was in the past. Even so, every adult experiences *some* of these changes, and every change requires a socialization process. The nature of this process is influenced by, among other things, the type of role change. For example, role changes may be voluntary or involuntary, may occur once or repeatedly, may or may not be reversible, may be made alone or along with other people, may occur quickly or gradually, and may occur alone or along with other role changes (Glaser and Strauss, 1971). All these factors influence the specific kind of socialization process that occurs with any given role change. For purposes of illustration, we shall examine the socialization processes that occur when you get a new job or start a family. Other situations requiring socialization are discussed in later chapters.

**Getting a Job** A good deal of socialization occurs when you begin your career. You must learn what it really means to be a teacher, a police officer, a lawyer, a salesperson, or an accountant. If the job was preceded by a period of training, you must learn what part of the training applies and what part doesn't. For many people starting out, it is distressing to hear "Forget everything you learned in ___________" (Fill in the blank with "education school," "police academy," "law school," "sales training," or whatever.) To survive in any career or profession, you must learn the norms of that career or profession and how to play the role in an acceptable way. To do so requires learning and accepting the profession's definition of that career as opposed to the public's. The meaning of a "good cop" from the viewpoint of other police officers may be different from the public's meaning of that term or from the meaning learned in the police academy. Similarly, a teacher who meets only the expectations of his or her students, and not those of other teachers, is not likely to feel accepted as a teacher and may doubt his or her success in that role.

This leads to a second point: Every place of employment has its own subculture, which must be learned by any new employee who wants to succeed. To be effective, even new supervisors must learn this subculture. To complicate matters further, there may be more than one subculture to which the new employee must accommodate. He or she must please not only co-workers, but also supervisors, whose norms may be quite different. For some, there are also customers, clients, voters, patients, or students to keep happy. In a very real way, all these different groups act as agents of socialization, and their messages concerning the work role are usually different.

**Marriage and Family Changes** No matter how much two people may be "in love," getting married or even cohabiting requires major adjustments that in turn require a good deal of socialization. Different ideas concerning such things as money, orderliness of the house, division of housework, and even food preferences can be major sources of conflict unless both parties can learn to compromise or find a mutually satisfactory way of doing things. Those who have lived on their own experience a loss of freedom. Those who have not run the risk of dependency. Some young people who have lived with their parents for all their lives until getting married risk becoming dependent on their spouses the same way they were dependent on their parents. Clearly the most important agent of socialization at this stage is the partner. However, to adjust successfully to this new reality, most young people also must interact with peers who are facing the same issues. Parents (and now in-laws) continue to act as agents of socialization at this stage and can be either helpful or a source of additional problems.

**BECOMING A PARENT** When people become parents, time management can become a critical issue, particularly if both parents are employed full time. Conflicts between spouses or with parents over child rearing can require additional adjustment. As noted, children are important agents of socialization concerning how to be a parent. Typically, parents and peers also play a major role in this socialization process, as do the media, with their abundant material on parenting techniques.

An increasing number of American women now enter the role of parent before marriage, in which case they must both raise and support the child by themselves. When teenagers become parents, this may be the first adult role to which they must become socialized, and they must learn this difficult role under highly adverse conditions.

**RETURN TO SINGLEHOOD** Another new role that large numbers of Americans now face is returning to singlehood after a divorce or the end of a "live-in" relationship. About half of all marriages in the United States now end in divorce, so this is an adjustment that a large number of people must make. This adjustment is the subject of Professor Diane Vaughan's "Personal Journey into Sociology." As Professor Vaughan illustrates, an important part of this socialization process is the development of a new (uncoupled) self-image or identity.

## Role Change, Adult Socialization, and Stress

While role changes like those described above always require adjustment and involve a socialization process, this is not entirely stressful. Learning a new role can be fun and exciting, and can offer an exit from a past, unsatisfactory role. Wheaton (1990) studied people who went through nine kinds of role transitions including new job, job loss, marriage, divorce, having a child, and having one's children move out, among others. For seven of the nine, the degree of stress in one's *old* role was important in determining whether learning the new role presented emotional difficulties. Similarly, marital happiness—and sometimes overall life satisfaction—improves with the arrival of the "empty nest" when the last child moves out of the home (White and Edwards, 1990). Thus, while there is a socialization process involved in learning a new role, it can lead to increased happiness.

# PERSONAL JOURNEY INTO SOCIOLOGY

## UNCOUPLING/DIANE VAUGHAN

I was married for twenty years. As I reflected on the relationship after our separation, the marriage seemed to have been coming slowly apart for the last ten. Certainly we had our good times, but I could retrospectively pick out turning points—moments when the relationship changed, times when the distance between us increased. These turning points did not hinge on arguments or the typical emotional catastrophes that beset any relationship. Instead, they appeared to be related to changes in each of our social worlds. For example, I started college because I realized I was never going to have the steady companionship of my partner and needed something of my own to do. This step, innocently taken, changed me—and us. As our marriage aged, we reacted to our difficulties by altering our relation to the world around us. Those changes, in turn, affected the relationship, changing us as individuals and our relationship to each other.

What's more, when I thought about our relationship in terms of our maneuverings in the social world, it seemed as if our marriage had eroded slowly and steadily over time in a regular, orderly way. Although we personally experienced the ending of the relationship as chaotic and disruptive, its ending took on a kind of social rhythm. That an experience could be orderly and disorderly at the same time was counterintuitive. Perhaps this orderliness was because ours was a long marriage, and thus its ending extended over a long period, giving the appearance of an orderly dissolution.

Perhaps it was a natural reflection of my occupation then: a graduate student in sociology, being trained to look for order.

During the same period, I came across an article describing marriage as a process in which two individuals renegotiate who they are with respect to each other and the world around them. They restructure their lives around each other. They create common friends, belongings, memories, and a common future. They redefine themselves as a couple, in their own eyes and in the eyes of others, who respond to the coupled identity they are creating.

They are invited out as a twosome, mail comes addressed to both, the IRS taxes them jointly. Single friends may hesitate to call, while the two people are readily incorporated into the social world of those who also are coupled.

The coupled identity they create is constantly reaffirmed, not only by the words and deeds of others, but also by the way others come to take the relationship for granted. This continual public confirmation gives them a stable location in the social world and validates their identity.

These ideas immediately captured my interest, for what appeared to have happened as my own relationship deteriorated was a reversal of this process: We slowly and over time began redefining ourselves as separate people. Rather than an abrupt ending, ours appeared to have been a gradual transition. Long before we physically separated, we had been separating socially—developing separate friends, experiences, and futures. We reacted to our changing relationship in ways that altered the definitions that we held of ourselves and that others held of us.

In order to answer the questions raised by my own experience, I began interviewing people about how their relationships ended. I wanted to learn about the relationships of people who had lived together as well as those who were married. Thus, my interest was not divorce, but uncoupling—how people living together in a sexually intimate relationship (gay and straight couples as well as the married) make transitions out of their relationships. I began collecting biographies of individual relationships. In interviews, I asked people to tell me about their relationships, beginning with the moment they first sensed something was wrong. I tape recorded their narratives, interjecting questions.

As a result of my inquiry, I discovered that uncoupling occurs in a uniform way—a describable pattern that is the same regardless of sexual preference or marital status. In a reversal of coupling, the partners redefine themselves, both in their own eyes and in the eyes of others, as separate entities once again. Getting out of a relationship entails a redefinition of self at several levels: in the private thoughts of the individual, between partners, and in the larger social context in which the relationship exists. Uncoupling is complete when the partners have defined themselves and are defined by others as separate and independent of each other—when being partners is no longer a major source of identity.

Typically, uncoupling happens like this: One person, the initiator, becomes discontented with the relationship. This person begins lobbying for change and, unable to achieve it, unintentionally begins responding to his or her personal problems in a way that begins to divide the couple. The initiator begins socially and psychologically leaving the relationship. At some point, what began unintentionally becomes intentional: The initiator, though deeply affected by the possibility of the loss, wants out.

By the time the partner realizes something is seriously wrong, the initiator has already gone in many ways. The initiator has mourned the relationship, thought about living apart, begun creating a separate lifestyle, and, in many cases, experimented with it. The partner, in contrast, has done none of these things. In fact, it is often at the moment of separation that the partner first realizes the relationship is in trouble. At this point, the initiator has been in transition for some time, and the partner's efforts to save the relationship are likely to fail. The rejected partner then begins the transition that the initiator began long before: acknowledging the problems, lobbying for change, mourning the relationship, developing separate friends, seeking alternatives to the relationship, and gradually preparing for a life alone.

When relationships come apart, both people make the same transition, but it starts and ends at different times for each. Consequently, understanding the impact of uncoupling hinges upon whether one is the initiator or partner in a relationship. Initiators have the advantage of time—time to think about and, in many instances, prepare for a life without the partner. When separation occurs, the partner is thrust into an unwanted new life for which he or she is socially and psychologically unprepared. Admittedly, identifying who is the initiator and who is being left behind is not so easy in some cases. Over the course of a long relationship, these roles may be passed back and forth, with one person assuming the role of initiator at one time and the other acting to end the relationship at another. How these roles get passed back and forth is, in fact, one of the more intriguing aspects of the uncoupling process.

## Resocialization in Total Institutions

A less ordinary type of adult socialization, which some experience and others do not, is resocialization in total institutions. The term **total institution**, developed by Irving Goffman (1961), refers to any group or organization that has almost total, continuous control over the individual and that attempts to erase the effects of the individual's previous socialization and instill a new set of values, habits, and beliefs. This process is referred to as **resocialization**. There are many examples of total institutions. One is the military, which takes people who generally believe that killing is wrong and seeks to convert them into fighting machines who will kill and risk their lives on orders, without asking questions. Prisons, which seek to eliminate criminal habits and tendencies and convert offenders into law-abiding citizens, are another example. Other examples are religious cults, "deprogramming" aimed at weaning people away from religious cults, prisoner-of-war camps, many boarding schools, orphanages, some residential substance-abuse programs, reform schools, some nursing homes, and the environments created by kidnappers.

**The Korean War: A Case Study** How do total institutions accomplish this? It is often said that they *brainwash* people. Thus, American prisoners of war on occasion defected to the North Koreans and

North Vietnamese; Patty Hearst joined her kidnappers in robbing a bank; peace-loving people have turned into fierce fighters after being drafted and put through boot camp. Actually, though, what goes on in total institutions—"brainwashing," if you will—bears some striking similarities to ordinary socialization processes. Consider, for example, studies of the "brainwashing" of American prisoners of war during the Korean War. It is said that the Chinese prisoner-of-war camps were especially effective at this. How did they do it?

Studies of Americans who returned from Chinese P.O.W. camps revealed several important findings (Bauer, 1957; Schein, 1957, 1961). First of all, reward and punishment were used. Those who behaved and expressed ideas consistent with the desires of their captors were given somewhat greater freedom, whereas those who rebelled were placed in solitary confinement and, in some cases, were physically punished. Second, selective exposure was used. Some P.O.W.s were allowed to spend as many hours as they wanted reading in libraries, as good a way as any to pass a very boring time. These libraries, of course, were stocked only with materials sympathetic to the Chinese and North Korean viewpoints. Contacts with their own culture were forbidden to the prisoners. Mail, for example, was not allowed to go through. The one exception was "bad mail"—unpaid bills, repossession notices, "Dear John" letters. The effect of this program, of course, was to foster a positive image of the Chinese and North Koreans while isolating P.O.W.s from all but the unpleasant aspects of their own background.

Most effective of all, perhaps, was the Chinese policy of "lenience" (Schein, 1961). This was intended to create an atmosphere of nurturance, a sense of obligation. Most American P.O.W.s had originally been captured in North Korea and were later taken to Chinese P.O.W. camps. Because they had been captured in the immediate war zone, conditions in Korea were harsh. Long forced marches were the rule, and they were fatal to many P.O.W.s. Scarce food and clothing went to Chinese and North Korean soldiers before it went to prisoners. In the Chinese prison camps behind the lines, however, conditions were somewhat better. Food and shelter were generally adequate, and forced marches were unnecessary. The Chinese military used this to considerable advantage. "Look how much better we treat you," they said. "We care about you and wouldn't treat you the way you were treated in Korea." Implicit, and sometimes explicit, was the threat that the prisoners could always be sent back to the far harsher conditions of Korea. This, of course, accomplished two things. First, many P.O.W.s became grateful for being treated better in China than in Korea and wanted to cooperate for that reason alone. Second, the fear of being sent back to Korea was enough to get most of the rest to cooperate, even if they didn't really want to.

We see, then, that the prisoner-of-war camp used some of the same techniques that are used in ordinary socialization processes—selective exposure and modeling, reward and punishment, and nurturance and identification.

**Ordinary Socialization versus Total Institutions** There are, however, four very important differences between resocialization in total institutions and ordinary socialization. First, the total institution seeks to eliminate the effects of previous socialization, whereas ordinary agents of socialization do not usually do this intentionally. Second, the total institution seeks to resocialize the individual strictly in accordance with its objectives. In short, the goal is to make a "good soldier," "communist sympathizer," or "cooperative inmate" out of the person. Thus, the objectives of the total institution, as opposed to the wishes or self-interests of the individual, are the entire purpose behind the process. Third, the total institution has complete, round-the-clock control of the individual and therefore does not have to compete with other agents of socialization. Finally, some total institutions, including the P.O.W. camps in the Korean War, use fatigue and physical brutality as additional ways of wearing people down. Endless questions and indoctrination and sleep deprivation are common. Eventually, the individual becomes so worn down that he or she has no energy left to resist the forced socialization, at least outwardly. Despite these very important differences, it remains true that there are important parallels between resocialization in total institutions and ordinary socialization.

# FUNCTIONALIST AND CONFLICT PERSPECTIVES ON SOCIALIZATION

While the theories of socialization discussed earlier in this chapter describe and analyze the *process* of socialization, we should also address the functions and purposes of socialization within the larger society. Let us take a closer look at two perspectives that help us understand the role and the importance of socialization. The *functionalist perspective* addresses ways in which the socialization process helps to preserve and meet the needs of society, while the *conflict perspective* sees the socialization process as a key mechanism for preserving social inequality, and ensuring that the wealthy and powerful can pass on their advantages to their children.

## The Functionalist Perspective

From a functionalist standpoint, there are several ways in which socialization preserves and meets the needs of society. It provides knowledge about adaptation to a society's physical and social environment. This knowledge, passed from generation to generation, helps the society survive and meet the demands of its environment. *Culture* carries this knowledge, and socialization is the means by which culture is passed from generation to generation. Culture, of course, also includes values and norms that are widely shared in a society, and as we have seen, functionalists see such shared values and norms as being essential to solidarity and cooperation.

On the other hand, society must be able to change in order to adapt to new situations. The fact that there are different agents of socialization, and that these agents often give somewhat different messages, offers a means by which this can occur. Because these agents of socialization offer different messages, the individual has the opportunity to choose the message that promotes change. The youthful peer group and the media may play particularly important roles in this process (Corsaro and Rizzo, 1988, 1990; Meyerowitz, 1985).

## The Conflict Perspective

From a conflict perspective, the socialization process helps the wealthy and powerful preserve and pass on their advantages. In general, the socialization process teaches people to accept, not challenge or question, the ways of their society. Recall that conflict theorists see the values, beliefs, and practices of society as serving the interests of the dominant group in society. To ask, "Do things have to be this way?" or "Isn't there a better way?" would be to challenge a status quo that works to the advantage of the wealthy and powerful. Rather than do this, socialization generally teaches children to value the greatness of their society: "This is a great country " and "Be grateful that you live here." Significantly, virtually all societies include such content in their socialization process.

Nonetheless, it is important to point out that opposition groups do sometimes form within and as a result of socialization processes. Black churches, for example, became organizing bases for the civil rights movement (Morris, 1984), and universities for the movement against the Vietnam War. Thus, agents of socialization *can* act as agents of social change, but that is probably not their usual or predominant effect.

Finally, conflict theory argues that socialization operates as a process of **social channeling** (Bowles and Gintis, 1976). It prepares the children of the wealthy and powerful for lives of wealth and power, by teaching them the values, beliefs, behaviors, and information they will need for such life. On the other hand, the children of the poor are channeled toward a life of poverty, and so on for other groups in between. Because of the linkages between social class and race, this process also helps perpetuate racial inequality. Finally, "sex role socialization," similarly prepares women and men for different and unequal roles, thereby helping pass from generation to generation the social and economic advantages enjoyed by males.

## SUMMARY

This chapter explained that social interaction is necessary for normal human development and that such interaction plays a central role in all theories about socialization. Besides meeting the need for interaction, socialization also teaches people the things they need to know in order to survive and develop in their physical and social environments. Particularly critical is the learning of social roles and norms.

Social scientists disagree about the roles nature and nurture play in human development. Interactionists see nurture—social interaction—as the dominant force, with personality being determined by the messages you get from others and your interpretation of those messages. As children develop, they learn the concept of roles, and they shift from interacting with individuals to playing roles and interacting with other roles. Freudian theory, in contrast, sees the expectations of society in fundamental conflict with basic drives such as aggression and sexuality. It holds that the ways in which these conflicts are resolved (or left unresolved) in childhood have a major impact on adult personality.

The cognitive-developmental approach, which focuses on reasoning processes, sees the child's physiological development as a factor limiting their cognitive development. But one's ability to reason also is affected by environmental or situational influences and experience. People develop through a series of stages with social interaction determining to a great degree how far a person proceeds and when. Closely related are theories concerning moral reasoning, such as those of Kohlberg. These theories see moral reasoning as progressing through a similar series of stages linked to reasoning ability. However, the ability to relate to the roles of others is necessary in order to move to higher stages. This, as well as a good part of the individual's reasoning ability, is gained through interaction with others.

The socialization process is carried out by agents of socialization, which include the family, schools, religion, peer groups, and the media. Although the family is probably the most influential of these agents, different agents predominate at different stages of life. To a greater or lesser extent, all of them shape behavior through processes of selective exposure and modeling, reward and punishment, and feedback and identification. Most agents of socialization also deliver messages to the individual that play a critical role in defining his or her self-image.

Socialization is a lifelong process, even though it occurs most intensively during the childhood period of primary socialization. In adulthood, people undergo a new socialization process each time they enter a new role, such as leaving their parents' home, starting college, getting a job, getting married or divorced, having children, retiring, or experiencing the death of a spouse. In extraordinary circumstances, they may experience resocialization in a total institution, which uses its complete control over the individual to erase old values and beliefs and instill new ones.

The functionalist and conflict theories offer different explanations of the meaning and purpose of the socialization process. To functionalists, the process helps people learn to participate in society, perpetuates social knowledge and culture, and supports consensus and solidarity. To conflict theorists, it tends to serve the interests of the dominant group by bringing about false consciousness and social channeling. Both perspectives, however, recognize that conflicting messages from different agents of socialization can act as an important source of social change. It is this social change that allows society to adapt to new conditions, and also offers a source of opportunity for disadvantaged groups to improve their position in society.

# GLOSSARY

**socialization** The process whereby new members of a society are taught to participate in that society, learn their roles, and develop a self-image.

**play stage** According to George Herbert Mead, a stage of socialization in which the child acquires language, recognizes the self as a separate entity, and learns norms from significant others.

**significant others** Specific individuals with whom a person interacts and who are important in that person's life.

**self** A distinct identity attached to a person; an awareness of that person's existence as a separate entity.

**role model** A significant other from whom a child learns to play a role.

**game stage** According to George Herbert Mead, a stage of socialization at which organized activity becomes possible.

**id** In Freudian theory, that part of the human personality that is a product of natural drives such as hunger, aggression, and sexual desire.

**superego** In Freudian theory, that part of the personality that internalizes the norms and expectations of society and of significant others.

**ego** In Freudian theory, that part of the personality that mediates between the id and the superego.

**cognitive-development theories** Theories of socialization that emphasize the development of reasoning ability.

**cognitive processes** Mental processes involved in reasoning and learning.

**agents of socialization** People and institutions that carry out the process of socialization; they act as important influences on the individual's attitudes, beliefs, self-image, and behavior.

**modeling** A process whereby the behavior of a significant other is observed and imitated.

**identification** A process whereby an individual develops strong positive feelings toward a person acting as an agent of socialization.

**total institution** An organization or group that has complete control over an individual and that usually engages in a process of resocialization.

**resocialization** A process occurring in total institutions designed to undo the effects of previous socialization and teach an individual new and different beliefs, attitudes, and behavior patterns. Social channeling A process whereby socialization prepares an individual for a particular role in life.

# FURTHER READING

BANDURE, ALBERT. 1986. *Social Foundations of Thought and Action: A Social Cognitive Theory.* Englewood Cliffs, NJ: Prentice Hall. Bandura's social cognitive theory stresses the socially based reciprocal relationship between the individual and his or her environment. A good supplement to the discussion in the chapter of Piaget's cognitive development theory.

CURTISS, SUSAN. 1977. *Genie: A Psycholinguistic Study of a Modern-Day "Wild Child"* New York: Academic Press. The story of a girl who was kept locked in a room for 12 years, as told by a social scientist who worked for several years trying to socialize her.

ELKIN, FREDERICK, and GERALD HANDEL. 1989. *The Child and Society,* 5th ed. New York: McGraw-Hill. A brief but thorough and well-written overview of childhood socialization, which draws on both sociological and social-psychological perspectives. Examines how race, sex, social class, place of residence, and other social characteristics relate to the socialization process.

GILLIGAN, CAROL. 1982. *In a Different Voice: Psychological Theory and Women's Development.* Cambridge, MA: Harvard University Press. A feminist analysis of the socialization process that considers differences in the ways males and females experience that process, as well as the consequences of those differences for women and men.

HEWITT, JOHN P. 1990. *Dilemmas of the American Self.* Philadelphia: Temple University Press. This is a well-written book characterized by traditional interactionist themes. It also addresses the impact of American culture and social structure on self.

MEYEROWITZ, JOSHUA. 1985. *No Sense of Place: The Impact of Electronic Media on Social Behavior.* An analysis of how telecommunications media such as television, VCRs, computers, telephones, and fax machines have altered the socialization process. They have weakened the influence of family, local, and community agents of socialization by offering everyone the same messages and choices regardless of place, and by facilitating communications among people separated by distance and social status.

ROSE PETER I. (ED.) 1979. *Socialization and the Life Cycle.* New York: St. Martin's Press. A collection of articles that explore the socialization process as it occurs throughout life.

# Chapter 6

# Sex, Gender, and Society

*Imagine two people, both born in 1960. Both are from upper-middle-class backgrounds, and both graduated in 1982 from a well-known state university. Both obtained full-time employment when they graduated; got married in 1984; and had two children between then and 1988. Both got divorced in early 1993. Both still work today for the employer that hired them when they graduated from college. So far, they seem alike in every regard. But there are important differences. Although both have the same education level and have been working full-time, one has an annual salary of $40,000, while the other makes only $28,000. The person with the higher salary also enjoys more autonomy and opportunity for creativity at work, while the one with the lower salary works in a more structured situation and is more closely supervised.*

*There are also differences in the amount of time these two people spend working and at leisure. For most of the time since college graduation, the one with the higher income had* more *leisure time than the one with the lower income. Despite the higher income, this person's total work week—employment and household work combined—was 63 hours per week, compared with 67 hours for the person with the lower income. When both people got divorced last year, another big difference in their situations developed. After the divorce, the standard of living of the person with the higher income* rose *by 42 percent, while the standard of living of the other person* fell *by 73 percent.*

*How could two people with such similar backgrounds and education have such different experiences in life? All of it can be explained by one thing: One of them is male and one of them is female. All the differences described above are based on average statistical differences between the situations of men and women in the United States. In other words, what happened to these two individuals reflects what happens to men and women in the United States* on average. *Even when their education and social background is identical, women on average are paid less, have less autonomy at work, spend more time working and less at leisure, and suffer financially from divorce (while men typically gain financially). In this chapter, we examine some of the reasons why.*

Boys and girls experience the socialization process different and are prepared for different roles in life. In this chapter, we shall explore how and why society defines the roles of men and women as being different and unequal, and we shall consider in greater detail the socialization processes that prepare men and women for these different roles. At the same time, we shall see that society's expectations concerning the roles of men and women have in some ways changed dramatically over the past 30 years. Indeed, this is one of the more profound social changes of our age. Nonetheless, we shall also see that a good deal has not changed, and that we cannot yet say that equality of the sexes has been attained in the United States or in most other industrialized countries.

## WHAT ARE SEX AND GENDER ROLES?

To begin our discussion, we should define several important terms. The chapter title mentions *sex* and by *gender*, but precisely what is the difference between the two? Basically, sex is biologically defined, whereas gender is socially defined. Thus, sex refers to the biological fact that a person is either a man or a woman. **Gender** refers to socially learned traits associated with, and expected of, men or women (Giele, 1988, p. 294). Therefore, to be *male* or *female* is a matter of sex, but to be *masculine* or *feminine* is a matter of gender. Gender, in short, refers to socially learned behaviors and attitudes, such as mannerisms, styles of dress, and activity preferences.

## Sex and Gender Roles

These socially learned behaviors often are specified by **gender roles.** Gender roles can be defined as roles society expects people to play on account of their sex. One example of gender roles can be seen in the world of work (Spence, Deaux, and Helmreich, 1985). Society expects women to fill certain occupations and men to fill others. Thus, male nurses and female firefighters are still the exception to the rule. Men wishing to be nurses and women wishing to be firefighters will discover that their wishes go against the expectations of many people, and that they can become the objects of ridicule or hostility.

Gender roles also exist with respect to interpersonal behavior (it is still more common for men to ask women for dates than vice versa), the family (the wife and mother is still expected to take primary responsibility for matters pertaining to the home, even if she is employed), and recreational activities (how many women are on your college football team, and how many men do you know who sew because they enjoy it?). In fact, men and women are expected to fill different roles in virtually every area of life. Even if these roles are less rigidly defined than in the past, they are still around.

## Sexism

Gender roles are not only different, they are often unequal. Structured inequality between men and women, and the norms and beliefs that support such inequality, are called **sexism.** Sexism takes a variety of forms. One form is *ideological sexism*, the belief that one sex is inferior to another. Ideological sexism is often used to justify *sexual discrimination*, unequal treatment on the basis of sex. Some men believe incorrectly that women are "too emotional" for certain jobs that require high levels of responsibility—an example of ideological sexism. They then use that belief as an excuse or justification for sexual discrimination—refusal to hire or promote women into jobs with high levels of responsibility. Today, however, the most important form of sexism is probably **institutional sexism.** This term refers to systematic practices and patterns within social institutions that lead to inequality between men and women. One such pattern, which will be discussed later in this chapter, is the relatively low pay of occupations in which most workers are women—even compared to predominantly male occupations with similar educational requirements and levels of responsibility.

## Traditional American Gender Roles

Different and unequal gender roles have long been a part of Western culture. In the United States and most other Western societies, social positions involving leadership, power, decision making, and interacting with the larger world have traditionally gone to men. Positions centering around dependency, family concerns, child care, and self-adornment have traditionally gone to women.

**The Male Role** These unequal gender roles mean that men and women are expected to behave differently in a number of situations (Broverman et al., 1972; Deaux and Lewis, 1983, 1984). Men are expected to be leaders, to take control, to make decisions, and to be active, worldly, unemotional, and aggressive. Through his actions, a man is said to determine his own status. At the same time, men are not expected to talk about (or even necessarily understand) their inner feelings. They are permitted to be blunt, loud, and a bit sloppy. In their relationships with women, men are expected to take the initiative, and sexual gratification is often a higher priority than interpersonal intimacy.

However, the most important characteristic of the male role in the United States is probably that it carries disproportionate power. It is this feature of the male role that allows men to be paid more for the work they do, while simultaneously enjoying more leisure time. As Barbara Reskin (1988) puts it, "Dominant groups remain privileged because they write the rules." She points out that as circumstances change, powerful groups such as men find new reasons to justify their advantage. When most breadwinners were male, men argued that their higher pay was justified because they had to support families. Today, with the large number of single female heads of households, the justification is different: Men's higher wages are justified on the basis that men are typically in different occupations than women (Reskin, 1988).

The male role carries power in a variety of ways—elected public offices and corporate boards and management positions are occupied mostly by males, while the higher income that most husbands receive often relegates wives to a position of economic dependency in the home. This was particularly true in the past when most middle-class women did not work outside the home, but women's lower pay perpetuates their dependency to a considerable extent. Even the emotional inexpressiveness of men has been seen by some sociologists as a source of power, because it is a mechanism many men use to withhold their true feelings from their partners (Sattel, 1989). In fact, such use of power is so much a part of the male role and the male subculture that men similarly withhold feelings from one another. They do this because they believe that to do otherwise would make them vulnerable and let other men gain advantage over them (Sattel, 1989).

**The Female Role** Women have traditionally been expected to be dependent, emotional, and unable to exercise leadership, think quantitatively, or make decisions. As a result, their status in life was often seen as a product not of their own actions but of the actions of the man to whom they were married. Women were also expected to be neater and more considerate than men, to have a better understanding of their own feelings and those of others, to have a higher standard of morality, and to be more appreciative of art, religion, and literature. In relationships, they were expected to view intimacy as more important than sexual gratification. Women who take the initiative have traditionally been regarded as "pushy."

Although a perception of basic differences in gender roles is deeply embedded in U.S. culture, some changes have occurred. In early American history, for example, property ownership and the right to vote were reserved for males. Even in the area of child rearing—where the day-to-day work was done by women—ultimate authority lay with males. Today, women in theory enjoy the same rights of voting and property ownership as men, although in reality both politics and material wealth remain disproportionately controlled by males. Our view of the female role has evolved greatly over the past two or three decades. As we shall see in much of the discussion in the rest of the chapter, though women may not have succeeded yet in ridding themselves of all aspects of the traditional female role (nor would they necessarily want to), they have expanded it to include behaviors that are much more self-determining.

**Gender Role Variations in the United States** While gender roles have always been unequal, there has been considerable variation in the specific nature of gender roles, both over time and among different groups within the United States. In early America, for example, both men and women were involved in producing salable goods—and both worked at home, farming or making products that could be sold (Degler, 1980). Although both men and women were involved in child rearing and home care, the majority of this work fell to women. The *authority* over children, however, as well as property rights, belonged to men.

Later, for middle-class women, the housewife role became predominant. As work moved outside the home, it was the men who moved with it—which preserved their economic control. The role of housewife was justified on the basis that it protected women from the harsh realities of the workplace, and many women saw it as a gain in that they no longer had responsibility for both taking care of the home and children and producing goods to be sold. In reality, however, it limited what women could become, by prohibiting them from taking on careers.

For working-class women and most African-American women, the situation was different. Economic realities forced them to work outside the home, so most of them never experienced an exclusive housewife role (Glenn, 1980, Jones, 1985; Seifer, 1973). Many of them worked at hard, low-paying jobs; in textile mills and other industries, and many others cleaned the houses and cared for the children of the more affluent.

Today, the situation has changed somewhat, with far fewer women in the housewife role. The change has been most notable for middle-class women, many of whom are moving into more challenging and lucrative careers. However, as we shall soon see in greater detail, women continue to be paid less than men with comparable education. In 1990, women employed full-time were paid only about 70 percent as much as men employed full-time. Women in the workplace often encounter a "glass ceiling" that limits their chances to move up in the organization; thus the jobs with the greatest status and power are usually occupied by males (De Prete and Soule, 1988). Moreover, there has been less change for women who lack a college education: They continue to be concentrated in low-paying clerical, household, and fast-food and other service jobs. Finally, women continue to shoulder most of the responsibility for household work and child rearing, which is the main reason men enjoy more leisure time.

## Cultural Variation in Gender Roles

**Gender Roles: A Cultural Universal?** As we have seen, gender roles in the United States, though they have changed over time, have always existed and have always been marked by inequality. Is this the case throughout the world? The answer appears to be that nearly all societies have gender roles, though the nature of those roles varies widely. In most societies, gender roles are unequal, though there are clear examples of societies in which this is not the case.

In a classic study, Murdock (1935) found that the overwhelming majority of societies do divide at least some tasks by sex. However, the content of those gender roles—that is, precisely what men and women are expected to do and to be—varies widely. Murdock found only a few tasks that are nearly always done by men or by women. In over eighty percent of the societies he studied, hunting, fishing, and trapping were predominantly or exclusively the jobs of males, whereas cooking, carrying water, grinding grain, and gathering roots and seeds were primarily female chores. However, most tasks were done by males in some societies, by females in others, and by both sexes in yet others. Examples of such tasks are various farming activities, constructing shelter, starting and maintaining care of fires, carrying objects, and preparing drinks and medicine.

The housewife role, once so ingrained in American society, is far from universal, even among modern industrial societies. In the former Soviet Union both men and women have long been expected to contribute to the financial support of the household through employment. In Japan, Thailand, and the Philippines, the majority of adult women are employed outside the home, and in China, virtually all women are. Similarly, patterns of occupational segregation vary considerably. In the former Soviet Union, for example, over two-thirds of all medical doctors are women. As we shall see shortly, however, all of the aforementioned societies have sexual inequality, despite the absence of the housewife role.

**Androgynous Societies** There are at least a few societies where the roles of men and women differ little, if at all. Social scientists refer to such societies as **androgynous societies**. Margaret Mead's (1935) famous studies of three societies in New Guinea present two such examples. In one of them, the Arapesh, both men and women play what in America would be considered a feminine role. Both are gentle, strongly child-oriented, and giving. In the second, the Mundugumor, both men and women play a role we would consider masculine. They are loud and aggressive, fight a great deal, and are very uninterested in children. In the third society she studied, the Tchambuli, sex roles exist, but they are the opposite of what we are familiar with. Economic production is the role of women, whereas men concern themselves with self-adornment and trying to gain favors and approval from women. In fact, this society could be defined as *female-dominant.*

At least as common as androgynous societies, however, are societies in which gender roles are different but relatively equal. One example of this can be seen in Native American groups that were primarily horticulturalist, including several Southeastern tribes. Among these groups, women were often responsible for raising crops and often provided the majority of the group's food—giving them power and status comparable to that of men in their societies. Studies of Native American societies reveal that the more women's roles involve production of the essentials of life, the higher their status has tended to be (Nordstrom, 1992).

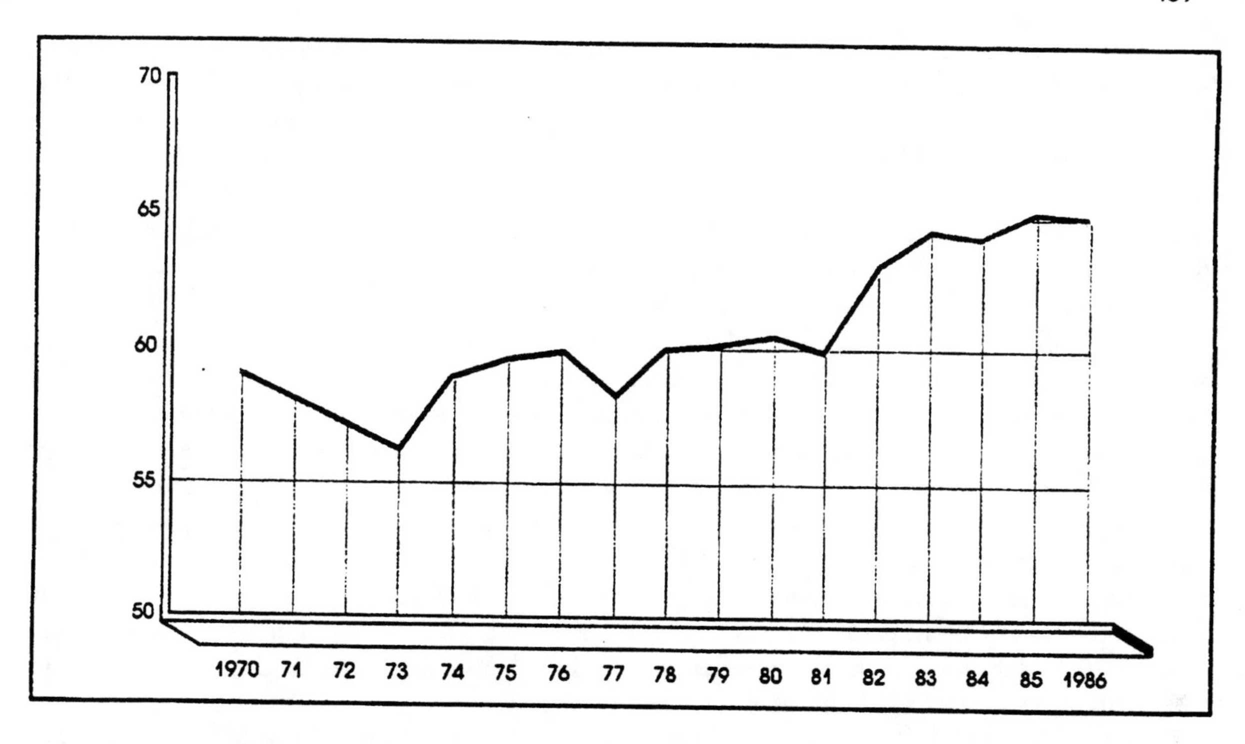


**FIGURE 6–1 Median Women's Income as a Percentage of Median Men's Income: Year-Round, Full-Time Workers, 1970–1986.**

SOURCE: U.S. Bureau of the Census. 1991. Current Population Reports: consumer Income. Series P-60, No. 174, Money Income of Households, Families, and Persons in the United States, 1990, Table 24.

**Are Societies Becoming More Androgynous?** There is evidence that many societies are becoming more androgynous than they were in the past. The proportion of women in the paid labor force has risen across much of the world over the past few decades. China today proclaims the legal equality of men and women, yet just two generations ago women were virtually the property of men and were expected to live for the purpose of serving their husbands. Although China is a dramatic case that undoubtedly changed more than most countries because of the revolution that occurred there after World War II, its direction of change parallels that of much of the world. In most countries, including the United States, modernization eventually has been accompanied by the large-scale entry of women into the paid labor force (see Figure 6-1), and by increased legal recognition of the rights of women. Dozens of countries today have laws forbidding sex discrimination in at least some areas of life. As recently as a century ago, such laws were unheard of in many of these countries.

While modernization usually leads toward greater gender equality, the influence of modern societies on less developed ones sometimes has the opposite effect. In the Third World, colonialism in its various forms, including the influence of multinational corporations, has often led to increased inequality between men and women (Boserup, 1970). When private property systems were introduced in land ownership, for example, women more often than men lost traditional land-use rights (Sen and Grown, 1987). Investment by multinationals has tended to displace women from their traditional occupations, while most of the new jobs created have gone to males (Ward, 1984).

**Male Dominance: A Cross-Cultural View** The vast majority of the world's societies have historically been male-dominant and remain so. Although many societies are becoming more androgynous, they have yet to eliminate either distinct gender roles or gender inequality. In the former Soviet Union, for example, where most doctors are women, that profession enjoys neither the prestige nor the high pay that it does in the United States. In Russian society, the leadership of both the national government and the republics have remained male domains. Women have been almost totally absent from important Soviet and Russian government posts. In China, which unlike the Soviet Union remains communist, women are not much better represented. The Scandinavian countries have long been regarded as leaders in the effort to bring about equality between the sexes, yet significant inequalities exist there, too. Their parliaments are three-quarters male, except in Norway, where the percentage of women is higher. Swedish and Norwegian women earn 75 to 80 percent of what men in those countries earn—better than women in the United States or Canada, but still not equality (Reimer, 1986; Rosenfield and Kalleberg, 1990).

In virtually all societies studied by Murdock (1935) and others, political structures are controlled more by males than by females. This remains true today even though women such as Indira Gandhi, Margaret Thatcher, and Golda Meir have been prominent world leaders, and even though the proportion of women in government has risen in a number of countries. The significance of these findings is that, in most societies, power is predominantly in the hands of males. In many societies, too, economic activities performed away from the home are largely a male domain, whereas the home and family are more the domain of women. Until the past few decades, whenever women did engage in economic production, it was usually in the home. Even today, when women are active in the labor force in many societies, they nearly always earn less on average than men. Taking all of these things into consideration, it is hard to avoid the conclusion that male dominance, though not universal, is much more the rule than the exception among the world's societies.

## GENDER-ROLE SOCIALIZATION: AN INTERACTIONIST ANALYSIS

Gender roles, like all social roles, are teamed through *socialization.* There are probably some behavioral differences between the sexes that reflect biological influences. Males may, for example, have a slight natural tendency to be more aggressive than females (Frieze et al., 1978; Gove, 1985). This tendency is almost a cultural universal (Whiting and Edwards, 1976), and even newborn males tend to be slightly more active than females. Part of the reason may be hormonal (Maccoby and Jacklin, 1974). However, some women are for more aggressive than some men; there are wide variations among societies in the levels of aggressiveness of both men and women; and male-female differences in aggression are highly situation-specific (Maccoby, 1980). When the norms of the situation support it, women can be as aggressive as men.

There may also be a slight biological basis for the development of different skills in men and women (Rossi, 1985). Girls usually develop somewhat earlier than boys, while boys have slightly better visual-spatial perception (Stockard and Johnson, 1992). These small differences may be the product of either hormonal differences or differences in brain hemisphere dominance (Halpern, 1986). Differences in verbal and mathematical achievement, on the other hand, seem to be socially induced, not the product of innate differences in ability. Such differences are not consistent across cultures (Tobias, 1978), and in the United States they have been decreasing to the point that on many tasks, there is no longer a gender difference (Hyde and Linn, 1988; Hyde, Fennema, and Lamon, 1990; Linn and Hyde, 1989).

Although the evidence conflicts concerning moral development, there is no evidence of innate differences between males and females in such areas as conformity, dependency, social orientation, and overall achievement. Thus, nurture, not nature, is the prime determinant of sex-linked behavior. (For a comprehensive analysis of the basis for this conclusion, see Fausto-Sterling, 1985.)

### How Gender Roles Develop

With so few biological differences between them, how do males and females learn such different roles? The values and expectations of society are transmitted through the socialization process. From infancy through adulthood, male and female human beings are treated differently and given different messages. The result is that small natural differences in behavioral predisposition become greatly exaggerated, and men and women come to think of themselves in different ways and to play different roles in life. The process by which different and, in many cultures, unequal, gender roles are transmitted is called **gender role socialization.** In this part of the chapter, we shall examine how gender roles are taught by four key agents of socialization: the family, the school, the media, and the peer group.

## Teaching Gender Roles in the Home

For the most part, parents in the United States today do not try to reach boys to be aggressive or girls to be submissive or dependent (Lytton and Romney, 1991; Johnson, 1988). However, there is gender-typing in how children are expected to play, what chores they are expected to do around the house, and toy choices. Significantly (since men are the group that stands to gain from gender inequality), these differences in gender-typing are greater among fathers than among mothers (Bradley and Gobbart, 1989; Lytton and Romney, 1991). There are also differences in how rooms are decorated (Rheingold and Cook, 1975) and in the amount of freedom given (boys get more, particularly in father-dominant families) (Hagan, Simpson, and Gilles, 1987).

Some gender role socialization also occurs through *modeling*—children see their parents in gender-typed roles and behavior. Fathers, for example, have less contact with their children on average than mothers, and the contact they have is more likely to involve play activities rather than directing activities such as brushing teeth or getting ready for school (Stockard and Johnson, 1992). Some research suggests that modeling of peers and media images may be a greater factor than modeling of parents, since there is not much correlation between the degree of gender-typing in parents and their children (Whiting and Edwards, 1988). Even so, gender roles seen in the home do tell children a good deal about how men and women are expected to behave, and thus may contribute to the long-term development of gender roles.

Some effects of gender role socialization develop quite early. By the age of five, boys and girls *prefer* different toys and can identify different occupations as being "men's jobs" and "women's jobs" (Garrett et al., 1977; Masters and Wilkinson, 1976). They can identify stereotypical male and female traits even earlier—sometimes as young as three (Reis and Wright, 1982).

## Teaching Gender Roles In the School

Gender role socialization continues when children reach school. The tendency to prefer different kinds of toys—which symbolize different roles in life—continues. One study, for example, showed that in kindergarten, girls are encouraged to play with dolls, and boys are encouraged to play with wheeled toys and building blocks (Best, 1983). Girls' toys thus come to represent a domestic, child-oriented role, whereas boys' toys represent going out into the world, doing and building. Children also see different images of males and females in their school books and materials. Studies of these materials indicate a number of ways they teach gender inequality. The main characters, for example, are much more likely to be male than female (Grauerholz and Pescosolido, 1989; Women on Words and Images, 1974). Male characters display creativity, bravery, achievement, and similar themes, while female characters display emotion, fear, and dependency (Key, 1975; Kolbe and LaVoie, 1981; Williams et al., 1987). Good things that happen to male characters result from their own efforts, while good things that happen to female characters result from luck or the actions of others (Penrod, 1986, p. 88). Sex stereotypes have been found in books ranging from math books (Federbush, 1974) to introductory sociology textbooks (Feree and Hall, 1990). Although stereotyping decreased somewhat during the 1970s and 1980s, recent studies show that it is far from gone (Feree and Hall, 1990; Vaughn-Roberson et al., 1989; Williams et al., 1987). One study found male lead characters still two to three times as common as female lead characters in the 1980s (Grauerholz and Pescosolido, 1989).

Children get a similar message from what they see firsthand in their schools. Although the teaching profession has historically been a largely female occupation, the proportion of women in the profession falls as the importance and status of the job increase. As you move from kindergarten through grade school, junior high school, high school, and on to college, there are progressively fewer female teachers and more male teachers. At every level of education, the proportion of women among principals and administrators is lower than it is among teachers (see, for example, Baker, 1980). The message children get from this is clear: The most important and highest-status jobs are for men.

Another process that takes place in schools is *subject channeling*. Boys are expected to excel in math, science, and logic; girls are expected to excel in reading, art, and music. These expectations occur in the home and in school. Parents frequently believe that learning math and science is more important for boys than for girls (Parsons et al., 1982) and thus do more to encourage boys to learn these subjects. In the school, teachers and counselors have similar beliefs. Thus, they encourage boys to take more math and science than girls, and they expect higher achievement from boys than from girls in these subjects (Coakley, 1972; Curran, 1980). One recent study found that, when boys do well in math, teachers attribute it to ability, whereas when girls do well, teachers attribute it to effort (Fennema et al., 1990). An important consequence of such channeling is that young men and women choose different college majors, which prepare them for different occupations (Table 6.1).

Such different treatment of children on the basis of gender sometimes combines with unequal treatment based on race, creating special problems for African-American girls. Observations of a first-grade classroom revealed that black female students, more than any other group, received attention based on their social skills rather than their academic skills. Similarly, they were the most likely to act as "go-betweens" in negotiations among teachers and students—particularly when the negotiators were of different race or gender. This may direct black females toward maintaining peace among others rather than developing their own skills—a stereotypical role of black women (Grant, 1984).

## Teaching Gender Roles on Television

Most children in the United States today spend more time watching television than they spend either in school or talking to their parents. What kinds of messages do they get from television about the roles of men and women? Whether we consider television entertainment or television advertising, the evidence is that they get highly stereotyped messages.

Television entertainment, for example, gives messages that reinforce the segregation of men and women into separate occupations. Between 1950 and 1980, 95 percent of doctors on television were men, and 99 percent of nurses were women (Kalisch and Kalisch, 1984). In general, television roles that involve leadership and decision making are played by men, whereas women's roles are likely either to be home-centered or, if at work, to involve following more than leading. There has undoubtedly been some change in these stereotypes over the past few decades. Women have appeared on television in recent years as tough cops, savvy lawyers, and private investigators. However, two important points must be made here. First, such portrayals remain the exception to the rule. Second, there is some evidence that although women are now sometimes portrayed in these roles, they are playing such roles differently than men play them (Roman, 1986). Female police officers, for example, may be portrayed as either more caring than male officers or more devious and conniving; male officers are shown as more aggressive and quicker to use force.

Although sex stereotyping may have become more subtle in television entertainment, it is hardly subtle in television advertising. Very attractive and often thinly clad females are used to sell everything from cars to shaving products to electronic gadgets. Sometimes the message is more about sex than about the product. When a woman is the lead in a commercial, the message is much more likely to be based on attractiveness than when a man is the lead (Downs and Harrison, 1985). In contrast, the voice of authority on most commercials is male (Klemesrud, 1981; Rak and McMullen, 1987). Significantly, male voice-overs are most common when the actors on the commercial are attractive women (Downs and

**TABLE 6.1 Percentage of Bachelor's Degrees Awarded to Women by Discipline, 1966, 1981,1985, and 1989 (Selected Fields)**

| Discipline | 1966 (%) | 1981 (%) | 1985 (%) | 1989 (%) |
|---|---|---|---|---|
| Agriculture | 2.7 | 30.8 | 31.1 | 31.1 |
| Architecture | 4.0 | 18.3 | 35.5 | 39.3 |
| Biological sciences | 28.2 | 44.1 | 47.8 | 50.2 |
| Business | 8.5 | 36.7 | 45.1 | 46.7 |
| Computer and information science | 13.0* | 32.5 | 36.8 | 30.7 |
| Education | 75.3 | 75.0 | 75.9 | 77.7 |
| Engineering | 0.4 | 10.3 | 14.5 | 13.6 |
| English and English literature | 66.2 | 66.5 | — | — |
| Foreign languages | 70.7 | 75.6 | 73.4 | 73.3 |
| Health | 76.9 | 83.5 | 84.8 | 84.9 |
| Home economics | 97.5 | 95.0 | 93.5 | 90.6 |
| Mathematics | 33.3 | 42.8 | 46.1 | 46.0 |
| Physical sciences | 13.6 | 24.6 | 28.0 | 29.7 |
| Psychology | 41.0 | 65.0 | 68.1 | 70.8 |
| Social sciences | 35.0 | 44.2 | 44.1 | 44.4 |
| Economics | 9.8 | 30.5 | — | — |
| History | 34.6 | 37.9 | — | — |
| Sociology | 59.6 | 69.6 | — | — |

*Data are for 1969, the earliest year available.

— Not available.

Note that women are most highly represented in home economics and health, which reflect the traditional female role, and are most underrepresented in such "technical" areas as engineering and architecture. However, note also the rapid changes in such areas as architecture, biology, and business.

SOURCES: U.S. Department of Health, Education and Welfare, Office of Education, "Earned Degrees Conferred: 1965-66"; U.S. Department of Education, National Center for Education Statistics, "Earned Degrees Conferred, 1980-81"; U.S. Department of Education, National Center for Education Statistics, "Trends in Bachelor's and Higher Degrees, 1975-1985;" U.S. Bureau of the Census, Statistical Abstract of the United States, 1992.

Harrison, 1985). The hidden message is that women are pretty and men are knowledgeable and authoritative. Besides being attractive, women are also portrayed as engaging in rather mindless behaviors, usually in the home. They frequently become excited about a small improvement in a detergent or floor cleaner or about the softness of facial tissues or toilet paper.

Under these circumstances, it is hardly surprising that social scientists have found that children who watch more television are more stereotyped in their own thinking than children who watch less (Beuf, 1974; Frueh and McGhee, 1975; see also Tan, 1979). Moreover, those who are exposed to stereotypical television become more stereotyped in their own thinking, whereas those who see counter-stereotypical television become less stereotyped (Geis et al., 1984; Johnson et al., 1980; Johnson and Davidson, 1981; McArthur and Eisen, 1976; Miller and Reeves, 1976). Taking all this into consideration, there is no doubt that television has been and remains an important means by which gender roles are taught.

## How Peers Teach Gender Roles

Some of the strongest pressures for gender role conformity come from peers. The peer group enforces the principle that boys and girls are supposed to enjoy different activities and play different roles. The reward for conforming to such norms is approval and inclusion; the costs of violating them include rejection, ridicule, and social isolation. In general, peer pressures for gender role conformity are stronger among boys than among girls (Hartley, 1974). It is worse for a boy to be labeled a "sissy" than for a girl to be labeled a "tomboy." The "tomboy," after all, is only seeking to move from what society has defined as an inferior role into one that society views more favorably; the "sissy" is doing the reverse. In fact, boys are sometimes so negative toward the traditional female role that even girls look down upon it as a result. Best (1983), for example, has noted cases in which girls became reluctant to be seen playing with dolls by the third grade. Why? Because boys made fun of them. The message here, of course, is that the traditional female role of domesticity is inferior and is therefore to be avoided.

Pressures for conformity to "boys' play" and "girls' play" start young; they have even been found among pre-schoolers as young as 3 (Lamb et al., 1980). However, these pressures increase as children move through their education, and by the third or fourth grade they are reinforced by a strong system of sex segregation in play: Boys play with boys and girls play with girls. Within each group, strong pressures exist for "sex-appropriate" behavior. Peer pressures for boys to be masculine and for girls to be attractive appear to be strongest in adolescence (Bernard, 1981, p. 137; Coleman, 1961).

# HOW GENDER ROLES ARE LEARNED

We have seen that the family, the school, the media, and the peer group all send children messages about the different roles of men and women. We shall now explore further the process by which these sex roles are learned, and we will see evidence that if the socialization process were different, girls and boys would not be channeled toward different roles in life in the ways that they are now.

## The Looking-Glass Self and Gender Role Socialization

According to Cooley, our self-image is a product of the messages we receive from others and the ways we understand and interpret those messages. When the messages are different and unequal, as messages given to boys and girls often are, it is hardly surprising that boys and girls come to see themselves differently. Girls are often told that they are understanding, attractive, well-behaved, and good in art and reading, while boys are told that they are hardy, mischievous, and good at math, science, and building things. On the other hand, girls are told that they are delicate and not so good at math and science, and boys are not expected to be understanding or good at art or creative writing. As a result of these different self-images, boys and girls do in fact become different kinds of people. Thus, for example, *boys become* better than girls at math and science. Although there is no difference in their ability test scores in the early grades, boys do score higher than girls by seventh or eighth grade, with the difference increasing until high school graduation (see Benbow and Stanley, 1980; Curran, 1980; Fairweather, 1976). However, these differences are smaller today than in the past (Stockard and Johnson, 1992).

Moreover, a variety of evidence suggests that when boys and girls are exposed to similar expectations and messages, such differences either do not develop or can be largely reversed (Coser, 1986; Newcombe et al., 1983; Tobias, 1978). There are at least three conditions under which this is the case. First, such differences do not develop in societies that do not channel girls away from jobs involving math, science, and reasoning, even if other types of sexual inequality exist. The former Soviet Union has been cited as one example of such a society (Tobias, 1978). Second, such differences do not develop in some schools even in the United States, quite possibly because these schools make efforts *not* to channel boys and girls toward separate occupations. Finally, girls who, for whatever reason, resist the message and develop a sufficiently strong interest in math and science to take advanced courses do just as well as the boys in these courses (College Entrance Examination Board, 1974).

We see, then, that when it comes to education, the looking-glass self is indeed at work. When boys and girls are given different messages about their abilities, they see themselves differently, and as a result they do develop different abilities. The beliefs of parents, teachers, and counselors become a *self-fulfilling prophecy*. In other words, their perceptions lead them to behave in ways that make their expectations about boys and girls come true. When, however, boys and girls are given similar messages about their abilities, they develop similar abilities. Thus, gender role socialization produces unequal opportunities for boys and girls, and elimination of some of these patterns of socialization could produce more equal opportunities. Although we have focused on subject channeling, much the same could be said of any of the other messages boys and girls get about themselves from significant others.

## Modeling and Gender Role Socialization

Repeated and selective exposure to a particular behavior pattern leads to modeling of that behavior pattern. This is particularly true when children identify with the model, as they do with their parents. It is clear from the foregoing discussion that in nearly every aspect of their lives, children are exposed to images of men and women in very different roles. Does this selective exposure lead to modeling, as we would expect? Evidence suggests that it does.

**Modeling and Occupations** One example of modeling can be seen in the occupational aspirations of boys and girls. Despite all the recent changes in the roles of men and women, most boys and girls still plan on seeking jobs that have traditionally been held by people of their sex. A study of eighth graders shows, for example, that boys are twice as likely as girls to plan on science, engineering, and technical careers, and seven times as likely to expect a skilled craft occupation. Girls, on the other hand, were three times as likely to expect clerical or sales work, service jobs, or work in the home (U.S. Department of Education, 1989, p. 30). Gender effects on job expectations interact with effects of race and class. Ladner and Gourdine (1984), for example, report a decline since around 1970 in expectations for success in any occupation among poor black teenage girls.

What happens when young people are *not* frequently exposed to gender-typed roles and behavior? Apparently, the answer is that they are less gender-typed in their own occupational plans. There is much evidence for this. In general, the more that children are exposed to sexual stereotypes at home or through the media, the more stereotyped their thinking is (Coltrane, 1988; Hoyenga and Hoyenga, 1979, pp. 214-218). Robb and Raven (1982), for example, found that children of mothers who are employed full-time see fewer sex-stereotyped roles in the home than other children, and that these children in fact become less stereotypical in their own thinking.

# STRUCTURED SEXUAL INEQUALITY: POWER

As was stated earlier, gender roles, as they exist in the United States, are not just *different*; they are also *unequal*. Whether you consider power, income, or occupational status, men in the United States are an advantaged group compared to women. Let us consider each of these areas in greater detail.

Although we shall examine the concept of *power* in considerably greater detail later, we shall briefly introduce and define it here, because it is an important area in which men and women experience social inequality. Power can be defined as the ability to get other people to behave in ways that you desire. Power is often exercised through the political system. It frequently rises from *authority*—the right to make certain decisions that is attached to a certain social position. We shall focus on power as it relates to men and women in two key areas: positions of authority, and power within the family.

**TABLE 6.2 Percentage of elected Offices in the United States filled by Women, 1979–1994**

| Office | 1979–80 | 1981–82 | 1983–84 | 1985–86 | 1987–88 | 1989–90 | 1991–92 | 1993–93 |
|---|---|---|---|---|---|---|---|---|
| U.S. Senators | 1.0 | 23.0 | 2.0 | 2.0 | 2.0 | 2.0 | 2.0 | 6.0 |
| Governors | 2.0 | 2.0 | 4.0 | 4.0 | 6.0 | 6.0 | 6.0 | 6.0 |
| U.S. Representatives | 3.7 | 4.4 | 4.8 | 5.3 | 5.3 | 5.7 | 6.7 | 10.8 |
| Lieutenant Governors | | | | 4.0 | 8.0 | 2.1 | | |
| State Treasurers | | | | 4.0 | 16.0 | 26.2 | | |
| Secretaries of State | | | | 4.0 | 22.0 | 32.6 | | |
| State Legislators | 10.3 | 12.4 | 13.5 | 15.7 | 15.8 | 16.9 | 18.1 | |

SOURCES: Taylor's World of Politics; *The New York Times;* U.S. Bureau of the Census, *Statistical Abstract of the United States;* World Almanac and Book of Facts, 1991; St. Louis Post-Dispatch; 1993 Information Please Almanac.

## Men, Women, and Positions of Authority

One way to judge the power of a social group is to gauge whether that group is well represented among people known to hold power. Clearly, power in the form of authority is held by people in certain positions in business and government. Chief executive officers (CEOs) of businesses, political officials, and certain public administrators such as city managers and school administrators have considerable power.

How well represented are women in these positions of power? Part of the answer can be found in Table 6.2. Even today, women are almost completely absent from the most important positions of power. Although more than one in ten elected officials overall are female, the percentage is smaller though growing, when we look at the most important positions such as governors and U.S. senators and representatives. When we consider the top political levels, we find that no woman has ever even been nominated for president by a major party, and the only woman ever nominated for vice president was Representative Geraldine Ferraro, the Democratic candidate in 1984 (her ticket lost in the general election). Women are almost totally absent from the ranks of CEOs of major corporations, as they are from corporate boards of directors. There has been some increase in the number of women in upper management in recent years, but very few of them have been selected for the *very* top positions.

## Women in Politics

It can no longer be said that the reason why women are underrepresented in positions of power is that relatively few women seek them. Women are still less likely than men to run for political office, but the number of female candidates has risen sharply in recent years. Yet, they often have a harder time getting elected than men. Of the thirteen women nominated to be governors or U.S. senators in 1986, only three won (Clements, 1987). One factor that perpetuates male dominance of politics is the advantage of *incumbency*. Incumbents usually win, and most incumbents are male. As a result, the limited number of women who are nominated to run for high offices usually run against male incumbents, and relatively few succeed in being elected. In addition, recent polls have indicated that many people are still reluctant to vote for a woman, though the number of people responding this way has fallen in recent years. Significantly, willingness to vote for women is greater when they are running for less-powerful positions such as city council and school board, but far lower when they seek more powerful positions such as governor or president. In 1987 about one voter in four indicated an unwillingness to vote for *any* woman for president (ABC News, 1987). By 1992, however, the number of women being elected to important offices was on the rise nonetheless, as discussed in the box on the following page.

## SOCIOLOGICAL INSIGHTS

### 1992: THE YEAR OF THE WOMAN?

In 1992, more women were elected to the U.S. House of Representatives and the U.S. Senate than ever before. For the first time, an African-American woman—Carol Moseley-Braun of Illinois—was elected to the U.S. Senate. Also for the first time, a state chose women to fill both of its U.S. Senate seats—Barbara Boxer and Dianne Feinstein of California. As a result of the 1992 elections, the number of women in the U.S. Senate rose to six, three times as many as before.

An important reason for the election of more women in 1992 was anger over the Senate's decision to confirm Clarence Thomas to the Supreme Court, in spite of testimony by law professor Anita Hill that she had been sexually harassed by Thomas when he was her supervisor. Part of what contributed to this anger was the Senate Judiciary Committee's harsh treatment of Professor Hill when she testified, with several senators in effect charging that she had made up the charges against Thomas out of personal or political motivations.

Senator Moseley-Braun was one of several women who decided to run because of anger over the handling of the Thomas case, and who were nominated for largely the same reason. In a tightly contested three-way race, she defeated incumbent Illinois Senator Alan Dixon in the Democratic primary. Dixon had voted to confirm Clarence Thomas, and that vote ultimately may have cost him his Senate seat. Moseley-Braun won the primary by combining the votes of African Americans in the city of Chicago with strong support from working women in the suburbs. The latter group, galvanized by their anger over Dixon's vote for Thomas, resulted in Moseley-Braun's receiving more support from white voters than is often the case when black candidates oppose white candidates in statewide elections. Helped by a sense that Illinois voters were about to make history, Moseley-Braun swept to an easy win in the general election in November.

Moseley-Braun was not the only woman who ran and received her party's nomination as a result of anger over the handling of the Thomas hearings. Democrats Lynn Yeakel of Pennsylvania and Jean Lloyd-Jones of Iowa ran for much the same reason, opposing Republican senators Arlen Specter and Charles Grassley, respectively, both of whom had questioned Professor Hill quite harshly during the hearings. Both women won their party's nomination, largely because of women's anger over the Thomas hearings. However, the disadvantages of running against a popular incumbent were too great for them to overcome, and both Yeakel and Lloyd-Jones lost in the general election.

Two important points should be kept in mind when thinking about the "Year of the Woman." First, while the Thomas hearings served to galvanize women candidates and voters, the growing number of women running for and winning public offices was a continuation of a trend already under way for several years. Second, even with the successes of Moseley-Braun, Boxer, Feinstein, and others, women remain severely underrepresented among public officeholders. Another way of looking at the statistics on the current Congress is that the Senate remains 94 percent male, and the House of Representatives more than 89 percent male.

## Women in the Business World

In the business world, the absence of women in part reflects the reluctance of male boards of directors to appoint women to top executive positions. Many men don't want to work under female supervisors, which may heighten this resistance. There are many women in lower-and middle-level management. Over half of all U.S. women, and almost 70 percent of women between the ages of 20 and 45, are in the labor force. By 1989 about 15 percent of full-time female workers were in executive or managerial work, compared to 16 percent of male workers (U.S. Bureau of the Census, 1990a). Yet very few of these women have been appointed to the top management positions that have real decision-making power. Too often, their opportunities to move into such positions have been blocked by an informal "glass ceiling" that limits how high women can move in the organization. Women in the corporate world encounter barriers that inhibit their opportunities to gain real power. In corporations with relatively few women managers, women in management are often responded to more as women than as managers, thus being deprived of the full opportunity to be evaluated and responded to on the basis of the work they do (Kanter, 1977). As the number of women increases, male managers become more accustomed to women and treat them more as they would any other employee—up to a point. However, when the number of women begins to approach a majority, male workers often feel threatened, which may inhibit opportunities for the women workers (Weiss, 1983). Until such attitudes change, women are not likely to fill many positions of real power.

What ultimately may lead to the placement of more women in such positions is the evident economic rationality of doing so. Increasing evidence suggests that women may be particularly effective as managers in today's changing workplace, because they may be more likely than men to break down hierarchy and involve workers in decision making (Helgeson, 1990; Holusha, 1991; Rosener, 1990). This style of management generally leads to increased productivity.

While well-educated, middle-class women are limited by the glass ceiling, it is economic survival, not career, that is the main concern of working-class and poor women. Virtually all of these women are employed out of sheer economic necessity; this is particularly the case for the lowest-income segment among women of color. The concentration of low-income black and Hispanic women in industries such as fast-food and hotel housekeeping has resulted in steadier employment than what has been available to inner-city men in recent years, but it is difficult and very low-paying work (Collins, 1991, Chapter 3). In an earlier era, when divorce and single parenthood were much less common than today, such women could combine their incomes with the somewhat higher incomes of their husbands to provide somewhat adequate support for their families. Today, when many women are the sole breadwinners for their families, however, the wages paid for such work—which remain well below the pay of men with comparably low levels of education—are woefully inadequate.

**Men, Women, and Power in the Home** The relative powerlessness of women in the worlds of government and business is largely mirrored in the home. Even in homes where both the husband and wife are employed full-time, several realities give greater power to the husband. For one thing, even when both partners work full-time, the husband typically provides 60 percent or more of the family's income, because men's wages substantially exceed those of women. Where the wife works only part-time or not at all, this discrepancy is even greater (Sorensen and McLanahan, 1987). The power of the purse within the family, then, is disproportionately in the hands of the male. Even today, women must often seek money from their husbands for various types of purchases. Until recently, married women usually could not borrow money unless they applied jointly for credit with their husbands. Today, the law has changed, but women's incomes are often too low for them to get substantial credit lines on their own, so they must still sometimes depend on their husbands.

Also limiting the power of women in the home is the continuing influence of the norm that providing income through employment is the first responsibility of the husband, while taking care of the household is the first responsibility of the wife. For one thing, even women who have good jobs must often put their husbands' jobs first when questions of relocation arise. (Bielby and Bielby, 1992). Families are far more likely to move for the husband's career opportunities than for the wife's. In addition, the wife, not the husband, is expected to miss work for such household emergencies as taking care of sick children and letting in repairpersons. (For a discussion of both of these issues, see Duncan and Corcoran, 1984, pp. 156-161.)

Finally, the primacy of the woman's responsibility for the home means that women employed full-time have a longer work week than men employed full-time. According to one study (Peskin, 1982), the total (employment and home) work week of a typical female full-time employee was 67 hours, compared with 63 hours for the typical male full-time employee. The difference: Women put in considerably more hours working around the house than men did. In 1981 dollars, the value of the uncompensated housework of the average woman was $10,000—compared with only $5,000 for the average man. Translated to 1991 dollars these figures become $15,000 for the average woman and $7,500 for the average man. Men *have* increased their work around the house, and such tasks as cooking, washing dishes, grocery shopping, and laundry are shared in far more households today than in the past. Thus, as women have entered the labor force, men have increased their share of household work to a certain extent. For many men, this is a dramatic role change from what they saw their fathers doing when they were children. In most households, however, men have still not increased their share of the household work to anywhere near an *equal* share, even when both husband and wife are employed full time (Hochschild, 1989). Husbands also tend not to take the initiative to do various household tasks—their wives usually have to ask. They tend not to be concerned with matters such as doctors' appointments, household tasks, clothing purchases, or scheduling their children's engagements, for instance, unless their wives direct them to do so (Stockard and Johnson, 1992, p. 63).

## STRUCTURED SEXUAL INEQUALITY: INCOME

We saw earlier that the average woman employed full-time receives only about 70 percent of the income of her male counterpart. As shown in Figure 6.2, this represents some narrowing of the gap since the early 1970s, when women received only 57 percent of the income of men when both worked full-time. The difference between men's and women's incomes is not the result of educational differences between men and women: As shown in Table 6.3, the difference in men's and women's wages is similar at all levels of education. It is true, as shown in Table 6.4, that gender differences in income are smaller among younger workers and greater among older workers. This fact could be interpreted in two ways. The optimistic interpretation is that sexual wage inequality is decreasing, and that young women now entering the labor market are receiving fairer treatment. A less optimistic interpretation is that women do not get advanced to higher-paying jobs as quickly as men do. We have already seen that women are often excluded from the top managerial jobs. Even more important, many women work in clerical and service occupations that offer little chance for promotion to substantially higher-paying jobs. Finally, even though younger women do better relative to men than older women in terms of income, they still earn considerably less than men in their age group.

### Some Possible Reasons for Women's Low Wages

Why do women continue to be paid so much less than men? A number of possibilities have been suggested, including the competing role of women in the home, wage inequality in the same job, hiring patterns, and occupational segregation. Let us consider each.

**Competing Expectations of Working Women** Certainly, part of the answer is to be found in women's role in the home. As we already saw, women are less able than men to move to take a job and are more likely to miss work because of household emergencies. Both of these things impede their ability to move up to better-paying positions. Moreover, women are more likely than men to leave the job market temporarily, especially to take care of young children. (Again, if anyone quits work for this reason in a family, it is usually the wife.)

How important are these factors as a cause of low income? They are part of the reason, but not most of it, and may be declining in importance. A national study by Duncan and Corcoran (1984) found that differences in work experience, work continuity, self-imposed limits on work hours and location, and absenteeism *combined* could explain only one-third of the difference in men's and women's

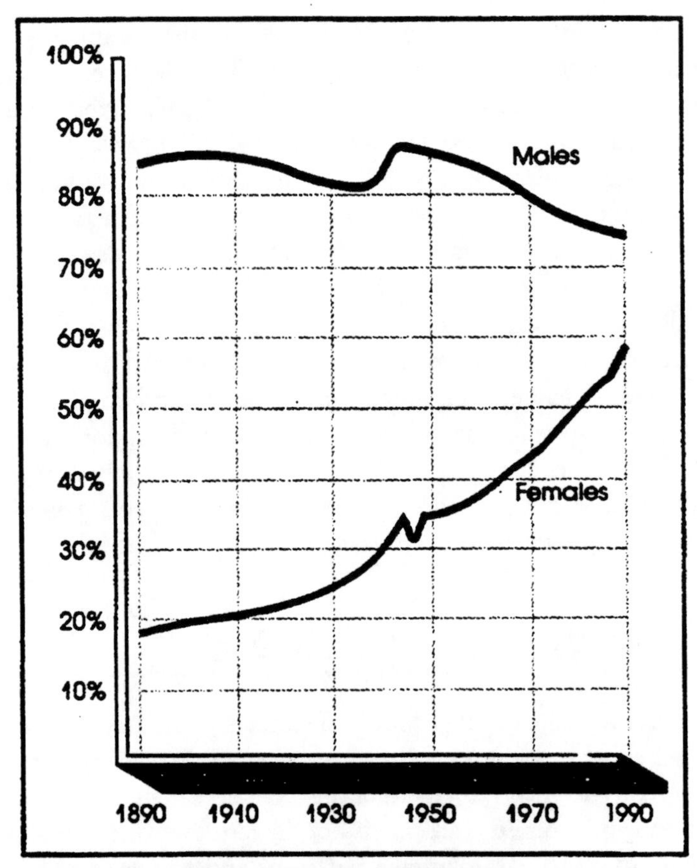


**FIGURE 6-2 Labor Force Participation Rates of Men and Women in the United States, 1890-1987.**
Note that, although rates for men still substantially exceed those for women, the gap has closed significantly. What implications does this hold for the U.S. economy in the twenty-first century?
SOURCE: Adapted from Francine D. Blau and Marianne A. Ferber, *The Economics of Women, Men, and Work*, 1986 (Englewood Cliffs, NJ: Prentice Hall), p. 70; and *Statistical Abstracts of the United States*, 1988, Table 608. U.S. Bureau of the Census. 1991. Statistical Abstract of the United States, 1991. Washington: USGPO, Table 635.

**TABLE 6.3 Median Income of Year-Round, Full-Time Workers, by Sex and Level of Education, 1990**

| Educational Level Completed | Males | Females | Percent of Male Income |
|---|---|---|---|
| All workers, 25 and over | $30,733 | $21,372 | 69.5% |
| 8th grade or less | 17,394 | 12,251 | 70.4 |
| 1-3 years high school | 20,902 | 14,429 | 69.0 |
| 4 years high school | 26,653 | 18,319 | 68.7 |
| 1-3 years college | 31,734 | 22,227 | 70.0 |
| 4 years college | 39,238 | 28,017 | 71.4 |
| 5 or more years | 49,304 | 33,750 | 68.5 |

SOURCES: U.S. Bureau of the Census. 1991. Current Population Reports, Consumer Income, Series P-60, No. 174, Table 24.

**TABLE 6.4 Median Income of Year-Round, Full-Time Workers, by Sex and Age, 1989**

| Age | Males | Females | Percent |
|---|---|---|---|
| All ages | $29,172 | $20,586 | 70.6% |
| 15-24 | 15,580 | 13,955 | 89.6 |
| 25-34 | 25,502 | 20,178 | 79.1 |
| 35-44 | 32,611 | 22,483 | 68.9 |
| 45-54 | 35,731 | 21,937 | 61.4 |
| 55-64 | 33,180 | 20,765 | 62.6 |
| 65 and over | 35,520 | 22,866 | 64.4 |

SOURCE: U.S. Bureau of the Census 1991, Current Population Reports, Consumer Income, Series P-60, No. 174, Table 24.

income. More recent research shows that women are *not* more likely than men to have jobs that allow them flexibility to meet family needs (Glass and Camanigg, 1992; see also Desai and Waite, 1991). With more employers offering family leave, and with the passage in 1993 of a law requiring such leave, fewer women will feel it necessary to give up their jobs to care for their families in crisis situations. The practice of leaving the labor force to care for young children is also becoming less common, as (1) fewer and fewer families can afford to give up the income, (2) growing numbers of mothers are single parents and the only source of their family's income, and (3) a career has become more important for those women who could afford to leave the work force. In fact, research has revealed that women devote *more* effort to their jobs than similarly situated men, not less (Bielby and Bielby, 1988).

**Wage Inequality Within Occupations** Even when they work in the same occupation, women are paid less than men (Bergmann, 1986; Kemp and Beck, 1986; Stockard and Johnson, 1992). There are a number of reasons for this. Because of employer stereotypes about women's commitment to the labor force, a woman is less likely to be offered on-the-job training—even when she has been with the firm for the same amount of time as a man (Duncan and Corcoran, 1984). Also, men are more likely to be given supervisory and/or hiring and firing authority than are women—and are paid better as a result (Hill and Morgan, 1979; Duncan and Corcoran, 1984). Women are also promoted less often, which also contributes to their lower pay. Within occupations, women are frequently channeled into lower-paying specialties. Female physicians are more likely to specialize in pediatrics or public health while male physicians more often specialize in cardiology or gastroenterology; female lawyers more often specialize in domestic relations and males in corporate or criminal law; and in construction, women are less likely than men to get on-site jobs such as operation of heavy equipment (Stockard and Johnson, 1992). In each case, the disproportionately "male" specialization is paid more, even though the occupation is the same. Such differences often reflect discrimination and gender channeling by mentors, employers, and, in some occupations, unions.

Finally, it appears that another reason for wage inequality reflects the relative powerlessness of women: They are often tied to a locality by their husband's occupational choice. As noted earlier, if a family relocates on the basis of job availability, it is usually the husband's job that determines where they will live (Bielby and Bielby, 1992). This means that women must take what is available in the locality of the husband's job. In the case of a one-university town, for instance, wives of faculty and administrators may be forced to take whatever is available there if they want a job. Because their job choices are limited, women must work for less (Blau and Ferber, 1986). Some firms take advantage of this, by hiring mostly women and paying them less than they would pay men in the same occupation. Currie and Skolnick (1984, p. 219), for example, have pointed out that accounting firms that hire mainly female accountants pay less than firms that hire mainly male accountants.

## Occupational Segregation

Although women typically receive lower wages than men even in the same occupation, a major cause of income inequality is **occupational segregation.** This term refers to the concentration of men and women into different occupations, even when they have similar levels of skill and training. Occupational segregation has significant impacts, in terms of both the incomes and the occupational choices and opportunities for men and women.

Considerable occupational segregation is evident even if we look at broad categories of jobs. Men are more likely to work in management and skilled labor (precision production and crafts), whereas women are more likely to work in clerical and service jobs. Significantly, management and skilled-labor jobs pay better than clerical and service jobs. In fact, managerial and executive workers are the best paid of any of the broad categories, while service workers are near the bottom.

However, even when men and women are evenly represented in one of these broad categories, they often work at different specific jobs *within* the category (Bielby and Baron, 1986). Women are slightly more likely than men to be employed in the "professional specialty" category, but within this category, they often work at lower-paying jobs than men. Most physicians, lawyers, engineers, dentists, and architects are men. These men are better paid than are nurses, teachers, and social workers—professional employees who are mostly women.

Such differences can exist even within the same industry. Currie and Skolnick (1984, pp. 222-223) have illustrated this point using the food and beverage industry. The highest-paid employees are brewery workers, who are 85 percent male. Their average pay in 1981 was $497 per week. At the opposite end are poultry workers, the majority of whom are women, many of them women of color. Their average pay in 1981 was only $169 per week. In general, it has been shown that the greater the number of women in an occupation, the lower the pay of that occupation (England et al., 1988; Mellor, 1984).

Why do jobs typically held by men so often pay better than jobs typically held by women? There seem to be several reasons. First, unequal pay is probably a carry-over from the days when it was widely believed that men should be paid more because they were more likely to be supporting a family. Although this is no longer true today and deliberate sexual pay discrimination by an employer *within the same occupation* is illegal, there is nothing to stop unequal pay in *different* occupations. Custom and bureaucratic inertia also seem to play a role in perpetuating such inequalities (Bridges and Nelson, 1989). When pressures for change are exerted on such organizations, they are more likely to change than when there is no such pressure (Baron, Mittman, and Newman, 1991).

Second, predominantly male occupations are more highly unionized than predominantly female occupations. As a result, their pay tends to be better. In part, these differences may reflect different attitudes among men and women toward unionization, but they probably also reflect the fact that, until recently, most unions were more interested in organizing predominantly male occupations.

Finally, Reskin (1988) has argued that predominantly male jobs are paid more than predominantly female jobs for the same reason that occupational segregation exists in the first place: Men—the more powerful group in society—benefit from both arrangements. She points out that in the past, when men were the main source of support for most families, that fact was used to justify their higher income. But today, when that is no longer the case, occupation has become the basis for assigning wages.

**Comparable Worth** Clearly, occupational segregation is an important cause of male-female income inequality. Even when they require similar levels of skill and training, "men's jobs" usually pay better than "women's jobs." One short-term measure that has been proposed to address this income inequality is *comparable worth* legislation. Comparable worth states that men and women who work in different occupations that require similar skills and education should receive similar wages. To implement such a policy, an employer must first conduct a comparable worth study to evaluate the relative education, skill, knowledge, and responsibility required for different occupations. This study establishes sets of occupations that are similar in these regards. The employer must then adjust the pay scale so that people in occupations that fall within the same category receive similar or equal wages.

Most of the employers that have instituted such policies are state and local governments. At least half the states have conducted comparable worth studies, but few states and municipalities have actually adjusted wages on the basis of these studies. Moreover, the adjustments that have taken place as a result have been smaller than anticipated, and the overall effect on wage differences between men and women has not been large (Bridges and Nelson, 1989; Acker, 1989). One reason may be that men continue to have power over the bureaucratic structures responsible for implementing comparable worth laws (Stockard and Johnson, 1992).

Over the longer run, many people feel that to deal with income inequality, we must address the question of occupational segregation itself. This view holds that occupational segregation would be a problem even if there were no inequalities in pay because it deprives women of opportunities to work in jobs that are more rewarding, challenging, and enjoyable. In general, jobs typically held by males offer greater autonomy and prestige than those held by women.

**Causes of Occupational Segregation** This leads to the question, of course, of *why* women are so absent from many of these jobs. One reason turns out to be the effect of gender role socialization—men and women are taught to aspire to different jobs and thus end up in different jobs. Another answer is that, until recently, open discrimination was common against women seeking to enter historically male occupations. This was true both of employers and of educational programs required for entry to an occupation. Although illegal today such discrimination has lingering effects. An occupation composed primarily of members of one sex can be quite uncomfortable for a person of the opposite sex to enter. Thus, male nurses and secretaries and female firefighters and auto mechanics may face reactions ranging from ridicule to resistance to ostracism. A more serious problem, dramatically illustrated during the confirmation hearings for Supreme Court Justice Clarence Thomas, is sexual harassment of women in predominantly male occupations and workplaces. This includes both unwanted sexual advances and creation of a hostile environment through sexual jokes and comments, display of nude pictures, and so forth (Ollenberger and Moore, 1992; Lewin, 1992). These attitudes alone tend to perpetuate occupational segregation, particularly when they operate in combination with the effects of gender role socialization. Also, as previously discussed, many young people still aspire to sex-typed occupations (Bain and Fottler, 1980; Barrett, 1979), although the extent to which this is true is declining, especially among women (Jacobs, 1989). As we would expect, occupational segregation appears to be most intense in the kinds of places where attitudes about gender roles are most traditional (Abrahamson and Sigelman, 1987).

Finally, there is evidence that occupational segregation may exist in part because it *does* perpetuate gender wage inequality (Reskin, 1988). From this view, it is a means by which men maintain their pay advantage. Several recent studies support this view (Bielby and Baron, 1986; Bielby and Bielby, 1989, tables 29 and 30). Strang and Baron (1990), for example, found that in a state civil service system, the more women there were in an area of similar job content such as civil engineering or legal counsel, the more job titles there were—which permitted more occupational segregation and thereby greater wage inequality. Reskin (1988) has argued that so long as men retain disproportionate power, wage inequality will persist. She points out that in occupations that have become gender-integrated, men have retained the more desirable and lucrative specializations. Also, changes in work content, autonomy, and/or pay had often taken place, which made these occupations less desirable prior to the time at which more women entered them. They then opened up to women as men looked elsewhere for work (Reskin and Roos, 1990).

As noted above, one thing that sometimes discourages women from entering predominantly male, high-status occupations is the increased risk of sexual harassment in such male-dominated work settings. This issue is explored further in this chapter's *Social Issues for the '90s* section.

## FUNCTIONALIST AND CONFLICT PERSPECTIVES ON GENDER ROLES

Thus far, our discussion of sexism has focused on the forces that maintain sexual inequality. Another fundamental question is this: *Why does sexism exist in the first place?* To understand the fundamental causes of sexism, it is useful to consider the functionalist and conflict perspectives. These perspectives address such questions as what purpose or purposes are served by sexism, why societies establish social roles and social inequality along the lines of gender, and why societies teach these unequal roles to succeeding generations.

### The Functionalist Perspective

One common school of thought among functionalist sociologists is that, whether or not gender roles perform any important functions for society today, they certainly did in the past. These sociologists note that until about a century ago, most women spent much of their young adult lives either pregnant or taking care of infants. Infant and child mortality was very high, and in order to have two or three children

## SOCIAL ISSUES FOR THE '90s

### SEXUAL HARASSMENT

The arrival of women in the work force, notably in fields previously dominated by men, and the collapse of the old code of manners between men and women, have led to a situation where the acceptable rules of behavior in an office, in the field, or on campus are not always clear and are frequently violated. As occupational segregation has lessened, awareness of sexual harassment has increased.

To what extent is sexual harassment a sexual issue or an attempt to keep women in their perceived place?
Is sexual harassment about power more than it is about sex?
Is sexual bantering OK in a work environment?
When a woman is bothered or offended by what she considers sexual harassment, should she complain to the authorities (campus authorities, her boss, or the courts) or confront the man harassing her—even at the risk of losing her job?

*Sexual harassment* is defined as deliberate or repeated unsolicited verbal comments, gestures, or physical contacts of a sexual nature that are unwelcome by the recipient and create an intimidating or hostile work environment. An employer or supervisor may threaten an employee with getting fired if he or she doesn't comply to his or her sexual request. Most often, however, there is not an explicit threat. Rather, harassment consists of repeated requests for dates or sexual favors, explicit sexual language, or fondling.

Three out of four victims of sexual harassment are women. A study of 23,000 U.S. government workers found that 42 percent of women and 15 percent of men have experienced some form of sexual harassment at work during the previous two years.

Harassment is most common when women enter traditionally all-male environments, like the military, medicine, or engineering. In a 1993 survey of young doctors at the University of California in San Francisco, three-fourths of the women and one-fifth of the men claimed that they had been sexually harassed during training. In a 1990 U.S. Defense Department study, 64 percent of women in the armed services reported sexual harassment. In one of the military's worst sexual harassment cases, 60 women aviators were sexually assaulted in a Las Vegas hotel in 1991 at the annual Tailhook Convention, a gathering of Navy fliers.

Victims of sexual harassment report feelings ranging from embarrassment and humiliation to depression, anxiety, powerlessness, and psychosomatic illnesses.

The issue of sexual harassment was first brought up in 1979 by the Working Women's Institute, a nonprofit organization established to support education and lobbying efforts on women's behalf. In 1980 the U.S. Equal Employment Opportunity Commission issued guidelines on sexual harassment, defining it as a form of sex discrimination and a violation of Title VII of the 1964 Civil Rights Act.

Ironically, it was while working at the Equal Employment Opportunity Commission that Anita Hill claims she was harassed by her then supervisor, Clarence Thomas. At Judge Thomas's Supreme Court confirmation hearings, Hill, now a law professor, accused Thomas of having repeatedly made sexual comments to her. Hill said she had not come forward while working at the EEOC for fear of losing her job. Thomas denied these allegations and was ultimately confirmed as a Supreme Court Justice. Another case, less publicized, involves 51-year-old neurosurgeon Frances Conley. As professor of medicine at Stanford University, she allegedly endured sexual harassment from male colleagues—lewd jokes and inappropriate touching. Like Anita Hill, Dr. Conley didn't report the sexual harassment when it was going on for fear of jeopardizing her career.

Why didn't these women stand up to the men sexually harassing them at the time of the harassment, even at the risk of losing their jobs? Isn't it a weaker stance to wait 10 years to invoke a feminist principle instead of fighting back on the spot?

One difficulty with this issue is the subjective nature of the offense: What one person calls sexual harassment may be considered flattery or harmless banter by another. In other words, it's only harassment if the victim (usually a woman) feels the behavior is inappropriate, and that might depend on her ethnic, religious, and/or cultural background and tolerance for outspoken sexual innuendos. Some men, on the other hand, may be unable or unwilling to understand where to draw the line between harmless sexual banter and grossly inappropriate or threatening behavior in a work environment. One young doctor at the University of California medical school complained of harassment when she was asked on dates by two doctors who were supposed to write letters of recommendation for her. Another woman might have felt flattered, or might have wanted to go out with the doctors. Some physical contact, like hugging or putting an arm around a colleague, can be viewed as harassment by women of a certain ethnic background or in certain circumstances, but may be considered a warm gesture or harmless flirting by other women. If a woman feels a colleague's behavior is inappropriate, then it is her obligation to say so, verbally or in writing. Once she has done so, the colleague is obligated to stop the behavior. However, in the atmosphere of intimidation that often accompanies sexual harassment, speaking out can be difficult to do. This is particularly the case because the person doing the harassing is usually more powerful than the person who is harassed. In such a situation, victims often fear that if they object to the harassment, they will be penalized.

Because of the ambiguities sometimes involved, it can be difficult for a court to determine if sexual harassment has actually taken place. Courts have generally determined that it is not necessarily the advances themselves that violate the Civil Rights Act, but the continuation of such advances once it is known that they are unwanted. The loss of tangible job benefits or the existence of an intimidating, hostile, or offensive work environment also have been recognized by courts as illegal sexual harassment.

Some analysts contend that sexual harassment is a way for some men who feel threatened by the emergence of women in the workplace to tell them: "You don't belong here. You're not welcome here." According to that theory, harassment isn't about sex, but about intimidation of women—making them feel unwelcome and undermining their job competence by treating them as sex objects. In fact, the most serious cases of harassment, involving threats of job loss or repeated sexual overtures, usually involve advances by a supervisor.

survive to adulthood, a woman often had to give birth to five or six. In those days, of course, there was no baby formula, so having babies meant breast-feeding. In short, these necessities meant that women simply weren't available to do things away from the home much of the time, which probably explains, among other things, why hunting is one of the few activities that has quite consistently been performed by males across different societies.

A second consideration is physical strength. Because of their larger physical size, men are—on average—more capable of tasks that involve heavy lifting or moving large objects. At a time when most work was physical in nature, this difference probably led to some gender role specialization. Thus, frequent pregnancy and long periods of breast-feeding, together with differences in physical strength, explain why gender role specialization was functional in the past. But what of today?

**Gender Roles as Cultural Lag** Some sociologists believe that gender roles exist today mainly as a result of *cultural lag*. Gender roles were functional in the past, but have no use to society today, according to this view. Nonetheless, they persist because society is slow to change. Gender roles, and the norms that support them, have become ingrained in our culture, which is passed from generation to generation through the socialization process. Thus, they disappear only gradually. This viewpoint suggests that if gender roles are no longer functional, they will persist for some time but will become weaker with each new generation, because they have no use in today's society. A case can be made that this is in fact happening. As we shall see in more detail later, there have been major changes in the gender role attitudes of Americans and people in many other modern societies. Nonetheless, many sociologists disagree with this interpretation. Some argue that gender roles are beneficial to society in other ways; others explain their existence from the conflict perspective. Let us consider the former group first.

**Are Gender Roles Still Functional?** Most functionalist arguments that support the usefulness of gender roles today focus on the family. Some argue that gender roles permit a desirable form of specialization within the family, and others argue that traditional gender roles are conducive to family cohesiveness.

**GENDER ROLES AND FAMILY SPECIALIZATION** The notion that gender roles facilitate specialization within the family is largely associated with the writings of Talcott Parsons and Robert Bales (1955). They based their arguments on research showing that in organizations and groups performing tasks, two types of leaders typically emerge: *instrumental leaders*, whose main concern is getting the job done, and *expressive leaders*, whose role is to address the feelings of people in the group and the relations among those people. Parsons and Bales argued that, as a small group, the family needs both instrumental and expressive leadership. They saw the traditional male role as filling the family's need for instrumental leadership and the traditional female role as providing expressive leadership. Thus, a role division that emphasizes the man's getting the jobs done and providing income and the woman's taking care of social and emotional needs is seen as functional for the family.

Parsons and Bales's functionalist explanation of gender roles has been strongly criticized by other sociologists for two reasons. First, even though the family might need both instrumental and expressive leadership, there is no clear reason why the instrumental leadership must come from the male and the expressive leadership from the female. It could just as well happen the other way around. Second, this functionalist explanation does not consider the possible *dysfunctions* of restricting women to the expressive role, which will be addressed shortly.

**GENDER ROLES AND FAMILY COHESION** A more contemporary functionalist argument centers around the cohesiveness of the family. This argument holds that traditional, male-dominated families experienced less divisiveness because women did not think and act independently of their husbands. Thus, as women have become more free and independent, family conflict has increased. Those who support this view often cite statistics showing that as women obtain work outside the home, the likelihood of their marriages ending through divorce rises. Finally, some people argue that when mothers work outside the home, their children suffer. These people claim that when children are in day care or must come home from school to an empty house, their mental health suffers, and they become at high risk for juvenile delinquency, drug and alcohol abuse, and teenage pregnancy.

Although some of these issues will be addressed in later chapters, several important facts relevant to these arguments can be noted here. First, time-budget studies indicate that full-time working mothers interact with their children about as much as do full-time housewives (Farley, 1977, pp. 197-202; Goldberg, cited in Hodgson, 1979; Robinson, 1977; Nock and Kingston, 1988; Benokraitis, 1993, pp. 318-319), although housewives may spend more time on care-related tasks (Hodgson, 1979; Vanek, 1973, pp. 138, 172). Women's satisfaction with their roles, whether in the home or at work, seems to be a much better predictor: Women who are more satisfied spend more time interacting with their children (Hodgson, 1979). Sometimes there are problems of supervision of children, these are largely the product of the limited availability of quality day care. In general, children in properly planned and supervised day-care centers do as well as children raised at home (Hayes and Kamerman, 1983; Hoffmann, 1989; McCartney et al., 1982; Berg, 1986). There may be an increasing tendency among adults to put their own concerns ahead of the welfare of their children (Popenoe, 1988). This tendency exists among both men and women, however, and cannot simply be attributed to changing gender roles.

## SOCIOLOGICAL INSIGHTS

### THE COSTS OF SEXISM TO MEN

Although men benefit from sexism in terms of income, wealth, and power, sexism exacts some high costs in other areas of their lives. Men as well as women are denied certain freedoms by sexism. In fact, the pressure to "be a man" that males experience from early childhood probably exceeds anything that women encounter. Those who do not conform to this pressure are labeled "sissies" or "wimps," with all the negative consequences that such labels carry.

More specifically, men are supposed to be in control of every situation (which is not always possible) and to avoid any public display of emotion. Neither expressions of tenderness nor emotional breakdowns or outbursts have been acceptable male behavior. Such pressures on men exact a high cost in terms of mental and physical health. In all likelihood, they are at least part of the reason why men are more likely than women to abuse alcohol and other drugs and are far more inclined to commit violence—the overwhelming majority of assaults and murders are committed by males, usually against other males. Many stress-related illnesses are also more common among men than among women, including heart disease, high blood pressure, and ulcers. Although men are often under less stress than women, they are expected to handle stress differently, always maintaining outward calm and control. Women, in contrast, have more opportunities to release the tension by expressing their emotions. Compared to men, women also receive much more encouragement to talk with their friends about feelings, emotions, and personal concerns and problems. Men, in contrast, are usually encouraged to keep such feelings inside, in order to appear "in control." Rather than viewing their friends as confidants, they are more likely to see them as "playmates"—e.g., golfing, bowling, or fishing buddies. These are among the reasons that women outlive men by six or seven years on average.

Thus, a move toward a more androgynous society could offer opportunities for men and risks for women. Men today undoubtedly feel freer to express their emotions than they did in the past. There is a growing recognition of the role of emotional expression in the mental health of both men and women. Conversely, as women move into traditionally male roles, they may experience some of the same pressures men feel.

With respect to family cohesion, it is true that women who work outside the home are at greater risk of divorce than housewives. This might be because dual-earner couples have less time to spend together (see Kingston and Nock, 1987). However, a more important reason is that working women are financially more able to leave an unhappy marriage. According to Thornton and Freedman (1984, pp. 27-28), social-science research provides no clear evidence that families with the wife in the labor force are any less happy than families where the wife remains at home. Thus, changing gender roles may have altered how women *respond* when they find themselves in an unhappy or troubled home situation, but there is no evidence that the actual incidence of such situations has increased.

**Dysfunctions of Gender Roles** Any functionalist analysis of gender roles must also consider their dysfunctions. In what ways do they *inhibit* the effectiveness of society, the family, or the individual? One area in which there is evidence of such dysfunctions is psychological well-being. Among both men and women, people with a *mix* of masculine and feminine personality traits have higher self-esteem and better mental health than those in whom traditional gender traits predominate (Deutsch and Gilbert, 1976; Lamke, 1982; Major et al., 1981; Orlovsky, 1977; Spence et al., 1975). Moreover, *androgynous* individuals—those with some of the traditional traits of each sex—display greater flexibility in various aspects of behavior (Ickes and Barnes, 1978; LaFrance and Carmen, 1980). These findings suggest that in terms of personal adjustment, self-esteem, and flexibility, adherence to a traditional gender role can be dysfunctional. These researchers conclude that women show better self-esteem, flexibility, and role performance when they have both masculine and feminine traits. Specifically in terms of roles, there is also evidence that women who are employed outside the home either part-time or full-time are happier on average and less at risk of depression than those who are full-time homemakers (National Center for Health Statistics, 1980; Hoffmann, 1989; Baruch, Barnett, and Rivers, 1983; Gallup, 1989, pp. 164-165, Hoyenga and Hoyenga, 1979).

From a broader functionalist perspective, one might raise serious questions about the benefits to society of denying half of its adult population the opportunity to develop fully their creativity, productive capacity, and freedom of choice. From a purely economic standpoint, the only thing that has saved the typical American family from a substantial decline in its standard of living over the past two decades has been the massive entry of women into the labor force (Olsen, 1990). Productivity growth and real hourly wages (hourly pay adjusted for the effects of inflation) have generally lagged since the mid-1970s. Millions of wives and mothers entered the labor force in part to compensate for the resultant loss of income. Had this not occurred, the standard of living of many Americans would have declined substantially.

## The Conflict Perspective

Conflict theorists ask, who benefits from gender roles as they exist in America? The answer, they believe, is that men benefit from them, (For comprehensive statements of this view, see Collins, 1971a; Reskin, 1988.) Conflict theorists also ask, Does the group that benefits have disproportionate power, so that it can arrange society to its advantage? With respect to gender roles, they note the great power of men, something we have already discussed in reference to the political system, the family, and the world of work. Thus, gender roles persist because men use their power to maintain a system from which they benefit.

*How* do men benefit from traditional gender roles? We have already seen many ways in this chapter. Men receive higher wages than women and have a better chance of getting jobs that offer status, autonomy, and authority. Men enjoy greater mobility and freedom in choosing how to spend their time—their jobs take them outside the home, and if the family owns just one automobile, it is likely to be the husband's. Even in today's typical two-worker, two-car family, men still enjoy advantages. For example, when both husband and wife are employed full-time, the total work week of men—on the job and in the home—is shorter than that of women. In terms of income, wealth, status, power, and free time, all indications are that traditional gender roles work to the advantage of men. As shown in the box entitled "The Costs of Sexism to Men," there are other areas in which men pay a price for these benefits. Even so, the material benefits of gender roles to men are real. Thus, it is hardly surprising that men would use their power to maintain such gender roles.

**Sources of Male Power** One question that conflict theorists ask is, How did males achieve unequal power in the first place? One explanation, which involves a combination of functionalist and conflict theory, is that male power is the outgrowth of a role specialization that was once useful to society. Although assigning roles to men that took them outside the home was originally useful, it also gave men certain power that women didn't have. It gave them greater freedom of movement and more contact with the outside world, and it made women dependent upon them for basic food supplies obtained through hunting. All this translated into male power, and once males had this power, they began to use it to their advantage, setting up a society that became increasingly male-dominated.

Some conflict theorists add a second line of reasoning to this. They argue that size and physical strength were sources of power that males used to get what they wanted from women, In the United States, China, and many other societies, wives used to be seen largely as their husbands' property.

Certainly, the use or threat of violence is an important source of power, and it probably played a major role in the establishment of male dominance.

Today, of course, the law forbids violence by men against women, although even now the courts and police are often reluctant to intervene if such violence occurs within the family. Physical strength is largely irrelevant to most jobs, so occupational specialization by sex is far less functional than it once was. Yet today, there are other mechanisms by which men retain disproportionate power. To a large extent, we have already seen what these are: disproportionate political power and control of money within the family.

## Feminism: A Challenge to Male Power

In the United States and many other societies throughout the world (particularly those with higher levels of industrialization), one of the major social changes of recent decades has been the emergence of **feminism** on a large scale. Essentially, the governing principles of feminism as an ideology and social movement are that women should enjoy the same rights in society as men and that they should share equally in society's opportunities and in its scarce resources, such as income, power, status, and personal freedom.

**Origins of Feminism in America** In the United States, feminism can be traced back nearly 150 years. The movement is generally regarded as having begun with an 1848 meeting in Seneca Falls, New York, which set forth a statement of women's rights modeled after the Declaration of Independence. For the next 70 years, the major objective of this movement was to obtain the vote for women (only men were allowed to vote in the national elections in the United States until 1920). The early feminist movement didn't succeed in changing other aspects of sex discrimination in America, however, for several reasons (Degler, 1980). First, women in that era saw advantages in the emerging housewife role. Second, just getting women the vote was a tremendous battle because opponents (as well as many supporters) of women's suffrage believed that if women got the vote, they would overturn the political order by voting in ways radically different from men. (They didn't.) After the suffrage battle was won, feminism as an issue faded for a time, only to resurface in the 1960s and 1970s in a form that amounted to a much wider and more fundamental challenge to traditional gender roles.

**Twentieth-Century Feminism** By the 1970s, U.S. feminists were challenging the housewife role in a way the earlier movement never did, and they had some real successes. For example, women have moved out of the home and into the paid labor force in unprecedented numbers over the past two decades. As shown in Figure 6–3, a clear majority of married women are in the paid labor force. Even among women with young children, more than half work outside the home for pay. In large part, this trend reflects economic necessity, as well as changed views about the role of women. For working-class and poor women, economic necessity is the main force behind the trend, while for wealthier, more educated women, the desire to have a career is more important. Among all classes, however, the notion that women should remain in the home has lost favor, particularly among younger women.

As more and more women left the role of housewife for that of paid worker, the feminist movement increasingly addressed other issues. The right to equal pay for equal (or comparable) work has been a major issue, as has been the right to be free from sexual harassment at work and at school. Issues outside the workplace have also taken on increased importance, as feminists have increasingly objected to the fact that women do a disproportionate share of housework. Feminists have also placed a high priority on reproductive freedom, emphasizing issues such as the right to choose whether to have an abortion and opposition to any restrictions on the availability of birth control.

Some feminist issues have been of particular concern among women of color and working-class women. For example, the issue of sexual harassment has had special importance for African-American women, because in addition to the risk of sexual harassment that all women face, African-American women have often been expected to submit to white males because of *racial* inequality as well as gender

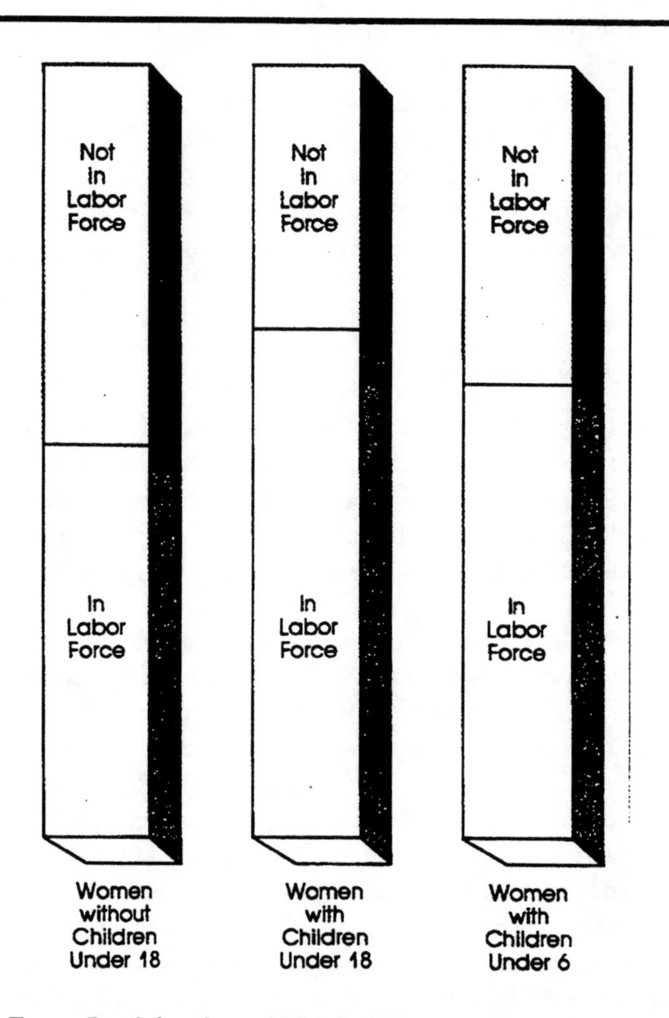


**FIGURE 6–3 Labor Force Participation of Married Women, by Presence and Age of Children**

SOURCE: U.S. Bureau of the Census, 1991. Statistical Abstract of the United States, 1991. Washington: USGPO, Table 644.

inequality. This, in turn, "contributed to images of black women as fair game for all men" (Collins, 1991, p. 54). African-American and Hispanic women must also face low-wage work—often in service occupations—that results from a lack of opportunity arising from both racial and gender inequality. The loss of jobs in many black and Hispanic neighborhoods has also resulted in a shortage of potential mates for inner-city black and Hispanic women (Wilson, 1987; forthcoming). The reason for this is that as manufacturing jobs have left inner cities, black and Hispanic men have experienced rising joblessness, rendering growing numbers of them unable to provide support for a family. In an era in which most unmarried adults are sexually active and in a population in which access to and knowledge of contraceptives is often limited, this shortage of men eligible for marriage has elevated the number of single parent, female householder families. At the same time, as low-paying service jobs have replaced the old manufacturing jobs, black and Hispanic women have often been hired for these low-paying jobs (Wilson; forthcoming). One consequence is that those women are more likely to be the sole support of their families—and the low-wage work available to them is often inadequate for this purpose. The result is the emergence of different modes of feminist thought among women of color and working-class women. While they emphasize some of the same issues that feminism has always stressed, these varieties of feminism also raise issues of particular concern to working-class women and women of color (Collins, 1991; Hooks, 1981, 1991; Davis, 1981; Lorde, 1992; Higgenbotham, 1992).

The growing influence of feminism has not been limited to the United States. Other countries had suffrage movements during the nineteenth century parallel to that of the United States (Flexner, 1975). Since the 1960s (and in some cases earlier), resurgent feminist movements have been important social forces throughout the industrialized world, and feminism has been a growing influence in the Third World as well (Ward, 1984, pp. 36 - 37).

### Social Origins of the New Feminism

Why has feminism become so influential? Although the reasons vary somewhat from country to country, certain conditions have appeared in a number of countries. First, traditional gender roles have become less functional in modern societies, for reasons noted earlier in this chapter. Conditions also developed in many countries that made women less satisfied with their traditional roles. Women were becoming more educated but were not getting the opportunity to use that education. During World War II, women were pressed into nontraditional roles in many countries, including performing manual labor in defense plants, and found that they could be effective in those roles. They also found that under the right conditions, they could be well rewarded for work outside the home. Although many women were happy to return to their traditional roles after the war, they realized that they could succeed in other roles, and this may have had the long-term effect of making them more interested in nontraditional roles. Also during this time, the growth of mass media throughout the world enhanced communication, which made it easier for feminist leaders to transmit their message to other dissatisfied women.

Finally, the 1960s was a period of worldwide social upheaval that witnessed the antiwar and civil rights movements in the United States, the student and labor upheavals in France, the Cultural Revolution in China, the struggle for political freedom in Czechoslovakia, the separatist movement among French-Canadians, the religious conflict in Northern Ireland, and the beginnings of long struggles for majority rule in South Africa and Zimbabwe (then Rhodesia). Women were involved in all of these struggles, but they often found themselves relegated to such nonleadership roles as preparing meals, stuffing envelopes, and running errands. This had three effects. First, involvement in these movements made women realize that they, too, could create a movement. Second, the limited role allowed to women in many of these social movements heightened their dissatisfaction. Third, these movements brought dissatisfied women together, so they could communicate with each other and organize a movement of their own (Freeman, 1973). Together, these conditions greatly accelerated the development of feminist movements in many countries.

## HOW ARE GENDER ROLES CHANGING IN AMERICA?

In this final section, I shall attempt to assess the meaning of recent changes in sex and gender roles in America and to address some information that may give us an idea where our society is headed. We shall begin by noting areas in which norms concerning relations between men and women have changed.

### Sexual Double Standard

Society's views concerning the sexual freedom of men and women have changed dramatically over the past few decades. The Victorian sexual double standard assumed that sex was to be enjoyed by men and that it was normal for unmarried men to want to "fool around." Women, however, were expected to remain pure and were considered "too good" to enjoy sex. As a result, sexual activity among unmarried males was largely taken for granted (even if somewhat disapproved of). For unmarried women, though, it was much more seriously forbidden, and a good deal less common. By the late 1960s, however, that system had changed (Christiansen and Gregg, 1970). Today, norms about sexual behavior are more similar for men and women than in the past, as are the behaviors themselves (Hunt, 1974).

## Employment Discrimination

Another area in which there has been major change is the law. The Civil Rights Act of 1964 forbade deliberate discrimination against women in hiring and wages. Since then, it has been illegal to refuse to hire a person because of sex, unless the employer can prove that sex is a bona fide factor in a person's ability to perform a particular job, which is rarely the case. Similarly, you cannot pay an employee less (or, for that matter, more) than other employees in the same job with similar qualifications simply because she is a woman. Moreover, the government has often interpreted this law as requiring employers to take affirmative action to ensure that women have the same opportunities as men to get the more desirable jobs. This policy was reversed under the Reagan and Bush administrations, which opposed affirmative action; the policy changed again under the Clinton administration, which favors affirmative action.

## Sexual Assault

At the level of state law, there have been important changes in the rules of evidence concerning sexual assault. In the past, a rape victim practically had to prove to the court that she did not bring on the rape by her own behavior. She was asked questions about her past sexual behavior, as well as her past relationship with the person charged with raping her. Often, if a woman indicated that she had been sexually active in the past or had previously been involved with the accused, it was assumed that she really had engaged in sex voluntarily, or at least had misled the accused person into thinking she really wanted to have sex. In some cases, assumptions were made about the victim's sexual availability simply on the basis of how she dressed. In a sense, the victim was on trial, and if her past or present behavior was found wanting, judges and juries rejected the possibility that a crime might have taken place. Most states, however, have recently passed laws restricting the kinds of questions that can be asked of rape victims. It can no longer be assumed in most states that if a woman once wanted to have sex, she always will in the future, which is about what the old patterns of questioning assumed. Still, rape victims are often subjected to personal and embarrassing questioning, and as a result, many rapes still go unreported and thus unprosecuted. Moreover, women who have raised issues of sexual harassment are particularly subjected to such questioning. As previously noted in this chapter, when Professor Anita Hill reported having been sexually harassed by Supreme Court nominee Clarence Thomas, she was subjected to intense questioning by the Senate judiciary Committee. In some ways, she was questioned more intensely than was Thomas, and several senators rather openly suggested that she had made up the accusations out of personal or political motivations. By 1993, however, there were signs that such questioning was becoming less acceptable. When the Senate Ethics Committee investigated charges of sexual harassment against Senator Bob Packwood, it prohibited consideration of any witness' sexual history—in that and all other sexual harassment cases.

## Limitations of Change

Despite some changes, women's efforts to improve their status have met with only limited success. The effect of civil rights legislation on the actual pay received by men and women, for example, has been limited. We have seen that there have been changes, but only modest ones, in the wages of women relative to those of men and in occupational segregation. Thus, the biggest actual change in the status of women, so far, has been the movement of many women out of the housewife role and into the labor force. Although this movement has given women a measure of freedom and independence they did not enjoy in the past, the low pay of employed women remains a major barrier to full sexual equality. In fact, when combined with the increased divorce rate and changes in divorce law, this low pay has led to a new problem. As is discussed in the box "The Feminization of Poverty," being a woman has increasingly become associated with being poor in the United States. At present, the sex of the primary wage earner is the best predictor of whether a family's income will fall below the federal poverty level.

## SOCIOLOGICAL INSIGHTS

### THE FEMINIZATION OF POVERTY: A NEW FORM OF SEXISM?

One highly disturbing trend in the United States is the *feminization of poverty* (Pearce, 1982). More than ever before in our history, being a woman has become associated with being poor. In 1991 the overall female poverty rate in the United States was 16.0 percent, compared to 12.3 percent among males (U.S. Bureau of the Census, 1992f, p. 10). Among adults, where virtually all the difference occurs, the poverty rate for women was 14.0 percent, compared to just 8.9 percent for men (computed from U.S. Bureau of the Census, 1992f, p. 10).

The difference becomes even more pronounced if we look at family data. Among families with a female householder, the poverty rate in 1991 was over 35 percent—more than three times the poverty rate among all families. Of course, the poverty rate among two-parent families is bound to be lower, because most of them have two earners. However, if we compare only single-parent families, the poverty rate was 13.0 percent among those with a male householder, compared to 35.6 percent among those with a female householder. In fact, the sex of the householder is more closely associated with family poverty than any other characteristic, including race, region of the country, or urban/rural location. Among people of color, the poverty rates of female-householder families are even higher. For both blacks and Hispanics, half of female-householder families had an income below the poverty level in 1991 (U.S. Bureau of the Census, 1991f, pp. 8-9).

Why is being a woman, or living in a family with a female householder, so strongly associated with poverty today? Essentially, the reasons involve the high divorce rate, the resolution of divorce cases by the legal system, and—most important—the low pay of women. With our high divorce rate—about one marriage out of two ends in divorce—far more women today than in the past must support themselves and one or more children solely on their own incomes. Partly because women are more likely than men to seek custody of children, and partly because the courts often favor the mother in custody battles, over 85 percent of all children in one-parent households live with their mothers. Many more female households today are also created by out-of-wedlock births than was the case in the past. One child out of four is born to a single mother, and it is nearly always the mother, not the father, who raises such children.

The courts play a role in the feminization of poverty for several reasons. First, alimony is rarely awarded today. Many judges assume that women are employed and therefore can support their families, an assumption that is incorrect because of women's low wages. Second, although child-support decrees are often awarded in divorce cases, they are poorly enforced. Thus, a large percentage of fathers stop paying child support rather quickly, and some never pay at all, despite court orders. Finally, any order to pay child support—much less enforcement—is very rare in cases of out-of-wedlock births. The result of all this is that the majority of fathers who do not live with their children do not contribute much, if anything, toward the support of those children.

All these things might not make such a great difference if women's wages were as high as men's, and if quality, low-cost day care were as available in the United States as it is in most other industrialized countries. With women's wages so low, however, and with affordable day care so hard to find, the conditions described in the preceding paragraphs make a huge difference. The reality is that when a divorce occurs, the husband usually experiences a substantial *increase* in his standard of living, whereas the wife and children experience an even larger *decline* in theirs (Weitzman, 1985). The net result of all this is what sociologists call the feminization of poverty.

## What Does the Future Hold?

What are the prospects for a move toward greater equality between American men and women in the future? There are a number of ways we can look for answers to this question. We can start with the attitudes of Americans. It does appear that, in many ways, American attitudes are supportive of gender equality. A poll by the Roper Organization (1980) showed that 72 percent of adult men and women believed that changes in American gender roles were of a permanent nature, and a smaller but still substantial majority of 57 percent said they *wanted* the changes to continue. In the decade after that poll, the American media placed considerable emphasis on the "losses" resulting from women being in the workforce. In what Faludi (1991) referred to as a backlash against the women's movement, it was suggested that many women were frustrated that their jobs took them away from their families. However, she points out that the polls for the most part did not support such a view: Women were no more likely than men to express such frustrations, and by a margin of more than 70 percent, women from the mid-1980s to 1990 indicated a preference for high-pressure jobs with advancement opportunities over low-pressure jobs with less opportunity, and rejected the so-called "mommy track"—less demanding work with shorter hours—because they saw it as a way of paying women less (Faludi, 1991, p. 91).

Of course, generalized support for equal opportunity does not always translate into the reality of equal opportunity. In the economic arena, for example, true equality of opportunity for men and women would require fundamental social changes. One such change would be a major change in current patterns of occupational segregation. Is there any sign that this is happening? In keeping with the finding noted earlier that gifted girls are most likely to aspire to traditionally male occupations, there has been a sharp rise in the number of women training for certain prestigious fields such as law and medicine (see Figure 6.4). However, *overall* occupational segregation has declined only modestly, and many occupations remain overwhelmingly male or female. As late as 1980, for example, over 95 percent of nurses, secretaries, receptionists, and kindergarten teachers were female, but less than 5 percent of construction workers, engineers, firefighters, and airplane pilots were (Blau and Ferber, 1986, p. 167).

Although full workplace equality probably cannot occur as long as occupational segregation persists, major reductions of *income* inequality could occur even without a change in occupational segregation. For this to happen, however, something similar to comparable worth legislation would have to be implemented. In other words, men and women with comparable skills, education, and experience would have to be paid equal wages, even when they work at *different* jobs.

Comparable worth is unlikely to happen voluntarily in the private sector, however, because any company that decided to pay women the same as comparably skilled and educated men would experience an increase in labor costs, and therefore would be at a disadvantage vis-à-vis companies that had no such policy. In this sense, a conflict theorist could argue that our economic system, with its profit orientation, is inhibiting the move toward economic equality of the sexes.

In noneconomic areas the prospects for change also remain uncertain. Although men have changed their thinking concerning their role in the home, it is not clear that they are willing to share fully in domestic chores. Moreover, different patterns of communication continue to both reflect and reinforce inequalities between men and women. Although there are serious questions about the adequacy of her sample, Hite's (1987) survey of American women does strongly suggest that lack of communication is one of the biggest complaints women have about their husbands. In general, men interrupt far more than women (Kollock et al., 1985; Zimmerman and West, 1975), and women are expected to spend more time listening while men talk (Kollock et al., 1985). Women also are more likely than men to use gestures associated with low status, such as nodding, smiling, and holding their arms close to their bodies (see McKenna and Denmark, 1978). So long as these patterns exist, men and women will not interact as equals, and it is unlikely that women will attain equal access to desirable roles in life. Thus, although gender roles have changed considerably in some ways, they have not changed much in other ways. More important, gender roles remain not only different, but also *unequal.*

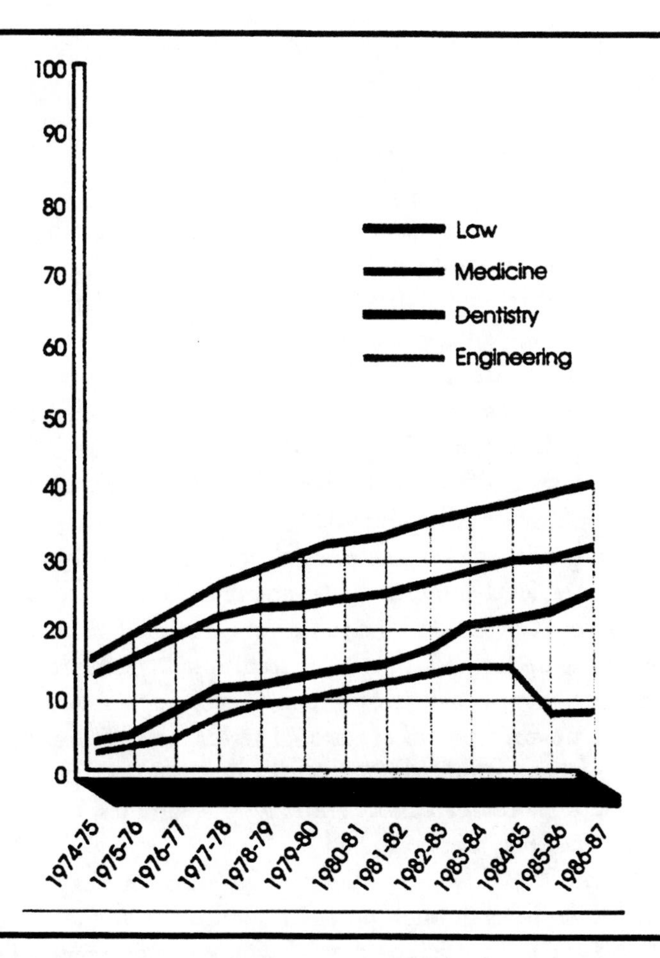


**FIGURE 6–4 Percentage of Women among Degree Recipients, Selected Professions, 1974–1987.**

SOURCE: Carpenter, 1987, pp. 38, 40, 47; National Center for Educational Statistics, U.S. Department of Education.

The likelihood that we will eliminate this inequality between the roles of men and women at any time in the foreseeable future appears dubious at best. Our society has moved in that direction, perhaps more dramatically in the past two decades than at any previous time in our history. However, it has a very long way to go before true sexual equality is attained.

## SUMMARY

*Sex* refers to the biological characteristic of being male or female, whereas *gender* refers to socially learned traits that are attached to sex in society. Most societies have a system of *gender roles*, in which men and women are expected to play different parts. In most societies, including the United States, these roles are unequal, and male dominance is the rule. Some societies, however, are androgynous, and a few are even female-dominant. Moreover, even though male dominance is widespread, its form varies from one society to another, and it changes over time. In the United States and other Western societies, for example, the housewife role that emerged with the Industrial Revolution faded in importance after World War II.

In the United States and other industrial societies, women are increasingly entering the paid labor force. However, women work at different jobs than men, usually for lower pay. Despite some improvements, the typical American woman still receives little more than two-thirds the wages of the typical man. Differences in the wages and salaries of men and women cannot be explained by differences in education or skills, or even by the greater tendency of women to work part-time and to leave the labor force temporarily. Rather, they are a product of the different jobs of women, their lesser opportunity to be promoted into jobs with supervisory authority, and their frequent need to subordinate their own careers to those of their husbands.

Some of this inequality is also the result of gender role socialization, the process by which men and women are taught to expect and seek different and unequal roles in life. Achievement, strength, and independence are stressed for boys, while girls are taught to be nice and to look attractive. Clothes, games, children's books, television, parents, and teachers all give these messages. Through the process of the looking-glass self, boys and girls are taught different self-images. They come to believe that their skills lie in different subjects, and by high school, this process has become a self-fulfilling prophecy. Children also see men and women in different jobs (in the media, in school materials, and in their own experiences), and as a result they aspire to different jobs themselves. Recent research suggests that these differences are decreasing, but they have not disappeared.

Some functionalists see gender roles as a case of cultural lag—something that was useful in the past but no longer is today. They predict that society will gradually move toward androgyny. Other functionalists, however, see gender roles as essential to the cohesiveness of the family and blame such problems as the soaring divorce rate on the declining influence of traditional gender roles. Conflict theorists argue that gender roles exist because men benefit from them. According to conflict theories, men use their disproportionate power to maintain a system of unequal gender roles. Feminism offers the possibility of changing this system of inequality. Conflict theorists also argue that families with traditional gender roles are no happier or more functional than are more androgynous families, and that the ability of working women to afford to get divorced may not be all bad.

Increasingly since World War II, women in a number of countries, including the United States, have challenged unequal gender roles through powerful feminist movements. These recent movements have been more broad-based and influential than earlier women's movements. They have been facilitated by the increased education of women, improved mass communication, and the participation of women in a number of other social movements. Feminism has not eliminated gender roles or sexual inequality, but it has brought significant legal changes in many countries, as well as some important changes in public opinion concerning the appropriate roles of men and women.

## GLOSSARY

**sex** The physical or biological characteristic of being male or female.

**gender** Socially learned traits or characteristics that are associated with men or women.

**gender roles** Social roles that people are expected to play because they are male or female, and that often carry unequal status, rewards, and opportunities.

**sexism** Structured inequality between men and women, and the norms and beliefs that support such inequality.

**institutional sexism** Systematic practices and patterns within social institutions that lead to inequality between men and women.

**androgynous societies** Societies in which the roles of men and women differ little, if at all.

**gender role socialization** The process by which gender roles are taught and learned.

**occupational segregation** A pattern whereby two groups—most often men and women—hold different types of jobs.

**feminism** An ideology or a related social movement advocating the ideas that social roles should not be assigned on the basis of sex, and thus that an equal share of scarce resources should go to women.

# FURTHER READING

BIANCHI, SUZANNE, and DAPHNE SPAIN. 1986. *American Women in Transition.* New York: Russell Sage Foundation. A comprehensive, data-based examination of the status of women in contemporary American society. A good source of statistical information on the relative positions of men and women with respect to income, employment, and family status.

BRADLEY, HARRIET. 1989. *Men's Work, Women's Work: A Sociological History of the Sexual Division of Labor in Employment.* Minneapolis: University of Minnesota Press. A documentation of the reasons for the persistence of gender-based occupational segregation. While focused on Great Britain, this book offers interesting cross-cultural comparisons. Includes a discussion of how contemporary definitions of masculinity and femininity have shaped new sex-typing of jobs.

COLLINS, PATRICIA HILL. 1991. *Black Feminist Thought: Knowledge, Consciousness, and the Politics of Empowerment.* New York: Routledge. This award-winning book examines how race and class have altered the ways in which sexism operates upon African-American women, and develops a specialized variety of feminist theory that addresses their particular situation. The book is also a prime example of how sociologists can learn from both personal experiences and more abstract theories and research methodologies.

DOYLE, JAMES A. 1983. *The Male Experience.* Dubuque, IA: William C. Brown. An examination of masculinity and the role of men in society, with emphasis on both historical development and cross-cultural comparison.

FALUDI, SUSAN. 1991. *Backlash: The Undeclared War Against American Women.* New York: Crown Publishers, Faludi points out and critically analyzes a number of arguments and issues raised in the mass media in recent years that have the effect of limiting women's gains from changing gender roles. She holds that these arguments reflect a backlash against women's gains by the male-dominated power structure, and points to the lack of valid social-scientific data for many of the arguments. This book is interesting methodologically, because it shows how uncritically incomplete, tentative, or erroneous social research findings are often repeated by the press (and, sometimes, other social scientists).

FRANKLIN, CLYDE W. 1988. *Men and Society.* Chicago: Nelson-Hall, Inc. This paperback offers a readable sociological analysis of the effects of culture in general and social structure in particular on men and their concept of masculinity.

JONES, JAQUELINE. 1985. *Labor of Love, Labor of Sorrow: Black Women, Work, and the Family from Slavery to Present.* New York: Basic Books. Although gender roles exist within all racial and ethnic groups, the nature of those roles is greatly influenced by the experiences of each group and by its position in the larger society. This book explores the female role as experienced by African-American women.

RESKIN, BARBARA F., and PATRICIA A. ROOS. 1990. *Job Queues, Gender Queues: Explaining Women's Inroads into Male Occupations.* Philadelphia: Temple University Press. Why do some traditionally male jobs open up to women? This book argues that the main reason is that they have changed in ways that make them less desirable to men. The authors use examples ranging from book editing and pharmacy to real estate sales and bartending to show how this has happened in various occupations. If the authors are correct, a decline in occupational segregation may bring smaller gains for women than is widely believed.

RICHARDSON, LAUREL. 1988. *The Dynamics of Sex and Gender: A Sociological Perspective.* New York: Harper and Row. This readable work on the subject of gender consists of four sections: learning the culture, institutions of social control (ideational elements), the structure of sex-based inequality, and social and political change.

# Chapter 7

## Forms of Social Life

*Human behavior is not random; it is patterned. Regularity and order can be found in the actions of all humans, whether they are Nepalese living in Katmandu, aborigines living in the outback of Australia, or New Yorkers living on the Upper East Side of Manhattan. Average people living anywhere will know how to relate to the people with whom they come in contact in their daily lives. Imagine what would happen, however, if we were to take a person from any one of these places and put him or her in another society. The results would vividly reveal how the patterns of behavior in a society must be learned.*

*Because many of the social patterns of our own society are so familiar, we often give them little attention. In this chapter we will examine a wide range of different patterns of social relations. We will begin with a general concept that sociologists often use when describing a pattern of social relationships (social structure). Then, beginning at the microscopic level, we will see how interaction between individuals produces patterned behavior even in a two-person relationship. Next we will move to the level of groups and then to organizations. The chapter will conclude with a discussion of societies.*

## SOCIAL STRUCTURES

Social Structures are regular patterns of social interaction and persistent social relationships. Social structures are constructed by the ongoing interaction of people, but at the same time, by observing these patterns of interaction, we can identify social structures. Social structures can be observed at any social level from the interaction between two people, through groups and organizations, to entire societies. To illustrate how a social structure is created through interaction, and, simultaneously, how social structures are observable in the regularities and patterns of everyday interaction, we will consider a familiar example.

Imagine a number of college students who come together at the beginning of a school year to live on the same corridor of a dormitory. When they first move in they are probably strangers, or perhaps they know each other only casually. Over a period of time, however, through their interaction, they will start sorting themselves into sets of people who spend time together. These sets of people will talk, go to meals together, help each other with homework, and so on. Some of the emerging groups are apt to have special interests and activities—sports, dorm politics, partying, practical jokes, or studying. Using the words of the social structure definition, we can say that regular patterns of social interaction and persistent social relationships will occur among these students.

When anthropologist Michael Moffatt (1989) lived among the residents of a dormitory at Rutgers University, he was able to observe the social structures that emerged during the first two months of the school year. He reports: "By late October, the residents of the floor had connected themselves together in the complex network of friendship [groups]" (Moffatt, 1989, p. 95). He describes some of the larger friendship groups and cliques, identifying their leaders, their special activities, and their differing styles. He also notes that there were some two- and three-person groups (see "Dyads and Triads," p. 105) that were either outside the larger groups, or in some cases connecting two different groups. Also, some first-year students "floated between this clique and others on the floor" (Moffatt, 1989, p. 96). These patterns of interaction (social structures) on a single dormitory floor were clearly identifiable after only two months of interaction. One can be quite certain that at the beginning of each academic year similar structures will emerge in dormitories and residence halls at every other college.

Because of the patterned nature of social structures, they can typically be sketched in diagrammatic form. For example, Figure 7-1 is a partial depiction of Moffatt's diagram of the student social structure that emerged on the dormitory floor where he made his observations. In Figure 7-1, the lines drawn between individuals are based on mutual friendship choices as expressed on a questionnaire that Moffatt gave to the residents of the floor in late October.

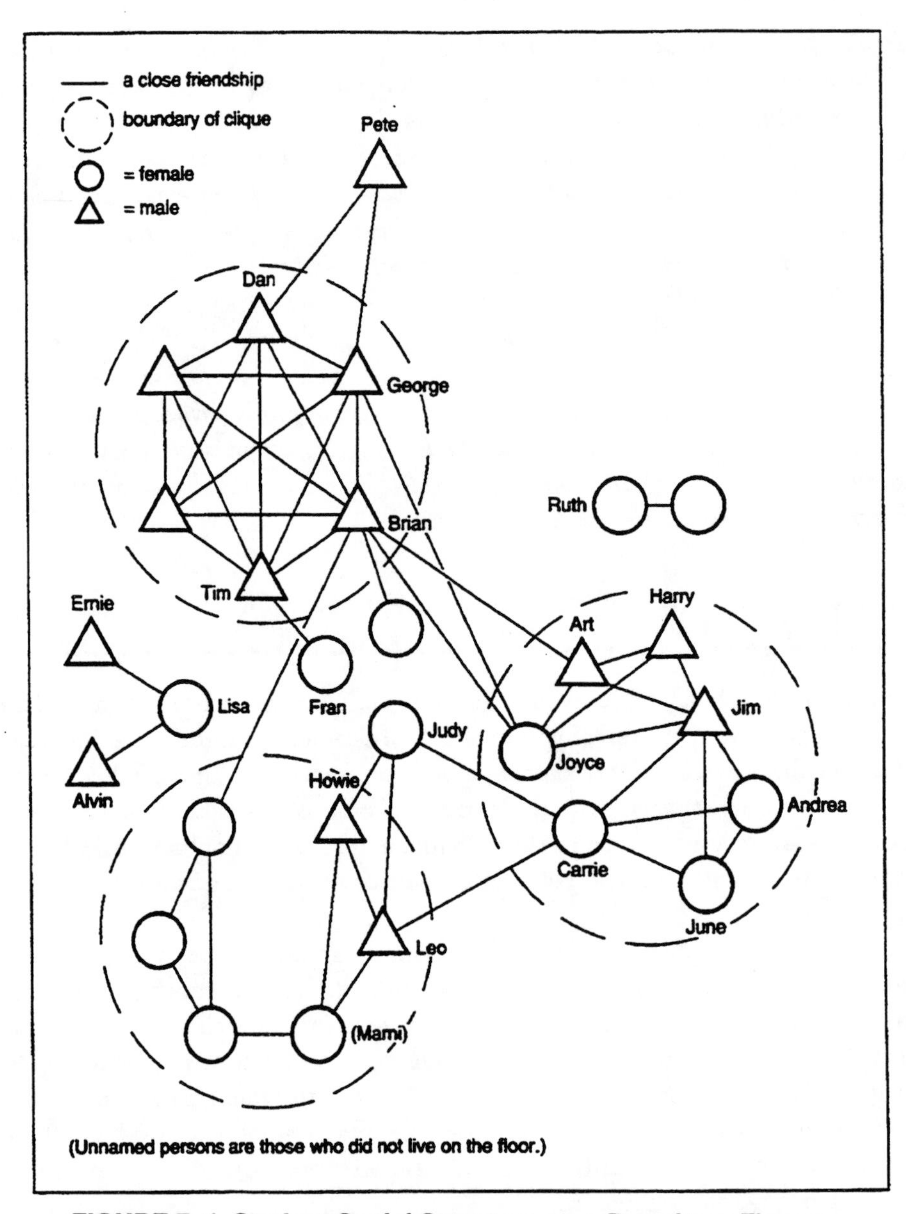


**FIGURE 7–1 Student Social Structure on a Dormitory Floor.**

SOURCE: Michael Moffat, *Coming of Age in New Jersey.* New Brunswick, N.J.: Rutgers University Press (1989), p. 97.)

Because social structures are created by people, they can change over time. But structures tend to have some persistence, and when sociologists speak of social structures they are talking about patterns of interaction and social relationships that persist over time. Included would be the major social structures found in societies, for they generally do not change rapidly. Examples in American society, to be examined later, are the socioeconomic-status system with its different social classes (Chapter 8) and the major racial and ethnic groups. These stratification systems are, of course, social structures. The social class structure of the society is observable through the way people interact with each other, and these patterns of interaction do not change much over time. The same is true with respect to the relationships between racial and ethnic groups in the United States. Racial discrimination, for example, which places blacks and other racial minorities in disadvantaged positions, has existed for centuries and persists today.

Throughout this chapter we will be describing social structures at the various levels of social life. We will begin with the interaction between individuals and then move on to groups and organizations. We will conclude, at the macroscopic end of the social continuum, with a consideration of societies.

## INTERACTION

The ability of humans to meet and interact with other humans is a high-level skill, but most of the time we do it with ease. In an average day a person typically interacts with a wide variety of people, including friends, relatives, lovers, acquaintances, and strangers. As long as we share the same language with these people, we can negotiate almost any kind of situation, whether it is friendly or hostile, comfortable or awkward, casual or formal.

As we saw in our consideration of symbolic interaction theory, the human mind, with its ability to understand and use symbols (both verbal and nonverbal), makes interaction possible between people. People interact primarily through verbal symbols, or words, not only with others but with themselves. By using symbols to interact with themselves, people are able to evaluate other people and situations, and decide what actions to take. Again, this is an important principle of symbolic interaction theory.

When interaction occurs between two people, two things happen, almost simultaneously. Each person in an interaction situation is *sending* words and cues and *receiving* and *processing* words and cues as they come in from the other person. The important feature of any interaction is the way people use their minds to interpret the words and cues of another person, deduce their meaning, and respond accordingly.

This abstract description of interaction makes it seem complex and unfamiliar, but if we take an everyday situation we can see how the process of interaction works. Consider a hypothetical yet commonplace situation in which a male and a female college student are getting acquainted. If they are in college and happen to sit next to each other in a class, over a period of time they may have a series of interactions that could ultimately result in their dating and becoming romantically involved. Their early interaction is important in this process. Two people seated side by side may rarely talk with each other at first. Gradually, however, they may start to interact. Of course, the very act of engaging in conversation when it is not necessary is in itself a symbolic act. When two people find themselves engaged in conversation they may recognize that their interaction could imply a mutual attraction. Even as they talk about something as mundane as the sociology professor or the next test, the young man might reflect to himself that he is attracted to the young woman and that she might be attracted to him.

As this interaction continues, different things might be happening at different levels simultaneously. Noncommittal ideas may first be exchanged, as the students talk about the professor or about studying for the next examination. The young woman may say she doesn't have anyone with whom to study, but if she makes this remark, the young man must interpret what it means. He has only a second or two to decide if she is saying that it might be pleasant for the two of them to get together outside of class, ostensibly to do some studying. At the same time, as he is assessing what her words really mean, he is formulating his response. If he responds to her objective statement inappropriately, he may look foolish. If he treats it as a suggestion that they get together outside of class and she did not mean it that way, he may be embarrassed. The young man must quickly select from his many possible choices: "I don't have anyone to study with either," or "I always find it helps to study with someone just before the test," or "Why don't we get together before the test?"

If the young man made the last of these statements, the young woman would have to decide exactly what his words meant. He could be asking for a date, or he could simply be suggesting that they study together. The woman must weigh all the evidence, again in just a second or two, and make some appropriate response. As a rule, a person in this situation will reply in such a way that the response will be appropriate regardless of the real intent of the statement. Or the young woman could simply say, "Are you asking me for a date or do you want to get together to study?" However, before doing so she will have to weigh the consequences of this response. Will the young man be shocked by her directness? Will her statement have the effect of acknowledging the previously unstated attraction between them?

The interaction just described goes on within the context of the cultural values and the social norms we discussed in the last chapter. In some societies, the norms of courtship would make it totally inappropriate for two young people to make a date of any kind. Often parents would have to be consulted and a chaperon obtained before two young people of the opposite sex could spend any time together. We can see from these normative constraints why human behavior is not random but is, as we said, patterned. The interaction between two people who are getting acquainted is partially open to their own creativity and inventiveness, but it is also patterned by the norms that prevail in a society. But there is another important social constraint on the interaction between the young man and woman we have been describing. Both people have social statuses, or positions, and attached to these statuses are social roles. Status and role are important sociological concepts because they reveal why there is a great amount of regular and patterned social behavior.

## STATUS AND ROLE

The words and actions of the young man and woman described above will certainly be influenced and shaped, especially in the early interaction, by the fact of their genders. Many American young people still believe it more appropriate for males to initiate invitations for dates than for females to do so. This view is changing, but many young women still say, "I think it is fine for a woman to ask a guy for a date, *but I wouldn't do it.*" This statement tells us that although some young women do not see anything wrong with a woman initiating a date, many still feel that it might be inappropriate behavior. But why is it viewed as inappropriate? To understand why someone would feel this way and why this feeling is shared by many other people—young and old, female and male—we have to examine the importance of the sociological concepts of status and role.

A **status** is a socially recognized position in a social system. A **role** is the behavior generally expected of one who occupies a particular status. Again we can use gender as an example of status and role. In all societies, males and females have socially recognized positions, with certain expectations, about what one will and will not do. However, males and females are not expected to act in the same way in every society. In Chapter 10 we will examine some societies in which men and women are expected to act in ways that are very different from those traditionally expected of them in U.S. society. But—and here is the important point—gender is always a status that carries with it some expected behaviors. Roles are always connected with gender.

Statuses can be of two types: ascribed and achieved. An **ascribed status** is one into which individuals move or are placed, irrespective of their efforts or capacities. Examples of ascribed statuses include being male or female, young or old, black or white, son or daughter. We have little control over our ascribed statuses. (An example of an effort to control ascribed status would be a person who undergoes a sex change.) In contrast, an **achieved status** is one that people acquire through their own efforts. Examples include becoming a college graduate, getting married, having children, becoming an astronaut, or even becoming a bank robber.

A related concept is that of master status. A **master status** refers to a position so important that it dominates and overrides all other statuses, both for the person and all other people. For example, a study of male college basketball players at a major university demonstrated that the status of being on the men's basketball team overwhelmed all other statuses of these young men (Adler and Adler, 1991). Even if these men wished to be seen as more than simply basketball players, everyone else on campus identified them in this way. For them, *basketball player* became a master status that overrode all other statuses.

Often in our society, a master status is related to one's occupation. A person who is a Supreme Court Justice, a nun, a college president, or an opera singer is likely to be seen primarily in terms of his or her major occupational role—a master role.

Another point about statuses and roles is that they have a reality of their own; they exist irrespective of the persons who fill them. Whoever occupies the status of the president of the United States, or is the center-fielder on a baseball team, or the anchorperson on a television news show must attend to certain expectations that accompany the status. In general, the people who fill a status understand the expectations and follow the behavior expected of them.

However, not everyone in a particular status behaves in exactly the same way. There are two reasons for this. First, the role expectations connected with a status are not fully detailed. Role expectations are not so precisely stated or understood that every detail of expected behavior is clear. Second, individuals who hold statuses may have their own orientations toward the role. Let us deal with each of these issues separately.

Roles do not specify every exact behavior that a person in a given status must follow. In fact, roles often have only broad requirements within which a person must operate. Airline pilots, for example, are expected to be competent to fly planes in all kinds of conditions and handle difficult and emergency situations in a calm and collected way. When pilots speak to the passengers, they generally present themselves as steady, serious, and relaxed, even though they may not always feel that way. However, some pilots will occasionally inject humor, irritation (with delays, for example), or other emotions into their public presentations. When they are not within hearing or sight of the passengers, their behavior may be even more at odds with the general role expectations for airline pilots. Behind the scenes they are able to introduce their unique, personal characteristics and still fulfill the role expectations connected with a status. In other words, people do not simply conform to role expectations; they also actively modify their roles. This ability of individuals to modify (at least to some degree) their own roles has been called **role-making** (Hewitt, 1984, p. 81).

Another way to see how individuals can vary their performance of a role is to note that the dominant view about what is expected of people in a given status need not be universal. Different orientations toward a role can exist. The college student role has broad outlines—enrolling, going to class, studying, taking exams—but different students might emphasize different features of the student role. These different emphases are called **role orientations**. Some students might emphasize the academic and intellectual aspect of the student role. With this orientation they would take advantage of college to become involved in intellectual pursuits. Their role orientation toward their college-student status has been called the *academic-intellectual* role orientation. In comparison, other college students are more oriented toward the vocational or professional training they receive in school. They see student life as an opportunity to learn a profession and gain entry into it. This orientation has been called the *vocational* role orientation. Some students see their college experience as an opportunity to engage in an active social life or to learn social skills. For them, college is a learning ground for their future social lives. The fraternity-sorority scene may be a forerunner of the country club life that they expect to enter later. This has been called the *social life* role orientation (Bolton and Kammeyer, 1967).

As we have seen, the roles connected with statuses do not make individuals in the same status behave in the same way, but enough similarity is evident in role performance to produce some general patterns of behavior. These patterns, found among males and females, airline pilots, and students, and a vast array of other statuses, are sufficiently consistent to produce identifiable patterns in social life. However, statuses and roles can always be modified and changed over time, through the continuing actions and interactions of people.

## DYADS AND TRIADS

When two people engage in interaction, it is called a **dyad**. When a third person is introduced into the interaction, it is called a **triad**. While both dyads and triads involve interaction, and both can be seen as groups, there are some interesting differences between two-person and three-person interaction. From a sociological and practical point of view, the triad is a much more complicated social arrangement (Simmel, 1950).

A dyad has only one relationship, but a triad has three (A and B, A and C, B and C). That in itself makes the triad more complicated. Consider, for example, the common situation of a husband and wife dyad becoming parents of a new baby, thus becoming a triad. The relationship between the husband and wife becomes more complicated because each will now have a relationship with the baby. It is a fairly common occurrence for a new mother to devote so much attention to her relationship with the baby that her husband feels neglected. A substantial amount of research shows that satisfaction with marital relationships declines when married couples have children. Part of the reason can probably be attributed to the changes in interaction when a married-couple dyad becomes a triad.

Similar problems often emerge in three-person friendship groups. Although three-person groups can maintain a cohesive "three-musketeers" relationship, a balance is difficult to maintain. All pairs of relationships in a triad must be about equal in time spent together, displays of friendship, conversation, and so on. If this equality is not maintained, then one of the pairs will dominate, leaving the third person relatively isolated. Many people who have been in three-person friendship groups have had the experience of two members drawing closer together and shutting out the third.

Although dyads and triads are frequent forms of social interaction, the social group brings us to a more purely sociological level. We turn to this level next.

## SOCIAL GROUPS

While the word *group* is used in various ways in everyday speech, and even in sociology, the technical sociological meaning focuses our attention on some important features of social life. A **group** may be defined as a relatively small number of people who interact with one another over time and thereby establish patterns of interaction, a group identity, and rules or norms governing behavior.

One key feature defining a group is the interaction among all members. A larger entity such as a society (for example, U.S. society) differs from a group in that all the members of a society cannot possibly interact with each other because of their large number.

Although a large number of people cannot technically constitute a social group, a small number of people will not necessarily constitute a group either. Several people who meet briefly on an elevator are not a group, because they lack a group identity and because they do not interact on the basis of patterns they have established.

### In-groups and Out-groups

According to our definition, a basic characteristic of a group is that the interacting individuals have a group identity. Therefore, to qualify as a group, the people who compose it must define themselves as members and, conversely, those outside the group must be defined as outsiders. The emphasis on group identity leads to the distinction between *in-groups* and *out-groups* (Sumner, 1904). An **in-group** is one that members are involved in and with which they identify, while an **out-group** is one to which outsiders belong. The importance of this distinction is the tendency for people to believe in the rightness and desirability of the in-group, and to reject the ways of the out-group. The in-group, out-group distinction usually takes on its greatest significance when two or more groups are in close proximity. Members of fraternities and sororities on a college campus may view members of other fraternities and sororities as out-groups. This can lead to an attitude of "us" against "them." In extreme cases, in-group, out-group attitudes may lead to conflict between groups. (See Sociology in the News, p. 195).

### Primary and Secondary Groups

Sociologists also differentiate between primary groups and secondary groups. The concept of **primary groups** was developed by Cooley (1909) to describe groups "characterized by intimate face-to-face association and cooperation." Primary groups are typically small and close-knit. The relationships among the members are very personal. They strongly identify with each other as well as with the group as a whole. As a result of the closeness of the relationships, the primary group often has a profound effect on its members. As examples of primary groups, Cooley cites the family, play groups of children, and neighborhood or community groups.

## SOCIOLOGY IN THE NEWS

### STREET GANGS AND GROUP IDENTITY

There are hundreds, probably thousands, of street gangs in the United States. In Los Angeles County alone there are an estimated 800 street gangs with more than 90,000 members (Lacy, 1991). While urban gangs have existed throughout this century, their numbers and the intensity of their activities today make them an important part of urban life. In Los Angeles, street gangs are estimated to have been responsible for 650 killings in 1990.

Gangs are generally found in areas of the city that are poor; slums and ghettos are the breeding grounds for gangs (Jankowski, 1991; Padilla, 1992). Particular gangs are likely to be of one racial, ethnic, or nationality group. There are gangs whose members are African American, Hispanic (Chicano, Puerto Rican, Dominican, Jamaican), Asian, and white (Irish, for example) (Jankowski, 1991).

Gangs have group identities that are displayed through their names, symbols, and activities. Often individual gangs will have a distinct type of clothing that sets them apart from other gangs. These symbols of identity give gang members a strong sense of in-group feeling, which commonly leads to hostility toward out-groups. In Los Angeles, two major groups who are arch rivals are the Bloods and the Crips. The identifying color of the Bloods is red; the Crips color is blue. The Bloods and the Crips are actually two major categories, with each having many neighborhood groups subsumed under their general labels: for example, the Grape Street Crips of Watts, the Hoover Street Crips, or the Inglewood and Avenue Piru Bloods (Rheinhold, 1988).

In areas of Los Angeles where gangs thrive, a gang member who strays into the neighborhood of a rival gang or is found in the street wearing the wrong color clothing might get beaten up or even killed. Because of the dangers associated with wearing the colors of the Bloods and Crips, many Los Angeles-area schools have, for years, enforced dress codes that prohibit students from wearing either red or blue bandanas, shoelaces, or belts (Lacey, 1991). But the gangs have a new clothing fad—the wearing of professional sports team jackets and hats—that is now endangering the lives of nongang members living in Los Angeles (Lacey, 1991).

The Los Angeles Raiders football team is known widely for its black and silver colors and its menacing pirate symbol. Many Los Angeles gangs have adopted the black athletic jacket of the Raiders—it is said to be the favored attire at funerals when a gang member is killed. The problem arises when school children (and even school teachers and staff members) wear the Raiders jackets simply because they like the football team. In many Los Angeles neighborhoods they may be mistaken for members of a rival gang, and their lives may be endangered. School administrators are now banning the wearing of Raiders jackets in their schools because they fear one of their students will be mistaken for a gang member and beaten or killed (Lacey, 1991).

JANKOWSKI, MARTIN SANCHEZ, *Islands in the Street; Gangs and American Urban Society,* Berkeley: University of California Press, 1991.

LACEY, MARC. "Danger Links for Fans as Gangs Adopt Pro Attire." *Los Angeles Times,* March 20, 1991.

PADILLA, FELIX M. *The Gang as an American Enterprise.* New Brunswick, N.J.: Rutgers University Press, 1992.

RHEINHOLD, ROBERT, "In the Middle of L.A.'s Gang Warfare." *New York Times Magazine,* May 22, 1988.

**Secondary groups**, in contrast to primary groups, are typically large and impersonal. Members do not know each other as intimately or completely as do the members of a primary group. Members' ties to a secondary group are typically weaker than the ties to primary groups. Secondary groups have a less profound impact on members. They are usually formed for a specific purpose, and the members rarely interact with each other outside of the activities that are oriented toward the group goal. The members of a local Parent-Teacher's Association or a labor union are examples of secondary groups.

## Reference Groups

Another sociological perspective on groups is revealed by thinking of how groups (both primary and secondary) serve as reference groups. **Reference groups** are any groups that a person takes into account when evaluating his or her actions or characteristics. As humans we are always trying to evaluate ourselves and our behavior. Am I attractive? Am I doing a good job? Should I wear these clothes tonight? One way we answer these questions for ourselves is to refer to the performance or the qualities of the members of some group. Although individuals often use groups of which they are members as reference groups, a person does not necessarily have to be a member of a group in order to use it as a reference group. Take, for example, a woman who is making reasonably good career progress and, after some years, becomes a manager in a major corporation. If this woman's reference group is made up primarily of the circle of friends with whom she went to high school, she will undoubtedly have positive feelings about her career progress. Many of her high school friends have probably not gone on to jobs in the corporate world; compared to them she is doing well. On the other hand, if this same woman manager takes as her reference group the fastest-rising executives in her own corporation, she will evaluate her career success more negatively.

As this example shows, a reference group can be used to make comparative evaluations about oneself and one's performance. But reference groups can also provide a normative function by supplying an individual's norms and values. Thus, a young manager may not yet be a member of top management, but the latter can be his or her reference group, supplying the aspiring executive with the relevant standards of behavior. For example, if an aspiring young female manager notices that the successful female executives wear tailored suits and silk blouses, she too might stock her wardrobe with these items.

Religious group membership often provides an important reference group that has a profound influence on individual behavior. A study of U.S. adults has shown that membership in different religious groups influences attitudes toward premarital sex, birth control, and abortion (Bock et al., 1983). Research evidence also reveals that religions as reference groups influence alcohol use (Cochran et al., 1988).

A person will likely have a number of reference groups, and those groups will probably change over time. Many college students have reference groups that include students who are socially popular figures, varsity athletes, and campus leaders. After graduation some of the characteristics and qualities of these types may seem superficial and irrelevant. Whatever one's reference groups are while in college, they are likely to change dramatically when one leaves the campus and enters the business or professional world.

## Conformity: Three Classic Experiments

As the discussion of reference groups suggests, individual behavior is influenced by the groups to which one belongs and the groups to which one aspires. The tendency of individuals to respond to social groups and to allow them to influence behavior is one of the most intriguing aspects of human behavior. Americans place great value on their individualism, and yet there is ample evidence that individuals have a tendency to *conform* to the behavior of other members of a group, even when no explicit demands are made to do so. That is, people seem to want to go along with the majority of group members even when those group members do not explicitly pressure them to conform.

**The Sherif Experiment** An important study in this line of research is Muzafer Sherif's (1935) famous experiment, "A Study of Some Social Factors in Perception." Sherif was interested in studying what people would do when presented with an ambiguous phenomenon—one lacking in stable reference points. The phenomenon Sherif presented to his subjects was a single point of light in a completely dark room. Because no other objects in the room could be seen, there were no reference points, and the light appeared to move (even though it was not moving). This phenomenon is known as the *autokinetic effect.* In one part of this study individuals were first shown the light alone and then again in the presence of a group of people. When individuals alone were presented with the light, each established a sense of the distance that the light had moved. When those individuals were then placed in the same situation with a group of people, each individual's judgment of the distance that the light moved tended to converge with the judgment of the group. It appears from this experiment that individuals prefer to be closer to the standards of the group; they preferred to be in conformity.

**The Asch Experiment** In another classic experiment, Solomon Asch (1952) studied groups of seven to nine college students to examine the effect of group pressure on individuals. In each group, all but one of the members (the subject) were confederates of the researcher. The group was shown pairs of cards—the first card with a single vertical line and the second with three vertical lines. One of the lines on the second card was equal in length to the line of the first card. The other two lines were sufficiently different that, when asked to match lines on the two cards, the vast majority of people making decisions alone chose the correct line.

In the crucial experiment, Asch had his confederates choose an incorrect line on the second card. These choices were made out loud, within hearing of the subjects, who were positioned toward the end of the group. Responding in turn, subjects showed that they were experiencing group pressure, even to the extent of making the same incorrect choice. In about one-third of the cases the subjects sided with the majority and made the incorrect choice. This tendency to conform to the majority opinion appeared even when the subjects apparently knew that they were making incorrect judgments. Although this experiment demonstrates the pressure to conform to group opinions, it is important to remember that in about two-thirds of the cases the subjects resisted the majority and made the correct decision.

**The Milgram Experiment** An experiment conducted by Stanley Milgram (1974) focused on a somewhat different aspect of conformity. He was able to demonstrate that many people will comply with the orders of someone who appears to be in a position of authority in an organization (the social form we will consider next). In the Milgram experiments subjects were asked to work with other individuals who, unknown to the subjects, were paid by Milgram to act out prearranged parts. The subjects always found themselves in the position of "teacher" in the study, while the confederates served as "learners." The learners were strapped into chairs and hooked up to electrodes. The teacher-subjects were placed in another room with a fake shock generator. Labels on the generator indicated the increasing intensity of its charge—from "Slight Shock" at the low end to "Danger: Severe Shock" and, finally, "XXX" at the other end. The shocks were not real, but the teacher-subjects did not know it. They were instructed to give the learner-confederates an electric shock for every wrong answer (intentional on the part of the confederate) and to increase the amount of shock each time. Learner-confederates reacted with screams, as if pained by the shocks. Almost two-thirds of the subject-teachers continued to administer shocks to the point marked "XXX"—a level they believed was potentially lethal. The researcher, dressed in white coat and projecting an aura of scientific respectability, was perceived by most subjects as an authoritative figure whose instructions were to be followed regardless of the resulting harm to other people.

Before the study, almost all of the subjects said they would never be able to bring themselves to inflict severe pain on someone in any foreseeable circumstances. The Milgram study indicates that, under certain conditions, many people, especially if they receive orders from authority figures, will violate their own moral norms and inflict pain, perhaps even at lethal levels, on other human beings.

These experimental studies reveal how people are influenced by the behavior of other members of groups and by authority figures in organizations. Furthermore, these reactions were produced in experimentally created groups and organizational settings. It is possible that the real groups and organizations to which individuals belong (families, friendship groups, schools, workplaces, and so on) may have even more influence on member behavior. Clearly, groups and organizations can and do exert an influence on the behavior of individuals.

We are now ready to take a closer took at organizations and how they work. Of special importance is the bureaucratic form of organization that is so pervasive today.

# ORGANIZATIONS AND BUREAUCRACIES

We live in a world that is increasingly characterized by large-scale organizations. Most of us were born in large hospitals or multipurpose medical centers; we have been educated in large school systems, have often worked for major corporations or businesses, and have dealt with complex governmental systems. Major portions of our lives are spent dealing with and working in large-scale organizations. We recognize increasingly that we cannot understand the society in which we live if we do not understand how organizations work and how the many different kinds of organizations—political, economic, and social—relate to each other (Clark, 1988).

To see just how enmeshed we are with large-scale organizations, we have only to open our wallets or purses. We carry social security cards, identification cards, registration cards, driver's licenses, medical insurance cards, credit cards, and a variety of other membership cards that verify that we belong to organizations. In other words, we live in an "organizational society" (Presthus, 1978).

Sociologists use the term **organization** to describe a deliberately constructed collectivity aimed at achieving specified goals with clearly delineated statuses, roles, and rules. Thus, the U.S. Postal Service is an organization of managers, supervisors, postal clerks, mail carriers, and many others whose task it is to deliver the mail. Handgun Control is an organization established to reduce the number of handguns in U.S. society. Any neighborhood improvement association, with officers, members, and meetings, is an organization created to do something positive for a neighborhood.

These three examples show that many different types of organizations exist. Some are government agencies; some are private enterprises. Organizations may focus on causes or have special interests and may be national or local in scope.

Another way to make distinctions among types of organizations is on the basis of how control is exerted over people who exist at or near the bottom of the organization, called the *lower participants.* Three types of organizations have been identified on this basis (Etzioni, 1961).

**Coercive Organizations** A **coercive organization** uses force to control those at the bottom of the structure. The major examples of coercive organizations are prisons and custodial mental hospitals. The lower participants in such organizations are prisoners and mental patients—people who have no personal commitment to these organizations. Because they are not deeply committed to the organization and, in fact, probably have negative feelings toward it, coercion is needed to get them to do what the organization wants.

A special name given to a certain extreme type of coercive organization is the total institution (Goffman, 1961). A **total institution** is an organization that is cut off from the rest of society, forming an all-encompassing social environment to meet all the needs of its members. Not all coercive organizations are total institutions, for example, some prisons and mental institutions allow inmates considerable flexibility (for example, weekend leaves, conjugal visits, open doors). On the other hand, some total institutions may not have the key characteristics of coercive organizations. For example, many large naval ships remain at sea for weeks and even months, providing the personnel on board everything they need for a full and complete life (food, personal and medical services, entertainment and recreation, religious services, and so on). Although these ships are total institutions, the people on board are not absolutely coerced into being there.

**Utilitarian Organizations** A second type of organization is the **utilitarian organization** that uses money to control the people at the bottom. Industries and businesses are the most common types of utilitarian organizations. All employees and workers, but especially those at the bottom (clerks and those who do menial labor), are in the organization primarily for the wages they receive. Such workers are not likely to be highly committed to their organizations, although they tend to have a higher level of commitment than the lower participants in coercive organizations. They do what the organization expects of them because they are paid for it.

**Normative Organizations** Finally, in **normative** or **voluntary organizations**, participants are controlled by the norms and values of the organization. Mothers Against Drunk Drivers, which was founded in 1980 by Cindy Lighter of Fair Oaks, California, after her 13-year-old daughter was killed by a hit-and-run driver, is an example of a normative organization (Weed, 1990, 1991). M.A.D.D. chapters appeared all around the United States because people in many communities shared a concern about the needless deaths caused by drunk driving and sought to do something about the problem. Other examples of normative organizations include those organized around environmental views (Greenpeace), animal rights, and political ideologies (Young Democrats, Young Republicans). Members are committed to the organization's purposes and beliefs, and do what they can to support their causes.

## THE CULTURES OF ORGANIZATIONS

Organizations, like societies, have cultures (Trice and Beyer, 1993). Organizational cultures have symbols, beliefs, values, and norms, just like societal cultures. Researchers of organizations are increasingly paying attention to these organizational cultures, because understanding the culture helps us to understand how an organization works and even how successful it is (Peters and Waterman, 1982).

While all organizations have cultures, the elements of such cultures can be seen vividly in some of the well-known direct-selling organizations (these include familiar names such as Amway, Avon, Mary Kay Cosmetics, and Tupperware). Direct-selling organizations often place a special emphasis on symbols, and these are very likely to reflect their values.

The Mary Kay Cosmetics organization, for example, uses the color pink as one of its primary symbols, perhaps because it is associated with femininity and, by extension, the use of cosmetics. The values of ambition and enthusiasm are expressed at Mary Kay meetings when the members sing special songs, such "I've Got That Mary Kay Enthusiasm" (sung to the tune of "I've Got That Old-time Religion"). The theme of financial success is also highlighted by frequent awards ceremonies at which top sellers are presented with gold and diamond pins, fur stoles, and the ultimate symbol of success, the pink luxury automobile (Trice and Beyer, 1993).

Every organization's culture is in some ways different from every other organization's culture. But almost all organizations, especially as they grow in size, tend to become bureaucracies. The bureaucracy has become the most common form of organization in contemporary life. Although the term is often used in a negative or derogatory way, it is necessary to take a more neutral and objective look at this form of organization.

### What Is a Bureaucracy?

A **bureaucracy** is an organization with a special set of characteristics:

1. A division of labor among the members, with everyone having specialized duties and functions;
2. A well-defined rank order of authority among members;
3. A system of rules covering the rights and duties of all members in all positions;
4. Rules and procedures for carrying out all tasks;
5. Impersonality in the relations among members;
6. Selection for membership, employment, and promotion based on competence and expertise.

These typical features of a bureaucracy are what sociologists call an ideal type. An ideal type is not, as it might seem, a best possible form of something. Rather, an **ideal type** is a logical, exaggerated, and "pure" model of some phenomenon that one wishes to study or analyze. It is a methodological tool developed by the German theorist Max Weber, whom we discussed in Chapter 1 (Weber, 1903-1917/

1949). Weber developed the ideal type as a tool for analyzing and studying real bureaucracies. By specifying the characteristics of the ideal-type bureaucracy, it is possible to see if, and to what, degree, actual organizations are bureaucratic.

As an ideal type, a bureaucracy consists of a hierarchy of positions, with each position under the control and supervision of the one above it. Each position is assigned the task of performing a set of official functions, and procedures in each position are defined by a set of official rules. The individual in each position is granted the authority to carry out the functions of that position, but that authority does not extend beyond it.

For bureaucrats to apply the rules attached to their positions, they must receive specialized training. In general, only those who are formally qualified through specialized training are entitled to hold positions within a bureaucracy. Bureaucrats do not own the means of production—the offices, desks, and machines; the organization owns them and provides them to the bureaucrats as needed. Bureaucrats are not self-employed; they are employees. The written word is the hallmark of a bureaucracy because administrative acts, decisions, and rules are all put into writing.

Only the highest authority within a bureaucracy can obtain his or her position without going through bureaucratic selection procedures such as testing or presenting certain educational credentials. Often in the federal government the heads of departments or agencies are political appointees, perhaps chosen more for their special relationship with the president than for their specialized skills. Although such appointees may obtain their positions through nonbureaucratic means, their authority, like that of those below them in the bureaucracy, is limited by the position they hold.

People become bureaucrats by their own choice, not because they have inherited a position in a bureaucracy. Bureaucrats are paid a salary, which is usually directly related to their positions in the bureaucratic hierarchy. The work associated with the official title is the sole, or at least the primary, occupation of the bureaucrat and is looked upon as a career. This opens up the possibility of moving to ever-higher positions within the organization. Upward mobility is based on merit and seniority. Promotion is determined by superiors within the organization.

Remember that this ideal—typical description may not pertain to any particular organization, but it should describe the characteristics that appear to some degree in any large organization (Blau and Meyer, 1987). One of these characteristics—the authority that is invested in the positions of a bureaucracy—requires some special attention.

**Authority** refers to "legitimate" power; it is the exercise of power that is accepted by those over whom it is exerted. It probably seemed quite natural when we stated above that people in the higher positions of an organization have authority over those in positions below them. But why is this true? How does a position in an organization give someone power over others in that organization? To understand the answer to this question we must examine how authority becomes legitimate (Weber, 1921/1968).

**Legitimation of Authority** In earlier times authority came primarily from the positions into which people were born. Kings and other royal family members in times past (and even in some places today) believed they were born with the *right* to exercise power over their subjects. But equally important is the fact that the people they ruled considered it their *duty* to obey the ruler's demands. This kind of authority is legitimized by **tradition**—the way things have been done for a long time in a society or social group. While traditional authority was more common in the past, tradition can also produce legitimacy for authority in some organizations today. Subordinates accept the position of a traditional leader because they have accepted it for a long period of time or their parents and grandparents accepted it.

A second way authority can be legitimized is by the charisma a leader claims—and is believed by followers to possess. **Charisma** is the extraordinary, sometimes supernatural, qualities of a person. Leaders of revolutionary social, political, and religious movements frequently derive their authority from their charismatic qualities. Examples of charismatic political leaders are Hitler, Mao Tze-tung, Castro, and Gandhi. Charismatic religious leaders include Jesus, Mohammed, and Reverend Sun Myung Moon of the Unification Church. Even some entertainment stars are sometimes believed by their fans to have charisma or a larger-than-life quality that gives them extraordinary power. Charisma is derived more from the beliefs of the followers than from the actual qualities of leaders. As long as a person believes he or she has special qualities, or it is believed by followers, authority can be derived from charisma.

Charisma is a very short lived form of authority, generally limited to the life span of the charismatic leader and perhaps a short while thereafter. Attempts are frequently made to extend a leader's charisma beyond his or her own lifetime. This process, called the **routinization of charisma**, is accomplished when the qualities originally associated with a charismatic individual are passed on and incorporated into the characteristics of a group or organization. As an example, even after the death of Martin Luther King, the civil-rights movement in the United States was able to keep his charismatic qualities alive in order to advance the movement's objectives. Once charismatic leadership is translated into an organizational form, however, it eventually evolves into either a traditional or a rational-legal form of domination (Weber, 1921/1968).

In a system of **rational-legal authority**, leaders are legitimized by the rule of law. They derive their authority from the rules and regulations of the system rather than from their personal qualities or from tradition. For example, the office of president of the United States is legitimized by the Constitution, which defines the president's rights and responsibilities. The president's authority generally does not stem from his personal charismatic qualities or from tradition, although it may in some cases. Presidential power is legitimized because people accept the rule of law and therefore accept the president's right to exercise the power of that office. When President Kennedy was assassinated, his Vice-President, Lyndon Johnson, immediately assumed the powers of the presidency. Whether people felt about Johnson the way they had felt about Kennedy was of no importance. The rule of law prevailed.

These ideas on the sources of authority relate closely to our concern with bureaucracy. Weber argued that each form of authority would manifest itself through some form of organizational structure. Rational-legal authority, with its emphasis on adherence to carefully defined rules and regulations, is conducive to the development of bureaucratic organization, while the other forms of authority spawned other types of organizational structures. Bureaucratization is the organizational form of rational-legal authority. Weber believed that as societies become increasingly rationalized, rational-legal authority will increasingly triumph over traditional and charismatic authority. In other words, the modern world would become increasingly bureaucratized.

In the early years of this century, before bureaucratic tendencies had reached nearly the proportions they have today, Max Weber predicted the triumph of bureaucracy in the modern world. His sociological prediction proved to be correct, but he would not have been pleased. He deplored the move toward bureaucratization, saying that we were creating an "iron cage" from which there would be no escape (Mitzman, 1969). Weber thought that individuality and creativity would disappear in the face of the inexorable advance of bureaucratization. In Weber's view of the future: "Not summer's bloom lies ahead of us, but rather a polar night of icy darkness and hardness . . ." (in Gerth and Mills, 1958, p. 128).

## The Realities of Bureaucracy

In the preceding section we have examined the ideal-typical features of bureaucracies: features that can be viewed as a rational system for accomplishing large numbers of tasks or great amounts of work. Indeed, bureaucracies do exactly that. Each year in the United States billions of pieces of mail are delivered, billions of checks are processed, and millions of student grade reports are placed on college transcripts. All these tasks and many billions of others are accomplished by the people and computers of bureaucratic organizations. These monumental amounts of work are completed because the people and machines of bureaucracies apply precise rules and procedures in a uniform manner to every case processed. Also, because of the high degree of specialization, each person in a bureaucracy is doing a limited range of things in a highly repetitive manner. These features of the bureaucracy make it efficient in dealing with large numbers of tasks.

As everyone who has encountered a bureaucracy knows, however, bureaucracies are not very good at handling unusual or unique cases. The customer, or client, or student who has an out-of-the-ordinary situation or case nonetheless has the rigid rules of the bureaucracy applied, even though they are inappropriate or inapplicable. Under such circumstances many people become frustrated with bureaucracies and find them unfair as well as inefficient. But this reality of bureaucracies is just one of many that conflict with the organizational model of rationality and efficiency. We will consider a few others next.

**The Impersonal Treatment of Clients** The ideal bureaucrat is supposed to perform in a formal and impersonal manner. When bureaucrats come into contact with clients, however, the clients often perceive this behavior style as disinterest or even hostility. The impersonal treatment of clients has been called "service without a smile" (Hummel, 1987, p. 27). The client feels like a nonperson in the face of this impersonal bureaucratic treatment. Of course, now that much bureaucratic work is done by computers there is literally no live person with whom the client can interact.

**Paperwork and Red Tape** As noted earlier, the written word is the hallmark of bureaucracies. Not only is this true for the bureaucrats who must maintain written records of their actions, but it is also true for the clients of bureaucracies. Clients are frequently asked to complete various elaborate and detailed forms. Anyone who has ever applied for admission to a college, applied for a credit card, or visited a doctor knows that the first step is to fill out an application. Bureaucracies ask for many different kinds of personal information, and through their computers they are easily able to retain files on massive numbers of people. Every adult in contemporary society has left a paper trail of his or her activities through encounters with bureaucracies.

**Rules and Regulations** Bureaucracies have exact rules that are supposed to cover all situations and cases. The rules are to be followed precisely so that clients and cases will be uniformly treated. In this way the bureaucracy does not engage in favoritism and special treatment. However, sometimes the rules of the organization actually get in the way of what the organization is supposed to accomplish. The following account of an incident in a post office illustrates this point:

> I overheard a clerk telling a customer that he couldn't rent a post-office box unless he had a permanent address.
>
> "But the reason I need a box is because I don't have a permanent address," the man explained. "When you get a permanent address," the clerk politely explained, "you can get the box." "But, then I won't need it . . . " (Greenberg, 1979).

This example may be called a "Catch 22," a term first used as the title of a novel by Joseph Heller (1955). In this novel about military life during World War II, the protagonist, a bomber pilot named Yossarian wanted to be excused from flying any more bombing missions by having the doctor declare him crazy. But the doctor explained that, even though there was a rule stating that a flier could be grounded if he were crazy, there was another rule—number 22—stating that anyone who wanted to get out of combat was not really crazy. This is the origin of the phrase "Catch 22."

The term **Catch 22** has become a part of the English language and is used for a wide range of encounters with bureaucracies. Generally, the term is applied to situations in which the rules of an organization make it impossible to do what these same rules require.

**The Bureaucratic Personality** Closely related to the issue of rules is the term **bureaucratic personality**, which is the tendency for bureaucrats to conform in a slavish manner to the rules of the organization. The person with a bureaucratic personality treats the rules as more important than the task or the objective of the organization. By adopting a bureaucratic personality, the bureaucrat can avoid guilt and personal conscience in dealing with clients (Hummel, 1987). The clerk who will not accept your check because the "company policy forbids accepting checks" can avoid personal blame or guilt when turning you down.

**The Informal System.** According to the ideal-type characterization, bureaucratic organizations are built on the principle of impersonal relations among members. Members are supposed to be judged on the basis of objective measures of their performances, and relationships are based on rational principles. However, in reality, bureaucratic organizations always contain personal relationships and often close-knit social groups—primary groups of the type we discussed earlier. Some of the classic studies of sociology have shown how the informal groups in organizations, such as manufacturing plants, employment agencies, and the U.S. Army, influence behavior in ways that either subvert or override the objectives of the organization (Roethlisberger and Dickson, 1939/1964; Blau, 1963; Little, 1970).

## The Tendency toward Oligarchy

Although positions in bureaucratic organizations, including leadership positions, are supposedly based on competence and expertise, such is not always the case. Even democratic organizations have a tendency to end up being undemocratic, or oligarchic. An **oligarchy** is characterized by a small group of people at the top of the organization having almost all the control and power. An early sociologist formulated the "iron law of oligarchy" to depict this tendency (Michels, 1915/1962).

To test out his thesis, Michels focused on the most unlikely places for oligarchies to arise—socialist political parties and labor unions. He felt that if he found oligarchical tendencies in such seemingly democratic organizations, he would find them anywhere and everywhere. In fact, Michels did find the existence of oligarchy in such organizations and concluded that the tendency toward oligarchy must be an "iron law" (Michels, 1915/1962, p. 50).

Michels attributed the oligarchic tendencies of organizations, in part, to the resources that come naturally to the people in positions of leadership. The leaders have higher-quality information and more information than is held by the membership. Leaders also control the flow of information throughout the organization, through the organization's news media and by an agenda they choose to present to the organization's membership. Leaders are also likely to have and develop a higher level of political skill—making speeches, writing editorials, and organizing group activities. Michels argued that leaders of organizations place their need to continue in a dominant position over the needs, interests, and values of the organization. In other words, power becomes more important to organizational leaders than does democracy. This means that the leaders of such organizations are perfectly willing to subvert the basic democratic principles of the organization in order to maintain their power.

## Conflict in Organizations

The ideal-typical description of bureaucracy does not include conflict between individuals or groups within organizations. Yet conflict within organizations is pervasive. Of course, much conflict in organizations occurs between individuals, perhaps because they have incompatible personalities or because they are in competition for some scarce goal or resource. However, sociologists are often more interested in conflict that grows out of the characteristics of the organizations themselves (Clark, 1988; Perrow, 1986).

A major form of conflict within bureaucracies occurs when professionals such as physicians, lawyers, and scientists are employed in bureaucratic organizations. Professionals generally assume that their actions and performances should be judged and controlled only by other professionals. However, professionals employed in bureaucratic organizations are often subject to the supervision of nonprofessional superiors.

One study of Canadian doctors employed by large companies found the doctors in conflict with managers over various medical and health issues. For example, preemployment physical examinations were given to prospective employees, and the doctors were pressed by the company to disqualify any doubtful cases, even for minor medical reasons. The company wanted to minimize future risks, but this created conflicts with doctors who felt they were being pressured to violate their medical ethics. A number of other areas—plant safety, pressures on workers to return to work after injuries, and compensation for illnesses and injuries—revealed management interests that were in conflict with the medical autonomy of company doctors (Walters, 1982).

We have presented only one of many instances in which individuals or a sector of an organization has a nearly inevitable conflict with some other sector. For example, conflict almost always exists between sales and production people in industrial firms, between administrators and faculty in colleges, between doctors and nurses and administrators in hospitals, and between treatment and custodial staffs in prisons (Perrow, 1986).

## Can Bureaucracy Be Eliminated?

While Max Weber was one of the first to fear and dislike the advance of bureaucracy, he was certainly not the last. Other scholars and intellectuals, as well as politicians and average citizens, have criticized the ever-larger bureaucracies and lamented the increasing number of bureaucrats (Blau and Meyer, 1987, pp. 194-195). Most contemporary observers, however, think that the clock cannot be turned back. "As much as we may wish otherwise . . . large organizations operating on bureaucratic principles will remain part of the social landscape for some time to come" (Blau and Meyer, 1987, p. 195).

Another view of the future of bureaucratic organizations, however, sees profound changes occurring (Hage, 1988; Heydebrand, 1989). According to this view, the mindless rigidity of large bureaucracies is being replaced by smaller organizations characterized by informality and flexibility. Even though large organizations may continue to exist, their working subunits will be smaller, less formal, and more democratically organized. These working units will be mission- or task-oriented. Two decades ago, Alvin Toffler (1970) coined the word *ad-hocracies* to suggest the idea of temporary work groups composed of a wide variety of highly skilled workers brought together to solve specific, nonroutine problems.

An example of an ad-hocracy can be seen in the way a movie might be produced by a set of creative and highly skilled people. Few rigid rules would guide their behavior, because most of the time they would be dealing spontaneously with emerging problems and questions. Some people believe that more and more circumstances will occur where these more informal and flexible work groups will emerge because they are best suited for the tasks at hand (Heydebrand, 1989; Toffler, 1970).

Although some social analysts foresee a future in which bureaucratic forms of organization will decline, the fact remains that the bureaucratization of life continues to expand. In the schools where we are educated, the organizations in which we work, and in virtually every other organization we encounter in our everyday lives, the form of organization is bureaucratic (Blau and Meyer, 1987; Meyer et al., 1985). On a worldwide basis the lives of more and more people are undoubtedly touched by governments and organizations that are increasingly bureaucratic. The bureaucratic form of organization may be modified, but it will not disappear in the foreseeable future.

Organizations of the type we have been considering are parts of larger social units called institutions. Institutions will be introduced briefly at this point.

# INSTITUTIONS

An **institution** is a set of groups and organizations with norms and values that center around the most basic needs of a society. The major institutions are the family, education, the economy, health and medicine, and the polity. All these institutions are found in one form or another in all societies because they carry out necessary societal tasks. As an example, societies must have some orderly way of ensuring that males and females produce enough offspring and care for them well enough so that a sufficient number will survive and the society can continue. The institution that accomplishes these tasks is, of course, the family. Following the definition offered above, the family as an institution has identifiable groups (families and kinship units); there are norms associated with the family (for example, rules specifying how many spouses one can have); and there are values associated with the family (loyalty to family members).

Descriptions of the major institutions help to define the nature of a society. Indeed, all of the institutions, taken together, give a fairly clear view of a society. We are now ready to consider this major social unit, the society.

## SOCIETY

Although sociologists sometimes focus on large portions of the world (Chirot, 1985) or on the relationships between parts of the world (Arrow and King, 1990; Sklair, 1991; Wallerstein, 1974, 1980), the largest social entity typically studied by sociologists is the society. A society typically is the most complete, the most all-encompassing unit of sociological analysis. A society is a population living in a given territory, with a social structure, and sharing a culture.

This definition covers a wide range of actual societies and therefore encompasses considerable diversity. For example, the population size of a society can vary greatly. With a 1994 population of approximately 260 million people, the United States is a society, but other societies in the world have only a few thousand people (the Yanomamo described in Chapter 4), and some have only a few hundred. Even China, with its population of over a billion people (1.3 billion in 1994), is described as a society, although great cultural differences exist from one part of China to another.

Societies are most commonly described in terms of their economic systems. The long history of human existence has had only a few basic types of economic arrangements. We will summarize them briefly:

### Hunting and Gathering Societies

Through hundreds of thousands of years of human existence, until about 7000 B.C., all humans lived by hunting and gathering their food. They hunted wild game or fished and gathered wild fruits and plants. Hunting and gathering societies were not permanently fixed in one place, because when the supply of food declined in a particular area it was necessary to move on to another. Only a few small hunting and gathering societies still survive in the world today. One, for example, is the !Kung[1] in the Kalahari Desert of Africa, a society that has been of great interest to anthropologists. The !Kung offer anthropologists an opportunity to study a hunting and gathering society and thereby gain insights into what the lives of prehistoric peoples might have been.

### Horticultural Societies

Beginning about 9000 years ago (7000 B.C.), some humans started growing part of their own food rather than gathering foods growing wild. In horticultural societies, food is typically grown in gardenlike plots, which may be somewhat temporary in nature. When people started to grow their own food, they also established more permanent communities and were not as likely to be nomadic.

Horticultural societies can still be found in the world today, as, for example, the Gahuku people of the New Guinea Highlands (Read, 1980). The Gahuku people have small personal garden plots that they cultivate with digging sticks. They raise mostly sweet potatoes, taro, and corn, though banana trees and other wild-growing fruits also provide food. These horticultural people also raise pigs, which provide food, especially for special ceremonial occasions.

---

1 The exclamation mark before the name Kung reflects the fact that the Kung use a clicking sound in their language that does not exist in English.

## CROSS-NATIONAL PERSPECTIVES

### SOMALIA: THE COLLAPSE OF A SOCIETY

A few years ago most Americans had not heard of Somalia, and those who had were probably unsure of exactly where it was on the African continent. Today, Somalia is known to most of us because of the horrible and disturbing photographs and television images of starving, emaciated children, women, and old people. Some Americans have learned about Somalia directly because they have been sent there as part of military units whose mission was to restore order and allow emergency food shipments to reach the starving people.

Somalia is one of those rare examples of a society breaking down, almost completely. The patterns of social interaction, the order that makes societal life possible, had very nearly disappeared in Somalia in 1992. What the world saw was a population where very little food, or anything else, could be produced and distributed. The people of Somalia were mostly huddled in refugee camps, waiting, often in vain, for relief supplies of food to be delivered.

But the food that reached the ports of Somalia could often not reach the starving people. Relief ships sometimes stayed offshore because when they docked they were likely to be overwhelmed by marauding, heavily armed males. These men and teenage boys had no reluctance to fire on anyone who stood in their way. Even when food was unloaded, it was almost always intercepted by these unorganized, but very dangerous, armed men and boys.

Somalia at its chaotic and anarchic worst provided the world with a glimpse of what life is like without an organized society. The only order that existed was based on raw firepower—rifles, grenades, and small artillery pieces. Those people with guns were able to eat; those without starved and died.

The question of how Somalia reached a state of nearly complete anarchy is complex and multifaceted. Unlike many African countries, almost all the Somali people speak the same language, and more than 90 percent are of the same religion (the Sunni version of Islam) (Perlez, 1992). This would suggest an organized society, but two intrusions from the outside have contributed to the present situation. The first was nineteenth-century colonialism, when Great Britain took the northern third of the country and Italy the south (Gregory, 1992). The people under British control were made citizens of Kenya, also a British colony, and the people of the south became a part of Ethiopia. The traditional political organization of the Somalis collapsed under these conditions.

About 30 years ago, colonial control ended, but then, in succession, first by the Soviet Union and then by the United States, Somalia was used as a military base in the Cold War. Since it was on the east coast of Africa near the oil fields of the Middle East, Somalia was strategically located. The United States poured millions of dollars into the country during the 1970s and 1980s, but by 1990 Somalia was no longer as strategically valuable as it once had been and it was abandoned (Gregory, 1992).

Along with being divided by European colonial powers and being a Cold War pawn, the Somalis engaged in a war with Ethiopia in which they were routed and, thereafter, they have had sporadic clan warfare within their country. It was the clan wars that eventually led to the near-complete breakdown of the society in the 1990s and brought about the famine. These events led the United Nations and United States to intervene, and it was then that we obtained a revealing look at what life is like when a society breaks down.

Gregory, Sophfronia Scott. "How Somalia Crumbled." *Time*, December 14. 1992, p 34.

Perlez, Jane. "Somali Clans Planning Last Grab for Advantage." *New York Times*. December 9, 1992, p. A9.

## Agrarian Societies

Agrarian societies appeared in about 3000 B.C. (5000 years ago). These societies differed from the horticultural societies by their larger scale of food production. Crops were regularly planted and harvested, often with the aid of plows pulled by draft animals. Generally, the production of foods in agrarian societies was at a subsistence level, which means that the farm produce of one growing season was consumed during that year. As agricultural methods improved, however, some surpluses were produced, allowing some people in the society to engage in other kinds of productive activity. Since communities in agrarian societies could grow to larger sizes, the first cities emerged during this era.

The most prominent, early agrarian societies were in ancient Egypt, the Middle East, and China, and later in medieval Europe. Agrarian societies exist today wherever most of the people rely on agriculture for their livelihood and subsistence.

## Industrial Societies

Industrial societies are those in which the predominant economic activity is the production of manufactured goods. The Industrial Revolution, which opened the way for industrialization, is usually placed in the last half of the eighteenth century. England led the way by introducing a variety of machines, powered by steam, that produced manufactured goods in factories. Agricultural production must, of course, continue in industrial societies, but in the most highly industrialized societies only a small proportion of the population is engaged in agriculture. In the United States today, the figure is about 2 percent.

## Postindustrial Societies

A recently introduced term for describing the economic base of a society is *postindustrial society* (Bell, 1973). The **postindustrial society** describes a society that was formerly industrial but is now primarily engaged in producing services and information rather than manufactured goods. In the United States today, most people in the labor force are providing services of some kind instead of producing things.

## A Sociological Classification of Societies

While the economic systems of societies have been widely used as a basis for classification, the classic sociological way describes societies in terms of the social relationships that predominate. A question that can be asked about societies is, How do people generally relate to one another? Or, looked at historically, Do people relate to each other differently in contemporary society (especially the large urban—industrial or postindustrial—societies) than they did in societies of the past? A nineteenth-century German sociologist named Ferdinand Toennies suggested that the relationships between people are different in modern societies than in societies of the past. He labeled historical societies *gemeinschaft* and modern societies *gesellschaft* (Toennies, 1887/1957).

**Gemeinschaft societies** are characterized by very personal face-to-face relationships such as those that exist in families, in rural villages, and perhaps in small towns. These highly personal relations between people are valued for their intrinsic qualities, not for the use they might be to us.

**Gesellschaft societies** are characterized by relationships that are impersonal and distant. People interact with each other only in limited ways. The relationships are entered into only for what they might provide. Social relationships in a *gesellschaft* society are seen as means to ends.

Obviously any modern, industrial society today has both *gemeinschaft* and *gesellschaft* relationships. No society exists in which close personal relationships are totally absent. Similarly, in historical, traditional societies, people did enter some relationships for self-interested reasons. Toennies's distinction calls attention to the *prevailing* or *predominant* patterns of social relations in a society.

## SUMMARY

The way the people of any society relate to each other and organize their social lives is not random but patterned. Social structures are regular patterns of interaction and persistent social relationships. At a societal level, structures often reflect distributions of wealth, power, or authority, but structures can also be described along ethnic or racial lines.

Interaction between individuals is a complex process, but people do it with ease in their everyday lives. Although interaction has a creative and spontaneous dimension, it is patterned to some degree by cultural values and social norms.

Patterns of behavior are also produced by the statuses and roles that people occupy. Statuses are positions, and roles are the expected behaviors for a person occupying a position. However, people do not simply conform to a rigid set of role expectations, but may actively modify their roles.

Two people engaging in interaction is a dyad. When a third person is added, the dyad becomes a triad, making relationships much more complicated.

A key feature of social groups is that they are composed of a number of people who interact over time and thereby establish patterns of interaction, a group identity, and norms. Identifying with a group often produces in-group attitudes maintaining that the ways of one's own group are right and those of out-groups are wrong. Primary groups are intimate, face-to-face groups, while secondary groups are larger and more impersonal. Reference groups are groups that people take into account in evaluating their behavior, even when they are not members of those groups. Experimental studies have shown that people tend to conform to the ways of groups they are in.

Organizations and bureaucracies are increasingly important in contemporary life. Organizations, divided according to how they control the members at the bottom, can be classified as coercive, utilitarian, normative—voluntary. Bureaucracies are organized along rational-legal lines, and in an ideal—typical sense are characterized by a division of labor, rank-ordered authority, a system of rules, impersonality, and membership based on competence or expertise.

The realities of bureaucracy include impersonal treatment of clients, paperwork and red tape, scrupulous observance of rules, a tendency toward oligarchy, and conflict. Although bureaucracies are often viewed negatively, they are not likely to disappear; however, the future may see modifications and changes in bureaucratic organization.

Institutions, such as the family, education, the economy, health and medicine, and the polity, are found in all societies. It is through the institutions that necessary societal tasks are accomplished.

Societies, the largest social entity typically studied by sociologists, are commonly distinguished by their economic systems: hunting and gathering, horticultural, agrarian, industrial, and postindustrial. Sociologically, societies can be described as *gemeinschaft* or *gesellschaft* types.

## CRITICAL THINKING

1. Draw a diagram of the social structure of some set of people you know (or have known). The people could be in your living unit, in your community, or in your high school class, for example.
2. What statuses do you hold in life? Give an example of an expected behavior associated with each.
3. Are the following statuses achieved or ascribed: teacher, grandparent, female, judge, baby, nurse? How do you make the determination?
4. Give examples of groups that illustrate the primary or secondary groups. Explain how the classification is made.
5. What reference groups are most important in your life? Explain how these groups may or may not influence your behavior.

6. Describe the Sherif, Asch, and Milgram experiments. What does each show us about human behavior in groups?
7. Use today's newspaper to identify two or three organizations (using the term *organization* as sociologists would define it). Classify each organization as coercive, utilitarian, or normative.
8. The authors agree that the modern world is becoming increasingly bureaucratized. Give examples from this chapter and from your own life to support or refute this idea.
9. Give examples of both *gemeinschaft* and *gesellschaft* relationships in contemporary society.

# Chapter 8

# Deviance and Social Control

*Sirens sliced through the night as police cruisers joined in angry pursuit of the 1988 Hyundai speeding through a suburban neighborhood in Los Angeles. As the black-and-white cars closed in on their quarry, a helicopter chattered overhead, its powerful floodlight bathing the sudden eruption in a shimmering brilliance.*

*Twenty-five-year-old Rodney Glen King, the lone occupant of the Hyundai, brought his car to a halt, opened his door, and scrambled into the street. In an instant, police swarmed around him, and a sergeant lunged forward, staggering King with the discharge of a fifty-thousand-volt Taser stun gun. Unarmed, King fell to the pavement and tried to get back on his feet. As a group of eleven police looked on, three officers took turns kicking King and striking him with their clubs. By the time the beating ended, King had sustained a crushed cheekbone, a broken ankle, damage to his skull, a burn on his chest, and internal injuries.*

*The beating of an unemployed construction worker by the police might have attracted little notice except for the resident of a nearby apartment building who had observed the event—through the eyepiece of his video camera. In a matter of hours, what appeared to be a flagrant abuse of power was being replayed on television screens across the United States (Lacayo, 1991; Morrow, 1991).*

*The King beating touched off a firestorm of debate. To some critics, the incident is all too familiar: a black man being brutalized by white police for little or no reason. Sociologist and law professor Jerome Skolnick explained the need for caution in asserting that the case was racially motivated. But he concluded that "racist police are more likely to be brutal and brutal police are more likely to he racist."*

*The officers involved in the King controversy were charged with assault with a deadly weapon and use of excessive force. In a first trial, the jury acquitted the four, sparking several days of rioting in Los Angeles in which fifty-three people died. Subsequently, a federal prosecution for violating King's civil rights brought convictions for two of the officers.*

Even as the furor over the Rodney King incident subsided, many people maintain that poor people, and especially minorities, find little justice in our legal system. Others wonder if we ask the impossible of police who try to hold back a rising tide of crime and drug abuse in cities wracked by poverty. Routinely risking personal harm for low pay, police officers often see themselves embroiled in a literal war on crime, in which atrocities are committed by people on both sides.

Every society struggles to establish some notion of justice, to reward people who play by the rules, and to punish those who do not conform. But, as the Rodney King incident so vividly demonstrated, the line that separates good and evil is no simple matter of black and white. This chapter investigates many of the questions that underlie this case: How do societies create a moral code in the first place? To what extent can societies control crime? Why are some people more likely than others to be charged with offenses? And what are the legitimate purposes of the criminal justice system? We shall begin by defining several basic concepts.

## WHAT IS DEVIANCE?

**Deviance** is *the recognized violation of cultural norms.* Norms guide virtually all human activities, and so the concept of deviance covers a correspondingly broad spectrum. One distinctive category of deviance is **crime**, *the violation of norms a society formally enacts into criminal law.* Even criminal deviance is extensive, ranging from minor traffic violations to serious offenses such as rape and murder. A subcategory of crime, **juvenile delinquency**, refers to *the violation of legal standards by the young.*

Some instances of deviance barely raise eyebrows; other cases command a swift and severe response. Members of our society pay little notice to mild nonconformity like left-handedness or boastfulness; we take a dimmer view of dropping out of school, and we dispatch the police in response to a violent crime like rape.

Not all deviance involves action or even choice. For some categories of individuals, just existing may be sufficient to provoke condemnation from others. To whites who are in the majority, the mere presence of people of color may cause some discomfort. Similarly, many people of all races consider the poor disreputable to the extent that they do not measure up to conventional middle-class standards. Gay men and lesbians also confront derision and even hostility from those who are intolerant of their sexual orientation.

Examples of nonconformity that come readily to mind—stealing from a convenience store, neglecting a pet, driving while intoxicated—involve overtly breaking some rule. But since we all have shortcomings, we sometimes define especially righteous people—those who never raise their voices or are enthusiastic about paying their taxes—as deviant, even if we accord them a measure of respect (Huls, 1987). Deviant actions or attitudes, then, can be negative or positive. In either case, deviance involves *difference* that causes us to react to another person as an "outsider" (Becker, 1966).

## Social Control

All societies target their members with efforts at social control. Like norms, social control takes many forms. Socialization is a complex process by which family, peer groups, and the mass media influence people's attitudes and behavior. Conforming to approved patterns earns people praise from parents, friends, and teachers; deviance, generally speaking, provokes criticism and scorn.

Many instances of deviance prompt only informal responses, such as a scowl or a bit of "friendly advice." Charges of more serious deviance, however, may propel an individual into the **criminal justice system**, a *formal reaction to alleged violations of law on the part of police, courts, and prison officials.*

In sum, deviance is much more than a matter of individual choice or personal failing. *How* a society defines deviance, *whom* individuals target as deviant, and *what* people decide to do about nonconformity are all issues of social organization. Only gradually, however, have people recognized this essential truth, as we shall now explain.

## The Biological Context

People a century ago understood—or, more correctly, misunderstood—human behavior as an expression of biological instincts. Understandably, early interest in criminality emphasized biological causes.

### *Early Research*

In 1876 Caesare Lombroso (1835-1909), an Italian physician who worked in prisons, suggested that criminals had distinctive physical features—low foreheads, prominent jaws and cheekbones, protruding ears, hairiness, and unusually long arms that made them resemble the apelike ancestors of human beings.

Although he later acknowledged the importance of social forces in criminality, Lombroso's early theory that some people were literally born criminals was extremely popular, especially among powerful people who dismissed the idea that flaws in social arrangements might account, in part, for criminal deviance (Jones, 1986).

But the defect in Lombroso's research was that the physical features he attributed to prisoners actually existed throughout the entire population. We now know that there are no physical attributes, of the kind described by Lombroso, distinguishing criminals and noncriminals (Goring, 1972; orig. 1913).

### *Delinquency and Body Structure*

Although Lombroso's theory had been discredited, William Sheldon (1949) suggested that body structure might be related to criminality. He categorized hundreds of young men in terms of body type and, checking for any criminal history, concluded that delinquency was most likely among boys with muscular, athletic builds.

Sheldon Glueck and Eleanor Glueck (1950) confirmed Sheldon's conclusion. They cautioned, however, that a powerful build is not necessarily a cause of criminality. Parents, they suggested, treat powerfully built males with greater emotional distance so that they, in turn, grow up to display less sensitivity toward others. Moreover, if people expect muscular, athletic boys to act like bullies, they may treat them accordingly, thereby prompting aggressive behavior in a self-fulfilling prophecy.

## GENETIC RESEARCH

To date, there exists no conclusive evidence that criminality is the product of any specific genetic flaw. What is likely, however, is that people's overall genetic composition, in combination with social influences, accounts for some variation in criminality. In other words, biological factors probably have a real, if modest, effect on whether or not individuals engage in criminal activity (Rowe, 1983; Rowe & Osgood, 1984 Wilson & Herrnstein, 1985: Jencks, 1987).

Sociobiologists continue to investigate possible connections between genetics and crime. They note, for example, that men commit far more violence than women and that parents are more likely to abuse disabled or foster children than healthy or natural children (Daly & Wilson, 1988).

**Critical Evaluation** Biological theories that try to explain crime in terms of rare physical traits of individuals can, at best, explain only a small proportion of all crimes. Recent sociobiological research is promising, but, at this point, we know too little about the links between genes and human behavior to draw firm conclusions.

In any case, an individualistic biological approach cannot address the issue of how some kinds of behaviors come to be defined as deviant in the first place. Therefore, although there is much to be learned about how human biology may affect behavior, research currently places far greater emphasis on social influences (Gibbons & Krohn, 1986; Liska, 1991).

### Personality Factors

Like biological theories, psychological explanations of deviance focus on cases of individual abnormality, this time involving personality. Some personality traits are hereditary, but psychologists think that temperament is mostly a product of social experiences. Therefore, they explain the outbreak of deviance as the result of "unsuccessful" socialization.

The work of Walter Reckless and Simon Dinitz (1967) illustrates a psychological approach to explaining juvenile delinquency. These researchers began by asking teachers to identify boys about age twelve who seemed likely and unlikely to engage in delinquent acts. Interviews with both categories of boys and their mothers provided information on each boy's self-concept—how he viewed himself and how he related to others. The "good boys" displayed a strong conscience (or *superego*, in Sigmund Freud's terminology), coped well with frustration, and identified positively with cultural norms and values. The "bad boys," by contrast, had a weaker conscience, displayed little tolerance for frustration, and identified less with conventional culture.

Over a four-year period, the researchers found that the "good boys" did have fewer contacts with the police than the "bad boys." Since all the boys studied lived in areas where delinquency was widespread, the investigator attributed staying out of trouble to a personality that reined in impulses toward deviance. Based on this conclusion, Reckless and Dinitz call their analysis *containment theory*.

**Critical Evaluation** Psychological research has demonstrated that personality patterns have some connection to delinquency and other types of deviance. Nevertheless, the value of this approach is limited by a key fact: The vast majority of serious crimes are committed by people whose psychological profiles are *normal.*

In sum, both biological and psychological approaches view deviance as an individual attribute without exploring how conceptions of right and wrong initially arise, why people define some rule breakers but not others as deviant, and the role of social power in shaping a society's system of social control. We now turn to these issues by delving into sociological explanations of deviance.

## The Social Foundations of Deviance

Although we tend to view deviance in terms of the free choice or personal failings of individuals, all behavior—deviance as well as conformity—is shaped by society. Three *social* foundations of deviance, identified below, are detailed in later sections of the chapter.

1. **Deviance varies according to cultural norms.** No thought or action is inherently deviant; it becomes deviant only in relation to particular norms. The life patterns of rural Vermonters, small-town Texans, and urban Californians differ in significant ways; for this reason, what people in each category prize or scorn varies also. Laws, too, differ from place to place. Texans, for example, can legally consume alcohol in a car, a practice that draws the attention of police in most other states. Casinos are a focal point in Atlantic City, New Jersey, Las Vegas, Nevada, and on a few Indian reservations elsewhere; such gambling is illegal everywhere else in the United States. Further, most cities and towns have at least one unique statute: Only in Seattle, for example, is a person suffering from the flu subject to arrest simply for appearing in public.

   In global context, deviance is even more diverse. Albania outlaws any public display of religious faith, such as "crossing" oneself; Cuba can prosecute its citizens for "consorting with foreigners"; police can arrest people in Singapore for selling chewing gum; U.S. citizens risk arrest by their own government for traveling to Libya or Iraq.

2. **People become deviant as others define them that way.** Each of us violates cultural norms, perhaps even to the extent of breaking the law. For example, most of us have at some time walked around talking to ourselves or "borrowed" supplies, such as pens and paper, from the work-place. Whether such activities are sufficient to define us as mentally ill or criminal depends on how others perceive, define, and respond to any given situation.

3. **Both rule making and rule breaking involve social power.** Karl Marx viewed norms, and especially law, to be a strategy by which powerful people protect their interests. For example, the owners of an unprofitable factory have a legal right to close their business, even if doing so puts thousands of people out of work. If workers commit an act of vandalism that closes the same factory for a single day, however, they are subject to criminal prosecution. Similarly, a homeless person who stands on a street corner denouncing the city government risks arrest for disturbing the peace; a mayoral candidate during an election campaign does exactly the same thing while receiving extensive police protection. In short, norms and their application are linked to social inequality.

# STRUCTURAL-FUNCTIONAL ANALYSIS

We now turn to exactly how deviance is inherent in the operation of society. The structural-functional paradigm examines how deviance makes important contributions to a social system.

## Emile Durkheim: The Functions of Deviance

Emile Durkheim's (1964a, orig. 1895; 1964b, orig. 1893) pioneering study of deviance began by noting that there is nothing abnormal about deviance since it performs four functions essential to society.

1. **Deviance affirms cultural values and norms.** Culture involves moral choices: People must prefer some attitudes and behaviors to others. Conceptions of what is morally right exist only in opposition to notions of what is wrong. Just as there can be no righteousness without evil, there can be no justice without crime. Deviance, in short, is indispensable to the process of generating and sustaining morality.
2. **Responding to deviance clarifies moral boundaries.** By defining people as deviant, a society sets the boundary between right and wrong. For example, a college marks the line between academic honesty and cheating by imposing disciplinary procedures on those who commit plagiarism.
3. **Responding to deviance promotes social unity.** People typically react to serious deviance with collective outrage. In doing so, Durkheim explained, they reaffirm the moral ties that bind them. For example, most members of our society joined together in condemning a rash of shootings of foreign tourists in Miami during 1993.
4. **Deviance encourages social change.** Deviant people, Durkheim claimed, patrol a society's moral boundaries, suggesting alternatives to the status quo and encouraging change. Today's deviance, he declared, may well become tomorrow's morality (1964a:71). In the 1950s, for example, many people denounced rock and roll music as a threat to the morals of youth and an affront to traditional musical tastes. Since then, however, rock and roll has been swept up in the musical mainstream and become a multibillion dollar industry perhaps more "all-American" than apple pie.

### *An Illustration: The Puritans of Massachusetts Bay*

Durkheim's functional analysis of deviance is supported by Kai Erikson's (1966) historical investigation of the early Puritans of Massachusetts Bay. This highly religious "society of saints," Erikson discovered, created deviance to clarify various moral boundaries. Durkheim explained this process using words that apply well to the Puritans.

> Imagine a society of saints, a perfect cloister of exemplary individuals. Crimes, properly so called, will there be unknown; habit faults which appear [insignificant] to the layman will create there the same scandal that the ordinary offense does in ordinary consciousness. . . . For the same reason, the perfect and upright man judges his smallest failings with a severity that the majority reserve for acts more truly in the nature of an offense. (1964a:68-69)

Deviance, in short, is inevitable in society, however righteous individuals may be.

The kind of deviance the Puritans created changed over time, depending on the moral issues they confronted. How much dissent to allow, how to respond to outsiders, what their religious goals should be—they resolved all these questions in the process of celebrating some of their members while condemning others as deviant.

Finally, Erikson discovered, although the reasons for deviance changed, the Puritans declared a steady proportion of their number as deviant over time. Erikson saw this stability as support for Durkheim's idea that deviants served as moral markers, outlining a society's changing moral boundaries. By constantly defining a small number of people as deviant, in sum, Puritan society ensured that the social functions of deviance were carried out.

## Merton's Strain Theory

While some deviance is inevitable in all societies, Robert Merton (1938, 1968) argues that excessive deviance arises from particular social arrangements. Merton's theory is concerned with cultural *goals* (such as financial success) and the *means* (such as schooling and hard work) available to achieve them. The essence of conformity, then, is pursuing conventional goals by approved means.

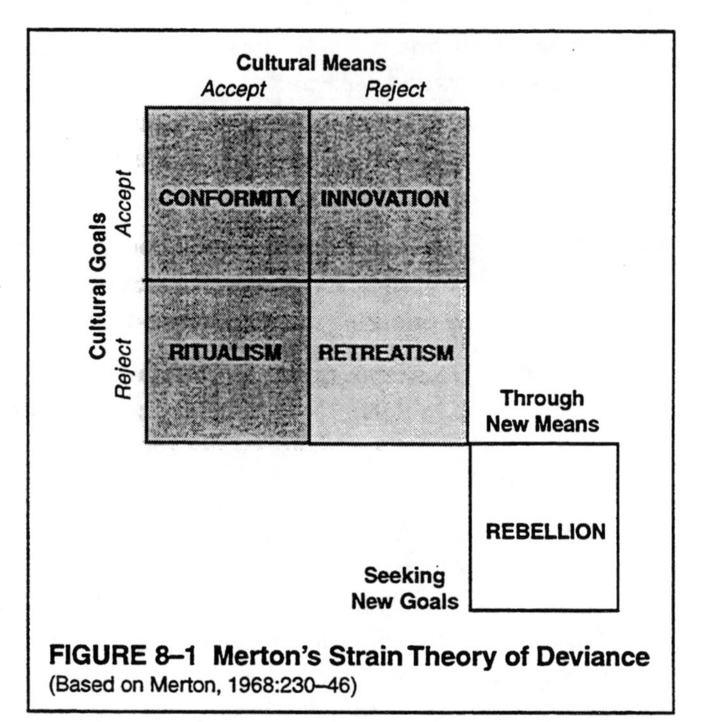


**FIGURE 8–1 Merton's Strain Theory of Deviance**
(Based on Merton, 1968:230–46)

But not everyone who desires conventional success has the opportunity to achieve it. Young people raised in poor inner-city neighborhoods, for example, may see little hope of becoming successful if they "play by the rules." As a result, they may seek wealth through one or another kind of crime—say, by dealing cocaine. Merton called this type of deviance *innovation*—the attempt to achieve a culturally approved goal (wealth) using unconventional means (drug sales). Figure 8-1 shows that innovation involves accepting the goal of success while rejecting the conventional means of becoming rich.

This kind of deviance, according to Merton, results from "strain" between our society's emphasis on material success and the limited opportunity it provides to become successful. The poor, especially, may respond to this dilemma by engaging in what we conventionally define as theft, selling illegal drugs, or other forms of street hustling. The box on page 219 highlights the life of mobster Al Capone to explain why, historically, Merton's "innovation" has been attractive to people at the margins of our society.

The inability to become successful by normative means may also prompt another type of deviance that Merton calls *ritualism* (see Figure 8-1). Ritualists resolve the strain of limited success by abandoning cultural goals in favor of almost compulsive efforts to live "respectably." In essence, they embrace the rules to the point that they lose sight of goals entirely. Lower level bureaucrats, Merton suggests, often succumb to ritualism as a way of gaining respectability.

A third response to the inability to succeed is *retreatism*—the rejection of cultural goals and means as a form of dropping out. Retreatist include some alcoholics and drug addicts, and some of the street people common to U.S. cities. The deviance of retreatists lies in unconventional living and, perhaps more seriously, accepting this situation.

The fourth response to failure is *rebellion*. Like retreatists, rebels reject both the cultural definition of success and the normative means of achieving it. Rebels, however, go one step further by advocating radical alternatives to the existing social order. They may promote unconventional values and norms using political or religious language and withdraw from society, forming a counterculture.

## Deviant Subcultures

Richard Cloward and Lloyd Ohlin (1966) extended Merton's theory in their investigation of delinquent youth. They maintain that criminal deviance results not simply from limited legitimate opportunity but also from available illegitimate opportunity. In short, deviance or conformity follow from the *relative opportunity structure* that young people face in their lives.

The life of Al Capone shows how ambitious individuals denied legitimate opportunity could take advantage of organized crime to forge a successful career. Where illegal opportunities predominate, Cloward and Ohlin predict the development of *criminal subcultures* that offer the knowledge, skills, and other resources people need to succeed in unconventional ways.

But, especially in poor and highly transient neighborhoods, even illegal opportunity may be lacking. Here, delinquency is likely to surface in the form of *conflict subcultures* where violence is ignited by frustration and a desire for fame or respect. Alternatively, those who fail to achieve success, even using

## SOCIAL DIVERSITY

### AL CAPONE: CRIME AND SOCIAL MARGINALITY

At the onset of Prohibition, which outlawed alcoholic beverages in the United States between 1920 and 1933, Al Capone seized the opportunity to build a vast criminal empire. For someone willing to take the risk, there was an enormous amount of money to be made in bootlegging.

Capone rose to power and gained great wealth during an era when U.S. cities bustled with millions of European immigrants, most poor but eager to share in the American Dream of success. Condemned by their backgrounds, their languages, and their religions to second-class citizenship, immigrants collided time and again with barriers of prejudice and discrimination. The vast majority nonetheless patiently remained "conformists," in Merton's terminology, hoping that their lives would improve with the passing of time.

But some saw in organized crime a means to achieve their goals. So it was that Alphonse Capone—a brilliant and ambitious man, yet socially handicapped by having grown up in an Italian slum in New York City—came to dominate one of the largest criminal empires of our history.

Capone's life exemplifies Merton's "innovator," an individual who pursues the culturally approved goal of success according to unconventional means. For people like Al Capone, this type of deviance is a product of ambition coupled to a lack of legitimate opportunity. In the words of one analyst of the criminal underworld:

> The typical criminal of the Capone era was a boy who had . . . seen what was rated as success in the society he had been thrust into—the Cadillac, the big bankroll, the elegant apartment. How could he acquire that kind of recognizable status? He was almost always a boy of outstanding initiative, imagination, and ability; he was the kind of boy who, under different conditions, would have been a captain of industry or a key political figure of his time. But he hadn't the opportunity of going to Yale and becoming a banker or broker; there was no passage for him to a law degree from Harvard. There was, however, a relatively easy way of acquiring these goods that he was incessantly told were available to him as an American citizen, and without which he had begun to feel he could not properly count himself as an American citizen. He could become a gangster. (Allsop, 1961:236)

But even those gangsters who managed to garner wealth and power lacked the prestige accorded to members of more "respectable" families. Thus many distanced themselves from their ethnic origins by, for example, changing their names. Capone's first employer was a fellow immigrant and reputed Mafia boss who called himself Mr. Frankie Yale and ran a speakeasy on Coney Island that he named the Harvard Inn. Similarly, as the leader of the Chicago rackets, Capone demanded that others address him as Anthony Brown and surrounded himself with men who displayed none of the ethnic traits he sought to leave behind.

Capone even engaged in the public generosity favored by many upper-class people when, during the Depression, he provided food to Chicago's poor. Later he enrolled his son Anthony at prestigious Yale University, and subsequently he celebrated the young man's wedding to a well-to-do woman from Nashville.

Surely one of the most notorious U.S. criminals of this century, "Scarface" Al Capone modeled his life on achieving the American Dream. His deviance—like that of thousands of young people dealing drugs in today's cities—was motivated by hunger for success amid limited opportunity.

SOURCES: Allsop (1961) and Baltzell (1964).

criminal means, may embrace *retreatist subcultures* that advocate dropping out through abuse of alcohol or other drugs.

Albert Cohen (1971) suggests that delinquency is most pronounced among lower-class youths because society offers them little opportunity to achieve success in conventional ways. Because conventional definitions of success call for achieving wealth and all its trappings, they find little basis for self-respect in their impoverished condition. In response, they may create a delinquent subculture that "defines as meritorious the characteristics [these youths] *do* possess, the kinds of conduct of which they *are* capable" (1971:66). For example, because the dominant culture values the calculated pursuit of wealth, a delinquent subculture may extol stealing "for the hell of it."

Walter Miller (1970) agrees that delinquent subcultures typically develop among lower-class youths who contend with the least legitimate opportunity. He describes six focal concerns of delinquent subcultures: (1) *trouble*, arising from frequent conflict with teachers and police; (2) *toughness*, the value placed on physical size, strength, and athletic skills, especially among males; (3) *smartness*, the ability to succeed on the streets, to outthink or "con" others, and to avoid being similarly taken advantage of; (4) *excitement*, the search for thrills, risk, or danger to gain needed release from a daily routine that is predictable and unsatisfying; (5) a concern with *fate*, derived from the lack of control these youths feel over their own lives; and (6) *autonomy*, a desire for freedom often expressed as resentment toward figures of authority.

## Hirschi's Control Theory

A final argument that builds on Durkheim's analysis of deviance is Travis Hirschi's (1969) *control theory*. Hirschi assumes that everyone finds at least some deviance tempting; what requires explanation is not deviance, but *conformity*. He suggests that conformity arises from four types of social controls.

1. **Attachment.** Strong social attachments to others encourage conformity; weak relationships in the family, peer group, and school leave people freer to engage in deviance.
2. **Commitment.** The higher one's commitment to legitimate opportunity, the greater the advantages of conformity. A young person bound for college, with good career prospects, has a high stake in conformity. In contrast, someone with little confidence in future success is more likely to drift toward deviance.
3. **Involvement.** Extensive involvement in legitimate activities—such as holding a job, going to school and completing homework, or pursuing hobbies—inhibits deviance. People with little legitimate involvement—who simply "hang out" waiting for something to happen—have time and energy for deviant activity.
4. **Belief.** Strong beliefs in conventional morality and respect for authority figures also restrain tendencies toward deviance; people with weak beliefs are more vulnerable to temptations toward deviance.

Hirschi's analysis explains many kinds of deviant behavior, and it has gained support from subsequent research. Here, again, a person's location in society as well as strength of moral convictions are crucial in generating a stake in conformity or allowing everyday temptations to cross the line into actual deviance (Wiatrowski, Griswold, & Roberts, 1981; Sampson & Laub, 1990; Free, 1992).

**Critical Evaluation** Durkheim's pioneering work in the functions of deviance remains central to sociological thinking. Even so, recent critics point out that a community does not always come together in reaction to crime; sometimes fear of crime drives people to withdraw from public life (Liska & Warner, 1991).

Derived from Durkheim's analysis, Merton's strain theory has also come under criticism for explaining some kinds of deviance (theft, for example) far better than others (such as crimes of passion or mental illness). In addition, not everyone seeks success in conventional terms of wealth, as strain theory implies. Members of our society embrace many different cultural values and are motivated by various notions of personal success.

The general argument of Cloward and Ohlin, Cohen, Miller, and Hirschi—that deviance reflects the opportunity structure of society—has been confirmed by subsequent research (Allan & Steffensmeier, 1989). However, these theories, too, fall short in assuming that everyone shares the same cultural standards for judging right and wrong. Moreover, we must be careful not to define deviance in ways that unfairly focus attention on poor people. If crime is defined to include stock fraud as well as street theft, criminals are more likely to include affluent individuals. Finally, all structural-functional theories imply that everyone who violates conventional cultural standards will be defined as deviant. Becoming deviant, however, is actually a highly complex process, as the next section explains.

## SYMBOLIC-INTERACTION ANALYSIS

The symbolic-interaction paradigm directs attention to how people construct reality in countless everyday settings. Applied to deviance, this theoretical orientation reveals that definitions of deviance and conformity are surprisingly flexible.

### Labeling Theory

The central contribution of symbolic-interaction analysis is **labeling theory**, *the assertion that deviance and conformity result, not so much from what people do, but from how others respond to those actions.* Labeling theory stresses the relativity of deviance, meaning the same behavior may be defined in any number of ways. Howard S. Becker claims that deviance is, therefore, nothing more than "behavior that people so label" (1966:9).

Consider these situations: A woman takes an article of clothing from a roommate; a married man at a convention in a distant city has sex with a prostitute; a member of Congress drives home intoxicated after a party. The reality of each situation depends on the response of others. We might define the first situation as borrowing or as theft. The consequences of the second case depend largely on whether the news of the man's behavior follows him back home. In the third situation, is the official an active socialite or a dangerous drunk? The social creation of reality, then, is a highly variable process of detection, definition, and response.

People sometimes contend with deviant labels for involvement in situations completely beyond their control. For example, victims of violent rape are sometimes subjected to labeling as deviants because of the misguided assumption that they must have encouraged the offender. Similarly, individuals with acquired immune deficiency syndrome (AIDS) sometimes find that they are shunned by employers, friends, and even family members.

#### *Primary and Secondary Deviance*

Edwin Lemert (1951, 1972) notes that many episodes of norm violation are insignificant and transitory, provoking little reaction from others and with little effect on a person's self-concept. Lemert calls such passing episodes *primary deviance.*

But what happens if other people take notice of someone's deviance and make something of it? If, for example, people begin to think of a boisterous friend as an unsuitable social companion, that person, feeling left out, might become angry, escalating criticism from others. Such a response is *secondary deviance*, which may take the form of defending deviant actions, lying about them, or getting used to them. In other words, in response to people's reaction to some earlier violation, an individual adopts secondary deviance as a role with far greater consequences for social identity and self-definition. Initial labeling, then, can encourage individuals to develop deviant identities, thereby fulfilling the expectations of others.

### *Stigma*

The onset of secondary deviance marks the emergence of what Erving Goffman (1963) called a *deviant career*. Typically, this occurs as a consequence of acquiring a **stigma**, *a powerfully negative social label that radically changes a person's self-concept and social identity*.

Stigma operates as a master status overpowering other dimensions of social identity so that an individual is diminished and discounted in the minds of others and, consequently, socially isolated. Sometimes an entire community formally stigmatizes individuals through what Harold Garfinkel (1956) calls a *degradation ceremony*. A criminal prosecution is one example, operating much like a high school graduation except that people stand before the community to be labeled in a negative rather than a positive way.

### *Retrospective Labeling*

Once people have stigmatized a person, they may engage in **retrospective labeling**, *the interpretation of someone's past consistent with present deviance* (Scheff, 1984). For example, after discovering that a priest who has worked for years with children has sexually molested a child, others rethink his past, perhaps musing, "He always did want to be around young children." Obviously, retrospective labeling involves a highly selective and prejudicial view of a person's biography, guided more by the present stigma than by any attempt to be fair. But this process may nonetheless deepen a person's deviant identity.

### *Labeling and Mental Illness*

Labeling theory is especially applicable to mental illness, since a person's mental condition is difficult to define. Psychiatrists often assume that mental disorders have a concrete reality similar to diseases of the body. There is truth to this, insofar as heredity, diet, stress, and chemical imbalances in the body do account, in part, for mental disturbances. However, what we call "mental illness" is also a matter of social definitions people sometimes make with the intention of forcing others to conform to conventional standards (Thoits, 1985).

Is a woman who believes that Jesus rides the bus to work with her every day seriously deluded or merely expressing her religious faith in a highly graphic way? If a man refuses to bathe, much to the dismay of his family, is he insane or simply unconventional? Is a homeless woman who refuses to allow police to take her to a city shelter on a cold night mentally ill or simply trying to live independently?

Psychiatrist Thomas Szasz charges that the label of insanity is widely applied to what is actually only "difference"; therefore, he claims, the notion of mental illness should be abandoned (1961, 1970; Vatz & Weinberg, 1983). Illness, Szasz argues, afflicts only the body, making mental illness a myth. Being "different" in thought or action may irritate others, but it is no grounds on which to define someone as sick. To do so, Szasz claims, simply enforces conformity to the standards of people powerful enough to get their way.

Szasz's views have provoked controversy; many of his colleagues reject the notion that all mental illness is a fiction. Others have hailed his work, however, for pointing out the danger of abusing medical practice in the interest of promoting conformity. Most of us, after all, have experienced periods of extreme stress or other mental disability at some time in our lives. Such episodes, although upsetting, are usually of passing importance. If, however, they form the basis of a social stigma, they may lead to further deviance as a self-fulfilling prophecy (Scheff, 1984).

## The Medicalization of Deviance

Labeling theory, particularly the ideas of Szasz and Goffman, helps to explain an important shift in the way we understand deviance. Over the last fifty years, the growing influence of psychiatry and medicine in the United States has encouraged the **medicalization of deviance**, *the transformation of moral and legal issues into medical matters*. In essence, medicalization amounts to a change in labels. Conventional moral judgment involves calling people or their behavior "bad" or "good." However, the scientific objectivity of modern medicine passes no moral judgment, instead utilizing clinical diagnoses such as "sick" and "well."

To illustrate, until the middle of this century, people generally viewed alcoholics as weak and morally deficient people easily tempted by the pleasure of drink. Gradually, however, medical specialists redefined alcoholism so that most people now consider alcoholism a disease, rendering individuals "sick" rather than "bad." Similarly, obesity, drug addiction, child abuse, promiscuity, and other behaviors that used to be a matter of morality are today widely defined as illnesses for which those afflicted need help rather than punishment.

### *The Complex Case of Homosexuality*

Some forms of behavior have been defined and redefined over time. For centuries, most women and men in the United States considered homosexuality a moral issue, a straightforward example of being "bad" against a heterosexual standard of "good." But the American Psychiatric Association (APA) in 1952 officially declared being gay or lesbian a "sociopathic personality disturbance." In the wake of this pronouncement by medical authorities, by 1970 two-thirds of adults agreed that homosexuality was a "sickness that could be cured."

More recently, however, homosexual and bisexual people have asserted that they may be *different* without being *deviant* at all. Supporters of this view note the lack of success in "curing" homosexuality and the growing evidence that sexual orientation is a matter of biology rather than personal choice. In 1974, the APA switched again, redefining homosexuality as simply a "form of sexual behavior" (Conrad & Schneider, 1980:193-209).

Furthermore, people who oppose all deviant labels for gays have countered traditional prejudices by defining hostility toward homosexuals as "homophobia." This strategy suggests that deviance may lie in "conventional" people and not those they victimize.

### *The Significance of Labels*

Whether we define deviance as a moral or medical issue has three profound consequences. First, it affects who *responds* to deviance. An offense against common morality typically provokes a reaction by citizens or police. Applying medical labels, however, places the situation under the control of clinical specialists, including counselors, psychiatrists, and physicians.

A second difference is *how people respond* to a deviant. A moral approach defines the deviant as an "offender" subject to punishment. Medically, however, "patients" need treatment (for their own good, of course). Therefore, while punishment is designed to fit the crime, treatment programs are tailored to the patient and may involve virtually any therapy that a specialist thinks will prevent future deviance (von Hirsh, 1986).

Third, and most important, the two labels differ on the issue of *the personal competence of the deviant person.* Morally, people take responsibility for their own behavior; we all do wrong, in other words, but at least we understand what we are doing and must face the consequences. Medically speaking, however, if we are sick we are no longer responsible for what we do. Defined as personally incompetent and unaware of what is in our own best interest, we become vulnerable to more intense, often involuntary, treatment. For this reason alone, attempts to define deviance in medical terms should be made only with extreme caution.

## Sutherland's Differential Association Theory

Related to the issue of how we view others' behavior is how we come to define our own. Edwin Sutherland (1940) suggested that we learn social patterns, including deviance, through association with others, especially in primary groups.

We all encounter forces promoting criminality as well as those supporting conformity. The likelihood that a person will engage in criminal activity depends upon the frequency of association with those who encourage norm violation compared with those who encourage conformity. This is Sutherland's theory of *differential association.*

Sutherland's theory is illustrated by a study of drug and alcohol use among young adults in the United States (Akers et al., 1979). Analyzing responses to a questionnaire completed by junior and senior high school students, researchers discovered a close link between the extent of alcohol and drug use and the degree to which peer groups encouraged such activity. The investigators concluded that young people embrace delinquent patterns as they receive praise and other rewards for defining deviance rather than conformity in positive terms.

**Critical Evaluation** Labeling theory links deviance not to *action* but to the *reaction* of others. Thus some people are defined as deviant while others who think or behave in the same way are not. The concepts of stigma, secondary deviance, and deviant career demonstrate how people sometimes incorporate the label of deviance into a lasting self-concept.

Yet labeling theory has several limitations. First, because this theory takes a highly relative view of deviance, it glosses over how some kinds of behavior, such as murder, are condemned virtually everywhere (Wellford, 1980). Labeling theory is thus most usefully applied to less serious deviance, such as sexual behavior and mental illness.

Second, the consequences of deviant labeling are unclear: Research is inconclusive as to whether deviant labeling produces subsequent deviance or discourages further violations (Smith & Gartin, 1989; Shermin & Smith, 1992).

Third, not everyone resists the label of deviance; some people may actually want to be defined as deviant (Vold & Bernard, 1986). For example, individuals may engage in civil disobedience leading to arrest to call attention to social injustice.

While Sutherland's differential association theory has had considerable influence in sociology, it provides little insight into why society's norms and laws define certain kinds of activities as deviant in the first place. This important question is addressed by social-conflict analysis, described in the next section.

## SOCIAL-CONFLICT ANALYSIS

The social-conflict paradigm links deviance to social inequality. This approach suggests that who or what is labeled as deviant depends on the relative power of categories of people.

### Deviance and Power

Alexander Liazos (1972) points out that the term "deviance" brings to mind "nuts, sluts, and 'preverts'" who share the trait of powerlessness. Bag ladies (not tax evaders) and unemployed men on street corners (not those who profit from wars) carry the stigma of deviance.

Social-conflict theory explains this pattern in three ways. First, the norms—including laws—of any society generally reflect the interests of the rich and powerful. People who threaten the wealthy, either by taking their property or by advocating a more egalitarian society, may be readily defined as "common thieves" or "political radicals." Karl Marx argued that all social institutions tend to support the capitalist economic system and protect the interests of the rich, capitalist class. Echoing Marx, Richard Quinney makes the point succinctly: "Capitalist justice is by the capitalist class, for the capitalist class, and against the working class" (1977:3).

Second, even if their behavior is called into question, the powerful have the resources to resist deviant labels. Corporate executives who might order the dumping of hazardous wastes are rarely held personally accountable for these acts. While such actions pose dangers for all of society, they are not necessarily viewed as criminal.

Third, the widespread belief that norms and laws are natural and good masks their political character. For this reason, we may condemn the *unequal application* of the law but give little thought to whether the *laws themselves* are inherently fair (Quinney, 1977).

## Deviance and Capitalism

Steven Spitzer (1980) argues that deviant labels are applied to people who impede the operation of capitalism. First, because capitalism is based on private control of property, people who threaten the property of others—especially the poor who steal from the rich—are prime candidates for labeling as deviants. Conversely, the rich who exploit the poor are unlikely to be defined as deviant. Landlords, for example, who charge poor tenants high rents and evict those who cannot pay are not considered a threat to society; they are simply "doing business."

Second, because capitalism depends on productive labor, those who cannot or will not work risk deviant labeling. Many members of our society think of people who are out of work—even if through no fault of their own—as deviant.

Third, capitalism depends on respect for figures of authority, so people who resist authority are generally labeled as deviant. Examples are children who skip school or talk back to parents and teachers; adults who do not cooperate with employers or police; and anyone who opposes "the system."

Fourth, capitalism rests on the widespread acceptance of the status quo; those who undermine or challenge the capitalist system are subject to deviant labeling. In this category fall antiwar activists, environmentalists, labor organizers, and anyone who endorses an alternative economic system.

To turn the argument around, people label positively whatever enhances the operation of capitalism. Winning athletes, for example, have celebrity status because they express the values of individual achievement and competition vital to capitalism. Additionally, Spitzer notes, we define using drugs of escape (marijuana, psychedelics, heroin, and crack) as deviant, while embracing drugs that promote adjustment to the status quo (such as alcohol and caffeine).

People who are a "costly yet relatively harmless burden" on society, says Spitzer, include Robert Merton's retreatists (for example, those addicted to alcohol or other drugs), the elderly, and people with physical disabilities, mental retardation, and mental illness. These people are subject to control by social welfare agencies. But those who directly threaten the capitalist system, including the inner-city "underclass" and revolutionaries—Merton's innovators and rebels—come under the purview of the criminal justice system and, in times of crisis, military forces such as the National Guard.

Note that both the social welfare and criminal justice systems apply labels that place responsibility for social problems on individuals rather than the social system. Welfare recipients are deemed unworthy free-loaders; poor people who vent their rage at their plight are labeled rioters; anyone who actively challenges the government is branded a radical or a communist; and those who attempt to gain illegally what they cannot otherwise acquire are called common thieves.

## White-Collar Crime

Until 1989, few people other than Wall Street stockbrokers had ever heard of Michael Milken. Yet Milken had accomplished a stunning feat, becoming the highest paid U.S. worker in half a century. With salary and bonuses in 1987 totaling $550 million—*about $1.5 million a day*—Milken ranks behind only Al Capone, whose earnings in 1927 reportedly reached $600 million in current dollars (Swartz, 1989). Milken has something else in common with Capone: The government accused him of criminality, in this case, breaching securities and exchange laws. Milken's activities exemplify **white-collar crime**, defined by Edwin Sutherland in 1940 as *crimes committed by persons of high social position in the course of their occupations* (Sutherland & Cressey, 1978). As the Milken case suggests, white-collar crime rarely involves uniformed police converging on a scene with drawn guns and does not refer to crimes such as murder assault, or rape that are committed by people of high social position. Instead, white-collar crimes are acts by powerful people making use of their occupational positions to enrich themselves or others illegally, often causing significant public harm in the process (Hagan & Parker, 1985; Vold & Bernard, 1986). For this reason, sociologists sometimes call white-collar offenses that occur in government offices and corporate board rooms crime in the suites as opposed to *crime in the streets.*

The most common white-collar crimes are bank embezzlement, tax fraud, credit fraud, bribery, and antitrust violations. Most cases of white-collar crime, like most street crimes, involve relatively little money and cause limited harm to individuals. But the occasional major crime—like the savings and loan scandal a few years ago—attracts a great deal of attention and causes substantial losses to many people (Weisburd et al., 1991). The government program to bail out the savings and loan industry will end up costing U.S. taxpayers $600 billion—$2,500 for every adult and child in the country.

Sutherland (1940) argued that most white-collar offenses provoke little reaction from others. When they do, however, they are more likely to end up in a civil hearing rather than in a criminal courtroom. *Civil law* regulates economic affairs between private parties while *criminal law* encompasses specific laws that define every individual's moral responsibility to society. In civil settlements, a loser pays for damage or injury, but no party is labeled a criminal. Further, since corporations have the legal standing of persons, white collar offenses commonly involve the organization as a whole rather than particular individuals.

And when white-collar criminals are charged and convicted, the odds are they will not go to jail. One accounting shows that fewer than three in ten embezzlers convicted in the U.S. District Court system spent a single day in prison; most were placed on probation (U.S. Bureau of Justice Statistics, 1992). Similarly, just ninety people were jailed for all federal environmental crimes between 1986 and 1991 (Gold, 1991).

The main reason for such leniency is that, as Sutherland noted years ago, the public voices less concern about white-collar crime than about street crime. Corporate crime, in effect, victimizes everyone—and no one. White-collar criminals don't stick a gun in anyone's ribs, and the economic costs are usually spread throughout the population.

**Critical Evaluation** According to social-conflict theory, the inequality in wealth and power that pervades our way of life also guides the creation and application of laws and other norms. This approach suggests that the criminal justice and social welfare systems act as political agents, controlling categories of people who threaten the capitalist system.

Like other approaches to deviance, however, social-conflict theory has its critics. First, this approach assumes that laws and other cultural norms are created directly by the rich and powerful. This assumption is, at least, an oversimplification, since many segments of our society influence, and benefit from, the political process. Laws also protect workers, consumers, and the environment, sometimes in opposition to the interests of capitalists.

Second, social-conflict analysis implies that criminality springs up only to the extent that a society treats its members unequally. However, according to Durkheim, all societies generate deviance, whatever their economic or political system.

We have presented various sociological explanations for crime and other types of deviance. Table 8.1 summarizes the contributions of each approach.

## DEVIANCE AND SOCIAL DIVERSITY

The shape of deviance in a society has much to do with the relative power and privilege of different categories of people. The following sections examine two examples: how gender is linked to deviance, and how racial and ethnic hostility motivates hate crimes.

**TABLE 8.1 Sociological Explanations of Deviance: A Summary**

| Theoretical Paradigm | Major Contributions |
|---|---|
| Structural-functional analysis | While what is deviant may vary, deviance itself is found in all societies; deviance and the social response it provokes serve to maintain the moral foundation of society; deviance can also direct social change. |
| Symbolic-interaction analysis | Nothing is inherently deviant but may become defined as such through the response of others; the reactions of others are highly variable; the label of deviance can lead to the emergence of secondary deviance and deviant careers. |
| Social-conflict analysis | Laws and other norms reflect the interests of powerful members of society; those who threaten the status quo are likely to be defined as deviant; social injury caused by powerful people is less likely to be defined as criminal than social injury caused by people who have little social power. |

## Deviance and Gender

Virtually every society in the world applies more stringent normative controls to women than to men. Historically, our society has limited the roles of women largely to the home. Even today, in the United States and many other societies, opportunities in the work-place, in politics, and in the military are limited for women. Elsewhere in the world, the normative constraints placed on women are even more glaring. In Saudi Arabia, women cannot legally operate motor vehicles; in Iran, women who dare to expose their hair or wear makeup in public can be whipped.

Given the importance of gender to the social construction of deviance, we need to pause a moment to see how gender figures in to some of the theories we have already discussed. Robert Merton's strain theory, for example, defines cultural goals in terms of financial success. Traditionally, however, this preoccupation with material things has dominated the thinking of men, while women have been socialized to define success in terms of relationships, particularly marriage and motherhood (Leonard, 1982). Only recently have women and men come to recognize the "strain" caused by the cultural ideals of equality clashing with the reality of gender-based inequality.

Labeling theory, the major approach in symbolic-interaction analysis, offers some insights into ways in which gender influences how we define deviance. To the extent that we judge the behavior of females and males by different standards, the very process of labeling involves sex-linked biases. Further, because society generally places men in positions of power over women, men often escape direct responsibility for actions that victimize women. In the past, at least, men engaging in sexual harassment or other assaults against women have been tagged with only mildly deviant labels; sometimes, they have suffered no adverse consequences and even have won societal approval.

By contrast, women who are victimized may have to convince an unsympathetic audience that they are not to blame for what happened. Research confirms an important truth: Whether people define a situation as deviance—and, if so, whose deviance it is—depends on the sex of both the audience and the

## SOCIAL POLICY

### DATE RAPE: EXPOSING DANGEROUS MYTHS

Completing a day of work during a business trip to the courthouse in Tampa, Florida, thirty-two-year-old Sandra Abbott* pondered how she would return to her hotel. An attorney with whom she had been working—a pleasant enough man—made the kind offer of a lift. As his car threaded its way through the late afternoon traffic, their conversation was animated. "He was saying all the right things," Abbott recalled, "so I started to trust him."

He wondered if she would join him for dinner; she happily accepted. After lingering over an enjoyable meal, they walked together to the door of her hotel room. The new acquaintance angled for an invitation to come in, but Abbott hesitated, sensing that he might have something more on his mind. She explained that she was old-fashioned about relationships but would allow him to come in for a little while with the understanding that talk was *all* they would do.

Sitting on the couch in the room, soon Abbott was overcome with drowsiness. Feeling comfortable in the presence of her new friend, she let her head fall gently onto his shoulder, and, before she knew it, she fell asleep. That's when the attack began. Abbott was startled back to consciousness as the man thrust himself upon her sexually. She shouted "No!" but he paid no heed. Abbott describes what happened next:

I didn't scream or run. All I could think of was my business contacts and what if they saw me run out of my room screaming rape. I thought it was my fault. I felt so filthy, I washed myself over and over in hot water. Did he rape me?, I kept asking myself. I didn't consent. But who's gonna believe me? I had a man in my hotel room after midnight. (Gibbs, 1991a:50)

Abbott knew that she had said "No!" and thus had been raped. She notified the police, who conducted an investigation and turned their findings over to the state attorney's office. But the authorities backed away from Abbott. In the absence of evidence like bruises, a medical examination, and torn clothes, they responded, there was little point in prosecuting.

The case of Sandra Abbott is all too typical. Even today, in most incidences of sexual attack, a victim makes no report to police, and no offender is arrested. The reason for such inaction is that many people have a misguided understanding of rape. Three inaccurate notions about rape are so common in the United States that they might be called "rape myths."

A first myth is that rape usually involves strangers. A sexual attack brings to mind young men who lurk in the shadow's and suddenly spring on their unsuspecting victims. But this pattern is the exception rather than the rule: Experts report that only one in five rapes involves strangers. For this reason, people have begun to speak more realistically about *acquaintance rape* or, more simply, *date rape*. A rape—legally speaking, the carnal knowledge of a female forcibly and against her will—is typically committed by a man who is known to, and even trusted by, his victim. But common sense dictates that being a "friend" (or even a husband) does not prevent a man from committing murder, assault, or rape.

A second myth about rape is that women provoke their attackers. Surely, many people think, a woman claiming to have been raped must have done *something* to encourage the man, to lead him on, to make him think that she really wanted to have sex.

In the case described above, didn't Sandra Abbott agree to have dinner with the man? Didn't she invite him into her room? Such self-doubt often paralyzes victims. But having dinner with a man—or even inviting him into her hotel room—is hardly a woman's statement of consent to have sex with him any more than she has agreed to have him beat her with a club.

A third myth is the notion that rape is simply sex. If there is no knife held to a woman's throat, or if she is not bound and gagged, then how can sex be a crime? The answer is simply that *forcing a woman to have sex without her consent is rape.*

To accept the idea that rape is sex one would also have to see no difference between brutal combat and playful wrestling. In the absence of consent, as Susan Brownmiller (1975) explains, rape is not sex but violence. "Having sex" implies intimacy, caring, communication, and, most important of all, consent—none of which is present in cases of rape. Beyond the brutality of being physically violated, date rape also undermines a victim's sense of trust.

The more people believe these myths about rape—that offenders are strangers, that victims provoke their attackers, and that rape is just spirited sex—the more women will fall victim to sexual violence. The ancient Babylonians stoned married women who became victims of rape, claiming that the women had committed adultery. To a startling extent, ideas about rape have not changed over thousands of years, which helps to explain why, even today, perhaps one in twenty rapes results in an offender being sent to jail.

Nowhere has the issue of date rape been more widely discussed than at colleges and universities. On the campus, students have easy access to one another, the collegiate setting encourages trust, and young people often have much to learn about relationships and about themselves. While this open environment encourages communication, it also permits sexual violence.

To counter the problem of sexual violence, we must begin by exposing the myths about rape. In addition, some critics have raised questions about the large role of alcohol in campus social life and the effect of cultural patterns that define sex as a sport. To address the crisis of date rape, everyone needs to understand two simple truths: Forcing sex without a woman's consent is rape, and when a woman says "no," she means just that.

* A pseudonym; the facts of this case are from Gibbs (1991a).
SOURCES: Gibbs (1991a, 1991b) and Gilbert (1992).

actors (King & Clayson, 1988). The box above takes a closer look at the issue of date rape, in which many women and men are standing up for an end to a double standard that has long threatened the well-being of women.

Finally, a notable irony is that social-conflict analysis—despite its focus on social inequality—has long neglected the importance of gender. If, as conflict theory suggests, economic disadvantage is a primary cause of crime, why do women (whose economic position is much worse than that of men) commit far *fewer* crimes than men do? The crime discussion, beginning on page 225, which examines crime rates in the United States, will provide an answer to this question.

## Hate Crimes

More than a decade ago the concept of **hate crime** came into our language to designate *a criminal act carried out against a person or that individual's property by an offender motivated by racial or other bias.* In addition to racial bias, a hate crime may express hostility based on religion, ancestry, sexual orientation, or physical disability.

Although hate crimes are nothing new, the federal government has only tracked them since 1990. While still a small share of all crime, their numbers are rising. A survey conducted by the National Gay and Lesbian Task Force (cited in Berrill, 1992:19-20) in eight U.S. cities found that one in five lesbians and gay men had been physically assaulted because of their sexual orientation; more than 90 percent claimed to have been at least verbally abused for this reason. Research indicates that hate-motivated violence is especially likely to target people who contend with multiple stigmas, such as gay men of color.

It is not the race or ancestry of the victim that qualifies an offense as a hate crime, it is the fact that such considerations *motivate* the offender. Such a crime, then, is an expression of hatred directed at some category of people. The box describes a recent case—the basis for a Supreme Court ruling upholding stiffer sentences for crimes motivated by hate.

## *Seeing Ourselves*

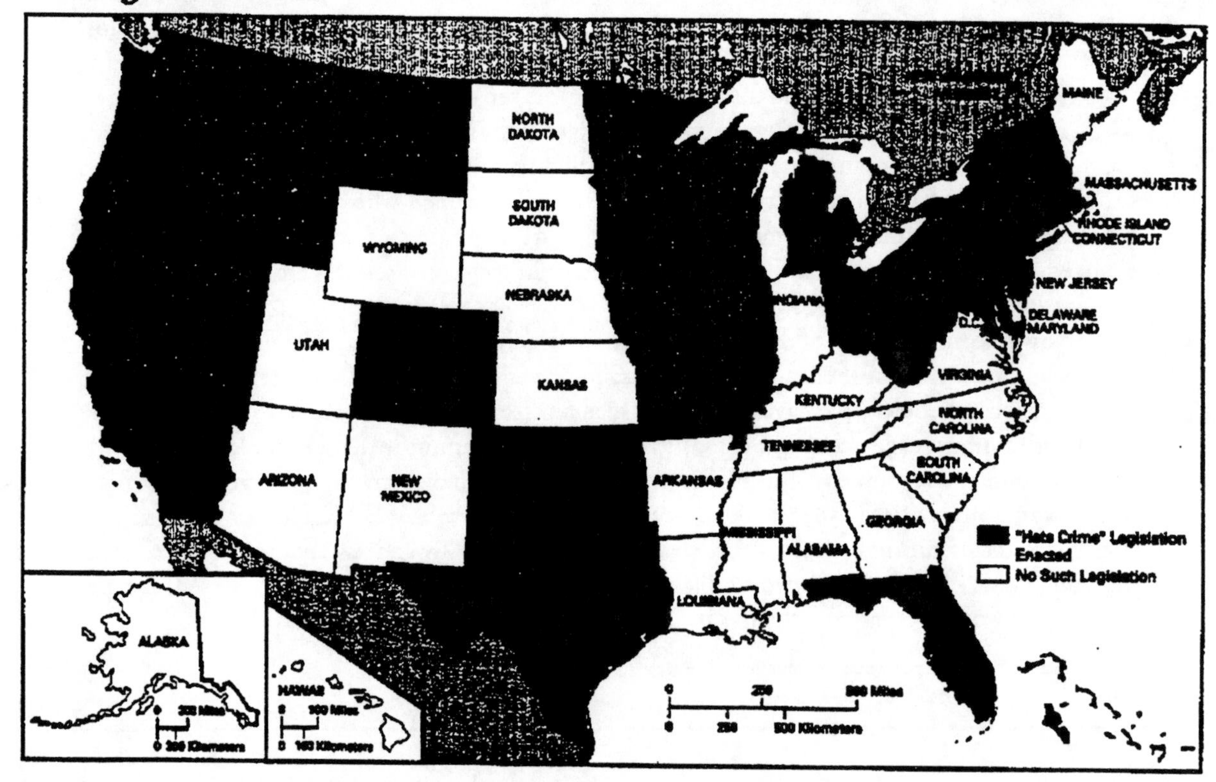


**NATIONAL MAP 8–1 Hate Crime Legislation Across the United States**

The states shown in black have legally mandated harsher penalties for crimes motivated by racial, ethnic, or other bias. Generally, laws of this kind are favored by political liberals. Can you see a pattern in the map? *Hint:* Most of the states that have enacted hate-crime laws supported Democrat Bill Clinton in the 1992 presidential election.



National Map 8-1 shows that, as of mid-1993, twenty-seven states had enacted hate-crime legislation. Based on current trends, it is likely that many more states will do so in the next few years.

# CRIME

All societies have a formal means for dealing with perceived violations of law, generally through statutes of criminal law enacted by local, state, or national government. Because various jurisdictions employ different legal standards, however, behavior that provokes a swift response in one time and place may merit barely a raised eyebrow in another.

In centuries past, for example, a Chinese commoner who simply looked at the Chinese emperor in public committed a serious crime. Today, a citizen of the People's Republic of China who expressed support for the nation's historic monarchy would likely face criminal charges. Closer to home, the U.S. judicial system has also undergone sweeping changes, supporting slavery for two centuries, for example, then condemning racial discrimination.

## SOCIAL POLICY

### HATE CRIMES: PUNISHING ACTIONS OR ATTITUDES?

On an October evening in 1989, Todd Mitchell, an African-American teenager, and a group of friends were milling about the front of their apartment complex in Kenosha, Wisconsin. They had just watched the film *Mississippi Burning* and were fuming over a scene in which a white man beats a young black boy kneeling in prayer.

"Do you feel hyped up to move on some white people?" asked Mitchell. Minutes later, a young white boy walked toward the group on the other side of the street. Mitchell commanded: "There goes a white boy; go get him!" The group surrounded the white boy, beating him to the ground and leaving him bloody and in a coma. They took his tennis shoes as a trophy of their conquest.

The black boys were identified and charged with the beating. At the trial of Todd Mitchell, who acted as the ringleader, the jury took the unusual step of finding the young man guilty of aggravated battery *motivated by racial hatred*. Instead of the typical two-year prison sentence, the jury committed Mitchell to jail for four years.

The enhancement of sentences for crimes motivated by bias is quickly becoming the law of the land. Supporters of hate-crime legislation make three arguments in favor of this trend. First, an offender's intentions have always been part of criminal deliberations, so this case represents nothing new. Second, crimes motivated by racial or other bias inflame the public mood more than those carried out for more common reasons like monetary gain. Third, supporters continue, such crimes are typically more harmful to the victims than those that involve other motives.

Critics, however, see in hate-crime laws a threat to free speech and expression. Under such a law, offenders are sentenced not for their actions, but for their underlying attitudes. As Harvard law professor Alan Dershowitz cautions, "As much as I hate bigotry, I fear much more the Court attempting to control the minds of its citizens." In short, according to the critics, hate-crime statutes open the door to punishing beliefs rather than behavior.

In 1993, the Supreme Court upheld the sentence handed down to Todd Mitchell. In a unanimous decision, the justices rejected the idea of punishing an individual's beliefs. At the same time, they reasoned, an abstract belief is no longer protected when it becomes the motive for a crime.

SOURCES: Greenhouse (1993) and Terry (1993).

## The Components of Crime

Technically, our society conceives of crime as having two distinct parts: the *act* itself (or, in some cases, the failure to do what the law requires) and *criminal intent* (in legal terminology, *mens rea*, or "guilty mind"). Intent is a matter of degree, ranging from a deliberate action to negligence in which a person acts (or fails to act) in a manner that may reasonably be expected to cause harm. Juries weigh the degree of intent in determining the seriousness of a crime and may find one person who kills another guilty of first-degree murder, second-degree murder, or negligent manslaughter. Alternatively, they may rule a killing justifiable.

## Type of Crime

In the United States, the Federal Bureau of Investigation gathers information on criminal offenses and regularly reports the results in a publication called *Crime in the United States*. Two major types of offenses contribute to the FBI "crime index."

**Crimes against the person** constitute *crimes against people that involve violence or the threat of violence.* Such "violent crimes" include murder and manslaughter (legally defined as "the willful killing of one human being by another"), aggravated assault ("an unlawful attack by one person upon another for the purpose of inflicting severe or aggravated bodily injury"), forcible rape ("the carnal knowledge of a female forcibly and against her will"), and robbery ("taking or attempting to take anything of value from the care, custody, or control of a person or persons by force or threat of force or violence and/or putting the victim in fear").

**Crimes against property** encompass *crimes that involve theft of property belonging to others.* "Property crimes" range from burglary ("the unlawful entry of a structure to commit a [serious crime] or a theft") to larceny-theft ("the unlawful taking, carrying, leading, or riding away of property from the possession of another"), auto theft ("the theft or attempted theft of a motor vehicle"), and arson ("any willful or malicious burning or attempt to burn the personal property of another").

A third category of offenses, not incorporated into major crime indexes, is **victimless crimes**, *violations of law in which there are no readily apparent victims.* So-called crimes without complaint include illegal drug use, prostitution, and gambling. "Victimless crime" is often a misnomer, however. How victimless is a crime when young people abusing drugs may have to steal to support a drug habit? How victimless is a crime if a young pregnant woman smoking crack causes the death or permanent injury of her baby? How victimless is a crime when a young runaway lives a desperate life of prostitution on the streets? And how victimless is a crime when a gambler falls so deeply into debt that he can no longer afford mortgage payments? In truth, the people who commit such crimes are themselves both offenders and victims.

Because public opinion about such activities varies considerably, the laws regulating victimless crimes differ from place to place. In the United States, gambling is legal only in a few locations, including Nevada and part of New Jersey; prostitution is legal only in part of Nevada; homosexual (and some heterosexual) behavior among consenting adults is still legally restricted in about half of the states. Where such laws do exist, enforcement is generally uneven.

## Criminal Statistics

Statistics gathered by the Federal Bureau of Investigation show that crime rates have generally risen in recent decades, despite increases in government spending on anticrime programs. During the 1980s, the police recorded some 8 million serious crimes annually, documenting a 23 percent jump in violent crime across the decade. Property crime, however, showed a modest trend in the other direction, falling by 3 percent (U.S. Federal Bureau of Investigation, 1991). Figure 8-2 illustrates the relative frequency and the trend for various serious crimes.

Always read crime statistics with caution, however, since they include only crimes known to the police. The police learn about almost all homicides, but assaults—especially among acquaintances—are far less likely to be reported. The police record even a smaller proportion of property crimes, especially those involving items of little value. Some victims may not realize that a crime has occurred, or they may assume they have little chance of recovering their property even *if* they notify the police.

As already noted, women do not report most cases of rape to the police. However, rising public support for rape victims has prompted more women to come forward, a trend reflected in a 25 percent increase in the number of forcible rapes reported to police during the 1980s (Harlow, 1991).

One way to evaluate official crime statistics is through a *victimization survey*, in which a researcher asks a representative sample of people about being victimized. These surveys indicate that actual criminality occurs at a rate three times higher than what official reports suggest.

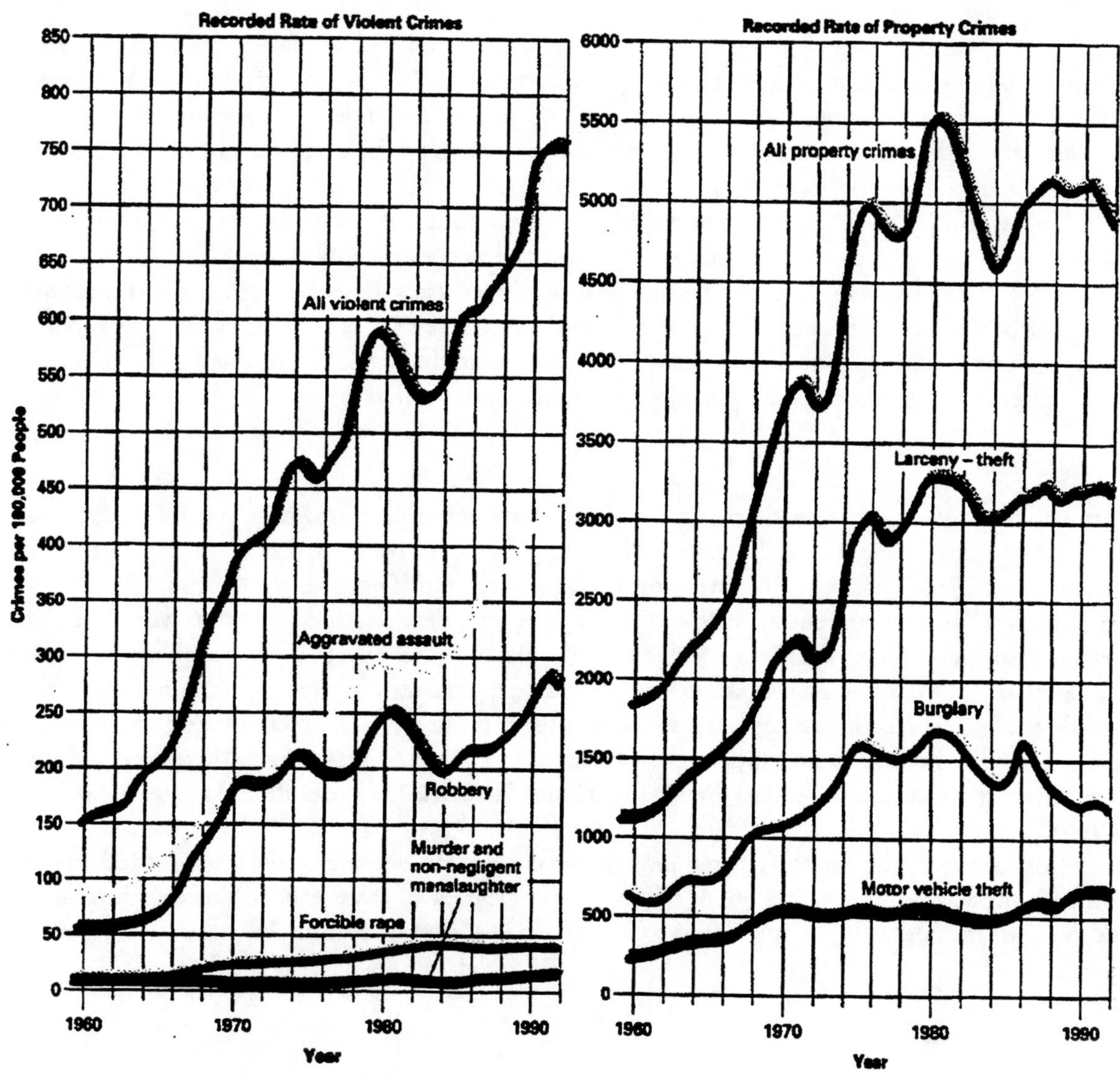


**FIGURE 8–2 Crime Rates in the United States, 1960–1992**

(U.S. Federal Bureau of Investigation, 1993)

## The "Street" Criminal: A Profile

Government statistics paint a broad-brush picture of people arrested for violent and property crimes. We now examine the breakdown of these arrest statistics by age, gender, social class, race, and ethnicity.

### *Age*

Official crime rates rise sharply during adolescence and peak at about age nineteen, falling thereafter. Although people between the ages of fifteen and twenty-four represent only 14 percent of the U.S. population, they accounted for 42.1 percent of all arrests for violent crimes in 1992 and 44.7 percent for property crimes (U.S. Federal Bureau of Investigation, 1993).

A notable—and disturbing—trend is that young offenders are committing crimes that are more serious. The number of adults arrested for murder, for example, has been dropping in recent years. At the same time, however, the number of teenagers charged with homicide has risen sharply.

### *Gender*

Official statistics suggest that the vast majority of crime is committed by males. Although each sex constitutes roughly half of the population, police collared males in 74.5 percent of all property crime arrests in 1992. This means that men are arrested three times as often as women for these crimes. In the case of violent crimes, the disparity is even greater: 87.5 percent of arrests involved males and just 12.5 percent were of females (a seven-to-one ratio).

Some of this gender difference stems from the reluctance of law enforcement officials to define women as criminals. Even so, the, arrest rate for women has been moving closer to that of men, which is probably one indication of increasing sexual equality in our society. Between 1983 and 1992, the *increase* in arrests of women was greater (37.5 percent) than that for men (16.9 percent) (U.S. Federal Bureau of Investigation, 1993). In global perspective, this pattern holds, with the greatest gender difference in crime rates marking societies that most limit the social opportunities of women.

### *Social Class*

Criminality is more widespread among people of lower social position; however, the matter is more complicated than it appears on the surface (Wolfgang, Figlio, & Sellin, 1972; Clinard & Abbott, 1973; Braithwaite, 1981; Thornberry & Farnsworth, 1982; Wolfgang, Thornberry, & Figlio, 1987).

In part, this pattern reflects the historical tendency to view poor people as less worthy than those whose wealth and power confer "respectability" (Tittle & Villemez, 1977; Tittle, Villemez, & Smith, 1978; Elias, 1986). But it is a mistake to assume that being socially disadvantaged means being criminal. While crime—especially violence—is a serious problem in the poorest inner-city neighborhoods, most people who live in these communities have no criminal records, and most crimes there are committed by a relatively few hard-core offenders (Wolfgang, Figlio, & Sellin, 1972; Elliott & Ageton, 1980; Harries, 1990).

Moreover, as John Braithwaite reminds us, the connection between social standing and criminality depends on what kind of crime one is talking about (1981:47). If we expand our definition of crime beyond street offenses to include white-collar crime, the "common criminal" has much higher social position.

### *Race and Ethnicity*

Both race and ethnicity have a strong influence on crime rates, although the reasons are many and complex. Official statistics indicate that 67.6 percent of arrests for index crimes in 1992 involved whites. However, arrests of African Americans were higher than for whites in proportion to their numbers; black people represent about 12 percent of the population and 31.8 percent of arrests for property crimes (versus 65.8 percent for whites) and 44.8 percent of arrests for violent crimes (53.6 percent for whites) (U.S. Federal Bureau of Investigation, 1993).

What accounts for African Americans experiencing a disproportionate level of arrests? Several factors are important. First, keep in mind that arrest records do not qualify as statements of proven guilt. To the degree that prejudice related to color or class prompts white police to arrest blacks more readily, and leads citizens more willingly to report black people to police as potential offenders, African Americans are overly criminalized (Liska & Tausig, 1979; Unnever, Frazier, & Henretta, 1980; Smith & Visher, 1981).

Second, race in the United States closely relates to social standing, which, as we have already explained, affects the likelihood of engaging in street crimes. Judith Blau and Peter Blau (1982) suggest that criminality is promoted by the sting of being poor in the midst of affluence as poor people come to perceive society as unjust. Because unemployment among African-American adults is double the rate among whites, and because almost half of black children grow up in poverty (in contrast to about one in six white children), no one should be surprised at proportionately higher crime rates for African Americans (Simpson, 1987).

Third, remember that the official crime index excludes arrests for crimes ranging from drunk driving to white-collar offenses. Clearly, this omission contributes to the view of the typical criminal as a person of color. If we broaden our definition of crime to include driving while intoxicated, insider stock trading, embezzlement, and cheating on income tax returns, the proportion of white criminals rises dramatically.

Finally, some categories of the population have unusually low rates of arrest. People of Asian descent, who account for about 3 percent of the population, figure in only 1 percent of all arrests. Asian Americans enjoy higher than average incomes and have a particularly successful record of educational achievement, which enhances job opportunities. Moreover, the cultural patterns that characterize Asian-American communities emphasize family solidarity and discipline, both of which serve to inhibit criminality.

## Crime in Global Perspective

By world standards, the United States has a lot of crime. The New York metropolitan area recorded 2,401 murders in 1992. Rarely does a day pass with no murder in New York; typically more New Yorkers are hit with stray bullets than are gunned down deliberately in cities elsewhere in the world.

The homicide rate in the United States stands at about five times that of Europe, the rape rate seven times higher, and the rate of property crime is twice as high. The contrast is even greater between our society and the nations of Asia, including India and Japan, where rates of violent and property crime are among the lowest in the world.

Elliott Currie (1985) suggests that crime stems from our culture's emphasis on individual economic success, frequently at the expense of family and community cohesion. The United States also has extraordinary cultural diversity, the legacy of centuries of immigration. Moreover, economic inequality is higher in this country than in most other industrial societies. Taken together, our society has a relatively weak social fabric, which, combined with considerable frustration among this country's have-nots, generates widespread criminal behavior.

Another contributing factor to violence in the United States is extensive private ownership of guns. Of 22,540 murder victims in the United States in 1992, 68.2 percent died from shootings. By the early 1990s, Texas and several other southern states reported that deaths from gunshots exceeded automobile-related fatalities. Rising public demand for gun control led Congress in 1993 to pass the so-called Brady Bill, named for President Ronald Reagan's press secretary who was shot along with the president a decade before. The law requires a seven-day waiting period for the purchase of handguns, with the purpose of discouraging impulsive buying and allowing police time to perform background checks on purchasers.

But there are already as many guns in the hands of private individuals as there are people in the United States. Further, guns represent only one piece in this nation's crime puzzle. As Elliott Currie notes, the number of Californians killed each year by knives alone exceeds the number of Canadians killed by weapons of all kinds. Most experts do think, however, that gun control will help curb the level of violence.

It is true that crime rates are soaring in some of the largest cities of the world like São Paulo, Brazil, which have rapid population growth and millions of desperately poor people. By and large, however, the traditional character of less economically developed societies and their strong family structure allow local communities to control crime informally (Clinard & Abbott, 1973; *Der Spiegel*, 1989).

One exception to this pattern is crimes against women. Rape is a rapidly growing problem throughout the world, especially in poor societies. Traditional social patterns that curb the economic opportunities available to women also promote prostitution. Global Map 8-1 shows the extent of prostitution in various world regions.

Finally, as noted in earlier chapters, a process of "globalization" is at hand by which various societies of the world are becoming more closely linked. This trend holds for crime as well. Some types of crime have always been multinational, including terrorism, espionage, and arms dealing (Martin & Romano, 1992).

## *Window on the World*

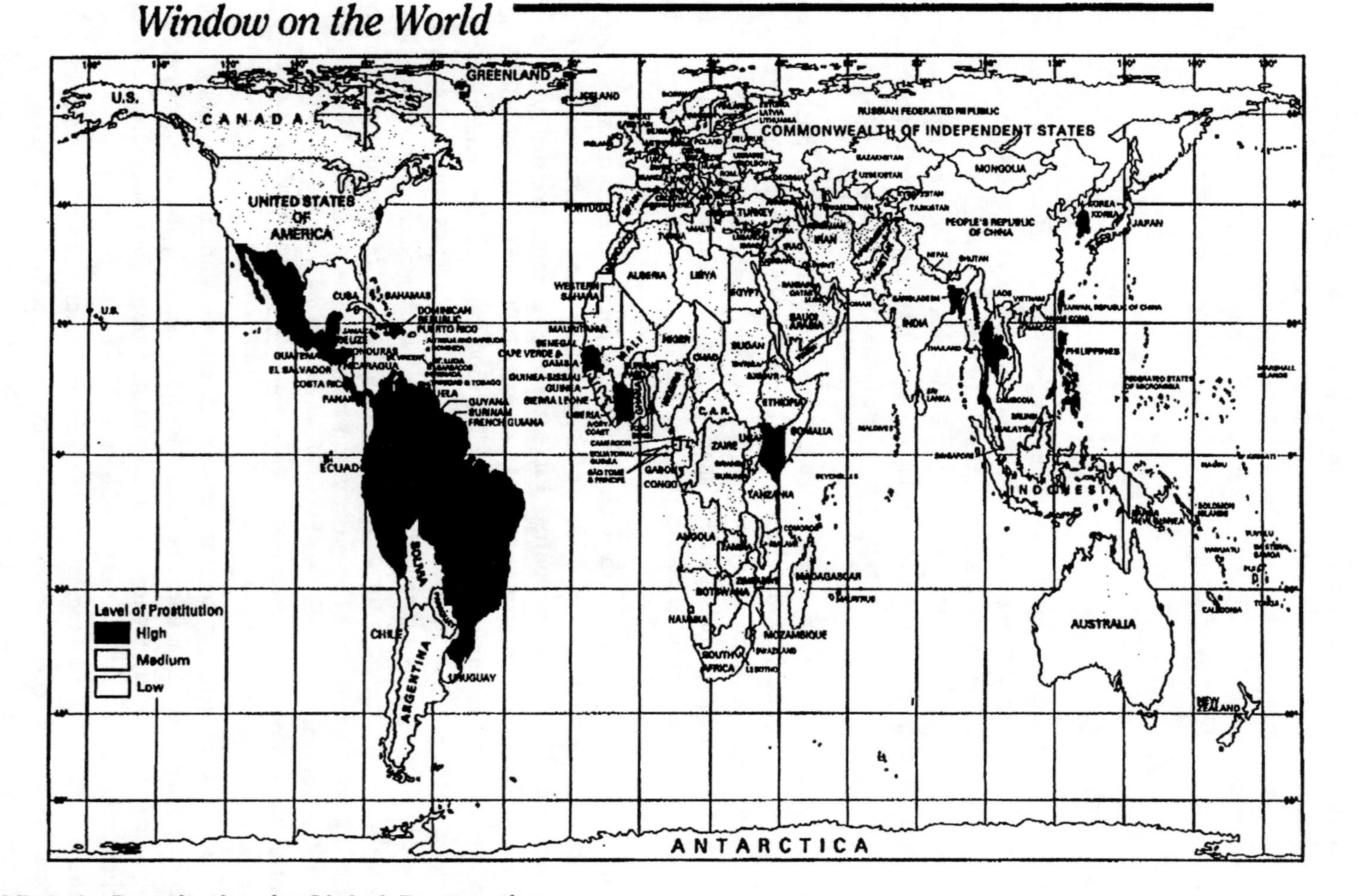


**GLOBAL MAP 8–1 Prostitution in Global Perspective**

Generally speaking, prostitution is widespread in societies of the world where women have low standing in relation to men. Officially, at least, the now-defunct socialist regimes in Eastern Europe and the former Soviet Union, as well as the People's Republic of China, boasted of gender equality, including the elimination of "vice" such as prostitution. By contrast, in much of Latin America, a region of pronounced patriarchy, prostitution is commonplace. In many Islamic societies patriarchy is also strong but religious forces restrain this practice. Western, industrial societies display a moderate amount of prostitution.

From *Peters Atlas of the World* (1990).

A more recent case in point is the illegal drug trade. In part, the problem of illegal drugs in the United States is a "demand" issue, since there is a very profitable market for cocaine and other drugs in this country, as well as legions of young people willing to risk arrest or even violent death by engaging in the lucrative drug trade. But the "supply" side of the issue is just as important. In the South American nation of Colombia, 20 percent of the people depend on cocaine production for their livelihood, and the rate is higher in the poorest regions of the country. Furthermore, not only is cocaine Colombia's most profitable export, but the drug outsells all other exports combined (including coffee). Clearly, then, understanding crimes such as drug dealing requires analyzing social conditions both in this country and elsewhere.

## THE CRIMINAL JUSTICE SYSTEM

The criminal justice system is a society's formal response to crime. We shall briefly introduce the key elements of this scheme: police, the courts, and the punishment of convicted offenders.

### Police

The police generally serve as the point of contact between the population and the criminal justice system. In principle, the police maintain public order by uniformly enforcing the law. In reality, 550,000 full-time police officers in the United States (in 1992) cannot effectively monitor the activities of 250 million people. As a result, the police exercise considerable discretion about which situations warrant their attention and how to handle them. Although police work demands some degree of discretion, the ability of police to pursue a situation as they see fit also fosters unequal treatment of some categories of people, as suggested by the Rodney King incident in Los Angeles, described at the beginning of this chapter.

How, then, do police carry out their duties? In a study of police behavior in five cities, Douglas Smith and Christy Visher (1981; Smith, 1987) concluded that, because they must act quickly, police rely on external cues to guide their actions. First, the more serious they perceive the situation to be, the more likely they are to make an arrest. Second, police assess the victim's preference as to how the matter should be handled. In general, if a victim demands that police make an arrest, they are likely to do so. Third, police more often arrest suspects who appear uncooperative. Fourth, they are more likely to arrest suspects whom they have arrested before, presumably because this suggests guilt. Fifth, the presence of bystanders increases the likelihood of arrest. According to Smith and Visher, the presence of observers prompts police to appear in control of the situation and also to use an arrest to move the interaction from the street (the suspect's turf) to the police department (where law officers have the edge). Sixth, all else being equal, police are more likely to arrest people of color than whites. Smith and Visher concluded that police generally consider people of African or Hispanic descent as either more dangerous or more likely to be guilty. In the researchers' view, this perception contributes to the disproportionately high arrest rates among these categories of people.

Finally, the concentration of police relative to population varies throughout the United States. Typically, the hand of law enforcement is heaviest in cities with high concentrations of nonwhites and with large income disparities between rich and poor (Jacobs, 1979). Looking nationally, as shown in National Map 8-2, on page 232, the concentration of police is several times higher in some states than in others.

### Courts

After arrest, a court determines a suspect's guilt or innocence. In principle, our courts rely on an adversarial process involving attorneys—who represent the defendant on the same side and the state on the other—in the presence of a judge who monitors adherence to legal procedures.

## Seeing Ourselves

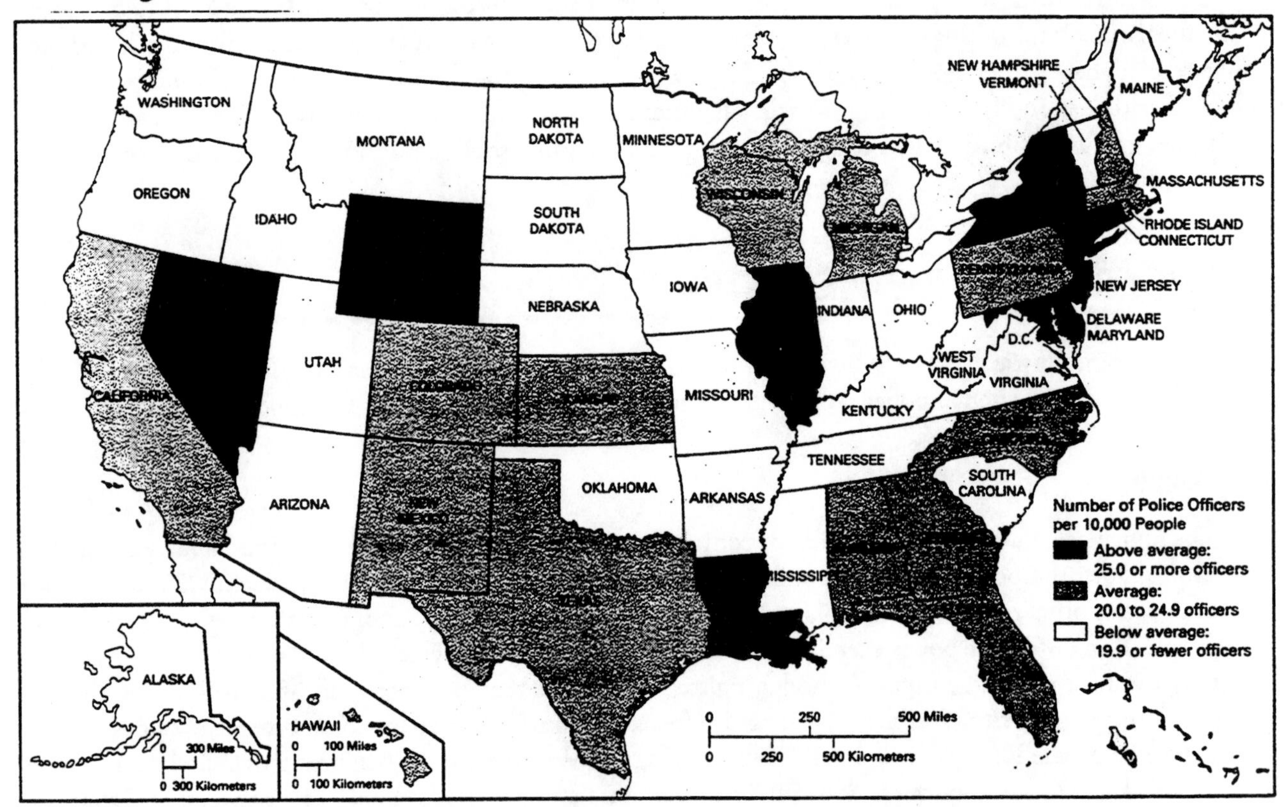


**NATIONAL MAP 8–2 The Concentration of Police Across the United States**

For the United States as a whole, there are 23 police officers for every 10,000 people. The range of police strength shows striking variation, however, from a high of 75.1 in Washington, D.C., to a low of 15.4 in South Dakota. What do states that have high concentrations of police have in common? What accounts for lower police power? Finally, Washington, D.C., not only has the highest concentration of police, it also leads the nation in homicide rates. What does this suggest about the ability of police to curb crime?

Prepared by the author using data from The U.S. Federal Bureau of Investigation.

In practice, however, about 90 percent of criminal cases are resolved prior to court appearance through **plea bargaining**, *a legal negotiation in which the prosecution reduces a defendant's charge in exchange for a guilty plea.* For example, a defendant charged with burglary may agree to plead guilty to the lesser charge of possession of burglary tools; another charged with selling cocaine may go along with pleading guilty to mere possession.

Plea bargaining is widespread because it spares the system the time and expense of court trials. A trial is usually unnecessary if there is little disagreement as to the facts of the case. By selectively trying only a small proportion of the cases, the courts can also channel their resources into those they deem most important (Reid, 1991).

But this process pressures defendants (who are presumed innocent) to plead guilty. A person can exercise the right to a trial, but only at the risk of receiving a more severe sentence if found guilty. In essence, say critics, plea bargaining undercuts the rights of defendants as it circumvents the adversarial process.

## Punishment

On January 5, 1993, a bound and hooded Westley Allan Dodd dropped through the trap door on a scaffold in Walla Walla, Washington, to his death. Few could feel compassion for a man who admitted raping, torturing, and then killing three young boys. But any such event causes people to reconsider the wisdom of legal execution and, more broadly, to ponder the purpose of punishment.

Scholars, too, reflect on the purposes of punishment. They commonly advance four justifications.

### *Retribution*

The celebrated justice of the Supreme Court, Oliver Wendell Holmes, stated "The first requirement of a sound body of law is that it should correspond with the actual feelings and demands of the community." Because people react to crime with a passion for revenge, Holmes continued, "the law has no choice but to satisfy [that] craving" (quoted in Carlson, 1976).

From this point of view, punishing satisfies a society's need for **retribution,** *an act of moral vengeance by which society subjects an offender to suffering comparable to that caused by the offense.* Retribution is based on a view of society as a system of moral balance. When criminality upsets this balance, punishment exacted in comparable measure restores the moral order, as suggested in the biblical dictum "An eye for an eye."

Retribution stands as the oldest justification for punishment. During the Middle Ages, most people viewed crime as sin—an offense against God as well as society—that warranted harsh punishment. Although sometimes criticized today because it offers little to reform the offender, retribution remains a strong justification for punishment.

### *Deterrence*

A second justification for punishment, **deterrence,** amounts to *the attempt to discourage criminality through punishment.* Deterrence is based on the Enlightenment notion that humans are calculating and rational creatures. From this point of view, self-interested people will forgo deviance if they perceive that the pains of punishment outweigh the pleasure of mischief.

Initially, deterrence represented reform of the system of harsh punishments based on retribution. Why put someone to death for stealing, critics asked, if that crime could be discouraged with a prison sentence? As the concept of deterrence became better accepted, execution and physical mutilation of criminals were replaced by milder forms of punishment such as incarceration.

Punishment may deter in two ways. *Specific deterrence* demonstrates to an individual offender that crime does not pay. Through *general deterrence,* the punishment of one person serves as an example to others.

### *Rehabilitation*

The third justification for punishment is **rehabilitation,** *a program for reforming the offender to preclude subsequent offenses.* Rehabilitation paralleled the development of the social sciences in the nineteenth century. According to early sociologists, crime and other deviance sprang from an unfavorable environment marked by poverty or a lack of parental supervision, for example. Proponents of rehabilitation argued that, just as offenders learned to be deviant, they learn to obey the rules if placed in the right setting. *Reformatories* or *houses of correction,* therefore, afforded offenders a controlled environment that might help them learn proper behavior.

Rehabilitation resembles deterrence in that both motivate the offender toward conformity. But rehabilitation emphasizes constructive improvement, while deterrence and retribution simply make the offender suffer. In addition, while retribution demands that the punishment fit the crime, rehabilitation focuses on the distinctive problems of each offender. Thus identical offenses might prompt similar acts of retribution but different programs of rehabilitation.

**TABLE 8.2 Four Justifications of Punishment: A Summary**

| | |
|---|---|
| Retribution | The oldest justification of punishment that remains important today. Punishment is atonement for a moral wrong by an individual; in principle, punishment should be comparable in severity to the deviance itself. |
| Deterrence | An early modern approach. Deviance is viewed as social disruption, which society acts to control. People are viewed as rational and self-interested, so that deterrence requires that the pains of punishment outweigh the pleasures of deviance. |
| Rehabilitation | A modern approach linked to the development of social sciences. Deviance is viewed as the product of social problems (such as poverty) or personal problems (such as mental illness). Social conditions are improved and offenders subjected to intervention appropriate to their condition. |
| Societal | A modern approach easier to implement than rehabilitation. If society is unable or unwilling to improve offenders or reform social conditions, protection from further deviance is afforded by incarceration or execution. |

## Societal Protection

A final justification for punishment is **societal protection,** *a means by which society renders an offender incapable of further offenses temporarily through incarceration or permanently by execution.* Like deterrence, social protection is a rational approach to punishment and seeks to protect society from crime.

Table 8.2 summarizes these four justifications of punishment.

**Critical Evaluation** We have identified four purposes of punishment. Assessing the actual consequences of punishment, however, is no simple task.

The value of retribution reminds us of Durkheim's theory of the functions of deviance, presented earlier in this chapter. Durkheim believed that punishing the deviant person increases people's moral awareness. To accomplish this objective, punishment was traditionally a public event. Public executions occurred in England until 1868; the last public execution in the United States took place in Kentucky in 1937. Even today, the mass media ensure public awareness of executions carried out inside prison walls (Kittrie, 1971).

Nonetheless, it is difficult to prove scientifically that punishment upholds social morality. Often it advances one conception of social morality at the expense of another, as when our government imprisons people who refuse to perform military service.

To some degree, punishment serves as a specific deterrent. Yet our society also has a high rate of **criminal recidivism,** *subsequent offenses by people previously convicted of crimes.* One 1991 study of state prison inmates found that 62 percent had been incarcerated before, and 45 percent had been sentenced three or more times (U.S. Bureau of Justice Statistics, 1991). Put in other terms, once released from jail, half of former inmates are returned to prison within several years. Such a high rate of recidivism raises questions about the extent to which punishment actually deters crime. Then, too, only about one-third of all crimes are known to police, and of these, only about one in five results in an arrest. The old adage that "crime doesn't pay" rings rather hollow when we consider that such a small proportion of offenses ever result in punishment.

General deterrence is even more difficult to investigate scientifically, since we have no way of knowing how people might act if they were unaware of punishments meted out to others. In the debate over capital punishment, permitted in thirty-six states, critics of the practice point to research suggesting that the death penalty has limited value as a general deterrent in the United States, which is the only Western, industrial society that routinely executes serious offenders (Sellin, 1980; van den Haag & Conrad, 1983; Archer & Gartner, 1987; Lester, 1987; Bailey & Peterson, 1989; Bailey, 1990; Bohm, 1991).

Efforts at rehabilitation spark controversy as well. Prisons accomplish short-term societal protection by keeping offenders off the streets, but they do very little to reshape attitudes or behavior in the long term (Carlson, 1976). Perhaps this result is to be expected, since according to Sutherland's theory of differential association, placing a person among criminals for a long period of time should simply strengthen criminal attitudes and skills. And because incarceration severs whatever social ties inmates may have in the outside world, individuals may be prone to suffer crime upon their release, consistent with Hirschi's control theory.

Finally, inmates returning to the surrounding world contend with the stigma of being ex-convicts, often an obstacle to successful integration. One study of young offenders in Philadelphia found that boys who were sentenced to long prison terms—those likely to acquire a criminal stigma—later committed both more crimes and more serious ones (Wolfgang, Figlio, & Sellin, 1972).

Ultimately, we should never assume that the criminal justice system—the police, courts, and prisons—can eliminate crime. The reason, echoed throughout this chapter, is simple: Crime—in fact, all kinds of deviance—is more than simply the acts of "bad people"; it is inextricably bound up in the operation of society itself.

## SUMMARY

1. Deviance refers to violations that span a wide range, from mild breaches of etiquette to serious violence.
2. Biological explanations of crime, from Caesare Lombroso's research in the nineteenth century to developing research in human genetics, has yet to produce much insight into the causes of crime.
3. Psychological explanations of deviance focus on abnormalities in the individual personality, which arise from either biological causes or the social environment. Psychological theories help to explain some kinds of deviance.
4. Social forces produce nonconformity because deviance (1) exists in relation to cultural norms, (2) results from a process of social definition, and (3) is shaped by the distribution of social power.
5. Sociology links deviance to the operation of society rather that the deficiencies of individuals. Using the structural-functional paradigm, Durkheim claimed that responding to deviance affirms values and norms, clarifies moral boundaries, promotes social unity, and encourages social change.
6. The symbolic-interaction paradigm is the basis of labeling theory, which holds that deviance arises in the reaction of others to a person's behavior. Labeling theory focuses on secondary deviance and deviant careers, which result from acquiring the stigma of deviance.
7. Following the approach of Karl Marx, social-conflict theory holds that laws and other norms reflect

the interests of the most powerful people in society. Social-conflict theory also spotlights white-collar crimes that cause extensive social harm, although the offenders are rarely defined as criminals.

8. Official statistics indicate that arrest rates peak in adolescence, then drop steadily with advancing age. Three-fourths of property crime arrests are of males, as are almost nine of ten arrests for violent crimes.
9. People of lower social position commit more street crime than those with greater social privilege. When white-collar crimes are included among criminal offenses, however, this disparity in overall criminal activity diminishes.
10. More whites than African Americans are arrested for street crimes. However, African Americans are arrested more often than whites in proportion to their respective populations. Asian Americans show lower than average rates of arrest.
11. The police exercise considerable discretion in their work. Research suggests that factors such as the seriousness of the offense, the presence of bystanders, and the accused being African American make arrest more likely.
12. Although ideally an adversarial system, U.S. courts predominantly resolve cases through plea bargaining. An efficient method of handling cases where the facts are not in dispute, plea bargaining nevertheless places less powerful people at a disadvantage.
13. Justifications of punishment include retribution, deterrence, rehabilitation, and societal protection. Because its consequences are difficult to evaluate scientifically, punishment—like deviance itself—sparks controversy among sociologists and the public as a whole.

## KEY CONCEPTS

**crime** The violation of norms a society formally enacts into criminal law.

**crimes against the person** (Violent crimes) crimes against people that involve violence or the threat of violence.

**crimes against property** (Property crimes) crimes that involve theft of property belonging to others.

**criminal justice system** A formal reaction to alleged violations of the law on the part of police, courts, and prison officials.

**criminal recidivism** Subsequent offenses by people previously convicted of crimes.

**deterrence** The attempt to discourage criminality through punishment.

**deviance** The recognized violation of cultural norms.

**hate crime** A criminal act carried out against a person or that individual's property by an offender motivated by racial or other bias.

**juvenile delinquency** The violation of legal standards by the young.

**labeling theory** The assertion that deviance and conformity result, not so much from what people do, as from how others respond.

**medicalization of deviance** The transformation of moral and legal issues into medical matters.

**plea bargaining** A legal negotiation in which the prosecution reduces a defendant's charge in exchange for a guilty plea.

**rehabilitation** A program for reforming the offender to preclude subsequent offenses.

**retribution** An act of moral vengeance by which society subjects an offender to suffering comparable to that caused by the offense.

**retrospective labeling** The interpretation of someone's past consistent with present deviance.

**societal protection** A means by which society renders an offender incapable of further offenses temporarily through incarceration or permanently by execution.

**stigma** A powerfully negative social label that radically changes a person's self-concept and social identity.

**victimless crimes** Violations of law in which there are no readily apparent victims.

**white-collar crime** Crimes committed by people of high social position in the course of their occupations.

## CRITICAL-THINKING QUESTIONS

1. How does a sociological view of deviance differ from the common sense notion that bad people do bad things?
2. Identify Durkheim's functions of deviance. From his point of view, would a society free from deviance be possible?
3. In general, how does social power affect deviant labeling? Suggest the importance of gender, race, and class in this process.
4. What do official crime statistics teach us about this form of deviance?

## SUGGESTED READINGS

### Classic Sources

Kai Erikson. *Wayward Puritans: A Study in the Sociology of Deviance.* New York: Wiley, 1966. This historical account of the Puritans of Massachusetts Hay finds strong support for Durkheim's functional theory of deviance.

Thomas Szasz. *The Myth of Mental Illness: Foundations of a Theory of Personal Conduct.* New York: Harper & Row, 1961. This influential and controversial treatise condemns the concept of mental illness as a fiction utilized to impose conformity on those who simply differ.

## CONTEMPORARY SOURCES

Allen E. Liska. *Perspectives in Deviance.* 4th ed. Englewood Cliffs, N.J.: Prentice Hall, 1995. This resource includes most of the issues raised in this chapter.

Gregory M. Herek and Kevin T. Berrill. Hate Crimes: *Confronting Violence Against Lesbians and Gay Men.* Newbury Park, Calif.: Sage, 1992. This collection of essays analyzes the legal, psychological, and social issues surrounding bias crimes against homosexual men and women.

Sally Engle Merry. *Getting Justice and Getting Even: Legal Consciousness Among Working-Class Americans.* Chicago: University of Chicago Press, 1990. Does our society live up to its stated ideal of "equal justice under the law?"

Edwin M. Schur. *Labeling Women Deviant: Gender, Stigma, and Social Control.* Philadelphia: Temple University Press, 1984. Why have women been virtually ignored in much analysis of deviance? This book offers an answer and tries to remedy the problem.

Robert Johnson. *Death Work: A Study of the Modern Execution Process.* Pacific Grove, Calif.: Brooks/Cole, 1990. This gripping account of a researcher's personal investigation of the ultimate punishment makes a strong case for its abolition.

ANNE CAMPBELL. *The Girls in the Gang.* 2d ed. Cambridge, Mass.: Basil Blackwell, 1991. Most research about youth gangs in the United States is about, and by men. Anne Campbell provides a rare and insightful account of yoking women in New York street gangs.

DONNA GAINES. *Teenage Wasteland: Suburbia's Dead End Kids.* New York: HarperCollins, 1992. Beginning as an exploration of a suicide pact among four New Jersey teenagers, this study probes the aspirations and fascination with deviance among troubled youth.

M. DAVID ERMANN and RICHARD J. LUNDMAN, eds. *Corporate and Governmental Deviance: Problems of Organizational Behavior in Contemporary Society.* 4th ed. New York: Oxford University Press, 1992. This collection of eleven essays investigates patterns of deviance by governmental and corporate elites.

THOMAS SZASZ. *A Lexicon of Lunacy: Metaphoric Malady, Moral Responsibility, and Psychiatry.* New Brunswick, N.J.: Transaction, 1993. In his latest book, a controversial medical activist argues that scientific diagnosis typically reflects cultural definitions.

FREDA ADLER and WILLIAM S. LAUFER, eds. *The Legacy of Anomie: Advances in Criminological Theory.* Vol. 6. New Brunswick, N.J.: Transaction Books, 1994. This collection of essays describes the continuing utility of anomie theory, with its roots in the thinking of Emile Durkheim and further developed by Robert Merton, for understanding deviant behavior.

## GLOBAL SOURCES

IKUYO SATO. *Kamikaze Biker: Parody and Anomy in Affluent Japan.* Chicago: University of Chicago Press, 1991. In the tradition of Emile Durkheim, this account of juvenile delinquency in Japan highlights the breakdown of traditional social controls that often accompanies material affluence.

JOHN M. MARTIN and ANNE T. ROMANO. *Multinational Crime: Terrorism, Espionage, Drug and Arms Trafficking.* Newbury Park, Calif.: Sage, 1992. The "globalization" trend is affecting even patterns of crime, as this book explains.

ROBERT Y. THORNTON with KATSUYA ENDO. *Preventing Crime in America and Japan.* Armonk, N.Y.: M. E. Sharpe, 1992. Based on comparative research in two cities, this report provides insights into the different strategies for controlling crime in Japan and the United States.

HANS-GUNTHER HEILAND, LOUISE I. SHELLEY, and HISAO KATOH, eds. *Crime and Control in Comparative Perspectives.* Hawthorne, N.Y.: Aldine de Gruyter, 1991. This broad comparison of global crime patterns includes both more- and less-developed nations as well as those with capitalist and socialist economies.

# Chapter 9

## Social Stratification: The Economic and Prestige Dimensions

*In 1991, Anthony O'Reilly, chief executive of H. J. Heinz, was paid $205,753. That was not his* annual *pay, however. That is how much he received* per day. *On an annual basis, Mr. O'Reilly received $75,100,000 in salary, benefits, and long-term compensation (*St. Louis Post-Dispatch, *1992). Although Mr. O'Reilly was the highest paid corporate executive in the United States in 1991, he certainly was not in a category by himself. Toys R Us chairman Charles Lazarus received $60 million in 1986; Lotus Development chairman Jim Manzi, $26 million in 1987; and UAL chairman Stephen Wolf, $18 million in 1990—even though his company's profits fell 71 percent. The highest pay in recent years was the $78.2 million paid to Steven Ross of Time-Warner in 1990. Overall, the* average *chief executive officer (CEO) of a major corporation was paid $1.4 million in 1990, and during the 1980s, CEO pay rose 212 percent—four times as fast as the pay of ordinary workers (Thomas and Reibstein, 1991;* St. Louis Post-Dispatch, *1992).*

*Meanwhile, most Americans struggled to keep up with inflation. Adjusted for inflation, the typical family's income declined by 3.2 percent between 1990 and 1991, and the typical household's income fell more than 5 percent between 1989 and 1991 (U.S. Bureau of the Census, 1992a). The number of people below the poverty level rose to 35 7 million in 1991 (U.S. Bureau of the Census, 1992f). The immense contrast between the wealthiest CEOs and the poorest Americans is hard to imagine. The combined* annual *income of 14 families of four living at the federal poverty level would be less than what Anthony O'Reilly received* every day *in 1991!*

Somewhere between Anthony O'Reilly and the family living at the poverty level are the great mass of middle-income Americans whose incomes have at best remained stable but whose share of the nation's total income has declined over the past decade or two (U.S. Bureau of the Census, 1990a, p. 6). Between 1980 and 1990, the income of this middle group rose by only about 7 percent after adjusting for inflation, and between 1988 and 1990, it declined. In contrast, the much higher incomes of those in the top 5 percent of the population rose by about 26 percent between 1980 and 1990, and unlike that of the middle-income group, the 1990 income of the wealthiest group remained above its 1988 level (U.S. Bureau of the Census, 1991f).

Clearly, these figures indicate the existence of great and increasing inequality in American society. Although inequality may be more extreme in the United States than in other industrialized nations, the United States has no monopoly on social inequality. In this chapter, we shall examine the nature, causes, and consequences of social *stratification*: structured inequality in the distribution of scarce resources. A *scarce resource* can be anything people want that is not abundant enough for all people to have as much as they want. Money, power, and fame are all examples of scarce resources.

## WHAT IS STRATIFICATION?

Some form of social stratification exists in all societies. These patterns of stratification can be thought of as *ranking systems* within societies. People can be ranked on the basis of how much of the society's scarce resources they own and control. Those with a large share of scarce resources rank high; those with a small share rank low.

### Dimensions of Stratification

Different kinds of scarce resources are distributed unequally in a society. On the basis of his or her share of one resource such as money, a person could hold a high rank, while on the basis of his or her share of another resource, such as status in the community, the same person might rank low. Consider, for example, a poorly educated rural family that by a stroke of luck comes into a great fortune—a situation humorously portrayed in the television show *Beverly Hillbillies.*

These different ranking systems, based on the distribution of different scarce resources, have been referred to by sociologists as **dimensions of stratification.** A major contribution of the classic social theorist Max Weber (1968 [orig. 1922]) was his recognition that most societies have three major dimensions of stratification: an *economic dimension* (wealth and income), a *political dimension* (power), and a *social prestige dimension* (status). Let us consider each.

## The Economic Dimension

The economic dimension of stratification concerns money and the things it can buy. It involves two key variables, *income* and *wealth,* which are related but are not the same.

**Income** refers to the amount of money that a person or family receives over some defined period of time, usually a calendar year. Essentially, it is what you report on your income-tax form in April. Data on income in the United States are readily available because the Census Bureau asks people about their incomes each year in its current population survey. More detailed data on income also are collected every 10 years, as part of the decennial Census.

**Wealth** refers to the total value of everything that a person or family owns, minus any debts owed. It is similar in meaning to "net worth." Thus, wealth refers not to what you *receive* over some time period, but to what you *have* at a particular point in time.

## The Political Dimension

As we saw in earlier chapters, *power* can be defined as the ability to get people to behave as you want them to behave. Power usually is exercised through the political system, at least to some extent. Thus, voting, office holding, lobbying, contributing to campaigns, boycotting, striking, and demonstrating are all means by which people can exercise power. Because power is an abstract concept and can be exercised in many different ways, there is no simple way of measuring it. Nonetheless, sociologists have developed some rather sophisticated ways of examining the distribution of power. For now, however, our main concerns are the economic and social prestige dimensions of stratification.

## The Social Prestige Dimension

The third dimension of stratification is social **prestige,** sometimes referred to as *status.* This dimension has to do with what people think of you. If people think highly of you and you are well known, you have a high level of status or prestige. If people think poorly of you, you have a low level of prestige. By definition, prestige is a scarce resource. Being "well regarded" is always a relative or comparative matter. It would be meaningless to be well regarded if everyone were equally well regarded. Then everyone would be the same, and nobody would stand out.

There are numerous ways to gain prestige or status. People can get status on the basis of their family name, if, for example, they happen to be a Rockefeller or a Kennedy, or, perhaps, a Fonda or a Jackson. They can get it on the basis of their education or occupation—as we shall see later, occupation is one of the most consistent determinants of status. Accomplishments, titles, and public exposure can be sources of status or prestige. Ultimately, however, prestige is a matter of what people think. Thus, the best way to measure it is to ask. Surveys of occupational prestige, most admired person, most recognized name, and so forth are important ways of measuring prestige.

# THE DISTRIBUTION OF WEALTH AND INCOME IN THE UNITED STATES

## The Distribution of Income

In 1991, the median family income in the United States was $35,353 (U.S. Bureau of the Census, 1992). Median family income is the income level that is in the middle of the distribution: Half of all families have incomes above the median; half have incomes below the median. For individual adults not married or living with their parents, the median income in 1991 was $15,008. Income is distributed quite unequally in the United States. In 1990, the top one-fifth of households received 46.6 percent of all income, or about *12 times* the share that went to the bottom fifth (3.9 percent) (U.S. Bureau of the Census, 1991f).

A limited number of families and individuals at the very top get an especially large share of the nation's income. For example, the richest 5 percent of American families receive about four times as big

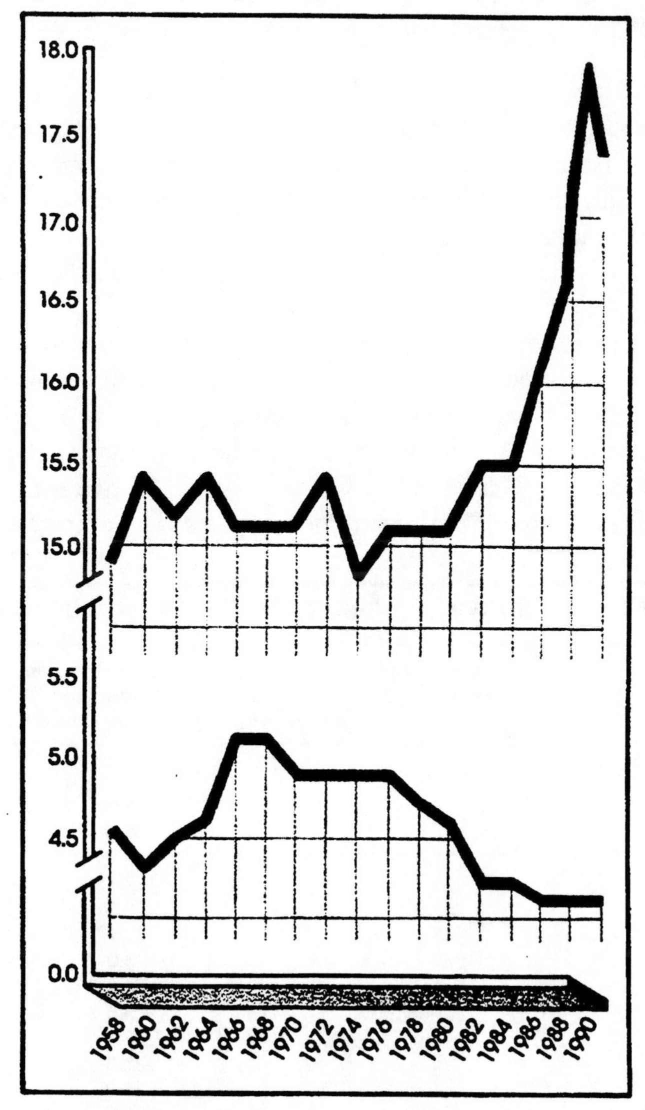


**FIGURE 9–1 Time Trend in the Distribution of Family Income, United States, 1958–1989**

Top line: Share of family income going to top 5 percent of all U.S. families. Bottom line: Share of family income going to bottom 20 percent of all U.S. families.

SOURCE: U.S. Bureau of the Census, 1990a, 1987a, 1985a, 1991f.

a share of the nation's income as is received by the poorest 20 percent of families. In fact, this 5 percent actually receive a larger share of the nation's family income than the lowest 40 percent of families do.

Among individuals, the difference is even more extreme: The richest 5 percent receive five and one-half times as much income as the poorest 20 percent (U.S. Bureau of the Census, 1990, p. 29), and more than one and one-half times as much as went to the bottom 40 percent. Thus, it is clear that income differences within the United States are very large.

**The Trend: More or Less Equal?** Do these figures represent more or less inequality than in the past? The answer is that, over the long run, there has not been a great deal of change, but since the mid-1970s, as is illustrated in Figure 9–1, the distribution has clearly shifted in the direction of inequality (Olsen, 1990; Burtless, 1990). Over the longer term of American history, there has been some limited change in the degree of inequality. There was some shift toward greater equality between about 1929 and 1944 (Fusfeld, 1976, p. 630)—a period roughly corresponding to Franklin Roosevelt's New Deal and World War II. For the next 30 years, there was little change. In the last 10 years, there appears to be some shift back to the pre-Roosevelt pattern, as the rich have gotten richer and the poor poorer. This is a fairly significant change, given the relatively small changes across the longer term of American history (Bartlett and Steele, 1992).

**Income Inequality: A Comparative View** How does the United States compare to other countries in its distribution of income? First, it is important to point out that *virtually all* industrialized countries distribute income more equally than most preindustrial, less economically developed countries (Fusfeld, 1976, p. 630). As countries industrialize and modernize, their inequality tends to decrease (Lenski, 1966). The appropriate standard of comparison for the United States, then, is other countries that have already industrialized.

The United States has greater income inequality than most of these countries. Table 9.1 shows that income inequality in the United States is above average for industrialized countries. The wealthiest 10 percent of Americans received a larger share of total income than the average for all the countries, and there is not one country among the 15 shown in the table where the poorest 20 percent received a smaller share of total income than in the United States. Overall, the top 10 percent of Americans received 5.3 times as much income as the bottom 20 percent; this compares to an average of 3.6 for the other coun-

**TABLE 9.1 Income Inequality in 15 Industrialized Countries**

| Country and Year | Percent of Income Received by Lowest 20% of Households | Percent of Income Received by Highest 10% of Households | Ration of Top 10% to Bottom 20% |
|---|---|---|---|
| Switzerland, 1982 | 5.2% | 29.8% | 5.7 |
| Spain, 1980–81 | 6.9 | 24.5 | 3.6 |
| Italy, 1986 | 6.8 | 25.3 | 4.4 |
| United Kingdom, 1979 | 5.8 | 23.3 | 4.0 |
| Japan, 1979 | 8.7 | 22.4 | 2.6 |
| Belgium, 1978–79 | 7.9 | 21.5 | 2.7 |
| Finland, 1981 | 6.3 | 21.7 | 3.4 |
| Netherlands, 1983 | 6.9 | 23.0 | 3.3 |
| Canada, 1987 | 5.7 | 24.1 | 4.2 |
| France, 1979 | 6.3 | 25.5 | 4.0 |
| West Germany, 1984 | 6.8 | 23.4 | 3.4 |
| Denmark, 1981 | 5.4 | 22.3 | 4.1 |
| United States, 1985 | 4.7 | 25.0 | 5.3 |
| Sweden, 1981 | 8.0 | 20.8 | 2.6 |
| Norway, 1979 | 6.2 | 21.2 | 3.4 |
| Average, 15 countries | 6.6 | 23.1 | 3.6 |

SOURCE: Reprinted by permission from The World Bank, *World Development Report, 1992*. New York: Oxford University Press. Copyright 1992 by the International Bank for Reconstruction and Development/The World Bank.

## EXECUTIVE SALARIES

The issue of the salaries of American CEOs came up during George Bush's 1992 trip to Japan with senior automobile executives: The Japanese blamed the high price of American cars on exorbitant U.S. executive salaries. Though executive salaries account for a relatively small part of the cost of a car, it is true the American executives are generally paid more than their counterparts in other countries.

According to Graef Crystal, an executive pay expert and professor at the University of California at Berkeley, the chief executives of America's biggest companies made an average of $3.2 million in 1992, while their Japanese counterparts averaged $525,000. Chrysler's CEO, Lee Iacocca, had a $4.6-million pay package that year (small potatoes compared to the late Time Warner chief Steve Ross's $78.2 million take in 1990, or Reebok International CEO Paul Fireman's $14.8 million).

An American pay package consists of a base salary (in 1992 Lee Iacocca's base salary was $976,378, for instance), to which a huge bonus is often added (depending on sales and performance of the company), and stock options, i.e., rights to buy shares of company stock at reduced cost. Some of these options are worth millions of dollars. These profitsharing incentives are supposed to focus an executive's energies on improving the company's performance.

In their defense, American CEOs contend that Japanese executives receive nontaxable perks that boost their salaries, such as company-supported luxury houses or apartments in exclusive neighborhoods, club memberships that would otherwise cost hundreds of thousands of dollars, and virtually unlimited expense accounts.

Still, compensation experts admit that U.S. executives are the best paid in the world. According to Honda North America spokesman Aki Kato, Honda's president, Nobuhiko Kawamoto, earned about $400,000 last year—less than one-tenth of Iacocca's compensation—and did not benefit from any extra executive perks. Douglas Ostrom, an economist at the Japan Economic Institute in Washington, estimates that U.S. CEOs are, on average, paid 80 times as much as their blue-collar employees earn. In contrast, Japanese top managers get about eight times the pay of their rank-and-file workers. While the high pay of CEOs may or may not be a substantial factor in the profit-loss situation of American companies, they do act as a drain on their resources and may hurt worker morale by heightening a sense of unfairness. At the very least, they are hard to justify on any basis of productivity, as some American executives have received large compensation increases even as companies were losing tens or hundreds of millions of dollars.

SOURCES: *Reuters*, October 15, 1992; *The New York Times*, April 11, 1992; *Newsweek*, February 10, 1992; *The Detroit News*, January 10, 1992.

tries. Thus, in the United States, the wealthy receive more income relative to the poor than in most industrialized countries.

In at least some cases, this has become a source of tension in international economic relations. As is discussed in the box "Executive Salaries," the high salaries of U.S. CEOs have been criticized by officials from Japan, where executive salaries are much lower.

## The Distribution of Wealth

As unequal as the distribution of income is in the United States, wealth is even more unequally distributed. A Census Bureau survey concerning household wealth found that, nationally, just 10 percent of the population owns half the wealth, and the top 20 percent owns two-thirds (Oliver and Shapiro, 1990).

The study also showed that the average white household was eleven times as wealthy as the average black household, and that about one in 10 white households and one in three black households had zero or negative net worth (National Research Council, 1989; Oliver and Shapiro, 1990).

Another survey, conducted by the University of Michigan's Institute for Social Research (ISR), is considered particularly useful because it included an oversampling of the very wealthy, a group so small that usually it is largely missed in surveys. This survey showed that just 0.5 percent of the population owned 27 percent of the wealth—a slightly larger share than 20 years earlier (Ericksen, 1988), but almost twice as much as in 1976 (*St. Louis Post Dispatch*, 1986). Both surveys showed that, overall, about one American household out of five has zero or negative net worth. Thus, ownership of wealth is highly concentrated in the United States. Moreover, recent research indicates that it became even more concentrated between 1983 and 1989 (Wolff, 1992).

Ownership of the types of wealth that produce income, such as corporate stock, is even more concentrated among the few (Blume, 1974; U.S. Bureau of the Census, 1986c). One study found that, for all wealth other than houses and cars, 90 percent is owned by just 20 percent of the population, and more than half is owned by the wealthiest 5 percent of the population (Oliver and Shapiro, 1990).

## SOCIOECONOMIC MOBILITY

Thus far, we have described the degree of economic inequality found in the United States. A separate, although related, question about the *degree* of inequality concerns **socioeconomic mobility**: the frequency with which people move up or down in the society's economic hierarchy. In a society with very high socioeconomic mobility, it would not be unusual (or a person to be born very poor and end up very wealthy as an adult—or the other way around. In sociological terms, a society such as this would have an **open stratification system**. In this type of system, *achieved statuses* have substantial influence over the social status a person attains in adulthood. In a society with very *low* mobility, those born poor nearly always stay poor, and those born wealthy nearly always stay wealthy. This type of society is said to have a **closed stratification system**. In a closed stratification system, *ascribed statuses* largely determine a person's social position throughout life.

Among all societies, there is generally greater mobility in societies that have less inequality. The main reason for this is that as preindustrial societies modernize and become industrialized societies, inequality declines and mobility increases over the long run. However, among societies at any given level of industrialization, the relationship between the degree of inequality and the amount of mobility is much weaker.

Sociologists have classified societies into three types, based on their degree of mobility. The least mobility is found in *caste systems*, with only modestly greater mobility in *estate* or *feudal systems*. Both of these types of society are typically found in preindustrial societies. *Class systems*, usually found in industrialized societies, have greater, but far from unlimited, mobility.

### Caste Systems

As noted above, the least mobility is found in a **caste system**. A caste system has legally or formally defined groupings that are assigned by birth and are not subject to change. In other words, a person is born into a particular group, called a **caste**, and must remain in that caste throughout life. In sociological terms, a person's position throughout life is entirely determined by the ascribed status of the caste into which he or she was born; achieved statuses have no influence over a person's life situation in a caste system.

**India: A Case Study** Although caste has existed in some form in many societies throughout history, the two best known examples of caste systems are those of India and South Africa. In India, a caste system based on religion has existed for thousands of years. Different roles have been assigned to different castes for centuries, ranging from the priestly religious functions of the highest, or Brahman, caste to the common labor performed by the lowest caste. The lowest castes are defined as "untouchable" by people in the higher castes, with contact of all types—even looking at one another—being forbidden. Of course, the castes also are required to live separately. As is generally true of caste systems, the caste into which one is born has traditionally determined one's status throughout life, whom one can marry, the jobs one can have, and the status of one's children and grandchildren throughout their lives. The caste system in India was officially abolished in 1949, but it continues to have considerable influence on social behavior, particularly in rural areas. In urban areas, however, its influence has waned, partly because of the legislation, but also partly because cities house such a variety of people who must do business and come into contact with one another that regulating who may speak to whom is far more difficult. Not only in India, but everywhere, formal and rigid closed systems of stratification become harder and harder to maintain as society urbanizes and modernizes.

**South Africa and Apartheid** About the same time that India was legally abolishing its caste system, South Africa was formally writing its caste system—called **apartheid**—into law. From 1948 until 1991, South Africa was a prime example of a **racial caste system**, in which the castes are defined on the basis of race. During this period, South Africa's apartheid laws defined four racial castes: European (white), African (black), coloured (mixed European and African ancestry), and Asian. Political and educational rights, types of jobs, and type and location of housing were all legally defined on the basis of these groupings. Until the late 1980s, people of different races were forbidden to marry, have sexual contact, or even *conspire* to have sexual contact. People had to carry passes identifying their race, which determined where and when they could travel. By 1991, all these laws had been repealed except for one crucial one: Africans—the vast majority of the country's population—still cannot vote in national elections, although negotiations on political rights were under way in 1993. Thus, *legally* speaking, many aspects of the racial caste system have been eliminated. However, as a practical matter, different groups have vastly different rights and standards of living. Still, the violent protest against apartheid from the 1960s on and the eventual elimination of formal, legally mandated segregation and race classification again illustrate the great difficulty of maintaining a caste system in a modernizing, urbanizing society.

The United States also has a racial caste system in its history, dating back to the beginnings of slavery. The "Jim Crow" laws that mandated segregation of blacks in the South from two decades after the Civil War until the mid-twentieth century continued a system in which race determined where one could go and what one could do, in many ways paralleling the laws that mandated segregation in South Africa. At one time, similar laws also existed in many parts of the North, though they were eliminated there earlier. Since the mid-1950s, federal court rulings and legislation also have eliminated segregation laws in the South, and today deliberate racial discrimination is illegal. However, vestiges of the old caste system remain in the form of substantial socioeconomic inequalities between African Americans and whites.

## Estate or Feudal Systems

The **estate system**, also called the *feudal system*, offers slightly more mobility than the caste system. In an estate system, status is determined on the basis of land ownership, often accompanied by some type of formal title. In general, the high-status groups are those who own land, and the rest of the population generally works for them. Some variety of the estate system has been found in most of the world at some point in history, including the feudal systems of medieval Europe and of China and Russia in the nineteenth and early twentieth centuries, and the hacienda systems of Latin America, some of which remain largely intact today. The American South before the Civil War, where wealth and power were concentrated in the hands of large-scale plantation owners, is often regarded as a form of feudal or estate system, although slavery also made it a type of racial caste system.

In a feudal system, your position throughout life is usually determined by the *ascribed status* of whether you were born into the landowning class. Occasionally, however, titles that permit entry into this elite class may be conferred. In the European feudal system, for example, a peasant could occasionally be knighted or admitted to the clergy, which gave him the privileges associated with these landowning classes. However, this was the exception to the rule. Because of their link to land ownership, estate systems are found in agricultural, preindustrial societies. When societies begin to urbanize, the feudal system almost inevitably breaks down.

## Class Systems

The highest degree of mobility is found in **class systems.** In a class system, both ascribed statuses and achieved statuses have significant effects on people's income, wealth, and social position. In other words, people who are born into affluent families generally enjoy a higher status as adults than people who are born into poorer families, but what people *do*—the amount of schooling they attain and the success of their personal and economic decisions—also influences their status as adults. Class systems are typically found in modern industrial societies. The present-day United States, Canada, Australia, New Zealand, Israel, and most countries in Europe are examples of class systems.

**Achieved and Ascribed Statuses** Many people have the misunderstanding that only achieved statuses matter in a class system. This is clearly not true. The difference between class systems and the other two systems (caste and estate) is not that ascribed statuses don't matter, but rather that achieved statuses do. This can be seen by examining studies of socioeconomic mobility in class societies. Most such studies look at **intergenerational mobility**; that is, they compare a person's status with that of his or her parents. The majority of these studies have compared the status of sons to that of their fathers, because in previous generations, mothers usually did not work outside the home and derived their social and economic status from their husbands. Recently, however, such studies have begun to include both women and men (e.g., DiPrete and Grusky, 1990). What all these studies show is that mobility is quite limited in class systems. In other words, most people have statuses quite close to those of their parents (Blau and Duncan, 1967; see also Featherman and Hauser, 1978). In most cases, the status of the offspring is slightly higher than that of the parent, but this mainly reflects what sociologists call **structural mobility**—there has been growth in better-paying, more pleasant, higher-status, white-collar jobs, and a decline in the number of blue-collar jobs (Featherman, 1979).

**Exchange Mobility** Although many people do move up slightly in status and a good number of sons of blue-collar workers (about one in three) have moved up to white-collar employment, two facts show the continuing influence of ascribed statuses. First, although many people move up a little because there are more of the "desirable" jobs today than in the past, people usually do not change their *relative* status a great deal (Rytina, 1989, 1992). A man who has a white-collar job in contrast to his father's blue-collar job may still have a job status and an income below those of 70 percent of the population, just as his father did. Sociologists refer to this situation as an absence of **exchange mobility**. People's absolute position may change, but their position *relative to others* is less likely to.

The second point to remember is that, even though people may move up or down slightly, they are not likely to move a great deal. We can see this by examining the proportion of sons of manual workers who attain *professional* employment—the more desirable jobs that require specific technical or professional education. In the United States, the most widely cited study of mobility found that only one out of ten sons of manual laborers attains professional employment—in contrast to *seven* out of ten sons of professional workers (Blau and Duncan, 1967). In other words, if your father is a professional worker, you have *seven times* as great a chance of getting that type of job as you have if your father is a laborer. Your chances of getting such a high-status job are even lower if you are born into a family with an income below the poverty level. If this is the case, you are a good deal more likely than the average person to experience poverty as an adult. Thus poverty as well as wealth is frequently passed from generation to generation. Recently, research has indicated that exchange mobility has increased, but as the economy has stagnated and good jobs have disappeared, structural mobility has decreased in the United States. The result is little overall change in occupational mobility (Hout, 1988).

Ascribed statuses such as race and sex also continue to be important in class societies. Women and racial or ethnic minorities receive lower pay and work at lower-status jobs than white males do, even when their parents have similar status. Among year-round, full-time workers in 1990, for example, black males received a median income only 71 percent as high as that of white males. The median income of white females was only 69 percent as high as that of white males, and black females and Hispanic males and females fared even worse (computed from U.S. Bureau of the Census, 1991f, p. 106). Thus, race and sex biases compound the influence of ascribed statuses in class societies. A final important point is that ownership of major, income-producing wealth is even more likely to be based on the luck of birth. For all these reasons, then, the status into which you are born makes a big difference, even in a class society.

## International Comparisons of Mobility

How does the United States compare to other class societies with regard to mobility? It is often argued that the greater class inequality of the United States is offset by greater mobility. The actual findings of research suggest that this may be true, but only to a very limited extent. In general, there is little difference in the degree of mobility in different class societies (Lipset and Bendix, 1960; Tyree, Semyonov, and Hodge, 1919; Ishida, Goldthorpe, and Erikson, 1991; Grusky and Hauser, 1984; Lin and Bian, 1991). All have some mobility, but in all of them, including the United States, movement from very low statuses to very high statuses is much more the exception than the rule. Movement within and out of the middle strata, in contrast, appears more common (Grusky and Hauser, 1984). Within this general observation, a case can be made that there is a little more mobility in the United States than in other industrialized countries (Krymkowski, 1991). For example, the proportion of people who move from manual labor to professional occupations—although a tiny minority everywhere—*is* higher in the United States than in most other countries. This may reflect high ***structural mobility*** owing to white-collar job growth rather than high ***exchange mobility*** (see Slomczynski and Krauze, 1987, p. 605; but also Hauser and Grusky, 1988).

A precise answer to the question of whether the United States has more mobility than other countries, however, depends on how you measure mobility and what countries you use for comparison. The United States does appear to have more mobility than Great Britain, for example (Yamaguchi, 1988), but that may be more a reflection of the unusually low level of mobility in Great Britain (Wong, 1990). Comparisons with Japan show conflicting results depending on the measure of mobility used (Yamaguchi, 1988), but overall the difference between the United States and Japan is not large (Wong, 1990). Wong's study found that Poland and Hungary also had levels of mobility similar to the United States and Japan; however, all these countries had more relative mobility than countries such as Great Britain and Brazil. Slomczynski and Krauze (1987, p. 608) compared 22 countries on two measures of relative or exchange mobility, and found that the United States had above-average levels of mobility by one measure but average mobility according to the other. At the very least, then, it would be inaccurate to say that the United States has much greater mobility than most other industrialized countries. The similarities—particularly for exchange or relative mobility—are much greater than the differences (Ishida, Goldthorpe, and Erikson, 1991), and different measures do not give highly consistent results.

Although the United States has little more mobility than most other industrialized societies, the fact remains that Americans *believe* we have considerable mobility. The Horatio Alger myth that anyone, no matter how poor, can succeed on a grand scale is alive and well. Seventy percent of Americans agree, for example, that "America is the land of opportunity where everyone who works hard can get ahead" (Kluegel and Smith, 1986, p. 44). Although over 80 percent agree that "people who grew up in rich families" have a better-than-average chance of getting ahead, two-thirds also think that "people who grew up in poor families" have an average or better-than-average chance of getting ahead (Kluegel and Smith, 1986, p. 49). The majority also believe the same about blacks and women, and over 90 percent feel that way about "people who grew up in working-class families." The fact is that all of these groups have a considerably poorer-than-average chance of getting ahead, yet most Americans persist in believing otherwise. In short, the reality is that there is significantly less mobility in American society than most Americans believe. The result of these beliefs is that many Americans oppose efforts to reduce poverty, because they incorrectly place most of the blame for poverty on poor people themselves (Kluegel, 1990; Kluegel and Smith, 1986).

## SOCIAL CLASS IN U.S. SOCIETY

Sociologists refer to a group of people who are similar in terms of level of income or wealth as a **social class**. Inequalities in income and wealth are called *class stratification*, and your position within that system of inequality is called your *social class*. A term similar in meaning to class is **socioeconomic status**. Social class and socioeconomic status are often taken to include not only your levels of income and wealth, but also the prestige of your occupation and the amount of education you have attained. Sociologists do not agree on the relative importance of these various factors in defining social class. Partly for this reason, they cannot agree on any uniform system for defining or identifying social classes. We shall focus on three common formulations of social class: the Marxian definition, the composite approach, and subjective class, recognizing at the start that none of these is accepted by all sociologists.

### The Marxian Definition of Social Class

Karl Marx made the most important early contribution to thinking about social class and made the study of social class a key item on the agenda for sociology. Marx's entire analysis of society centers around social class. He believed that all aspects of a society are an outgrowth of -but also help to perpetuate—the society's **class structure**. To Marx, there were only two classes in any type of society that really mattered—the *ruling class*, who owned the means of production, and the *subordinate class*, who did not.

In a feudal agricultural society, the landowners are the ruling class, and the subordinate class consists of peasants, serfs, tenant farmers, sharecroppers, or slaves—those who work land they do not own and turn over the products of their labor to the landowning class. When urbanization and industrialization arrive, such an economy is replaced by a new system with a new class structure. In a capitalist society—any industrial society where the means of production are privately owned—the ruling class is the bourgeoisie: the class that owns capital. By capital, we mean productive capacity—factories, mineral resources, land, or money that can be converted into these things.

Most of the population, however, belongs not to the bourgeoisie but to the proletariat: those who do not own capital but work for those who do. Much of the value of what is produced by the proletariat goes not to the proletariat, but to the bourgeoisie. The only thing that really matters in the Marxian definition of class is ownership of the means of production. No matter how much money salaried employees earn, they still do not belong to the ruling class because they do not own the means of production and hence do not gain the benefits of wealth and income produced by the labor of others. At the time Marx wrote, most people who worked for wages or salaries had very low incomes, so the exclusion of this group from the ruling class was probably more obvious than it is today. Nonetheless, modern Marxist theorists argue that this definition continues to be appropriate for two reasons. First, even today most of those who work for wages and salaries have relatively low incomes compared with the owners of capital. Second, even those with high salaries do not receive most of their income from the work of others, unless they use their high salaries to purchase capital on a large scale.

According to this definition of social class, even today the ruling class is very small and the subordinate class is very large. One problem with using Marx's definition is deciding how to classify what he called the *petit bourgeoisie*; people, such as "ma and pa" convenience store owners, who own small businesses that produce only marginal income. Most Marxist sociologists exclude this group from the true ruling class because their wealth produces a limited amount of income and, usually, little additional wealth. Today, most wealth that generates income and additional wealth is to be found in the corporations—large-scale organizations with multiple owners. Moreover, although many people own *some* corporate stock, the great bulk of corporate wealth is held by a tiny fraction of the population. Recall, for example, studies cited earlier showing that a small percentage of the population owns most of the nation's wealth. The great majority of the U.S. population work for those who do own capital, and even most of those with a relatively high income have a standard of living far below that of the tiny elite that owns most of the corporate wealth. In this regard, the Marxian definition of social class continues to make sense, despite the great diversity in income and lifestyle among those who work for wages and salaries.

## The Composite Definition of Social Class

One problem with the Marxian definition of social class is that it places a salaried person receiving $125,000 a year in the same social class with a person working for the minimum wage (whose income would be less than $9,000 per year). Clearly, these two people would have very different life experiences as a result of their large difference in income, although neither would live in the style of a Ford or a Rockefeller. Moreover, income is not the only thing that defines social class. Should an assembly-line worker with a high-school degree and an income of $40,000 per year be placed in a higher social class than a college professor with a doctorate who earns $35,000? Many would say no, because the college professor has the advantage of a much greater education and enjoys far more freedom, autonomy, and opportunity for creativity on the job. In fact, this case illustrates the ambiguities of social class: The assembly-line worker enjoys an advantage in some areas of life, and the professor does in others.

Sociologists have attempted to deal with this problem by developing a *composite approach* to defining social class that considers wealth, income, prestige, education, job status, and other factors. This approach is consistent with Max Weber's view, discussed earlier in this chapter, that there are different dimensions of stratification that vary independently of one another. The composite approach does not use hard-and-fast rules for placing people into categories, and the boundaries between categories are often vague. What it does do is create groupings of people who, on the basis of a variety of considerations, are relatively similar. The first such effort, which has guided all subsequent efforts, was that of W. Lloyd Warner and colleagues (1949), in a study of a community they nicknamed "Yankee City." Warner's categories, defined on the basis of wealth, income, prestige, possessions, lifestyle, and community participation, defined six classes: upper-upper, lower-upper, upper-middle, lower-middle, upper-lower, and lower-lower. The majority of the population fell into the two lower groups, about 40 percent into the two middle groups, and just 3 percent into the two upper groups. Since then, sociologists have used a variety of classification systems, most of which have involved five or six classes, labeled in different ways, always with unclear boundaries. Some of these studies have indicated a shrinkage of the lower categories and a growth of the middle ones, partly as a result of the decline in blue-collar employment and the growth of white-collar employment. The truly wealthy elite, however, has changed little in size since the time of Warner's study. Roughly speaking, the use of this type of classification system today would yield something like the six groupings shown in the box entitled "American Social Classes in the 1990s."

## The Subjective Definition of Social Class

A third way to approach social class is to let people define their own social class. We refer to this self-defined social class as **subjective class**. In the United States, people do not like to think in terms of class distinctions and tend to place themselves and nearly everyone else in or around the middle. Thus, most studies of subjective class, including a survey I have done in my own classes dozens of times, reveal that around 50 to 60 percent of Americans consider themselves "middle class," and about 30 to 40 percent

## SOCIOLOGICAL INSIGHTS

### AMERICAN SOCIAL CLASSES IN THE 1990s

In the 1990s, Americans can be roughly classified into six social classes, each of which is described briefly below.

#### CORPORATE ELITE

Making up about 1 percent of the population, this is the group that owns the bulk of the country's corporate wealth. Usually owning assets in excess of $1 million, people in this group enjoy a standard of living far beyond that of the rest of the population. They are largely the "old rich," whose names alone are a source of great prestige, and who have been wealthy for generations. Such families include the Rockefellers, Fords, Carnegies, Mellons, and Danforths. A few in this elite are "new rich," having gained corporate wealth as a result of skillful investment, foresight, and often, an element of luck. Examples include the late Sam Walton (founder of Wal-Mart), with a net worth that stood at $7 billion *after* he lost $1 billion in one day in the 1987 stock marker crash, and Apple Computer founder Steven Jobs. Though the new rich are as wealthy as the old rich, the old rich do not accept them as members of the true elite, and their prestige remains a notch below that of the Fords and Rockefellers.

#### UPPER CLASS

Amounting to about 2 to 5 percent of the population, people in this group differ from the corporate elite in that they are less wealthy and more likely to have gained their wealth as a result of a high salary or investment of earned income than by ownership of key corporate capital. The successful rock singer and professional athlete would fall into this diverse group, as would many corporate executives and some owners of smaller-scale businesses. Although this group includes a good number of millionaires, it is made up mostly of "new rich," and to a significantly lesser extent than the corporate elite, its income comes from its own labor rather than from the labor of others.

#### UPPER-MIDDLE CLASS

Accounting for perhaps 15 to 20 percent of the U.S. population, this group is made up of better-paid management and professional employees: doctors, lawyers, airline pilots, middle and upper corporate management, and owners of the more successful small businesses. Most people in this group are college educated, and many have graduate or professional degrees. It is taken for granted that their children will attend college and, increasingly, graduate or professional school. This group is likely to live in bigger-than-average homes in the more prestigious suburbs. Incomes run above the median family income of $35,000, but generally not into the hundreds of thousands of dollars typical of the lower rungs of the upper class.

#### LOWER-MIDDLE CLASS

This group, amounting to about 25 to 30 percent of the population, holds the lower-status white-collar jobs, which may or may not require a college degree. Some of the best-paid blue-collar workers, such as skilled building crafts workers and auto workers, could also be included in this group, largely because of their relatively high incomes. In general, the incomes in this group are fairly close to the median family income of about $35,000. People in this group tend to own their own homes and live in "good" suburbs, but not in the most prestigious areas. As in the upper-middle class, it is common for both the husband and wife to be employed full-time, but here it is more likely that the wife will be working out of economic necessity and less likely that she will be "moving up" in her career. Though still diverse, this group tends to be a bit more conservative than the upper-middle class, particularly when it comes to "social issues" such as abortion, sexual freedom, and freedom of expression. The children of this group are often expected to attend college, but it is more likely to be a two-year school or the local commuter university, and fewer go on to graduate or professional school.

## WORKING CLASS

This group, around 30 to 35 percent of the population, works at blue-collar or clerical jobs and has incomes at or, more often, below the average level. More often than not, both the husband and wife must work in order to support the family. They typically have high-school diplomas but no college training. They often own homes in older and less prestigious suburbs, small towns, or the nonpoor areas of the central city, although many rent. They live an adequate, though by no means extravagant, lifestyle, but they must worry more often than middle- and upper-class people about how to pay their bills. Although their attitudes may be liberal on economic issues, they tend to be conservative socially and are sometimes fearful of losing economic ground to other groups. Their children are less likely to go to college. In some families, however, where education is seen as the hope for upward mobility for the next generation, the children do attend college, particularly two-year and commuter schools in their local area. For this group, a crisis such as a divorce or the loss of a job can mean falling into poverty, and there is in general less feeling of security about life than in the middle class.

## LOWER CLASS

Amounting to 15 to 20 percent of the population, this group is always struggling just to make it. Depending on such factors as being employed, marital status, and wage level, people in this group have incomes around the poverty level or a little above it. Finding adequate food, shelter, clothing, and medical care ranges from difficult to impossible for them. Many people in this group lack even a high-school education, and although their children have a better chance of completing high school than they did, many do not, and very few go on to college. Most rent rather than own their own homes, and they more frequently live in a central city, rural area, or small town than in the suburbs. Divorce and separation rates are high, as are the number of single-parent families. At the bottom of this group is the chronically poor and unemployed underclass, whose children rarely know anyone who has a stable job, a decent education, or the opportunity for upward mobility. Thus, they are psychologically prepared to be the next generation of poor and near-poor.

"working class" (National Opinion Research Center, 1983; Hodge and Trieman, 1968). Very few—certainly well under 10 percent—ever admit to being "upper class" or "lower class." In my own classes, I have had people who reported family incomes as high as $150,000 label themselves "middle class," even though such a figure at the time the students were surveyed put them in the upper 2 or 3 percent of all families. Because nearly all Americans call themselves "middle class" or "working class," this method obviously has the disadvantage of classifying people less precisely than the composite method. However, it does tell us a good deal about how Americans think about class.

What factors determine how people define themselves? The answer appears to be a combination of income, education, and occupation. Those with high incomes, a college education, and a white-collar occupation nearly always answer "middle class," whereas those with a below-average income, a high-school education or less, and a blue-collar job generally answer "working class." Men and women define class in somewhat different ways. Men nearly always define their social class on the basis of their own characteristics, while married women define their social class partly according to their own characteristics and partly according to those of their husbands (Simpson, Stark, and Jackson, 1988). However, more women today define their class on the basis of their own characteristics (Davis and Robinson, 1988).

The least predictable answers come from those with *status inconsistencies*—people who rank high in one area but low in another. In my class survey, for example, people from blue-collar families with incomes at or above the median family income are about as likely to call themselves "middle class" as "working class." This is because while their parents' occupations are typical of the working class, their family income is typical of the middle class.

Another group experiencing status inconsistencies is the so-called *new class*, a rapidly growing group of young professionals who are well educated, but, partly because of a labor market flooded by baby boomers born in the 1950s and early 1960s, have experienced relatively low pay and a significant risk of unemployment or underemployment (Harrington, 1979, pp. 135-137). This group tends to have middle-class tastes and expectations and the education to go with them. Moreover, many are people who deal in the production of ideas, such as professors, journalists, publishers, entertainers, planners, and policymakers. Thus, they tend to be independent thinkers and distrustful of conventional beliefs and traditions (Bruce-Briggs, 1979; Kristol, 1978). At the same time, their incomes are too small to live up to their high expectations, as illustrated by studies showing falling real family incomes among young workers (*St. Louis Post-Dispatch*, 1985). As a result, many of them are finding that it takes two incomes to attain a standard of living that could once be obtained by one breadwinner.

Some experts have predicted that this group may become highly dissatisfied and a major source of dissent in America and other modern societies (Gouldner, 1979; Harrington, 1979). Recent research in the Netherlands has confirmed that this group has to a large extent become the source of leadership for social movements, particularly ones dealing with cultural and environmental issues (Kriesi, 1989). It may also have played an important role in the election of President Bill Clinton in 1992.

**Occupational Prestige** Closely related to subjective class is occupational prestige. In fact, we already saw that occupation is one of the key factors that determines how people see their own social class. Different occupations clearly carry different levels of prestige, and the work people do has a major effect on the entire prestige or status dimension of stratification. Significantly, the relative prestige of various jobs has remained similar over time and across different places. Surveys done over half a century in the United States have consistently shown that the jobs that had high status in the 1920s and 1930s continue to have high status today; indeed, the relative status of a wide range of jobs has changed very little over the past 50 years (National Opinion Research Center, 1983; Hodge, Siegel, and Rossi, 1964). About the only source of change is in the creation of new jobs or the elimination of old ones. In 1920, for example, there was no such thing as a computer programmer or a television camera operator. Similarly, technology has largely eliminated other jobs, such as keypunch and elevator operators.

Additionally, studies comparing job status across different societies have shown that the relative status of different jobs is quite similar in a number of different industrialized societies (see Hodge, Trieman, and Rossi, 1966). Thus, a doctor, a lawyer, or an airline pilot has high status not only in the United States, but in Canada, Sweden, and Great Britain as well. A janitor or taxi driver, in contrast, has low status in all these societies. In addition, the relative status of these jobs in all these societies is about the same today as it was decades ago. Even in some less industrialized countries, the same patterns hold. Recent research by Nan and Wen (1988) has revealed that the prestige of jobs in China is very similar to the prestige of jobs in other countries.

What determines the prestige of a job? As is true of subjective class, several factors are relevant. In general, better-paid jobs have higher prestige. Prestige also depends on the educational requirements of the job and the amount of physical labor it entails. Thus, even though college professors are often paid less than many assembly-line workers, they consistently rank near the top in occupational prestige. The very highest ranked jobs, such as physician and airline pilot, are professional occupations associated with both high incomes and high levels of education. Similarly, the jobs with lowest-prestige, such as garbage collector, janitor, and shoe shiner, involve hard physical work, require little or no education, and pay poorly. A list of some jobs and their occupational prestige ratings from surveys in the United States and other countries is presented in Table 9.2.

## Class Consciousness in the United States

One important aspect of class in America is the extent to which Americans are aware of, and identify with, the social classes to which they belong. Such awareness and identification is called *class consciousness.* Americans seem to be less class-conscious than people in many other societies. We have already noted that nearly all Americans think of themselves as "middle class" or "working class." This contrasts with some other societies where, for example, the wealthy readily identify themselves as upper class. United States society was founded as a result of a rebellion against title and monarchy and was based on the principle that "all men are created equal." Although, as we have seen, the reality is that there is great social inequality in America, most Americans prefer not to acknowledge that openly. Rather, we prefer to believe that people have similar statuses and similar situations in life—that we are all pretty much alike (DeMott, 1990). America's entertainment media abet this belief as they either gloss over social-class differences, or present them as easily surmountable. The Horatio Alger myth that anyone who tries can succeed, and the assertion that love will easily overcome social-class differences, is still popular, as we can see in such movies as *Pretty Woman*, *Dirty Dancing*, and *White Palace* (DeMott, 1991).

Two other reasons have been suggested to explain why Americans are less class-conscious than people in other industrialized countries. First, education has been more accessible in the United States than elsewhere. The great majority of Americans graduate from high school, and more go on to college than in other industrialized countries. Although we do have sizable educational differences based on class, we have not formalized these differences as other countries such as Great Britain have done. This leads us to think of ourselves as being more similar to one another.

The other reason is that, until the 1970s, the United States experienced more economic expansion and therefore more structural mobility than other countries. As a result, people's standards of living improved, and people saw class boundaries as less real and more permeable. An end to this high structural mobility could mean a rise in class consciousness in America. As higher paying jobs disappeared in the 1980s and job growth occurred mainly in lower-paying jobs, the opportunities associated with structural mobility began to disappear and the perception of people trapped in the underclass grew.

There are already signs that this has led Americans to become somewhat more class-conscious. Class-related issues played a more prominent role in the 1992 presidential election, as Democrats Bill Clinton and Al Gore hit hard on the failure of the "trickle-down" notion that tax breaks for the wealthy would create better jobs for the middle class and the poor. Unlike other recent elections, the 1992 election saw changes in the distribution of income become an important issue, as Clinton and Gore repeatedly and successfully sounded the theme that the wealthiest few were getting even wealthier while everyone else was losing income relative to inflation.

# POVERTY IN THE UNITED STATES

The extremes of social and economic stratification are the easiest to see—and the most difficult to deny. We turn our attention now to those at the bottom of the economic stratification system: the poor. We shall begin our discussion of poverty by examining some different ways of defining poverty; then we shall see how poverty is officially defined and measured in the United States.

**TABLE 9.2 Occupational Prestige Ratings: United States Compared to 60-Country Average**

| Occupation | Average, 60 Countries | United States |
|---|---|---|
| University president or dean | 86 | 82.4 |
| Physician | 78 | 81.5 |
| University professor | 78 | 78.3 |
| Physicist | 76 | 73.8 |
| Member, board of directors | 75 | 71.8 |
| Lawyer | 73 | 75.7 |
| Architect | 72 | 70.5 |
| Dentist | 70 | 73.5 |
| Chemist | 69 | 68.8 |
| Sociologist | 67 | 65.0 |
| Airline pilot | 66 | 70.1 |
| High-school teacher | 64 | 63.1 |
| Clergy member | 60 | 70.5 |
| Personnel director | 58 | 57.8 |
| Artist | 57 | 57.0 |
| Classical musician | 56 | 55.0 |
| Social worker | 56 | 52.4 |
| Journalist | 55 | 51.6 |
| Professional nurse | 54 | 61.5 |
| Secretary | 53 | 45.8 |
| Actor or actress | 52 | 55.0 |
| Union official | 50 | 41.2 |
| Real-estate agent | 49 | 44.0 |
| Professional athlete | 48 | 51.4 |
| Farmer | 47 | 43.7 |
| Motor-vehicle mechanic | 44 | 35.8 |
| Policeman or policewoman | 40 | 47.8 |
| Railroad conductor | 39 | 40.9 |
| Telephone operator | 38 | 40.4 |
| Jazz musician | 38 | 37.2 |
| Carpenter | 37 | 42.5 |
| Dancing teacher | 36 | 32.3 |
| Firefighter | 35 | 33.2 |
| Sales clerk | 34 | 27.1 |
| Truck driver | 33 | 31.3 |
| File clerk | 31 | 30.3 |
| Assembly-line worker | 30 | 27.1 |
| Construction worker | 28 | 26.2 |
| Gas-station attendant | 25 | 21.6 |
| Waiter | 23 | 20.3 |
| Janitor | 21 | 16.1 |
| Farm worker | 20 | 21.4 |
| Garbage collector | 13 | 12.6 |
| Shoe shiner | 12 | 9.3 |

NOTE: In a limited number of instances, there were slight differences in job titles between Appendix A (worldwide average) and Appendix D (United States). In these instances, the closest job title was used.

SOURCE: Reprinted by permission from Appendices A and D in Donald J. Trieman, *Occupational Prestige in Comparative Perspective*. Copyright 1977, by Academic Press.

## How Poverty Is Defined

Generally, statistics on poverty are based on the federal government's poverty level. To make sense of these statistics, we must understand (1) what is meant by the term *poverty* and (2) how the federal poverty level is determined.

**Relative versus Absolute Concepts of Poverty** Poverty can be defined as the condition of having a very low income and standard of living. However, such a definition immediately raises a question: What do we mean by low? Low could mean "low compared with almost everyone else," or it could mean "below the level sufficient to buy necessities." For this reason, poverty can be defined in either a relative (low compared with others) or an absolute (lacking necessities) manner. In the case of *relative poverty*, a person's standard of living is low compared with that of others who enjoy a higher standard of living. By this definition, every society with social inequality will have *some* poverty. However, some societies have greater degrees of poverty than others. In the United States, where the poorest 10 percent of the population has one-fifteenth the income of the richest 10 percent, poverty in a *relative* sense is more extreme than in Sweden, where the poorest 10 percent has one-seventh the income of the richest 10 percent (Thurow, 1977).

Now, consider the *absolute* definition of poverty. By this definition, poverty exists whenever people lack some basic necessities of life. Thus, it is possible, at least in theory, for a country to have no poverty at all, even if it has considerable social inequality. If everyone gets all the basic necessities, there is no poverty.

**The Official Definition of Poverty in the United States** The U.S. government's official definition of poverty is intended to delineate poverty in the *absolute* sense. In other words, it is meant to represent a level of income below which people are unlikely to be able to buy all of the necessities of life. The official definition of poverty in the United States originated in the 1950s, when the government estimated the cost of the minimum diet necessary to get a person or a family through a limited period of financial difficulty in good health. As a result of a 1961 government study showing that the average low-income family spent one-third of its income on food, the poverty level was set at roughly three times the cost of this minimum diet. (Because of differences in their cost of living, this multiplication factor is a little more than three for individuals and smaller families, and a little less than three for rural families.) Since 1961, the poverty level has been adjusted upward each year to take account of inflation. In 1991, the poverty level for a family of four was $13,924. For one nonelderly individual living alone, it was about $6,900. Questions have been raised about the extent to which this standard correctly measures poverty. Although some critics disagree, the dominant opinion among economists, home economists, and sociologists is that the official definition *fails* to include many people who are poor in the absolute sense. (See Rodgers, 1978; U.S. Bureau of the Census, 1976.)

## Poverty in America: The Current Situation

In 1991, the most recent year for which data are available, 35.7 million Americans, or 14.2 percent of the population, were living below the poverty level (U.S. Bureau of the Census, 1992a). This amounts to almost one person out of every seven living in the United States today. Just how large a group is this? It is twice the population of New York State and more than three times that of Illinois. Clearly, we are talking about a very large number of people.

Is the number of poor people growing or getting smaller? The answer to this question is found in Figure 9–2. This figure indicates that both the number and the percentage of Americans living below the poverty level fell from 1960 until around 1970, reached a low point in 1973, and fluctuated irregularly from then until 1978. Between 1978 and 1983, poverty rose sharply. By 1983, there were again over 35 million poor people in the United States, the highest number since before 1964, when President Lyndon

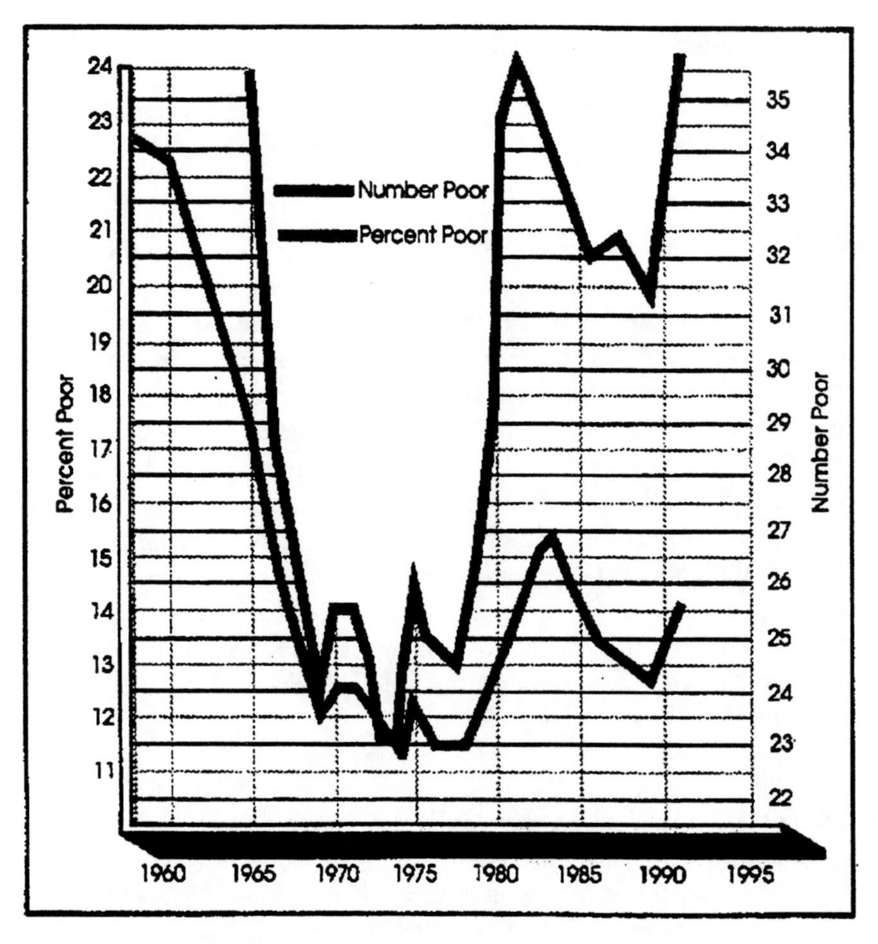


**FIGURE 9–2 The Trend in Poverty, 1960–1989**
Note the dramatic rise in the incidence of poverty since the late 1970s.

SOURCE: U.S. Bureau of the Census, Current Population Reports, Series P–60, No. 168, p. 15 (September, 1990).

Johnson proclaimed his "War on Poverty." The poverty rate had increased to over 15 percent. Between 1983 and 1989, poverty again declined modestly, but it rose again after 1989 as the economy slipped into recession, and by 1991 there were more poor people than the 1983 peak.

In a direct sense, the rise in poverty after 1978 reflects two things. First is a general increase in social inequality in the United States (Jencks, 1991). As we have already seen from the income and wealth data, the rich got richer and the poor got poorer during this period. To a very large extent, this trend resulted from policies of the Reagan administration: the deregulation of business, the decrease in tax rates for the wealthy, and cutbacks in government antipoverty programs (Bartlett and Steele, 1992).

Second, the growth in poverty between 1978 and 1983 was partly the result of a lack of real economic growth and productivity growth in the American economy. Real (that is, adjusted for inflation) family incomes fell between 1973 and 1984, even though more wives entered the work force (*St. Louis Post-Dispatch*, 1985), and there was little or no growth in productivity during this period. Since productivity rose again in the mid-l980s, and since there has still been growth in real per-capita income, largely because of women entering the labor force (Jencks, 1991; Olsen, 1990), we would expect a sizable drop in poverty to have taken place since about 1984. In fact, there was only a small decline in poverty in the 1980s, and that was wiped out by the 1990–1992 recession. Thus, lack of economic growth is only part of the cause of today's high poverty rates; the rest lies in rising economic inequality.

Because it has more economic inequality than other industrialized countries, the United States has more poverty, even by the standard of absolute poverty. Smeeding, Torrey, and Rein (1988) compared the

United States to seven other industrialized countries, using the U.S. government's methods for comparing poverty rates. In five of the seven countries, the poverty rates averaged a full five percentage points lower than in the United States. Perhaps most disturbing is the difference in poverty among children: The United States had the highest child poverty rate of any of the countries, and was about 10 percentage points above the poverty rates of most of the other countries (Peterson, 1991).

## Who Is Poor?

A number of social characteristics increase the risk that people will be poor. In general, the groups with disproportionate amounts of poverty are blacks, Hispanics, and American Indians; women; people living in female-headed families; children; and people who live in central cities and rural areas (as opposed to suburbs). To a large extent, this reflects the lower status accorded to these groups by society and their relative lack of power. The number of poor people and the poverty rates of people with various characteristics is shown in detail in Figure 9–3 and Table 9.3. Note that although the poverty rate of blacks is three times that of whites and the Hispanic poverty rate is more than double that of non-Hispanic whites, the majority of all poor people in the United States are non-Hispanic whites. This is because the large majority of the population is white and non-Hispanic. The single biggest risk factor for poverty is living in a

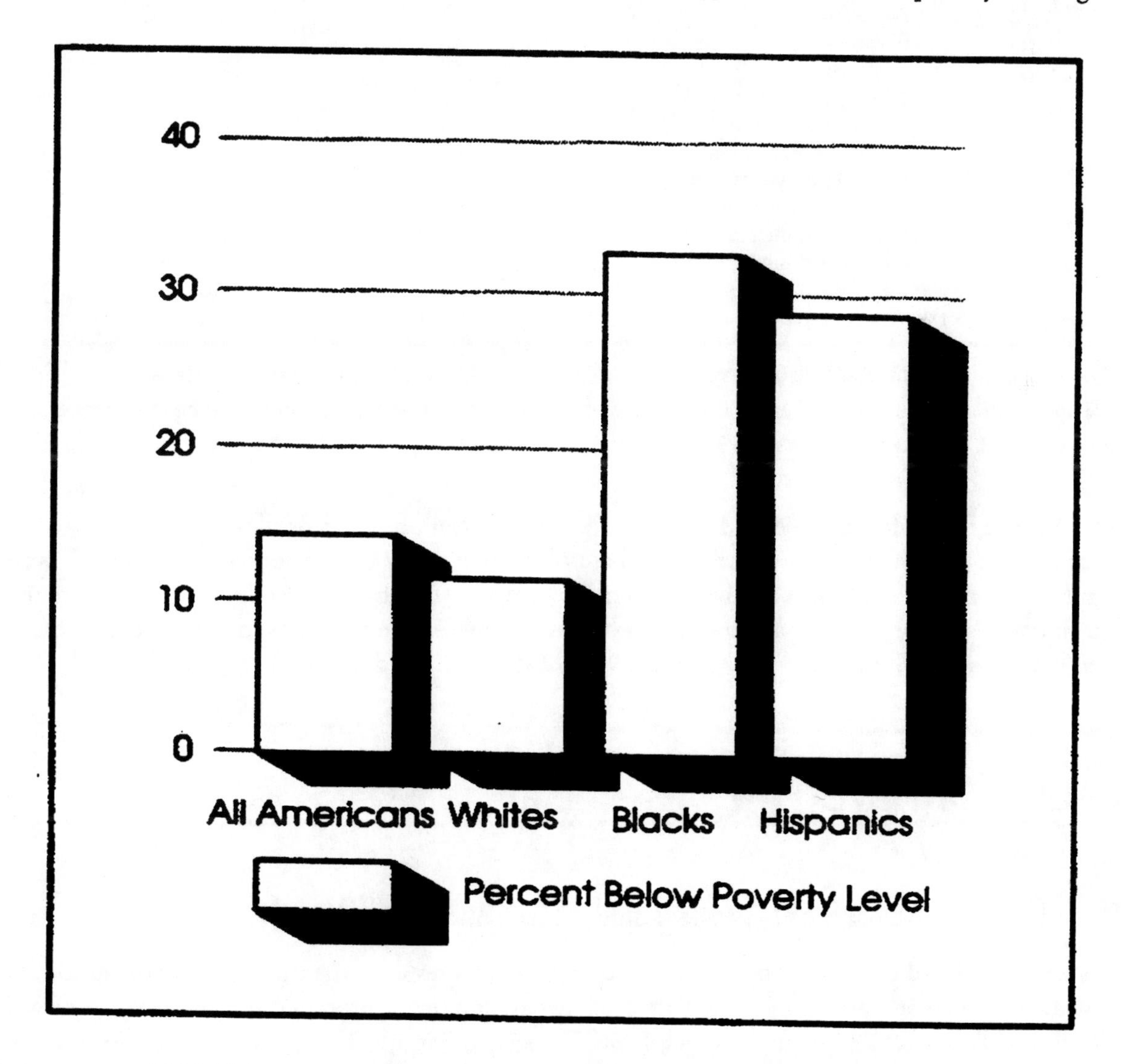


**FIGURE 9–3 Poverty Rates by Race and Hispanic Origin, 1991.**
SOURCE: U.S. Bureau of the Census Press Release, Sept. 3, 1992.

**TABLE 9.3 Number of People below Poverty Level, and Poverty rates for Selected Groups in the U.S. Population, 1991**

| Population Subgroup | Number of People below Poverty Level (in millions) | Poverty Rate |
|---|---|---|
| Total U.S. Population | 35.7 | 14.2% |
| White Americans | 23.7 | 11.3 |
| Black Americans | 10.2 | 32.7 |
| Americans of other races[1] | 1.7 | 17.6 |
| Hispanic Americans[2] | 6.3 | 28.7 |
| Children under 18 | 14.3 | 21.8 |
| White children under 18 | 8.8 | 16.8 |
| Black children under 18 | 4.8 | 45.9 |
| Hispanic children under 18[2] | 3.1 | 40.4 |
| Married-couple families | 3.2 | 6.0 |
| Female-householder families | 4.2 | 35.8 |
| People in female-householder families | 13.8 | 39.7 |
| White | 6.8 | 31.5 |
| Black | 6.6 | 54.8 |
| Hispanic | 2.3 | 52.7 |
| Central-city residents | 15.3 | 20.2 |
| Suburban residents | 11.5 | 9.6 |
| Nonmetropolitan residents | 8.9 | 16.1 |
| People 18 to 64 years of age | 17.6 | 11.4 |
| People 65 years of age and over | 3.7 | 12.4 |
| People living in the Northeast | 6.2 | 12.2 |
| People living in the Midwest | 8.0 | 13.2 |
| People living in the South | 13.8 | 16.0 |
| People living in the West | 7.8 | 14.3 |

[1] Does not include Hispanics. This group consists mainly of Asian Americans and American Indians.

[2] Hispanics are regarded by the Census Bureau as an ethnic group, not a race, and thus may be of any race.

SOURCE: U.S. Bureau of the Census, 1992f.

family with a female householder and no husband present. Over one-third of all poor people live in such families, even though fewer than one American out of seven lives in a female householder family. It is also significant that children have a relatively high risk of poverty (Duncan and Rodgers, 1991). More than one in five were poor in 1991, and more than one in three will experience poverty at some time during their childhood (U.S. Bureau of the Census, 1990a, 1992a; Ellwood, 1987).

# CAUSES OF POVERTY

## Poor People Themselves? Work, Family Structure, and Poverty

It is widely believed that people often experience poverty as a result of their own actions or inactions—unwillingness to work, drunkenness, welfare dependency, and sexual promiscuity leading to out-of-wedlock births (Feagin, 1972; see also Kluegel, 1990; Kluegel and Smith, 1986; Schuman, 1975). A careful examination of the characteristics of the poor, however, indicates that these factors are relatively unimportant as causes of poverty.

**Work Experience of the Poor** One relevant set of characteristics can be seen in Figure 9–4, which shows the work experience of poor people over age 15 in 1989. At first glance, the data in the figure appear to support the "unwillingness to work" explanation—over half of poor people over 15 did not, in fact, work during 1989. However, if we examine the *reasons* these people did not work, we get a different picture. To begin with, nearly two-thirds of those who did not work were ill, disabled, retired, or attending school—all of which are generally regarded as legitimate reasons for being out of the work force. In fact, these groups combined account for about one-third of *all* poor people over 15.

Another sizable group (5 percent) of the nonworking poor had looked for work but were unable to find it. Almost all of the rest of the nonworking poor—19 percent of all poor people—fell into the "keeping house" category. About half of these were female single parents with children, and most of the rest were nonemployed wives with children. In addition to the fact that a mother staying home to take care of her children has always been acceptable in American society (and until recently was the norm), we must consider here the cost of day care and medical care. As we shall see later, many poor people have no employment available except minimum-wage jobs, most of which include no medical benefits. By the time a poor mother pays for day care for her children (which can cost well over $200 per month per child), she may already have used up all the income from a minimum-wage job. And in most states, if she remains employed, she must give up Medicaid, which means she must pay for medical care for herself and her family as well, or let her family go without needed care. In many cases, she literally can't afford to take a job—the costs of day care and medical care are simply too great.

We have now accounted for all but 2 percent out of the 58 percent of poor people who did not work in 1989. In other words, the number of poor people who did not work in 1989 and did not have what would generally be regarded as a good reason for not working was just 2 percent of the U.S. population—hardly a great mass of people. These statistics are consistent with research findings reported by Tienda and Stier (1991). In a study of Chicago's poorest neighborhoods, they found that only 6 percent of the population could be characterized as shiftless; that is, unwilling to work. The rest were either employed, caring for children, disabled, students, or looking for work.

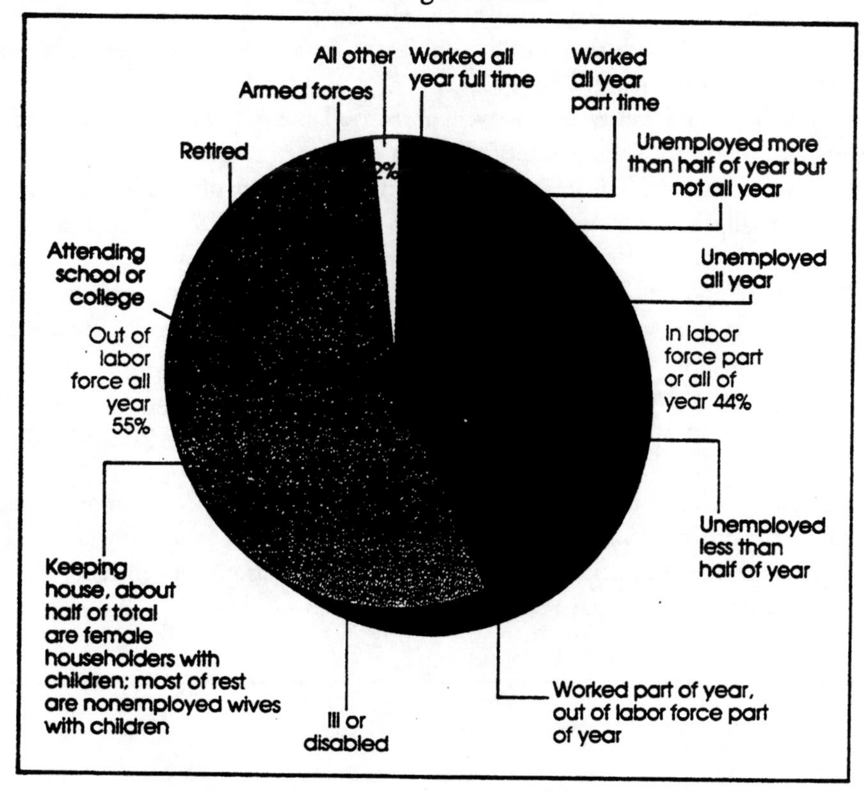


**FIGURE 9–4 Labor-Force Status of Poor People 15 and Over, 1989**
SOURCE: U.S. Bureau of the Census, 1990a, p. 65.

## COMPARING CULTURES AND SOCIETIES

### AMERICAN POVERTY AND TEENAGE PREGNANCY IN GLOBAL PERSPECTIVE

Poverty is more widespread and severe in the United States than in other industrialized countries, and children are more likely than other Americans to be poor. One possible reason: American teenagers are more likely to get pregnant and have a baby out-of-wedlock than teenagers in other industrialized countries. When this happens, their children often experience poverty. In fact, more than 90 percent of American children who live in a single-parent home through the first 10 years of life will experience poverty (Ellwood, 1987). About two-thirds of these children will be poor for the entire 10 years.

The fact that American teens are more likely to become parents than their counterparts in other industrialized countries was shown in a study comparing the United States, Canada, France, Great Britain, the Netherlands, and Sweden (Jones et al., 1986). The United States had by far the highest rates of teenage pregnancies, births, and abortions of any of these countries. Although some of the difference was the product of the higher poverty rate in the United States and the relatively high incidence of teenage pregnancy among American minority groups, these factors were not by any means the whole answer. White U.S. teenagers, for example, have pregnancy rates far above those found in any of the other countries. The differences also could not be explained by differences in sexual activity: U.S. teenagers are no more likely than teenagers in the other countries (except possibly Canada) to be sexually active.

Why, then, do American teenagers get pregnant so much more often than teenagers in other countries? At least part of the answer is that they are less likely to use contraceptives (Jones et al., 1986). Part of the reason for that, in turn, is that it is harder for American teenagers to get contraceptives. Many Americans believe that making contraceptives available to teenagers will encourage them to have sex, so we have avoided doing so.

What would happen if contraceptives were more available to U.S. teenagers? We don't have all the answers, but we do have some. Experiments in cities such as Baltimore provided teenagers with contraceptives, along with information concerning human sexuality and advice that they did not have to be sexually active if they didn't want to be (Hayes, 1987). In such a context, the provision of contraceptives did not increase teenage sexual activity; if anything, the total effect of the program was the opposite (Schorr, 1988, p. 53). Moreover, those teenagers who did have sex were more likely to use contraception, and the pregnancy rate fell—meaning fewer teenage births and fewer teenage abortions.

Thus, the common American belief that making contraceptives more available will lead more teenagers to have sex appears not to be true, at least if school health programs are properly designed. The Jones et al. study suggests another reason for Americans' opposition to contraceptives for teenagers: Americans, more than people in other countries, may favor more sexual restrictions because of religious beliefs. However, since American teens are as sexually active as teens in other industrialized countries, the main effect of American restrictions on contraceptives seems to be a higher teenage pregnancy rate relative to other countries.

**Out-of-Wedlock Births** Single-parent, female-headed families are at a very high risk for poverty. As the percentage of such families has risen, the poverty rate also has risen (Eggebeen and Lichter, 1991). Many female-householder families are the result of out-of-wedlock births, although many others are the result of divorces and separations. However, to say that out-of-wedlock childbearing (or, for that matter, divorce) is one of the most important causes of poverty is to ignore several key realities. First, the rate of out-of-wedlock births is far higher among people who are *already* poor or who grew up in poverty than among the general public (see Hayes, 1987b). Thus, poverty appears to be at least as much a *cause* of out-of-wedlock births as a *consequence*. One reason for this is that poor people are less likely to be familiar with, or have access to, birth control, which increases their nonmarital birth rates. In addition, because of high unemployment, urban minority poor women—the ones most likely to give birth out of wedlock—have a strikingly small pool of employed, marriageable men (Wilson, 1987, pp. 95–100; see also Mare and Winship, 1991; Lichter, LeClere, and McLaughlin, 1991). As a result, a larger proportion of these women never marry, and those who do marry later and wait longer to remarry after a divorce. This means that more of them are at risk of a nonmarital pregnancy. Like the great majority of nonmarried women of all socioeconomic levels, they are usually sexually active—but they are unmarried for a longer part of their-lives, and they know less about contraception.

Research also shows that poverty affects self-image and attitudes in ways that increase the likelihood of out-of wedlock pregnancy, especially among teenagers (Anderson, 1991). Poor people experience less control over their lives and may feel less able to control whether they get pregnant—so they are less likely to try. To an impoverished teenage girl, a baby can sometimes be a source of self-esteem, a way of feeling grown-up. Among poor teenage boys, sexual conquest (which is valued to some extent among young males of all social classes) may be one of the few ways of feeling a sense of accomplishment, when most legitimate opportunities for achievement are blocked. Thus, however much out-of-wedlock childbirth may perpetuate poverty, it is probably more a *consequence* of poverty than a cause. Moreover, as shown in the box entitled "American Poverty and Teenage Pregnancy in Global Perspective," there is much that we could do to prevent teenage pregnancy but have chosen not to do as a result of misperceptions about the likely consequences, as well as religious objections. Finally, the low wages of women are a major reason for the high poverty rate among female-householder families.

These findings clearly indicate that poor people themselves are not, by and large, the cause of their own poverty. Most of them either are employed, are looking for work, or have a good reason not to be working. Although they do have high rates of divorce, separation, and nonmarital childbearing—and thus a high incidence of female-householder families—this appears to be much more a *consequence* than a cause of poverty. Moreover, the economic situation of female-householder families would be far less difficult if women were simply paid at the same rate for their work as men are, and if day care and health care were publicly funded, as they are in nearly all other industrialized countries.

What, then, *are* the causes of poverty, and why has poverty increased so much since the mid-1970s? Among the explanations are unemployment and low wages, both of which have become more prevalent as socioeconomic inequality has increased in the United States since the 1970s. In addition, certain public policies have contributed to the spread of poverty or to worsening its impact.

## SOCIAL ISSUES FOR THE '90s

### Does Welfare Cause Poverty?

Some argue that the supposedly generous welfare benefits of the past two or three decades have made it too easy for people not to work, and that many people are poor simply because they would rather collect welfare than get a job. They argue that, by discouraging people from working, welfare causes them to become detached from the labor force—in other words, to get in the habit of *not* working. As a result, they argue, welfare actually causes an *increase* in poverty, as people become less attached to the labor force and chronically out of work. Such arguments have led social scientists to ask a number of questions:

*Do most people who fall below the poverty level and/or receive welfare become chronically poor and dependent on welfare?*

*When more people are on welfare or when welfare benefits are increased, does long-term poverty increase?*

*Does welfare cause people to have children out of wedlock, to avoid marriage, or to get divorced?*

Intuitively, one might think that the answers to the above questions would be "yes." However, actual research results suggest that the answers are not that simple. For one thing, we have already seen that most non-working poor people have good reasons not be working. In addition, research relating to the questions posed above points to additional flaws in the argument that welfare increases poverty by discouraging work.

First, poverty is less often chronic and long-term than is commonly believed; relatively few poor people remain on welfare year after year. A long-term survey by Duncan et al. (1984), for example, showed that of all the people who were poor at some time between 1969 and 1978, about half were poor for two years or less. Only one in ten was persistently poor for eight or more of the 10 study years, which amounts to less than 3 percent of the total population of the United States. Only about 4 percent of the U.S. population used welfare persistently over the decade, and of these, fewer than half used it as their main source of income. Thus, the number of people who consistently use welfare to avoid work is small, probably not larger than 2 percent of the entire population.

It is true, however, that a sizable share of the poor in *any given year* are people who are experiencing long periods of poverty (Bane and Ellwood, 1983a). Additionally, evidence suggests that the proportion of persistently poor people increased somewhat during the first half of the 1980s (Adams, Duncan, and Rogers, 1988; Duncan and Rogers, 1989). But, there are other explanations that better account for this poverty than the welfare incentive.

Charles Murray (1984) made the argument in his controversial book *Losing Ground* that the expansion of welfare benefits has led to a growth in poverty by encouraging people to accept welfare benefits rather than to work. However, there are clear problems with this argument. One of the most important is that, during the period from 1978 to 1983 when poverty grew most rapidly, real (inflation-adjusted) welfare benefits were *falling*, not rising (see, for example, Wilson, 1987). In fact, real welfare benefits fell steadily and substantially from 1972 on, and by 1984, the combined, inflation-adjusted value of welfare and food stamps was 22 percent lower than it had been in 1972 (Wilson, 1987, p. 94). According to Murray's argument, there should have been fewer poor people and less unemployment in 1984 than in 1972; in fact, the opposite was true. There *had been* an improvement in welfare benefits, but it came earlier, when poverty was on the way down, not up.

Research has been conducted on the extent to which the incentive to collect welfare leads people to have children, to avoid marriage, or to get divorced. Comparisons between states with high and low levels of welfare show no effect of welfare levels on birth rates among the poor, and only very small effects on the divorce/separation rate (Ellwood and Bane, 1984; Rank, 1989; Wilson, 1987, pp. 77-81). If there is any effect, it is that where welfare levels are higher, young single mothers with children are more likely to live independently and less likely to live with their parents (Ellwood and Bane, 1984; Holden, 1987).

It may be that welfare requirements that no man be present in the household of a mother receiving welfare do contribute to family disruption, however. If a husband/father is unable to find work, the family may well be better off economically if he leaves, because it may then be eligible for welfare. In some cases, this probably does disrupt families and encourage welfare dependency. However, this is an issue unrelated to the presence or amount of welfare: it is a product of a specific policy attached to some welfare programs that no able-bodied partner be present in the household, regardless of the availability of work.

## PERSONAL JOURNEY INTO SOCIOLOGY

### HOW SOCIETAL CHANGES HELP SHAPE MY VIEWS ON RACE RELATIONS AND URBAN POVERTY / William Julius Wilson

Unlike many who enter a field of specialization on the basis of graduate training, I did not pursue race and ethnic relations and urban poverty as major fields of study in graduate school at Washington State University. My graduate study focused mainly on sociological theory and the philosophy of the social sciences. However, my concentration on these fields of study could not be sustained in a period dominated by events in the black protest movement.

In my last two years as a graduate student in the mid-1960s I, like most blacks, was caught up in the spirit of the civil rights revolution and was encouraged by the changes in social structure that led to increasing opportunities for black Americans. I also followed with intense interest the ghetto riots in Watts, Newark, and Detroit. And although at this point I had not developed a serious academic interest in the field of race and ethnic relations, my intellectual curiosity for the subject, fed by the escalating racial protest and my sense of the changing social structure for blacks in America, was rising so rapidly that by the time I accepted my first full-time academic job as an assistant professor of sociology at the University of Massachusetts, Amherst, in the fall of 1965, I had firmly decided to develop a field of specialization in that area.

My first major publication in the field of race relations was *Power, Racism and Privilege: Race Relations in Theoretical and Sociohistorical Perspectives*, published by Macmillan in 1973 and by Free Press in a paperback version in 1976. This study presents a comprehensive theoretical framework that is applied to race relations in the United States and the Republic of South Africa. However, by the time the book was in press my thinking about the field of race relations in America had already begun to change. I regretted not only that I had paid so little attention to the role of class in understanding issues of race, but also that I tended to treat blacks as a monolithic socioeconomic group in most sections of the book.

It was not until after I moved to Chicago and joined the sociology faculty at the University of Chicago in 1972 that my views on the intersection of class with race in the United States sufficiently crystallized. My thinking about intraracial divisions in America during the 1970s was in no small measure shaped by my perception of the changing social environments in Chicago's variegated ethnic neighborhoods. At one extreme were the upper-middle-class black professional neighborhoods in parts of the South Side; at the other extreme were the communities of the ghetto poor, plagued by long-term joblessness, in other parts of the South Side and on the West Side. The widening gap between the haves and have-nots among African Americans would have been obvious to any student of urban life who cared to take the time to drive around the Chicago neighborhoods at different points in time, as I did in the early to mid 1970s.

It is one thing to recognize and describe these intragroup differences; it is quite another thing to account for their evolution and relate them not only to the problems of intergroup relations, but, more importantly, to the broader problems of societal organization in America. The stimulating intellectual environment of the University of Chicago helped me develop a broader vision on race. The university encourages interdisciplinary contact and thereby afforded me the opportunity to confront questions about racial interaction from students of varied disciplinary backgrounds. The net result was the development of a holistic approach to race relations in America that directed the writing, particularly the theoretical writing, of *The Declining Significance of Race.*

The theoretical framework of this book relates problems associated with race to the broader issues of societal organization. To study problems of race in terms of societal organization entails an investigation of not only the political, economic, and other institutional dimensions of societal organization that affect intra- and intergroup experiences, but the technological dimensions as well. The basic theoretical argument presented in *The Declining Significance of Race* is that different systems of production in combination with different policies of the state impose different, constraints on racial group relations by producing dissimilar contexts, not only for the manifestation of racial antagonisms but also for racial-group access to rewards and privileges.

I had hoped that my major academic contribution would be to explain racial change by applying this framework to historical developments of race relations in the United States. But there was another contribution I had wished to make—I wanted to highlight the worsening condition of the black underclass, in both absolute and relative terms, by relating it to the improving position of the black middle class.

*The Declining Significance of Race* generated an even greater controversy than I had originally anticipated. At the time of its publication, heightened awareness of racial issues had been created not only because changing social structures altered many traditional patterns of race relations, but also because the state was inextricably involved in the emerging controversy over affirmative action.

In the initial months following the book's publication, it seemed that critics were so preoccupied with what I had to say about the improving conditions of the black middle class that they virtually ignored my more important arguments about the deteriorating position of the black urban poor. The view was often expressed that since all blacks from all socioeconomic class backgrounds are suffering there is no need to single out the black poor.

During the controversy over *The Declining Significance of Race* I committed myself to doing two things: (1) I would address the problems of the ghetto poor in a comprehensive analysis; and (2) I would spell out, in considerable detail, the policy implications of my work. These two commitments provided direction for the writing of *The Truly Disadvantaged: The Inner City, The Underclass, and Public Policy*, published in 1987 by the University of Chicago Press.

The first commitment grew out of my personal and academic reaction to the early critics' almost total preoccupation with my arguments concerning the black middle class. It was only after I began writing *The Truly Disadvantaged* that serious scholars began to focus on my previous analysis of the underclass in *The Declining Significance of Race*, particularly those scholars who are working in fields such as urban poverty, social welfare, and public policy.

The second commitment stemmed from my reaction to those critics who either labeled me a neo-conservative or directly or indirectly tried to associate *The Declining Significance of Race* with the neo-conservative movement. Although I am a social democrat, and probably to the left politically of the overwhelming majority of these critics, and although some of the most positive reviews and discussions of *The Declining Significance of Race* have come from those of the democratic left, the title of my book readily lends itself to an assumption that I am a black conservative. Nonetheless, because I did not spell out the policy implications of *The Declining Significance of Race* in the first edition, it was possible for people to read selectively my arguments and draw policy implications significantly different from those that I would personally espouse. In the second edition of *The Declining Significance of Race*, published in 1980, I wrote an epilogue in which the policy implications of my work were underlined in sharp relief, but by then the views of many readers of the first edition had already solidified.

If the idea for *The Truly Disadvantaged* grew out of the controversy over *The Declining Significance of Race*, the former also generated controversy. *The Truly Disadvantaged* challenges liberal orthodoxy in analyzing inner-city problems; discusses in candid terms social dislocations of the inner city; establishes a case for moving beyond race-specific policies to ameliorate inner-city social conditions to policies that address the broader problems of societal organization, including economic organization; and advances a social democratic public-policy agenda designed to improve the life chances of truly disadvantaged groups such as the ghetto underclass by emphasizing programs to which the more advantaged groups of all races can positively relate.

*The Truly Disadvantaged* enjoys the unique distinction of generating a lot of attention both within and outside academia. And in contrast to *The Declining Significance of Race*, the scholarly attention it has attracted is not focused mainly on controversy but on the theoretical and substantive arguments raised in the book. Indeed, *The Truly Disadvantaged* has generated a new research paradigm that has stimulated studies not only in sociology, but in economics, psychology, anthropology, education, social work, history, philosophy, and political science as well.

The notion that poor people have more babies in order to collect welfare simply isn't supported by research findings. This is not surprising, as the costs associated with having and raising a child are *far greater* than additional welfare benefits that child might bring. Finally, Jencks (1991, pp. 56-62) suggests that availability and level of welfare have little effect on the proportion of single mothers who are employed. (For further discussion, see Ellwood, 1987.)

It may be true, as William Julius Wilson has argued in *The Truly Disadvantaged*, that detachment from the labor force does perpetuate poverty. However, research does not support the notion that welfare in and of itself causes either detachment from the labor force or an increase in poverty. Rather, Wilson and others point out, labor force detachment is better explained by long-term losses of jobs—particularly jobs that pay well—from inner city areas. When jobs are chronically difficult or impossible to find, and are only temporary and pay poorly on the rare occasions when they are available, people eventually give up on work. This condition has become increasingly common in America's central cities since the 1960s, but structural changes leading to job loss, not welfare, appear to be the main causes of persistent poverty.

## Unemployment

Consider again Figure 9.4., which shows that only 6 percent of poor people were unemployed all year. But now look at the number who were unemployed for more than half of the year (4 percent) and the number who were unemployed for less than half of the year (9 percent). This adds up to one poor adult out of five who experienced some unemployment over the course of the year, and nearly one out of two of those who actually sought employment. In addition, some of those who worked part-time did so because they could not find a full-time job. Thus, unemployment plays an important role as a cause of poverty.

**Recent Unemployment Trends** Unemployment has been more prevalent since around 1980 than it was in earlier decades. In the best years of the 1980s, it averaged 6 or 7 percent, and in the recession of the early 1980s, it exceeded 10 percent. By the early 1990s, unemployment was on the rise again. In addition, these official unemployment figures understate true unemployment, because they do not include people who have given up looking for work.

One reason for rising unemployment can be tied to rising numbers of people entering the labor force: baby boomers who reached working age in the 1970s and 1980s, and women who entered the labor force in many cases because their family income could not keep up with inflation without two incomes. However, other factors are more important than the growth of the labor force.

**Deindustrialization** A cause of declining wages, as well as rising unemployment, is **deindustrialization** (Harrison and Bluestone, 1988; Wilson, 1987), a decline in the importance of heavy industry as a source of employment. Deindustrialization is a result of automation, international competition, and relocation of jobs—sometimes out of the United States. Because of more efficient operations and, in some cases, lower wages, many countries can produce cars, televisions, machine tools, and other products comparable or superior to American producers at lower cost. American companies also have contributed to deindustrialization in the United States. In search of low wages, American companies often have moved assembly operations to Third World countries, depriving Americans of jobs in the process (Harrington, 1984). Thousands of manufacturing jobs have been shifted from the United States to northern Mexico for this reason. Of the 1,400 manufacturing plants in Mexico near the border in 1988, for example, 90 percent were American-owned (Rohan, 1989). By eliminating higher-paying jobs, deindustrialization has resulted in growing inequality and rising poverty since the late 1970s.

The effects of deindustrialization have been particularly devastating for central cities, particularly manufacturing cities in the Midwest and Northeast (Kasarda, 1990; Wilson, 1987, 1991a, 199lb). The increasing African-American and Hispanic populations in these cities, devastated by the loss of jobs, also find it difficult to move into the still segregated suburban areas, where jobs are often more readily available (Farley, 1987b; Kasarda, 1980, 1985, 1989; Massey and Eggers, 1990). A recent experiment in Chicago shows the impact of such exclusion: When poor blacks were given the opportunity to move from the city to the suburbs, their employment rose relative to others who remained behind in the city (Rosenbaum and Popkin, 1991). As a result of job losses, the proportion of blacks and Hispanics in older cities who live in neighborhoods of highly concentrated poverty has risen. This phenomenon may further perpetuate poverty by undermining neighborhood institutions and depriving young people of successful role models (Anderson, 1991; Crane, 1991a, 1991b; Wilson, 1987, 199la).

In some cities, manufacturing employment losses have been offset by growth of employment in the service and administrative sectors (Kasarda, 1990). However, this has been of limited benefit, for two reasons. First, these industries were highly automated and computerized and often did not employ as many people relative to their size as manufacturing had. Second, many of the jobs they did offer required a high level of education, so they were not available to displaced industrial workers or the inner-city poor (Wilson, 1987, pp. 39-42). Moreover, the service jobs that did not have high educational requirements paid much lower wages than the industrial jobs that had been lost. As a result of these changes, portions of our older cities have increasingly become the home of a chronically poor and often unemployed *underclass* (Wilson, 1987; Jencks and Peterson, 1991).

Finally, we must recognize that today's relatively high unemployment is partly the result of government policy. In the 1980s, the government chose to place a higher priority on fighting inflation than on fighting unemployment. As a result, the rate of inflation fell, the unemployment rate rose, and more people slipped into poverty.

## Low Wages

One striking feature of Figure 9.4 is the number of people who worked but were poor anyway. In fact, about one poor adult in 10 worked full-time all year. How is it possible for these people to be poor? A little math will show you. Begin with the $4.25 minimum wage in effect in 1992. Assume that someone works at the minimum wage 40 hours a week, 52 weeks a year. Such a person would earn $8,840. If this person is the sole source of support for a family as small as two people (including the wage-earner), his or her earnings will not be enough to lift that family above the 1991 poverty level. For a family of four, the annual pay based on the 1991 minimum wage falls more than $4,000 below the poverty level.

Low-wage jobs were among the fastest-growing areas of employment. During the 1980s. In fact, most of the job growth during this decade occurred either in dead-end, low-wage jobs or in well-paid, high-tech jobs that required a high level of education. There was little job growth in between, which meant there were far fewer opportunities for a person with a limited education to get a decent-paying, stable industrial job.

## Government Policy

Both low wages and rising unemployment during the 1980s resulted partly from policies pursued by the federal government. Specifically, the government during this period chose to fight inflation rather than unemployment and refused for years to adjust the minimum wage for inflation. Also contributing to poverty during this period was a very substantial cutback in government antipoverty programs. Beginning in the late 1970s, and to a greater extent under the Reagan administration in the 1980s, benefits in government poverty programs were curtailed as part of an effort to reduce both federal spending and the budget deficit. (Actually both government spending and the deficit increased because of a massive increase in military spending in the early 1980s.) Benefits in many programs were not adjusted to keep up with inflation, and standards of eligibility were tightened. Significantly, subsequent research has shown that those who were most severely hurt by these cutbacks were the working poor and the near-poor (Institute for Social Research, 1983). Many people were forced into poverty, and for many others, the impact of poverty became more severe as they were no longer able to supplement their meager incomes with government benefits such as food stamps.

Finally, it must be noted that the failure of the American public sector to provide certain necessities taken for granted in most industrialized countries also increases the extent and impact of poverty. Virtually all other industrialized countries, for example, use tax revenues to fund health care and day care for all who need them. One consequence is that other industrialized countries do not have 12 to 16 percent of their population totally lacking health insurance, as did the United States in the early 1990s. And we have already addressed the role day care expenses play in making it hard for impoverished single parents to seek employment. Thus, not only does the United States have more poverty than other modern industrialized countries, but because of lack of governmental support for health care and day care, the impact of poverty in the United States is greater than in other industrialized countries. This could, of course, change if proposals by the Clinton administration to establish universal health coverage are enacted.

In summary, the relatively high level of inequality in the United States compared with other countries results in a high level of poverty. This situation worsened in the 1980s and early 1990s, as deindustrialization, the growth of low-wage employment, and government policies resulted in greater inequality and more poverty. Finally, the impacts of poverty are greater in the United States than in other industrialized countries, because the United States provides far less assistance than other countries in areas such as health care, day care, and housing.

## CONSEQUENCES OF POVERTY

If the causes of poverty are complex, its consequences are clear. In virtually every way imaginable, life is more difficult for poor people. They are ill more often, receive poorer and more limited medical care, and live shorter lives. They also have a higher rate of mental illness, particularly for the more serious illnesses such as depression, schizophrenia, and personality disorders (Dohrenwend, 1975; Warheit, Holzer, and Schwab, 1973). They also report lower levels of personal happiness than the nonpoor (Campbell, Converse, and Rogers, 1976). The children of the poor are at greater risk of dying in infancy, and if they survive, they have a greater risk than nonpoor children of getting in trouble with the law or becoming pregnant as teenagers. They will receive a much poorer education than nonpoor children, and they are far less likely to complete high school. One study showed that in Chicago's public schools, where a large proportion of the students are from poverty-stricken families, fewer than half of all 1980 ninth-graders graduated on time in 1984—and of those who did graduate, only one out of three could read at a twelfth-grade level (Wilson, 1987, p. 57).

Poor people will spend more of their income on food and housing than the nonpoor, but they still will be less adequately fed and housed. A study of housing in southern Illinois by Quinn (1984) revealed that poor people were several times as likely as the general public to live in overcrowded housing, yet 80 to 90 percent of these poor people were paying more than the government standard of 25 percent of their incomes for rent.

Poor people are more likely both to commit street crimes and to be the victims of such crimes (Barlow, 1993). Crime rates are highest in poor neighborhoods, for criminals tend to victimize those who are close by and available. As a result, a highly disproportionate number of robbery, assault, and homicide victims are poor. So high is the incidence of crime in some poor neighborhoods that poor people are afraid to venture outside their homes (Rainwater, 1966). Summer after summer in several major cities, elderly poor people have died from heat-related illnesses because they could not afford air conditioning and were afraid to open their windows because of crime.

In the winter, the risks become cold and fire. Dozens of poor people die every winter as a result of fires started by makeshift heating arrangements, some of which were attempted after their gas or electricity had been turned off because they could not pay the bill.

**Homelessness** Probably those most severely affected by poverty are America's hundreds of thousands of homeless. We cannot count the exact number of homeless, partly because it is hard to define exactly who is homeless (Rossiet al., 1987). Most would agree that a person who has a place to stay for only one or two nights before having to return to the streets or seek another place is homeless, but what about a person who has a place to stay for several weeks? Experts do not agree on exactly who is homeless, and hence they do not agree on how many homeless people there are. The 1990 Census, the first to attempt a systematic count of homeless people, found about 230,000 homeless people (Haub, 1991). This is clearly the low end of the possible range (see Haupt, 1990); an estimate by the Urban Institute in 1989 placed the number of homeless at 600,000. Other estimates have ranged as high as 3 million.

We do know that the number of homeless people rose during the 1980s (U.S. Conference of Mayors, quoted in *St. Louis Post-Dispatch*, 1987), and that in much of the county, this trend continued into the early 1990s (Hart, 1991; *The Washington Post*, 1992). While most homeless people are adult males (Rossi et al., 1987), the number of homeless families and homeless women and children is increasing. A Temple University study found that 15 percent of the homeless were under the age of 5 (King, 1989), and a 1990 study of 30 cities estimated that 40 percent of the homeless were families with children (Toth, 1991). People become homeless in a wide variety of ways: Eviction, job loss, fires and other disasters, mental illness, chemical dependency, and divorce are among the more common (Henslin, 1990; Rossi, 1987). Tragically, some are "throwaway" children who have been forced out of their homes or otherwise abandoned by their parents, and some are runaways, many of whom are seeking to escape from physical or sexual abuse. According to Rossi et al. (1987), the median annual income of Chicago's homeless was just $1,200, and most of them had been unemployed for years—typically for up to two years *before* becoming homeless. Moves during the 1980s to "deinstitutionalize" the mentally ill also resulted in many of these people becoming homeless (Rossi et al., 1987) because they were too sick to take care of themselves, lacked someone to help them, or both.

Whatever its causes, the physical and psychological consequences of homelessness are devastating. Children grow up with inadequate or no schooling, the homeless are at constant risk of being victimized, and homelessness becomes a source of stigma that is highly destructive to self-esteem. And, of course, the homeless must always face the variable weather. In the bitter January of 1988, for example, homeless people died of exposure to the cold in a number of cities. Yet, so great was their fear of crime in the homeless shelters that some of the homeless nonetheless chose to remain on the streets.

While the problem of homelessness is more severe in the United States than in most industrialized countries, it exists to some extent nearly everywhere. There are both similarities and differences between countries in the causes of homelessness, as is illustrated in the box, "Japan's Homeless."

## FUNCTIONALIST AND CONFLICT PERSPECTIVES ON STRATIFICATION

In this final section, we turn to the larger sociological issue of why economic inequality and poverty exist in society. As with other questions of this nature, the two macrosociological perspectives, functionalist and conflict theories, offer starkly different answers. Let us first consider the functionalist answer.

## COMPARING CULTURES AND SOCIETIES

### JAPAN'S HOMELESS

Despite its rapid economic growth, high productivity, and relatively limited degree of socioeconomic inequality, Japan still has its homeless. Their numbers are fewer; there are, for example, only a few hundred homeless in Yokohama, a city of 3 million. Still, the thousands of homeless people in Japan live a life much like that of homeless people everywhere. They sleep on cardboard in alleys, seek warmth in tunnels and train stations, and are widely ignored by the rest of Japanese society. In fact, they are probably ignored even more than their counterparts in the United States. The Japanese census bureau and the National Police Agency do not publicly reveal their estimates of how many homeless live in Japan. As in the United States, Japan's homeless are sometimes even worse off when they are *not* ignored: In 1983, three homeless me were killed by a group of rock-throwing high-school students, in an event hauntingly similar to attacks in the United States.

Some of the causes of homelessness are the same in Japan as in the United States: Many homeless have only part-time work, and are plagued by unemployment and low wages. The homeless generally live in the part of town where large numbers of laborers line up for part-time, low-paying construction jobs, often at shape-ups run by organized crime. Racial and ethnic minorities are overrepresented among the homeless, as are the physically disabled. Many homeless Japanese also are debilitated by alcohol abuse, though abuse of other drugs is less common than in the United States.

There are, however, some important differences. Although mental illness contributes to homelessness in Japan as elsewhere, Japan has not emptied its mental institutions onto the streets as has the United States. Undoubtedly, this accounts in part for the lower incidence of homelessness in Japan than in the United States. Also unlike the United States, there are very few homeless families in Japan. Finally, it is uncommon in Japan for anyone with ongoing, full-time employment to be homeless—a phenomenon that is on the rise in the United States because of fires, evictions, divorces, and other personal catastrophes.

Characteristic of Japan's culture stressing self-help and responsibility, homeless people in Japan are extremely reluctant to accept assistance. One homeless man told a social worker that he would not go to a shelter because "I just don't like to beg for help." The same night, a homeless couple in a part turned down an offer of a blanket. According to volunteers who work with Japan's homeless, many homeless people are reluctant to have anyone know their names and, for that reason, the volunteers often do not ask.

SOURCE: The material in this box is based largely on Steven B. Weisman, "Japan's Homeless: Seen Yet Ignored," *The New York Times*, January 19, 1991, p. 4.

## The Functionalist View: Davis and Moore

In one of the most widely cited and debated pieces ever to appear in a sociology journal, Kingsley Davis and Wilbert Moore presented a functionalist theory of socioeconomic inequality in their 1945 article "Some Principles of Stratification." Davis and Moore argued that economic stratification exists because it meets society's needs for productivity by motivating people. Davis and Moore started with the notions that some jobs are more critical to society's needs than others, and that some jobs—often the most critical ones—require longer and more difficult training than others. Such jobs also carry greater responsibility, are frequently very stressful, and often require people to work longer hours than other jobs. If the highly capable people needed to fill such jobs are to get the extra training and work the extra hours required, Davis and Moore argued, they must be motivated by the prospect of higher pay. Otherwise, why would people want these jobs, with all the training, stress, and extra hours they entail? More specifically, would people sacrifice current income in order to get the years of training some of these jobs require? Suppose a person could get the same money as a doctor by working seven or eight hours a day sweeping streets—with no after-hours responsibility and no long, expensive period of training, including four years of college, four years of medical school, and four years of internship/residency. Would it not be harder to get people to become doctors if they could earn just as much money doing something much easier—and earn it now, rather than 12 years from now?

## The Conflict View

Although conflict theorists generally acknowledge that socioeconomic inequality occurs in nearly all societies, they do not think it exists because it meets a social need for productivity. They note, for example, that more economically developed and productive societies generally have less inequality than others, not more (see Lenski, 1966). In general, conflict theorists see socioeconomic inequality as existing because the wealthy and powerful—usually a small group in any society—benefit from it and have enough power to make the social system work to protect their interests.

As a result of this great inequality, conflict theorists—in the tradition of Karl Marx—see a tendency in most societies for *class conflict*: conflict between the wealthy and those who lack wealth. It is in the interest of the wealthy to keep things as they are, whereas those without wealth have an interest in social change. Marx predicted that this conflict of interest would eventually lead to the overthrow of most capitalist societies, as the subordinate class realized its own interest and seized the wealth from the ruling class.

In fact, this has not happened, for many reasons. One of the most important is that the expansion of economies under capitalism, at least until recently, raised the standard of living of the working classes substantially, despite continued inequality. Another is that democratic reforms curtailed the more blatant excesses of the owners of wealth and afforded some protection to the rights of even those with little wealth and power. Marxists would argue that a third reason is that the wealthy use their influence over government, the media, and other key institutions to promote beliefs and ideologies that inhibit class consciousness. According to the conflict perspective, then, the interests of the wealthy—not the needs of the society as a whole—are served by inequality.

## Is Stratification Really Functional?

In an article that is among the most widely cited in sociology, conflict theorist Melvin Tumin pointed out what he saw as several shortcomings in the logic used by Davis and Moore (Tumin, 1953; see also Tumin, 1970). First, he questioned whether some of the better-paying and more prestigious jobs are really more critical to society than others. For example, is the physician really more essential to the health of the public than the garbage collector? Without garbage collectors, the hazard of contagious disease would be tremendous. Significantly, historical demographers agree that public sanitation systems were able to increase people's life expectancies at an earlier point in history than were medical doctors. The treatment of illness was too unscientific to accomplish much before about 1900. Only then, for example, was the practice of washing one's hands before performing surgery becoming widespread. The establishment of garbage-collection systems and sanitary sewers, however, had replaced the common practice of throwing garbage and human waste in the nearest street or river by around 1850 in many areas, and it was certainly a key factor in the steady fall in American and European mortality rates between 1800 and 1900. (For more discussion of the effects of medicine and public sanitation on mortality, see Thomlinson, 1976, pp. 98-107.) In a similar vein, Tumin points out that if factories had all managers and engineers and no line workers, they could produce nothing. Thus, low-status, poorly paid workers can be as essential as those whose jobs carry status, power, and big paychecks.

Second, *wealth* is distributed more unequally than *income,* and a large share of wealth is inherited rather than earned (Barlow, Brazer, and Morgan, 1966; Lundberg, 1968). It is hard to see how inherited wealth could motivate people to do anything except be born into rich families, something that we have yet to figure out a way to control! About half of America's 400 wealthiest people in 1989 became wealthy through either inheritance or investment of inherited wealth (Queensman, 1989). To the extent that wealth is concentrated through inheritance, it is very difficult to see how it could serve to motivate people to enter critical jobs. A related point is that parental income has a substantial effect on a person's ability to obtain the education necessary to do the most demanding jobs. If stratification were really to work the way Davis and Moore argued it did, ability and motivation would have to be the main factors determining the amount of education obtained. In fact, family income plays a large role, making it easy for the wealthy to educate their children for the best jobs and hard for the poor to do so.

Third, the training required for getting better-paying jobs often is far from unpleasant; many people, for example, find college a highly rewarding time of their lives. In addition, attending college—and even more so, attending law, medical, or graduate school—gives a person a certain prestige. At the least, there is a good side as well as a bad side to the training that people must go through to get the better jobs, and that in itself can serve to motivate them.

Finally, Tumin points out that although the highest paying jobs often require great training and long hours, they also carry considerable nonmaterial rewards, including autonomy, sense of accomplishment, prestige, and—in many cases—the ability to set your own hours. This has been confirmed by recent research by Jeucles, Perman, and Rainwater (1988), who found that there are many rewards to a good job besides high pay. We do, moreover, have no shortage of people in certain occupations that require great training but pay relatively poorly—for example, social workers and college professors. There are a number of jobs people with a high-school degree can get that pay as well as that of a college professor, which requires four years of college and, typically, four to six years after that to obtain a Ph.D. Even so, the supply of recent Ph.D.s has continued to outstrip the number of new college faculty positions available. Clearly, a major reason for this is that the job carries considerable nonmonetary rewards.

## Synthesis

To conclude our discussion of the debate between functionalist and conflict sociologists about the causes of economic stratification, it may be useful to examine the relationship between social inequality and productivity among industrialized societies. This information is provided in Table 9.4. As a measure of inequality, the table shows the ratio of income going to the top 10 percent of the population to the share going to the bottom 20 percent. The larger this ratio, the greater the inequality of a society. As a measure of productivity, the table shows gross national product (GNP) per capita for 1990. The table indicates there is little relationship between the inequality measure and the productivity measure. The two countries with the highest degree of inequality, Switzerland and the United States, were among the countries with the highest productivity—but so were the two countries with the least inequality, Japan and Sweden. Overall, analysis of the data for these countries by the author showed that variation in inequality accounted for less than 10 percent of the variation in GNP per capita, and inequality was *negatively* correlated with productivity growth. Thus, the conclusion is unavoidable that, among these industrialized countries, the degree of economic inequality has little to do with the level of productivity.

**The Dysfunctions of Inequality** From a functionalist viewpoint, we also must consider the possible dysfunctions of a condition such as social inequality along with its possible functions. Functionalists see a need for order and cooperation in society—yet economic inequality is one of the most important causes of conflict and disorder in society (Tumin, 1953). Beyond this, those who are at the bottom often become hopeless and alienated and thus "drop out" of any economically productive role. Thus, whatever benefits inequality may have, it also clearly has its costs, to the larger society as well as to those at the bottom of the stratification system.

**TABLE 9.4 Economic Inequality and Economic Productivity, Selected Industrialized Countries, 1990**

| | Inequality, 1990 | Productivity, 1990 | Average Annual Growth |
|---|---|---|---|
| Country | Ratio of Income of Top 10% to that of Bottom 20%, Most Recent Data Available in 1990 | Per Capita Gross National Product, 1990 | Growth in Per Capita GNP 1965–90 |
| Ireland | 3.49 | $9,950 | 3.0% |
| Spain | 3.55 | 11,020 | 2.4 |
| Italy | 4.36 | 16,830 | 3.0 |
| United Kingdom | 4.02 | 16,100 | 2.0 |
| Japan | 2.57 | 25,430 | 4.1 |
| Belgium | 2.72 | 15,420 | 2.6 |
| Finland | 3.44 | 26,040 | 3.2 |
| Netherlands | 3.33 | 17,320 | 1.8 |
| Canada | 4.23 | 20,470 | 2.7 |
| France | 4.05 | 19,490 | 2.4 |
| Germany* | 3.44 | 22,320 | 2.4 |
| Denmark | 4.13 | 18,450 | 1.8 |
| United States | 5.32 | 21,790 | 1.7 |
| Sweden | 2.60 | 23,660 | 1.9 |
| Norway | 3.42 | 23,120 | 3.4 |
| Switzerland | 5.73 | 32,680 | 1.4 |

SOURCE: The World Bank, 1992, World Development Report 1992. New York: Oxford University press.

•Data refer to West Germany before unification.

Does all this mean that the functionalist explanation of inequality is simply wrong? Probably not. For one thing, all of the countries in Table 9.4 do have a significant amount of inequality, although the levels vary widely. In Japan, with the least inequality, the wealthiest 10 percent still receive two-and-a-half times as much income as the poorest 20 percent. The fact that economic inequality exists in all modern countries—even socialist ones—is certainly consistent with the functionalist viewpoint. What the data do suggest, though, is that although inequality may be functional up to a point, most countries have far more of it than they need. This is especially true of the United States, which had over twice as much economic inequality (by the measure in Table 9.4) as either Japan or Sweden, and also more than Norway, yet did no better in terms of productivity in 1990. As Lenski (1966) put it, the functionalist theory probably explains a certain amount of stratification, but it cannot account for anywhere near all of it. Undoubtedly, much of the rest exists for the reasons outlined by conflict theorists—the disproportionate power of the wealthy, and their use of that power to keep their economic advantage.

The wealthy are not the only people among the nonpoor who benefit from poverty, and therefore have a stake in the confirmation of poverty. To see how others benefit—as well as to get some enlightening insights about functionalist and conflict theories—see the box, "Herbert Gans and the Functions of Poverty."

## SOCIOLOGICAL INSIGHTS

### HERBERT GANS AND THE FUNCTIONS OF POVERTY

A discussion of functionalist and conflict analyses of stratification could not be complete without a review of the writings of Herbert Gans (1971, 1972) concerning the functions of poverty. Gans's insights are useful not only for understanding poverty but also for seeing the similarities between functionalist and conflict theories. In an article titled "The Positive Functions of Poverty," Gans listed a number of ways in which poverty is "functional," some of which are given here:

It provides people to do unpleasant "dirty work" that others don't want to do.

It provides a source of employment for police and penologists, Pentecostal ministers, pawnshop owners, social workers, heroin pushers, and other legal and illegal occupations that depend upon the poor.

It provides people to buy spoiled and damaged goods at a reduced price that otherwise would have to be thrown out.

It provides a convenient group of people to punish in order to uphold society's rules.

It reassures the nonpoor of their status and worth.

It enhances educational opportunities for the middle class by ensuring that a sizable part of the population will not compete with them.

It is a source of popular culture that others enjoy and make money on. Jazz, blues, rock, gospel, and country music all had their origins among the poor.

It provides people to absorb the costs of social change in the form of unemployment, cheap labor, and residential displacement—so others won't have to.

Although some people have interpreted this article as making a functionalist argument—and Gans certainly wrote it to sound that way—it has more commonly been seen as a spoof of functionalist theory written by someone who really identifies with the conflict perspective. An earlier and similar article by Gans, "The Uses of Poverty: The Poor Pay All" (1971), supports this interpretation. However, whether Gans identifies with functionalist theory or conflict theory, his articles make a key point: *A good many Americans—nonpoor and often wealthy—benefit from the continued existence of widespread poverty.* Thus, the fact that influential special-interest groups benefit from poverty may be one reason that poverty persists. In essence, this is what conflict theorists have always argued: Inequality exists because some group benefits from it. It would appear that this is true to some extent, not only of overall socioeconomic inequality, but also of the widespread poverty existing amid affluence in the United States.

## SUMMARY

Sociologists use the term *stratification* to refer to the unequal distribution in society of scarce resources. Stratification has an economic dimension (the distribution of income and wealth), a political dimension (the distribution of power), and a social prestige dimension, sometimes called *status*. In the United States, income (what a person receives annually) is distributed more unequally than in most other industrialized countries, and the distribution of wealth (the total value of everything a person owns) is even more unequal. Although the distributions of income and wealth in the United States have not changed dramatically over time, there has recently been a shift toward greater inequality.

Another area in which stratification systems vary is mobility. Open stratification systems have relatively high mobility—people can move "up" or "down"—whereas closed systems have low mobility. The most closed type of stratification system is the caste system; the estate or feudal system has slightly greater mobility. The highest level of mobility is found in class systems, but even there, ascribed statuses—those into which we are born—play an important role. The mobility that does exist is frequently structural—that is, a result of an increase in the number of better-paying jobs rather than of some people moving up while others move down. Although it is widely believed that the United States has high mobility compared with other class systems, the fact is that industrialized countries do not vary widely in their degree of mobility. The degree of mobility found in the United States is similar to that of most other industrialized societies.

Social class can be defined in a number of ways. To Karl Marx, there were only two classes: those who owned the means of production and those who did not. Many modern sociologists prefer a composite approach, which considers such factors as income, wealth, education, and occupational status. Another approach—subjective class—is to allow people to classify themselves. In the United States, most people call themselves "middle class" or "working class," because Americans don't like to divide themselves into classes, and thus tend to identify with the middle.

Poverty can be defined in either a relative sense (being poor compared with others in the same society) or an absolute sense (lacking necessities). By either definition, there are a large number of poor people in the United States, despite its relative affluence, and this number has increased since the late 1970s. Most poor people are non-Hispanic whites, but blacks and Hispanics have disproportionately high poverty rates, as do female-headed families and people who live in either central cities or rural areas. Among the key causes of poverty are unemployment, low wages, and the inability of single mothers to earn sufficient wages to pay the costs of day care and medical care and support their families. It appears that relatively few people are poor because they prefer welfare to work. Although welfare dependency does occur, it is less widespread than is commonly believed, and most of the nonworking poor have good reasons to be out of the labor force. During the late 1970s and particularly the 1980s, government policies both raised the poverty rate (by allowing unemployment to increase in order to fight inflation) and made the impact of poverty more severe (by cutting back aid to the poor). The effects of poverty are devastating in nearly every aspect of life, ranging from educational opportunities to life expectancy to the likelihood of being a victim of crime.

Functionalist and conflict theorists disagree about the causes of social stratification. In the view of functionalists, stratification exists because it is useful for society. It motivates people to get the training and work the long hours required for certain critical and difficult jobs. Conflict theorists, however, argue that stratification exists mainly because those with wealth and power benefit from it. At the least, it does appear that there is greater inequality in most societies than can be explained purely on the basis of the need for motivation. In the United States, with its particularly high degree of economic inequality, this seems to be especially true.

## GLOSSARY

**dimensions of stratification** The different bases on which people in a society are unequally ranked, including economic (wealth and income), political (power), and prestige (status).

**income** The dollar value of that which a person or family receives during a specified time period, including wages and return on investment.

**wealth** The total value of everything that a person or family owns, less any debts.

**prestige** The degree to which a person is respected and well regarded by others.

**socioeconomic mobility** The movement of people to higher or lower positions within the stratification system.

**open stratification system** A system of inequality in which opportunities to move to a higher or lower status are relatively great.

**closed stratification system** A system of inequality in which opportunities for mobility are relatively limited.

**caste system** A very closed stratification system in which the group or caste into which a person is born determines that person's status on a lifelong basis.

**caste** A grouping into which a person is born that determines that person's status in a caste system.

**apartheid** Now abolished by law, the official name for the racial caste system in South Africa, where political and economic rights are defined according to which of four official racial groupings—white, black, coloured, and Asian—a person belongs to.

**racial caste system** A closed stratification system in which castes are established on the basis of race.

**estate system** A relatively closed stratification system, also called a feudal system, found in agricultural economies, in which a person's status is determined on the basis of land ownership and, frequently, formal title.

**class system** A system of social inequality, usually found in modern industrial societies, in which a person's position in life is influenced by both achieved and ascribed statuses.

**intergenerational mobility** Attainment by people of a socioeconomic status higher or lower than that of their parents.

**structural mobility** A type of socioeconomic mobility that occurs because of an increasing proportion of jobs in the higher-status, white-collar categories.

**exchange mobility** A type of socioeconomic mobility that occurs when some people move to higher positions in the stratification system, while others move to lower positions.

**social class** A group of people with similar socioeconomic status in an industrialized society.

**socioeconomic status** A person's overall position within the stratification system, reflecting such things as income, wealth, educational level, and occupational prestige.

**class structure** The distribution of wealth and other scarce resources in society.

**subjective class** The class to which people perceive that they belong.

**poverty** The condition of having an extremely low income and standard of living, either in comparison with other members of society (relative poverty) or in terms of the ability to acquire basic necessities (absolute poverty).

**deindustrialization** A decline in the importance of heavy industry as a source of employment in the United States and other modern economies. Automation, job decentralization, and the transition to a postindustrial economy all play a role in this process.

## FURTHER READING

BARTLETT, DONALD L., and JAMES B. STEELE. 1992. *America: What Went Wrong?* Kansas City: Andrews and McMeel. This easy-to-read book by two Pulitzer Prize-winning journalists documents the extent to which inequality in income grew in the United States during the 1980s—resulting in growing poverty and a shrinking middle class. It also identifies specific government policies that led to increased inequality and loss of higher-paying jobs.

DANZINGER, SHELDON, and DANIEL H. WEINBERG (eds.). 1986. *Fighting Poverty: What Works and What Doesn't.* Cambridge, MA: Harvard University Press. This is a collection of articles by experts on various aspects of poverty. It addresses the successes and failures of past efforts to fight poverty, and it lays out a research agenda to identify more effective ways to do so.

DEMOTT, BENJAMIN. 1990. *The Imperial Middle: Why Americans Can't Think Straight About Class.* New York: William Morrow. Although America is very much a class society, Americans are less aware of class distinctions than people in almost all other industrialized countries. This book examines the reasons why that is the case and looks at how and why our leaders and our media encourage us to downplay the influence of class.

DUNCAN, GREG J., et al. 1984. *Years of Poverty, Years of Plenty: The Changing Economic Fortunes of American Workers and Families.* Ann Arbor: Institute for Social Research, The University of Michigan. This book presents the results of a study of family income conducted over a period of 10 years. It is written to be understood by people who do not have advanced training in sociology and statistics. Duncan and his colleagues present fascinating findings concerning family economic mobility, the extent of persistent poverty, and the causes of low wages among women.

EHRENREICH, BARBARA. 1991. *Fear of Falling: The Inner Life of the Middle Class.* New York: HarperCollins Publishers. This book offers a look at the middle class in America from the 1960s through the 1980s. It describes the prevailing attitudes and values that govern this lifestyle and also challenges prevailing myths about middle-class behavior.

EITZEN, D. STANLEY, and MAXINE BACA ZINN (eds.). 1989. *The Reshaping of America.* Englewood Cliffs, NJ: Prentice-Hall. This book contains 42 articles by a variety of analysts examining how and why stratification is changing in the United States. Among the forces for change examined are electronic technology, the emergence of a worldwide economy, the increased mobility of capital throughout the nation and world, and the transition from an economy based primarily on manufacturing to one based primarily on information and services.

HARRINGTON, MICHAEL. 1984. *The New American Poverty.* New York: Penguin. This book examines the growth of poverty in the United States during the early 1980s. It identifies the diverse groups affected by this poverty, and it examines the various social, economic, and political conditions that led to the increase in poverty. The book is written from a conflict perspective by the author of *The Other America*, a 1962 book that made many Americans aware that they were living in the midst of poverty.

JENCKS, CHRISTOPHER, and PAUL E. PETERSON. 1991. *The Urban Underclass.* Washington, D.C.: Brookings Institution. A series of essays by leading researchers on urban poverty, reporting and discussing the latest findings on the extent and causes of the worsening conditions of America's urban poor. Several authors discuss forces that perpetuate poverty and make it hard to escape, and explore the extent of persistent poverty in urban America.

ROSSI, PETER. 1989. *Down and Out in America: The Origins of Homelessness.* Chicago: University of Chicago Press. This book offers a descriptive analysis of homelessness in Chicago. Findings are compared to those obtained from earlier generations of research and those recently obtained elsewhere. Contains an interesting comparison of today's homeless with the Great Depression and the skid row era poor.

SOBEL, RICHARD. 1989. *The White-Collar Working Class: From Structure to Politics.* New York: Praeger. A well-written book that attempts to locate the white-collar professional and technical workers in the existing class structure. The author reviews theories of a "new middle class," then follows with his contention that white-collar employees are part of a stratified working class.

TUMIN, MELVIN. 1985. *Social Stratification: The Forms and Functions of Social Inequality*, 2nd ed. Englewood Cliffs, NJ: Prentice Hall. A thorough and readable introduction to stratification, by a sociologist who is recognized as a leading theorist in this area.

# Chapter 10

## Stratification: The Political Dimension

*Think for a minute about people who have had political power in the United States. What names come to mind? Perhaps you thought of Ronald Reagan or Bill Clinton, or perhaps senators Ted Kennedy or Jesse Helms. Probably you did not think of David K. Aylward. Who, you might ask, is David K. Aylward? He is a former congressional staffer who joined a lobbying company that worked for an organization called the Alliance for Capital Assets from the mid-1980s until 1991. The purpose of this organization was to block any legislation that would take away the unlimited and restricted tax deduction for corporate interest expenses. Specifically, the Alliance wanted to be certain that interest on junk bonds being used to buy out other companies remained tax-deductible. For six years, the Alliance wanted to be certain that interest on junk bonds being used to buy out other companies remained tax-deductible. For six years, the Alliance succeeded in blocking any legislation that would have limited the tax-deductibility of corporate interest expenses. To accomplish this, the Alliance spent $4.9 million between 1985 and 1990 to wine, dine, and otherwise influence members of Congress.*

*In 1991, the Alliance disbanded because, in Mr. Aylward's words, "There's no legislative activity on the horizon that would justify people contributing to that kind of organization anymore" (Bartlett and Steele, 1992, p. 191). In other words, there was no longer even a threat that Congress would place any restrictions on corporate interest tax deductions.*

*This was true in spite of the fact that corporate takeovers financed by junk bonds and similar tax-free mechanisms—and reorganizations designed to thwart them—resulted in the elimination of thousands of jobs, and in dozens of plant closures throughout the United States. Examples include a Florsheim Shoe factory in Herman, Missouri, that had been profitable ever since 1902; it was closed when Florsheim's parent company borrowed $2.9 million to fight off a takeover by two corporate raiders and could not repay the debt. In addition to this, the tax revenue the federal government lost because of the interest write-off grew as corporations borrowed more and more in the 1980s—over $90 billion a year during that decade. This was one reason why the share of taxes paid by corporations fell from 39 percent in the 1950s to 17 percent in the 1980s. Individuals picked up the slack (Bartlett and Steele, 1992).*

*But there's still more to the story. While it was David K. Aylward who successfully lobbied Congress to protect the unlimited corporate interest deduction, the person behind the Alliance for Capital Assets has a name you might recognize—Michael Milken, the "junk bond king" since convicted of fraud. Two of the three directors of the Alliance for Capital Assets were executives of companies that had been part of Milken's junk bond network, and of the 120 companies that contributed to the Alliance, more than half had ties to Milken (Bartlett and Steele, 1992). Thus, to understand the true sources of power, you need to consider the influence of people like Reagan, Clinton, Kennedy, and Helms, but also of people like Aylward and Milken.*

As the opening vignette illustrates, there are many routes to power. Elected officials have power, but one also can gain power through wealth (as illustrated by Milken) and through personal connections (as illustrated by Aylward). Power also can arise from personal skills, including the ability to lead and influence others, as well as the ability to identify and use circumstances that favor one's agenda. It has been noted, for example, that civil rights leaders were wise in choosing the 1950s and 1960s as a time to push for greater rights and opportunities for African Americans, because the economic growth that occurred then made it possible to offer greater opportunities to blacks without taking opportunities away from whites (Broom and Glenn, 1969, p. 24; Wilson, 1973, Chap. 7).

In this chapter, we shall address the question of power—something that is distributed very unequally in many societies. Among the issues we shall address are who has power and who doesn't; how people get power, how power is distributed in American society; and how closely power is related to the economic dimension of stratification, which includes wealth and income. We shall begin that discussion by expanding more clearly what we mean by power.

## WHAT IS POWER?

When we talk about the political dimension of stratification or social inequality, we are, for the most part, talking about inequality in the distribution of **power.** What do sociologists mean when they use that word? Simply put, they mean the ability to affect the actions of others, even when those others resist. If you can get people to do what you want them to do, you are exercising power (Dahl, 1957). Power may be exercised on an individual, a group, or a societal level. On the societal level, power means the ability make to decisions that affect the direction in which the entire society moves.

To a large extent, power is exercised through the political system (Weber, 1946). However, there are many other ways people obtain and exercise power. In fact, many sociologists believe that in almost every situation in which people interact, unequal power exists. Proponents of exchange theory, for example, contend that even interpersonal relationships such as friendship and courtship display unequal power (Blau, 1964; Emerson, 1972; Molm, 1987). This unequal power leads to unequal exchanges, which shape every aspect of the social interaction, including who starts conversations, who gives in during disputes, who touches whom, and who terminates contacts.

In this chapter, our main concern is the use and distribution of power in the political power in the political system. However, before we can narrow our discussion to that extent, we must say a bit more about the various ways in which people get power.

## SOURCES OF POWER

Recall that power means the ability to affect the actions of others. This includes the idea that if you have power over others. This includes the idea that if you have power over others, you can get them to do what you want even if that is not what they want to do. However, an even more effective form of power is getting people to want to do what you want them to do. If you can do this, you can exercise power without resorting to conflict. Thus, it is important to recognize that power is often exercised without any use of force, threat, or coercion. Sometimes the people involved do not even realize that they have been influenced by the will of another. Let us consider some of the ways that power is obtained and used.

### Authority

At about this point in my introductory sociology classes, I frequently ask my students to stand up. Every time I have done this, all of them or nearly all of them have done so. Because I am the professor, I have authority in the classroom. **Authority** is power that is attached to a social position (in this case, professor) or to an individual, and that people accept as legitimate. Hence, when I asked them to stand up, they do so—for no other reason than that I wanted them to. This example also illustrates the fact that a given person's authority often exists only within a limited sphere of activity. In the classroom, I, as the professor, have authority, and my request to stand up is obeyed. Were I to make the same request of a group of strangers sitting on a bench at a bus stop, I would likely get a very different response because I have no authority in that situation.

Individuals who have authority possess **legitimate power.** In other words, people accept the idea that it is proper for the individual with authority to have power. Hence, they will do what that person wants them to do, simply because he or she wants them to do it.

There are at least four important ways in which people get authority. The first three—traditional authority, charismatic authority, and legal-rational authority—were first pointed out by Max Weber and have long been recognized by sociologists. The fourth—expertise—is largely a product of the important and growing role of science and technology in modern industrial societies.

**Traditional Authority** The authority of a king or queen is perhaps the best example of **traditional authority**, which is based on long-standing, institutionalized, and largely unquestioned customs and practices. It often has a sacred element, so the person who challenges it is defined as evil, heretical, or ungodly. It is obtained by birth and passed on to offspring according to a long tradition that says authority rests in a royal family, with a set procedure for succession to the throne. In many countries, monarchs play a key role in the established religion, and—at least in the past, when monarchs had much greater power than most do today—their rule was supposed to reflect the will of God.

Many religions also operate on the basis of traditional authority. In the Roman Catholic Church, for example, the pope is seen as a divinely inspired successor to St. Peter, who delivers the word of God and, under certain specified conditions, is infallible on matters of faith and morals.

Because this type of authority is based on tradition, it generally remains with the person once that person has attained the position of authority. Thus, because tradition specified that Queen Victoria was to be monarch and to rule the British Empire, she retained that title and the authority to rule from the time she ascended the throne to the end of her life.

**Legal-Rational Authority** In contrast to a king or queen, a prime minister or president—elected by a parliament or by the public—is chosen for the express purpose of carrying out policies desired by the people, as expressed by their votes. Such authority, which is attached to a position and is established to accomplish certain ends, is called legal-rational authority. He or she will appoint numerous administrators who also have **legal-rational authority**, but their authority is derived from their appointment by a president or prime minister chosen to carry out the will of the people. Like traditional authority, legal-rational authority often has the backing of law. However, law has a very different meaning in this case: rather than being based on tradition and unchangeable, law is established for specific purposes and can be changed.

Legal-rational authority is tied to the position, not the person. Whereas a king, a pope, or an emperor normally rules for life, a president or a prime minister does not. When his or her policies are perceived as no longer meeting public objectives, a new leader is chosen, and the authority of the position transfers to the new leader. Unlike Queen Victoria, British Prime Minister John Major belongs to a political party that must face the voters periodically in order to continue to rule. When the majority of voters decide that some other political party could do a better job of running the country, Mr. Major's authority will disappear.

The anecdote about the professor's authority in the classroom is an example of legal-rational authority. I have authority in my classroom, given to me for the express purpose of teaching my students about sociology; I have no authority in matters unrelated to the class. Similarly, should I be perceived as failing in the objective for which I was given authority, I could be stripped of that authority. In this respect, legal-rational authority is fundamentally different from traditional authority.

**Charismatic Authority** **Charismatic authority** derives from an individual's personal characteristics. Charismatic leaders have authority because they excite and inspire people. The Reverend Jesse Jackson, for example, has been able to gain a large political following in part because many people like not only what he has to say, but also how he says it. True, he is a well-educated minister, and as such exercises a certain amount of both legal-rational and traditional authority. However, the main basis of his appeal lies in his ability to get his points across in a style that affects people. In the 1988 campaign for the Democratic presidential nomination, in which he finished second out of a large field, his success was based largely on the fact that his exciting and emotional speaking style presented a stark contrast to the drier approaches of most of his competitors.

Charismatic leadership, which often arises during periods of social conflict, can be an important source of social change. It frequently offers a major challenge of traditional or legal-rational authority. Revolutions usually have charismatic leaders (Corazon Aquino and Mao Tze-tung, for example), as do many of the more successful social movements. Such movements always have underlying causes and grievances, of course, but their success if often a result, at least partly, of a charismatic leader who can inspire and mobilize people.

Because charismatic authority lies within the person and not the position, it differs from traditional and legal-rational authority in that it cannot be institutionalized. Attempts are sometimes made to do so, but they usually fail. When charismatic leaders die, for example, their leadership cannot be replaced simply by appointment another person to their position. For example, no civil rights leader could fill Martin Luther King's shoes at the time of his death, and the movement lost some of its dynamism as a result. The death of a charismatic national leader such as Mahatma Gandhi in India or Mao in China almost inevitably leaders to a period of power struggle, often followed by substantial changes in the direction of national policy.

Although charisma always involves exceptional leadership capabilities, charismatic leaders do not always use their power justly or wisely. Hitler most certainly was a charismatic leader, as was Iran's Ayatollah Khomeini. Such leaders have used their power brutally to suppress opposition. Hitler succeeded in convincing the German people that their problems were largely caused by Jews and other "non-Aryan" peoples and introduced a policy of genocide to wipe these peoples out. These cases illustrate the potential for danger in charisma. Because charismatic authority arises largely from the personal appeal of the leader, the change it brings about can be highly unpredictable. The nature of the change depends largely on the intentions and objectives of the leader. Charismatic leaders can either renew and revitalize a society or take it in self-destructive directions. A recent example of the self-destructive direction may be seen in David Koresh, who led 85 of his followers to a fiery death at the Branch Davidian compound near Waco, Texas in 1993.

**Expertise** A final source of authority, not included in Weber's original formulation, is **expertise.** People often exercise authority because they possess special knowledge that others need or value. This is especially true in modern industrial societies that place a high value on scientific knowledge (Wilensky, 1967). People such as Carl Sagan, Jonas Salk, and Marian Wright Edelman, for example, are valued for their knowledge of science, medicine, and child welfare, respectively. As we shall see in more detail later in this chapter, social and natural scientists affiliated with universities, research institutions, and "think tanks" play a crucial role in the formulation of government policy in the United States. Expertise also is relied upon in the courts, private business, and in virtually every other place where important decisions are made. In the courts, for example, expert witnesses are used for such purposes as to assist in determining whether a defendant is insane, or whether an action taken by an organization was racially motivated, which would constitute illegal discrimination. Businesses use demographers and market researchers to determine what product lines to develop and how to market these products.

A problem with expertise, of course, is how to decide who can legitimately claim it. Because of the power and prestige associated with expertise, many people claim to be experts when in fact they are not. For this reason, **credentials** have come to play a key role in distinguishing those with true expertise. Credentials include such indicators as graduate or professional degrees, occupation, reputation, professional certification, and evidence of acceptance in the form of scientific publications. Credentials, like expertise, are not universal but are subject-specific. That is, there are clear boundaries on the areas in which a person can claim expertise.

## Voting

Besides authority, a key source of power in any democratic society is voting. Votes can be a source of power in several ways. First, voters do determine who gets elected, and this is a direct exercise of power.

## COMPARING CULTURES AND SOCIETIES

### WHY DO SO MANY AMERICANS NOT VOTE?

Voting can operate as a source of power only if people actually vote. In fact, many Americans do not vote. Consider Ronald Reagan's "landslide" victory in the 1984 election. With over 60 percent of the popular vote, Reagan won by one of the most lopsided margins ever, and he took that victory as a great popular mandate for his agenda. There is, however, another way to look at it. Although Reagan won a big majority of *those who voted*, he, as well as all other recent presidents, got a distinct minority of *those who were eligible to vote*. In the 1984 presidential election, only 53 percent of voting-age citizens actually voted. Of that 53 percent, only 60 percent, or about 33 percent of eligible voters, actually voted for Reagan. Thus, despite Reagan's landslide win, only one out of three voting-age Americans actually voted for him.

The 1984 voting pattern was not unusual. As shown in Figure 10–1, turnout in U.S. presidential elections has fluctuated between 50 and 65 percent over the past 50 years. In other words, one-third to on-half of all Americans have consistently not voted in presidential elections during the twentieth century. Congressional elections in nonpresidential years have drawn even lower turnouts; never in the past 50 years have as many as half the eligible voters turned out for such elections.

Voter turnout in the United States fell steadily from 1960 to 1990. One reason is the addition of 18- to 20-year-olds to the electorate in 1972. This age group has a lower turnout than any other. However, the addition of young voters merely accelerated a trend that was already under way. In the 1992 presidential election, voter turnout did increase—for the first time in more then 30 years. The 55 percent turnout that year was the highest since the 1972 election (when 18-year-olds first got to vote). The increase in turnout was particularly strong among voters under the age of 30: Post-election estimates indicated that turnout in this age group increased by one-third to one-half over the 1988 election.

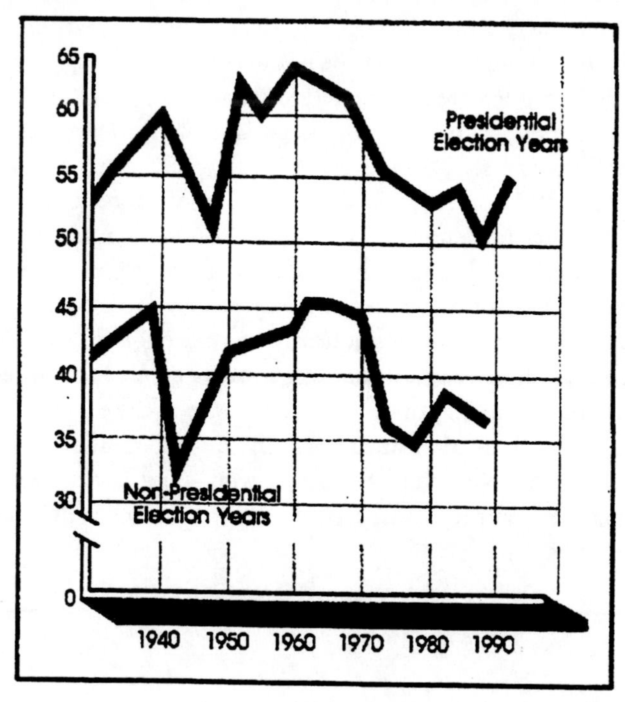


**FIGURE 10–1 American Voter Turnout: 1932–1990**

SOURCE: U.S. Bureau of the Census, 1987, p. 243: Brownstein, 1990; Burnham, 1987; *St. Louis Post-Dispatch*, 1992b.

Even with this increased turnout, however, citizens of the United States remain less likely to vote than citizens of almost all other industrialized countries (see Figure 10.2). Why? One reason is that many other countries maintain address registers and automatically update voter registration when people move. In the United States, people must re-register to vote whenever they move, and they are purged from voter rolls if they do not vote within a specified time. As a result, polls have shown that Americans who have recently moved are less likely to vote (Toner, 1990a). Another reason for the lower turnout in the United States is that it has proportionately more poor people than most European democracies, and poor people vote at lower rates than the nonpoor.

Some of the low turnout can be attributed to the American two-party system. While many European countries allocate seats in parliament to various parties in proportion to their share of the vote, American elections are "winner take all." This discourages votes for "fringe" parties, as voters perceive such votes as wasted. With just two viable political parties, each tries to appeal to a broad range of groups because no one group is big enough to make a majority. This makes the parties less ideological and more similar to one another as they seek "swing votes" in the middle. It thus makes less difference who wins than it does in countries with three, four, or five parties, each representing distinct viewpoints and interest groups (Downs, 1957). The fact that voter turnout increased in 1992, when Ross Perot ran for president as an independent, seems to support this interpretation.

The two-party system leaves the poor particularly unrepresented, because they are a relatively small minority. A party appealing strongly to the poor would lose votes with the much larger group of nonpoor—a fatal error in a two-party system. Thus, the United States has no labor or socialist party such as most European countries have. Therefore the poor are not represented strongly by any political party, and they have less incentive to vote (Burnham, 1987; Devine, 1972; Hartz, 1955). Hence, it is not surprising that poverty is more strongly linked to low voter turnout in the United States than in countries with multiparty systems (Burnham, 1987). Polls also show that poor people in the United States are more likely than others to believe that "things will go on as before no matter who is elected" (Toner, 1990a).

Another reason for low turnout in the United States is the high proportion of "safe seats." Incumbents usually win: In 1988 and 1990, only 2 to 4 percent of U.S. representatives running for reelection lost (Mann, 1987; Toner, 1990b). In 1992, over 100 seats changed hands, but in many cases, the reason was that incumbents chose not to run again, though some lost in primaries. However, of the 349 who ran and were nominated for reelection, only 24—less than 7 percent—lost. One reason is that the political parties, who draw legislative boundaries, try to protect their elected representatives. But when so few races are in doubt, the incentive to vote is reduced.

Finally, E. J. Dionne (1991) has argued that the falling voter turnout in recent decades has been caused in part by both parties' emphasis on "cultural" issues such as school prayer, gay rights, the Pledge of Allegiance, abortion, "family values," and so forth. He argues that while a minority of voters are very concerned about these issues, the majority are more concerned about economic issues. As the parties battled over these issues in nearly every election from 1972 through 1988, he says, the majority of voters—those who did not feel strongly about such issues—were turned off and voter turnout declined. In contrast, in 1992 the poor state of the economy played a bigger role in the election. The Republications tried unsuccessfully to turn attention to cultural issues. Ultimately, voter turnout increased, and the Democrats won—and both facts are consistent with Dionne's argument. But U.S. voter turnout, even in 1992, remained well below that of nearly all other industrial democracies.

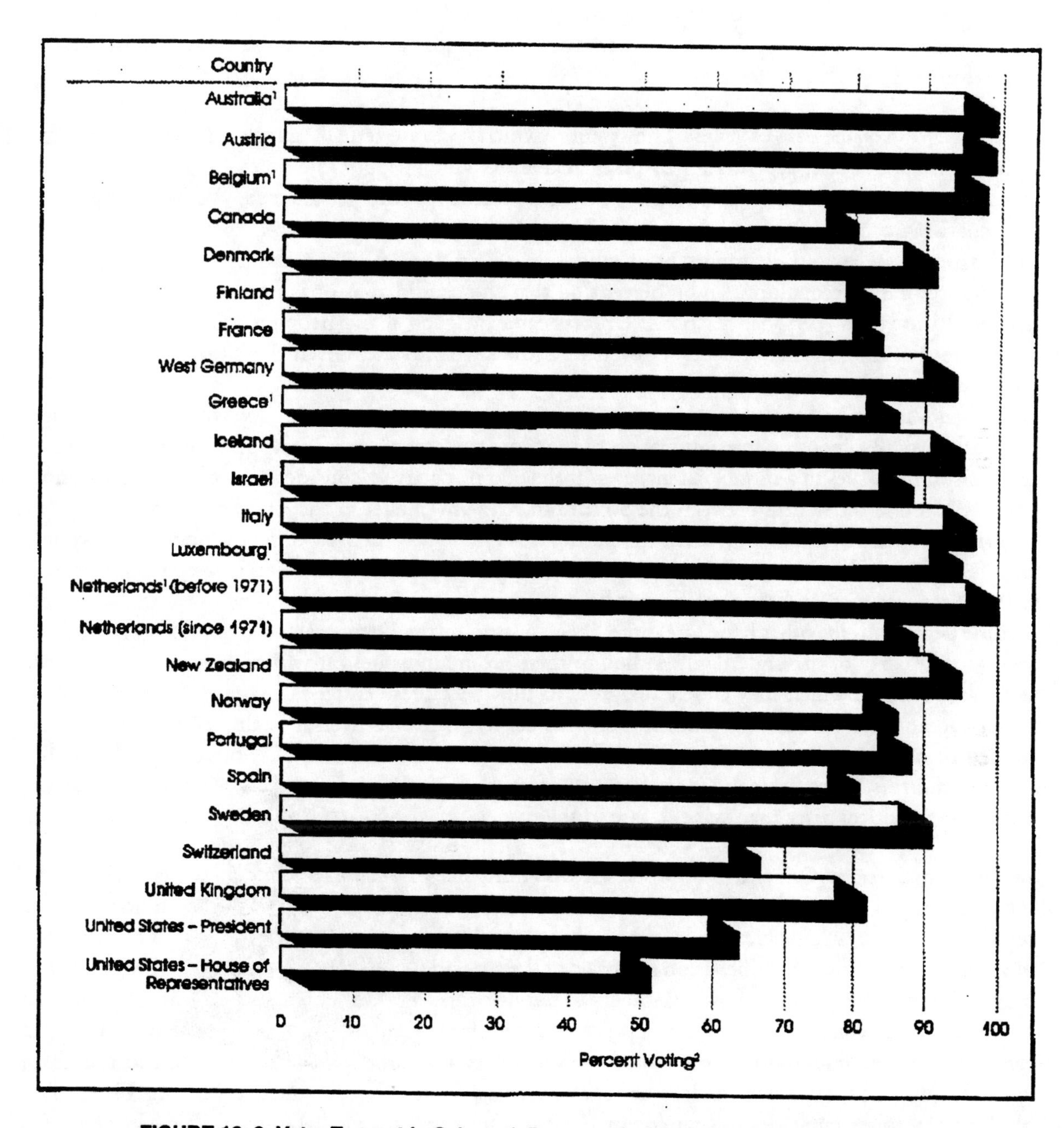


**FIGURE 10–2 Voter Turnout in Selected Democratic Countries, Average, 1945–1980**

All except the United States are percentage of registered voters who vote. United States is percentage of voting-age population who vote. This distinction has little practical consequence because registration is mandatory in virtually all countries except U.S. and France. In general, 95 percent or more of voting-age population is registered in countries other than the United States, except France, where about 90 percent is registered.

SOURCE: Vernon Bogdanor, 1987, *The Blackwell Encyclopedia of Political Institutions* (New York: Basil Blackwell, p. 623).

If voters are dissatisfied with how things are going under a particular set of elected officials, they can turn out those officials and replace them with new ones—as voters did in record numbers in the 1992 primaries and, to a lesser extent, in the general election. After an official has been elected to office, his or her behavior also can be influenced by the opinion of the voters. Politicians want to be reelected, and thus they do not usually say and do things that they think are likely to cost them votes. If they get a clear message that the majority of their constituents favor or oppose a given policy, they might vote accordingly (Burstein, 1981, pp. 293-294).

**Do People Vote on the Basis of Issues?** The extent to which votes are actually translated into influence over public policy, of course, depends largely on the extent to which people vote on the issues. Clearly, many things besides the candidates' positions on the issues influence who gets elected. We have already seen that charisma can be important. More broadly, evidence indicates that people's personal reaction to a candidate can be at least as important as where that candidate stands on the issues. Speaking ability, appearance, name recognition, and a perception that the candidate is or is not honest and competent influence the voters' personal reactions. Unfortunately, a good many people do not know where the candidates stand on the major issues, or even what the key issues are. Given this situation, the extent to which votes are translated into influence over public policy is clearly limited.

One way in which people may indirectly vote on the basis of the issues is by voting on the basis of political party. By choosing the political party that comes closer to their viewpoints, people do vote on the basis of the issues to a certain extent, even if they do not actively consider a candidate's views on the issues. Although differences between the political parties are smaller in the American two-party system than in European multiparty systems, the parties do represent somewhat different political viewpoints and somewhat different interest groups. In general, support for the Republication is greater among people with higher incomes, and the Republicans have long been perceived as the "party of business." Lower-income people, on the other hand, are more likely to support the Democrats, who have historically been seen as the "party of the underdog." Although there are many issues on which the parties differ little, there are some on which they clearly disagree. In the 1992 presidential primaries, for example, every major Democratic presidential candidate favored some form of universal health care coverage either funded or mandated by government, while both major Republican candidates opposed such a policy. Having said this, however, it also is important to note that people's votes today are less influenced by a candidate's political party than was the case in the past.

**Interest-Group Voting** One situation which votes do influence public policy occurs when large, organized interest groups vote as a bloc. This does not happen as often as most people believe, but it does occur in certain situations. One such example is the "ethnic vote." When a racial or ethnic group is concentrated in an area, it may chose its officials on the basis of their position on issues of concern to the group, or it may seek power by electing its own members to public office. This influence is most important in local elections, where concentration of a group is sometimes large enough to determine the outcome of an election. It is less important on the national level, where no one group is in a position to dominate. However, it can be important in close national elections. Were it not for the overwhelming support of black voters, for example, John Kennedy in 1960 and Jimmy Carter in 1976 would have lost narrowly instead of winning narrowly, and the 1992 election would have been a virtual dead heat between Bill Clinton and George Bush. However, the black vote did not influence the outcome of presidential elections in 1964, 1968, 1972, 1980, 1984, or 1988. At roughly 10 percent of the electorate, it simply is not large enough to determine the outcome unless the vote is otherwise close.

In recent years, gender has also played a bigger role in voting patterns. Since women gained the vote in 1920, men and women have voted quite similarly, but in the 1980s, a "gender gap" began to appear. Women began to vote somewhat more than men for politically liberal candidates. The influence of women was particularly pronounced in the 1992 U.S. Senate primaries, in which women such as Lynn Yeakel in Pennsylvania, Carol Moseley-Braun in Illinois, and Jean Lloyd-Jones in Iowa ran and were

## SOCIOLOGICAL INSIGHTS

### EMILY'S LIST

EMILY's List, an acronym for Early Money Is Like Yeast (it makes the dough rise) is a campaign donor network that raises money for pro-choice Democratic women candidates. It was founded in 1985 by Ellen Malcolm, a veteran of Washington politics who had worked with the National Women's Political Caucus.

1992 signaled a dramatic increase in women's political fund-raising involvement. In just one year, EMILY's List saw its membership skyrocket from 3,500 to 24,000 and its receipts increase from $1.5 million to $6 million. It is fast becoming one of the most envied and sought-after campaign donors. Of the 55 women it bankrolled in November 1992, EMILY's List candidates won five Senate seats, including those of Barbara Boxer and Dianne Feinstein of California and Carol Moseley-Braun of Illinois, and 21 of 50 House seats. Women now account for one-third of the freshman Democrats in the 103rd Congress.

EMILY's List describes itself as a fund-raising group rather than a political action committee. Its members make their contribution checks payable directly to a candidate's campaign, but they send the checks to EMILY's List, which then "bundles" the checks to a certain candidate and presents them. EMILY's List officials insist they are not a "special-interest" group and do not lobby members of Congress on legislative issues.

There is a pro-life, conservative counterpart to EMILY's List: WISH (Women in the Senate and House) List was founded in December 1991. It has approximately 1,500 members and raised $400,000 for the 1992 GOP campaign.

SOURCES: Gannett News Service, February 22, 1993; *Los Angeles Times*, January 20, 1993; *Common Cause*, October 1992.

nominated for the Senate in order to oppose senators who had supported the nomination of Clarence Thomas for Supreme Court (despite charges of sexual harassment made by law professor Anita Hill). These women won their party's nomination largely because of strong support from women in the primaries. When gender-related issues such as the Thomas nomination become prominent politically, the influence of gender on voting patterns often increases.

## Force and Coercion

Another way to influence the behavior of others is through force and coercion. If I have the power to fail you in your introductory sociology course if you do not do what I tell you to do—and you see no way to prevent me from doing so—chances are you will do what I say. The reason is not that you really want to do what I say, but that I can impose real costs or ham on you if you do not. In effect, I have used coercion—I have created a situation where if you do not do what I want, you will suffer some undesirable consequence.

**Legitimate versus Illegitimate Coercion** Coercion, like some other forms of power, can be either *legitimate* or *illegitimate*. In general, people accept the principle that the police should be able to use coercion as a way of enforcing the law. Thus, if a person attempts to rob a bank, it is accepted that a police officer has the right to use force (the threat of arrest and physical force, if necessary) to prevent that person from robbing the bank. This is a legitimate use of coercion. The bank robber, on the other hand, in threatening to shoot bank employees if they refuse to turn over the bank's money, is using a form of coercion that most of us would regard as illegitimate.

Governments, businesses, and private citizens all resort to coercion on occasion, and in each case, that coercion can be seen as either legitimate or illegitimate. In the case of government action, most of us would recognize the legitimacy of calling the police to prevent a violent crowd from burning down a building or attacking an individual. However, what if the police are called in to shut down tables where students are peaceably handing out literature in a public place on a university campus? That happened at the University of California at Berkeley in 1964, and it was perceived by most of the students there as illegitimate coercion by the university aimed at stifling free speech. The result was the beginning of the "student protest" era of the 1960s.

We should not, however, think of coercion as something done only by governments. Businesses use coercion in a variety of ways, including the threats to fire employees or to close a plant and relocate to an area with a "friendlier business climate." Many businesses have private security forces, and the advent of the computer has produced a boom in electronic spying on employees, as bosses "listen in" to find out what their workers are saying and doing (Marx and Sherizen, 1987). The possibility that such spying may be going on, of course, is enough to prevent many employees from saying or doing anything they wouldn't want their bosses to know about. Finally, coercion has been extended to employees' private lives, as many employers have begun to require applicants to pass polygraph and drug tests in order to be hired. By 1988, for example, about one out of three major U.S. corporations required employees or applicants to take drug tests (Finny, 1988).

When ordinary citizens lack or become frustrated with traditional channels of influence over either the political system or private businesses, they, too, turn to coercion. Coercion may occur in the form of legal activities such as strikes and boycotts, nonviolent civil disobedience such as sit-ins, or violent actions such as riots and sabotage. All of these actions are attempts to influence authorities by imposing costs upon them if they do not change their ways. Thus, a boycott threatens a company with the loss of income until it stops dumping raw sewage into a river; a restaurant that will not serve blacks is faced with a racially mixed crowd that refuses to leave until all are served; or a country occupying foreign territory is faced with continuous rioting until it gives up or democratizes that territory.

**Limits of Coercion** With all forms of coercion, people comply not because they want to but because they *have* to. The problem is that as soon as the coercer loses the ability to coerce, he or she has lost power, and others may no longer behave as he or she wishes. Also, coercion nearly always requires more effort and energy than other ways of exercising power. Thus, authority, persuasion, voting, and other means of power are generally seen as preferable to coercion because they generally get people to *want* to do what the person exercising power desires them to do. In general, when the exercise of power is seen as legitimate, coercion is less likely. Legitimate authority, for example, is usually obeyed. Thus, there is little need for those holding such authority to resort to coercion. Those who oppose legitimate authority also are less likely to use coercion because even if they disagree with the policies being pursued by political authorities, they do recognize their right to pursue those policies.

Perhaps such considerations explain why coercion and attempts at coercion are more common in societies that are deeply divided. In such a situation, other forms of power are less likely to work, and people and governments turn to coercion as an alternative. South Africa, the Israeli-occupied Arab territories, Northern Ireland, Lebanon, and former Yugoslavia are probably all good examples of this principle. In less divided societies such as the United States, coercion is most likely to occur when divisive issues such as the Vietnam War arise, or when social movements fail to achieve their objectives through other methods. That was the case with the civil rights movement, which had little alternative to civil disobedience given the refusal of southern states in the 1950s to allow blacks to exercise their constitutional rights.

## Control of Information

Particularly in modern societies with mass communications, the *control of information* is an important source of power. To some extent, everyone's behavior is influenced by the information available to him or her. Suppose, for example, that you have been told repeatedly that your chances of getting a job are better if you get a degree in business administration than if you get a degree in English, mathematics, or anthropology. To the extent that you are working toward a degree in order to get a job, you are likely to seek a degree in business administration. Thus, your behavior has been influenced by the information that you have been given. One important implication of this is that power of influence over your behavior has been exercised by those who have been given you this information. Another is that it does not really matter, in terms of your behavior, whether the information you have been given is accurate. If you have consistently gotten the same message, you have probably trusted it and acted upon it. If it turns out to be right, you have been influenced in a way that will you get what you want; if it turns out to be wrong, you have been what is commonly called a "victim of poor advice."

Who has control over the type of information that influences people's behavior? To help answer this question, think for a few moments about where you would look to find out which majors are most likely to land you a job. You would probably turn to placement counselors, and you also might choose to read a couple of studies of the job-finding experiences of recent college graduates. If you did these things, you would be influenced by expertise. Indeed, expertise is one important source of control over information. You also might try to find some magazine or newspaper articles on job prospects in different areas of employment. You also might watch the television schedule for any news specials dealing with this topic. In doing this, you would be obtaining information from the *mass media;* that is, popular broadcast and published means of communication that reached a substantial segment of the public. The mass media are one of the most important sources of information in modern societies.

**Media Control of Information** In what they choose to include and to exclude in their articles and programming, the mass media exercise great influence over the information that becomes available to the average citizen. Also, the tone and emphasis of media presentations of an issue or a topic have considerable influence over what people have the opportunity to learn. In presidential campaigns, for example, it is easy to find out who is three points ahead or behind in the polls in any given week. In fact, the media often treat the campaign as if it were a horse race, focusing mainly on who is ahead or behind and who is gaining or losing ground (Hunt, 1987, pp. 63-68; Patterson, 1980). However, try to find out by reading the paper or watching the television news which candidates favor taxing capital gains at the same rate as wages and which ones favor different rates of taxation. In most recent elections, the media had given greater coverage to who is ahead in the race than to the positions of the candidates. However, preliminary analyses of the 1992 campaign suggest that somewhat more coverage was given to the issues, perhaps in response to criticism of "horse race" coverage of earlier campaigns. Nonetheless, the question of who was ahead still received extensive coverage. When the press focuses mostly on who is ahead, it makes it easier for people to vote on the basis of who is expected to win than on the basis of candidate positions on the issues. Thus, the media exercise power over your choice by the kind of information they give you.

The importance of the mass media in shaping people's decisions can be seen especially clearly in the way dictatorships act to control the media. In virtually all dictatorships, the government controls the media to prevent people from getting information that challenges the legitimacy or policies of the government. Democratic countries typically define a free press as a constitutional right, and any blatant attempt to regulate the press—such as censorship of programs about Northern Ireland on the government-owned British Broadcasting Corporation (BBC)—instantly generates a major controversy. Both dictators and civil libertarians recognize that control of information is a source of power, and they act accordingly. Significantly, when a society moves toward democratization, information usually becomes more available.

**Government Control of Information** Control of the press it not the only means by which governments can control information. Merely because they are in the center of the decision-making process, governments have access to a great deal of information that ordinary citizens do not. By choosing what to make public and by stressing the fact that they have more information than ordinary citizens, government decision makers are able to influence public perceptions of controversial issues. According to Wilensky (1967, p. 144), such secrecy "obscures great issues of public policy and permits sustained masking of blunders." Such a process was used during the Vietnam War. Presidents Johnson and Nixon repeatedly maintained that if the public had all the information that top government decision makers had, they would support the government's policy. The government insisted that such information couldn't be made public because it would provide the enemy with intelligence that might threaten the lives of American fighting men. As it turned out, this was not the only reason the information wasn't made public. Another key reason was much of this information showed that the Viet Cong and North Vietnamese were stronger than widely believed, and that American prospects were poorer than the government publicly acknowledged (Karnow, 1983, pp. 423-426, 498-514). By keeping this information secret, government leaders were able to contain opposition to the war and continue their policy longer than they would have had the true situation been understood by the American public. More recently, the Reagan administration withheld information from the public in the Iran-contra scandal, again on the basis of "national security."

## Wealth and Income

Besides lying at the core of economic stratifications, wealth and income are an important source of power. Money can be translated into political power in a number of ways. For one thing, it provides access to the mass media by enabling a person to buy advertising, publish books, and make movies and television programs. Such media access is important because it determines what information and viewpoints the public will and will not be exposed to. Thus, the people who control information are likely to be wealthy. Money also is of obvious importance in getting elected. In this era of media campaigns, running for public office is expensive. Campaigns for governor and U.S. senator inevitably cost *millions* of dollars. In 1992, Ross Perot spent $60 million of his own money to run for president. The cost of campaigns is significant for two reasons. First, it means you usually need a lot of money to run for any office. Note that around one-half of all U.S. senators are millionaires (Barnes, 1990). Second, because even millionaires don't have enough personal wealth to finance an expensive campaign, candidates must nearly always raise a lot of money in campaign contributions in order to stand a chance of getting elected. Thus, people who are in a position to make large campaign contributions also are in a position to influence the votes, decisions, and policies of public officials.

An increasing proportion of these contributions come from political action committees (PACs) representing special interests. The majority of these PACs represent corporations or trade associations. Their contributions paid 41 percent of campaign costs in 1988, up from 14 percent a decade earlier (Eagleton, 1990). The role of the PACs is explored further in this chapter's "Social Issues for the '90s" section, "PACs and Lobbyists."

# ECONOMIC AND POLITICAL INEQUALITY: HOW CLOSELY RELATED?

How much does money influence the making of public policy? Social scientists have been debating this question for at least a century. One viewpoint—arising from the theories of Karl Marx—is that money and power are virtually synonymous: If you want to know who has power, find out who has money. Another view—based on the work of Max Weber—is that wealth and power, although not totally

## SOCIAL ISSUES FOR THE '90s

### PACs AND LOBBYISTS

During the 1992 election campaigns, there was much talk of changing the campaign financing laws and regulating lobbying. In his first speech in front of Congress, President Bill Clinton said: "We must begin again to make government work for ordinary taxpayers, not simply for organized interest groups, and that beginning must start with real political reform." The issue is, of course, that of the lobbies and political action committees (PACs), which, according to many people, unduly influence or even corrupt the democratic process.

*In what ways do PACs influence democratic system?*
*What are the advantages and disadvantages of outlawing PACs?*
*Would it be legal to outlaw lobbying and financing of PACs?*
*How could PACs be regulated?*

The word lobby refers to the lobby or antechamber outside the room where legislators vote on public bills. It is here that the people seeking to influence their votes would meet with legislators; thus the name lobbyists. Today, lobbies are associations or federations representing businesses, citizens, or special-interest groups, formed in order to influence the decisions of elected legislators by pushing them to pass or defeat certain bills. Some of the major lobbies are the American Association of Retired Persons (34 million members), the National Association of Realtors (800,000 members), the National Auto Dealers Association, and the American Medical Association. Lobbying is a way for organized groups to make their wishes known to legislators. Strictly speaking, there is nothing corrupt or undemocratic about the system. In fact, it would be unconstitutional to outlaw lobbying because the Constitution guarantees citizens the right of free speech and the right to petition legislators.

Lobbying can become corrupt when a lobbyist tries to influence a legislator by offering favors or money. In order to control corruption, lobbying is regulated by federal and state laws and lobbying practices are made public.

But lobbies do not need to bribe a legislator outright. They can buy his or her vote in a more subtle and legal way: by financing the candidate's campaign.

The way they do this is through PACs. Federal law prohibits corporations and labor unions from making direct political contributions to candidates. So, in order to circumvent the law, these same corporations, unions, and various organizations have established panels called political action committees, which collect voluntary contributions from the organizations' employees or members and give the money to a favored candidate.

During the 1992 election cycle, House incumbents raised $190 million for their campaigns. Nearly half of that money came from PACs, representing private industry and other interest groups.

Most members of Congress oppose the outlawing of PAC contributions, for the obvious reason that they usually have been elected with the help of political action committees. Nathan Deal, a Florida Democrat elected in 1992, thinks that PACs are necessary because "they, in effect, represent nothing more than smaller interest groups that pool their clout to be more effective."

Lobbyists, of course, are quick to defend the role of PACs. They say PACs enable a wide array of business people to become politically involved, and that eliminating PACs would only eliminate disclosure. (PACs must disclose which candidates their money is going to and in what amount.) Others say that because individual contributions are legally limited to $5,000 (and there's talk of limiting contributions to $1,000), PACs are more democratic than millionaire contributors of the past, and they allow the average citizen to participate in the political arena.

Larry Sabato, a professor of government at the University of Virginia who has written extensively about PACs, is against outlawing them. "If we abolish PACs," he says, "industry, labor and trade groups will merely find other ways of using their influence."

Still, it can be argued that the actual power of lobbies and PACs in the United States in effect hampers the democratic system of representative elections: Instead of answering only to the people who elected them, legislators are more inclined to satisfy the special interests whose money helped elect them and might elect them next time. A reform of campaign financing might alter this situation. One option that has been suggested is publicly-funded campaigns. Under such an arrangement, candidates for Congress would not have to rely on special interests to get money for their campaigns.

Cries of corruption have accompanied the meteoric jump in the number of PACs—from 608 in 1974 to 4, 172 in 1990, with contributions growing from $12.5 million to more than $159 million. These contributions give undue influence to special interests, which expect something (a bill passed or defeated) for the money given a candidate. As a result, PAC financing may push through agendas that shortchange the ordinary citizens who have no PACs to represent them.

Cleaning up the PAC system might not be enough. Susan Manes, vice president of issues for Common Cause, the Washington-based citizens' interest lobby, believes that "if we want a more representative government, we have to deal with the entire spectrum of influence money." That includes campaign-spending caps and controls on "soft money" (money that skirts the technical boundaries on contributions).

The greatest concern about PACs today, experts say, is the advantage they give incumbents. Of the $100 million in PAC contributions that went to House candidates in 1990, more than 80 percent went to incumbents. Giving by PACs now favors incumbents over challengers by about 10 to 1.

unrelated, can exist independently of each other. Wealth is no guarantee of power, and power is no guarantee of wealth. We shall now explore this debate in greater detail and evaluate it in terms of the findings of contemporary social research.

## Origins of the Debate: Marx and Weber

As noted, the debate about the relationship between wealth and power is a long-standing one, dating back to the early sociological writings of Marx and Weber. Although these two important social thinkers lived in different generations, Weber's writings have been described as a "debate with the ghost of Marx," and both men have shaped subsequent sociological debates on the issue.

**Marx: Wealth Determines Power** Karl Marx saw wealth and power as essentially the same. Marx has often been described as an economic determinist because he felt that in any society, those who own the means of production determine virtually all the characteristics of that society. This group uses its wealth to control all social institutions—government, education, law, science, the arts, and the media. With respect to government policy, the wealthy use their power to ensure that government operates in their interests. They can do this directly, by placing their own members in positions of power. An example was the feudal era, when land ownership was the equivalent of wealth, and royal families always owned great amounts of land. The wealthy also can control policy indirectly by using their wealth either to put others in places of power to do their bidding or to influence whoever is in positions of power. Marx and his coauthor Friedrich Engels believed so strongly that government was inevitably a tool of the wealthy that they predicted that after economic inequality was eliminated through common ownership of the means of production, government would "wither away."

**Weber: Wealth and Power as Distinct Dimensions** Writing about half a century after Marx, when the benefits of industrialization were beginning to spread beyond the owners of capital, Max Weber (1968 [orig. 1922]) saw wealth and power as distinct from each other. Although Weber did not deny that wealth often contributes to power, he argued that wealth, power, and social prestige are all distinct dimensions of stratification. Although your position along one of these dimensions can influence your position along another, it does not determine it. Thus, for example, being wealthy may increase your chance of having political power, but it is no guarantee of power (Orum, 1988, p. 398). According to Weber, some people have great wealth but little political power, and others have great political power but limited wealth. Rather than simply being an outgrowth or manifestation of wealth, power and prestige exist in their own rights, sometimes independently of wealth. An example of this may be seen in Bill Clinton. He came from a single-parent family and a modest economic background. Yet he attended prestigious colleges and was elected president.

## The Debate Today

**Modern Weber: The Pluralist Theory** A modern interpretation of Weber's thinking can be found in the **pluralist model** of power distribution, represented by such social thinkers as David Riesman (1961), Seymour Martin Lipset (1959), and Robert Dahl (1961, 1981, 1982). Pluralists argue, in effect, that the wealthy cannot have a monopoly on power in modern democratic societies because power is not concentrated in the hands of any one group, but rather is divided among many competing groups (Pampel and Williamson, 1988). These groups include business, labor, ethnic, racial, regional, and religious interests—all of which try to influence the decisions of political authorities. According to pluralists, all of these various groups (or at least their leaders) have some power, and none has complete power. Often they act as **veto groups**; that is, they are strong enough to prevent decisions that seriously threaten their interests, but not strong enough to bring about a decision that some other group opposes.

In one sense, the pluralist theory resembles the conflict perspective in that it addresses what happens when groups composed of people with opposing self-interests or policy orientations attempt to influence political decision making. However, in more important ways, the pluralist theory is functionalist, because it sees modern democracies as working well. They balance the interests of various groups so that every group gets some representation and some protection against harmful government decisions. Pluralism also is seen as functional in the sense that it keeps conflicts under control. Any one person may identify with several different interest groups depending on the issue. For example, the same person might at times identify with whites, females, born-again Christians, trade unionists, and environmentalists (Lipset, 1959). Hence people in a pluralist society enter into different coalition on different issues, win some battles and lose others, and rarely, if ever, divide themselves into long-standing, hostile, opposing factions. Riesman even goes so far as to argue that what often protects the interests of a group is not the reality of its power, but the *perception* by others that it can exercise power through voting, lobbying, or other means. If politicians believe that a group has power, they will treat it as though it does, even if in reality it controls fewer votes than the politicians believe.

A final important point about pluralist theory is that it does not necessarily imply that a large number of ordinary citizens directly influence the political process. Rather, the idea is that they are represented by *leaders* of the interest groups they belong to (Knocke, 1981; see also Dahl, 1961; Riesman, 1961). The leadership of labor unions looks out for workers, the Chamber of Commerce looks out for small businesses, and leaders of civil rights organizations look out for the interests of blacks and Hispanics. In this way, pluralists argue, everyone's interests are represented.

**Modern Marx: Power-Elite Theory** Standing in opposition to pluralist theory is a modern descendant of Marx's theory known as *power-elite theory*. The best-known modern American sociologists supporting this viewpoint are C. Wright Mills (1956) and G. William Domhoff (1967, 1978, 1983). Although this theory is not strictly Marxist, it does share many of Marx's assumptions. First, it directly opposes pluralist theory by arguing that real political power is concentrated among a small group (called the *power elite*), rather than divided up among competing groups. Second, it argues that this power elite is made up mainly or entirely of the very wealthy. Power-elite theory stresses that much of the real decision making is done behind the scenes, and that you therefore *cannot* necessarily judge who has power by looking at who holds elected offices or who lobbies public officials. Rather, real power and influence may lie with appointed officials who work quietly behind the scenes, or with research foundations that are funded by, and act on behalf of, specific wealthy interests, such as multinational corporations (Domhoff, 1983; Mills, 1956). According to power-elite theorists, these processes often go on without any appearance of public conflict. The power elite makes its important decisions behind the scenes so that they do not become controversial public issues. Because it portrays the political system as dominated by a small and wealthy interest group power-elite theory is generally regarded as a type of conflict theory.

Power-elite theory also bears some similarity to a set of theories developed decades earlier by several European social theorists: Michels (1967 [orig. 1911]), Pareto (1935 [orig. 1915-1919]), and Mosca (1936 [orig. 1896]). Like Marxism and power-elite theory, these theories hold that societies tend to be dominated by a small ruling elite. However, unlike the other approaches, these theories argue that elite dominance is a product of the very nature of collective decision making, not of a particular distribution of wealth. Thus, Michels, Pareto, and Mosca maintained that power elites were inevitable. In contrast, both Marxists and the modern power-elite theorists see concentration of power as largely the product of concentration of wealth, and they deny that either type of concentration is inevitable.

## WHO HAS POWER IN AMERICA TODAY?

Which theory comes closer to describing reality in the United States today—the pluralist theory or the power-elite theory? To answer this question, we must determine who really *has* power. This is not easy to do, because power is the type of abstract concept, or construct, that cannot be measured directly. Domhoff (1983) has proposed three questions to help sociologists determine who really has power. One way to measure power is to ask the question "*Who governs*?" In other words, what are the socioeconomic characteristics of the people who hold elective and appointive offices? A second question is "Who benefits from government decisions?" Presumably, if a group of people consistently benefits from government decisions, this group is exercising some degree of power in shaping those decisions. Finally, we can get an idea of who has power by asking "*Who wins*?" when controversial issues arise. Again, if the same group usually wins when various groups compete to influence public policy, we can assume that group is exercising power. If, however, different groups win on different issues, or if most decisions are actually compromises that take everyone's concerns into consideration, power is probably dispersed among a number of groups, as suggested by the pluralist theory (Banfield, 1962; Banfield and Wilson, 1963).

Besides Domhoff's three ways of measuring power, there is the *reputational approach*. This approach assumes that when someone repeatedly exercises power, others know about it. Thus, one way to find out who has power is by asking people involved in politics who is powerful (Hunter, 1955, 1980). This method has two shortcomings: (1) People do not always *know* who has power. (2) Asking people "Who is powerful?" may lead them to assume that someone *must be* powerful and thus to answer the question in ways that confirm the existence of a power elite (Cousins and Nagpaul, 1979; Polsby, 1980; Walton, 1966, 1977).

### Interest Groups in American Politics

To answer such questions as "Who governs?" or "Who wins?" we must have some sense of which interest groups are trying to influence public policy. There are literally thousands of such groups. On the federal level, there were about 6,800 official lobbying groups in 1990, up from 4,000 in 1980 (Hey, 1990). To attempt to rate the relative influence of all these groups would require a lifetime of study. Fortunately, from the standpoint of research, many of these groups represent similar interests with similar policy orientations. In fact, Domhoff (1983) argues that the majority of these groups can be grouped under three broad coalitions, each of which represents a major identifiable interest group or coalition of interest groups; the multinational corporate-interest group, the small-business interest group, and the labor-liberal coalition.

**The Multinational Corporate-Interest Group** The first group includes the largest **multinational corporations** and, in some cases, the families that own them. This group influences public policy through a variety of foundations, "think tanks," and "good government" groups. Included are the Ford, Rockefeller, and Carnegie foundations; the Committee for Economic Development (CED); the Council on Foreign Relations (CFR); the Trilateral Commission; and the Business Roundtable. Most of the members of these organizations have a direct link to one or more of the largest multinational corporations, and the foundations receive their funding from these same corporations. With a few exceptions, these organizations present themselves not as lobbyists ostensibly representing particular interests but rather as policy groups seeking to develop policies that are best for the nation as a whole.

However, careful study of the positions advocated by this group reveals that they follow a fairly consistent political or ideological orientation, which might be classified as "moderate conservative" or "middle of the road." Furthermore, these positions are largely aimed at eliminating sources of upheaval and threats to the activities of the multinationals, preserving international free trade, and preserving other policies that allow the multinationals to operate safely and profitably. A recent example of successful influence is the U.S. government's support of Mexico's Maquiladora program, which encourages the assembly in Mexican plants near the border of components used in American products. Under this program, major American companies have employed over half a million workers in Mexico since 1965—at wages sharply lower than they would have had to pay in the United States (Bartlett and Steele, 1992, p. 35). Another example is corporate foundation support for the world population control movement. This appears motivated in part by a desire to prevent upheavals resulting from overpopulation, which could threaten governments that are friendly to the multinationals (Dye, 1983).

Increasingly, the corporate group has also wielded influence through PAC contributions. Research by Clausen and Neustadtl (1989) has shown that corporate PAC contributions generally go to conservative candidates.

**The Small-Business Interest Group** This group is represented by such organizations as the Chamber of Commerce and the national organizations of professions that operate largely as small businesses—the American Medical Association (AMA), American Bar Association (ABA), American Dental Association (ADA), and the National Farm Bureau. It also includes some smaller corporations, but not generally the large multinationals. This group tends toward a more conservative political orientation, and unlike the multinational corporate group, it opposes virtually all governmental regulational regulation of business. Although more openly a lobbying group and less supportive of research institutes and "good government" groups, the small-business interest group does have some involvement in this area. The most notable examples of such conservative "think tanks" are the American Enterprise Institute and the Hoover Institute.

**The Labor-Liberal Coalition** The third group or coalition identified by Domhoff is the loosest coalition of the three and includes the widest variety of interest groups, It includes labor groups, minority groups, environmentalists, consumer groups, feminists, liberal intellectuals, and a variety of groups linked to the public sector, such as educators and public employees. It includes such organizations as the National Association for the Advancement of Colored People (NAACP), Urban League, National Organization for Women (NOW), National Education Association (NEA), the Ralph Nader organizations, and a variety of labor unions. Because of its greater variety, this group cannot always present a consistent and unified political front. However, there is sufficient cooperation and similarity of political orientation among the various elements of this coalition to identify it as a loose political alliance. Unlike the other two groups, this coalition is strongly oriented toward the Democratic party. However, it is more liberal in its orientation than most Democratic officeholders, and it is not necessarily better represented than the other two groups within Democratic administrations.

## The Distribution of Power: The National Level

We turn now to the question of how power is actually distributed among these groups. We shall seek to discover this by considering the three questions raised by Domhoff that we introduced earlier: "Who governs?" "Who benefits" and "Who wins?"

**Who Governs?** The wealthy are greatly overrepresented among those who hold public office. Mills (1956) was among the first to note that top positions in the executive branch of government and the military were overwhelmingly in the hands of a power elite who shared a background of having served on large corporate boards of directors, to which they often returned after completing their public service. This group also had a common cultural and educational background. They attended a relatively small group of elite schools and belonged to the same private clubs and organizations. Burch (1980-81) studied Cabinet members, diplomats, and Supreme Court appointees in every administration from George Washington's through Jimmy Carter's. This study defined the economic elite as executives or owners of large companies or law firms, or as members of families that either were very wealthy or were closely associated with corporate executive positions. By this definition, the elite held between 60 and 90 percent of Cabinet and diplomatic appointments throughout the entire period, except during Franklin Roosevelt's New Deal, when they held only 47 percent. It is striking that presidents as politically divergent as Kennedy, Nixon, Carter, and Reagan chose their Cabinet officers from the same places (Domhoff, 1983; see also Dye, 1983; Mintz, 1975). Most people who get such appointment belong to the first of the three interest groups identified by Domhoff—the multinational corporations.

**THE MAKEUP OF THE CONGRESS** Congress is not very different. If the Senate were representative of the U.S. population in terms of wealth, there would be one or two millionaire senators instead of the 40 or 50 that there are.

Of course, those who govern are unrepresentative not only in terms of wealth, but also in terms of race and sex—even though record numbers of minorities and women were elected to Congress in 1992. It took until 1992 for the first African-American woman (Carol Moseley-Braun) and the first Native American (Ben Nighthorse Campbell) to be elected to the U.S. Senate—and Braun is the first black of either gender to serve in the Senate since 1978. In the House of Representatives, the numbers of blacks and Hispanics rose to 38 and 17, respectively, in 1992, the most ever (St. Louis Post-Dispatch, 1992d). However, less than 9 percent of representatives are black and 4 percent Hispanic, compared with 12 and 8 percent of the population, respectively. The 47 women in the House and six women in the Senate after the 1992 elections are both record numbers, but are still a tiny proportion of the 51 percent of the population that is female. Blacks, Hispanics, and woman also have been extremely rare among Cabinet officials and top presidential advisers, though the Clinton administration departs from this pattern. In general, the characteristics of top officeholders are much like what would be predicted by the power-elite theory.

The House of Representatives is more diverse than the Senate. Compared with the Senate, the House has more blacks, Hispanics, and women, and few millionaires. Because it represents smaller districts, some of which vary greatly from one another, the House includes people from a wider range of backgrounds than either the Senate or the executive branch. Thus, the composition of the House conforms more closely to the pluralist model. Despite this greater diversity, however, white males and the wealthy are still greatly overrepresented. Moreover, the influence of the diverse population of the House can be offset to a large extent by the elite's highly disproportionate representation in the Senate in the executive branch.

## COMPARING CULTURES AND SOCIETIES

### A SOCIETY WHERE WOMEN HAVE POLITICAL POWER

Imagine a society in which the prime minister and half her Cabinet are women. One in which the leaders of both of her opposition parties are women. One in which both candidates for mayor of the nation's largest city are women. And one in which 59 of the 165 members of Parliament are women. Actually, you don't have to imagine, because such a society exists—it is Norway. While many countries have had a woman in one of the roles mentioned above, there are few, if any where, as in Norway, women hold offices throughout the political system in proportions that approach their share of the population. In the United States, for example, 10.8 percent of congressional representatives and 6 percent of senators are women. In Great Britain, only 7 percent of members of Parliament are women. Why is Norway so different?

The reasons seem to lie in both Norway's culture and its social and political structure. Norway, like other Scandinavian countries, has long placed a high value on human social equality. Norway's prime minister, Gro Harlem Brundtland, argues that this led the feminist movement to be accepted as a part of ordinary people's everyday lives in a way that it was not in other countries, where it took on something more of the air of an intellectual debate. At the same time, there are features of Norway's society that probably improved its chances of attaining sexual equality. For one, Norway is prosperous, and its long commitment to social equality has largely eliminated poverty as a major social problem. And it is a racially homogeneous country. Thus, debates on equality that have focused on economics or race in many other countries have been able to focus more strongly on gender in Norway. And finally, reforms were made in Norway's political structure that ensured that women would participate on a meaningful level. In 1983, the majority Labor Party adopted rules specifying that between 40 and 60 percent of its nominees were to be women, and other major political parties quickly followed suit. This institutional reform virtually guaranteed that a substantial proportion of Norway's political decision makers would be women.

Lest one be misled into thinking that Norway has totally resolved issues of gender inequality, however, we must consider one other explanation offered in a 1987 study by a Norwegian research institute. This study concluded that one other reason for the rising number of women in Norwegian politics is that social changes have led Norwegian men to become less interested in politics. As Norway's economy internationalized, real power shifted from politics to the private sector's multinational corporations, and men followed, losing some of their political involvement along the way. Notably, women are less involved in the private sector than in politics.

Nonetheless, it remains true that women have greater political power in Norway than almost anywhere else. And this has made a difference—according to Prime Minister Brundtland, it has led to increased emphasis on issues such as child care, education and family life.

**THE MAKEUP OF ADVISORY GROUPS** A look at those who have close access to policy makers also is revealing. Members of Congress do represent a variety of districts and constituencies, and the composition of their personal staffs largely reflects this reality. However, the advisers of executive-branch officials are distinctly less diverse. The fact is that both the executive branch and the legislative leadership rely heavily on a fairly limited number of policy organizations, "think tanks," research centers, foundations, and professors from elite universities for advice on policy. These groups, in turn, have strong connections to the multinational corporate-interest group.

One sign of the influence of these organizations is that they supply most of the members of governmental advisory commissions. The extent of corporate influence on such commissions is illustrated by a study of one ongoing government commission by Charles Schwartz (1975). This study found that over half the professors who served on the President's Science Advisory Commission between 1957 and 1973 had been directors of large corporations. If you add consultants to large corporations and directors of smaller ones, the percentage rises to two-thirds. Because most professors do not serve on corporate boards of directors, it is clear that professors who directly influence government policy are far more connected to corporate interests than are professors as a whole. Moreover, Robin Stryker's (1990) study of the role of social science in two government agencies showed that when such experts support the interests of the wealthy, their involvement becomes institutionalized, but when they oppose such interests, their role is likely to be eliminated.

Of course, the fact that most high officials and their advisers are drawn from the wealthy and the corporate elite does not mean they always support policies favored by that group. There are, for example, some very important differences between the political positions of millionaire Edward Kennedy and millionaire Ronald Reagan. Pluralists, in fact, argue that such fundamental differences over public policy prove that millionaires are not really a power elite (Dahl, 1982). Moreover, argue the pluralists, politicians have to worry about getting reelected, which limits their power to act on behalf of their own interest group (Riesman, 1969). Thus, although the answer to "Who governs?" at the national levels seems to be more consistent with the power-elite view than with the pluralist view, we cannot definitively answer that question until we take up the questions "Who benefits?" and "Who wins?"

**Who Benefits?** The question of who benefits from government decisions is probably the hardest of Domhoff's three questions to answer. Sociologists who try to answer this question use such indicators as the distributions of wealth and income, the recipients of government money, and the share of income that people at different income levels pay in taxes. With respect to the distributions of income and wealth, we already saw that a large share of income, and an even larger share of wealth, are in the hands of a small minority of the American population. We also saw that income is distributed more *unequally* in the United States than in most industrialized democracies. While it is very difficult to determine to what extent this concentration of income and wealth results from government policies as opposed to other influences, the government has done nothing to break up this concentration: In fact, both wealth and income became more concentrated during the 1980s. In this sense government could be seen as acting on behalf of the wealthy.

Determining who benefits from government taxing and spending policies is a more difficult problem. With a budget exceeding *$1 trillion*, the federal government is collecting money from all segments of society and spending it on a wide variety of programs. Nonetheless, many of these expenditures clearly do benefit the wealthy.

**THE MILITARY-INDUSTRIAL COMPLEX** One example of spending that benefits the wealthy is the massive military budget. The United States, as a superpower, has a larger military budget than most industrialized countries, even though its military budget has been modestly reduced since the end of the Cold War. A large share of that budget goes to purchases of increasingly complex and expensive weapons systems from the multinational corporations. Most large corporations are involved to some degree in sales to the military, and some—one in 10 of the 50 largest corporation—*rely primarily* on sales to the military. The eight biggest Pentagon contractors had sales in the early 1980s that exceeded the gross national product of the entire country of Norway (Skolnick, 1984). The fact that such a large segment of the economy depends on military spending is probably the biggest reason that the military budget has not been cut more since the end of the Cold War. Today, we spend as much as we do on the military not so much because of military threats, which greatly decreased with the demise of the Soviet Union, but because cutting the military budget would have an impact on an important and powerful segment of American industry. All this is particularly significant in the context of Mill's (1956) finding that the top leaders of the military, the executive branch, and the major corporations have common backgrounds and often move back and forth among these power centers.

Clearly, the government's expenditures are heavily influenced by the interests of this **military-industrial complex.** In many cases, such expenditures do more for the profits of these giant companies than for the country's true security needs. This is particularly true of expenditures for the procurement of weapons systems. Many experts, for example, have made this observation about the Strategic Defense Initiative (SDI), popularly known as "Star Wars." Though research and development costs alone for this project amount to billions of dollars, there is great doubt that it could ever stop a full-scale nuclear attack. Nor, following the demise of the Soviet Union, is it clear where such an attack might come from. Nonetheless, the budget for fiscal year 1993 continued to include money for the development of this system, even as the projected budget soared to $350 billion or more.

**ANTIPOVERTY PROGRAMS** At the other end of the scale, we can learn something more about who benefits from government spending by examining the share of the budget that goes to antipoverty programs. Although it is widely believed that the government spends massive amounts of money on welfare, the actual share of the federal budget that goes to programs for low-income people is quite small (Shirk, 1992). In 1984, for example, total means-tested assistance (assistance for which only low-income people were eligible) amounted to about $100 billion (Burtless, 1986, p. 22), or about 10 percent of the federal budget. If you add labor- and job-training programs, the total rises to around $115 billion (Burtless, 1986, p. 35), about 12 percent of the federal budget. Thus, it is *not* true that a massive share of the federal government is going to antipoverty programs. In fact, the amount is quite small, and most of these programs suffered substantial cuts during the 1980s (Levitan, 1985).

**FEDERAL TAXES** The federal income tax is, on paper, a **progressive tax:** The rates are designed so that the proportion of income paid in taxes increases as income increases—though to a far lesser extent than was the case a quarter-century ago. However, in reality the tax system often does not work this way. Because the wealthy have more power, tax laws—even reforms—tend to favor them.

The 1986 Tax Reform Act, touted as an effort to make the tax system work in a more progressive manner, is a prime example of how government action often benefits the wealthy. Though its sponsors claimed it would make the system more progressive, it did not in reality do so. The tax reform act did close some loopholes, and specified that income from all sources, whether salary or capital gains, would be taxed at the same rate. These changes made it somewhat harder for the wealthy to escape taxation. However, the law also lowered the tax rates in the highest income brackets, and this largely offset the other changes. By 1988, several studies showed that most income groups were paying about the same share of taxes they paid before tax reform (Bradshaw and McKenzie, 1989; Klott, 1988, Koratz, 1988). More recent data indicate that the share of taxes paid by the wealthy fell rather than rose. Bartlett and Steele (1992, p. 48) report that while middle-income taxpayers got a 7 percent tax cut, taxpayers in the $500,000-to-$1 million bracket got a 31 percent tax cut—more than four times as much. Especially hurt were many two-earner middle-income couples who lost deductions (Klott, 1988).

At the same time as upper-income taxpayers benefited because their tax rates fell, many loopholes were not closed. Because the home mortgage deduction may be taken on mortgages up to $1 million, most of the tax subsidy from this deduction goes to the wealthy. In the first year after tax reform, the wealthiest 17 percent of the population received over half of all federal housing subsidies, mainly from the tax deduction for mortgage interest (Mariano, 1987).

Another stated objective of the 1986 Tax Reform Act was to lower the taxes of the poor by increasing the personal exemptions and the standard deduction. This did bring an 11 percent reduction in taxes for households with incomes below $10,000. However, the wealthy benefited more. Those in income brackets above $1000,000 received at least a 22 percent reduction. Because of their bigger incomes, the wealthy got much bigger dollar savings. Tax reform saved the average household in the $100,000-to-$200,000 bracket $7,203. The average household with an income below $10,000 saved $37 (Bartlett and Steele, 1992, p. 6).

Finally, tax reform was supposed to shift $120 billion in taxes from individuals to corporations between 1987 and 1992. It didn't. At first, corporate taxes rose as expected, but taxes paid by corporations quickly fell below projections (Bradley, 1990; Rosenbaum, 1990; Stout, 1990). By 1992, it was apparent that the ultimate shift in taxes was from corporations to individuals, not the other way around as had been promised. In 1980, before tax reform, 21 percent of all federal income taxes were paid by corporations. By 1992, corporations were paying 17 percent of all income taxes—4 percent less than a decade earlier.

The experience of tax reform suggests that, whatever its intent or promise may have been, the biggest beneficiaries were wealthy individuals and corporations. This experience, like such indicators as the distribution of wealth and income and the beneficiaries of government spending, suggests that government policies very often do benefit the wealthy to a disproportionate extent. This seems to have been the case particularly in the 1980s, when the wealth distribution, the income distribution, and the distribution of taxes paid all shifted in directions favorable to the wealthy. Thus, the answer to "Who benefits?" seems largely to fit the power-elite model.

**Who Wins?** Perhaps most critical in assessing the nation's power structure is the question "Who wins when competing interest groups attempt to influence public policy?" Domhoff (1983) reviewed much of the research on this question, focusing on the relative influence of the three coalitions he identified—the multinational corporate-interest group, the small-business group, and the labor-liberal coalition. His review showed that when there is substantial policy disagreement among these three groups, the corporate group nearly always gets its way (see also Neustadtl and Clawson, 1988). A recent example of this is the inability of doctors and hospitals to block cost controls desired by corporations in the 1980s (Imershein, Rand, and Mathis, 1992). Over a period of about five decades, the corporate group had only one clear defeat—the passage of the pro-labor National Labor Relations Act in 1935. Even this law was later modified to make it more acceptable to the corporations.

With respect to the other two groups, small business appears to have a fair amount of veto power; it could usually stop something that was threatening to it. It regularly defeated initiatives of the liberal group that it found threatening, and in some cases it was able to modify, although it could not block, initiatives of the corporate group. It fared less well with its own initiatives, usually winning only when it had the support of the corporate moderates.

Least powerful was the labor-liberal coalition. It could act as an effective veto group only when it had the support of the corporate group to stop an initiative of the small-business conservatives. Rarely did it succeed in passing its own initiatives, and when it did, it was usually with the support of the corporate group. Significantly, its power increased during periods of social conflict and upheaval, as the corporate group sought to maintain order by making concessions (see, for example, Gilbert and Howe, 1991, pp. 215-216; Jenkins and Breuts, 1989, 1991). Why, according to Domhoff, did this group have the least ability to win? First, it was a looser and more diverse coalition, and thus suffered from less unity and more divisiveness. Second, it had fewer economic resources than either of the other groups. Third, it had less access to governmental officials.

Hence, the answer to the question "Who wins?" indicates limited pluralism. One group nearly always wins, another wins only sometimes, and the third usually can win only with help and under certain conditions. There is a power elite that has important advantages in any public-policy conflict at the national level.

Much of what we know about the American power structure has been influenced by the research of G. William Domhoff. In his "Personal Journey into Sociology," (p. 274) Domhoff tells us how he started out as a researcher on dreams and became a student of power structure.

## Interest Groups at the Local Level

The important interest groups at the local level are harder to describe than those at the national level, because they vary, depending on the locality. However, certain types of groups are usually involved at this level. One such group consists of established, wealthy, and prestigious families in the community (Levy, 1979; Lynd and Lynd, 1937). Such families exist in large and small cities. They may be founders of local industries (the most frequent type), families associated with major local cultural or educational institutions, or even descendants of the founders of the community. These families frequently overlap. A second important group, often overlapping with the first, consists of corporations and financial or industrial concerns with major operations in the locality. In many cities, ethnic groups and religious groups are organized and actively involved in city politics (Dahl, 1961). In some cities, too, poor people are well organized and seek to influence policy through groups such as ACORN (Association of Community Organizations for Reform Now), a poor people's organization with chapters in many medium-to-large cities.

However, in most local areas, the business interests are the most politically powerful group. This group—banking, construction, real estate, and insurance interests—depends on growth and new construction for their profits. Many cities are so dominated by these interests that their local governments function as "growth machines": Their main purpose is to promote growth and new development that benefits these interests (Molotch, 1976; Lyon et al., 1980). In such cases, the power of this "growth lobby" exceeds that of any other group. In some cities, however, antigrowth interests also are heavily involved in local politics. These groups represent citizens who see growth as a threat to the quality of life, bringing more crowds, noise, pollution, and traffic jams. In some cities, antigrowth lobbies have successfully challenged the notion that "bigger is better" and have succeeded in implementing policies that restrict growth. Most often this has happened in cities with affluent, educated, and highly involved citizens, located in rapidly growing areas such as California, Oregon, and parts of New England.

## The Distribution of Power: The Local Level

We have already mentioned the difficulties of describing local power structures arising from place-to-place variations. Another problem is that even experts studying the same city cannot always agree on its distribution of power. In New Haven, Connecticut, for example, studies by Dahl (1961) and Polsby (1959) concluded that the city's power structure was pluralist, whereas a later study by Domhoff (1978) concluded that the city was dominated by a power elite. How did this happen? In this case, it happened partly because different researchers examined who was involved and who won on different sets of issues. Political nominations on school policies, two of the areas studied by Dahl, did not appear to be dominated by any one group, perhaps because the wealthy in New Haven made little effort to influence them. Their children attended private schools, and they appeared more concerned with influencing whatever policy was implemented than with who got elected. Domhoff, on the other hand, focused mainly on urban renewal, a development issue in which the affluent growth lobby dominated, as predicted by Molotch's (1976) "growth machine" theory. Domhoff's study emphasized an issue where the wealthy did have a clear economic stake, and on this issue they were both highly active and, according to Domhoff, successful in getting their way.

The general approach you choose in studying local power distributions also can affect your conclusions. Studies using the *reputational approach,* for example, tend to find a power elite: If you ask people who has power in a community, you will frequently get similar answers from many different people. Studies of *who wins* in controversial issues, however, frequently find a pluralist power distribution. Again, there may be a bias: Issues only become controversial when they are debated publicly and when two ore more organized interest groups contend over them. If the power elite exercises its power behind the scenes, it might prevent issues of concern to it from being controversial (Molotch and Lester, 1973). Even when issues do become controversial, and even if elected officials do represent a variety of backgrounds, they may still make their decisions under the influence of powerful unelected elites. This principle is vividly illustrated in the film *Poletown Lives* and in a book by Jeanie Wylie (1989), both of which show how a working-class Polish and black neighborhood in Detroit was destroyed to permit expansion of a General Motors plant. Despite the fact that the mayor and much of the city council had backgrounds in labor and civil rights activism, they were virtually unanimous in doing the bidding of the automaker, apparently because they feared loss of employment if they did not.

Studies of *who benefits* from local government decisions often support the power-elite view. City after city offers massive *tax abatements* and other subsidies to industries to entice them to locate there. This means that large developers and corporations pay no property tax, or a much-reduced property tax, for a substantial period of time after building a new factory, business office, or apartment building. This policy is designed to encourage development and attract jobs, yet many studies have found that it is not very effective in doing so (Harrison and Kantner, 1978; Kieschnick, 1981; Wolkoff, 1982, 1983) and that the main result for tax abatement and other community development efforts is to subsidize the wealthy by reducing taxes paid by corporations (Ravitz, 1988). Abatements fail to attract jobs for several reasons. First, virtually every area offers such abatements to any company willing to locate there, so the policy does little to encourage development in any particular city. Second, considerations other than taxes generally play a bigger role in corporations' decisions about where to locate. Typically, local taxes are only 2 to 3 percent of the costs a company faces (Wolkoff, 1983). Third, many firms have little choice about where to locate because of established markets or business ties in local areas.

**Some General Observations** If different studies tend to give different answers to the pluralist versus power elite question, we do know that certain characteristics of cities predispose them toward either a pluralist or a power-elite orientation. Cities with partisan elections (except ones overwhelmingly dominated by one party) tend to conform more to the pluralists model (Aiken, 1970, p. 505) because there is always an organized opposition. Moreover, to some extent, one party may represent business and another labor, ethnic, or environmental concerns. In cities with nonpartisan elections, in contrast, the political and ideological orientations of the candidates are often less clear, and once elected, officials have no automatic opposition. This probably increases the behind-the-scenes influence of elites, because officials are less likely to be called to task for responding to special interests when there is no organized opposition. The city manager system also contributes to behind-the-scenes decision making, and cities with this system of government tend to resemble the power-elite model more closely than those with an elected mayor as the only executive leader (Aiken, 1970, pp. 499-500).

Cities with one major industry (such as Detroit) have a tendency to operate according to the power-elite model, reflecting the great power of that industry. This is especially true if the industry is locally owned or headquartered, so that its leaders are present and concerned with city issues. In contrast, cities with diverse industries are more likely to follow a pluralist model, as are cities with absentee-owned or-operated industries, because the leaders live elsewhere and are thus less likely to become involved in local affairs (Aiken, 1970).

Cities with large, diverse, and well-organized ethnic or religious groups or labor unions also are more likely to operate according to the pluralist model (Aiken, 1970; Alford, 1969).

## The Importance of Local versus National Power

Before concluding our discussion of the distribution of power in America, we should note one more important point. Regardless of the nature of the local power structure, the national power structure, which seems to come closer to the power-elite pattern, has important impacts at the local level.

One example of this can be seen in the federal government's treatment of poverty. American poverty today is heavily concentrated in large central cities. Federal decisions that have the consequence of increasing the poverty rate will have serious impacts on such cities regardless of their power structures. This impact will be compounded if the federal government simultaneously reduces aid to cities in order to

## PERSONAL JOURNEY INTO SOCIOLOGY

### HOW I BECAME A PROFESSOR OF DREAMS AND POWER

G. WILLIAM DOMHOFF

Nothing about my background predisposed me to become a political sociologist interested in uncovering the power structure of American society. My family was average in every way and took no interest in politics. While growing up I played sports and wrote for the high-school newspaper, and I thought I might be a journalist when I left the Midwest to go to college in the South.

Still, I always had a strong dislike for injustice and unfairness. The poverty I saw as a child when we drove downtown always puzzled and upset me. But my inclination to question injustice manifested itself only in crusading articles in my high-school and college newspapers. Then, too, one of my early college term papers concerned the famous muckraking journalists of the Progressive Era. Their investigations into the rise of the "money trusts" and giant corporations fascinated me.

In college my interest in journalism slowly gave way to a liking for the mysteries of human psychology. I became interested in motivation, in what makes people I read case histories of patients, interpretations of myths and rituals, and studies of the unconscious. After much hesitation and soul searching, I decided to go to graduate school to become a psychoanalyst or professor, even though many aspects of psychology bored me. I had to steel myself for the fact that some of what I would study would not be enjoyable to me and that I would have to suffer through this material to attain my goal.

I gradually became involved in systematic studies of dreams, the revealing picture stories of the night. This was because I had a change to work with one of the few well-known psychologists who studied that almost-taboo topic: the late Calvin S. Hall, best known for such books as *Theories of Personality, The Primer of Freudian Psychology*, and *The Primer of Jungian Psychology*. My dissertation had the rather grandiose title "A Quantitative Study of Dream Content Using an Objective Indicator of Dreaming." That title sounds too strained to me now, for later research showed that such objective indicators of dreaming as rapid eye movements (REM) and unique brain wave patterns were not as good as we originally thought they were.

But questions of power were creeping up on me, too, sometimes in very roundabout ways. Traveling in Europe the summer after my second year of graduate school, I met a woman from California, and the next summer we were married. It was her family that started me reading and thinking about power, for they were all political activists and avid readers. When I read a book by C. Wright Mills called *The Power Elite*— published in 1956, a year of complacency and celebration in America—I was more than interested; I was mildly hooked. Here was a world of power below the surface of society that was just as new and surprising to me as the private motives underneath our individual behavior.

Even so, I might not have switched my research interest from dreams to power if it had not been for the excitement and hopefulness stirred in me by the rising civil rights movement. That movement started to gain national attention just as I was finishing graduate school in Florida and taking my first teaching job at a state college in California. I was intrigued by the way the civil rights movement used research on local and national power structures to help its cause.

I still wouldn't have made the transition to power-structure research if I hadn't come across another sociology book, this one by E. Digby Baltzell: *Philadelphia Gentlemen: The Making of a National Upper Class.* Baltzell's book was crucial to me because it contained a list of "indicators" of upper-class standing, meaning that we could tell who was and was not part of the social elite by listings in the *Social Register*, attendance at expensive private schools, and membership in exclusive social clubs. His book enabled me to think in terms of systematic research that traced networks of power from the social upper class and the corporations to policy-forming groups, political parties, and government.

In other words, I immediately saw ways that I could use Baltzell's upper-class indicators to test the ideas of the aforementioned C. Wright Mills as well as those of various Marxists and pluralists. It has always been my tendency to try to test the most exciting ideas I can find with the most respectable and solid methods that can be used. I also like to synthesize the ideas of different people, so my first book, *Who Rules America?*, began by saying that it would build on the works of four very different people—Mills, Baltzell, the Marxist Paul Sweezy, and the pluralist Robert Dahl. It was written in a direct and graphic way, thanks to all my journalism experience in my background, and it was loaded with what we like to call empirical information. It also named names.

When I finished that book I honestly thought I would go back to dream research. I was not prepared for the book's great success. It had hit at just the right time, the late 1960s, when civil rights activism had combined with anti-war and other movements to create tremendous ferment in the country. My book sold by the tens of thousands each year. It made sense to people because they were watching the power structure I described continue to fight the war in Vietnam even though growing numbers of people opposed it.

Even academic reviewers were not only negative toward my book, which was surprising in an era when just about everyone in academia denied the existence of a power structure. Moreover, I felt that I could do more research to answer the kinds of questions that did get raised about the book. So I plunged back into research on power, writing more books, which in turn led critics to raise more questions. I was caught up in an exciting dialogue, and the result has been eight authored or co-authored books and three edited books in 25 years of research.

However, some of the fun went out of it for me in the late 1970s as the social movements of the 1960s disappeared and interest in the study of power structures declined. Moreover, a new breed of young Marxists began to claim that my books were part of the problem. I supposedly discouraged potential activists by writing that there is a power structure rooted in a small social upper class that owns and controls the large banks and corporations. I was making it seem hopeless. Thus, after being seen as useful in the 1960s, helping people to focus their actions and formulate the perspective within which they were operating, I now was viewed as a hindrance. This change from one decade to the next showed me that research such as mine has only a limited effect, and that is often interpreted in terms of the atmosphere within which it is being read.

I think my research into power has been useful to democratic activists interested in opening up the power structure, but I also know from letters and conversations that it has been used by upwardly mobile social climbers to find the "right" schools or summer resorts and by young members of the upper class who have not yet grasped the overall nature of the complex power structure they are destined to enter. My work has been of interest to these diverse people because it is first and foremost an attempt to describe and understand, letting the chips fall where they may.

At the same time, even though there is little in my books that is judgmental or prescriptive, my research has been "radical" in that it attempts to get at the heart of the matter when it comes to understanding the great wealth and income inequality in the United States. It also is radical in a sense nicely stated by Mills in an answer to those hand-wringing social scientists who worried that he might be some sort of dangerous subversive rather than a proper sociologist. "When little is known," replied Mills, "or only trivial items publicized, or when myths prevail, then plain description becomes a radical fact—or at least is taken to be radically upsetting."

If my work has been radical, or radically upsetting, or useful, it is because so little is known about how power operates in a country where a mere one-half of one percent of the people own about 25 percent of *all* privately held wealth.

finance a tax cut or a military buildup. This is not an academic example; it is exactly what happened in the early 1980s. The result was that in city after city across the country, the poverty rate rose and federal assistance fell at the same time. The rise in the poverty rate meant that cities simultaneously collected less in taxes and paid more in costs associated with poverty, such as health services and crime control—and lost some of their federal aid.

In many large cities, the results were devastating. City governments had to raise taxes and cut services at the same time. Aging streets and bridges could not be repaired, and sewers constructed a century ago collapsed and could not be replaced. In some cities, recent efforts to improve minority employment by hiring more blacks and Hispanics as city workers were largely undone when fiscal crisis forced layoffs according to seniority. Significantly, these things happened independently of the local power structure.

For cities dominated by a power elite at the local level, there is another significant consideration. Very often, local elites are closely linked to national elites (Domhoff, 1978; Hunter, 1980; Kourvetaris and Dobratz, 1982). One example of this that we have already seen is the power of the auto companies in Detroit. As members of the corporate coalition, they are part of the power elite at the national as well as the local level. Thus, their influence on decisions made in Detroit is both indirect, through their influence over federal decisions that affect Detroit, and direct, through their influence over local decision making.

## SUMMARY

Power can be defined as the ability to get others to behave as you want them to. By its very nature, power is distributed unequally. When others accept a person's power as legitimate, that person is said to hold authority. Authority takes several forms. Legal-rational authority is attached to a position that a person holds and is linked to the tasks and responsibilities attached to that position. Traditional authority also may be linked to a position, but it is neither as limited nor as task-specific as legal-rational authority. Rather, it is based on long-standing and unquestioned ways of doing things, is often lifelong, and may have a scared or mystical aspect. Charismatic authority arises out of the attractive or inspirational qualities of a particular individual and cannot be attached to a position. Finally, authority may be gained through expertise and credentials. Authority of this last type is linked not just to position but to knowledge, and it is limited to areas relevant to that knowledge.

There are several other important sources of power besides authority. One is voting, though the extent to which voting is translated into power depends on the extent to which people vote on the basis of issues (or, in fact, vote at all). Another form of power is coercion—attempting to force people to behave in a particular way by threatening them with undesirable consequences if they do not do so. Like other forms of power, coercion may be either legitimate or illegitimate. When coercion or any other form of power is legitimate, people accept the principle that the person exercising power has the right to do so. When power is illegitimate, people perceive its exercise as improper, unauthorized, or violating their rights.

Control of information is another important source of power. Those who possess or control information can manipulate public opinion by selectively making information public. They also can argue that they should make the decisions because they have information the general public doesn't.

Finally, wealth and income are important sources of power, largely because they can so easily be converted into influence over public officials and control of information.

One key issue is the relationship between money and power. How closely related are economic stratification and power inequalities? A closely related issue is whether power is concentrated in the hands of a few or is widely dispersed among different groups. Power-elite theory holds that power is concentrated and that the few who hold it come mainly from the ranks of the very wealthy. An opposing theory holds that the power structure is pluralist, containing a number of competing centers of power arising from competing interest groups, many of which are outside the ranks of the very wealthy. In general, power-elite theory arises from assumptions made by the conflict perspective, and pluralist theory is more closely aligned with the functionalist perspective.

Sociologists have devoted considerable effort to studying power in the United States in an attempt to determine whether this country more closely resembles the power-elite or the pluralist model. Research has concentrated on discovering who governs, who benefits from government policy, and who wins when debates arise over alternative policies. In general, research at the national level is more supportive of the power-elite than the pluralist model, although it does not completely support either. A policy group dominated by large corporations has sought to influence national decision making throughout this century, has had more access to the policy-making process than anyone else, and has occasionally compromised but rarely lost. In contrast, policy groups dominated by small business and by a coalition of labor and liberal groups have had far less access and success. The labor-liberal group, in particular has been able to win only when it has been supported by the corporate group.

At the local level, power structures are more variable, depending on such factors as the type of government of a city, its ethnic makeup, and the number and size of major businesses in the community. Regardless of a city's local power structure, two facts remain. First, the largely elite nature of the national power structure has important impacts at the local level because federal policy and federal spending have major consequences for virtually every major locality. Second, those who hold power at the local level are often the same groups who hold power at the federal level, which broadens the scope of their power and influence.

## GLOSSARY

**power** The ability o a person or group to get people to behave in particular ways, even if they do not wish to do so.

**authority** A right to make decisions and exercise power that is attached to a social position or to an individual and is accepted because people recognize and acknowledge its legitimacy.

**legitimate power** Power that others accept as proper.

**traditional authority** Authority based on long-standing custom, often reinforced by a sacred element.

**legal-rational authority** Authority that is tied to a position rather than to an individual and is based on principles of law or on an individual's proper appointment to a position.

**charismatic authority** Authority that is based on the personal qualities of an individual, such as the ability to excite, inspire, and lead other people.

**expertise** An individual's specialized knowledge concerning some specific topic, issue, or scientific discipline.

**credentials** Items of information used to document or support the claim that an individual has certain capabilities.

**political parties** Organizations, usually with different viewpoints or ideologies, that run slates of candidates for elective office.

**coercion** An exercise of power that forces people to recognize and obey a group or an individual whose legitimacy they did not accept.

**mass media** Popular published and broadcast means of communication that reach a substantial segment of the population.

**pluralist model** A theory holding that power is dispersed among a number of competing power centers, each representing a different interest group.

**veto groups** Interests groups that possess the power to block policy changes or proposed laws that threaten their interests.

**multinational corporation** A large corporation that produces or sells its products, and usually owns property, in a large number of countries.

**military-industrial complex** A grouping of powerful individuals and organizations that share a common interest in large military expenditures.

**progressive tax** A tax that requires those with higher incomes to pay a greater percentage of their income in taxes.

## FURTHER READING

DAHL, ROBERT. 1961 *Who Governs?* New Haven, CT: Yale University Press. This book, based on a study of the power structure of New Haven, is a classic and remains one of the most influential statements of the pluralist theory of local power distributions.

DOMHOFF, G. WILLIAM. 1983. *Who Rules America Now?* Englewood Cliffs, NJ: Prentice Hall. Probably the best place to get an overview of research on the American power structure by the author of the "Personal Journey into Sociology" box that appears in this chapter. This book addresses who has had power and influence at the national level in the United States under every president from Franklin Roosevelt through Ronald Reagan.

DYE, THOMAS R. 1990. *Who's Running America? The Reagan years*, 5th ed. Englewood Cliffs, NJ: Prentice Hall. An excellent introduction to research on the American power structure, updated to reflect changes and continuities that took place under Ronald Reagan. It addresses methodological issues in power research, describes the concentration of power in a variety of American institutions, and examines the social networks and interaction of leaders. Includes profiles of many leaders of the 1980s.

HUNTER, FLOYD. 1980. *Community Power Succession: Atlanta's Policy Makers Revisited.* Chapel Hill: University of North Carolina Press. An update of a highly influential reputational study of local power structure first published by Hunter in 1955; a statement of the power-elite viewpoint on local community power structures.

LO, CLARENCE Y. 1990. *Small Property versus Big Government: Social Origins of the Property Tax Revolt.* Berkeley: University of California Press. A history of the grass-roots tax revolt supported by middle-income homeowners in California during the 1970s. Most of the tax relief went to business property owners. The book explains how this antielitist movement ended up reinforcing existing inequality and privilege.

MILLS, C. WRIGHT. 1956. *The Power Elite.* New York: Oxford University Press. The classic American sociological work on power structure, this book remains one of the most influential statements of the power-elite thesis.

REISMAN, DAVID. 1961. *The Lonely Crowd.* New Haven, CT: Yale University Press. One of the more influential sociological descriptions of American society in the late 1950s, this work also is one of the most frequently cited examples of the pluralist view of power in industrial democracies.

SMITH, HEDRICK. 1988. *The Power Game: How Washington Works.* New York: Ballantine Books. This book describes how the political transformations since the mid-1970s have rewritten the rules of the "power game" in Washington, D.C. Smith argues that new sets of rules, new ways of achieving power leverage, and the "new breed" of politicians has contributed to a more wide-open "power game" that's played at the national level of government.

# Chapter 11

## Race and Ethnicity

*The 200 or so people gathered in the farmyard slowly formed a corridor, and, as they gave Nazi salutes and shouted "White Power!," 300 hooded figures walked through the human corridor, formed a circle around the giant wooden cross, and after a short speech by the Grand Wizard, lit their torches one by one. Earlier, the group had been whipped into a frenzy by another, longer speech by the same man, in which he shouted that the Revolutionary War had not been fought to protect the rights of "race-mixers" and "queers," and that America had been founded as a "white Christian nation"—not for the "Japs, Mexicans, Negroes, Jews, or queers." All the while he spoke, a group of 40 protesters stood across the street, behind a line of wary sheriff's deputies, chanting "Down with the Klan, up with love!" In response to every "White Power!" chant, they replied "People Power!" Now it was late, the protesters had left, and the Klan rally was nearly over—but not until the hooded Klan members set the cross on fire and, surrounding it, tossed their torches in a pile at its base.*

*The scene described above did not take place in the South. It did not take place in the 1920s, 1940s, or 1950s. It occurred near Alton, Illinois, in September 1992. According to a reporter on the scene, nearly every car in the parking lot bore Illinois license plates. It was one more ugly reminder of the deep racial divisions that continue to affect America in the 1990s. Other reminders included the bloodiest urban violence of the 20th century in Los Angeles after four white police officers were acquitted of the videotaped beating of Rodney King, and a near-riot at City Hall by New York City police officers, in which news reporters overheard some participants refer to Mayor David Dinkins as a "nigger."*

*The problem of racial and ethnic conflict, however, is global. In Germany, mobs of right-wing, nativist thugs repeatedly attacked hostels housing immigrants in 1992, resulting in deaths, many injuries, and much homelessness. In what once was Yugoslavia, Serbs bent on "ethnic cleansing" committed atrocities against Bosnians and Croatians, and repeatedly attacked civilian targets, raping Muslim women and girls and then killing them. Scenes of their concentration camps brought chilling memories of the Holocaust, in which millions of Jews, Gypsies, homosexuals, and others were murdered by the Nazis in World War II. Old ethnic and racial conflicts continue between Armenians and Azerbaijanis in the former Soviet Union, Arabs and Jews in the Middle East, Irish-ancestry Catholics and British-ancestry Protestants in Northern Ireland, Kurds and Muslims in Iraq, blacks and whites in South Africa. Despite hope a year earlier of a peace agreement, some of 1992's worst violence occurred in South Africa, as police on several occasions fired into unarmed crowns of anti-*apartheid *demonstrators, resulting in scores of deaths.*

In this chapter, we shall explore some of the reasons that racial and ethnic conflicts have been so widespread throughout history. In order to address this issue, we must first understand what is meant by race and ethnic group.

## RACIAL AND ETHNIC GROUPS: WHAT IS THE DIFFERENCE?

Some of the examples discussed above involve *racial* conflict, others involve ethnic conflict, and yet others involve both. There are similarities between a race and an ethnic group. Both are socially defined categories of people who share a common ascribed status. Membership in both is hereditary. However, there are also differences. A **race** can be defined as a category of people who (1) share some socially recognized physical characteristic (such as skin color or facial features) that distinguishes them from other such categories, and (2) are recognized by themselves and others as a distinct status group (Cox,

1948, p. 402). An **ethnic group**, in contrast, is a category of people who are recognized as a distinct status group entirely on the basis of social or cultural criteria such as nationality or religion. There is no reliable way to identify a person's ethnic group by his or her physical appearance.

Although physical characteristics play a role in identifying races, race is much more a social concept than a biological one. A crucial part of the definition of *both* races and ethnic groups is that they must be *socially recognized* as distinct groups. Human societies choose to pay attention to a particular physical characteristic, which then becomes the basis for defining a race. In fact, there is no good scientific basis for even saying how many races there are. There is no one gene for race, and different genes affect different aspects of physical appearance (Thernstrom, Orlov, and Handlin, 1980, p. 869). For this reason, social scientists and biologists have never been able to agree on the number or races—different schemes have identified as few as three or more than 100 races. Moreover, racial clarifications vary in different societies. In the United States, for example, you are considered black if you have any identifiable African-American ancestry or physical appearance. However, many people considered African-American in the United States would be placed in a mixed group, often identified as "mulatto" or "colored," in many other countries.

For both races and ethnic groups, membership is usually involuntary and lifelong; in other words, it is an *ascribed* status. In addition, it is usually passed from parent to child, although in some instances it may change for the offspring of marriages whose partners are of different races or ethnic groups. The characteristics used to define races are usually ones that are consistently and reliably passed from generation to generation, which explains, for example, why skin color is commonly used to define races and eye color is not.

### Majority and Minority Groups

As we have seen, many societies that have two or more races or ethnic groups experience inequality and conflict. One or more groups are in an advantaged or dominant position with the power to discriminate, while other groups are in disadvantaged or subordinate positions and are often the victims of discrimination. Those in the advantaged or dominant positions are called **majority groups;** those in disadvantaged or subordinate positions are called **minority groups.** Often the majority group in this sociological sense is also a majority in the numerical sense, as with whites in the United States and people of British ancestry in Canada and Northern Ireland. However, a numerical minority can be a majority group in the sociological sense, and vice versa. One example is South Africa where about 5 million whites dominate more than 25 million native South Africans in politics, economics, and every other aspect of life. Hence, many sociologists believe the terms *dominant group* and *subordinate group* are more accurate, but the majority group/minority group terminology is still more commonly used.

Besides race and ethnicity, minority groups may be defined on the basis of other ascribed social characteristics such as sex, physical handicap, or sexual orientation. While these minority groups are discussed in other chapters, it is significant to note that prejudice and discrimination against them is often closely linked to racial and ethnic bias, as illustrated by the actions of the Nazis and Klan members discussed in the opening vignette

## RACISM

Whenever prejudice, discrimination, or systematic social inequality occurs along the lines of race or ethnicity, we have an example of *racism.* Social scientists have used the term in so many ways that some have questioned its very usefulness (cf. Wilson, 1987, p. 12). Still, the reality of racial and ethnic conflict and inequality is so pervasive in the world that some underlying processes must be responsible for it. Thus, we shall select a broad definition of racism and then specify some distinct types of racism. For our purposes, **racism** is any attitude, belief, behavior, or social arrangement that has the intent or the ultimate effect of favoring one racial or ethnic group over another. As we shall see, this definition implies that although racism is often open, conscious, and deliberate, it can also exist in subtler forms. Sometimes, in fact, people can be racist without even being aware of it.

## Ideological Racism

At one time, the term *racism* referred to the belief that one race or ethnic group is naturally superior (or inferior) to another. Today, in recognition of the variety of forms that racism can take, this type of belief is referred to as **ideological racism**, or *racist ideology*. It includes such notions as Hitler's concept of a "master race," the belief of slaveholders that blacks were uncivilized and incapable of anything more than physical labor (Jordan, 1968, Chap. 2; Wilson, 1973, pp. 76-81), and the conviction among southwestern Anglos of the late nineteenth century that the partial Indian ancestry of Mexican Americans predisposed them to "savagery" and "banditry" (Mirande, 1987). Ideological racism can become institutionalized to the point where it has the status of an unquestioned "truth" that few people (in the majority group, at least) challenge.

An important function of ideological racism is to justify the exploitation of the minority group (Cox, 1948). As Davis (1966) has pointed out, to enslave a human being like yourself is a terrible thing that most people cannot accept. If you can convince yourself and others that the one you are enslaving is less than fully human, however, then you can probably convince yourself and others that slavery is not so bad. This helps to explain why, for example, racist ideologies against blacks became more extreme and were invoked more frequently *after* slavery was established in the U.S. South than *before* (Wilson, 1973. pp. 76-81).

## Racial and Ethnic Prejudice

Still in the realm of racist *thinking* (as opposed to action) is racial and ethnic **prejudice:** any categorical and unfounded overgeneralization concerning a group. It can take the form of beliefs about a group, negative feelings toward a group, or the desire to discriminate against a group. In each of these cases, prejudice involves an automatic reaction to a group or to a person's group membership. If I automatically don't like you because you are white, if I want to discriminate against you because you are black, or if I think you are greedy because you are Jewish, I am prejudiced, because I am responding to you entirely on the basis of your race or ethnicity. I am choosing to ignore or disbelieve the influence of everything else about you except the fact that you are white, black, or Jewish.

One common type of prejudice is the **stereotype,** an exaggerated belief concerning a group of people. A stereotype assumes that anyone in a group is very likely to have a certain characteristic. American culture is full of stereotypes, such as the narrow-minded and authoritarian German; the greedy Jew, the lazy, musical, or sports-minded black; the hard-drinking Irish; the gang-prone Chicano, and the bigoted southern white. Every one of these stereotypes, like all others, is a gross overgeneralization. Undoubtedly, some people in any group do fit the stereotype, but many others do not. The point is not that stereotypes do not apply to *anyone* in the group at which they are aimed, but that they are never true for *everyone* in that group.

Stereotypes can be positive or negative, but even the positive ones are a mixed blessing. It is, for example, undoubtedly good to be musical, athletic, or a good dancer, which are common stereotypes about African Americans. However, if whites believe that these are the only areas in which blacks can achieve, then they will probably behave in ways that close off opportunities for African Americans in professions other than sports and entertainment. Equally significant, if young African Americans internalize the message that the areas for them to get ahead in are sports and music, they can be directed away from other areas in which they could be equally successful (see the vignette in Chapter 4 by Harry Edwards).

### Individual Discrimination

Although prejudices of any type concern what people think, *discrimination* concerns what they *do*. **Individual discrimination** is any behavior that treats people unequally on the basis of race, ethnicity, or some other group characteristic. Individual discrimination is usually conscious and deliberate. Examples are a restaurant owner who refuses to serve a Chinese person, or a taxi driver who passes a man by because he is black. In the United States, most discrimination on the basis of race, sex, religion, or disability is illegal. Nonetheless, some types of individual discrimination are hard to prove, and in some areas, such as housing, this kind of discrimination remains common.

### Institutional Discrimination

The most subtle form of racism, yet perhaps the one with the most serious consequences today, is institutional racism, or **institutional discrimination** on the basis of race (Carmichael and Hamilton, 1967; Farley, 1978; Feagin and Feagin, 1978). This form of discrimination occurs whenever widespread practices and arrangements within social institutions have the intent or effect of favoring one race (usually the majority group) over another (usually the minority group). Institutional discrimination can be very deliberate, as in the system of school segregation and denial of voting rights to blacks that existed throughout the U.S. South until the early 1960s. A more contemporary example of deliberate institutional discrimination is the widespread practice in the real estate industry of *racial steering*—showing white customers houses in white neighborhoods and black customers houses in racially mixed or all-black neighborhoods (Lake, 1981; Pearce, 1976).

Today, institutional discrimination is often unconscious and unintentional, though its consequences can be just as devastating as if it were deliberate. In the educational system, for example, teachers often expect less achievement from black and Hispanic students than they do from white students (Brophy, 1983; Brophy and Good, 1974; Hurn, 1978; Harvey and Slatin, 1975; Leacock, 1969; Moore and Pachon, 1985). In schools that are predominantly black or Hispanic, such low expectations often become generalized to the entire student body. When teachers *expect* less, they *demand* and *get* less, and achievement falls (Brophy, 1983). As a result, black and Hispanic students frequently learn less, are graded lower, get a poorer education, and consequently lose out on job opportunities when they grow up. Although none of this may be intentional discrimination, its consequences are every bit as serious.

Another important example of institutional discrimination is the movement of jobs out of predominantly black and Hispanic central cities and into predominantly white suburbs. This trend takes job opportunities away from the minority groups and gives them to whites (Squires, 1989). Evidence shows that where jobs have become suburbanized in this manner, black and Hispanic men have higher unemployment rates than white men (Farley, 1987b; Lichter, 1988), and that when blacks do get opportunities to move to the suburbs, their unemployment rate declines (Rosenbaum and Popkin, 1991). To compound the problem, institutional discrimination within the real estate industry makes it very difficult for minorities to follow the jobs to all-white suburbs. In addition, the lack of automobiles in many black and Hispanic households, combined with poor mass transit, often makes commuting next to impossible (see Alexis and DiTomaso, 1983).

## THEORIES ABOUT THE CAUSES OF RACIAL AND ETHNIC INEQUALITY

We now turn to a more detailed exploration of the causes of racial and ethnic discrimination, conflict, and inequality. Social scientists offer three general explanations for these behaviors. One set of theories is based on social psychology, the other two are sociological in nature, arising, respectively, from the functionalist and conflict perspectives. We turn our attention first to social-psychological theories.

## PERSONAL JOURNEY INTO SOCIOLOGY

### THE ARAB IMAGE / JACK G. SHAHEEN

America's bogeyman is the Arab. Until the nightly news brought us pictures of Palestinian youths being punched and beaten, almost all portraits of Arabs seen in America were threatening. Arabs were either billionaires, bombers, bedouin bandits, belly dancers, or bundles in black—rarely victims. They were hardly ever seen as ordinary people practicing law, driving taxis, singing lullabies, or healing the sick. Though some TV newscasts may portray them more sympathetically now, the absence of positive media images nurtures suspicion and stereotype.

Historically, the Arab lacks a human face. Media images are almost invariably hostile and one-sided. They articulate, perhaps are even responsible for, the negative stereotype Americans have of Arabs. As an Arab American, I have found that ugly caricatures have had an enduring impact on Americans of Arab heritage. For the prejudiced, during the Gulf War, all Arabs—including some of the three million Americans with Arab roots—became "camel jockeys," "ragheads," and "sand suckers." Whenever there is a crisis in the Middle East, Arab Americans are subjected to vicious stereotyping and incidents of violence and discrimination.

I was sheltered from prejudicial portraits at first. My parents came from Lebanon in the 1920s; they met and married in America. Our home in the steel city of Clairton, Pennsylvania, was a center for ethnic sharing—black, white, Jew, and gentile. There was only one major source of screen images then, at the State movie theater where I was lucky enough to get a part-time job as an usher. But in the late 1940s, Westerns and war movies were popular, not Middle Eastern dramas. Memories of World War II were fresh, and the screen heavies were the Japanese and the Germans. True to the cliché of the times, the only good Indian was a dead Indian. But when I mimicked or mocked the bad guys, my mother cautioned me. She explained that stereotypes hurt; that they blur our vision and corrupt the imagination "Have compassion for all people, Jackie," she said. Experience the joy of accepting people as they are, and not as they appear in films, she advised.

Mother was right. I can remember the Saturday afternoon when my son, Michael, who was seven, and my daughter, Michele, six, suddenly called out: "Daddy, Daddy! They've got some bad Arabs on TV." They were watching that great American morality play, professional wrestling. Akbar the Great, who liked to hear the cracking of bones, and Abdullah the Butcher, a dirty fighter who liked to inflict pain, were pinning their foes with "camel clutches." From that day on, I knew I had to try to neutralize the media caricatures.

I believe most researchers begin their investigations because they have strong feelings in their gut about the topic. To me, the stereotyping issue was so important I had to study it. For years I watched hordes of Arabs prowl across TV and movie screens. Yet, a vacuum existed in the literature: Research on TV and movie Arabs did not exist. My research began with television because visual impressions from the tube indoctrinate the young. Once a stereotypical image becomes ingrained in a child's mind, it may never wither away.

Investigating television's Arabs began as a solo effort. But members of my family, friends, and colleagues assisted by calling attention to dramas I might otherwise have missed. For several years, I examined *TV Guide* and cable and satellite magazines. Daily, I searched for Arab plots and characters, then taped, studied, and categorized them. To go beyond personal observations, I interviewed more than 30 industry leaders, writers, and producers in New York and Los Angeles. In the spirit of fair-mindedness, I invited image makers, those influential purveyors of thought and imagination, to offer sparks of decency that illuminate, rather than distort, our perception of others.

It hasn't been easy. Images teach youngsters whom to love, whom to hate. With my children, I have watched animated heroes Heckle and Jeckle pull the rug from under "Ali Boo-Boo, the

Desert Rat," and Laverne and Shirley stop "Sheik Ha-Mean-ie" from conquering "the U S and the world." I have read more than 250 comic books like the "Fantastic Four" and "G.I. Combat" whose characters have sketched Arabs as "lowlifes" and "human hyenas." Negative stereotypes were everywhere. A dictionary informed my youngsters that an Arab is a "vagabond, drifter, hobo, and vagrant." Whatever happened, my wife wondered, to Aladdin's good genie?

To a child, the world is simple: good versus evil. But my children and others with Arab roots grew up without ever having seen a humane Arab on the silver screen, someone to pattern their lives after. To them, it seems easier for a camel to go through the eye of a needle than for a screen Arab to appear as a genuine human being. Recent movies suggest that Americans are at war with Arabs, forgetting the fact that out of 21 Arab nations, America is friendly with 19 of them.

Audiences are bombarded with rigid, repetitive, and repulsive depictions that demonize and delegitimize the Arab. One reason is that since the early 1900s more than 500 feature films and scores of television programs have shaped Arab portraits.

I recently asked 293 secondary school teachers from five states—Massachusetts, North Carolina, Arkansas, West Virginia, and Wisconsin—to write down the names of any humane or heroic screen Arab they had seen. Five cited past portraits of Ali Baba and Sinbad; one mentioned Omar Sharif and "those Arabs" in *Lion of the Desert* and *The Wind and the Lion.* The remaining 287 teachers wrote "none."

Nicholas Kadi, an actor with Iraqi roots, makes his living playing terrorists in such films as the 1990 release "Navy Seals." Kadi laments that he does "little talking and a lot of threatening—threatening looks, threatening gestures." On screen, he and others who play Arab villains say "America," then spit. "There are other kinds of Arabs in the world," says Kadi. "I'd like to think that some day there will be an Arab role out there for me that would be an honest portrayal."

The Arab remains American culture's favorite whipping boy. In his memoirs, Terrel Bell, Ronald Reagan's first secretary of education, writes about an "apparent bias among mid-level, right-wing staffers at the White House" who dismissed Arabs as "sand niggers."

Sadly, the racial slurs continue. Posters and bumper stickers display an Arab's skull and an atomic explosion. The tag: "Nuke their ass and take their gas."

At a recent teacher's conference, I met a woman from Sioux Falls, South Dakota, who told me about the persistence of discrimination. She was in the process of adopting a baby when an agency staffer warned her that the infant had a problem. When she asked whether the child was mentally ill, or physically disabled, there was silence. Finally the worker said: "The baby is Jordanian "

To me, the Arab demon of today is much like the Jewish demon of yesterday. We deplore the false portrait of Jews as a swarthy menace. Yet a similar portrait has been accepted and transferred to another group of Semites—the Arabs. Print and broadcast journalists have started to challenge this stereotype. They are now revealing more humane images of Arabs, a people who traditionally suffered from ugly myths. Others could follow that lead and retire the stereotypical Arab.

The civil rights movement of the 1960s not only helped bring about more realistic depictions of various groups, it curbed negative images of the lazy black, the wealthy Jew, the greasy Hispanic, and the corrupt Italian. These images are mercifully rare on today's screens. Conscientious imagemakers and citizens worked together to eliminate the racial mockery that had been a shameful part of the American cultural scene.

It would be a step in the right direction if movie and TV producers developed characters modeled after real-life Arab Americans. We could then see a White House correspondent like Helen Thomas, whose father came from Lebanon, in "The Golden Girls," a lawyer patterned after Ralph Nader on "L.A. Law," or a Syrian American playing tournament chess like Yasser Seirawan, the Seattle grandmaster.

Politicians, too, should speak out against the cardboard caricatures. They should refer to Arabs as friends, not just as moderates. And religious leaders could state that Islam, like Christianity and Judaism, maintains that all mankind is one family in the care of God. When all imagemakers rightfully begin to treat Arabs and all other minorities with respect and dignity, we may begin to unlearn our prejudices. The ultimate result would be an image of the Arab as neither saint nor devil, but as a fellow human being, with all the potentials and frailties that condition implies.

## Social-Psychological Theories of Race Relations

Most social-psychological theories about race relations center around the concept of prejudice (Wilson and See, 1988, p. 226). Recall that *prejudice* refers to unfounded and inflexible overgeneralizations concerning a racial or ethnic group. Social-psychological theories argue that people's situations and social experiences influence their attitudes and beliefs. These experiences lead some people to develop prejudiced attitudes and beliefs, usually through *personality need* or *social learning*.

**Personality Need** The theory of **personality need** arises largely from the work of Theodor Adorno and his colleagues (1950). In his content analysis of speeches and writings of right-wing extremists such as Nazis and Ku Klux Klan members, Adorno uncovered a number of themes that were not logically related but nonetheless appeared repeatedly. Sensing that these themes might reflect a certain personality type, he developed a personality measure to rate nine distinct attitudes and beliefs, including excessive respect for authority, superstition, aggression against nonconformers, cynicism, worry about sexual "goings-on," opposition to looking inward to understand oneself, and a belief that the world is a dangerous place. Moreover, Adorno's research found that this personality type scored a good deal higher on anti-Semitic and antiblack prejudice than did others. Thus, having a certain personality type—which Adorno called the **authoritarian personality**—does indeed appear to be associated with prejudice.

**SCAPEGOATS** Why are such people prejudiced? It appears that prejudice meets two kinds of personality need in such people. The first of these needs refers back to our discussion of Sigmund Freud. Recall Freud's (1962 [orig. 1930]) theory that society's expectations, the superego, are in conflict with the child's natural drives, the id. If the superego is so powerful that it represses natural drives, these drives can surface later in other forms. Adorno applied this notion to prejudice. He found, from questions he asked his subjects, that adults with authoritarian personalities usually had experienced harsh discipline as children. As a result, they built up a good deal of frustration and aggression because they did not have the necessary outlets for their natural drives. However, because respect for authority was so deeply ingrained in them, they could not take out their aggression on the true source of their anger —their parents and other authority figures. Instead they took it out on **scapegoats**—racial, ethnic, or religious minorities, or other groups who displayed nonconformity in their dress or lifestyle. These scapegoats were not the true source of prejudiced people's anger, but they did serve as effective targets.

**PROJECTION** The second personality need met by prejudice is also related to childhood experiences. Prejudiced people had been taught that the world is made up of good and bad people, and you must always think, act, and behave as the good people do. People who adopt this good/ bad world view cannot admit any fault in themselves, be cause to do so would be to put themselves in the "bad" category. Using open-ended questions, Adorno and his colleagues (1950) found that prejudiced people were much less willing than nonprejudiced people to admit faults in either themselves or their parents. Moreover, their prejudices helped them to deny their faults. By exaggerating the faults of others, they could deny or minimize their own. In particular, they tended to exaggerate the faults of minority groups. Thus, they could deny or minimize their own greed by pointing to "greedy Jews" or forget about their own violent tendencies by talking about "Mexican gangs." This process is called **projection**. As with scapegoating, other researchers besides Adorno have confirmed its presence among many prejudiced people. (Allport, 1954, Chaps. 21 and 24; Simpson and Yinger, 1985, pp. 73-78).

**Social Learning** Although personality-need theories explain why some people are prejudiced, they do not explain all cases of prejudice. One need only look at the U.S. South during the 1950s to see this. Although the overwhelming majority of southern whites displayed relatively high levels of antiblack prejudice, the incidence of authoritarian personalities in the South was not much higher than that found in the rest of the country (Pettigrew, 1971, Chap. 5; Prothro, 1952). Clearly, something other than personality need was responsible for antiblack feelings. A large part of the answer is to be found in culture and **social learning**. The social-learning theory of prejudice is much like the subcultural theory of deviance. According to this view, people are prejudiced because they grow up in prejudiced environments where they learn prejudice from their significant others. This learning occurs through the processes of selective exposure and modeling, reward and punishment, and identification. When your family, neighbors, and playmates are all prejudiced, you will probably be prejudiced, too. If you are exposed only to prejudiced attitudes and beliefs, they seem like unquestioned truths. You are informally rewarded when you express such attitudes but laughed at or teased if you express contrary attitudes. Finally, if all the people you respect and love hold prejudiced beliefs, could such beliefs really be wrong?

All of these social-learning processes do tend to produce prejudice. Research has shown that those whose parents and other childhood significant others were prejudiced tend themselves to be more prejudiced as adults (Ehrlich, 1973). However, this type of prejudice is different in an important way from prejudice based on personality need in that it is easier to change. Very often, when people whose prejudices are based on social learning move to environments where their significant others are relatively unprejudiced, their prejudice levels fall. In other words, people can conform to nonprejudice as well as to prejudice (DeFleur and Westie, 1958; Ewens and Ehrlich, 1969; Fendrich, 1967). For people who have a personality need to be prejudiced, however, that need remains regardless of their social environment.

**The Relationship Between Prejudice and Discrimination** The relationship between prejudice and discrimination is not always clear. As illustrated in Table 11.1, sociologist Robert Merton (1949) has shown that not everyone who is prejudiced discriminates, and some people who are not prejudiced do discriminate. Social pressures and the costs of discriminating or not discriminating determine whether racial attitudes will be translated into behavior. If the costs of discriminating are great (complaints, legal hearings, and penalties), prejudiced people will often not discriminate. Similarly, relatively unprejudiced people may discriminate if pressured to do so by, say, the threat of losing white customers if they welcome black customers.

Attitudes may be changed by behavior. Prejudice, at least as measured by people's responses to questionnaires, fell considerably in the U.S. South after desegregation was ordered by federal law. In general, it was more satisfying for southerners to say "We know now that segregation is wrong" than to say "We did what those Yankee bureaucrats in Washington told us to do." This is very consistent with a social-psychological theory called **cognitive-dissonance theory**, which states that if behavior changes, attitudes will often change to become consistent with the new behavior (Festinger, 1957; Festinger and Carlsmith, 1959).

Thus, we cannot assume that behavior is always the result of attitudes. However, this does not mean that prejudiced attitudes are unrelated to actual racial discrimination. Prejudice has decreased considerably in the United States (R. Farley, 1984, 1977; Farley and Frey, 1992; Firebaugh and Davis, 1988; National Opinion Research Center, 1983, 1991; Owen, Eisner, and McFaul, 1981), but it has not disap-

**TABLE 11.1 Robert Merton's Typology on Prejudice and Discrimination**

| | Does Not Discriminate | Discriminates |
|---|---|---|
| **Unprejudiced** | 1. All weather liberal | 2. Fair-weather liberal |
| **Prejudiced** | 3. Timid bigot | 4. All-weather bigot |

SOURCE: John E. Farley, *Majority-Minority Relations*, 2nd ed. © 1988, p. 41, by permission of Prentice Hall, Englewood Cliffs, NJ.

peared. In fact, many researchers believe that modern prejudices have taken on a subtle form called **symbolic racism** (Kinder and Sears, 1981; Kluegel and Smith, 1986, 1982, McConahay et al., 1981).

Symbolic racism refers to a pattern in which people do not express overtly prejudiced or racist ideas, but oppose any social policy that would eliminate or reduce racial inequality, such as affirmative action, government spending to assist minorities, school busing, and minority scholarships. Surveys show that the majority of whites do oppose most such policies (Kluegel and Smith, 1986; National Opinion Research Center, 1991; Schuman and Bobo, 1988). There has been only slight change in these attitudes over the past 20 years (Kluegel, 1990). Why do so many people oppose such policies? They believe that the system is fair, that there is equal opportunity, and that minorities are mainly at fault for whatever disadvantages they suffer (Kluegel, 1990).

This belief, however, is not supported by the facts. With 45 percent of black children and 38 percent of Hispanic children living below the poverty level—compared with just 16 percent of white children (U.S. Bureau of the Census, 1991d)—minority children do not grow up with the same opportunities as white children. Children cannot be blamed for high poverty rates, and both poverty and institutional discrimination keep many of these children from enjoying the opportunities that the average non-Hispanic white child enjoys.

**Conflict Theories** It is probably fair to say that the conflict perspective is the predominant approach today among sociologists specializing in race and ethnic relations. In fact, there are at least three important contemporary conflict theories about intergroup relations, which we shall explore shortly. These theories share certain elements. Unlike the functionalist approach, they do not see racial or ethnic inequality as resulting, simply from cultural differences and ethnocentrism. Rather, they believe the critical factor is that *one group benefits by subjugating another.* When groups are in competition for scarce resources, or when one group has something, (land, labor, wealth) that another wants, an essential condition for inequality exists. However, this by itself does not produce intergroup inequality. A second condition must also be present: *unequal power,* which means one group can take what it wants from another (Noel, 1968). Without this condition, inequality does not occur, and conflict may even be less likely, because groups often calculate their chances of winning before initiating a fight. However, when both competition or opportunity for gain and unequal power between groups exist, racial or ethnic inequality is likely to occur (Semyonov, 1988; see also Belanger and Pinard, 1991). This is especially likely when the conditions noted by functionalists—ethnocentrism and cultural differences—are also present.

Although conflict theorists share the belief that competition and unequal power play key roles in racial and ethnic inequality, they disagree about the nature of that competition. Most societies experience competition along both racial/ethnic and economic lines, and different conflict theories offer different ideas about the precise roles of race and economics.

**INTERNAL COLONIALISM THEORY** One conflict theory of race and ethnic relations is *internal colonialism.* Most of us are familiar with the concept of *colonialism* in its traditional meaning—a powerful country establishes control of a foreign area and its people. Typically, the native people of the colony are assigned a status lower than that of the colonizers. The natural resources of the colony are taken and used, often along with its people's labor, to enrich the colonizing country. In the case of internal colonialism, much the same thing happens, but within the borders of the colonizing country. In both cases, the colonized groups are placed under the colonizing country's control *involuntarily* (Blauner, 1972).

Once the colonized group takes on the status of a conquered people, certain things occur. Colonized minorities are subjected to intense attacks on their culture. Because they are defined as inferior, they are subjected either to isolation or to forced assimilation. They are also kept outside the mainstream of economic activity to ensure that they will not compete with members of the colonizing groups. Blauner (1972) points out that these experiences of colonized minorities make them different from immigrant minorities. The latter enter a society voluntarily and are not subjected to the same levels of attack on their culture or economic isolation as are colonized minorities.

The four major groups who became "American" involuntarily are black Americans, Chicanos, Puerto Ricans, and American Indians. The experiences of these groups generally fit those of colonized minorities, which helps to explain why even today they occupy the most disadvantaged positions of all American racial and ethnic groups, including immigrant groups whose arrival is much more recent (Zweigenhaft and Domhoff, 1991, Chapter 7).

Internal-colonialism theory is different from other conflict theories of race and ethnic relations in one important regard—it focuses almost exclusively upon conflicts that occur between (rather than within) racial groups. Two other important conflict theories of intergroup relations focus in part upon economic conflicts *within the majority group*, pointing out that such conflicts may have an important effect on majority-minority relations. Let us examine these theories.

**SPLIT-LABOR-MARKET THEORY** The first such theory is *split-labor-market theory*, which lists three economic interest groups: employers (owners of capital), higher-paid labor, and lower-paid labor (Bonacich, 1972). In multiethnic or multiracial societies, higher paid labor is often made up of majority-group members, while minority group members are concentrated in the lower-paid labor category (Bunacich, 1975, 1976; Wilson, 1978). According to this theory, the majority-group members who hold the higher-paying jobs attempt to protect their position by demanding hiring discrimination against minorities. In the United States, for example, white workers have demanded discrimination against African Americans, Chicanos, and Asian Americans. Certain jobs were defined as white men's work," and any minority person who aspired to them encountered blatant hostility from white workers. (For a personal account of such discrimination, see Wright, 1937, pp. 5-15).

It is significant in this regard that the Ku Klux Klan and similar groups have always drawn the bulk of their support from working-class whites, who feel economically threatened by blacks and other minority groups. In the early twentieth century, labor unions demanded hiring discrimination (Bonacich, 1975, p. 38; Wesley, 1927, pp. 254-281), and in at least some instances, employers refused to hire blacks *because they were afraid of the reaction of white workers* (Brody, 1960, p. 186). Between 1850 and 1890, white workers in California rioted against Chinese, Japanese, and Chicano workers, protesting their presence in mining, shoemaking, and other industries (Barth, 1964; Ichihashi, 1969; Kitano, 1985, p. 220; Mirande, 1987, Chap. 3; Olzak, 1989).

According to split-labor-market theory, majority group workers demand and benefit from discrimination because it protects their favored position in the labor force. Employers, on the other hand, are often hurt by discrimination, both because it drives up wages by reducing the labor pool and because it deprives them of the opportunity to hire the best worker. (On this point, see Becker, 1971.)

How accurate is this view? Many white workers undoubtedly *believe* that discrimination works to their advantage. However majority-group workers can only benefit from discrimination if they (rather than their employers) control the hiring process. To a certain extent, white workers did this in the late nineteenth and early twentieth centuries by threatening to "cause trouble" if minorities were hired. However, when the costs of discrimination became high enough, employers resorted to hiring tactics that used racism to the disadvantage of both majority- and minority-group members. The reality is that, except in occupations with union hiring halls, workers do not control the hiring process. Hence, most sectors of the economy operate more in accordance with a third theoretical model, to which we now turn.

**MARXIST THEORY** The *Marxist theory of racism* holds that racism exists mainly because it benefits the ruling economic class (Cox, 1948). Today's Marxist theorists see two key economic interest groups, not three, as envisioned in split-labor-market theory. Marxist theory denies that there is any real conflict of interest between higher-paid and lower-paid labor. Rather, as wage laborers, both groups share a common interest that is in conflict with that of the owners of capital. Marxists believe that racial antagonisms are primarily a mechanism that is used by the owners of capital to divide the working class. Thus, they argue that employers encourage white workers to think that they are threatened by blacks and other minorities, because they then come to see the minority workers rather than the employer as their enemy.

This divides the working class along the lines of race and ensures that employers will not have to confront a unified work force.

The labor history of the early twentieth century in the United States offers considerable support for this viewpoint. Between 1910 and 1920, all-while labor unions struck in the railroad, meat-packing, aluminum, and steel industries. The employers played upon racial antagonisms to break these strikes. Through a combination of deception (southern blacks were offered "good jobs up North" without being told they would be strikebreakers) and skillful exploitation of black antagonism toward all-white unions, thousands of blacks were recruited to break these strikes (Bonacich, 1976; Foster, 1920; Kloss et al., 1976; Rudwick, 1964) . These tactics, of course, hurt both blacks and whites over the long run: White strikers were defeated, and black workers were restricted to low-paying nonunion jobs. These incidents of strikebreaking, along with a general fear of black economic competition, led to perhaps the worst wave of race riots in American history. Between 1906 and 1921, mobs of whites in a number of cities attacked and murdered at least 125 African Americans (Farley, 1988, p. 129). A study by Susan Olzak (1989) has confirmed that much of this antiblack violence was linked to labor conflict.

By the 1930s, white workers increasingly realized that their approach of demanding discrimination was hurting them more than it was helping them. Industrial workers formed the Congress of Industrial Organizations (CIO), which, especially in the North, frequently supported policies, laws, and labor contracts forbidding racial discrimination. Even today the evidence suggests that racial inequality hurts white workers more than it helps them. Comparisons of states and metropolitan areas by Reich (1981, 1986a) and Szymanski (1976) in 1970 and 1980 showed that those with greater racial inequality were also characterized by lower wages for white workers, higher corporate profits, and weaker unions. Since 1980, as the minority poor and working class have lost ground, inequality has also grown within the white population. The white working class and much of the middle class have lost income as the wealthiest whites have gained. These trends are consistent with Marxist theory.

## RACIAL AND ETHNIC RELATIONS: AN INTERNATIONAL PERSPECTIVE

Most societies with racial and ethnic diversity experience some degree of racial conflict and inequality. Discrimination and social inequality are encountered by Chinese in Vietnam; Aborigines in Australia; Catholics in Northern Ireland; Arabs in Israel; Jews in much of Eastern Europe; blacks, Pakistanis, and East Indians in Great Britain; Asians in several African countries, French-speaking people in Canada; native Indians in several Latin American countries; and a variety of immigrant groups in Germany. In many places, violence has erupted between racial or ethnic groups.

### Ethnic Inequality and Conflict: How Universal?

Does this mean that ethnic inequality and conflict are inevitable whenever different groups come into contact? It does not. In Switzerland, a variety of ethnic and language groups have gotten along in relative harmony for years. In Hawaii, racial diversity is greater than anywhere else in the United States—no race is a majority there—and interracial relations, though far from perfect, are in general more harmonious than elsewhere in the United States. British Protestants and Irish Catholics, who hate one another in Northern Ireland, get along in the United States. Ethnic and racial conflict then are not inevitable; rather, they are the product of certain social conditions We have already identified some of them. One is colonization, which is as evident in other societies as it is in the United States. Other examples of societies that must cope with racial and ethnic diversity arising from a history of colonization are South Africa, several countries in Eastern Europe, and Latin America.

## Racial Caste in South Africa

Recall our discussion of caste systems of stratification, including South Africa's racial caste system. Until very recently, South African law spelled out where people could live, who they could marry, what jobs they could have, even where they could travel—on the basis of legally codified racial categories. In many regards, this system resembled the U.S. South prior to the civil rights movement. There, too elaborate rules of segregation and denial of the vote were used to keep blacks in a separate and subordinate position.

In both the U.S. South prior to the 1950s and South Africa prior to the 1990s, long periods of social upheaval were the result of legally-mandated segregation and inequality. Such upheavals demonstrate that caste systems are very difficult to maintain in modern urban societies without great conflict. The greater diversity and weaker social control of the city, along with mass communications, make it more likely that people will rise up in protest against oppression (Blumer, 1965; Morris, 1984; Tilly, 1974; Williams, 1977). If the system continues to resist change, the conflict can become quite violent, as illustrated by the 2,100 deaths that resulted in South Africa between the summers of 1984 and 1986 (Cowell, 1986). However, as Blumer (1965) has pointed out, this process of increasing upheaval does not always lead to the same outcome. From a legal standpoint, the U.S. civil rights movement brought dramatic change. Virtually all forms of deliberate or official segregation were banned, and the Voting Rights Act of 1965 guaranteed the right to vote to millions of African Americans in the South. In South Africa, however change, has been more limited.

While many South African laws requiring segregation have recently been repealed, there are no laws *against* segregation in many areas of South African life, and the country remains highly segregated. Most important, black South Africans continue to be denied the vote, preserving a system of white minority rule. While there were encouraging talks between the government and the African National Congress in the early 1990s, those talks bogged down for a time in 1992, and renewed attacks by police upon unarmed protesters took dozens of lives. In 1993, however, a tentative agreement was reached to hold elections in 1994.

Why has change been limited in South Africa? One of the most important reasons is that black South Africans are the majority of the population. When the subordinate group is a numerical majority, they are seen as much more threatening by the dominant group; as a result, they encounter more resistance and discrimination (Blalock, 1967). If black South Africans get the right to vote, it will mean the end to white rule, since over 80 percent of the population is black. Contrast this with the United States, where the African-American vote poses little threat to the ability of whites to control the political system: There is not one state where the majority of the population is black.

Another reason for the limited change is the relatively limited political and economic pressure from the outside on South Africa, and little military pressure on it from either within or outside. This can be contrasted with Zimbabwe, formerly Rhodesia, a white-ruled African country. Unlike South Africa, a strong guerrilla movement by native Africans there pushed the country into the early stages of a civil war in the 1970s. Fearing a communist takeover if the rebels won, the United States and Great Britain put intense pressure on Rhodesia's white minority government to negotiate a settlement with the rebels. This settlement brought about black majority rule, with certain protections for the whites who remained. Most important from the U.S. and British standpoint, it preserved a government friendly to Western interests. In contrast, in South Africa, where there was no risk of a pro-Soviet government, the Western countries put only mild pressure on the government, in the form of economic sanctions. However, not all countries honored the sanctions, and their objectives were limited, focusing on the release of political prisoners such as Nelson Mandela rather than on majority rule. Nonetheless, economic difficulties resulting from sanctions did play some role in South Africa's decision to negotiate on the question of majority rule in the early 1990s.

## Ethnic Conflict In Eastern Europe

In the early 1990s, violent ethnic conflict spread throughout the former Soviet bloc countries in Eastern Europe, taking thousands of lives. From Azerbaijan, Armenia, and Uzbekistan in the former Soviet Union to the former Yugoslav republics of Croatia, Serbia, and Bosnia-Herzegovina to eastern Germany, violence and mayhem among ethnic groups became the rule. In a somewhat different way than in South Africa or the United States, the roots of the violence in many of these areas can be linked to colonialism. Both the Soviet Union and Yugoslavia could be described as empires dominated by one ethnic group—Russians in the Soviet Union and Serbs in Yugoslavia (Mestrovic and Letica, 1992). Under the strong hand of authoritarian rule, the ambitions for self-rule among the various subordinated ethnic groups were kept in check. But when that rule weakened, various groups, beginning with Lithuanians, Latvians, and Estonians in the Baltic republics of the Soviet Union, began to seek independence. One by one, virtually every ethnic republic and enclave in the Soviet Union and Yugoslavia sought independence.

However, as is discussed further in the next chapter, the boundaries of the republics often did not coincide with ethnic enclaves. The Armenian enclave of Nagorno-Karabakh existed within Azerbaijan; there are many Serbian enclaves within Bosnia-Herzegovina, one of the Yugoslavian republics that declared independence. As these enclaves rebelled against newly independent republics controlled by another ethnic group, civil war broke out in Azerbaijan and Bosnia. As this was being written, the worst violence has been in Bosnia, where Serbs who objected to being in a Bosnian (Muslim) nation promoted a policy of "ethnic cleansing": forcing Bosnians and Croatians out of their territories, then seeking to align themselves with Serbia. In many cases, Croatians and Bosnians who would not leave were killed or put in concentration camps. Thousands of women were raped, and Bosnian cities were destroyed by Serbian shelling. The result was the largest wave of refugees in Europe since World War II.

Many of these refugees went to Germany. Soon, however, these and other immigrants, many of them Turks who had lived in Germany all their lives, became the targets of nightly attacks by right-wing mobs, particularly in what had been East Germany. One reason this occurred was the ailing German economy, brought about in large part by the effects of absorbing the unproductive economy of East Germany. Two other factors also played a role in fueling ethnic tensions. In the eastern part of the country, there were dashed expectations: The hope had been that, once free from communism, the country would enjoy immediate economic prosperity. It didn't, and people became disappointed and angry. At the same time, the upheavals in Eastern Europe led to massive immigration. The combination of a declining economy, disappointing economic growth in eastern Germany, and massive immigration was explosive, and the immigrants became the scapegoat for all the problems and dashed hopes of Germans, particularly in the eastern part of the country.

## Racial Assimilation in Latin America

A number of Latin American countries present a striking contrast to race relations in the United States. Like the United States, they were colonized by Europeans who imported blacks from Africa to serve as slave labor and who took land from the Indians (Van den Berghe, 1978; pp. 63-65). Yet, the outcome has been ultimately very different. Both culturally and racially, such countries as Mexico and Brazil experienced a two-way assimilation that produced new cultures and ethnic groups that are neither European, African, nor Indian. A key element of this process was **amalgamation**—repeated intermarriage and interbreeding between racial groups to the point that the various groups became largely indistinguishable. In both Mexico and Brazil, a large portion of the population is of mixed European, Indian, or African ancestry. As a result, relatively few people can be identified as strictly European, black, or Indian. The great majority belong to a mixed group that is often thought of as simply "Brazilian" or "Mexican."

Why did this happen in Mexico and Brazil and not in the United States? One factor is population composition. The overwhelming majority of the Portuguese who came to the colony of Brazil were male. This led to widespread intermarriage early on, which became sufficiently accepted to continue when more European women did arrive. In the United States, by contrast, more English colonists came as families, which discouraged intermarriage. Whites in North America did, of course, have sexual contacts with Indians and black slaves—often highly sexist and exploitative ones. However, the children that resulted from these contacts were designated as part of the minority group, whereas in Brazil, they became part of the majority group.

Religious differences further contributed to these patterns (Kinloch, 1974). The Catholic religion of the Spanish and Portuguese emphasized conversion and the winning of souls (Harris, 1964). Thus, black slaves and especially Indians were incorporated into the dominant culture. In the United States, the Protestant religion of the early colonists placed a greater emphasis on predestination, the belief that people were either chosen to be saved or not, and not too much could be done for those who were not chosen. Thus efforts to convert and integrate were less common, particularly in the case of Indians.

Other cultural attributes of both the dominant and minority groups also made a difference. In Brazil, many Portuguese of Moorish (North African*) ancestry were dark complexioned and viewed such a complexion as a standard of beauty (Pierson, 1942). This further encouraged intermarriage with Indians and Africans. In Mexico, the native Aztec Indians had a highly developed urban culture. Their largest city, with a population of 300,000, was one of the biggest in the world. Thus, in some ways, the Mexican Indians were culturally more similar to the Europeans, and therefore could more easily adjust to European ways. In Mexico, the blend of European (Hispano) and native (Indio) culture became a symbol of national unity.

Although assimilation and amalgamation have been the rule in Mexico and Brazil, neither country is a racial paradise. In both countries, having a lighter skin is associated with a higher social and economic status (Bastide, 1965; Mason, 1971). Even so, the different cultural and demographic histories have produced very different patterns of race relations in Mexico and Brazil than in the United States.

## RACIAL AND ETHNIC GROUPS IN AMERICA

Because the United States is a nation of immigrants, it is one of the most diverse nations of the world in terms of race and ethnicity. No ethnic group in the United States accounts for more than about a quarter of the population, and—depending on how you count them—there are between 15 and 30 nationalities that are claimed by at least half a million Americans (see U.S. Bureau of the Census, 1983a). About three-quarters of the U.S. population is of European ancestry; about one-quarter is of African, Asian, Latin American, or Native American ancestry. Although many of these groups entered American society voluntarily through immigration, some did not (Blauner, 1972). Africans were brought here as slaves, and the Mexican-American group was created by the conquest of a large area of northern Mexico (now California, Texas, Nevada, Colorado, New Mexico, and Arizona). Puerto Rico became a U.S. colony after the Spanish-American War of 1898, and the entire United States was Indian territory before the arrival of the Europeans. Because we have such great racial and ethnic diversity, and because a number of groups became "American" involuntarily, the United States has experienced greater racial and ethnic inequality and conflict than many other countries.

## MINORITY GROUPS

### African Americans

The largest American racial and ethnic group that fits the definition of a minority is clearly Black (African) Americans. The 1990 census counted 30 million blacks, or 12.1 percent of the U.S. population—the same percentage as in 1980. The history of African Americans has been a history of exploitation, social inequality, and discrimination. Roughly speaking, it may be divided into three periods: slavery, segregation, and the modern era (Wilson, 1978, 1973).

**Slavery** The first period, slavery, dated from the arrival of blacks in 1619 until the end of the Civil War in 1865. During this period, most blacks lived in the South and were slaves, although there were some free blacks, mainly in the North. Slavery was a creation of the wealthy, landowning elite of the South, which sought a cheap and reliable source of labor to maximize profits in a highly labor-intensive plantation system. As Noel (1968), Boskin (1965), and Jordan (1968) have pointed out, blacks did not become slaves simply because the British colonists in America were prejudiced against them. Rather, Africans were one of many groups against whom the colonists were prejudiced, and antiblack prejudices became much stronger *after* slavery became institutionalized (Cox, 1948; Noel, 1972). Black slavery was a product of economic motivations and of the fact that blacks were in a weaker position to resist it than were other groups (Noel, 1968). The role of the economic interests and the power advantage of the southern "planter class" can be clearly seen by looking at what happened in the North. Slavery was, for a time, legal there too—but it never became widespread because no economic elite depended upon it for their wealth. Between 1780 and 1804, the northern states that had once allowed slavery outlawed it, but it took the Civil War to get rid of slavery in the South. This is a rather clear example of the conflict theorists' argument that social inequality occurs because it benefits a wealthy and powerful group.

**Segregation** The second period in African-American history is often referred to as *segregation* because that was the dominant reality experienced by blacks during this period. Segregation is generally seen as lasting from shortly after the Civil War until the period following World War II, although it was the dominant pattern in the North even before the Civil War. Under segregation, forced separation of the races and social isolation of African Americans was the rule. Segregation existed in both the North and the South, although it broke down somewhat sooner in the North and was stricter and more formal in the South. Segregation meant separation of the races in everything from bathrooms, bus and theater seats, lunch counters, and waiting rooms to—in some places—fishing lakes and public baseball diamonds. By law, black and white children attended separate schools in many states, and housing segregation was enforced by general policy and by deed covenants forbidding the sale of property to blacks (and in many cases Jews, Asians, Hispanics, and other "unwanted" groups). The races actually became more separated from one another in the South after the end of slavery. Though the master-slave relationship disappeared with the Thirteenth Amendment, whites sought to preserve the role of a master race by excluding blacks entirely from their social and economic world. This exclusion was enforced with deadly violence; about 3,000 blacks were lynched between the end of the Civil War and around 1930. These lynchings, which drove many blacks from the South, were especially likely to occur in hard economic times, when whites felt that their advantages were threatened (Beck and Tolnay, 1990; Tolnay and Beck, 1992).

**The Modern Era** For a variety of reasons, a powerful black civil rights movement emerged in the 1950s and grew in the 1960s. Through legal action and civil rights demonstrations—often including nonviolent civil disobedience—African Americans attacked the system of segregation and eventually succeeded in making nondiscrimination the law of the land. Many whites supported these actions, and whites as well as blacks participated in the lawsuits, marches, sit-ins, and "Freedom Rides."

Despite the success of the civil rights movement in outlawing open and deliberate racial discrimination, blacks have not come even close to attaining social and economic equality in the United States (Farley and Allen, 1987). Open and deliberate discrimination has been replaced to some extent by subtler forms of institutional discrimination that perpetuate the old inequalities (Farley. 1988; Feagin and Feagin, 1978). However, recent research suggests that overt prejudice and discrimination remain fairly common and that, to a large extent, they are a product of stereotypes that many whites continue to hold about African Americans (Feagin. 1991; Kirschenman and Neckerman, 1991; National Opinion Research Center, 1991). In addition, many of the manufacturing industries that employed blacks in the

## COMPARING CULTURES AND SOCIETIES

### INFORMAL SEGREGATION: THE "INVISIBLE WALL" AND THE "BLACK TABLE"

Informal racial segregation remains pervasive in American society today. At the university where I teach, our president has spoken of the "invisible wall" in the cafeteria. In the article below from *The New York Times,* New York attorney Lawrence Otis Graham explores this issue. He describes how he realized that, while African Americans and other minorities are often seen as choosing such informal segregation, the reality is that *both* majority and minority groups choose such segregation, and that people segregate themselves on the basis of all kinds of social characteristics. In fact, such informal segregation is an almost inevitable outgrowth of a society in which our neighborhoods, our schools, our social clubs, and our churches are made up mostly of people who are "our kind"—no matter who we are. Unless this societal segregation is reduced, the "black table" will continue to be a part of our social reality.

#### The 'Black Table' Is Still There

**by Lawrence Otis Graham**

During a recent visit to my old junior high school in Westchester County, I came upon something that I never expected to see again, something that was a source of fear and dread for three hours each school morning of my early adolescence; the all-black lunch table in the cafeteria of my predominantly white suburban junior high school.

As I look back on 27 years of often being the first and only black person integrating such activities and institutions as the college newspaper, the high school tennis team, summer music camps, our all-white suburban neighborhood, my eating club at Princeton, or my private social club at Harvard Law School, the one scenario that puzzled me the most then and now is the all-black lunch table.

Why was it there? Why did the black kids separate themselves? What did the table say about the integration that was supposedly going on in home rooms an in gym classes? What did it say about the black kids? The white kids? What did it say about me when I refused to sit there, day after day, for three years?

Each afternoon, at 12:03 P.M., after the fourth period ended, I found myself among 600 12-, 13-, and l4-year-olds who marched into the brightly lit cafeteria and dashed for a seat at one of the 27 blue formica lunch tables.

No matter who I walked in with—usually a white friend—no matter what mood I was in, there was one thing that was certain: I would not sit at the black table.

I would never consider sitting at the black table.

What was wrong with me? What was I afraid of?

I would like to think that my decision was a heroic one, made in order to express my solidarity with the theories of integration that my community was espousing. But I was just 12 at the time, and there was nothing heroic in my actions.

I avoided the black table for a very simple reason: I was afraid that by sitting at the black table I'd lose all my white friends. I thought that by sitting there I'd be making a racist, anti-white statement.

Is that what the all-black table means? Is it a rejection of white people? I no longer think so.

At the time, I was angry that there was a black lunch table. I believed that the black kids were the reason why other kids didn't mix more. I was ready to believe that their self-segregation was the cause of white bigotry.

Ironically, I even believed this after my best friend (who was white) told me I probably shouldn't come to his bar mitzvah because I'd be the only black and people would feel uncomfortable. I even believed this after my Saturday afternoon visit, at age 10, to a private country club pool prompted incensed white parents to pull their kids from the pool in terror.

In the face of this blatantly racist (anti-black) behavior, I still somehow managed to blame only the black kids for being the barrier to integration in my school and my little world. What was 1 thinking?

I realize now how wrong I was. During that same rime, there were at least two tables of athletes, an Italian table, a Jewish girls' table, a Jewish boys' table (where I usually sat), a table of kids who were into heavy metal music and smoking pot, a table of middle class Irish kids. Weren't these tables just as segregationist as the black table? At the time, no one thought so. At the time, no one even acknowledged the segregated nature of these other tables.

Maybe it's the color difference that makes all-black tables or all-black groups attract the scrutiny and wrath of so many people. It scares and angers people; it exasperates. It did those things to me, and I'm black.

As an integrating black person, I know that my decision not to join the black lunch table attracted its own kind of scrutiny and wrath from my classmates. At the same time that I heard angry words like "Oreo" and "white boy" being hurled at me from the black table, I was also dodging impatient questions from white classmates: "Why do all those black kids sit together?" or "Why don't you ever sit with the other blacks?"

The black lunch table, like those other segregated tables, is a comment on the superficial inroads that integration has made in society. Perhaps I should be happy that even this is a long way from where we started. Yet, I can't get over the fact that the 27th table in my junior high school cafeteria is still known as the "black table" —14 years after my adolescence.



1950s and 1960s have cut back, closed down, or moved out (Farley, 1987b, Waquant and Wilson, 1989; Wilson, 1987). As a result, the civil rights movement did not improve the day-to-day lives of many African Americans.

Although the racial gap in incomes of *employed* workers has narrowed (but black workers still get only about three-fourths the wages of white workers), high black unemployment and differences in family structure have held black family incomes down to the point where there has been virtually no gain relative to whites (Bianchi 1981; R. Farley, 1984; U.S. Bureau of the Census, 1992a, 1985). In the 1940s, median black family income was about half that of whites; by 1989, it was still only 58 percent (U.S. Bureau of the Census, 1991d). The black unemployment rate has been between two and two-and-one-half times the white unemployment rate ever since World War II, and the poverty rate of blacks has consistently been about three times that of whites.

Significantly poor blacks became poorer relative to the rest of the population and more isolated in urban ghettos during the 1980s (Waquant and Wilson, 1989; Massey and Eggers, 1990, Wilson, 1987). As their poverty has worsened, federal programs to help them have been cut. Although the educational gap between blacks and whites has narrowed somewhat, whites remain twice as likely as blacks to obtain a college degree, and about one black youth in five fails to get a high school diploma by his or her early twenties (Crews and Cancellier, 1988; U.S Bureau of the Census, 1992b). Black college enrollment actually fell between the late 1970s and the mid-1980s, especially among males, though it has risen slightly since then. Although housing discrimination is now illegal, the laws are not well enforced, and blacks and whites live almost as separately today as they did 30 years ago (Farley and Frey, 1992: O'Hare and Usdansky, 1992; Denton and Massey, 1988; Farley, 1987c; Jakubs, 1986; Massey and Denton, 1987, 1988). One effect of this segregation can be seen in the box, "Informal Segregation." Black people are more likely than whites to lack health insurance and to receive inadequate medical care, and they are at greater risk of malnutrition, infant mortality, on-the-job injury, and criminal victimization. For these reasons, the average black life expectancy is six and a half years less than the average white life expectancy.

## Hispanic Americans

The rapidly growing segment of the American population known as Hispanics or Latinos is actually made up of several distinct groups that share Latin American or Spanish ancestry. By 1990, the Hispanic population of the United States had reached 22.4 million, or 9 percent of the total U.S. population (U.S. Bureau of the Census, 1991b). This represented an increase of over 7 million since 1980. Of this total, 13.5 million, or nearly two-thirds, are Mexican Americans (see Figure 11–1). Other large groups are Puerto Ricans, Cubans, and Central and South Americans. Mexican Americans, or Chicanos, live mostly in the Southwest, though there are many in the Midwest also. Once primarily rural, Mexican Americans today, like other Hispanic groups and blacks, live disproportionately in large central cities. Puerto Ricans are concentrated in the Northeast, especially in and around New York City, and Cuban Americans are concentrated in Florida. Because of their high birth rate and high rates of immigration, it is likely that sometime within the next 20 years the Hispanic population will surpass the black population, making Hispanics the nation's largest minority group.

**Mexican Americans** As noted above, both Mexican Americans and Puerto Ricans came under American rule through military conquest. As a result, both groups have experienced severe discrimination and disproportionate poverty. Chicanos were subjected to segregation and job discrimination much like that experienced by blacks, and in many areas, non-Hispanic whites (often called Anglos) still look upon them primarily as a source of cheap labor. When northern Mexico was made a part of the United States by the treaty ending the Mexican-American War, many Mexicans in the territory were ranchers who owned large tracts of land. A protocol accompanying the treaty guaranteed that Mexican landowners would keep their land, but most lost it anyway (Mirande, 1987). Afterward, many formerly wealthy ranchers were reduced to impoverished farmhands, working in one of the very few occupations to which U.S. federal law has never given the right to union representation and to which it has only recently extended minimum-wage protection. In some states, laws required school segregation for Mexican-American children, just as they did for blacks. White workers often saw Chicanos as a threat to their jobs, and they campaigned to stop immigration from Mexico and sometimes rioted against Chicanos. The worst instance of anti-Chicano rioting occurred in Los Angeles in 1943 and continued for about a week (McWilliams, 1949).

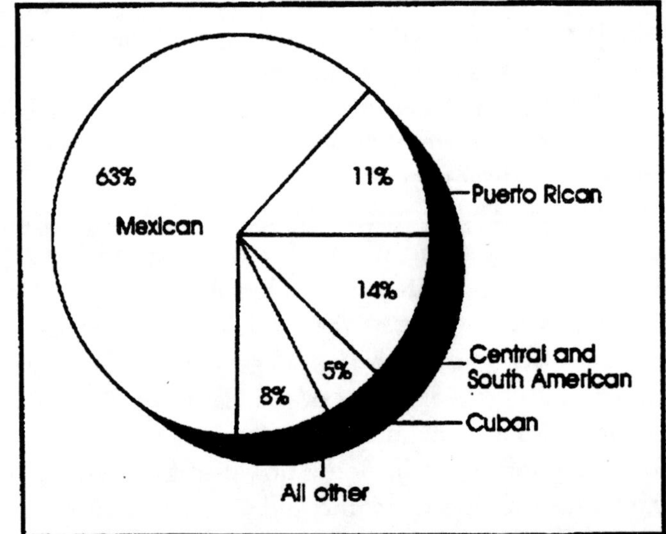


**FIGURE 11–1 Nationality Composition of the U.S. Hispanic Population, 1988**

SOURCE: U.S. Bureau of the Census, 1988f, p. 2.

**Puerto Ricans and Cuban Americans** In the Northeast, some Puerto Ricans have experienced double discrimination. Because of their substantial African ancestry, they have been discriminated against not only as Hispanics but also as blacks. In general, Puerto Ricans are the poorest and most segregated of the various Hispanic groups. Their median income is barely half that of non-Hispanic whites (U.S. Bureau of the Census, 1991e). Cuban Americans, on the other hand, have fared somewhat better than either Chicanos or Puerto Ricans because many of them were affluent and educated refugees from Fidel Castro's communist revolution. Those who came in the Mariel boatlift of the 1970s are distinctly poorer.

Like blacks, many Hispanics expected the civil rights movement to make substantial improvements in their lives. However, the same factors that have kept blacks disadvantaged have also worked against Hispanics. Even more so than blacks, Hispanics have suffered from a lack of educational opportunities. Half of all Hispanic adults lack a high school diploma, and even among people in their early twenties, who normally would benefit from recent advancements in education, 40 percent of Hispanics lack a diploma (U.S. Bureau of the Census, 1992b). Hispanics formerly were more likely to find well-paying jobs in heavy industry than anywhere else, but they lost many opportunities when those industries fled the central cities. Consequently, the unemployment rate of Hispanics is more than 50 percent above that of non-Hispanic whites. Their poverty rate has also risen steadily over the past decade; it is now two-and-one-half times that of white Anglos. In 1990, the typical Hispanic family's income was less than two thirds that of the typical white Anglo family (U.S Bureau of the Census, 1991e, p. 7).

## American Indians

When most Americans think of genocide, the first thing that comes to their minds is the extermination by the Nazis of millions of Jews during World War II. However, the United States also has a clear case of genocide in its own history. Although we have no way of knowing for certain how many Indians were present when the first Europeans arrived in North America, most experts estimate a million or more (Collier, 1947; Garbarino, 1976; Josephy, 1968; Spicer, 1980a). By 1900, actions by white people had reduced that population to about 240,000 (Spicer, 1980a, p. 59). A number of Indian tribes were completely wiped out, and others lost up to 90 percent of their population. How and why did this happen? Many Native Americans died in wars with the whites, and many others were murdered. Many Indians died of European diseases to which they had no immunity. (In some cases, whites deliberately exposed them to such diseases.) In the early to mid-1700s, colonial governments sometimes offered bounties for Indian scalps, including those of women and children. In a number of instances, whites who were victorious in battles with Indians killed them rather than taking them prisoner. Thousands of other Indian people died as a result of forced moves, such as the "Trail of Tears" between Georgia and Oklahoma.

The major reason for these attacks against Indian people was whites' desire for their land. As long as only limited numbers of whites were present in any given area, they usually coexisted peacefully with the Indians. However, when larger influxes of whites increased the demand for land, Native Americans were repeatedly attacked and pushed aside. Treaties were made specifying certain areas as "Indian territory," but whenever farmland was in short supply or precious metals were discovered on those lands, the whites violated the treaties (Lurie, 1985; Spicer, 1980b). In 1871, Congress abolished the concept of treaties altogether. Official U.S. practice became one of placing Indian reservations on remote tracts of undesirable land that bore little ecological resemblance to the Indians' original homeland. As a result, farming, fishing, hunting, or gathering methods that worked in the original homeland often became useless.

**Forced Assimilation** Once on the reservations, the surviving Indians were subjected to forced assimilation, particularly in the later nineteenth century. The idea was to remake the Indians in the image of white Americans. Their children were taken from them and placed in boarding schools, where they were forbidden to speak their native languages. A policy known as *allotment* was established in 1887 with the intent of giving each Indian a plot of land to become a small farmer, "just like the American family farmer." Although this policy may have been well intended, it was a miserable failure for several reasons.

First, it was applied without regard to whether a tribe had a history and knowledge of agriculture, which many did not. Second, it was based on white concepts of land ownership, which were different from Indian concepts of commonly owned land. Third, it was contrary to long-held patterns of sex roles in some tribes, which specified cultivation by women and hunting or warrior roles for men. Finally, whites widely encouraged Indian landowners who used the program to become indebted, then took their land for payment when they could not pay the debts. The result of this misguided attempt at assimilation was that Indians lost about two thirds of their land (Guillemin, 1978; Lurie, 1985; Spicer, 1980b, p. 117).

**The Situation Today** In general, Native Americans showed remarkable tenacity in resisting attempts at assimilation, and many today continue to speak their native languages and to maintain their tribal traditions. Over the past century, the Indian population has recovered to the point that the 1990 Census counted 1.9 million Native Americans (U.S. Bureau of the Census, 1991b). There are today about 200 different Indian tribes or nations, each with its own traditions and distinct social and economic history. Thus, even more so than Hispanic Americans, Native Americans are not one group but many.

Indians remain the least urbanized of any major American racial or ethnic group, with just over half living in urban areas. Most rural Indians live on or near reservations. As of 1980, more than one Native American out of four lived below the federal poverty level—about three times the white poverty rate for that year. On reservations, where Indian poverty is most intense, about half of the population lives below the poverty level. The 1980 unemployment rate for Indians was 13.2 percent, and on reservations it was higher yet.

Despite these difficulties, Indians have won some significant legal victories in recent years. Over the past decade, the courts have begun to take seriously the provisions of treaties that were negotiated long ago and then broken. Some tribes have been awarded monetary damages in the millions of dollars, and several states have been compelled to recognize Indian hunting and fishing rights guaranteed by treaties. Also, there has been growing recognition by non-Native Americans of the wrongs that have been done to Indian people. Undoubtedly, public awareness of the plight of American Indians was heightened by a series of militant Indian protests during the 1970s, including takeovers of closed federal institutions at Alcatraz Island in San Francisco Bay and Fort Lawton in Washington State that were based on an 1868 treaty stating that surplus federal property could be claimed by the Sioux. Perhaps the best-known incidents were a 1972 sit-in at the Bureau of Indian Affairs in Washington, D.C., and the 1973 occupation of Wounded Knee, South Dakota, which led to a confrontation with federal authorities and two fatalities.

One indicator of change in American thinking about Indian people is the fact that more Americans of mixed ancestry have come to identify with Indians as their racial or ethnic group. The number of people reporting their race as American Indian nearly doubled between the 1970 and 1980 Censuses, and rose by another 40 percent between 1980 and 1990. Not all of this change reflected real population growth; some of it occurred because people were willing to identify themselves as Indians (Johnson, 1991). On another 1980 Census question, over 6.7 million Americans listed American Indian as one of their two primary ancestry groups (U.S. Bureau of the Census, 1983).

## INTERMEDIATE STATUS GROUPS

Although African Americans, Hispanic Americans, and Native Americans most clearly fit the sociological definition of a minority group, there are a number of other American racial and ethnic groups that occupy an intermediate status between a minority group and a majority group. Most of these groups can be gathered together under two broad groupings—Asian Americans and "white ethnics" from Eastern and Southern Europe. Jewish Americans are also an example of a group with an intermediate status.

## Asian Americans

The most rapidly growing segment of the American population since about 1970 has been Asian Americans. The Asian-American population increased from 1.4 million in 1970 to 7 3 million, or about 3 percent of the population, in 1990. This rapid growth has taken place because of high rates of immigration and, to a lesser extent, relatively high birth rates. Like Hispanic Americans, Asian Americans are not one group but several, each with its own distinct history, social structure, culture, and (unlike Hispanics) language. The five largest Asian-American groups are shown in Table 11.2. Asian Americans are concentrated very heavily on the West Coast and in Hawaii, although there are also significant numbers in a few large eastern and midwestern cities such as New York, Boston, Washington, and Chicago.

**History of Asian Americans** Unlike the groups discussed in the preceding section, most Asian Americans came to the United States voluntarily, which has given them advantages in American society that other minority groups have not enjoyed. At the same time, however, they have experienced considerable prejudice and discrimination. Like Mexican Americans, Asian Americans were valued in the nineteenth century primarily as a source of cheap labor. Chinese and Japanese were encouraged for a time to immigrate to the United States to meet labor needs in the railroad and mining industries. Before long, however, they were seen by white laborers as a threat to jobs and wages, and they became the victims of riots and lynchings. Whites resented the fact that Asians, who were often in debt for passage to the United States, were sometimes willing to work for less than whites, and vicious anti-Asian stereotypes and prejudices replaced earlier, more positive, stereotypes.

By the early twentieth century, anti-Asian racism had been written into law, as first Chinese and then Japanese were forbidden to immigrate to the United States. In 1924, the government adopted a quota system that forbade all Asian immigration, except by Filipinos, who were treated as Americans because the Philippine Islands at that time were an American territory. However, when the Philippines be came independent after World War II, Filipinos were also subjected to the quotas, which effectively banned Asian immigration until the mid-1960s.

**Internment** One of the ugliest incidents of governmental racial discrimination in U.S. history occurred during World War II when 110,000 Japanese Americans were rounded up and put in prison camps after the government decided that they constituted a security threat because the United States was at war with Japan. They remained there for more than two years, even though very many of them were American citizens and there was no evidence that they had done anything to undermine the U.S war effort. As a result of this imprisonment, many of them lost their jobs and all that they owned. The role that race played in this process can be seen by the fact that there was no such imprisonment of German Americans, even though the United States was at war with Germany at the same time. (For a viewpoint on the Japanese-American experience that is at once personal and sociological, see Harry H. L. Kitano's "Personal Journey into Sociology.")

**TABLE 11.2 Approximate Population of Selected Asian American Groups in 1990**

| Group | Population |
|---|---|
| Chinese Americans | 1,645,000 |
| Filipino Americans | 1,407,000 |
| Japanese Americans | 848,000 |
| Asian Indian Americans | 815,000 |
| Korean Americans | 799,000 |
| Vietnamese Americans | 615 000 |

SOURCE: U.S. Bureau of the Census, 1991g, p. 3.

**The Recent Years** Despite these very real and serious cases of abuse and discrimination, Asian Americans never experienced, on a prolonged basis, the isolation and powerlessness endured by black slaves or reservation Indians. Moreover, as noted, they entered American society voluntarily and thus have not been treated as a conquered people. Finally, since Asian immigration reopened in the 1960s, immigration laws have favored people trained in occupations in which labor shortages exist, including scientific, technical, and medical occupations. As a result, most Asian immigrants in recent decades, with the important exception of Vietnamese refugees, have been relatively well educated.

For these reasons, Asian Americans recently have fared quite well economically and educationally—in some cases, even better than whites. However, they continue to be the target of much fear, resentment, and, sometimes, violence, from both white and minority Americans. Increasingly "Japan-bashing" —anger over Japanese competition among American workers—has been turned against Japanese Americans. In the 1980s, the Ku Klux Klan attacked Vietnamese fishermen in Texas. Korean Americans were targeted by black and Hispanic rioters in Los Angeles in 1992, because of both resentment of their higher income and anger arising from their ownership of ghetto and barrio stores. There have been similar resentments in the past against Italian and Jewish shopkeepers, but the recent immigrant status of the Koreans, combined with cultural differences and worsening inner-city conditions, made for an explosive combination.

## Jewish Americans

People of the Jewish faith have been present in the United States since 1654. Although there has been some immigration of Jews to the United States continuously for over 300 years, the major periods of immigration were from around 1880 to 1924, when immigration quotas were imposed, and again around World War II (Goren, 1980). In the latter period, far more European Jews could have escaped Nazi genocide had the immigration quota been lifted. Before the Civil War, most Jewish immigrants came from Germany and Spain, but in the subsequent large-scale immigration, most came from Eastern Europe, with the largest numbers arriving from Poland and Russia, and from Germany around World War II.

The Jewish experience in the United States has been indelibly shaped by centuries of persecution in Europe. The Nazi Holocaust was only the most violent of a series of systematic attacks that date back for about 1,000 years. In the thirteenth, fourteenth, and fifteenth centuries, Jews were expelled from England, France, and Spain (Goren, 1980). Many Christians viewed Jews as "Christ-killers," a view that only began to fade in the past century or so. The exclusion of European Jews from most of the desirable jobs forced many of them to work at occupations other groups didn't want, such as tax and bill collection and lending, which only had the effect of further increasing resentment against them. Unfortunately, many of these prejudices carried over into the United States. As the Jewish population grew in the early twentieth century, colleges and universities imposed quotas limiting Jewish enrollment. Entire communities banned Jewish residents, and restrictive deed covenants forbade the sale of houses to Jews. Many hotels and other businesses were "restricted"—in other words, Jews and various other racial and ethnic groups were banned. Forms of discrimination against Jews that were once widespread were made illegal by the civil rights laws of the 1960s.

**Jews and Asian Americans** The status of Jewish Americans today resembles that of Asian Americans in many ways. Educational levels among Jewish Americans are above the national average, and a high proportion of Jewish workers are in professional and managerial positions. Yet, like Asian Americans, Jewish Americans continue to encounter a good deal of prejudice and discrimination, and neither group has a major presence in the top echelons of American corporate or political life. Today there are about 6 million Jewish Americans, representing about 40 percent of the world's Jewish population (Goren, 1980). The population growth rate of Jewish Americans is lower than that of the white population as a whole. Jewish Americans are one of the most urban ethnic groups, with over 95 percent living in cities or suburbs.

## PERSONAL JOURNEY INTO SOCIOLOGY

### RACE, ETHNICITY, AND THE SOCIOLOGICAL PERSPECTIVE / HARRY H. L. KITANO

I grew up in San Francisco, surrounded by a variety of different ethnic groups. My parents were from Japan, but I lived in Chinatown, which was also close to the Italian section. So I had acquaintances from a rich variety of backgrounds. Names that I can remember from early school days were Padilla, Derrivan, Wong, Francesconi, and Lee. I remember how we jeered a new student from France named Donat—he came to school in a shirt, tie, and knickers and therefore warranted the name of "frog." We practiced prejudice and discrimination, but we were totally unfamiliar with these terms.

Being Japanese in the middle of Chinatown certainly made for differences. There was an elementary school right across the street from where I lived, but it was for "Chinese students" only. I therefore had to walk to a school several blocks away. But although I had many contacts with children from a variety of backgrounds, my close friends were of Japanese ancestry. There were about a dozen Japanese families living in the area; birthday parties, family gatherings, and the like were with my own ethnic group. Later, as I grew up, I joined a Boy Scout troop composed of Japanese Americans that was located in the Japanese section of San Francisco, a reasonable distance from my home. Concepts such as pluralism acculturation, and integration had little meaning for me, although my behaviors were surely actual experiences of these terms.

The first time that I remember hearing the term *sociology* was in a World War II concentration camp for people of Japanese ancestry. It should be recalled that after the Japanese attack on Pearl Harbor in 1941, all people of Japanese ancestry residing, along the West Coast, whether citizens or not, were sent to "relocation camps" scattered throughout the United States. I was a high-school student at the time, and during one of our endless discussions concerning our internment, I remember one fellow saying that a "sociological perspective" would give us insight into why we were imprisoned in such camps. My guess is that none of us knew what that meant, but, as was typical of many of our discussions, we all nodded wisely and agreed.

By that time I was dimly aware of terms such as *prejudice, discrimination*, and *racism*, but my main concern was to "gripe" about a system that put us into the camps. We blamed the Hearst press, greedy farmers, and "bad" politicians, as well as our parents, some members of our own ethnic community, the Japanese military, and even ourselves for our plight. We heard that university anthropologists, psychologists, and sociologists were studying the camps. Again, I didn't know what that meant, and only years later when monographs about the internment were published did I understand that these were "scientific studies" about us.

I was released with government clearance and relocated to the Midwest. Here I encountered racial and religious prejudice that differed from the West Coast variety where the Japanese were the main targets. I became a jazz musician and replaced a black musician in an all-white orchestra. At that time I must have thought that I was a better musician, but upon reflection, it is clear that the black player (who was one of the best musicians at his instrument and later gained fame with orchestras such as Duke Ellington's) was far superior, but that his color was less acceptable than mine. I was also surprised to hear violent discussions among my fellow musicians concerning anti-Semitism; one constant topic was to question the religion of Harry James, a famous trumpet player and band leader of the Big Band era. One young trumpet player argued that if Harry James was Jewish, then he would not serve as a role model, while there were constant jokes about Jews, Negroes (as they were politely referred to at that time), and Indians. I was sure that when I was not there, there would also be pointed jibes concerning Orientals (as we were known at that time).

These and other background experiences shaped my interest in questions of race and ethnicity. Although my initial training was in psychology, I found that psychological variables were limited in terms of understanding questions of racial stratification. I remember one argument that split the Japanese-American students while I was at the University of California in Berkeley. Evidently there was a house for Japanese American students at that campus prior to the wartime evacuation; the house was to reopen, and the question was whether to retain it for the ethnic group or to provide a more open-door policy without ethnic restrictions. I tried to make some sense out of this dilemma through understanding some of the personalities that were involved, but it did not make any sense. However, if the question were framed in terms of an assimilation versus a pluralistic model, then the issue became clearer.

The most important influence on my concentration on ethnic groups, especially the Japanese and other Asian Americans, was a historian, Roger Daniels, who was also studying Asian American groups, but through a historical perspective. We collaborated on a number of publications, starting with a book titled *American Racism,* then co-editing (with Sandra Taylor) *Japanese Americans: From Relocation to Redress,* and *Asian Americans: Evolving Minorities.* My own writings attempt to cover issues of race and ethnicity through an "insider's" perspective; that is, I try to emphasize the experiences of an individual who has gone through many of the events that I write about. I believe that studying in areas where your own life experiences are involved can make for a meaningful career.

### "White Ethnics"

The term *white ethnics* has been applied to a wide variety of groups from Eastern and Southern Europe, including Italian, Polish, Czech, Hungarian, Greek, and Ukrainian Americans. Besides their geographic origin, two other important features distinguish these groups from the rest of the white population. First, they are more recent immigrants. Most of them came between the late nineteenth century and the imposition of immigration quotas in 1924. Northern and Western European immigrants, in contrast came a good deal earlier. Second, unlike earlier immigrants, almost none of the "white ethnics" was Protestant, the dominant religious group in the United States.

These differences had several significant impacts. First, because the earlier immigrants already held most of the desirable jobs, more recent immigrants had to "work their way up" from less desirable positions. Second, the newer immigrants were subjected to considerable prejudice and discrimination because they were seen as a threat both of the jobs of those already here and to the rural Protestant culture that predominated at the time of their arrival. In the mind of the "established" Americans of their time, they were associated with "rum, Romanism, and rebellion."

Most of the Eastern and Southern European groups settled in the Northeast and the industrial cities of the Great Lakes region. The booming growth of American industry in the first half of the twentieth century opened up opportunities despite widespread discrimination. Thus, the history of white ethnics in America has generally been one of upward mobility. Today the socioeconomic status of Americans of Eastern and Southern European descent is quite similar to that of Americans descended from "older" immigrant groups from Western and Northern Europe, with one important exception: White ethnics have not yet moved into the upper echelons of government or business. Because their healthy position in the American economy is newer and less secure than that of other groups, white ethnics have frequently perceived efforts to create opportunities for blacks and Hispanics as a threat.

## THE MAJORITY GROUP

In the United States, the most advantaged societal position has always been occupied by whites from Northern and Western Europe. These groups include Americans of British, German, Irish, Scandina-

## SOCIOLOGICAL INSIGHTS

### RACIST REMARKS SHOULD THEY BE BANNED?

Racial incidents are occurring more frequently on American campuses. This may result in part from the increasing presence of minorities in higher education, and students' having difficulty handling the ethnic diversity. According to Howard J. Ehrlich of the National Institute Against Prejudice and Violence, racial slurs increased during the 1980s, "at a time when issues related to civil rights [were] devalued."

The *Dartmouth Review*, published by a group of students at Dartmouth College, is notorious for its slurs against every minority, ranging from a column in "black English," to comparing a black music teacher to a "brillo pad," and culminating with an anti-Semitic quote from Hitler's *Mein Kampf*. But Dartmouth is not unique. Most campuses report similar incidents.

Following a racist remark by its student association president (he had privately called a fellow student "nigger"). George Washington University sponsored an all-campus meeting to discuss race relations at the university. Racist fliers posted at Arizona State University and other campuses have sparked freedom-of-speech and censorship debates. Following 152 racial incidents, the University of Wisconsin took a more radical step: It decided to ban racist comments, pledging to give students an environment free of hostility and intimidation. But some students, backed by the American Civil Liberties Union, denounce the ban as a restriction of free speech. They argue that no one should be told what words are proper to use, and they worry that the ban might stifle classroom discussion, lead to censorship, and ultimately fail to discourage racism.

The National Institute Against Prejudice and Violence, a nonprofit research group based at the University of Maryland's Baltimore campus, has been urging college presidents to confront ethnic tensions, but their recommendations do not include banning racist remarks. Rather, their report urges colleges to both create a study group on human relations to measure students' attitudes on race and ethnicity and document the racial incidents. The report also recommends training programs for freshmen and key people on campus.

In a similar spirit, the University of Wisconsin became one of the first colleges to require every student to take ethnic classes, and it organizes workshops to sensitize students about racism. Since the late 1980s, hundreds of U.S. colleges have mandated some type of intergroup relations course for all of their students.

SOURCES: *The Washington Post*, November 3, 1992; *The New York Times*, October 11, 1990; *The New York Times*, October 7, 1990; *The New York Times*, June 2, 1990.

vian, French, and Dutch ancestry. They are predominantly Protestant, except for the Irish and French, most of whom are Catholic. Although virtually all of these groups except the British met with at least some prejudice and discrimination, it was less intense than that encountered by more recent immigrants, with the exception of Irish Catholics. Even they, however, are no longer the object of significant prejudice or discrimination, and they are thoroughly integrated into the population and culture of the United States. Northern and Western European groups have intermixed and intermarried so much that today most of them are of mixed ancestry and no longer identify exclusively with any one country of origin (U.S. Bureau of the Census, 1983, pp. 12-14.)

Besides enjoying high educational levels and desirable managerial and professional occupations, the majority group to a large extent controls the politics and business of the United States. Most corporate executives are males of Western and Northern European ancestry, as has been every president of the United States from George Washington to Bill Clinton.

There is very little growth in the majority group because of a low birth rate and because few people today immigrate from that part of the world. Thus, in the future, the numerically dominant position of this group in American society will fade.

## CURRENT ISSUES IN U.S. RACE RELATIONS

We shall conclude this chapter by examining two current issues concerning U.S. race and ethnic relations. The first is the growing debate over the relative importance of race versus class as causes of the disadvantaged position of many African and Hispanic Americans. The second is the appropriateness of affirmative action as a means of improving opportunities for minority group members.

### The Significance of Race versus Class

In 1978, William Julius Wilson published one of the most influential and controversial sociology books written in recent years, *The Declining Significance of Race.* In 1987, he elaborated on his ideas in another book, *The Truly Disadvantaged.* Wilson argued that current racial discrimination has become relatively unimportant as a cause of the economic disadvantages experienced by many blacks (and Hispanics). Rather, these groups are disadvantaged by their disproportionate presence in the **underclass**, a chronically impoverished group whose position has been worsened by recent changes in the American economy. So many blacks and Hispanics are part of this underclass largely because of disadvantages resulting from *past* racial discrimination. However, Wilson argues, their continued presence in this class results not so much from current racial discrimination as from aspects of the American economy that make it hard for members of this class to escape.

**Changes in the Job Market** One of the key reasons that escape from the underclass is so difficult today is the fact that well-paying jobs that do not require an advanced education are disappearing from the American economy, especially from the inner cities of the Midwest and Northeast where blacks are most concentrated (Wilson, 1987, p. 148) . At one time, heavy industry provided many such jobs and was an important source of mobility, first for immigrant groups, and more recently for blacks and Hispanics. However, in the 1970s, American industry began to lose jobs, and thus a promising opportunity for blacks and Hispanics with limited education was lost (Kasarda, 1989). This trend, known as *deindustrialzation.*

Such processes first create an underclass and then work to sustain it. As unemployment in the ghettoes and barrios rises, so does street crime, and many young males are arrested and imprisoned. Many more, of course, are not, but are unemployed. Wilson (1987, pp. 83-92) points out that this situation raises the incidence of separation and divorce and reduces the pool of appropriate marriage partners in the black community (see also Anderson, 1991; Bennett, Bloom, and Craig, 1989; Lichter, LeClere, and McLaughlin, 1991; Mare and Winship, 1991; Schoen and Kluegel, 1988). This pattern has become much more pronounced over the past 20 years, and as a result, black women have far less opportunity to get married than white women. Moreover, because over 90 percent of unmarried adult women of either race are sexually active, many black children are born outside of marriage. This, of course, produces more female-householder black families, which have a very high risk of poverty.

Finally, Wilson (1987, pp. 46-62) points out that black and Hispanic poor people are much more likely to live in neighborhoods with large concentrations of poor people than are poor whites (see also Massey and Eggers, 1990). Thus, they are less exposed to successful role models and more prone to see illegal activities as their only hope for upward mobility (see, for example, Anderson, 1991; Crane, 1991a, 1991b; Greenstone, 1991).

For all these reasons, Wilson sees the growing disadvantage of poor blacks and Hispanics as a product of the lack of stable, well-paying job opportunities. He argues that we must create large numbers of decent-paying jobs and provide the support poor people need to get and keep such jobs. He also sees a need for job training and for providing day care and medical insurance to employed low-income workers.

Although Wilson has made a major contribution to our understanding of the forces that have perpetuated and worsened the conditions of poor blacks and Hispanics, some critics have questioned his claim that race is declining in significance as a cause of poverty among inner city blacks (Hill, 1978; Willie, 1979). In his own recent work, he has placed greater emphasis on hiring discrimination against blacks resulting from stereotypes about poor, inner city blacks (Wilson, forthcoming. As noted earlier, several recent studies have documented the continuing effect of prejudice and discrimination (Feagin, 1991; Kirschenman and Neckerman, 1991; National Opinion Research Center, 1991). In his recent work, Wilson also places greater emphasis on the concentration of blacks and Hispanics in areas that are losing jobs while whites are more likely to be in areas of job growth. This pattern, arising in large part from racial housing segregation and discrimination, tends to elevate the unemployment rates of blacks and Hispanics (Farley, 1987b, Kasarda 1989; Lichter, 1988; see also Rosenbaum and Popkin, 1991).

## Reverse Discrimination?

Affirmative action is controversial because many whites (especially white males) see it as reverse discrimination. As predicted by split-labor-market theory, working-class whites, whose economic position is often insecure, have been particularly opposed to affirmative action, which they view as creating unfair competition for scarce jobs. Is a preference in hiring, promotion, or admission for minorities or women unfair to a white male who may have better qualifications? In some law and medical schools, white males with higher grade averages or admissions test scores have been turned down in favor of minorities with lower scores (Sindler, 1978). Because these white males are often not themselves guilty of discrimination, they are unfairly being made to pay for someone else's discrimination. Furthermore, it is argued, these policies hurt overall societal achievement by considering factors other than who is most qualified (Glazer, 1976).

## Is Affirmative Action the Only Remedy?

Those who support affirmative action are equally strong in their belief that *not* to have affirmative action would be unfair to minorities and women. They argue that just getting rid of active discrimination is not enough to create truly equal opportunity, for two reasons. First is the lingering effects of past discrimination. Even those who see current black disadvantages as resulting from disproportionate poverty rather than from current discrimination acknowledge that this poverty itself is the effect of *past* discrimination (Wilson, 1978, 1987). Thus, people who are poor because of past discrimination find it harder to gain the qualifications necessary for admission or hiring. Second is the effect of current institutional discrimination, especially in elementary and secondary education. Factors such as segregation, low teacher expectations, tracking, and the use of biased tests prevent many minority students from learning and achieving on the same level as whites. Similar problems exist in the employment arena, and were worsened by a series of 1989 Supreme Court rulings holding that employment practices that exclude minorities are legal so long as their *purpose* is not to exclude minorities. Legislative attempts to rectify this through a new civil rights law were vetoed by President Bush in 1990 and initially opposed by him again in 1991 on the grounds that the law was a "quota bill"—even though it explicitly banned use of quotas (Clymer, 1991). Later, Bush changed his mind and signed the bill into law. The argument for affirmative action is explored further in the box "What Makes a Fair Footrace?"

Some opponents of affirmative action say that reforming the schools so that they come closer to the ideal of creating equal opportunity is a better approach than affirmative action. Some approaches to doing this, including desegregation of schools through busing, will be discussed. However, those who

## SOCIAL ISSUES FOR THE '90s

### THE AFFIRMATIVE ACTION DEBATE

Racial inequality has persisted in the United States even though deliberate racial discrimination has been illegal for more than 20 years. This fact has convinced many Americans that steps beyond mere nondiscrimination are necessary to undo the effects of centuries of racial discrimination. One such step is affirmative action. In general, **affirmative action** refers to any special effort by an employer to increase the number of minority or female employees or to upgrade their positions, or by a college to increase the number of minority or female students. Affirmative action can include efforts to recruit more minority or female applicants, or it could involve hiring or admission preferences for underrepresented minorities or women.

Often affirmative action involves the use of *goals and timetables;* for example, "By 1996 we will try to have 12 percent blacks and 8 percent Hispanics among our supervisory staff." Contrary to popular conception, however, affirmative action goals are *not* usually firm quotas, and affirmative action does *not* mean hiring, promoting, or admitting unqualified applicants to meet the goal. In fact, such goals are missed more often than they are met.

Affirmative action has become a "hot button" social issue that evokes strong and sometimes emotional responses from people on both sides. This is the case in part because it involves race, an issue that has deeply divided the United States throughout its history. It is also the case partly because affirmative action raises basic questions about what is fair. Some questions key to the affirmative action debate include:

*Is affirmative action reverse discrimination that is unfair to white males?*

*Is it fair to minorities and women not to have affirmative action giving the continuing influence of past discrimination and the continuing presence of institutional discrimination?*

*As a practical matter, is there any other way to bring about equal opportunity for minorities in a reasonable amount of time?*

*Does the consideration of the race or gender of an applicant get in the way of choosing the most qualified applicant? How well do we actually measure who is best qualified?*

Federal policy toward affirmative action has varied sharply under different administrations. The concept originated in 1965 when the Johnson administration issued an executive order to government contractors requiring them to take "affirmative action" to be sure that they were not discriminating. Under the Johnson, Nixon, Ford, and Carter administrations, companies and universities having contracts with the federal government were required to establish goals and timetables. The Reagan and Bush administrations, however, opposed racial or sexual preferences and backed off on enforcement of affirmative action. This position was reversed again under the Clinton administration, which returned to earlier policies in support of affirmative action

support affirmative action point out that school reform is a long-term effort that will not help the current generation of disadvantaged adults.

Supporters of affirmative action also contend that some of the tests used to assess people's qualifications contain racial or sexual biases. Moreover, these tests are not very accurate predictors of future success. Law school admission criteria, for example, typically explain only about 25 percent of the variation in first-year academic performance of law students (Sindler, 1978, pp. 115-116), and college admissions tests are only about half that accurate (Owen, 1985; Slack and Porter, 1980). Thus, determining who is "best qualified" is a haphazard process subject to great error. In fact, the National Academy of

## SOCIOLOGICAL INSIGHTS

### WHAT MAKES A FAIR FOOTRACE?

Imagine two runners in a 20-mile race. One of the runners must start with a 10-pound weight on each of her feet. As a result, she cannot run as fast, tires more quickly, and falls far behind. Almost anyone would agree that this is not a fair race. So, halfway through the race, the judges decide that she can take off the weights. Is this enough to make the race fair? Does she have any realistic chance to win from her present position? Would it not be fairer to allow her to move ahead to the position of the other runner to compensate for the disadvantage of wearing the weights for the first half of the race?

This analogy has been used to illustrate the reasoning behind affirmative action (Farley, 1988, pp. 265, 336). The runner represents a minority or female individual seeking a good job or entry into graduate or professional school. The weights represent the effects of both past discrimination and the institutional discrimination she encountered in her elementary and secondary education. Examples of such discrimination, which may or may not be intentional, include low teacher expectations, tracking, biased tests and classroom materials, lack of minority and female role models, and underfunded and segregated schools. Just as the other runner was not encumbered by weights in the first half of the race, the white male applicant was not burdened by these disadvantages in early life. Most people would agree that it would not be fair to expect the runner to catch up after having to run half the race with weights. Could the same argument be made in the case of the minority or female applicant who often has to run the first half of the "race" of life with the "weights" of poverty and educational disadvantage? Is it fair, when that minority person applies for college or employment, to say "Now the weights are gone, so it's a fair race"?

Sciences concluded that testing unadjusted for possible racial biases was a poor predictor of employment performance, and excluded capable black and Hispanic applicants (Kilborn, 1991).

## How Effective is Affirmative Action?

Has the policy of affirmative action actually changed things to the point that minority group members and women enjoy an advantage over white males? Examination of income figures does *not* support this. Among young adults, white males continue to enjoy higher incomes than black and Hispanic males and women of any race, and black and Hispanic unemployment rates remain well above those of whites. Moreover, whites continue to graduate from college and enter medical, law, and graduate schools at double or more the rate of blacks and Hispanics. Women also remain underrepresented in law and medical schools, although their presence there has increased significantly. All these things suggest strongly that the effects of past and institutional discrimination outweigh any advantage affirmative action may bring to minorities or women. Even when we consider only those who complete college, minorities and women *still* do not appear to enjoy any overall advantage owing to affirmative action. Among recent college graduates working full-time in 1990, black and Hispanic males as well as females of all races still earned less than white males. In all cases except that of Hispanic males, the income gap with white males was at least $5,000 annually (U.S. Bureau of the Census, 1991f, Table 29).

Even so, it does appear that affirmative action has helped certain segments of the minority and female populations a good deal. A definite narrowing of the income gap between blacks and whites has occurred among people who do have jobs, particularly those with relatively high education levels. Law and medical schools are enrolling significantly more blacks, Hispanics, and women than they did before affirmative action, even though most of their students are still white males. Firms with government contracts, which are covered by federal affirmative action requirements, have nearly twice the percentage of minority employees as firms without government contracts (Pear, 1983).

Still, it is mainly the more educated segments of the minority and female populations that have truly benefited from affirmative action (Wilson, 1978). So far, affirmative action has done little for the chronically impoverished underclass, many of whom are lucky to get a high-school diploma. Affirmative action has probably contributed to a trend that was already under way in the black and Hispanic populations: The middle class is rising in status, while the situation of the poor is worsening (Wilson, 1978, 1987). For this reason, Wilson (1978, 1987) has argued that to achieve racial equality we must implement policies to improve the situation of the chronically poor, which affirmative action does not do.

Another, highly practical reason for having affirmative action is that our future productivity as a nation may depend upon it. The vast majority of new entrants into the labor force in coming decades will be people of color and women (U.S. Department of Labor, 1987). If these new employees do not get the opportunity to develop their skills and make important contributions in the workplace, the entire economy will likely suffer, becoming less able to keep up with international competitors. Some companies, such as Corning and Monsanto, have responded to this reality by combining affirmative action programs with programs to make the workplace more hospitable to minorities and women—with striking success. At Corning, for example, nearly two-thirds of recently hired salaried employees are minorities and/or women, as are well over a third of all salaried employees (Kilborn, 1990). According to the company's chairman, this was not only the right thing to do, but it served the company's interest by giving it new sources of managers when the pool of white males, the traditional group from which such employees were drawn, was shrinking.

## The Legal Status of Affirmative Action

Between 1978 and 1987, the U.S. Supreme Court ruled on at least eight major cases concerning affirmative action. In all but one of these cases, the Court approved some form of preferences for underrepresented minorities or women. The one circumstance under which preferences were *not* approved was in the case of layoffs of present employees where there was no proof that the employer had previously discriminated against minorities. However, the Court approved the use of racial preferences (though not quotas) in public higher education in the 1978 *Bakke* case, and it approved hiring preferences for minorities and women in private industries in a series of cases such as *Weber* in 1979. In both public and private hiring decisions, the Court has even approved the use of quotas under certain specified conditions. (More detailed discussion of the legal status of affirmative action can be found in Farley, 1988, pp. 340-343.)

In general, then, the U.S. Supreme Court until 1989 asserted that hiring and admissions preferences for underrepresented minorities and women were legal. The key was that they be *inclusionary*—their purpose must be to include the underrepresented or to make the student body or work force more diverse. It should be noted that many of these rulings were made by a five-vote majority of the Court—the bare minimum. Moreover, in 1989 the Court restricted the practice of setting aside a percentage of local government contracts for minority businesses (*Time*, 1989). Later, the court issued decisions making it harder for minorities and women to prove discrimination and easier for white males to challenge affirmative action plans (Freivogel, 1989). Hence, it appears that in the 1990s, "affirmative action programs will be harder to justify" (Tribe, 1989). This is especially the case because several Supreme Court justices who favored affirmative action have retired and were replaced with more conservative justices during the Reagan and Bush administrations.

# SUMMARY

Races are defined according to a combination of physical appearance and social criteria, whereas ethnic groups are defined on a purely cultural basis. Some of these groups occupy a dominant position in society and are called *majority groups,* while others occupy a subordinate position and are called *minority groups.* Racism takes a number of forms, including racist thought (racial prejudice) and racist behavior (racial discrimination). Ideological racism refers to the belief that one group is in some way naturally superior to another. The most subtle, but often the most important, form of racism is institutional racism, which occurs when social institutions operate in ways that favor one group (usually the majority group) over another. This process is also called *institutional discrimination.*

Social psychologists emphasize prejudice in their studies of race and ethnic relations. For some people, prejudice meets personality needs that may date to childhood experiences, while other people are prejudiced largely out of conformity to the attitudes of significant others in their past or present social environment. The functionalist and conflict perspectives see prejudice and discrimination as arising from society rather than from the experiences of individuals. Functionalists view prejudice as largely the outgrowth of cultural differences and ethnocentrism. They see assimilation as the solution because it eliminates the cultural differences that form the basis of prejudice and discrimination. Conflict theorists see racial inequality as an outgrowth of economic conflict, both within and between racial groups.

Much can be learned about the conditions that produce and alter patterns of racial and ethnic relations by examining other societies such as the former Soviet Union, South Africa, Yugoslavia, and various Latin American countries. Each of these areas has its own set of social conditions that shape its pattern of intergroup relations.

The United States is one of the most diverse nations of the world in terms of race and ethnicity. The largest minority group in the United States is African Americans, but the rapidly growing Hispanic population may soon catch up. Hispanics are not really one group but several, of which Mexican Americans, or Chicanos, are the largest. Blacks, Chicanos, and Puerto Ricans, along with Native Americans, have each in their own way endured conquest and internal colonization. As a result, they have experienced prejudice and discrimination far beyond that encountered by most American groups.

Groups whose status falls between majority and minority include Asian Americans, Jewish Americans, and "white ethnics" from Eastern and Southern Europe. All have experienced discrimination, yet all are largely middle class today. The educational and professional achievement of Asian and Jewish Americans is particularly notable. Even so, most of America's political and economic elite continues to be drawn from the long-standing American majority group, whites from Northern and Western Europe.

In the United States, current sociological debates on race relations concern the relative importance of racial discrimination and social-class inequality, and the use of affirmative action as a means of bringing about racial equality.

## GLOSSARY

**race** A category of people who share some common physical characteristic and who are regarded by themselves and others as a distinct status group.

**ethnic group** A group of people who are recognized as a distinct group on the basis of cultural characteristics such as common ancestry or religion.

**majority group** A group of people who are in an advantaged social position relative to other groups, often having power to discriminate against those other groups.

**minority group** A group of people who are in a disadvantaged position relative to one or more groups in their society, and who are often the victims of discrimination.

**racism** Any attitude, belief, behavior, or institutional arrangement that has the intent or effect of favoring one race over another.

**ideological racism** The belief that one racial or ethnic group is inherently superior or inferior to another.

**prejudice** A categorical and unfounded attitude or belief concerning a group.

**stereotype** An exaggerated belief concerning a group of people that assumes that nearly everyone in the group possesses a certain characteristic.

**discrimination** Behavior that treats people unequally on the basis of an ascribed status such as race or sex.

**individual discrimination** Behavior by an individual that treats others unequally on the basis of an ascribed status such as race or sex.

**institutional discrimination** Behaviors or arrangements in social institutions that intentionally or unintentionally favor one race, sex, or ethnic group—usually the majority group—over another.

**institutional racism** Institutional discrimination on the basis of race.

**personality need** A psychological need for a particular attitude, belief, or behavior that arises from the particular personality type of an individual.

**authoritarian personality** A personality pattern believed by social psychologists to be associated with a psychological need to be prejudiced.

**scapegoat** A person or group upon whom an individual displaces feelings of anger or frustration that cannot be expressed toward the true source of the individual's feelings.

**projection** A process by which a person denies or minimizes personal shortcomings by exaggerating the extent to which these same shortcomings occur in others.

**social learning** A process by which attitudes, beliefs, and behaviors are learned from significant others in a person's social environment or subculture.

**cognitive-dissonance theory** A social-psychological theory that claims that people often adjust their attitudes to make them consistent with their behavior in order to eliminate the stress that results when attitudes and behaviors are inconsistent.

**symbolic racism** A modern type of racial prejudice that does not express overtly prejudiced attitudes but does blame minority groups for any disadvantages they experience.

**assimilation** A process by which different ethnic or cultural groups in a society come to share a common culture and social structure.

**pluralism** A process whereby different racial, ethnic, or cultural groups in a society retain some of their own cultural characteristics while sharing others with the large society.

**amalgamation** A process whereby different racial or ethnic groups in a society gradually lose their identities and become one group as a result of intermarriage.

**underclass** Poor people who are chronically unemployed or underemployed and who lack the necessary skills to obtain stable, quality employment.

**affirmative action** Any effort designed to overcome past or institutional discrimination by increasing the number of minorities or females in schools, jobs, or job-training programs.

## FURTHER READING

ANDERSON, ELIJAH. 1990. *Streetwise: Race, Class, and Change in an Urban Community.* Chicago: University of Chicago Press. This book describes systematic observations conducted by the author while he lived in a racially and culturally diverse, but mostly middle-income, neighborhood that adjoined a mostly black neighborhood of concentrated poverty. In examining how the two neighborhoods got along and how each was affected by the other, Anderson offers important insights about race relations in 1990s America.

FARLEY, JOHN E. 1988. *Majority-Minority Relations,* 2nd ed. Englewood Cliffs, NJ: Prentice Hall. An introduction to the field of race and ethnic relations, written by the author or your textbook. Attention is given to the social-psychological and sociological perspectives on race and ethnic relations outlined in this chapter, as well as to the historical development of intergroup relations in the United States and the role of institutional discrimination today.

KITANO, HARRY H. L. 1991. *Race Relations,* 4th ed. Englewood Cliffs, NJ: Prentice Hall. This textbook, written by the author of one of the vignettes in this chapter, devotes separate chapters to each of a variety of racial and ethnic groups in the United States.

LEMANN, NICHOLAS. 1991. *The Promised Land: The Great Black Migration and How It Changed America.* New York: Vintage Books. This highly readable book chronicles one of the great movements of American population: the northward migration of African Americans between 1940 and 1970. By following the experiences of individual families, the author shows how—and some of the reasons why—the promise of prosperity "up north" was unfulfilled.

PARILLO, VINCENT N. 1990. *Strangers to These Shores,* 3rd ed. New York: Macmillan. The first four chapters provide the reader with a sociological framework of analysis. The following sections discuss the "old" European immigrants (Northern and Western Europeans), the "new" European immigrants (Southern, Central, and Eastern Europeans), racial minorities (Native Americans, Asian immigrants, and African Americans), Hispanics, religious minorities, and other non-Western immigrants (i.e., Arab Americans, Syrian-Lebanese, and Iranians).

RINGER, BENJAMIN B., and ELINOR R. LAWLESS. 1989. *Race-Ethnicity and Society.* New York: Routledge. This book places particular emphasis on the ways nation-states have incorporated racial hierarchy into their social and cultural fabric. The authors contend that there is a need today for more sociological analysis of the ways that the dominant group perpetuates the existing hierarchical structure of racial and ethnic groups.

SIMPSON, GEORGE EATON, and J. MILTON YINGER. 1985. *Racial and Cultural Minorities: An Analysis of Prejudice and Discrimination,* 5th ed. New York: Plenum. Probably the most detailed and comprehensive textbook available on race and ethnic relations. Excellent reference source for issues concerning race and ethnic relations.

WILSON, WILLIAM JULIUS. 1980. *The Declining Significance of Race: Blacks and Changing American Institutions,* 2nd ed. Chicago: University of Chicago Press. A discussion of American race relations during the slavery era, the segregations era, and the modern era. Notes the effects of changing economic structures on race relations and posits the controversial view that social class has become more significant than race in defining the opportunities available to black Americans.

WILSON, WILLIAM JULIUS (ed.). 1989. *The Ghetto Underclass: Social Science Perspectives.* Special issue of *The Annals of the American Academy of Political and Social Science,* Vol. 501. Newbury Park, CA: Sage Publications. Contains analyses of the social and economic conditions that perpetuate poverty among inner-city blacks and Hispanics by leading social-science experts on race relations and poverty. Considerable attention is given to issues relating to social policy toward the inner-city minority poor.

# Chapter 12

## Education

*The United States has a long history of educating its citizens. The educational system of the nation was built on the principles of Thomas Jefferson, who proclaimed that an educated electorate is necessary for a democratic society. Americans value education and often look to the schools to solve social problems or to straighten out "wayward" youth. The statistics also tell us that educational opportunities are nearly universally available and that the actual percentage of youth enrolled in schools is as high as any other country in the world.*

*However, almost daily we hear or read criticisms of the schools. Critics say that schools are failing to educate our young people, and because the educational system is not doing its job the United States is falling behind in economic and technical competition with other countries. Still other critics say the schools are teaching the wrong things or are not intellectually rigorous enough. Complaints continue to arise about how the schools are run badly or how the teachers teach poorly. Concerns are voiced about too much violence in the schools, too many drugs, and not enough discipline. The list of concerns and complaints about the school system is never-ending.*

*The paradox is that in the United States, in a country where education is valued and universally provided, the educational system is often seen as a failure. In this chapter we take a sociological look at educational systems. We will direct most of our attention to the educational system of the United States, but comparisons will be made with other countries, especially Japan and Great Britain. We will see both the problems and the successes of educational systems, but, more important, we will see how educational systems are closely tied to the culture and the structure of the societies in which they exist.*

## A BRIEF LOOK AT THE HISTORY OF EDUCATION IN THE UNITED STATES

In the earliest settlements of colonial America, most youngsters were educated in the "real world" instead of the classroom. In 1647, however, more than a century before the American Revolution, the first mandatory school systems were established in the Massachusetts Bay Colony (Monroe, 1940). Education in the United States initially emphasized the four R's: reading, 'riting, 'rithmetic, and *religion.* Later, schools began to replace the emphasis on religion with a variety of occupational and economic concerns. This change reveals a feature of education that we consider more fully below, namely, the tendency for the educational system to reflect the needs and desires of those who control the society. Early in American history a major purpose of education, as defined by colonial leaders, was to serve religious needs. Later, however, economic leaders and economic interests took priority in defining the objectives of the educational system.

Between colonial times and the 1870s, elementary education 'became more democratized, that is, more widely available to all children. Following the principles of universal education advocated by Jefferson, a free public school system emerged by the mid-1800s. The widespread education of girls at the elementary level also became a reality during this era. By the middle of the nineteenth century, the first public high schools had been founded. This description of a universal and democratic American education has been labeled the *traditional view*: The **traditional view** of the *history* of American education is that the United States was founded on democratic political principles, which required an educated and informed electorate. The United States also had a social and economic philosophy that was highly democratic. According to the ideal, every person, regardless of origins or social background, should have an equal opportunity to achieve and succeed. A school system that is available to all the children of the society, that is, a free and open system of mass education, is the major means by which equality is assured.

The traditional view of the history of American education still prevails today. Politicians, educators, and most citizens see the system of free and mass education as a way of ensuring that the society will have an informed citizenry, capable of making decisions in a democratic society. The educational system is seen as the key to success and achievement in the United States. However, among historians of education, this view has been challenged by the revisionist view.

The **revisionist view** of the history of American education emphasizes that the economic and social elites of the society will develop an educational system that meets their needs, not the needs of the masses of people. This view is a more critical, a less idealistic, perspective on education, based on the assumption that a fundamental conflict of interests always exists between the elites and masses of the society (Bowles and Gintis, 1976; Katz, 1968, 1987; Mennerick and Najafizadeh, 1987).

The revisionist historians of education contend that a major goal of mass education in the nineteenth century was to socialize the working-class and immigrant children so that they would be better workers in the nation's factories and businesses. The children were not learning the skills necessary for work as much as they were learning proper work habits. The educational system was teaching future workers the importance of punctuality, regular attendance, submission to authority, cleanliness, and order. Nowhere was the link between the needs of industrialization and those of the educational system more vividly revealed than in the Lancaster system.

The **Lancaster system**, named after its founder Joseph Lancaster, was a school system based on the principles of efficiency and order. Although the Lancaster system was found primarily in urban places, near industries and factories, it became the model for centralized and efficient school systems emerging around the country. In the Lancaster system careful attention was devoted to every detail of student behavior and classroom procedures. Teaching in the classrooms of a Lancaster school was always conducted in precisely the same way: the emphasis was on rote memorization of facts and on strict discipline. The way in which students were seated and even the way in which they wore their hats were carefully regulated. The hats were to be attached by strings to shirt collars, slipped off at the proper signal, and left resting on the students' backs (Parelius and Parelius, 1978, p. 60).

As a way of increasing the efficiency of the system, the Lancaster schools made maximum use of a minimum number of teachers; only one teacher was assigned to every 400 to 500 students. To manage such large numbers of students, the system relied heavily on student "monitors" who had previously been taught the lesson by the teacher. The huge classes were divided into groups of ten, each of which was headed by a monitor.

Lancaster schools were like factories, except that their product happened to be students. It is easy to see how students who were often headed for work in factories were well prepared by a school system that was itself a factory. This interpretation is consistent with the revisionist view of education, since it would obviously be in the interests of factory owners to have well-socialized workers.

In some ways, the traditional and revisionist views of the history of education resemble two competing sociological interpretations of education: functional and conflict theory. Functional theory offers an explanation of education that has some of the same elements as the traditional view. Conflict theory picks up key features of the revisionist view.

## FUNCTIONAL THEORY AND EDUCATION

One aspect of functional theory emphasizes that societies are made up of separate institutions that are integrated and interdependent. Thus, in an urban, industrial society, where families are less able to socialize their children for the work force, the educational system will take over some of the socializing functions. The educational system, according to functional theory, will ensure the social, political, and economic stability of the society. The schools can transform heterogeneous ethnic and religious groups into informed and productive citizens who have common values. Viewed in this way, the educational system contributes to an integrated, stable, and smooth-running society (Mennerick and Najafizadeh, 1987).

From a functionalist perspective, the schools perform more than an educational function; they provide a moral function as well. The **moral function** of the educational system is to teach children and young people the norms and values of the society. The norms and values are taught, in part, through the day-to-day activities of classrooms and schools, and, in part, through the content of what is taught to the young people. For example, even at the kindergarten level, children are being taught that they must conform to the expectations of those in authority and respect the rights of others. Kindergarten teachers organize the lives of the children in a way that prepares them for the order and conformity necessary at higher grades (Gracey, 1967).

Because schools transmit a society's norms and values, many students will internalize and accept as proper most of the values and rules that guide the larger society. For example, competition and achievement are two widely accepted American values. The school is instrumental in conveying the idea that it is fair to give different rewards for different levels of achievement (Parsons, 1959). Children soon learn that those who get their lessons done quickly and accurately will be praised and rewarded with good grades. Furthermore, and this is a very important lesson, the highest achievers will be given additional rewards—being allowed to carry out special errands for the teacher, becoming room monitors, engaging in recreational activities, and receiving honors and recognition. The winners not only get the intrinsic reward of accomplishing their school work but they get the additional external rewards as well.

This familiar classroom experience teaches a variety of lessons that apply again and again throughout life. The lesson that most activities are competitive is reinforced later in dating, making athletic teams, winning college scholarships, being admitted to the best colleges, getting into a professional or graduate school, and getting the best jobs.

Functional theorists view this part of the school's teaching in a positive light because it provides a shared set of values for all the people of the society who have gone through the school system. The moral function of the schools helps to integrate and stabilize the society. Conflict theorists, as we will see below, view this matter somewhat differently.

Functional theory also emphasizes that an educational institution, especially one that rewards students for their ability and the quality of their work, provides an equal opportunity for every individual. The task of the schools is, therefore, to evaluate and sort the students according to their ability and performance (Mennerick and Najafizadeh, 1987).

## CONFLICT THEORY AND EDUCATION

Conflict theory stresses that in any social system or society, conflicts of interests will exist between different groups or categories of people. This theory also stresses that some groups will have more power than others and that the most powerful groups will take advantage of their position to maximize their interests. Thus, conflict theorists agree that the schools teach and gain acceptance for the prevailing norms and values of the society, but these are the norms and values that especially serve the needs of the advantaged and powerful people of the society.

When children in the schools learn that competition and achievement are the routes to economic rewards and high status, the positions of those who already have wealth and high status are legitimized. It is in the best interests of those who are already in advantaged and powerful positions to get the largest number of people agreeing that they have a right to be there. It is especially important that people who are in lower-status positions, and are likely to remain there, accept the legitimacy of a system of inequality.

Not only do children learn in school that competition and achievement are the routes to reward but, more important, they also learn to believe in the correctness of this method of obtaining rewards. For nearly everyone the method learned is so right that it seems natural or even instinctive. Even those who do not win the competition and thus do not get the rewards generally believe in and accept the system. Often losers blame themselves for not getting the rewards. Rarely do they question the legitimacy of the norms and values of the system (Sennett and Cobb, 1972).

Conflict theorists also see the educational system as organized to favor the interests of the most powerful members of the society in another way that is similar to the revisionist historical view of education: the educational system will produce the kinds of workers needed by the dominant economic interests of the society (Useem, 1986). The schools often do this, as we have seen, by providing well-socialized workers who have learned to be responsible and to carry out the assignments they have been given.

Another point of dispute between conflict and functional theorists concerns the fairness of the educational system. Conflict theorists see the schools as organized and operated in ways that give the children of the advantaged groups a better chance of succeeding, and thus the schools perpetuate inequalities in the social structure. The sharpest continuing dispute between conflict and functional theorists rests on this last point. Instead of an educational system that gives everyone equal opportunities for success, conflict theorists argue that the system favors the children of higher-status families and works against the lower-status youngsters (Bowles and Gintis, 1976).

The differences between the views of functional theorists and conflict theorists regarding the educational system may be summarized around three issues:

1. Functionalists view the teaching of cultural norms and values as an integrating function of schools; conflict theorists view these norms and values as favoring the already dominant groups in the society.
2. Functionalists see the educational system as providing the skilled and trained workers needed by the economy; conflict theorists see the educational system as providing a docile work force that will be used by the dominant economic interests.
3. Functionalists view the educational system as fair and equitable—a system that gives everyone a chance at success, based on individual ability, hard work, and diligence; conflict theorists see unfairness and inequity in the educational system—a system that operates to keep lower-status youngsters in their place at the bottom of the social structure and that gives the children of the advantaged groups a greater likelihood of success.

Throughout this chapter, as we examine different aspects of educational systems and schools, we will see these issues reflected at several points: at the elementary, secondary, and college levels, and in educational systems of the United States and other countries of the world.

## EDUCATION AND EDUCATIONAL SYSTEMS WORLDWIDE

Universal schooling for all children in a society has become the ideal and the practice for countries throughout the world (Meyer et al., 1992). Universal or mass schooling, which started early in the history of the United States, has not always been found in the histories of other countries (Maynes, 1985; Melton, 1988), but, by 1985, laws in support of compulsory education were found in 80 percent of the countries of the world. According to UNESCO data, "Over 90 percent of the world's children spend some time enrolled in schools, and over 20 percent of the world's population is enrolled in elementary or secondary schools" (Meyer et al., 1992).

While the worldwide education picture has been improving during the last half of the twentieth century, it is far from perfect. Many children, especially in developing countries, receive only minimal schooling, and national expenditures on education are often inequitably distributed. In some African and Asian countries, only about one-quarter of the children are in primary and secondary schools. The largest of these developing countries with low enrollments are Afghanistan (17 percent), Ethiopia (28 percent), and Pakistan (29 percent). Furthermore, the schools that the children attend in developing countries are often seriously inadequate. For example, the developed countries have an average of one teacher for every 28 students; the developing countries have only one teacher for every 87 students. Yearly per capita expenditures on education in developed countries average $477; in developing countries the average is only $79 (Najafizadeh and Mennerick, 1988).

Even the limited amount of money that the developing countries are able to put into education is not equitably distributed. The monies are often concentrated in urban areas, and among the social and economic elites. Subsidies for education are given more to upper-class youth. In a study of ten selected Asian and Latin American countries, youths from the richest 20 percent of the population received from 38 percent to 83 percent of the educational subsidies (World Bank, 1988). Developing countries also use more of their economic resources to support students in higher education than they do for primary and secondary students. This policy, too, benefits the elites of these countries more than people in the lowest socioeconomic classes.

In most countries around the world, females are not enrolled in primary and secondary schools as frequently as males. Again, major differences exist between the developed and the developing countries. In the developed countries of the world, the numbers of males and females enrolled in primary schools are nearly equal (the number of enrolled females is 97 percent of the number of enrolled males). At the secondary level in the developed countries, the number of enrolled females is 78 percent of the enrolled males. However, in the developing countries as a whole, at the primary level, 86 percent of the male children are enrolled compared to only 71 percent of the female children. At the secondary level in the developing countries, 35 percent of the males, but only 29 percent of the females, are enrolled. Although some exceptions do exist, the developing countries are more likely to educate their males than their females (Najafizadeh and Mennerick, 1988).

The introduction of mass education may have many different influences on a society, but one that is especially significant is its relationship to childbearing. The larger the proportion of children in school, the smaller the number of children born to women in the society (London, 1992). This is a very important relationship, because large numbers of children lead to high levels of population growth, which is a problem in many countries of the world. A population theory by Caldwell (1982) explains this relationship. This theory states that, as the economic *value* of children declines, the number of children per family will decrease.

Before countries have mass education systems, children tend to be producers of wealth; through their work, both as children and adults, they will contribute economic resources to their parents' families. After countries introduce mass education, especially when it is compulsory, children become an expense for their parents. In Caldwell's terms, mass education starts to move the flow of wealth from parents to their children. As children become costly, parents will have smaller families.

The Caldwell hypothesis has been supported in specific less-developed countries (London and Hadden, 1988) and in cross-national studies of developing countries (London, 1988; 1992). A recent study found that, when the education level of females increases, childbearing is lower (London, 1992). This is probably because a higher proportion of girls attending elementary and secondary schools, especially in developing nations, is an indication of the changing status of women in these societies. More education for females probably means greater equality with males and this generally leads to lower rates of childbearing (see Chapter 17).

## National Systems of Education

Many differences in the educational systems of different nations can be noted, but one of the most fundamental is the degree to which systems are differentiated and rigid. A **differentiated school system** is one in which different programs, tracks, or streams lead to different educational outcomes (Bidwell and Friedkin, 1988). In the United States a typical high school will have several different programs, usually including vocational, college preparatory, and perhaps a commercial or business curriculum. Obviously, students in the college preparatory program are aimed toward college to earn a degree. Vocational and commercial students are much more likely to go directly into the work force, although they may get additional training at technical or vocational institutes. Differentiation can also be found at the elementary school level, where different tracks are available for students with different ability levels.

The **rigidity** of an educational system refers to the ease or difficulty of moving from one educational track or program to another (Bidwell and Friedkin, 1988). For example, the United States is often thought of as a less rigid system than the systems of many other countries. As a cultural ideal, that is true, but in practical terms the United States' system is more rigid than we might suppose. It is certainly possible for a student who has graduated from a vocational or commercial high school program to enter college at some later date. Such a student might be limited initially in the type of college he or she could enter, but it is possible to make a change in educational and career paths. Also, anyone can choose to go on for more education at a later point in life. Moreover, one important value of American society is that everyone has the right to a higher education, at any time in life. For example, it is not uncommon at graduation exercises for elderly graduates to be given special recognition, and news stories delight in describing how an older person has returned to college and earned a degree.

Although the American cultural value supports an open educational system, actual practice is a different matter. Again, this point illustrates the considerable difference between a cultural ideal and reality. Probably few students probably begin in a vocational track in high school and then later go on to a college or university to earn a degree. Such a student would probably have to find a way to make up courses that are prerequisites for college admission or would have to find a college that would waive them. These and other kinds of barriers make the American system of education more rigid in fact than the cultural ideals would lead us to believe.

Nonetheless, the educational system in the United States is generally less rigid, both in the ideal and in practice, than are educational systems in some other societies. Many Asian and European countries have very rigid educational systems. Great Britain and Japan are examples of more rigid systems, although they are somewhat different in nature. Both, however, place great emphasis on special examinations administered to all students at critical stages in their educational careers. Since these examinations are often given at very young ages, educational careers, and often occupational fates as well, are determined early in life.

**The British Educational System** Until about 1970, the British school system had three types of state-supported high schools: grammar schools, technical schools, and secondary modern schools. Since 1970 a new type of school, called the comprehensive high school, has been added (Kerckhoff, 1986; 1990).

The most prestigious British high schools have traditionally been the grammar schools. (Of course, Britain has also had very prestigious private secondary schools—called public *schools*—whose students are almost entirely the children of higher-status parents who can afford the tuition and boarding costs.) The British technical schools are for talented students who are aiming for technical colleges and, later, technical occupations. The secondary modern schools, in contrast, are attended by students who have shown the lowest level of academic promise. The recently established comprehensive high schools of Britain are similar to American high schools in that all ability groupings attend the same school. However, within the comprehensive high school the children are still put in tracks, or "streams," on the basis of ability levels. The comprehensive school now enrolls about 60 percent of British students and 90 percent of Scottish students (Kerckhoff, 1986).

The introduction of the comprehensive high school in Great Britain may have made their system less rigid, but it remains more rigid than the educational system of the United States. British students who have been chosen for either an elite school or a higher ability track are consistently and effectively moved toward better colleges and universities, and later to more prestigious occupations and professions (Kerckhoff, 1986, p. 857).

**The Japanese Educational System** The education of Japanese children has been the subject of much discussion and comment in the United States because it appears to be so successful and, because it is distinctly different in a number of ways from the American school system. Many Americans think of the Japanese system as rigorous, highly disciplined, and very examination oriented. This view is correct in some ways, but wrong in others.

The preschool education of Japanese children begins the process of introducing them to the responsibilities of group membership (Peak, 1991). When they are in their homes, young Japanese children may be demanding and selfish, but when they enter the school they are expected, by their teachers and their parents, to understand that they must conform to the expectations of the group. The Japanese have a term in their language that emphasizes that a person's behavior must be different outside the home especially when it is part of *life in a group* (Peak, 1991, p. 11).

The Japanese educational system is built around a series of examinations, each one determining admission for the next level in the system. The culminating examination occurs at the end of high school and is the one that determines admission to Japan's colleges and universities. The Japanese examination system, especially at the end of high school, is so intense it has been labeled "examination hell" or "examination war" (Duke, 1988; Rohlen, 1983).

The process of gaining admission to one of Japan's prestigious universities begins for some parents and children at the kindergarten level. Five-year-old kindergartners will sometimes take entrance examinations for the elementary schools that have the best records for getting their students into the most successful junior high schools. The ranking of junior high schools is determined, in turn, by their success in placing students in the best high schools. The examination hell near the end of high school allows a select few to be admitted to Tokyo University or to one of the major Japanese medical schools (White, 1987).

The Japanese educational system requires that students spend considerably more time in school each year than U.S. students. The school day typically begins at 8:30 A.M. and ends at 3:30 P.M., with a short lunch break. However, elementary school children often remain in school for another hour or more for additional class activities. Japanese children also attend school for a half day on Saturdays. Summer vacation is limited to the month of August, so the Japanese school year is 240 days, compared to the average of 180 days in American schools (Duke, 1986; White, 1987).

In 1992, Japan's Education Ministry announced a reduction in the school week by giving students one Saturday off each month (Reid, 1992a). However, the Education Ministry has published a 225-page book describing appropriate activities for the students on their open Saturday morning.

In addition to the regular schools, the Japanese have developed a private educational or tutoring system especially designed to prepare students for the next level of entrance examinations. These "examination cram" schools, called **juko**, drill the students on subjects that will be on the entrance examinations. Since about 80 percent of entering high school students aspire to a college or university education, almost all students attend *juko* schools after regular school hours. Furthermore, many Japanese students take 1, 2, or even 3 years off from their regular schools in order to attend the examination cram schools full time (White, 1987).

After all of this intense preparation, the Japanese students take the critically important university entrance examination. It is one of the ironies of Japanese education that the pace of work at the college and university level is rather leisurely, and very few students fail. Japanese students tend to see their college years as a time to enjoy life and indulge themselves.

## WHO SUCCEEDS IN THE AMERICAN SCHOOL SYSTEM?

Functional theorists view the American educational system as fair and equitable, a system that gives everyone a chance at success. In an abstract way, it may be true that everyone enters the educational system with an equal opportunity, limited only by his or her intellectual ability and a willingness to work hard. But there is ample evidence that children from the disadvantaged strata in society do less well in the school system. One sociologist of education sums up the matter clearly:

> By almost any criterion, and with few exceptions, students from working class and ethnic/minority backgrounds do poorly in school. They drop out at a higher rate than do their middle-income and ethnic-majority contemporaries. (Mehan, 1992, p. 3)

**TABLE 12.1 Schooling Completed among 25- to 29-Year Olds: Whites, Blacks, and Hispanics, 1991**

| | | High school graduates completing: | |
|---|---|---|---|
| | Completed high school | Some college | Completed college |
| Whites | 89.8% | 54.9% | 29.7% |
| Blacks | 80.7% | 42.5% | 13.6% |
| Hispanics | 55.9% | 41.3% | 16.4% |

SOURCE: U.S. Department of Education, National Center for Educational Statistics. *The Condition of Education, 1992*, Washington, D.C., 1992.

One way to examine the unequal success of American youth in educational attainment is to see how far the major racial and ethnic groups get in school. Table 12.1 shows what percentages of Americans (white, black, and Hispanic) aged 25 to 29 have completed various levels of education. About 90 percent of white Americans complete high school, somewhat over 80 percent of black Americans complete high school, and about 56 percent of Hispanics do.

Among those who complete high school, the percentages who have some college ( I to 3 years) is about 55 percent for whites, but drops to just over 40 percent for blacks and Hispanics (42.5 and 41.3 percent, respectively). The percentages of high school graduates who complete college is about 30 percent for whites, but is only 13.6 percent for blacks and 16.4 percent for Hispanics.

These statistics show that, for every 100 children in these racial-ethnic categories, about 27 whites, 11 blacks, and 9 Hispanics graduate from college. It is clear from the numbers that, compared to white Americans, black Americans and Hispanics have a much smaller chance of succeeding in the American educational system.

The high school drop-out rate of black Americans is higher than the rate of white Americans, especially in many urban areas of the United States. A study of the drop-outs of black Americans was the focus of a long-term study in the Woodlawn area of South Chicago, a poor, 97 percent black community of that city. More than 1100 students were followed from the time they were in the first grade (in 1966-1967) until the time they graduated from high school, or would have if they hadn't dropped out of school (Ensminger and Slusarcick, 1992).

The students who were the subjects of this study were assessed three times during their first year of school (their teachers provided much of the information). In the spring of their first school year, their mothers, or mother surrogates, were interviewed. In 1975-1976, when the children were teenagers, about 75 percent of the mothers, or mother surrogates, were reinterviewed.

In 1982, the scheduled year of graduation for these students, only 43 percent of the males and 55 percent of the females graduated. This is a high drop-out rate, but not greatly higher than the rates for Chicago as a whole in 1982 and drop-out rates found in other studies of disadvantaged young people (Ensminger and Slusarcick, 1992).

Those who dropped out of school before graduating were more likely to have had certain personal and family characteristics when they were in the first grade, many years earlier. Drop-outs, especially the boys who quit school before graduating, were more likely to have exhibited aggressive behavior and had poor grades in the first grade. They were also more likely to have come from poverty level homes where the mother did not have a high school education.

Several family characteristics proved to be "protective factors," which means that they protected some of those students who had negative first-grade characteristics (poor grades and aggressive behavior). When males with poor grades in the first grade had mothers who had graduated from high school, they were more likely to graduate than other boys who had low grades. Being from a mother-father family was protective for girls who had early negative characteristics. Coming from a home with strict rules regarding school was also a factor that kept girls from dropping out, even when their early school grades were low (Ensminger and Slusarcick, 1992).

This study of school drop-outs suggests that, even within a minority group, certain danger signs can be identified in the early years of a student's educational career. Furthermore, there are family characteristics that can counteract some of these early warning signs (Ensminger and Slusarcick, 1992).

A recent study has examined the educational, occupational, and economic conditions of young U.S. adults and has identified 20 million 16 to 24-year-olds as "the forgotten half" (William T. Grant Foundation, 1988). The forgotten half of American young adults are those who have not finished high school and high school graduates who are not college bound. Today, according to this report, even those who have high school degrees are often destined for low-paying jobs with limited chances for future economic advancement.

In the past a high school education was generally adequate for a reasonably well-paying job and an economically secure future. But recent technological and economic changes have altered the prospects for today's young adults who do not have college educations. Their economic futures are not bright, because even with a healthy economy, their opportunities are limited and their vulnerabilities great. In the years between 1973 and 1986, the median income of households headed by persons under 25 declined 26.3 percent. These households are largely made up of the young people who have not gone on to get a college education, but have married and entered the labor force. The drop in income for this group has been greater than that experienced by Americans between 1929 and 1933— critical years of the Great Depression in the United States (William T. Grant Foundation, 1988).

## Economic Background and College Attendance

Children from economically disadvantaged backgrounds, along with children from racial and ethnic minority groups, are also less likely to succeed in the educational system. The combined effect of these two disadvantages can be seen in Figure 12–1, which shows a larger proportion of children from better-off families attending college; but when the children are from minority families, they are less likely at almost all economic levels to attend college.

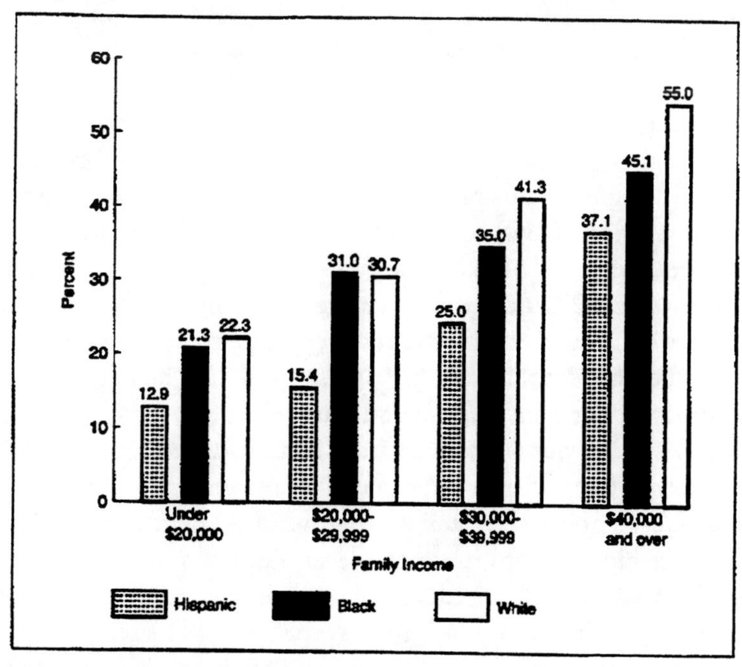


**FIGURE 12–1 Percentage of Households with at Least One Primary Family Member, 18 to 24 Years Old, in College, by Family Income, Race, and Origin.**

SOURCE: United States Bureau of the Census, *Current Population Reports*, Series P-20, No. 460, 1992, Table 16.

## The Importance of an "Elite" College Education

Today it is nearly a necessity to have a college education if one aspires to a high-status position in any relatively large corporate business in the United States. The same is true of the other developed societies of the world. However, not all colleges are equal because the degrees they grant are not considered equal. Colleges and universities in the United States are hierarchically ordered, with a small set of elite schools at the top that have the best reputations for academic excellence, distinguished faculties, and carefully selected, intellectually talented students. Disagreements may arise about the rank order of particular schools, but a typical list of elite colleges in the United States includes Harvard (also the oldest), Yale, Princeton, Columbia, and Stanford, just to name a few.

A question often asked by the public as well as by sociologists is "Does the college that one attends make a difference in one's career opportunities and occupational advancement?" The question is more complicated than it first seems, for several reasons. The college one attends is associated with a number of other characteristics that can also influence career opportunities and occupational advancement. These other characteristics include family background, personal ability, academic performance, and motivation to succeed (Alwin, 1974).

One study found that, even when all these factors were controlled, some independent effect of the college attended still prevailed (Alwin, 1974). Furthermore, a study conducted among Japanese males also found that the graduates of the most elite colleges of Japan attained higher lifetime incomes and higher positions in organizations than men who had graduated from less prestigious colleges. Although this study was not able to rule out family background as a contributing factor, the author argues that in Japan the status of the college from which one graduates does make a difference in the occupational careers of males (Miyahara, 1988).

In a study of over 2729 senior managers and executives of 208 major corporations in the United States, researchers tried to determine if getting a degree from one of the elite schools of the country influenced the chances of attaining the very topmost levels of corporate America (Useem and Karabel, 1986). The researchers were especially interested in whether the social (family) backgrounds of these top corporate leaders could account for their positions, or whether degrees from elite schools were more influential. The researchers considered not just bachelor's degrees but also master's of business administration degrees and law degrees. Thus, they came up with somewhat different lists of elite schools for each type of degree.[1]

This study concluded that the main portion of these 2729 senior managers and executives who made it to the very top of the corporate and business structure were helped by their educational credentials. Holding a bachelor's degree from a prestigious school made it more likely that a person would be chosen as a chief executive officer (CEO) of one of the major U.S. corporations. A bachelor's degree from an elite school made the chances of becoming a CEO twice as great as a noncollege graduate in this group. (About 15 percent of the 2729 corporate managers had not gone to college or had not completed college.) Master's degrees in business administration from elite business schools, and especially law degrees from one of the elite law schools, also gave these corporate managers a better chance of being selected for the top corporate positions (Useem and Karabel, 1986).

However, elite social background—coming from a family listed in the *Social Register* or attending one of the nation's exclusive prep schools—also aided in moving up in the higher levels of corporate management. In particular, an upper-class family background led more often to the boards of directors of corporations and to leadership positions in the top-level business associations. Of course, combining a high-status social background with an elite education made it even more likely that these highest levels of corporate management and leadership in the business world would be reached.

Since these managers were almost all middle-aged and older, and thus had received their college and professional degrees many years earlier, it is not clear why the status of their schools should continue to aid them in their careers. It seems unlikely that what they learned in college would still be an influential factor. It may be that their personalities or styles, which had been developed or cultivated in elite schools,

## SOCIOLOGY IN THE NEWS

# "POLITICAL CORRECTNESS" ON THE CAMPUS

The latest controversy associated with U.S. colleges and universities has been labeled the "political correctness" issue. This label, it should be noted, is a critical and negative label, generally used by those who wish to emphasize the excesses and dangers of this activity on U.S. campuses (Coleman, 1991; D'Sousa, 1991; Henry, 1991; Taylor, 1991).

Critics who are concerned about efforts to achieve "political correctness" attack the efforts of certain students and many faculty members who believe sexism, racism, ethnocentrism, and homophobia (among other things) are inherently bad and therefore should be eradicated in speech, in academic courses, in writing, and sometimes as subjects of scientific inquiry. These same students and faculty members are at the same time trying to awaken and sensitize people to points of view other than what they feel is the white-male-dominated, elitist, conservative point of view that now prevails.

It should be obvious that some of these objectives are partially linked to the subject matter of sociology. Throughout this book we have been considering concepts such as ethnocentrism, sexism, racism, the social class system, ageism, and others. We have seen, for example, that sexism and racism are deeply rooted in U.S. society and that they lead to unequal and unfair treatment for women and racial minorities.

As one dimension of the "political correctness" trend there are the efforts to eradicate language and speech that reflect sexist or racist views. Professors on many campuses, for example, would never get away with using derogatory slang terms for women or minority groups in their classrooms. But often, and perhaps inevitably, attempts to eliminate sexist or racist language, or any other language that offends any ethnic group, religion, or nationality will begin to encroach on freedom of speech and the free expression of individual opinion.

A number of colleges and universities have initiated policies that are trying to improve the sensitivity of students and faculty to these issues. Students are often required to take courses that will broaden their views of other cultures, nationalities, ethnic groups, women, racial minorities, gay males, and lesbians. Faculty members are challenged by students when they display sexist, racist, or homophobic tendencies. Student conduct rules are passed that make it an offense for students to make derogatory statements about groups or categories of people.

Political correctness gets its negative label from those cases where individuals or groups use extreme methods, or take extreme positions, in their efforts to eradicate intolerance or insensitivity. Students are not allowed to express their opinions in class, or they are penalized for "inappropriate" views; professors are accused, sometimes on flimsy grounds, of being racist or sexist in their classes; speakers are picketed, shouted down, or harassed; research projects are stopped because their scientific questions are considered by some to be unacceptable. Critics see these actions as dangerous encroachments on free speech, intellectual debate, academic freedom, and scientific autonomy.

The debate about political correctness is, as is so often the case, a conflict between two important sets of values. In this case one side is trying to eradicate intolerance and broaden perspectives (about the rights of women, racial minorities, gays and lesbians, and so on), while the other side sees these activities as infringements on individual freedom and academic or scientific autonomy.

COLEMAN, JAMES S. "A Quiet Threat to Academic Freedom." *National Review 43* March 18, 1991.

D'SOUZA, DINESH. "Illiberal Education." *The Atlantic 267 1991.*

HENRY, WILLIAM A. III. "Upside Down in the Groves of Academe." *Time* April 1, 1991.

Taylor, John. "Are You Politically Correct?" *New York* 24 January 21 1991.

gave them an advantage in the corporate world. It may also be that at the highest level of corporate management a great deal of uncertainty prevails, and trust is a critical factor. Thus, the top level of promotions go to people who are most like those already in power, both educationally and socially (Useem and Karabel, 1986, p. 198).

Getting a degree from an elite institution continues to be important at the level of graduate degrees (Ph.D.s, for example) and professional degrees (law and medicine). A study of Ph.D.s in psychology found that the best academic jobs, in the most prestigious research universities, went to the Ph.D. graduates who had gone to the most prestigious schools (Hurlbert and Rosenfeld, 1992). However, getting a Ph.D. from a prestigious school was only important for getting good first jobs and had no effect on the quality of later career jobs (Hurlbert and Rosenfeld, 1992).

An example of how important it can be to get a degree from an elite school is found in the case of Harvard Law School graduates (Granfield, 1992; Granfield and Koenig, 1992). By almost any objective standard (test scores or grades of students admitted, quality of the faculty, eminence of its graduates) and by its reputation, Harvard Law School is at or near the top of the elite law schools in the United States.

In their second and third years, the graduates of Harvard Law are heavily recruited by as many as 800 large, national law firms. Each student may have as many interviews with prospective employers as he or she wishes, since recruiters are required to meet with anyone who requests an interview. Some students report having as many as 90 interviews, but such a large number only reflects their stamina (Granfield and Koenig, 1992, p. 512).

As part of the recruitment process, Harvard Law students are often invited to visit the law firms recruiting them. These "fly-outs" are often very lavish and include eating in the best restaurants and staying in first-class hotels at the law firm's expense. Students describe their fly-out experiences in these words:

> On campus I had about 25 interviews. I flew out for about 15 of those. It was real cushy.
>
> I got a lot of fly-outs and spent a month on the road racking up frequent flyer points.
>
> It [recruiting] was beyond my wildest dreams.
>
> (Granfield and Koenig, 1992, p. 513)

All Harvard Law School graduates, even those who do not graduate with top grades, expect and get the best and generally highest paying law jobs in the country. It is clearly a major benefit of graduating from an elite school.

### Effects of Beginning at a Community College

At the opposite extreme from the elite colleges and universities are the community colleges of the United States. Nearly half of all college students at any given time are attending community colleges (Monk-Turner, 1990). The most likely students at community colleges are women, minorities, and students from working-class backgrounds. Many of these community college students go on to graduate from four-year colleges, but their occupational achievement is not as great as students who begin at four-year colleges (Monk-Turner, 1990).

## PERFORMANCE OF THE AMERICAN SCHOOL SYSTEM

The task of the schools is to educate the children and young people of the society, and widespread concern exists about how the school system is performing its primary responsibility. The schools have many critics who have pointed to failures and shortcomings in various areas. In the early 1980s, a government report on the educational system was ominously titled *A Nation at Risk* (1983). The crux of this report emphasized that the American educational system was mediocre, and the threat that our schools

## CROSS-NATIONAL PERSPECTIVES

### INTERNATIONAL COMPETITION IN MATHEMATICS AND SCIENCE

In 1991 the Educational Testing Service conducted its second international test to determine the mathematics and science skills of 9- and 13-year-olds in the United States compared to the students in five other countries. The first test was conducted in 1988, and at that time the relative performance of United States students was below that of the students of most other countries (LaPointe et al., 1989). The 1991 tests have not shown much improvement for American students (U.S. Department of Education, 1992).

In these international tests, the students in all countries are given the same questions in mathematics and science. For example, the students might be asked to calculate the average age of five children aged 13, 8, 6, 4, and 4. More complicated questions might require the students to understand the meaning of the radius of a circle and how to use it in a calculation. In the science test, they might have to know how a plant responds to artificial light (LaPointe et al., 1989).

In the 1991 tests, the students came from the United States, South Korea, Taiwan, the former Soviet Union, Spain, and Canada. In the mathematics tests the United States' students ranked lower than the students in the other five countries. Both at ages 9 and 13, their average for the percent of correct answers was the lowest. At 9 years of age the U.S. students had an average of 58.4 percent of the answers correct. Korean students had an average of 74.8 percent correct; Taiwanese students had an average of 68.1 percent correct. At age 13, the Korean and Taiwanese students had widened the gap between themselves and the American students (U.S. Department of Education, 1992).

In the science test the 9-year-old Americans did better than the 13-year-olds in comparisons with the students from the five other countries. Among the 9-year-olds, the United States students ranked near the middle, with only Korean and Taiwanese students having higher averages. By age 13, however, the United States students had fallen to the bottom again with lower averages than the students in the other five countries (U.S. Department of Education, 1992).

The relatively poor performances of American students, compared to those of other countries, are disturbing when considering the competitive economic world of the future. The mathematics and science skills of our 9- and 13-year-olds today are a critical component of the nation's competitiveness. "Twenty years from now the youth of today will be competing in the global marketplace. They will depend on [what they have] learned in this decade to succeed in the complex business and technological environment of 2012" (U.S. Department of Education, 1992, p. 50).

LAPOINTE, ARCHIE E.; MEAD, NANCY A.; and PHILLIPS, GARY W. *A World of Differences: An International Assessment of Mathematics and Science.* Princeton, NS: Educational Testing Service, 1989.

U.S. Department of Education, National Center for Educational Statistics. *The Condition of Education, 1992.* Washington, D.C.: 1992.

posed for our national well-being and security was as great as any external threat. Many of the problems identified in *A Nation at Risk* are still in evidence. We will review some of the most important of these problems, including functional illiteracy in the United States and achievement levels of U.S. students. We will also consider the problems of teachers in the contemporary school systems.

## Functional Illiteracy

To be illiterate is to be totally unable to read and write. Illiteracy in this sense is not a widespread problem in the United States today, at least compared to other countries of the world. But some adults who have gone through the elementary school system and even beyond have not yet learned to read, even though they are capable of doing so. The number of functionally illiterate adults is not easy to ascertain because people often successfully hide their inability to read and write. (A professional football player gained considerable attention by announcing that he was unable to read even though he attended a state university for four years.) Despite the difficulty of determining the number, one writer claims that 25 percent of the American labor force is functionally illiterate (Mathews, 1992, p. A19).

## Performance on Achievement Tests

When *A Nation at Risk* was published in 1983, some disturbing trends were noted in the achievement levels of U.S. children, at both the elementary and high school levels. In international comparisons, especially with the Japanese, U.S. students were losing ground. Equally disturbing was the fact that U.S. students as a whole were averaging lower scores in the late 1970s and early 1980s than they had been a decade before. On standard IQ tests the scores of Japanese students had increased by more than ten points in a generation. The average Japanese student had a score of 111 compared to 100 for an average student in the United States. More striking was the fact that over 10 percent of Japanese had IQs above 130, while in the United States only 2 percent of students had IQs that high.

As a result of these concerns and others dating back to the 1960s, the Congress of the United States mandated that periodically the knowledge, skills, and attitudes of U.S. children and youth be assessed. Beginning in 1970-1971, schools initiated periodic assessments of U.S. students through a program called the National Assessment of Educational Progress (NAEP). The NAEP has measured reading achievement of 9-year-old, 13-year-old, and 17-year-old students six times since 1970–1971. Over the 20 years, between 1970- 1971 and 1990-1991, there has been almost no measurable improvement in reading proficiency among American students. The reading scores for 9-year-olds, 13-year-olds, and 17-year-olds were virtually unchanged; the 17-year-olds made a slight improvement (U.S. Department of Education, 1992, p. 42). The most encouraging improvements were made by black and Hispanic students. While both of these minorities still had lower reading proficiency scores than white students, they did close the gap over the last 20 years (U.S. Department of Education, 1992, p. 42). Over the entire 20-year period, females, at all three ages, have always had higher average scores than males.

This testing program started to measure mathematics proficiency in 1973, and there have been four subsequent tests (the latest in 1990). Overall, at ages 9 and 13, average mathematics proficiency improved somewhat, but scores for 17-year-olds showed no improvement (U.S. Department of Education, 1992, p. 46).

Writing proficiency has been tested since 1984, and as recently as 1990, when the last examination was given, there had been no improvement (U.S. Department of Education, 1992, p. 44).

## Changing SAT Scores

Another measure of academic performance that has been closely watched are the average Scholastic Aptitude Test scores of high school students who wish to attend college. Between 1967 and 1980 the average SAT verbal scores dropped more than 40 points, and mathematics scores dropped by 26 points.

One possible cause of the decline in average SAT scores may have been that a larger proportion of high school seniors were choosing to take the examinations. Perhaps due to the greater numbers of less-qualified students, the average scores were being depressed.

During the first half of the 1980s the combined mathematics and verbal scores did increase from 890 to 906, which seemed to be an encouraging sign (Stern and Chandler, 1987). That trend was short-lived, however, since the combined average started dropping again in the mid-1980s and was down to 896 in 1991 (U.S. Department of Education, 1992). Verbal scores in particular have shown a decline, going down each year between 1986 and 1991 (Cooper, 1991). The 1991 verbal score average of 422 is the lowest in the history of the SAT examination. The mathematics scores, after remaining fairly steady through the 1980s, also declined in 1991 (Cooper, 1991). These declines have given support to the critics of American education who charge that the school system is not meeting the nation's needs.

## SOCIAL DIMENSIONS OF SCHOOLS AND CLASSROOMS

Schools and their classrooms are not just places for teaching and learning; they are also social settings. As with all other social settings there are roles, norms, values, and status hierarchies. From a sociological perspective it is important to see how social factors influence what happens in schools and classrooms—both to the students and to the teachers. We will begin our consideration of social dimensions of schools by examining the most basic of all relationships—the relationship between teachers and students.

### Teacher-Student Relationships

Without a doubt, the relationship between a teacher and a student can have a great influence on the student's academic performance and, ultimately, on his or her academic achievements. Many successful people are asked if any teachers influenced them, and usually they can recall one or two who had a significant effect on their lives. This kind of anecdotal evidence showing that teachers "make a difference" is supported by a growing body of research that identifies how teachers' attitudes and behavior can and do influence the academic performances of children. Sometimes, however, the teachers themselves are unaware of just how much their attitudes and personal values can influence their evaluations of student performances.

For example, as children go through a school system teachers in that system often become aware of the qualities and characteristics of many students even before they are directly responsible for teaching them. Teachers are likely to communicate with each other about particular students and may form judgments on the basis of siblings or other relatives. Teachers may reach conclusions about ability levels and expect corresponding performances in class work or behavior. Thus, if teachers expect a poor academic performance or a good performance from a student, the student may be evaluated in a way consistent with that expectation. This is an example of the self-fulfilling prophecy. A **self-fulfilling prophecy** is an initial expectation that may be based on a *false* definition of the situation; it can actually produce a behavior that makes the original expectation become true (Merton, 1968). A teacher's self-fulfilling prophecy might be illustrated by the following instances. If a boy is told that he is good at arithmetic, he develops ideas about himself (expectations) consistent with the evaluation. These ideas lead him to behave in ways that make the evaluations come true. The boy who believes that he is good at arithmetic, for example, will try hard to do problems in arithmetic. This assumption, of course, is just as likely to operate in the opposite way: students who are expected to perform poorly tend to live up to those expectations.

In addition to forming expectations for specific children, teachers also develop positive or negative expectations for whole groups of children. One consequence is that members of the group tend to live up to these expectations, whatever a member's individual level of ability is. The following advice was given to a new teacher by a fellow teacher at an all-black California high school:

"Jim, you ever work with these kids before?"

"No," I admitted.

"I thought so. Well, now, the first thing is, you don't ever push 'em, and you don't expect too much . . . you take them as they are, not as you and me [sic] would like them to be. That means, you find out what they can do, and you give it to them to do."

(Cited in Silberman, 1970, p. 84.)

Rosenthal and Jacobson (1968) have done the best-known research study on the effect of teacher expectations on the performance of groups of students. At "Oak School," the site for the study, all the students were given IQ tests. At the beginning of the next school year, each of the 18 teachers in grades one through six were given the names of students (about 20 percent of the population) who, researchers told them, could be expected to show dramatic intellectual growth in the coming academic year. These predictions were supposedly based on the students' IQ scores of the previous year. In fact, the names of the 20 percent had actually been drawn at random from the school population as a whole; there were no differences between them and the other students. As Rosenthal and Jacobson (1968, p. 196) put it: "The difference between the special children and the ordinary children, then, was only in the mind of the teachers."

The crucial finding in this research was that teacher expectations made a difference: the IQs of the "special" children increased much more than the IQs of the control group (Rosenthal and Jacobson, 1968, p. 176). Rosenthal and Jacobson's research was admittedly limited; it was only one study of a single school. Subsequent efforts to replicate their study at other schools (for example, Elashoff and Snow, 1971) have failed to produce such dramatic findings. Nevertheless, a variety of additional studies have supported the general notion that teacher expectations have an important effect on student performance (Boocock, 1980, pp. 154–160).

A somewhat different way of seeing the impact of teachers on the performances of their students comes from the study of a large and diverse sample of beginning first graders in the Baltimore, Maryland, public schools. Many of the schools in this study are inner-city schools serving minority (primarily black) populations. This study set out to see if it makes a difference when the teachers and parents of a student have different attitudes about what constitutes "good" and "bad" student behavior (Alexander et al., 1987a). The main hypothesis of the study was that if a student's teacher and parent had the same notion of a good student (or bad student), the student would perform better in the first grade. This hypothesis was *not* supported by the research, but something equally important was found. *The values of the teachers were related to the performances of the students in their classes.*

The researchers were especially interested in the way teachers' values were negatively related to the report card grades of black first graders. The researchers speculate that "Teachers who place a premium on 'proper values' and on 'following the rules' may be especially frustrated when their expectations for how pupils ought to behave are not fulfilled in the context of predominantly black inner-city schools, and they may find themselves, whether consciously or not, grading these students down as a result" (Alexander et al., 1987a, p. 74).

In another analysis with this same sample of Baltimore first graders, the researchers found that minority students performed less well when their teachers were from high socioeconomic backgrounds. The same findings occurred among nonminority students who came from low-socioeconomic-status backgrounds. Both nonminority, low-status students and minority students had their greatest difficulties with teachers when the teachers had high-socioeconomic-status backgrounds. The high-status teachers were more apt to evaluate their students as less mature and to hold lower performance expectations for them. These high-status teachers were also the ones who had especially low scores when asked to evaluate the general climate of their schools. The picture that comes through is one of teachers who are not satisfied with their teaching settings and are, in the process, turning out low-achievement students. The sociological point of considerable significance is that the social origins of teachers can influence student academic achievement (Alexander et al., 1987a; Alexander et al., 1987b).

## Long-term Effects of Elementary School Teachers

The early evaluations that teachers make of particular students may have a long-term impact on academic performance. In a follow-up study of students who had been first, second, and third graders some four to nine years earlier, evidence showed that the early influences of teachers (and parents) were continuing to affect academic performance. When these students were first studied in the early grades, their grades and achievement levels were found to be closely related to the influences of their teachers (for some students) or their parents (for other students). The teachers and parents influenced the performances of the students even when their cognitive or intellectual abilities were the same. Four to nine years later, these effects of "significant others" were still related to the school performances of these youngsters (again, among students with the same levels of cognitive ability).

Different interpretations might be made of these long-term effects of early experiences in school, but one possibility is that children incorporate as a part of their self-image a view given to them by their early teachers or by their parents. Furthermore, in school systems the grades earned one year may influence the grades earned the next year. In the researchers' words, "a 'paper person' is created that follows the child from grade to grade. Cumulative records that follow children through the school could support the children's high performance in later grades by affecting subsequent teachers' expectations" (Entwisle and Hayduk, 1988, p. 158).

## Tracking and Later School Performance

One of the hotly debated topics of education is the impact that **tracking** (grouping children by ability level) has on the subsequent academic performances of students. The underlying assumption about tracking is that, when students with similar ability levels are placed in classes together, the academic gains for all students will be maximized. High-ability students will not be slowed down by the less competent students, while students with less ability will be taught at a level and pace that will be more appropriate and thus beneficial for them (Kerckhoff, 1986).

Tracking is used widely in the United States and many other countries, sometimes at the elementary school level but especially at the junior and senior high school levels. The system appears to be widely accepted by teachers and administrators, but it has also developed a corps of critics (Oakes, 1985; Rosenbaum, 1976). One basic criticism cites tracking as a system that perpetuates inequality.

There is a concern among many critics about the fairness of the placement process. Some studies have found inconsistencies between the abilities of students and the tracks in which they are placed (Rehberg and Rosenthal, 1978). Kilgore (1991) has studied the factors that influence placement, and while her research does not find any arbitrariness, she does find that white students are able to match their educational aspirations with the appropriate track better than black and Hispanic students.

A second concern is that students who are placed in low-ability tracks will come to define themselves as poor students, unable to do academic work, and consequently they will do poorly. In other words, the tracking system also tends to become a self-fulfilling prophecy (Eder, 1981); being placed in a high track tends to elicit high-quality performance, while being placed in a low track tends to produce poor academic performance. The following statement by a student illustrates the negative effects a tracking system can have:

> I felt good when I was with my class, but they went and separated us—that changed us. That changed our ideas, our thinking, the way we thought about each other and turned us into enemies toward each other—because they said I was dumb and they were smart.
>
> (Schaefer, Olexa, and Polk, 1970, p. 12)

In a participant observation study of "Suburban High School," Finley (1984) examined the ways in which teachers shape and maintain a tracking system. Looking at English courses, Finley found four tracks—gifted, advanced, average, and remedial. Middle-class white children tended to be placed in the two highest tracks, while lower-class children, especially from minority groups, tended to be overrepresented in the lower tracks. The teachers defined high-track classes as desirable places in which to work, while low-track classes were regarded as undesirable. As a result, the teachers competed among themselves to teach the high-track classes and to avoid low-track classes.

Teachers evaluated themselves on the basis of the ratio of high-track to low-track classes they taught; the higher the ratio, the more positive the self-evaluation. This fact led teachers to create more higher-track classes, in which they could teach and thus increase their ratio. The key point is that the dynamics of the status system within the school led teachers to create and maintain a tracking system. In sum, "teachers created ability groupings for their own reasons," and the educational needs and fates of their students were affected by the ambitions of the teachers (Finley, 1984, p. 242).

Other studies of students in different tracks have found that students in lower tracks were likely to be more alienated, distant, and punitive toward each other. Lower-track students also had more negative attitudes about themselves, were less attentive in classes, and were more negative about their futures. Lower-track classes were more apt to be disrupted, which contributed to lower reading levels. Teachers of lower-track students had lower expectations for their students (Oakes, 1982; Eder, 1981; Femlee and Eder, 1983).

The critical question about tracking is whether it does, in fact, improve the academic achievements of *all* students, as its supporters claim. Does it improve the academic performances and achievement levels of the students in the low ability tracks as well as those in the high-ability tracks? On this question, studies coming from the United States, Great Britain, and Israel all support the same conclusion: students who are in the high-ability track generally improve their academic and intellectual performances over what they would otherwise be, but students in low-ability tracks are more likely to lower their performances (Kerckhoff, 1986; Rowan and Miracle, 1983; Shavit and Featherman, 1988).

In the Israeli study, these effects of tracking were found on cognitive intelligence tests administered to young males when they were tested for military service (Shavit and Featherman, 1988). This study finds that the experience of having been in a high-ability track in high school actually improved a person's cognitive *intelligence* level between ages 13 and 17. Students in high-track classes apparently had certain kinds of intellectual stimulation that raised their intelligence, while students in low-track classes did not. The measured intelligence of students in the low track remained the same at age 17 as it had been at age 13.

The impact of tracking on students in British schools was measured by achievement-test performances in both reading and mathematics. The evidence from this study left little doubt that students in the low-ability tracks lost ground when compared to students who had the same earlier academic performance but who were not placed in ability tracks. The opposite occurred for students in high-ability tracks: they increased their average performance level relative to comparable students in ungrouped schools. Thus, tracking improves the education of only the students who get in the high track, while it lowers the achievement levels of the students in the low track (Kerckhoff, 1986).

At least three possible reasons can be given as to why the different ability tracks produce opposite results for students in the low and high tracks: (I) students in the high-ability track are provided with a different, and better, educational program; (2) teachers assigned to the high-ability track are more competent and more highly motivated; (3) students are influenced by their peers, so that students at each level adopt the standards of their classmates (Kerckhoff, 1986).

## Order and Control in the Classroom

Classroom discipline and school violence are viewed by most teachers, as well as much of the public, as a critical problem in the schools. One-third of a sample of teachers said that discipline was the biggest problem in the schools (Dworkin, 1987).

Disruptions in the classroom can be of many different types, but their underlying characteristic is that they distract from the educational task. In the following vignette the student's behavior is not unruly or aggressive, but, nonetheless, it disrupts the class and is the kind of problem that teachers must confront.

> Pauline was in another part of the school picking up her year-book pictures when the bell rang, signalling the beginning of the period. She arrived in her English class late; and placing her books on her desk, immediately left the room. Ten minutes later she returned. . . . Once in class she devoted her attention to trying to close her purse, while her teacher presented a lesson from the textbook. Then she sashayed to the front of the room, casually sharpened a pencil, and returned at the same leisurely pace.
>
> Being a physically attractive young lady in an extremely short skirt, this jaunt captured the attention of everyone in the room, the teacher included. In her seat, she shortly began a whispered conversation with those around her, even though text work had been given. Pauline started hers, which was to write a business letter, but suddenly decided she needed something from her purse. After a few minutes' search, she dumped its contents onto the desk with a clatter, picked out an eraser, whisked everything else back into her purse, and resumed her work. Five minutes later she began another conversation with one of her neighbors. (Stebbins, 1977, pp. 45–46)

Such disruptions are not unusual, and indeed they often take a more serious and dramatic form. Maintaining order in a classroom is, from a teacher's perspective, frequently difficult. In his study of classroom discipline, Wegmann (1976, p. 77) concludes: "Regardless of what may be written in state law or school board regulations, the actual exercise of teacher authority is an uncertain, precarious enterprise."

The problem of maintaining discipline in the classroom, especially at the high school level, has been labeled by one researcher as "defensive teaching" (McNeil, 1986, p. 157). Defensive teaching occurs when teachers reduce the difficulty of academic work in order to keep the support and goodwill of the students, and thus the harmony and control of their classrooms can be maintained. Another way to describe what happens in many classrooms is to see it as an implicit "bargain" between teachers and students. The teachers, on their side of the bargain, keep the academic demands low, while the students, in return, are reasonably well behaved and passive (Sedlak et al., 1986). By "spoon-feeding" easy academic material, teachers are able to keep peace in their classrooms and avoid behavior problems.

Different explanations may be given as to why defensive teaching is necessary in today's schools. One reason already given is that life for the teacher can be easier by striking a bargain with the students. If the material is simple and can be evaluated as right or wrong through objective examinations and quizzes, classroom teaching is easier. But probably a more important reason, one that most teachers quickly learn, is that if discipline is not maintained in one's classroom, the repercussions are serious. School superintendents and principals judge classroom performance largely on the absence of problems. As one observer has noted:

> A teacher will rarely, if ever, be called on the carpet or denied tenure because his [or her] students have not learned anything; he [she] will certainly be rebuked if his [her] students are talking or moving about the classroom, or even worse—found outside the room. . . .
>
> (Silberman, 1970, p. 140)

The obvious result of defensive teaching and the classroom bargain is that educational quality is lowered. Knowledge is sacrificed for control, and the students are sold short in their educations (McNeil, 1986; Sedlak et al., 1986).

## SUMMARY

Government-supported education on the American continent had its beginnings in 1647. The first formal schools were influenced by religious interests, but later occupational and economic factors became predominant influences. In the 1800s a universal education system emerged, a system, which, from a *traditional* view, was important for a democratic society and provided equal opportunities for all children. An alternative historical view, labeled *revisionist*, emphasizes that the economic and social elites of the society develop an educational system that meets their needs. The Lancaster system of education is an example of a system that produced workers suited for the industrial workplace.

Functionalist theory, paralleling the traditional view of education, emphasizes how education is an integrating institution. Education helps to socialize children coming from diverse backgrounds, presenting them with an ideal version of the society and culture. Functional theory takes a positive view of education, emphasizing how students are rewarded for their ability and hard work.

Conflict theory, recognizing the conflicts of interest among different groups and categories of people, stresses that powerful interest groups in the society will control the educational system for their own ends. The educational system serves the powerful by providing the workers needed by the economic interests of the society. Conflict theorists also see the educational system as favoring the children of the advantaged groups over the disadvantaged.

The worldwide picture with respect to education has improved dramatically since the 1950s. Although great advances have been made, some areas of the world, notably in Africa and parts of Asia, many children receive only minimal schooling, and educational funds are often inequitably distributed. In many countries, especially the less developed ones, females receive less education than males. One important side effect of mass education is its effect on childbearing. When children are required to go to school, they become less valuable to their parents and parents have fewer children.

School systems of nations vary in their differentiation and rigidity. Differentiation refers to different schools, tracks, or streams for different students, and rigidity refers to the ease of moving from one to another. The United States' educational system, especially from the perspective of cultural values, is less rigid than many European and Asian countries. Great Britain and Japan provide illustrations of more rigid systems in which universal examinations are key determinants of educational and occupational opportunities.

The educational system does not serve different groups in the population equally. Blacks, Hispanics, and students from lower socioeconomic backgrounds tend to succeed less often in the educational system than those from the dominant white population. A college education today gives a great advantage in the occupational world and therefore the economic world. An education from one of the elite colleges or universities is a key to top corporate management in both the United States and Japan. Graduate and professional degrees from the elite schools (Harvard Law School, for example) get the best and generally the highest paying jobs. By contrast, students who begin at community colleges are at a disadvantage in the job market.

In recent decades, many people have been critical of the performance of the U.S. educational system. A substantial number of Americans continue to be functionally illiterate. Over 20 years, there has been no measurable improvement in reading proficiency among American students, although minorities did make some improvements. Mathematical proficiency did improve somewhat for the 9- and 13-year-olds, but not for 17-year-olds. Writing proficiency has not changed since 1984.

A key social aspect of the educational system is the relationship between teachers and students. The evaluations that teachers make of students, even if based on false assumptions, can influence how they grade students. The values and social class origins of teachers also are related to how teachers grade students. The influence of teachers at elementary grade levels tends to be long-lasting.

Tracking students according to ability level is supposed to maximize the academic performances of all students, but the evidence shows that it has a positive effect on the high-track students and a negative effect on the low-track students.

Order and control in schools and in the classrooms is an important problem in American education. Many teachers lower their educational standards as a way of maintaining control of the students in their classrooms.

## CRITICAL THINKING

1. Compare and contrast the traditional view of the history of U.S. education with that of the revisionists. Which view does the Lancaster example support?
2. Assume, as the functionalists do, that the education system serves a moral function. Give examples of norms and values you have learned in school.
3. Compare and contrast the conflict and functional sociological interpretations of educational systems.
4. To what extent is U.S. education differentiated and rigid? Compare your conclusions with the educational systems found in Japan and England.
5. How would you explain the fact that reading proficiency among American students has not increased in the last 20 years?
6. Does our educational system provide equal opportunity for all individuals in society? Use information from the chapter to support your conclusion.
7. In what ways might schools serve the needs of the advantaged and powerful people in society?
8. Does tracking perpetuate inequality? Use evidence from the chapter to support your conclusion.
9. What effect does defensive teaching have on the quality of education? What suggestions can you make to reverse this situation?

## ENDNOTE

1. The elite schools for bachelor's degrees were Columbia, Cornell, Dartmouth, Harvard, Johns Hopkins, Massachusetts Institute of Technology, Pennsylvania, Princeton, Stanford, Williams, and Yale. Elite schools for master's degrees in business administration were Columbia, Dartmouth. Harvard, M.I.T., Northwestern, Stanford, California—Berkeley, California—Los Angeles, Chicago, Michigan, and Pennsylvania. Elite schools for law degrees were Columbia, Harvard, New York University, Stanford, California—Berkeley, Chicago, Michigan, Pennsylvania, and Yale.

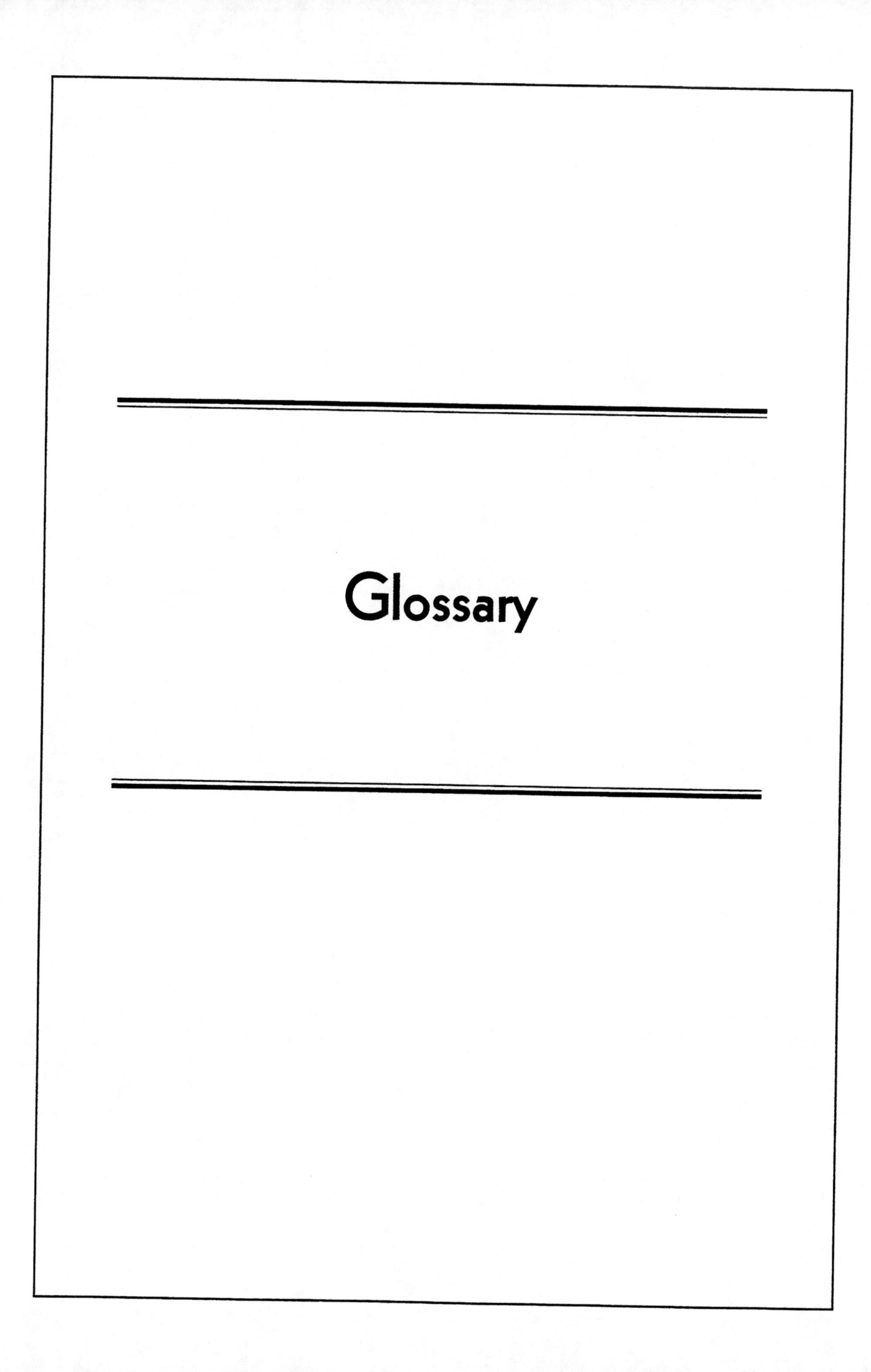

# Glossary

**absolute poverty** a deprivation of resources that is life threatening

**achieved status** a social position that someone assumes voluntarily and that reflects personal ability and effort

**acid rain** precipitation that is made acid by air pollution and destroys plant and animal life

**activity theory** the proposition that a high level of activity enhances personal satisfaction in old age

**Afrocentrism** the dominance of African cultural patterns in people's lives

**ageism** prejudice and discrimination against the elderly

**age-sex pyramid** a graphic representation of the age and sex of a population

**age stratification** the unequal distribution of wealth, power, and privileges among people at different stages in the life course.

**agriculture** the technology of large-scale farming using plows harnessed to animals or more powerful sources of energy

**alienation** the experience of isolation resulting from powerlessness

**animism** the belief that elements of the natural world are conscious forms of life that affect humanity

**anomie** Durkheim's designation of a condition of society in which individuals receive little moral guidance

**anticipatory socialization** the process of social learning directed toward gaining a desired position

**ascribed status** a social position that someone receives at birth or involuntarily assumes later in life

**assimilation** the process by which minorities gradually adopt patterns of the dominant culture

**authoritarianism** a political system that denies popular participation in government

**authority** power that people perceive as legitimate rather than coercive

**beliefs** specific statements that people who share culture hold to be true

**bilateral descent** a system tracing kinship through both females and males

**blue-collar occupations** lower-prestige work involving mostly manual labor

**bureaucracy** an organizational model rationally designed to perform complex tasks efficiently

**bureaucratic inertia** the tendency of bureaucratic organizations to perpetuate themselves

**bureaucratic ritualism** a preoccupation with organizational rules and regulations to the point of thwarting an organization's goals capitalism an economic system in which natural resources and the means of producing goods and services are privately owned

**capitalists** people who own factories and other productive enterprises

**caste system** a system of social stratification based on ascription

**cause and effect** a relationship between two varieties in which change in one (the independent variable) causes change in another (the dependent variable)

**charisma** extraordinary personal qualities that can turn an audience into followers

**charismatic authority** power legitimized through extraordinary personal abilities that inspire devotion and obedience

**church** a type of religious organization well integrated into the larger society

**civil religion** a quasi-religious loyalty binding individuals in a basically secular society

**class conflict** antagonism between entire classes over the distribution of wealth and power in society

**class consciousness** the recognition by workers of their unity as a social class in opposition to capitalists and to capitalism itself

**class society** a capitalist society with pronounced social stratification

**class system** a system of social stratification based on individual achievement

**cohabitation** the sharing of a household by an unmarried couple

**cohort** a category of people with a common characteristic, usually their age

**collective behavior** activity involving a large number of people, often spontaneous, and typically in violation of established norms

**collectivity** a large number of people whose minimal intention occurs in the absence of well-defined and conventional norms

**colonialism** the process by which some nations enrich themselves through political and economic control of other countries

**communism** a hypothetical economic and political system in which all members of a society are socially equal

**concept** a mental construct that represents some part of the world, inevitably in a simplified form

**concrete operational stage** Piaget's term for the level of human development at which individuals first perceive causal connections in their surroundings

**conglomerates** giant corporations composed of many smaller corporations

**control** the ability to neutralize the effect of one or more variables in order to assess the relationships among other variables

**conversion** a personal transformation resulting from adopting new religious beliefs

**corporation** an organization with a legal existence, including rights and liabilities, apart from those of its members

**correlation** a relationship between two (or more) variables

**counterculture** cultural patterns that strongly oppose those widely accepted within a society.

**credentialism** evaluating a person on the basis of educational degrees

**crime** the violation of norms a society formally enacts into criminal

**crimes against the person** (violent crimes) crimes against people that involve violence or the threat of violence

**crimes against property** (property crimes) crimes that involve theft of property belonging to others

**criminal justice system** a formal response to alleged violations of the law on the part of police, courts, and prison officials

**criminal recidivism** subsequent offenses by people previously convicted of crimes

**crowd** a temporary gathering of people who share a common focus of attention and whose members influence one another

**crude birth rate** the number of live births in a given year for every thousand people in a population

**crude death rate** the number of deaths in a given year for every thousand people in a population

**cult** a religious organization that is substantially outside the cultural traditions of a society

**cultural ecology** a theoretical paradigm that explores the relationship between human culture and the physical environment

**cultural integration** the close relationship among various elements of a cultural system

**cultural lag** the fact that cultural elements change at different rates, which may disrupt a cultural system

**cultural relativism** the practice of judging a culture by its own standards

**cultural transmission** the process by which one generation passes culture to the next

**cultural universals** traits that are part of every known culture

**culture** the beliefs, values, behavior, and material objects that define a people's way of life

**culture shock** personal disorientation that accompanies exposure to an unfamiliar way of life

**Davis-Moore thesis** the assertion that social stratification is a universal pattern because it has beneficial consequences for the operation of a society

**deductive logical thought** reasoning that transforms general ideas into specific hypotheses suitable for scientific testing

**democracy** a type of political system that views power as exercised by the people as a whole

**democratic socialism** an economic and political system that combines significant government control of the economy with free elections

**demographic transition theory** a thesis linking population patterns to a society's level of technological development

**demography** the study of human population

**denomination** a church, independent of the state, that accepts religious pluralism

**dependency theory** a model of economic and social development that explains global inequality in terms of the historical exploitation of poor societies by rich societies

**dependent variable** a variable that is changed by another (independent) variable

**descent** the system by which members of a society trace kinship over generations

**deterrence** the attempt to discourage criminality through punishment

**deviance** the recognized violation of cultural norms

**direct-fee system** a medical care system in which patients pay directly for the services of physicians and hospitals

**discrimination** an action that involves treating various categories of people unequally

**disengagement theory** the proposition that society enhances its orderly operation by disengaging people from positions of responsibility as they reach old age

**division of labor** specialized economic activity

**dramaturgical analysis** Erving Goffman's term for the investigation of social interaction in terms of theatrical performance

**dyad** a social group with two members

**eating disorder** an intense focus on dieting or other forms of weight control in order to become very thin

**ecclesia** a church that is formally allied with the state

**ecology** the study of the interaction of living organisms and the natural environment

**economy** the social institution that organizes the production, distribution, and consumption of goods and services

**ecosystem** the system composed of the interaction of all living organisms and their natural environment

**education** the social institution guiding a society's transmission of knowledge—including basic facts, job skills, and also cultural norms and values—to its members

**ego** Freud's designation of a person's conscious attempt to balance pleasure-seeking drives and the demands of society

**empirical evidence** information we are able to verify with our senses

**endogamy** marriage between people of the same social category

**environmental deficit** the situation in which negative, long-term consequences of decisions about the natural environment outweigh whatever short-term benefits may accrue

**ethnicity** a shared cultural heritage

**ethnocentrism** the practice of judging another culture by the standards of one's own culture

**ethnomethodology** Harold Garfinkel's term for the study of the way people make sense of their everyday lives

**Eurocentrism** the dominance of European (especially English) cultural patterns

**euthanasia** (mercy killing) assisting in the death of a person suffering from an incurable disease

**exogamy** marriage between people of different social categories

**experiment** a research method for investigating cause and effect under highly controlled conditions

**expressive leadership** group leadership that emphasizes collective well-being

**extended family** (consanguine family) a family unit including parents and children, but also other kin

**fad** an unconventional social pattern that people embrace briefly but enthusiastically

**faith** belief anchored in conviction rather than scientific evidence

**false consciousness** Marx's term for explanations of social problems in terms of the shortcomings of individuals rather than flaws of society

**family** a social institution, found in all societies, that unites individuals into cooperative groups that oversee the bearing and rearing of children

**family unit** a social group of two or more people, related by blood, marriage, or adoption, who usually live together

**family violence** emotional, physical, or sexual abuse of one family member by another

**fashion** a social pattern favored for a time by a large number of people

**female infanticide** the practice of aborting female fetuses and neglecting, or even actively killing, infant girls by parents who would prefer to raise boys

**feminism** the advocacy of social equality for the sexes, in opposition to patriarchy and sexism

**feminization of poverty** the trend by which women represent an increasing proportion of the poor

**fertility** the incidence of childbearing in a society's population

**folkways** norms that have less moral significance than mores

**formal operational stage** Piaget's term for the level of human development at which individuals use highly abstract thought to imagine alternatives to reality

**formal organization** a large secondary group organized to achieve its goals efficiently

**functional illiteracy** reading and writing skills insufficient for everyday living

**fundamentalism** a conservative religious doctrine that opposes intellectualism and worldly accommodation in favor of restoring a traditional, otherworldly spirituality

***Gemeinschaft*** a type of social organization by which people are bound closely together by kinship and tradition

**gender** the significance a society attaches to biological categories of female and male

**gender identity** traits that females and males, guided by their culture, incorporate into their personalities

**gender roles** (sex roles) attitudes and activities that a culture links to each sex

**gender stratification** a society's unequal distribution of wealth, power, and privilege between the two sexes

**generalized other** George Herbert Mead's term for widespread cultural norms and values we use as references in evaluating ourselves

**genocide** the systematic annihilation of one category of people by another

**gerontocracy** a form of social organization in which the elderly have the most wealth, power, and privileges

**gerontology** the study of aging and the elderly

***Gesellschaft*** a type of social organization by which people have weak social ties and considerable self-interest

**global economy** interconnected economic activity throughout the world that pays little regard to national borders

**global perspective** the study of the larger world and our society's place in it

**gossip** rumor about the personal affairs of others

**government** formal organizations that direct the political life of a society

**greenhouse effect** a rise in the earth's average temperature (global warming) due to an increasing concentration of carbon dioxide in the atmosphere

**groupthink** the tendency of group members to conform by adopting a narrow view of some Issue

**hate crime** a criminal act carried out against a person or personal property by an offender motivated by racial or other bias

**Hawthorne effect** a change in a subject's behavior caused by the awareness of being studied

**health** a state of complete physical, mental, and social well-being

**health care** any activity intended to improve health

**health maintenance organization** (HMO) an organization that provides comprehensive medical care to subscribers for a fixed fee

**hermaphrodite** a human being with some combination of female and male internal and external genitalia

**hidden curriculum** subtle presentations of political or cultural ideas in the classroom

**high culture** cultural patterns that distinguish a society's elite

**holistic medicine** an approach to health care that emphasizes prevention of illness and takes account of a person's entire physical and social environment

**homogamy** marriage between people with the same social characteristics

**horticulture** technology based on using hand tools to cultivate plants

**humanizing bureaucracy** fostering an organizational atmosphere that recognizes and encourages the contributions of everyone

**hunting and gathering** simple technology for hunting animals and gathering vegetation

**hypothesis** an unverified statement of a relationship between variables

**id** Freud's designation of the human being's basic drives

**ideal culture** as opposed to real culture, the social patterns mandated by cultural values and norms

**ideal type** an abstract statement of the essential characteristics of any social phenomenon

**ideology** cultural beliefs that, directly or indirectly, justify social stratification

**incest taboo** a cultural norm forbidding sexual relations or marriage between certain kin

**income** occupational wages or salaries and earnings from investments

**independent variable** a variable that causes change in another (dependent) variable

**inductive** logical thought reasoning that builds specific observations into general theory

**industrialism** technology that powers sophisticated machinery with advanced sources of energy

**infant mortality rate** the number of deaths among infants under one year of age for each thousand live births in a given year

**ingroup** a social group commanding a member's esteem and loyalty

**institutional discrimination** discrimination that is a normative and routine part of the economy, the educational system, or some other social institution

**instrumental leadership** group leadership that emphasizes the completion of tasks

**intergenerational social mobility** upward or downward social mobility of children in relation to their parents

**interview** a series of questions administered personally by a researcher to respondents

**intragenerational social mobility** a change in social position occurring during a person's lifetime

**juvenile delinquency** the violation of legal standards by the young

**kinship** a social bond, based on blood, marriage, or adoption, that joins individuals into families

**labeling theory** the assertion that deviance and conformity result, not so much from what people do, as from how others respond

**labor unions** organizations of workers seeking to improve wages and working conditions through various strategies, including negotiations and strikes

**language** a system of symbols that allows members of a society to communicate with one another

**latent functions** consequences of any social pattern that are unrecognized and unintended

**least-developed countries** societies with little industrialization in which severe poverty is the rule

**less-developed countries** societies characterized by limited industrialization and moderate-to-low personal income

**liberation theology** a fusion of Christian principles with political activism, often Marxist in character

**life expectancy** the average life span of a society's population

**looking-glass self** Cooley's assertion that the self is based on how others respond to us

**macro-level orientation** a focus on broad social structures that characterize society as a whole

**mainstreaming** integrating special students into the overall educational program

**manifest functions** the recognized and intended consequences of any social pattern

**marriage** a legally sanctioned relationship, involving economic cooperation as well as normative sexual activity and childbearing, that people expect to be enduring

**mass behavior** collective behavior among people dispersed over a wide geographical area

**mass hysteria** a form of dispersed collective behavior by which people respond to a real or imagined event with irrational, frantic, and often self-destructive behavior

**mass media** impersonal communications directed toward a vast audience

**mass society** a society in which industry and bureaucracy have eroded traditional social ties

**master status** a status that has exceptional importance for social identity, often shaping a person's entire life

**material culture** tangible products of human society, such as clothing and cities

**matriarchy** a form of social organization in which females dominate males

**matrilineal descent** a system tracing kinship through females

**matrilocality** a residential pattern in which a married couple lives with or near the wife's family

**mean** the arithmetic average of a series of numbers

**measurement** the process of determining the value of a variable in a specific case

**mechanical solidarity** Durkheim's term for social bonds, based on shared moral sentiments, that unite members of preindustrial societies

**median** the value that occurs midway in a series of numbers arranged in order of magnitude or, simply, the middle case

**medicalization of deviance** the transformation of moral and legal issues into medical matters

**medicine** a social institution concerned with combating disease and improving health

**megalopolis** a vast urban region containing a number of cities and their surrounding suburbs

**meritocracy** a system of social stratification based on personal merit

**metropolis** a large city that socially and economically dominates an urban area

**micro-level orientation** a focus on patterns of social interaction in specific situations

**migration** the movement of people into and out of a specified territory

**military-industrial complex** the close association among the federal government, the military, and defense industries

**minority** a category of people, distinguished by physical or cultural traits, who are socially disadvantaged

**miscegenation** the biological process of interbreeding among racial categories

**mob** a highly emotional crowd that pursues some violent or destructive goal

**mode** the value that occurs most often in a series of numbers

**modernity social** patterns linked to industrialization

**modernization** the process of social change initiated by industrialization

**modernization theory** a model of economic and social development that explains global inequality in terms of differing levels of technological development among societies

**monarchy** a type of political system that transfers power from generation to generation within a single family

**monogamy** a form of marriage involving two partners

**monopoly** domination of a market by a single producer

**monotheism** belief in a single divine power

**mores** norms that have great moral significance

**mortality** the incidence of death in a society's population

**most-developed countries** relatively rich, industrialized societies

**multiculturalism** an educational program recognizing past and present cultural diversity in U S. society and promoting the equality of all cultural traditions

**multinational corporation** a large corporation that operates in many different countries

**natural environment** the earth's surface and atmosphere including various living organisms and the air, water, soil, and other rescuers necessary to sustain life

**neocolonialism** a new form of global power relationships that involves not direct political control but, rather, economic exploitation by multinational corporations

**neolocality** a residential pattern in which a married couple lives apart from the parents of both spouses

**network** a web of social ties that links people who may have little common identity and interaction

**nonmaterial culture** intangible creations of human society, such as values and norms

**nonverbal communication** communication using body movements, gestures, and facial expressions rather than speech

**norms** rules and expectations by which a society guides the behavior of its members

**nuclear family** (conjugal family) a family unit composed of one or two parents and their children

**nuclear proliferation** the acquisition of nuclear-weapons technology by more and more nations

**objectivity** a state of personal neutrality in conducting research

**oligarchy the** rule of the many by the few

**oligopoly** domination of a market by a few producers

**operationalizing a variable** specifying exactly what one is to measure in assigning a value to a variable

**organic solidarity** Durkheim's term for social bonds, based on specialization, that unite members of industrial societies

**organizational environment** a range of factors external to an organization that affects its operation

**other-directedness** a receptiveness to the latest trends and fashions, often expressed in the practice of imitating others

**outgroup** a social group toward which one feels competition or opposition

**panic** a form of localized collective behavior by which people react to a threat or other stimulus with irrational, frantic, and often self-destructive behavior

**participant observation** a research method in which researchers systematically observe people while joining in their routine activities

**pastoralism** technology that supports the domestication of animals

**patriarchy** a form of social organization in which males dominate females

**patrilineal descent** a system tracing kinship through males

**patrilocality** a residential pattern in which a married couple lives with or near the husband's family

**peace** a state of international relations devoid of violence

**peer group** a social group whose members have interests, social position, and age in common

**personality** a person's fairly consistent patterns of thinking, feeling, and acting

**personal space** the surrounding area to which an individual makes some claim to privacy

**plea bargaining** a legal negotiation in which the prosecution reduces a defendant's charge in exchange for a guilty plea

**pluralism** a state in which racial and ethnic minorities are distinct but have social parity

**phiralist model** an analysis of politics that views power as dispersed among many competing interest groups

**political action committee** (PAC) an organization formed by a special-interest group, independent of political parties, to pursue specific aims by raising and spending money

**political revolution** the overthrow of one political system in order to establish another

**politics** the social institution that distributes power, sets a society's agenda, and makes decisions

**polyandry** a form of marriage joining one female with two or more males

**polygamy** a form of marriage uniting three or more people

**polygyny** a form of marriage joining one male with two or more females

**polytheism** belief in many gods

**popular culture** cultural patterns that are widespread among a society's population

**population** the people who are the focus of research

**positivism** understanding the world based on science

**postindustrial economy** a productive system based on service work and high technology

**postindustrialism** technology that supports an information-based economy

**postmodernity** social patterns characteristic of postindustrial societies

**power** the ability to achieve desired ends despite resistance from others

**power-elite model** an analysis of politics that views power as concentrated among the rich

**prejudice** an attitude involving a rigid and irrational generalization about an entire category of people

**preoperational stage** Piaget's term for the level of human development in which individuals first use language and other symbols

**presentation of self** the effort of an individual to create specific impressions in the minds of others

**primary group** a small social group in which relationships are both personal and enduring

**primary labor market** occupations that provide extensive benefits to workers

**primary sector** the part of the economy that generates raw materials directly from the natural environment

**primary sex characteristics** the genitals, used to reproduce the human species

**profane** that which is defined as an ordinary element of everyday life

**profession** a prestigious white-collar occupation that requires extensive formal education

**proletariat** people who provide labor necessary for the operation of factories and other productive enterprises

**propaganda** information presented with the intention of shaping public opinion

**qualitative research** inquiry based on subjective impressions

**quantitative research** inquiry based on the analysis of numerical data

**questionnaire** a series of written questions a researcher prepares for subjects to answer

**race** a category composed of men and women who share biologically transmitted traits that members of a society deem socially significant

**racism** the belief that one racial category is innately superior or inferior to another

**rain forests** regions of dense forestation, most of which circle the globe close to the equator

**rationality** deliberate, matter-of-fact calculation of the most efficient means to accomplish a particular goal

**rationalization of society** Max Weber's term for the historical change from tradition to rationality as the dominant mode of human thought

**rational-legal authority** (also **bureaucratic authority**) power legitimized by legally enacted rules and regulations

**real culture** as opposed to ideal culture, the actual social patterns that only approximate cultural expectations

**recycling** programs to reuse resources that we would otherwise discard as "waste"

**reference group** a social group that serves as a point of reference in making evaluations or decisions

**rehabilitation** a program for reforming the offender to preclude subsequent offenses

**relative deprivation** a perceived disadvantage arising from a specific comparison

**relative poverty** the deprivation of some people in relation to those who have more

**reliability** the quality of consistent measurement

**religion** a social institution involving beliefs and practices based upon a conception of the sacred

**religiosity** the importance of religion in a person's life

**replication** repetition of research by others in order to assess its accuracy

**research method** a strategy for systematically conducting research

**resocialization** deliberate control of an environment intended to radically alter an inmate's personality

**retribution** an act of moral vengeance by which society subjects an offender to suffering comparable to that caused by the offense

**retrospective labeling** the interpretation of someone's past consistent with present deviance

**riot** a social eruption that is highly emotional, violent, and undirected

**ritual** formal, ceremonial behavior

**role** behavior expected of someone who holds a particular status

**role conflict** incompatibility among the roles corresponding to two or more different statuses

**role set** a number of roles attached to a single status

**role strain** incompatibility among roles corresponding to a single status

**routinization of charisma** the transformation of charismatic authority into some combination of traditional and bureaucratic authority

**rumor** unsubstantiated information spread informally, often by word of mouth

**sacred** that which is defined as extraordinary, inspiring a sense of awe, reverence, and even fear

**sample** a part of a population researchers select to represent the whole

**Sapir-Whorf hypothesis** a hypothesis stating that people perceive the world through the cultural lens of language

**scapegoat** a person or category of people, typically with little power, whom people unfairly blame for their own troubles

**schooling** formal instruction under the direction of specially trained teachers

**science** a logical system that bases knowledge on direct, systematic observation

**secondary analysis** a research method in which a researcher utilizes data collected by others

**secondary group** a large and impersonal social group devoted to some specific interest or activity

**secondary labor market** jobs that provide minimal benefits to workers

**secondary sector** the part of the economy that transforms raw materials into manufactured goods

**secondary sex characteristics** bodily development, apart from the genitals, that distinguishes biologically mature females and males

**sect** a type of religious organization that stands apart from the larger society

**secularization** the historical decline in the importance of the supernatural and the sacred

**segregation** the physical and social separation of categories of people

**self** George Herbert Mead's term for a dimension of personality composed of an individual's self-awareness and self-conception

**sensorimotor stage** Piaget's term for the level of human development in which individuals experience the world only through sensory contact

**sex** the biological distinction between females and males

**sexism** the belief that one sex is innately superior to the other

**sex ratio** the number of males for every hundred females in a given population

**sexual harassment** comments, gestures, or physical contact of a sexual nature that are deliberate, repeated, and unwelcome

**sexual orientation** the manner in which people experience sexual arousal and achieve sexual pleasure

**sick role** patterns of behavior defined as appropriate for those who are ill

**social change** the transformation of culture and social institutions over time

**social character** personality patterns common to members of a particular society

**social conflict** struggle between segments of society over valued resources

**social-conflict paradigm** a framework for building theory based on the assumption that society is characterized by inequality and conflict that generate change

**social construction of reality** the process by which people creatively shape reality through social interaction

**social control** various means by which members of a society encourage conformity to norms

**social dysfunction** the undesirable consequences of any social pattern for the operation of society

**social epidemiology** the study of how health and disease are distributed throughout a society's population

**social fact** any pattern that is rooted in society rather than the experiences of individuals

**social function** the consequences of any social pattern for the operation of society

**social group** two or more people who identify and interact with one another

**social institution** a major sphere of social life organized to meet a basic human need

**social interaction** the process by which people act and react in relation to others

**socialism** an economic system in which natural resources and the means of producing goods and services are collectively owned

**socialization** the lifelong social experience by which individuals develop human potential and learn patterns of their culture

**socialized medicine** a health care system in which the government owns and operates most medical facilities and employs most physicians

**social marginality** the state of being excluded from social activity as an "outsider"

**social mobility** change in people's position in a system of social stratification

**social movement** organized activity that encourages or discourages social change

**social stratification** a system by which society ranks categories of people in a hierarchy

**social structure** a relatively stable pattern of social behavior

**societal protection** a means by which society renders an offender incapable of further offenses temporarily through incarceration or permanently by execution

**society** people who interact in a defined territory and share culture

**sociobiology** a theoretical paradigm that explores ways in which biological forces affect human culture

**sociocultural evolution** the Lenskis' term for the process of change that results from a society's gaining new cultural information, particularly technology

**socioeconomic status** (SES) a composite ranking based on various dimensions of social inequality

**sociology** the scientific study of human society

**special-interest group** a political alliance of people interested in some economic or social issue

**spurious correlation** an apparent, although false, relationship between two (or more) variables caused by some other variable

**state capitalism** an economic and political system in which companies are privately owned although they cooperate closely with the government

**state terrorism** the use of violence, generally without support of law, against individuals or groups by a government or its agents

**status** a recognized social position that an individual occupies

**status consistency** the degree of consistency of a person's social standing across various dimensions of social inequality

**status set** all the statuses a person holds at a given time

**stereotype** a set of prejudices concerning some category of people

**stigma** a powerfully negative social label that radically changes a person's self-concept and social identity

**structural-functional paradigm** a framework for building theory based on the assumption that society is a complex system whose parts work together to promote stability

**structural social mobility** a shift in the social position of large numbers of people due more to changes in society itself than to individual efforts

**subculture** cultural patterns that distinguish some segment of a society's population

**suburbs** urban areas beyond the political boundaries of a city

**superego** Freud's designation of the presence of culture within the individual in the form of internalized values and norms

**survey** a research method in which subjects respond to a series of questions in a questionnaire or an interview

**sustainable ecosystem** the human use of the natural environment to meet the needs of the present generation without threatening the prospects of future generations

**symbol** anything that carries a particular meaning recognized by people who share culture

**symbolic-interaction paradigm** a theoretical framework based on the assumption that society is the product of the everyday interactions of individuals

**technology** knowledge that a society applies to the task of living in a physical environment

**terrorism** violence or the threat of violence employed by an individual or group as a political strategy

**tertiary sector** the part of the economy involved in services rather than goods

**theoretical paradigm** a set of assumptions that guides thinking and research

**theory** a statement of how and why specific facts are related

**Thomas theorem** W. I. Thomas's assertion that situations we define as real become real in their consequences

**total institution** a setting in which people are isolated from the rest of society and manipulated by an administrative staff

**totalitarianism** a political system that extensively regulates people's lives

**totem** an object in the natural world collectively defined as sacred

**tracking** the assignment of students to different types of educational programs

**tradition** sentiments and beliefs passed from generation to generation

**traditional authority** power legitimized through respect for long-established cultural patterns

**tradition-directedness** rigid conformity to time-honored ways of living

**transsexuals** people who feel they are one sex though biologically they are the other

**triad** a social group with three members

**underground economy** economic activity generating income that one does not report to the government as required by law

**urban ecology** the study of the link between the physical and social dimensions of cities

**urbanization** the concentration of humanity into cities urban renewal government programs intended to revitalize cities

**validity** the quality of measuring precisely what one intends to measure

**values** culturally defined standards by which people judge desirability, goodness, and beauty, and which serve as broad guidelines for social living

**variable** a concept whose value changes from case to case

**victimless crimes** violations of law in which there are no readily apparent victims

**war** armed conflict among the people of various societies, directed by their governments

**wealth** the total amount of money and valuable goods that a person or family controls

**white collar crime** crimes committed by people of high social position in the course of their occupations

**white-collar occupations** higher-prestige work involving mostly mental activity

**zero population growth** the level of reproduction that maintains population at a steady state

# Readings and Articles

# Invitation to Sociology

*Peter L. Berger*

*Using the sociological perspective changes how we perceive the surrounding world, and even ourselves. Peter Berger compares thinking sociologically to entering a new and unfamiliar society—one in which "things are no longer what they seem." This article should lead you to re-think your social world, so that you become aware of truths that you may never before have realized.*

. . . It can be said that the first wisdom of sociology is this—things are not what they seem. This too is a deceptively simple statement. It ceases to be simple after a while. Social reality turns out to have many layers of meaning. The discovery of each new layer changes the perception of the whole.

Anthropologists use the term "culture shock" to describe the impact of a totally new culture upon a newcomer. In an extreme instance such shock will be experienced by the Western explorer who is told, halfway through dinner, that he is eating the nice old lady he had been chatting with the previous day—a shock with predictable physiological if not moral consequences. Most explorers no longer encounter cannibalism in their travels today. However, the first encounters with polygamy or with puberty rights or even with the way some nations drive their automobiles can be quite a shock to an American visitor. With the shock may go not only disapproval or disgust but a sense of excitement that things can *really* be that different from what they are at home. To some extent, at least, this is the excitement of any first travel abroad. The experience of sociological discovery could be described as "culture shock" minus geographical displacement. In other words, the sociologist travels at home—with shocking results. He is unlikely to find that he is eating a nice old lady for dinner. But the discovery, for instance, that his own church has considerable money invested in the missile industry or that a few blocks from his home there are people who engage in cultic orgies may not be drastically different in emotional impact. Yet we would not want to imply that sociological discoveries are always or even usually outrageous to moral sentiment. Not at all. What they have in common with exploration in distant lands, however, is the sudden illumination of new and unsuspected facets of human existence in society. This is the excitement and, as we shall try to show later, the humanistic justification of sociology.

People who like to avoid shocking discoveries, who prefer to believe that society is just what they were taught in Sunday school, who like the safety of the rules and the maxims of what Alfred Schuetz has called the "world-taken-for-granted," should stay away from sociology. People who feel no temptation before closed doors, who have no curiosity about human beings, who are content to admire scenery without wondering about the people who live in those houses on the other side of that river, should probably also stay away from sociology. They will find it unpleasant or, at any rate, unrewarding. People who are interested in human beings only if they can change, convert, or reform them should also be warned, for they will find sociology much less useful than they hoped. And people whose interest is mainly in their own conceptual constructions will do just as well to turn to the study of little white mice. Sociology will be satisfying, in the long run, only to those who can think of nothing more entrancing than to watch men and to understand things human. . . .

To ask sociological questions, then, presupposes that one is interested in looking some distance beyond the commonly accepted or officially defined goals of human actions. It presupposes a certain awareness that human events have different levels of meaning, some of which are hidden from the consciousness of everyday life. It may even presuppose a measure of suspicion about the way in which human events are officially interpreted by the authorities, be they political, juridical, or religious in character. If one is willing to go as far as that, it would seem evident that not all historical circumstances are equally favorable for the development of sociological perspective.

It would appear plausible, in consequence, that sociological thought would have the best chance to develop in historical circumstances marked by severe jolts to the self-conception, especially the official and authoritative and generally accepted self-conception of a culture. It is only in such circumstances that perceptive men are likely to be motivated to think beyond the assertions of this self-conception and, as a result, question the authorities. . . .

Sociological perspective can then be understood in terms of such phrases as "seeing through," "looking behind," very much as such phrases would be employed in common speech—"seeing through his game," "looking behind the scenes"—in other words, "being up on all the tricks."

. . . We could think of this in terms of a common experience of people living in large cities. One of the fascinations of a large city is the immense variety of human activities taking place behind the seemingly anonymous and endlessly undifferentiated rows of houses. A person who lives in such a city will time and again experience surprise or even shock as he discovers the strange pursuits that some men engage in quite unobtrusively in houses that, from the outside, look like all the others on a certain street. Having had this experience once or twice, one will repeatedly find oneself walking down a street, perhaps late in the evening, and wondering what may be going on under the bright lights showing through a line of drawn curtains. An ordinary family engaged in pleasant talk with guests? A scene of desperation amid illness or death? Or a scene of debauched pleasures? Perhaps a strange cult or a dangerous conspiracy? The facades of the houses cannot tell us, proclaiming nothing but an architectural conformity to the tastes of some group or class that may not even inhabit the street any longer. The social mysteries lie behind the facades. The wish to penetrate to these mysteries is an analogon to sociological curiosity. In some cities that are suddenly struck by calamity this wish may be abruptly realized. Those who have experienced wartime bombings know of the sudden encounters with unsuspected (and sometimes unimaginable) fellow tenants in the air-raid shelter of one's apartment building. Or they can recollect the startling morning sight of a house hit by a bomb during the night, neatly sliced in half, the facade torn away and the previously hidden interior mercilessly revealed in the daylight. But in most cities that one may normally live in, the facades must be penetrated by one's own inquisitive intrusions. Similarly, there are historical situations in which the facades of society are violently torn apart and all but the most incurious are forced to see that there was a reality behind the facades all along. Usually this does not happen, and the facades continue to confront us with seemingly rocklike permanence. The perception of the reality behind the facades then demands a considerable intellectual effort.

A few examples of the way in which sociology "looks behind" the facades of social structures might serve to make our argument clearer. Take, for instance, the political organization of a community. If one wants to find out how a modern American city is governed, it is very easy to get the official information about this subject. The city will have a charter, operating under the laws of the state. With some advice from informed individuals, one may look up various statutes that define the constitution of the city. Thus one may find out that this particular community has a city-manager form of administration, or that party affiliations do not appear on the ballot in municipal elections, or that the city government participates in a regional water district. In similar fashion, with the help of some newspaper reading, one may find out the officially recognized political problems of the community. One may read that the city plans to annex a certain suburban area, or that there has been a change in the zoning ordinances to facilitate industrial development in another area, or even that one of the members of the city council has been accused of using his office for personal gain. All such matters still occur on the, as it were, visible, official, or public level of political life. However, it would be an exceedingly naive person who would believe that this kind of information gives him a rounded picture of the political reality of that community. The sociologist will want to know above all the constituency of the "informal power structure" (as it has been called by Floyd Hunter, an American sociologist interested in such studies), which is a configuration of men and their power that cannot be found in any statutes, and probably cannot be read about in the newspapers. The political scientist or the legal expert might find it very interesting to compare the city charter with the constitutions of other similar communities. The sociologist will be far more concerned with discovering the way in which powerful vested interests influence or even control the actions of officials elected under the charter. These vested interests will not be found in city hall, but rather in the executive suites of corporations that may not even be located in that community, in the private mansions of a handful of powerful men, perhaps in the offices of certain labor unions, or even, in some instances, in the headquarters of criminal organizations. When the sociologist concerns himself with power, he will "look behind" the official mechanisms that are supposed to regulate power in the community. This does not necessarily mean that he will regard the official mechanisms as totally ineffective or their legal definition as totally illusionary. But at the very least he will insist that there is another level of reality to be investigated in the particular system of power. In some cases he might conclude that to look for real power in the publicly recognized places is quite delusional. . . .

Let us take one further example. In Western countries, and especially in America, it is assumed that men and women marry because they are in love. There is a broadly based popular mythology about the character of love as a violent, irresistible emotion that strikes where it will, a mystery that is the goal of most young people and often of the not-so-young as well. As soon as one investigates, however, which people actually marry each other, one finds that the lightning-shaft of Cupid seems to be guided rather strongly within very definite channels of class, income, education, [and] racial and religious background. If one then investigates a little further into the behavior that is engaged in prior to marriage under the rather misleading euphemism of "courtship," one finds channels of interaction that are often rigid to the point of ritual. The suspicion begins to dawn on one that, most of the time, it is not so much the emotion of love that creates a certain kind of relationship, but that carefully predefined and often planned relationships eventually generate the desired emotion. In other words, when certain conditions are met or have been constructed, one allows oneself "to fall in love." The sociologist investigating our patterns of "courtship" and marriage soon discovers a complex web of motives related in many ways to the entire institutional structure within which an individual lives his life—class, career, economic ambition, aspirations of power and prestige. The miracle of love now begins to look somewhat synthetic. Again, this need not mean in any given instance that the sociologist will declare the romantic interpretation to be an illusion. But, once more he will look beyond the immediately given and publicly approved interpretations. . . .

We would contend, then, that there is a debunking motif inherent in sociological consciousness. The sociologist will be driven time and again, by the very logic of his discipline, to debunk the social systems he is studying. This unmasking tendency need not necessarily be due to the sociologist's temperament or inclinations. Indeed, it may happen that the sociologist, who as an individual may be of a conciliatory disposition and quite disinclined to disturb the comfortable assumptions on which he rests his own social existence, is nevertheless compelled by what he is doing to fly in the face of what those around him take for granted. In other words, we would contend that the roots of the debunking motif in sociology are not psychological but methodological. The sociological frame of reference, with its built-in procedure of looking for levels of reality other than those given in the official interpretations of society, carries with it a logical imperative to unmask the pretensions and the propaganda by which men cloak their actions with each other. This unmasking imperative is one of the characteristics of sociology particularly at home in the temper of the modern era. . . .

## CRITICAL-THINKING QUESTIONS

1. *How can we explain the fact that people within any society tend to take their own way of life for granted?*
2. *What does Berger think is the justification for studying sociology?*
3. *What is involved in sociological "debunking"? How are others likely to respond to sociological insights?*

# Knowing About Things

## *Jonathan Turner*

The goal of all science is to produce theory. Since the word "theory" has such unsavory connotations, perhaps I should clarify just what theory is. Theory is *not* wild-eyed speculation. It can, initially, involve creative speculation but in the end theory is formal and rather sedate. Theory is *not* pie-in-the-sky ideas. True, it is abstract but the purpose of theory is to help us explain real events in the actual world. Theory is *not* dull or hard to understand. Students often think that it is because it is often removed from everyday events and the concrete world.

What, then, is theory? Theory is nothing more or less than formal statements that tell us how and why events in the world occur. Scientific theory has a special characteristic. It is designed to be proven *wrong*. Yes, wrong. The whole idea is to make statements that tell us how and why events occur and then try to show them to be wrong. This is done by collecting information or data on empirical events to see if things do indeed work as the theory says they should.[1] If a theory stands intact after repeated assaults, then it is considered plausible and is accepted for the time being as the explanation of the way things are. A theory is actually never proven; it can only be disproven. Tomorrow, someone might collect data to show that it is wrong, forcing us to reject or revise the theory. Yet, when theories stand the test of time—that is, repeated efforts to disprove them—then they become provisionally accepted as truth, as the way things are.

This is the way all science works. It is not an efficient process, but it is the way we keep our theories tied to real events. We hold theories skeptically and constantly check them against the facts.

Just how is theory checked? This is done by following some general procedures, often termed "scientific method." The general idea behind the methods of science is to develop unbiased procedures for collecting data and then to specify clearly the procedures we have used, so that others can come along and check up on us and verify that we were honest and didn't make any dumb mistakes. Without data that we can trust, or have confidence in, we do not know if the data really do bear on the theory we are testing.

The reason sociologists are concerned with methodology is that they, like all scientists, want to be sure that the procedures, or methods, used in collecting information are not biased, inappropriate, or faulty.[2] Otherwise, we cannot be sure that our data are any good and we cannot test our theory with it.

The use of statistics is simply a way of manipulating data once we have it in hand for interpretation. Without statistics, our capacity to interpret the world would be very limited. We would miss much and make lots of mistakes just because we could not get at the facts in sufficient detail.

Science, then, involves a constant interplay among theory, methods (data collection), and analysis (statistics in our case). If we relied only on our intuition, we could create theories that were "confirmed" simply by selective perception. We need to subject our hunches to a more rigorous scrutiny than that. Only by so doing can we begin to understand the social world and how it operates. . . .

But there is a broader issue to consider, besides merely getting a job. If we want to realize our humanism—and this motive is what gets most of us started in sociology—we need to be skilled at gathering and interpreting information about situations we want to change and people we want to help. We also need to understand *why* and *how* the situations operate. And we need to be able to anticipate the consequences of any changes we initiate and to collect accurate information on these changes. We cannot rely on intuition and our personal ideologies in these matters. We need formal theory that has withstood efforts to disprove it to tell us how and why things operate, and we need to use this theory in ascertaining what needs to be done to improve a situation. We will also need to collect accurate information and analyze it carefully to know just what exists in a situation and just what the consequences of our theoretically informed actions are.

If we have no theory, we have no framework to understand and interpret the social world. Hence, we do not know what we have done or what to expect. If we do not have methods and statistics, we cannot have confidence in our theories, since they have not been tested, and we cannot know exactly what in a situation needs to be changed. We can use our familiarity with a situation and our creative intuition to bring to bear relevant theories and to develop ways of gathering information. But our intuition cannot substitute for formal theory, carefully constructed methods, and detailed statistical analysis. Those who think it can are more likely to hurt than help people, despite their voiced concern for a more humane world.

## NOTES

1. For the most authoritative account of this argument, read Karl R. Popper, *The Logic of Scientific Inquiry* (New York: Basic Books, 1959). For a readable analysis of the interplay between theory and empirical data, see Bernard P. Cohen's *Developing Sociological Knowledge: Theory and Method* (Englewood Cliffs, N.J.: Prentice-Hall, 1980).
2. See Earl Babbie's *The Practice of Social Research* (Belmont, Calif.: Wadsworth, 1979) for a readable discussion of methods in sociology. Also, see volumes in Prentice-Hall's "Methods and Theories in the Social Sciences." In particular, I recommend Neil J. Smelser's *Comparative Methods in the Social Sciences,* H. W. Smith's *Strategies of Social Research.* Leonard Schatzman and Anselm Strauss's *Field Research,* Jarnes A. Davis's *Elementary Survey Analysis,* and Carol H. Weis's *Evaluation Research.* All are very readable and in paperback. Still the best book on the general issues surrounding research is Abraham Kaplan, *The Conduct Inquiry* (Scranton, Penn.: Chandler, 1964).

## DISCUSSION QUESTIONS

1. How does Turner show that theory and methods are related to each other?
2. Using the material by Turner, show how methodology helps science establish its knowledge base.

# The Positive Functions of Poverty

*Herbert J. Gans*

Some twenty years ago Robert K. Merton applied the notion of functional analysis to explain the continuing though maligned existence of the urban political machine: If it continued to exist, perhaps it fulfilled latent—unintended or unrecognized—positive functions. Clearly it did. Merton pointed out how the political machine provided central authority to get things done when a decentralized local government could not act, humanized the services of the impersonal bureaucracy for fearful citizens, offered concrete help (rather than abstract law or justice) to the poor, and otherwise performed services needed or demanded by many people but considered unconventional or even illegal by formal public agencies.

Today, poverty is more maligned than the political machine ever was; yet it, too, is a persistent social phenomenon. Consequently, there may be some merit in applying functional analysis to poverty, in asking whether it also has positive functions that explain its persistence.

Merton defined functions as "those observed consequences [of a phenomenon] which make for the adaptation or adjustment of a given [social] system." I shall use a slightly different definition; instead of identifying functions for an entire social system, I shall identify them for the interest groups, socioeconomic classes, and other population aggregates with shared values that "inhabit" a social system. I suspect that in a modern heterogeneous society, few phenomena are functional or dysfunctional for the society as a whole, and that most result in benefits to some groups and costs to others. Nor are any phenomena indispensable; in most instances, one can suggest what Merton calls "functional alternatives" or equivalents for them, i.e., other social patterns or policies that achieve the same positive functions but avoid the dysfunction. [In the following discussion, positive functions will be abbreviated as functions and negative functions as dysfunctions. Functions and dysfunctions, in the planner's terminology, will be described as benefits and costs.]

Associating poverty with positive functions seems at first glance to be unimaginable. Of course, the slumlord and the loan shark are commonly known to profit from the existence of poverty, but they are viewed as evil men, so their activities are classified among the dysfunctions of poverty. However, what is less often recognized, at least by the conventional wisdom, is that poverty also makes possible the existence or expansion of respectable professions and occupations, for example, penology, criminology, social work, and public health. More recently, the poor have provided jobs for professional and para-professional "poverty warriors," and for journalists and social scientists, this author included, who have supplied the information demanded by the revival of public interest in poverty.

Clearly, then, poverty and the poor may well satisfy a number of positive functions for many nonpoor groups in American society. I shall describe 13 such functions—economic, social, and political—that seem to me most significant.

*First,* the existence of poverty ensures that society's "dirty work" will be done. Every society has such work: physically dirty or dangerous, temporary, dead-end and underpaid, undignified and menial jobs. Society can fill these jobs by paying higher wages than for "clean" work, or it can force people who have no other choice to do the dirty work—and at low wages. In America, poverty functions to provide a low-wage labor pool that is willing—or, rather, unable to be *un*willing—to perform dirty work at low cost. Indeed, this function of the poor is so important that in some Southern states, welfare payments have been cut off during the summer months when the poor are needed to work in the fields. Moreover, much of the debate about the Negative Income Tax and the Family Assistance Plan has concerned their impact on the work incentive, by which is actually meant the incentive of the poor to do the needed dirty work if the wages therefrom are no larger than the income grant. Many economic activities that involve dirty work depend on the poor for their existence: restaurants, hospitals, parts of the garment industry, and "truck farming," among others, could not persist in their present form without the poor.

*Second,* because the poor are required to work at low wages, they subsidize a variety of economic activities that benefit the affluent. For example, domestics subsidize the upper-middle and upper classes, making life easier for their employers and freeing affluent women for a variety of professional, cultural, civic, and partying activities. Similarly, because the poor pay a higher proportion of their income in property and sales taxes, among others, they subsidize many state and local governmental services that benefit more affluent groups. In addition, the poor support innovation in medical practice as patients in teaching and research hospitals and as guinea pigs in medical experiments.

*Third,* poverty creates jobs for a number of occupations and professions that serve or "service" the poor, or protect the rest of society from them. As already noted, penology would be minuscule without the poor, as would the police. Other activities and groups that flourish because of the existence of poverty are the numbers game, the sale of heroin and cheap wines and liquors, pentecostal ministers, faith healers, prostitutes, pawn shops, and the peacetime army, which recruits its enlisted men mainly from among the poor.

*Fourth,* the poor buy goods others do not want and thus prolong the economic usefulness of such goods—day-old bread, fruit and vegetables that would otherwise have to be thrown out, second hand clothes, and deteriorating automobiles and buildings. They also provide incomes for doctors, lawyers, teachers, and others who are too old, poorly trained, or incompetent to attract more affluent clients.

In addition to economic functions, the poor perform a number of social functions.

*Fifth,* the poor can be identified and punished as alleged or real deviants in order to uphold the legitimacy of conventional norms. To justify the desirability of hard work, thrift, honesty, and monogamy, for example, the defenders of these norms must be able to find people who can be accused of being lazy, spendthrift, dishonest, and promiscuous. Although there is some evidence that the poor are about as moral and law-abiding as anyone else, they are more likely than middle-class transgressors to be caught and punished when they participate in deviant acts. Moreover, they lack the political and cultural power to correct the stereotypes that other people hold of them and thus continue to be thought of as lazy, spendthrift, etc., by those who need living proof that moral deviance does not pay.

*Sixth,* and conversely, the poor offer vicarious participation to the rest of the population in the uninhibited sexual, alcoholic, and narcotic behavior in which they are alleged to participate and which, being freed from the constraints of affluence, they are often thought to enjoy more than the middle classes. Thus many people, some social scientists included, believe that the poor not only are more given to uninhibited behavior (which may be true, although it is often motivated by despair more than by lack of inhibition) but derive more pleasure from it than affluent people (which research by Lee Rainwater, Walter Miller, and others shows to be patently untrue). However, whether the poor actually have more sex and enjoy it more is irrelevant; so long as middle-class people believe this to be true, they can participate in it vicariously when instances are reported in factual or fictional form.

*Seventh,* the poor also serve a direct cultural function when culture created by or for them is adopted by the more affluent. The rich often collect artifacts from extinct folk cultures of poor people; and almost all Americans listen to the blues, Negro spirituals, and country music, which originated among the Southern poor. Recently they have enjoyed the rock styles that were born, like the Beatles, in the slums; and in the last year, poetry written by ghetto children has become popular in literary circles. The poor also serve as culture heroes, particularly, of course, to the left; but the hobo, the cowboy, the hipster, and the mythical prostitute with a heart of gold have performed this function for a variety of groups.

*Eighth,* poverty helps to guarantee the status of those who are not poor. In every hierarchical society someone has to be at the bottom; but in American society, in which social mobility is an important goal for many and people need to know where they stand, the poor function as a reliable and relatively permanent measuring rod for status comparisons. This is particularly true for the working class, whose politics is influenced by the need to maintain status distinctions between themselves and the poor, much as the aristocracy must find ways of distinguishing itself from the *nouveaux riches.*

*Ninth,* the poor also aid the upward mobility of groups just above them in the class hierarchy. Thus a goodly number of Americans have entered the middle class through the profits earned from the provision of goods and services in the slums, including illegal or non-respectable ones that upper-class and upper-middle-class businessmen shun because of their low prestige. As a result, members of almost every immigrant group have financed their upward mobility by providing slum housing, entertainment, gambling, narcotics, etc., to later arrivals—most recently to blacks and Puerto Ricans.

*Tenth,* the poor help to keep the aristocracy busy, thus justifying its continued existence. "Society" uses the poor as clients of settlement houses and beneficiaries of charity affairs; indeed, the aristocracy must have the poor to demonstrate its superiority over other elites who devote themselves to earning money.

*Eleventh,* the poor, being powerless, can be made to absorb the costs of change and growth in American society. During the nineteenth century, they did the backbreaking work that built the cities; today, they are pushed out of their neighborhoods to make room for "progress." Urban renewal projects to hold middle-class taxpayers in the city and expressways to enable suburbanites to commute downtown have typically been located in poor neighborhoods, since no other group will allow itself to be displaced. For the same reason, universities, hospitals, and civic centers also expand into land occupied by the poor. The major costs of the industrialization of agriculture have been borne by the poor, who are pushed off the land without recompense; and they have paid a large share of the human cost of the growth of American power overseas, for they have provided many of the foot soldiers for Vietnam and other wars.

*Twelfth,* the poor facilitate and stabilize the American political process. Because they vote and participate in politics less than other groups, the political system is often free to ignore them. Moreover, since they can rarely support Republicans, they often provide the Democrats with a captive constituency that has no other place to go. As a result, the Democrats can count on their votes, and be more responsive to voters—for example, the white working class—who might otherwise switch to the Republicans.

*Thirteenth,* the role of the poor in upholding conventional norms (see the *fifth* point, above) also has a significant political function. An economy based on the ideology of laissez-faire requires a deprived population that is allegedly unwilling to work or that can be considered inferior because it must accept charity or welfare in order to survive. Not only does the alleged moral deviancy of the poor reduce the moral pressure on the present political economy to eliminate poverty, but socialist alternatives can be made to look quite unattractive if those who will benefit most from them can be described as lazy, spendthrift, dishonest, and promiscuous.

## THE ALTERNATIVES

I have described 13 of the more important functions poverty and the poor satisfy in American society, enough to support the functionalist thesis that poverty, like any other social phenomenon, survives in part because it is useful to society or some of its parts. This analysis is not intended to suggest that because it is often functional, poverty *should* exist, or that it *must* exist. For one thing, poverty has many more dysfunctions than functions; for another, it is possible to suggest functional alternatives.

For example, society's dirty work could be done without poverty, either by automation or by paying "dirty workers" decent wages. Nor is it necessary for the poor to subsidize the many activities they support through their low-wage jobs. This would, however, drive up the costs of these activities, which would result in higher prices to their customers and clients. Similarly, many of the professionals who flourish because of the poor could be given other roles. Social workers could provide counseling to the affluent, as they prefer to do anyway; and the police could devote themselves to traffic and organized crime. Other roles would have to be found for badly trained or incompetent professionals now relegated to serving the poor, and someone else would have to pay their salaries. Fewer penologists would be employable, however. And pentecostal religion could probably not survive without the poor—nor would parts of the second- and third-hand-goods market. And in many cities, "used" housing that no one else wants would then have to be torn down at public expense.

Alternatives for the cultural functions of the poor could be found more easily and cheaply. Indeed, entertainers, hippies, and adolescents are already serving as the deviants needed to uphold traditional morality and as devotees of orgies to "staff" the fantasies of vicarious participation.

The status functions of the poor are another matter. In a hierarchical society, some people must be defined as inferior to everyone else with respect to a variety of attributes, but they need not be poor in the absolute sense. One could conceive of a society in which the "lower class," though last in the pecking order, received 75 percent of the median income, rather than 15–40 percent, as is now the case. Needless to say, this would require considerable income redistribution.

The contribution the poor make to the upward mobility of the groups that provide them with goods and services could also be maintained without the poor's having such low incomes. However, it is true that if the poor were more affluent, they would have access to enough capital to take over the provider role, thus competing with, and perhaps rejecting, the "outsiders." (Indeed, owing in part to antipoverty programs, this is already happening in a number of ghettos, where white storeowners are being replaced by blacks.) Similarly, if the poor were more affluent, they would make less willing clients for upper-class philanthropy, although some would still use settlement houses to achieve upward mobility, as they do now. Thus "Society" could continue to run its philanthropic activities.

The political functions of the poor would be more difficult to replace. With increased affluence the poor would probably obtain more political power and be more active politically. With higher incomes and more political power, the poor would be likely to resist paying the costs of growth and change. Of course, it is possible to imagine urban renewal and highway projects that properly reimbursed the displaced people, but such projects would then become considerably more expensive, and many might never be built. This, in turn, would reduce the comfort and convenience of those who now benefit from urban renewal and expressways. Finally, hippies could serve also as more deviants to justify the existing political economy—as they already do. Presumably, however, if poverty were eliminated, there would be fewer attacks on that economy.

In sum, then, many of the functions served by the poor could be replaced if poverty were eliminated, but almost always at higher costs to others, particularly more affluent others. Consequently, a functional analysis must conclude that poverty persists not only because it fulfills a number of positive functions but also because many of the functional alternatives to poverty would be quite dysfunctional for the affluent members of society. A functional analysis thus ultimately arrives at much the same conclusion as radical sociology, except that radical thinkers treat as manifest what I describe as latent: that social phenomena that are functional for affluent or powerful groups and dysfunctional for poor or powerless ones persist; that when the elimination of such phenomena through functional alternatives would generate dysfunctions for the affluent or powerful, they will continue to persist; and that phenomena like poverty can be eliminated only when they become dysfunctional for the affluent or powerful, or when the powerless can obtain enough power to change society.

## AUTHOR'S POSTSCRIPT, JULY 22, 1987

Over the years, this article has been interpreted as either a direct attack on functionalism or a tongue-in-cheek satirical comment on it. Neither interpretation is true. I wrote the article for two reasons. First and foremost, I wanted to point out that there are, unfortunately, positive functions of poverty which have to be dealt with by antipoverty policy. Second, I was trying to show that functionalism is not the inherently conservative approach for which it has often been criticized, but that it can be employed in liberal and radical analyses.

# Manifest and Latent Functions

Robert A. Merton

*Robert Merton made a major contribution to structural-functional theory by pointing out that social patterns have both manifest and latent functions. Manifest functions are those consequences that are familiar, planned, and generally recognized. Latent functions, on the other hand, are unfamiliar, unplanned, and widely overlooked. For this reason, Merton argued, comprehending latent functions is a special responsibility of sociologists. Merton illustrates this process by offering observation about the pattern of conspicuous consumption.*

. . .Armed with the concept of latent function, the sociologist extends his inquiry in those very directions which promise most for the theoretic development of the discipline. He examines the familiar (or planned) social practice to ascertain the latent, and hence generally unrecognized, functions (as well, of course, as the manifest functions). He considers, for example, the consequences of the new wage plan for, say, the trade union in which the workers are organized or the consequences of a propaganda program, not only for increasing its avowed purpose of stirring up patriotic fervor, but also for making large numbers of people reluctant to speak their minds when they differ with official policies, *etc.* In short, it is suggested that the *distinctive* intellectual contributions of the sociologist are found primarily in the study of unintended consequences (among which are latent functions) of social practices, as well as in the study of anticipated consequences (among which are manifest functions).

## [Illustration:] The Pattern of Conspicuous Consumption

The manifest purpose of buying consumption goods is, of course, the satisfaction of the needs for which these goods are explicitly designed. Thus, automobiles are obviously intended to provide a certain kind of transportation; candles, to provide light; choice articles of food to provide sustenance; rare art products to provide aesthetic pleasure. Since these products *do* have these uses, it was largely assumed that these encompass the range of socially significant functions. Veblen indeed suggests that this was ordinarily the prevailing view (in the pre-Veblenian era, of course): "The end of acquisition and accumulation is conventionally held to be the consumption of the goods accumulated. . .This is at least felt to be the economically legitimate end of acquisition, *which alone it is incumbent on the theory to take account of.*"[1]

However, says Veblen in effect, as sociologists we must go on to consider the latent functions of acquisition, accumulation, and consumption, and these latent functions are remote indeed from the manifest functions. "But, it is only when taken in a sense far removed from its naive meaning [*i.e.* manifest function] that the consumption of goods can be said to afford the incentive from which accumulation invariably proceeds." And among these latent functions, which help explain the persistence and the social location of the pattern of conspicuous consumption, is [the fact that] it. . . *results in a heightening or reaffirmation of social status.*

The Veblenian paradox is that people buy expensive goods not so much because they are superior but because they are expensive. For it is the latent equation ("costliness = mark of higher social status") which he singles out in his functional analysis, rather than the manifest equation ("costliness = excellence of the goods"). Not that he denies manifest functions *any* place in buttressing the pattern of conspicuous consumption. These, too, are operative. . . *It is only that these direct, manifest functions do not fully account for the prevailing patterns of consumption. Otherwise put, if the latent functions of status-enhancement or status-reaffirmation were removed from the patterns of conspicuous consumption, these patterns would undergo severe changes of a sort which the "conventional" economist could not foresee.*

## CRITICAL-THINKING QUESTIONS

1. *Why, according to Merton, is the study of latent functions one of the important tasks of sociologists?*
2. *Distinguish between the manifest and latent functions of owning designer clothing, a fine car, or a large home.*
3. *According to Thorstein Veblen, whom Merton cites in his analysis, does the higher cost of various goods typically attest to their higher quality? Why or why not?*
4. *Identify some of the manifest and latent functions of (a) a primary school spelling bee, (b) sports, and (c) attending college.*

## NOTE

1. Thorstein Veblen, *Theory of the Leisure Class* (1899) (New York: Vanguard Press. 1928). p. 25.

# Manifesto of the Communist Party

*Karl Marx and Frederick Engels*

*Karl Marx, collaborating with Friedrich Engels, produced the "Manifesto" in 1848. This document is a well-known statement about the origin of social conflict in the process of material production. The ideas of Marx and Engels have been instrumental in shaping the political lives of more than one-fifth of the world's population, and of course, they have been instrumental in the development of the social-conflict paradigm in sociology.*

## BOURGEOIS AND PROLETARIANS[1]

The history of all hitherto existing society[2] is the history of class struggles.

Freeman and slave, patrician and plebeian, lord and serf, guild-master[3] and journeyman, in a word, oppressor and oppressed, stood in constant opposition to one another, carried on an uninterrupted, now hidden, now open fight, a fight that each time ended, either in a revolutionary reconstitution of society at large, or in the common ruin of the contending classes.

In the earlier epochs of history, we find almost everywhere a complicated arrangement of society into various orders, a manifold gradation of social rank. In ancient Rome we have patricians, knights, plebeians, slaves; in the Middle Ages, feudal lords, vassals, guild-masters, journeymen, apprentices, serfs; in almost all of these classes, again, subordinate gradations.

The modern bourgeois society that has sprouted from the ruins of feudal society, has not done away with class antagonisms. It has but established new classes, new conditions of oppression, new forms of struggle in place of the old ones.

Our epoch, the epoch of the bourgeoisie, possesses, however, this distinctive feature; it has simplified the class antagonisms. Society as a whole is more and more splitting up into two great hostile camps, into two great classes directly facing each other—Bourgeoisie and Proletariat.

From the serfs of the Middle Ages sprang the chartered burghers of the earliest towns. From these burgesses the first elements of the bourgeoisie were developed.

The discovery of America, the rounding of the Cape, opened up fresh ground for the rising bourgeoisie. The East Indian and Chinese markets, the [colonization] of America, trade with the colonies, the increase in the means of exchange and in commodities generally, gave to commerce, to navigation, to industry, an impulse never before known, and thereby, to the revolutionary element in the tottering feudal society, a rapid development.

The feudal system of industry, under which industrial production was monopolized by closed guilds, now no longer sufficed for the growing wants of new markets. The manufacturing system took its place. The guild-masters were pushed on one side by the manufacturing middle class; division of labor between the different corporate guilds vanished in the face of division of labor in each single workshop.

Meantime the markets kept ever growing, the demand ever rising. Even manufacture no longer sufficed. Thereupon, steam and machinery revolutionized industrial production. The place of manufacture was taken by the giant, Modern Industry, the place of the industrial middle class, by industrial millionaires, the leaders of whole industrial armies, the modern bourgeois.

Modern industry has established the world-market, for which the discovery of America paved the way. This market has given an immense development to commerce, to navigation, to communication by land. This development has, in its turn, reacted on the extension of industry; and in proportion as industry, commerce, navigation, railways extended, in the same proportion the bourgeoisie developed, increased its capital, and pushed into the background every class handed down from the Middle Ages.

We see, therefore, how the modern bourgeoisie is itself the product of a long course of development, of a series of revolutions in the modes of production and of exchange.

Each step in the development of the bourgeoisie was accompanied by a corresponding political advance of that class. An oppressed class under the sway of the feudal nobility, an armed and self-governing association in the medieval commune[4] here independent urban republic (as in Italy and Germany), there taxable "third estate" of the monarchy (as in France), afterwards, in the period of manufacture proper, serving either the semi-feudal or the absolute monarchy as a counterpoise against the nobility, and, in fact, cornerstone of the great monarchies in general, the bourgeoisie has at last, since the establishment of Modern Industry and of the world market, conquered for itself, in the modern representative state, exclusive political sway. The executive of the modern State is but a committee for managing the common affairs of the whole bourgeoisie.

The bourgeoisie, historically, has played a most revolutionary part.

The bourgeoisie, wherever it has got the upper hand, has put an end to all feudal, patriarchal, idyllic relations. It has pitilessly torn asunder the motley feudal ties that bound man to his "natural superiors," and has left no other bond between man and man than naked self-interest, than callous "cash payment." It has drowned the most heavenly ecstasies of religious fervor, of chivalrous enthusiasm, of philistine sentimentalism, in the icy water of egotistical calculation. It has resolved personal worth into exchange value, and in place of the numberless indefeasible chartered freedoms, has set up that single, unconscionable freedom—Free Trade. In one word, for exploitation, veiled by religious and political illusions, it has substituted naked, shameless, direct, brutal exploitation.

The bourgeoisie has stripped of its halo every occupation hitherto honoured and looked up to with reverent awe. It has converted the physician, the lawyer, the priest, the poet, the man of science, into its paid [wage-laborers].

The bourgeoisie has torn away from the family its sentimental veil, and has reduced the family relation to a mere money relation.

The bourgeoisie has disclosed how it came to pass that the brutal display of vigour in the Middle Ages, which Reactionists so much admire, found its fitting complement in the most slothful indolence. It has been the first to show what man's activity can bring about. It has accomplished wonders far surpassing Egyptian pyramids, Roman aqueducts, and Gothic cathedrals; it has conducted expeditions that put in the shade all former Exoduses of nations and crusades.

The bourgeoisie cannot exist without constantly revolutionizing the instruments of production, and thereby the relations of production, and with them the whole relations of society. Conservation of the old modes of production in unaltered form, was, on the contrary, the first condition of existence for all earlier industrial classes. Constant revolutionizing of production, uninterrupted disturbance of all social conditions, everlasting uncertainty and agitation distinguish the bourgeois epoch from all earlier ones. All fixed, fast-frozen relations, with their train of ancient and venerable prejudices and opinions, are swept away, all new-formed ones become antiquated before they can ossify. All that is solid melts into air, all that is holy is profaned, and man is at last compelled to face with sober senses, his real conditions of life, and his relations with his kind.

The need of a constantly expanding market for its products chases the bourgeoisie over the whole surface of the globe. It must nestle everywhere, settle everywhere, establish [connections] everywhere.

The bourgeoisie has through its exploitation of the world-market given a cosmopolitan character to production and consumption in every country. To the great chagrin of Reactionists, it has drawn from under the feet of industry the national ground on which it stood. All old-established national industries have been destroyed or are daily being destroyed. They are dislodged by new industries, whose introduction becomes a life and death question for all civilized nations, by industries that no longer work up indigenous raw material, but raw material drawn from the remotest zones; industries whose products are consumed, not only at home, but in every quarter of the globe. In place of the old wants, satisfied by the productions of the country, we find new wants, requiring for their satisfaction the products of distant lands and climes. In place of the old local and national seclusion and self-sufficiency we have intercourse in every direction, universal interdependence of nations. And as in material, so also in intellectual production. The intellectual creations of individual nations become common property. National one-sidedness and narrow-mindedness become more and more impossible, and from the numerous national and local literatures there arises a world-literature.

The bourgeoisie, by the rapid improvement of all instruments of production, by the immensely facilitated means of communication, draws all, even the most barbarian, nations into civilization. The cheap prices of its commodities are the heavy artillery with which it batters down all Chinese walls, with which it forces the barbarians' intensely obstinate hatred of foreigners to capitulate. It compels all nations, on pain of extinction, to adopt the bourgeois mode of production; it compels them to introduce what it calls civilization into their midst, i.e., to become bourgeois themselves. In a word, it creates a world after its own image.

The bourgeoisie has subjected the country to the rule of the towns. It has created enormous cities, has greatly increased the urban population as compared with the rural, and has thus rescued a considerable part of the population from the idiocy of rural life. Just as it has made the country dependent on the towns, so it has made barbarian and semi-barbarian countries dependent on the civilized ones, nations of peasants on nations of bourgeois, the East on the West.

The bourgeoisie keeps more and more doing away with the scattered state of the population, of the means of production, and of property. It has agglomerated population, centralized means of production, and has concentrated property in a few hands. The necessary consequence of this was political centralization. Independent, or but loosely connected provinces, with separate interests, laws, governments, and systems of taxation, became lumped together into one nation, with one government, one code of laws, one national class interest, one frontier, and one customs-tariff.

The bourgeoisie, during its rule of scarce one hundred years, has created more massive and more colossal productive forces than have all preceding generations together. Subjection of Nature's forces to man, machinery, application of chemistry to industry and agriculture, steam-navigation, railways, electric telegraphs, clearing of whole continents for cultivation, canalization of rivers, whole populations conjured out of the ground—what earlier century had even a presentiment that such productive forces slumbered in the lap of social labour?

We see then: The means of production and of exchange, on whose foundation the bourgeoisie built itself up, were generated in feudal society. At a certain stage in the development of these means of production and of exchange, the conditions under which feudal society produced and exchanged, the feudal organization of agriculture and manufacturing industry, in one word, the feudal relations of property became no longer compatible with the already developed productive forces; they became so many fetters. They had to be burst asunder; they were burst asunder.

Into their places stepped free competition, accompanied by a social and political constitution adapted to it, and by the economic and political sway of the bourgeois class.

A similar movement is going on before our own eyes. Modern bourgeois society with its relations of production, of exchange and of property, a society that has conjured up such gigantic means of production and of exchange, is like the sorcerer, who is no longer able to control the powers of the nether world whom he has called up by his spells. For many a decade past the history of industry and commerce is but the history of the revolt of modern productive forces against modern conditions of production, against the property relations that are the conditions for the existence of the bourgeoisie and its rule. It is enough to mention the commercial crises that by their periodical return put on trial, each time more threateningly, the existence of the entire bourgeois society. In these crises a great part not only of the existing products, but also of the previously created productive forces, are periodically destroyed. In these crises there breaks out an epidemic that, in all earlier epochs, would have seemed an absurdity—the epidemic of over-production. Society suddenly finds itself put back into a new state of momentary barbarism; it appears as if a famine, a universal war of devastation had cut off the supply of every means of subsistence; industry and commerce seem to be destroyed; and why? Because there is too much civilization, too much means of subsistence, too much industry, too much commerce. The productive forces at the disposal of society no longer tend to further the development of the conditions of bourgeois property; on the contrary, they have become too powerful for these conditions, by which they are fettered, and no sooner do they overcome these fetters than they bring disorder into the whole of bourgeois society, endanger the existence of bourgeois property. The conditions of bourgeois society are too narrow to comprise the wealth created by them. And how does the bourgeoisie get over these crises? On the one hand, by enforced destruction of a mass of productive forces; on the other, by the conquest of new markets, and by the more thorough exploitation of the old ones. That is to say, by paving the way for more extensive and more destructive crises, and by diminishing the means whereby crises are prevented.

The weapons with which the bourgeoisie felled feudalism to the ground are now turned against the bourgeoisie itself.

But not only has the bourgeoisie forged the weapons that bring death to itself; it has also called into existence the men who are to wield those weapons—the modern working class—the proletarians.

In proportion as the bourgeoisie, i.e., capital, is developed, in the same proportion is the proletariat, the modern working class, developed—a class of laborers who live only so long as they find work and who find work only so long as their labor increases capital. These laborers, who must sell themselves piecemeal, are a commodity, like every other article of commerce, and are consequently exposed to all the vicissitudes of competition, to all the fluctuations of the market.

Owing to the extensive use of machinery and to division of labor, the work of the proletarians has lost all individual character, and, consequently, all charm for the workman. He becomes an appendage of the machine, and it is only the most simple, most monotonous, and most easily acquired knack that is required of him. Hence, the cost of production of a workman is restricted, almost entirely, to the means of subsistence that he requires for his maintenance, and for the propagation of his race. But the price of a commodity, and therefore also of labor, is equal to its cost of production. In proportion, therefore, as the repulsiveness of the work increases, the wage decreases. Nay more, in proportion as the use of machinery and division of labor increases, in the same proportion the burden of toil also increases, whether by prolongation of the working hours, by increase of the work enacted in a given time, or by increased speed of the machinery, etc.

Modern industry has converted the little workshop of the patriarchal master into the great factory of the industrial capitalist. Masses of laborers, crowded into the factory, are organized like soldiers. As privates of the industrial army they are placed under the command of a perfect hierarchy of officers and sergeants. Not only are they slaves of the bourgeois class, and of the bourgeois State, they are daily and hourly enslaved by the machine, by the over-looker, and, above all, by the individual bourgeois manufacturer himself. The more openly this despotism proclaims gain to be its end and aim, the more petty, the more hateful and the more embittering it is.

The less the skill and exertion of strength implied in manual labor, in other words, the more modern industry develops, the more is the labor of men superseded by that of women. Differences of age and sex have no longer any distinctive social validity for the working class. All are instruments of labor, more or less expensive to use, according to their age and sex.

No sooner is the exploitation of the laborer by the manufacturer, so far, at an end, that he receives his wages in cash, than he is set upon by the other portions of the bourgeoisie, the landlord, the shopkeeper, the pawnbroker, etc.

The lower strata of the middle class—the small tradespeople, shopkeepers, and retired tradesmen generally, the handicraftsmen and peasants—all these sink gradually into the proletariat, partly because their diminutive capital does not suffice for the scale on which Modern Industry is carried on, and is swamped in the competition with the large capitalists, partly because their specialized skill is rendered worthless by new methods of production. Thus the proletariat is recruited from all classes of the population.

The proletariat goes through various stages of development. With its birth begins its struggle with the bourgeoisie. At first the contest is carried on by individual laborers, then by the workpeople of a factory, then by the operatives of one trade, in one locality, against the individual bourgeois who directly exploits them. They direct their attacks not against the bourgeois conditions of production, but against the instruments of production themselves; they destroy imported wares that compete with their labor, they smash to pieces machinery, they set factories ablaze, they seek to restore by force the vanished status of the workman of the Middle Ages.

At this stage the laborers still form an incoherent mass scattered over the whole country, and broken up by their mutual competition. If anywhere they unite to form more compact bodies, this is not yet the consequence of their own active union, but of the union of the bourgeoisie, which class, in order to attain its own political ends, is compelled to set the whole proletariat in motion, and is moreover, yet, for a time able to do so. At this stage, therefore, the proletarians do not fight their enemies, but the enemies of their enemies, the remnants of absolute monarchy, the landowners, the non-industrial bourgeois, the petty bourgeoisie. Thus the whole historical movement is concentrated in the hands of the bourgeoisie; every victory so obtained is a victory for the bourgeoisie.

But with the development of industry the proletariat not only increases in number; it becomes concentrated in greater masses, its strength grows, and it feels that strength more. The various interests and conditions of life within the ranks of the proletariat are more and more equalized, in proportion as machinery obliterates all distinctions of labor and nearly everywhere reduces wages to the same low level. The growing competition among the bourgeois, and the resulting commercial crises, make the wages of the workers ever more fluctuating. The unceasing improvement of machinery, ever more rapidly developing, makes their livelihood more and more precarious; the collisions between individual workmen and individual bourgeois take more and more the character of collisions between two classes. Thereupon the workers begin to form combinations (Trade Unions) against the bourgeoisie; they club together in order to keep up the rate of wages; they found permanent associations in order to make provisions beforehand for these occasional revolts. Here and there the contest breaks out into riots.

Now and then the workers are victorious, but only for a time. The real fruit of their battles lies, not in the immediate result, but in the ever expanding union of the workers. This union is helped on by the improved means of communication that are created by modern industry, and that place the workers of different localities in contact with one another. It was just this contact that was needed to centralize the numerous local struggles, all of the same character, into one national struggle between classes. But every class struggle is a political struggle. And that union, to attain which the burghers of the Middle Ages, with their miserable highways, required centuries, the modern proletarians, thanks to railways, achieve in a few years.

This organization of the proletarians into a class, and consequently into a political party, is continually being upset again by the competition between the workers themselves. But it ever rises up again, stronger, firmer, mightier. It compels legislative recognition of particular interests of the workers, by taking advantage of the divisions among the bourgeoisie itself. Thus the ten-hours' bill in England was carried.

Altogether collisions between the classes of the old society further, in many ways, the course of development of the proletariat. The bourgeoisie finds itself involved in a constant battle. At first with the aristocracy; later on, with those portions of the bourgeoisie itself, whose interests have become antagonistic to the progress of industry; at all times, with the bourgeoisie of foreign countries. In all these battles it sees itself compelled to appeal to the proletariat, to ask for its help, and thus, to drag it into the political arena. The bourgeoisie itself, therefore, supplies the proletariat with its own elements of political and general education, in other words, it furnishes the proletariat with weapons for fighting the bourgeoisie.

Further, as we have already seen, entire sections of the ruling classes are, by the advance of industry, precipitated into the proletariat, or are at least threatened in their conditions of existence. These also supply the proletariat with fresh elements of enlightenment and progress.

Finally, in times when the class-struggle nears the decisive hour, the process of dissolution going on within the ruling class, in fact within the whole range of old society, assumes such a violent, glaring character, that a small section of the ruling class cuts itself adrift, and joins the revolutionary class, the class that holds the future in its hands. Just as, therefore, at an earlier period, a section of the nobility went over to the bourgeoisie, so now a portion of the bourgeoisie goes over to the proletariat, and in particular, a portion of the bourgeois ideologists, who have raised themselves to the level of comprehending theoretically the historical movements as a whole.

Of all the classes that stand face to face with the bourgeoisie today, the proletariat alone is a really revolutionary class. The other classes decay and finally disappear in the face of modern industry; the proletariat is its special and essential product.

The lower-middle class, the small manufacturer, the shopkeeper, the artisan, the peasant, all these fight against the bourgeoisie, to save from extinction their existence as fractions of the middle class. They are therefore not revolutionary, but conservative. Nay more, they are reactionary, for they try to roll back the wheel of history. If by chance they are revolutionary, they are so, only in view of their impending transfer into the proletariat, they thus defend not their present, but their future interests, they desert their own standpoint to place themselves at that of the proletariat.

The "dangerous class," the social scum, that passively rotting mass thrown off by the lowest layers of old society, may, here and there, be swept into the movement by a proletarian revolution; its conditions of life, however, prepare it far more for the part of a bribed tool of reactionary intrigue.

In the conditions of the proletariat, those of old society at large are already virtually swamped. The proletarian is without property; his relation to his wife and children has no longer anything in common with bourgeois family-relations; modern industrial labor, modern subjection to capital, the same in England as in France, in America as in Germany, has stripped him of every trace of national character. Law, morality, religion, are to him so many bourgeois prejudices, behind which lurk in ambush just as many bourgeois interests.

All the preceding classes that got the upper hand, sought to fortify their already acquired status by subjecting society at large to their conditions of appropriation. The proletarians cannot become masters of the productive forces of society, except by abolishing their own previous mode of appropriation, and thereby also every other previous mode of appropriation. They have nothing of their own to secure and to fortify; their mission is to destroy all previous securities for, and insurances of, individual property.

All previous historical movements were movements of minorities, or in the interest of minorities. The proletarian movement is the self-conscious, independent movement of the immense majority, in the interest of the immense majority. The proletariat, the lowest stratum of our present society, cannot stir, cannot raise itself up, without the whole superincumbent strata of official society being sprung into the air.

Though not in substance, yet in form, the struggle of the proletariat with the bourgeoisie is at first a national struggle. The proletariat of each country must, of course, first of all settle matters with its own bourgeoisie.

In depicting the most general phases of the development of the proletariat, we traced the more or less veiled civil war, raging within existing society, up to the point where that war breaks out into open revolution, and where the violent overthrow of the bourgeoisie, lays the foundation for the sway of the proletariat.

Hitherto, every form of society has been based, as we have already seen, on the antagonism of oppressing and oppressed classes. But in order to oppress a class, certain conditions must be assured to it under which it can, at least, continue its slavish existence. The serf, in the period of serfdom, raised himself to membership in the commune, just as the petty bourgeois, under the yoke of feudal absolutism, managed to develop into a bourgeois. The modern laborer, on the contrary, instead of rising with the progress of industry, sinks deeper and deeper below the conditions of existence of his own class. He becomes a pauper, and pauperism develops more rapidly than population and wealth. And here it becomes evident, that the bourgeoisie is unfit any longer to be the ruling class in society, and to impose its conditions of existence upon society as an overriding law. It is unfit to rule, because it is incompetent to assure an existence to its slave within his slavery, because it cannot help letting him sink into such a state, that it has to feed him, instead of being fed by him. Society can no longer live under this bourgeoisie, in other words, its existence is no longer compatible with society.

The essential condition for the existence, and for the sway of the bourgeois class, is the formation and augmentation of capital; the condition for capital is wage-labor. Wage-labor rests exclusively on competition between the laborers. The advance of industry, whose involuntary promoter is the bourgeoisie, replaces the isolation of the laborers, due to competition, by their involuntary combination, due to association. The development of Modern Industry, therefore, cuts from under its feet the very foundation on which the bourgeoisie produces and appropriates products. What the bourgeoisie therefore produces, above all, are its own grave-diggers. Its fall and the victory of the proletariat are equally inevitable.

## CRITICAL-THINKING QUESTIONS

1. *What are the distinguishing factors of "class conflict"? How does this differ from other kinds of conflict, as between individuals or nations?*
2. *Why do Marx and Engels argue that understanding society in the present requires investigating the society of the past?*
3. *On what grounds did Marx and Engels* praise *industrial capitalism? On what grounds did they* condemn *the system?*

## NOTES

1. By *bourgeoisie* is meant the class of modern capitalists, owners of the means of social production and employers of wage-labor. By proletariat, the class of modern wage-laborers who, having no means of production of their own, are reduced to selling their labor-power in order to live.
2. That is, all written history. In 1847, the prehistory of society, the social organization existing previous to recording history, was all but unknown. Since then, Haxthausen discovered common ownership of land in Russia. Maurer proved it to be the social foundation from which all Teutonic races started in history, and by and bye village communities were found to be, or to have been, the primitive form of society everywhere from India to Ireland. The inner organization of this primitive Communistic society was laid bare, in its typical form, by Morgan's crowning discovery of the true nature of the gens and its relation to the tribe. With the dissolution of these primeval communities society begins to be differentiated into separate and finally antagonistic classes. I have attempted to retrace this process of dissolution in: "Der Ursprung der Familie des, Privatelgenthums und des Staats," 2d ed., Stuttgart 1886.
3. Guild-master, that is a full member of a guild, a master within, not a head of, a guild.
4. "Commune" was the name taken, in France, by the nascent towns even before they had conquered from their feudal lords and masters, local self-government and political rights as "the Third Estate." Generally speaking, for the economical development of the bourgeoisie, England is here taken as the typical country, for its political development, France.

# Alienated Labor

## *Karl Marx*

*The human species, argues Karl Marx, is social by nature and expresses that social nature in the act of production. But within the capitalist economic system, Marx claims., the process of production does not affirm human nature but denies it. The result is what he terms "alienated labor."*

. . . [We] have shown that the worker sinks to the level of a commodity, and to a most miserable commodity; that the misery of the worker increases with the power and volume of his production, that the necessary result of competition is the accumulation of capital in a few hands, and thus a restoration of monopoly in a more terrible form; and finally that the distinction between capitalist and landlord, and between agricultural laborer and industrial worker, must disappear, and the whole of society divide into the two classes of property *owners* and *propertyless* workers. . .

Thus we have now to grasp the real connexion between this whole system of alienation—private property, acquisitiveness, the separation of labor, capital and land, exchange and competition, value and the devaluation of man, monopoly and competition—and the system of *money*. . . .

We shall begin from a *contemporary* economic fact. The worker becomes poorer the more wealth he produces and the more his production increases in power and extent. The worker becomes an ever cheaper commodity the more goods he creates. The *devaluation* of the human world increases in direct relation with the *increase in value* of the world of things. Labor does not only create goods; it also produces itself and the worker as a *commodity*, and indeed in the same proportion as it produces goods.

This fact simply implies that the object produced by labor, its product, now stands opposed to it as an *alien being*, as a *power independent* of the producer. The product of labor is labor which has been embodied in an object and turned into a physical thing; this product is an *objectification* of labor. The performance of work is at the same time its objectification. The performance of work appears in the sphere of political economy as a *vitiation*[1] of the worker, objectification as a *loss* and as *servitude to the object*, and appropriation as *alienation.*

So much does the performance of work appear as vitiation that the worker is vitiated to the point of starvation. So much does objectification appear as loss of the object that the worker is deprived of the most essential things not only of life but also of work. Labor itself becomes an object which he can acquire only by the greatest effort and with unpredictable interruptions. So much does the appropriation of the object appear as alienation that the more objects the worker produces the fewer he can possess and the more he falls under the domination of his product, of capital.

All these consequences follow from the fact that the worker is related to the *product of his labor* as to an *alien* object. For it is clear on this presupposition that the more the worker expends himself in work the more powerful becomes the world of objects which he creates in face of himself, the poorer he becomes in his inner life, and the less he belongs to himself. It is just the same as in religion. The more of himself man attributes to God the less he has left in himself. The worker puts his life into the object, and his life then belongs no longer to himself but to the object. The greater his activity, therefore, the less he possesses. What is embodied in the product of his labor is no longer his own. The greater this product is, therefore, the more he is diminished. The *alienation* of the worker in his product means not only that his labor becomes an object, assumes an *external* existence, but that it exists independently, *outside himself* and alien to him, and that it stands opposed to him as an autonomous power. The life which he has given to the object sets itself against him as an alien and hostile force.

Let us now examine more closely the phenomenon of *objectification*; the worker's production and the *alienation* and *loss* of the object it produces, which is involved in it. The worker can create nothing without *nature*, without the sensuous *external world*. The latter is the material in which his labor is realized, in which it is active, out of which and through which it produces things.

But just as nature affords the *means of existence* of labor, in the sense that labor cannot *live* without objects upon which it can be exercised, so also it provides the *means of existence* in a narrower sense; namely the means of physical existence for the *worker* himself. Thus, the more the worker *appropriates* the external world of sensuous nature by his labor the more he deprives himself of *means of existence*, in two respects: First, that the sensuous external world becomes progressively less an object belonging to his labor or a means of existence of his labor, and secondly, that it becomes progressively less a means of existence in the direct sense, a means for the physical subsistence of the worker.

In both respects, therefore, the worker becomes a slave of the object; first, in that he receives an *object of work*, i.e. receives *work*, and secondly, in that he receives *means of subsistence*. Thus the object enables him to exist, first as a *worker* and secondly, as a *physical subject*. The culmination of this enslavement is that he can only maintain himself as a *physical subject* so far as he is a worker, and that it is only as a *physical subject* that he is a worker.

(The alienation of the worker in his object is expressed as follows in the laws of political economy: The more the worker produces the less he has to consume; the more value he creates the more worthless he becomes; the more refined his product the more crude and misshapen the worker; the more civilized the product the more barbarous the worker; the more powerful the work the more feeble the worker; the more the work manifests intelligence the more the worker declines in intelligence and becomes a slave of nature.)

*Political economy conceals the alienation in the nature of labor insofar as it does not examine the direct relationship between the worker (work) and production.* Labor certainly produces marvels for the rich but it produces privation for the worker. It produces palaces, but hovels for the worker. It produces beauty, but deformity for the worker. It replaces labor by machinery, but it casts some of the workers back into a barbarous kind of work and turns the others into machines. It produces intelligence, but also stupidity and cretinism for the workers.

*The direct relationship of labor to its products is the relationship of the worker to the objects of his production.* The relationship of property owners to the objects of production and to production itself is merely a *consequence* of this first relationship and confirms it. We shall consider this second aspect later.

Thus, when we ask what is the important relationship of labor, we are concerned with the relationship of the *worker* to production.

So far we have considered the alienation of the worker only from one aspect; namely, *his relationship with the products of his labor.* However, alienation appears not merely in the result but also in the *process of production,* within *productive activity* itself. How could the worker stand in an alien relationship to the product of his activity if he did not alienate himself in the act of production itself? The product is indeed only the *résumé* of activity, of production. Consequently, if the product of labor is alienation, production itself must be active alienation—the alienation of activity and the activity of alienation. The alienation of the object of labor merely summarizes the alienation in the work activity itself.

What constitutes the alienation of labor? First, that the work is *external* to the worker, that it is not part of his nature; and that, consequently, he does not fulfill himself in his work but denies himself, has a feeling of misery rather than well-being, does not develop freely his mental and physical energies but is physically exhausted and mentally debased. The worker, therefore, feels himself at home only during his leisure time, whereas at work he feels homeless. His work is not voluntary but imposed, *forced labor.* It is not the satisfaction of a need, but only a *means* for satisfying other needs. Its alien character is clearly shown by the fact that as soon as there is no physical or other compulsion it is avoided like the plague. External labor, labor in which man alienates himself, is a labor of self-sacrifice, of mortification. Finally, the external character of work for the worker is shown by the fact that it is not his own work but work for someone else, that in work he does not belong to himself but to an other person. . . .

We arrive at the result that man (the worker) feels himself to be freely active only in his animal functions—eating, drinking and procreating, or at most also in his dwelling and in personal adornment—while in his human functions he is reduced to an animal. The animal becomes human and the human becomes animal.

Eating, drinking, and procreating are of course also genuine human functions. But abstractly considered, apart from the environment of human activities, and turned into final and sole ends, they are animal functions.

We have now considered the act of alienation of practical human activity, labor, from two aspects; (1) the relationship of the worker to the *product of labor* as an alien object which dominates him. This relationship is at the same time the relationship to the sensuous external world, to natural objects, as an alien and hostile world; (2) the relationship of labor to the *act of production* within *labor*. This is the relationship of the worker to his own activity as something alien and not belonging to him, activity as suffering (passivity), strength as powerlessness, creation as emasculation, the *personal* physical and mental energy of the worker, his personal life (for what is life but activity?), as an activity which is directed against himself, independent of him and not belonging to him. This is *self-alienation* as against the [afore]mentioned alienation of the *thing*.

We have now to infer a third characteristic of *alienated labor* from the two we have considered.

Man is a species-being not only in the sense that he makes the community (his own as well as those of other things) his object both practically and theoretically, but also (and this is simply another expression for the same thing) in the sense that he treats himself as the present, living species, as a *universal* and consequently free being.

Species-life, for man as for animals, has its physical basis in the fact that man (like animals) lives from inorganic nature, and since man is more universal than an animal so the range of inorganic nature from which he lives is more universal. Plants, animals, minerals, air, light, etc. constitute, from the theoretical aspect, a part of human consciousness as objects of natural science and art; they are man's spiritual inorganic nature, his intellectual means of life, which he must first prepare for enjoyment and perpetuation. So also, from the practical aspect, they form a part of human life and activity. In practice man lives only from these natural products, whether in the form of food, heating, clothing, housing, etc. The universality of man appears in practice in the universality which makes the whole of nature into his inorganic body: (1) as a direct means of life; and equally (2) as the material object and instrument of his life activity. Nature is the inorganic body of man; that is to say nature, excluding the human body itself. To say that man *lives* from nature means that nature is his *body* with which he must remain in a continuous interchange in order not to die. The statement that the physical and mental life of man, and nature, are interdependent means simply that nature is interdependent with itself, for man is a part of nature.

Since alienated labor (1) alienates nature from man; and (2) alienates man from himself, from his own active function, his life activity; so it alienates him from the species. It makes *species-life* into a means of individual life. In the first place it alienates species-life and individual life, and secondly, it turns the latter, as an abstraction, into the purpose of the former, also in its abstract and alienated form.

For labor, *life activity, productive life*, now appear to man only as *means* for the satisfaction of a need, the need to maintain his physical existence. Productive life is, however, species-life. It is life creating life. In the type of life activity resides the whole character of a species, its species-character; and free, conscious activity is the species-character of human beings. Life itself appears only as a *means of life*.

The animal is one with its life activity. It does not distinguish the activity from itself. It is *its activity*. But man makes his life activity itself an object of his will and consciousness. He has a conscious life activity. It is not a determination with which he is completely identified. Conscious life activity distinguishes man from the life activity of animal. Only for this reason is he a species being. Or rather, he is only a self-conscious being, i.e., his own life is an object for him, because he is a species-being. Only for this reason is his activity free activity. Alienated labor reserves the relationship, in that man because he is a self-conscious being makes his life activity, his *being*, only a means for his *existence*.

## CRITICAL-THINKING QUESTIONS

1. *Does Marx argue that work is inevitably alienating? Why does work within a capitalist economy produce alienation?*
2. *In what different respects does labor within capitalism alienate the worker?*
3. *Based on this analysis, under what conditions do you think Marx would argue that labor is not alienating?*

## NOTE

1. Debasement.

SOURCE: "Alienated Labor" by Karl Marx in *Karl Marx: Early Writings*, trans. and ed. T. B. Bottomore (New York: McGraw-Hill, 1963), pp. 120–27. Reprinted by permission of McGraw-Hill.

# The Presentation of Self

*Erving Goffman*

*Face-to-face interaction is a complex process by which people both convey and receive information about each other. In this selection, Erving Goffman presents basic observations about how everyone tries to influence how others perceive them. In addition, he suggests ways in which people can evaluate how honestly others present themselves.*

When an individual enters the presence of others, they commonly seek to acquire information about him or to bring into play information about him already possessed. They will be interested in his general socioeconomic status, his conception of self, his attitude toward them, his competence, his trust worthiness, etc. Although some of this information seems to be sought almost as an end in itself, there are usually quite practical reasons for acquiring it. Information about the individual helps to define the situation, enabling others to know in advance what he will expect of them and what they may expect of him. Informed in these ways, the others will know how best to act in order to call forth a desired response from him.

For those present, many sources of information become accessible and many carriers (or "sign-vehicles") become available for conveying this in information. If unacquainted with the individual, observers can glean clues from his conduct and appearance which allow them to apply their previous experience with individuals roughly similar to the one before them or, more important, to apply untested stereotypes to him. They can also assume from past experience that only individuals of a particular kind are likely to be found in a given social setting. They can rely on what the individual says about himself or on documentary evidence he provides as to who and what he is. If they know, or know of, the individual by virtue of experience prior to the interaction, they can rely on assumptions as to the persistence and generality of psychological traits as a means of predicting his present and future behavior.

However, during the period in which the individual is in the immediate presence of the others, few events may occur which directly provide the others with the conclusive information they will need if they are to direct wisely their own activity. Many crucial facts lie beyond the time and place of interaction or lie concealed within it. For example, the "true" or "real" attitudes, beliefs, and emotions of the individual can be ascertained only indirectly, through his avowals or through what appears to be involuntary expressive behavior. Similarly, if the individual offers the others a product or service, they will often find that during the interaction there will be no time and place immediately available for eating the pudding that the proof can be found in. They will be forced to accept some events as conventional or natural signs of something not directly available to the senses. In Ichheiser's terms,[1] the individual will have to act so that he intentionally or unintentionally *expresses* himself, and the others will in turn have to be *impressed* in some way by him.

The expressiveness of the individual (and therefore his capacity to give impressions) appears to involve two radically different kinds of sign activity: the expression that he *gives*, and the expression that he gives *off*. The first involves verbal symbols or their substitutes which he uses admittedly and solely to convey the information that he and the others are known to attach to these symbols. This is communication in the traditional and narrow sense. The second involves a wide range of action that others can treat as symptomatic of the actor, the expectation being that the action was performed for reasons other than the information conveyed in this way. As we shall have to see, this distinction has an only initial validity. The individual does of course intentionally convey misinformation by means of both of these types of communication, the first involving deceit, the second feigning.

. . . Let us now turn from the others to the point of view of the individual who presents himself before them. He may wish them to think highly of him, or to think that he thinks highly of them, or to perceive how in fact he feels toward them, or to obtain no clear-cut impression; he may wish to ensure sufficient harmony so that the interaction can be sustained, or to defraud, get rid of, confuse, mislead, antagonize, or insult them. Regardless of the particular objective which the individual has in mind and of his motive for having this objective, it will be in his interests to control the conduct of the others, especially their responsive treatment of him. This control is achieved largely by influencing the definition of the situation which the others come to formulate, and he can influence this definition by expressing himself in such a way as to give them the kind of impression that will lead them to act voluntarily in accordance with his own plan. Thus, when an individual appears in the presence of others, there will usually be some reason for him to mobilize his activity so that it will convey an impression to others which it is in his interests to convey. Since a girl's dormitory mates will glean evidence of her popularity from the calls she receives on the phone, we can suspect that some girls will arrange for calls to be made, and Willard Waller's finding can he anticipated:

> It has been reported by many observers that a girl who is called to the telephone in the dormitories will often allow herself to be called several times, in order to give all the other girls ample opportunity to hear her paged.[2]

Of the two kinds of communication—expressions given and expressions given off—this report will be primarily concerned with the latter, with the more theatrical and contextual kind, the non-verbal, presumably unintentional kind, whether this communication be purposely engineered or not. As an example of what we must try to examine, I would like to cite at length a novelistic incident in which Preedy, a vacationing Englishman, makes his first appearance on the beach of his summer hotel in Spain:

> But in any case he took care to avoid catching anyone's eye. First of all, he had to made it clear to those potential companions of his holiday that they were of no concern to him whatsoever. He stared through them, round them, over them—eyes lost in space. The beach might have been empty. If by chance a ball was thrown his way, he looked surprised; then let a smile of amusement lighten his face (Kindly Preedy), looked round dazed to see that there *were* people on the beach, tossed it back with a smile to himself and not a smile *at* the people, and then resumed carelessly his nonchalant survey of space.
>
> But it was time to institute a little parade, the parade of the Ideal Preedy. By devious handlings he gave any who wanted to look a chance to see the title of his book—a Spanish translation of Homer, classic thus, but not daring, cosmopolitan too and then gathered to together his beach-wrap and bag into a neat sand-resistant pile (Methodical and Sensible Preedy), rose slowly to stretch at ease his huge frame (Big-Cat Preedy), and tossed aside his sandals (Carefree Preedy, after all).
>
> The marriage of Preedy and the sea! There were alternative rituals. The first involved the stroll that turns into a run and a dive straight into the water, thereafter smoothing, into a strong splashless crawl towards the horizon. But of course not really to the horizon. Quite suddenly he would turn on to his back and thrash great white splashes with his legs, somehow thus showing that he could have swum further had he wanted to, and then would stand up a quarter out of water for all to see who it was.
>
> The alternative course was simpler, it avoided the cold-water shock and it avoided the risk of appearing too high-spirited. The point was to appear to be so used to the sea, the Mediterranean, and this particular beach, that one might as well be in the sea as out of it. It involved a slow stroll down and into the edge of the water—not even noticing his toes were wet, land and water all the same to *him!*—with his eyes up at the sky gravely surveying portents, invisible to others, of the weather (Local Fisherman Preedy).[3]

The novelist means us to see that Preedy is improperly concerned with the extensive impressions he feels his sheer bodily action is giving off to those around him. We can malign Preedy further by assuming that he has acted merely in order to give a particular impression, that this is a false impression, and that the others present receive either no impression at all, or, worse still, the impression that Preedy is affectedly trying to cause them to receive this particular impression. But the important point for us here is that the kind of impression Preedy thinks he is making is in fact the kind of impression that others correctly and incorrectly glean from someone in their midst. . . .

There is one aspect of the others' response that bears special comment here. Knowing that the individual is likely to present himself in a light that is favorable to him, the others may divide what they witness into two parts; a part that is relatively easy for the individual to manipulate at will, being chiefly his verbal assertions, and a part in regard to which he seems to have little concern or control, being chiefly derived from the expressions he gives off. The others may then use what are considered to be the ungovernable aspects of his expressive behavior as a check upon the validity of what is conveyed by the governable aspects. In this a fundamental asymmetry is demonstrated in the communication process, the individual presumably being aware of only one stream of his communication, the witnesses of this stream and one other. For example, in Shetland Isle one crofter's wife, in serving native dishes to a visitor from the mainland of Britain, would listen with a polite smile to his polite claims of liking what he was eating; at the same time she would take note of the rapidity with which the visitor lifted his fork or spoon to his mouth, the eagerness with which he passed food into his mouth, and the gusto expressed in chewing the food, using these signs as a check on the stated feelings of the eater. The same woman, in order to discover what one acquaintance (A) "actually" thought of another acquaintance (B), would wait until B was in the presence of A but engaged in conversation with still another person (C). She would then covertly examine the facial expressions of A as he regarded B in conversation with C. Not being in conversation with B, and not being directly observed by him, A would sometimes relax usual constraints and tactful deceptions, and freely express what he was "actually" feeling about B. This Shetlander, in short, would observe the unobserved observer.

Now given the fact that others are likely to check up on more controllable aspects of behavior by means of the less controllable, one can expect that sometimes the individual will try to exploit this very possibility, guiding the impression he makes through behavior felt to be reliably informing.[4] For example, in gaining admission to a tight social circle, the participant observer may not only wear an accepting look while listening to an information, but may also be careful to wear the same look when observing the informant talking to others; observers of the observer will then not easily discover where he actually stands. A specific illustration may be cited from Shetland Isle. When a neighbor dropped in to have a cup of tea, he would ordinarily wear at least a hint of an expectant warm smile as he passed through the door into the cottage. Since lack of physical obstructions outside the cottage and lack of light within it usually made it possible to observe the visitor unobserved as he approached the house, islanders sometimes took pleasure in watching the visitor drop whatever expression he was manifesting and replace it with a sociable one just before reaching the door. However, some visitors, in appreciating that this examination was occurring, would blindly adopt a social face a long distance from the house, thus ensuring the projection of a constant image.

This kind of control upon the part of the individual reinstates the symmetry of the communication process, and sets the stage for a kind of information game—a potentially infinite cycle of concealment, discovery, false revelation, and rediscovery. It should be added that since the others are likely to be relatively unsuspicious of the presumably unguided aspects of the individual's conduct, he can gain much by controlling it. The others of course may sense that the individual is manipulating the presumably spontaneous aspects of his behavior, and seek in this very act of manipulation some shading of conduct that the individual has not managed to control. This again provides a check upon the individual's behavior, this time his presumably uncalculated behavior, thus re-establishing the asymmetry of the communication process. Here I would like only to add the suggestion that the arts of piercing an individual's effort at calculated unintentionality seem better developed than our capacity to manipulate our own behavior, so that regardless of how many steps have occurred in the information game, the witness is likely to have the advantage over the actor, and the initial asymmetry of the communication process is likely to be retained. . . .

In everyday life, of course, there is a clear understanding that first impressions are important. Thus, the work adjustment of those in service occupations will often hinge upon a capacity to seize and hold the initiative in the service relation, a capacity that will require subtle aggressiveness on the part of the server when he is of lower socioeconomic status than his client. W. F. Whyte suggests the waitress as an example:

> The first point that stands out is that the waitress who bears up under pressure does not simply respond to her customers. She acts with some skill to control their behavior. The first question to ask when we look at the customer relationship is, "Does the waitress get the jump on the customer, or does the customer get the jump on the waitress?" The skilled waitress realizes the crucial nature of this question. . . .
>
> The skilled waitress tackles the customer with confidence and without hesitation. For example, she may find that a new customer has seated himself before she could clear off the dirty dishes and change the cloth. He is now leaning on the table studying the menu. She greets him, says, "May I change the cover, please?" and, without waiting for an answer, takes his menu away from him so that he moves back from the table, and she goes about her work. The relationship is handled politely but firmly, and there is never any question as to who is in charge.[5]

When the interaction that is initiated by "first impressions" is itself merely the initial interaction in an extended series of interactions involving the same participants, we speak of "getting off on the right foot" and feel that it is crucial that we do so. Thus, one learns that some teachers take the following view:

> You can't ever let them get the upper hand on you or you're through. So I start out tough. The first day I get a new class in, I let them know who's boss. . . . You've got to start off tough, then you can ease up as you go along. If you start out easy-going, when you try to get tough, they'll just look at you and laugh."[6]

. . . In stressing the fact that the initial definition of the situation projected by an individual tends to provide a plan for the cooperative activity that follows—in stressing this action point of view—we must not overlook the crucial fact that any projected definition of the situation also has a distinctive moral character. It is this moral character of projections that will chiefly concern us in this report. Society is organized on the principle that any individual who possesses certain social characteristics has a moral right to expect that others will value and treat him in an appropriate way. Connected with this principle is a second, namely that an individual who implicitly or explicitly signifies that he has certain social characteristics ought in fact to be what he claims he is. In consequence, when an individual projects a definition of the situation and thereby makes an implicit or explicit claim to be a person of a particular kind, he automatically exerts a moral demand upon the others, obliging them to value and treat him in the manner that persons of his kind have a right to expect. He also implicitly foregoes all claims to be things he does not appear to be[7] and hence foregoes the treatment that would be appropriate for such individuals. The others find, then, that the individual has informed them as to what is and as to what they *ought* to see as the "is."

One cannot judge the importance of definitional disruptions by the frequency with which they occur, for apparently they would occur more frequently were not constant precautions taken. We find that preventive practices are constantly employed to avoid these embarrassments and that corrective practices are constantly employed to compensate for discrediting occurrences that have not been successfully avoided. When the individual employs these strategies and tactics to protect his own projections, we may refer to them as "defensive practices"; when a participant employs them to save the definition of the situation projected by another, we speak of "protective practices" or "tact." Together, defensive and protective practices comprise the techniques employed to safeguard the impression fostered by an individual during his presence before others. It should be added that while we may be ready to see that no fostered impression would survive if defensive practices were not employed, we are less ready perhaps to see that few impressions could survive if those who received the impression did not exert tact in their reception of it.

In addition to the fact that precautions are taken to prevent disruption of projected definitions, we may also note that an intense interest in these disruptions comes to play a significant role in the social life of the group. Practical jokes and social games are played in which embarrassments which are to be taken unseriously are purposely engineered.[8] Fantasies are created in which devastating exposures occur. Anecdotes from the past—real, embroidered, or fictitious—are told and retold, detailing disruptions which occurred, almost occurred, or occurred and were admirably resolved. There seems to be no grouping which does not have a ready supply of these games, reveries, and cautionary tales, to be used as a source of humor, a catharsis for anxieties, and a sanction for inducing individuals to be modest in their claims and reasonable in their projected expectations. The individual may tell himself through dreams of getting into impossible positions. Families tell of the time a guest got his dates mixed and arrived when neither the house nor anyone in it was ready for him. Journalists tell of times when an all-too-meaningful misprint occurred, and the paper's assumption of objectivity or decorum was humorously discredited. Public servants tell of times a client ridiculously misunderstood form instructions, giving answers which implied an unanticipated and bizarre definition of the situation.[9] Seamen, whose home away from home is rigorously he-man, tell stories of coming back home and inadvertently asking mother to "pass the fucking butter."[10] Diplomats tell of the time a near-sighted queen asked a republican ambassador about the health of his king.[11]

To summarize, then, I assume that when an individual appears before others he will have many motives for trying to control the impression they receive of the situation.

## CRITICAL-THINKING QUESTIONS

1. How does the "presentation of self" contribute to a definition of a situation in the minds of participants? How does this definition change over time?
2. Apply Goffman's approach to the classroom. What are the typical elements of the instructor's presentation of self? A student's presentation of self?
3. Can we evaluate the validity of the people's presentations? How?

## NOTES

1. Gustav Ichheiser, "Misunderstandings in Human Relations," supplement to *The American Journal of Sociology,* 55 (Sept. 1949), 6–7.
2. Willard Waller, "The Rating and Dating Complex," *American Sociological Review,* 2, 730.
3. William Sansom, *A Contest of Ladies* (London: Hogarth, 1956), pp. 230–32.
4. The widely read and rather sound writings of Stephen Potter are concerned in part with signs that can be engineered to give a shrewd observer the apparently incidental cues he needs to discover concealed virtues the gamesman does not in fact possess.
5. W. F. Whyte, "When Workers and Customers Meet," chap. 7, *Industry and Society,* ed. W. F. Whyte (New York: McGraw-Hill, 1946), pp. 132–33.
6. Teacher interview quoted by Howard S. Becker, "Social Class Variations in the Teacher-Pupil Relationship," *Journal of Educational Sociology,* 25, 459.
7. This role of the witness is limiting what it is the individual can be as been stressed by Existentialists, who see it as a basic threat to individual freedom. See Jean-Paul Satre, *Being and Nothingness,* trans. Hazel E. Barnes (New York: Philosophical Library, 1956), pp. 356ff.

8. Goffman, op. cit., pp. 319–27.

9. Peter Blau, "Dynamics of Bureaucracy" (Ph.D. dissertation, Department of Sociology, Columbia University, forthcoming, University of Chicago Press), pp. 127–29.

10. Walter M. Beattie, Jr., "The Merchant Seaman" (unpublished M. A. Report, Department of Sociology, University of Chicago, 1950), p. 35.

11. Sir Frederick Ponsonby, *Recollections of Three Reigns* (New York: Dutton, 1952), p. 46.

# How Cultures Collide

## *Elizabeth Hall*

**Elizabeth Hall** (*for pt*): For years, you've been saying that our ignorance of non-verbal communication threatens international relations, trade, and even world peace. Your new book, *Beyond Culture,* makes your warnings stronger and more specific. Just how, for example, does our ignorance of the silent language of behavior affect our relations with the People's Republic of China?

**Edward T. Hall:** All human beings are captives of their culture. When dealing with the Chinese, we are apt to try to read their true intentions from what they do rather than what they say. But in so doing, and by assuming that behavior means pretty much the same around the world, we anticipate their actions as if they were Americans—whereas they read our behavior with strong Chinese overtones. That could lead to serious misunderstandings.

One difference between us and the Chinese is in the way action chains are handled. An action chain is a set of events that resembles a dance, except that it is a dance with a goal. If any of the basic steps of the dance are omitted or distorted, the chain is broken and the action must begin all over again. The goal may be sex, marriage, corporate mergers, peace treaties—or something as simple as shaking hands or buying a gallon of paint. I doubt if any human social action exists that does not involve action chains.

In this culture, chains have clearly defined steps and stages; in China, the steps are not as clear to us. Faced with a troublesome situation, the Chinese will often act as though nothing has happened. They believe that once one acknowledges an event then one must take action—and action may be very, very serious. This is why the Chinese may seem to ignore our actions in one instance and be hypersensitive in another. We misread their intentions both in Korea and in Vietnam.

*pt:* And we misread them because we couldn't decipher the steps in their action chains?

**Hall:** In part, yes. In Vietnam we misread Chinese intentions by thinking they were motivated the way we were and took them too seriously; in Korea we didn't take them seriously enough. They told us where the line was, but we didn't believe them. In the same way, the Chinese may fail to see when we are very serious, and they misread the signs in our action chains. Whenever the members of one culture believe that another possesses no subtlety, as some Chinese apparently believe of us, it is a clear sign that the first culture has grossly misunderstood the second; I know of no culture without subtlety.

*pt:* We were warned that allowing the North Vietnamese to win would topple the first in a chain of dominoes, that Vietnam would lead to a solidly Communist Asia, just as Munich led toward a Nazi Europe.

**Hall:** When we went into Asia, we tried to fit events into a pattern that we have seen work in Europe. We confused Vietnam with Munich. The parallels were nonexistent. For we shared a history as well as political and social institutions with the Czechs; we shared none of these with the South Vietnamese. When Hitler marched on Czechoslovakia, it was an authoritarian government opposing a democratic regime; in Vietnam there were two authoritarian regimes.

*pt:* Do you think that with a better knowledge of the Chinese culture we would have known that some of the actions we took with trepidation would not provoke the Chinese into sending troops?

**Hall:** Possibly. But with a better knowledge of other peoples, we might not have fallen for our own propaganda. And might have avoided Vietnam in the first place. Clearly we had no idea of what we were getting into.

*pt:* And if you have a Secretary of State who meets every international situation as if it were an episode in 19th-century European politics . . .

**Hall:** You have a problem. But it runs deeper than that, for we avoid knowing. Our Department of State rotates its overseas employees every two years. According to one undersecretary in charge of personnel, our policy assumes that when a U.S. citizen knows a country too well, he begins to represent them, not us. This is, of course, a head-in-the-sand attitude.

As far as China goes, we eliminated the old China hands in Joe McCarthy's heyday. When men like John Stewart Service and John Carter Vincent told us what was happening in China, that Mao's Communists were winning, they were drummed out of the State Department as disloyal.

But to return to action chains. Americans, if they are sophisticated, watch other people's behavior to anticipate events. The Chinese do not ignore behavior entirely, but they are apt to pay more attention to where the other person is placed in a social system. They believe that the system will ultimately dictate behavior. This is because China is a high-context culture and we're a low-context culture.

*pt:* Just what do you mean by high- and low-context cultures?

**Hall:** Context and communication are intimately interrelated. In some cultures, messages are explicit; the words carry most of the information. In other cultures, such as China or Japan or the Arab cultures, less information is contained in the verbal part of a message, since more is in the context. That's why American businessmen often complain that their Japanese counterparts never get to the point. The Japanese wouldn't dream of spelling the whole thing out. To do so is a put-down; it's like doing your thinking for you.

*pt:* Like talking down to someone, or explaining something to a child.

**Hall:** Exactly. This sort of misunderstanding is so common that a few Americans picked up one reliable cue that shows when Japanese diplomats, having tried to get across an important point, realize they've failed. When this happens, they start slugging down Scotch. Remember, however, that in situations such as these, expectations may have significant unconscious overtones. Since much of culture operates outside our awareness, frequently we don't even know that we know. We pick them up in the cradle. We unconsciously learn what to notice and what not to notice, how to divide time and space, how to walk and talk and use our bodies, how to behave as men or women, how to relate to other people, how to handle responsibility, whether experience is seen as whole or fragmented. This applies to all peoples. The Chinese or the Japanese or the Arabs are as unaware of their assumptions as we are of our own. We each assume that they're part of human nature. What we think of as "mind" is really internalized culture.

*pt:* Let's explore some of the differences between high and low context. How does a high-context culture handle personal responsibility?

**Hall:** The difference is built in, shared, preprogrammed information as it relates to the transmitted, public part of the message. In general, high-context cultures can get by with less of the legal paperwork that is deemed essential in America. A man's word is his bond and you need not spell out the details to make him behave. One depends more on the power and influence of established networks of friends and relatives. Even in rather mundane matters, the two systems can be seen in contrast. For instance, several years ago I was traveling in Crete and wanted to visit the ruins at Knossos. My traveling companion, who was from low-context, fast-moving New York, took charge of the arrangements. He bargained with a taxi driver, agreed on a price, and a deal was made. We would take his taxi. Without warning, just as we were entering the cab, he stopped, got out and asked another driver if he would take us for less money. Since the second driver was willing, my friend said, "Let's go." The first taxi driver felt he had been cheated. We had made a verbal agreement and it had been violated. But my friend, coming from a low-context opportunistic culture, felt no moral obligation at all. He had saved the equivalent of 75¢. I can still see the shocked and horrified look on the face of the first taxi driver.

*pt:* Your friend was accustomed to getting three bids for a job.

**Hall:** Yes, and insisting on competitive bidding can also cause complications overseas. In a high-context culture, the job is given to the man who will do the best work and whom you can control. In a low-context culture, we try to make the specifications so precise that a builder has trouble doing a bad job. A builder in Japan is likely to say, "What has that piece of paper got to do with the situation? If we can't trust each other enough to go ahead without it, why bother?"

There are further implications of this pattern. A friend of mine in the Middle East was out one evening with a large group of Lebanese men. He happened to mention casually that if he only had some money, he could make a bundle. Much later as the group was breaking up, one of the men whom he didn't know gave him his card and asked him to drop by the next day. When my friend called, the man asked him how much money he needed and for how long, stating that he had some extra money. Upon hearing the amount, he proceeded to write out a check. The Lebanese businessman did not know my friend personally, but knew that he was part of a particular group, and therefore trustworthy.

*pt:* In other words, he didn't have to run a credit check.

Hall: No. Our low-context approach frequently ties the hands of American bankers in the Middle East. Several years ago, before things deteriorated out there, I interviewed a number of bankers. I was told they just couldn't compete with the local banks. For every loan over a certain amount, the Americans had to send a profit-and-loss statement to New York for an OK. By the time New York passed on the loan, the customer had gone elsewhere.

*pt:* That would mean that only high-risk loans would be left for American banks. Members of a high-context culture would know by a man's group whether he was a good risk.

Hall: Precisely.

*pt:* A number of corporations have gotten into hot water by paying bribes to foreign officials.

Hall: Bribery, as far as I know, is not condoned anywhere in the world, even in countries where it is a general practice. For a long time, civil servants in many countries simply did not earn enough to live on. They made a living wage by accepting a little extra to do their official tasks. But it's a long way from tipping an agent for stamping your visa to passing out a million dollars for an aircraft contract.

*pt:* From what you have been saying, the high-context culture functions on the basis of whom you know, while the American culture functions according to rules of procedure. Maybe American companies who pay off so-called agents are merely trying to buy the friendship network.

Hall: You are so right. However, any American could establish the same network that he tries to buy, but it would take him longer to do it. Most companies are not willing to invest that much time. Instead of building a solid foundation of relationships against the time when we will need them, we take a short cut and use money instead.

*pt:* How would a high-context culture like Japan have handled Watergate?

Hall: Again there are some interesting differences. In Japan, the man at the top is responsible. Nixon would have committed suicide. In the case of the My Lai massacre, Westmoreland would have taken the rap. In low-context systems, responsibility is kicked as far down the system as possible. In a high-context culture, the top man shoulders the blame.

*pt:* So the sign on Harry Truman's desk, "The Buck Stops Here," was really a high-context sign. He did take responsibility; he always said that dropping the bomb was purely his own decision.

Hall: Truman had a deep moral sense, a sense of continuity, and was deeply conversant with the presidency as an institution. He came out of the Old West, a man's word was his bond in this country, in part because everyone really did know everyone else. Truman belonged to this tradition. Recently our culture has been becoming noticeably more low-context.

*pt:* I can't disagree. We've had the rise of experts who tell us how to do everything from having sex to rearing children to being assertive—things one would assume people did as a part of being human. And the new marriage contracts specify everything about the bond from who washes dishes to how many nights out a week each partner has.

Hall: One of the complications of a low-context culture is the fragmenting of experience. The plethora of experts testifies to that. The marriage contracts may mean that our commitment to each other is diminishing. Commitment is greater in a high-context culture because the mass of the system is so great that you literally cannot escape, and it's almost impossible to change the rules.

*pt:* Nearly everything we have said shows up the advantages of a high-context culture. What are its disadvantages?

Hall: We've just said that they're very hard to move. Reforms come slowly. They're also likely to have rigid class structures and a family structure that holds people in a vise. You can't escape. The only way for a Japanese woman to get back at her mother-in-law is to wait until her own son marries. There's less mobility. Your occupation may be determined by what your father did. Or you may sign up with an employer for life as they do in Japan. High-context cultures are more group-oriented, and they sacrifice individualism. Individuals outside the group are apt to be helpless.

*pt:* Can you lay out some of the major cultures in terms of their context?

**Hall:** I would begin with the German-Swiss. They are low-context, falling somewhere near the bottom of the scale. Next the Germans, then the Scandinavians, as we move up. These cultures are all lower in context than the U.S. Above Americans come the French, the English, the Italians, the Spanish, the Greeks and the Arabs. In other words, as you move from northern to southern Europe, you will find that people move toward more involvement with each other. Look at the difference between a Swedish and an Italian movie.

*pt:* Sometimes people will discuss a Bergman movie and each will have a completely different motivation for the characters.

**Hall:** The first thing to remember about a Bergman movie is that no matter what it means to you, it means something else to a Swede. We can't possibly interpret all that's going on there.

*pt:* You said earlier that each culture also has its own way of dividing up space.

**Hall:** With space, of course, one has to mentally shift gears. Space is a communication system, and it's one of the reasons that many North Europeans and Americans don't like the Middle East. Arabs tend to get very close and breathe on you. It's part of the high sensory involvement of a high-context culture. If an Arab does not breathe on you, it means that he is consciously withholding his breath and is ashamed.

*pt:* For the Arabs, then, this part of culture doesn't operate outside awareness.

**Hall:** For us, much of it does—for the Arabs it's different. They say, "Why are the Americans so ashamed? They withhold their breath." The American on the receiving end can't identify all the sources of his discomfort but feels that the Arab is pushy. The Arab comes close, the American backs up. The Arab follows, because he can only interact at certain distances. Once the American learns that Arabs handle space differently and that breathing on people is a form of communication, the situation can sometimes be redefined so the American relaxes.

*pt:* In *The Hidden Dimension,* you wrote that each of us carries a little bubble of space around with us and that the space under our feet belongs to us.

**Hall:** Again, the things we take for granted can trip us up and cause untold discomfort and frequently anger. In the Arab world you do not hold a lien on the ground under foot. When standing on a street corner, an Arab may shove you aside if he wants to be where you are. This puts the average territorial American or German under great stress. Something basic has been violated. Behind this—to us—bizarre or even rude behavior lies an entirely different concept of property. Even the body is not sacred when a person is in public. Years ago, before all the fighting, American women in Beirut had to give up using streetcars. Their bodies were the property of all men within reach. What was happening is even reflected in the language. The Arabs have no word for *trespass,* no word for *rape.* The ego and the id are highly developed and depend on strong controls of the type few Europeans are accustomed to providing.

Space, of course, is one way of communicating; even at home, our language shows it. We say of an intimate friend that he is "close" and that someone who does not get emotionally involved is "standoffish" or "distant." Once I heard a hospital nurse describing doctors. She said there were beside-the-bed doctors who were interested in the patient, and foot-of-the-bed doctors who were interested in the patient's condition. They unconsciously expressed their emotional involvement—or lack of it—by where they stood.

*pt:* We're all becoming aware that the body does communicate. Books on body language have become popular. You can buy books that tell you how to succeed in business, be a smashing success at a cocktail party, or become popular with the opposite sex, all by reading body cues. Are these books generally helpful?

**Hall:** I think they are dreadful. Unfortunately, a few writers have exploited things that some of us have discovered about human behavior, and have managed to give the field a bad name. When a popularizer writes that sitting with your legs crossed has a certain specific meaning, he's just complicating life for everyone. In the final analysis, human beings have to deal with each other on a real-life basis.

*pt:* Are you implying that people who read these books will try to change their behavior?

**Hall:** That's the idea. It's manipulative, and I think it's not good for people to manipulate each other. Women don't like to be regarded as sex objects, because it involves manipulation.

*pt:* Besides the ethical objections, what about the practicality of such advice?

**Hall:** It's grotesque, and besides it just doesn't work. People are being taken advantage of, and they should feel quite angry when they find out.

*pt:* Does the problem lie in the fact that these books take the meaning of body language out of context?

**Hall:** You've put your finger on the crux of the matter. When body signals are not seen in context, their meaning can only be distorted. The popularizers of body language take a low-context, manipulative, exploitative view of high-context situations. When I speak of silent language, I mean more than body language. I refer to the totality of behavior as well as the products of behavior—time, space, materials, everything.

*pt:* One of the major differences in behavior you've found comes from a culture's way of handling time. How does time affect the shape of a culture or a person's view of the world?

**Hall:** Time, like space, communicates. It is not merely a convention, it's an organizing system. Our culture happens to organize most activities on a time base. We talk about time as if it were money; we spend it, save it or waste it. Time patterns are so deeply embedded in our central nervous system that we can't imagine getting along without them. The Western world couldn't function without its linear, one-thing-at-a-time system. Technology requires a monochronic approach. Railroads and airlines couldn't be integrated or run without schedules.

Of course, in the U.S. we don't begin to approach the Swiss in their slavery to time. Wherever a Swiss railroad stops, no matter how far into the mountains, passengers can look out the window at the nearest telegraph pole. On the pole will be a small white sign with a line down the middle and an arrow pointing in each direction, telling how many minutes—not kilometers—it is from the last station and how many it is to the next.

*pt:* It's apparently no accident that the Swiss are great watchmakers. But what is another way of handling time?

**Hall:** The Hopi Indians provide us with an excellent contrast because they don't have a single system that integrates everything. They believe that every living thing has its own inherent system and that you must deal with each plant or animal in terms of its own time. Their system is what I call polychronic, which hasn't always worked to their advantage. For example, if the Hopi had a slow-maturing variety of corn that would barely produce edible ears by the end of the growing season, they were apt to accept it. White Americans would be more apt to develop new strains that matured sooner; the old-time Hopi wouldn't think of altering a living time system.

*pt:* A bit of that polychronic time would help American mothers who become nervous if their children don't walk or talk at a certain age. They've been told each child has its own rate of maturation, but they don't believe it.

**Hall:** That's because we are wedded to some distant standard against which everything is measured. Even so, housewives have more experience with polychronic time than the rest of us. They must get husbands off to work, children to school, babies bathed and fed, meals ready, and clothes washed and dried. Each of those has its own time system, and it's one reason women have reacted so strongly to their life. A polychronic system tends to minimize individuality at the expense of group needs while a monochronic system can restore feelings of identity sometimes to the extent of narcissism. But if your identity comes from the group, as a Pueblo Indian's does, a monochronic system can be quite destructive because it interferes with group cohesiveness.

*pt:* Does this difference in time systems contribute to cross-cultural conflicts?

**Hall:** Of course. It can and has generated all sorts of tension between peoples. For example, 40 years ago when I worked with the Hopi, they were building dams paid for by the taxpayers. The government knew how long it takes to build dams and expected them to be finished in a set period of time. The Hopi felt that a dam had no built-in schedule, and they would not be hurried. Now, if it had been possible to convince the Hopi that inherent in the dam's structure was the fact that it was supposed to be completed in 90 days, for example, the problem would have been solved. But we didn't know enough then.

*pt:* Do all Western countries run on monochronic time?

**Hall:** Not entirely. Latin American and Mediterranean countries tend to be polychronic. It goes with high-context cultures. This has caused American businessmen and diplomats some trouble. Both have made appointments with Latin Americans and been kept waiting. Typically the Latin American, left to his own way of doing things, would have an office full of people, each there for a different purpose, showing no favoritism. He fails to devote himself to the North Americans who happen to be there to see him. The North American, running on a monochronic system, almost inevitably believes that the Latin American is telling him that he is not important. The Latin interprets the American's resentment as narcissism.

*pt:* How does this affect the manufacturing plants that American companies opened in Latin America?

**Hall:** For years I worked with an American company that tried to run a plant in Mexico. They finally gave up. They had a high-quality product and just couldn't get the Mexicans to produce to their standards. You should understand that the problem was not just time. It was a case of not developing a system that the local people could understand in terms of their own culture.

There's always a solution. Unfortunately Americans frequently fail to find it. Aramco, for example, was losing money on one of their trucking operations in Saudi Arabia. Finally, an Arab was able to buy the franchise and set up his own system. Knowing his own people, he worked out a series of complex reinforcement schedules for each truck and driver. He even penalized them for every valve cap that was missing and rewarded drivers when nothing that was supposed to be there was missing. Oil levels in the crankcase, maintenance schedules, time schedules, everything was examined and recorded. The cost per ton-mile dropped to a third of what it had been under American management.

*pt:* Sounds as if he simply imposed a behavior-shaping schedule on the drivers.

**Hall:** Yes, but he also organized a way of getting quality that the people understood and would accept. You couldn't set up such an arrangement with American drivers. It would be infringing on their territory to tell them how to take care of their trucks. We think of ourselves as successful managers, but the only people we can manage are other Americans, and we frequently don't do too well at that.

*pt:* How does all this affect our foreign relations in the Middle East?

**Hall:** Monochronic people tend to get their information from one or two sources, whereas polychronic people gather information from all over. The Arabs read several New York newspapers, *The Washington Post, Foreign Affairs,* everything they can get their hands on, and put the whole thing together. They come up with what they believe is the policy of the U.S. Once when I was in the Middle East during a crisis, I tried to tell Arabs that they had been reading the expression of several special-interest groups, which bore little or no resemblance to the policy of the U.S., but I didn't get very far. Instead of reacting to the policy of the State Department or Kissinger or Ford, they're reacting to some curious amalgam of the views of Kissinger, James Reston, various U.S. senators, the oil companies, the Anti-Defamation League, and goodness knows where else.

Another difference between Europeans and Arabs concerns disputes and how they are handled. Arabs depend on outsiders to intervene in disputes. In Arab societies, if two people are arguing and one of them gets hurt, the bystander who failed to stop the fight is the guilty party.

*pt:* Is that why Egypt is open to Kissinger's diplomacy?

**Hall:** Kissinger has a healthy male ego. Not only is there a meshing of personalities, but Arabs understand personal diplomacy. Remember that the first Arab-Israeli accord came about when Ralph Bunche got both parties isolated on an island and put each on a separate floor of a hotel. He carried messages back and forth between the floors until, finally, things began to work. He was very persuasive. Kissinger has done something similar, but I am under the impression that he didn't design it in that way.

*pt:* Do the different cultural backgrounds of the Arabs and the Israelis complicate the situation?

**Hall:** Naturally. The Middle East is a village culture, and village land is sacred in a way that is impossible to describe in the U.S. For example, about 25 years ago, a friend of mine conducted a census of a Lebanese village. The villagers claimed several times as many people as actually inhabited the village. People who had emigrated to Mexico and New York and Brazil and who hadn't been back for generations were counted and were still considered members of the village.

Europeans and Americans think in terms of nation states. Israel is a nation state in the midst of a village-culture complex. We're not talking about mere convention. The Palestinian Arabs who were displaced from their land have not forgotten, and they will never forget. They still consider as their sacred home that village their fathers were driven out of 30 years ago.

On top of that, Zionism is a European thing. Israel has some of the same problems with her Yemenite Jews that she has with the Arabs. Indigenous Jews, as you know, have to be enculturated into a new European tradition.

*pt:* So before you even begin to talk about religion, you begin with two incompatible traditions.

**Hall:** It took the Arabs 20 years to discover that. They finally woke up and discovered that they were not fighting Jews, because they had gotten along with Jewish villages for centuries. They were fighting Europeans.

*pt:* In *The Hidden Dimension,* you have a photograph of a house built by an Arab to punish a neighbor. Do Arab spite patterns affect the conflict between Israel and the Arab States?

**Hall:** They haven't yet, but they could. That house looks like a big wall, four stories high. The man who built it owned a narrow strip of land along the road, and the man behind him pushed too hard in trying to buy the land, and told the owner his land wasn't worth anything because no one could build a house on it. The owner of the land said, "I'll show you," and he built this house about six-feet thick—and furthermore built it high enough to cut off his neighbor's view of the Mediterranean.

If the Arabs are pushed too far and a Holy War is declared, there will be a disaster. I don't even like to think about it because once an Arab is in the spite response, he's apt to do anything—wreck his life—the lives of his children—he's past caring. No warning is given and, once the spite pattern takes over, nobody can intervene successfully until it runs its course.

*pt:* Do the cultural differences between blacks and whites in this country cause misunderstandings?

**Hall:** The data we have show that they do. The black culture is considerably higher in context than the white culture. I'm not talking about middle-class blacks; they're likely to be as low-contexted, compulsive and obsessional as whites.

But take the matter of the way we listen or show that we are paying attention when someone is talking. I once got a young black draftsman a job with an architectural firm, where he almost got fired. He did his work well but his employer complained about his attitude. This mystified me until once when I was talking to him and noticed I wasn't getting any feedback. He just sat there, quietly drawing. Finally I said, "Are you listening?" He said, "Man, if you're in the room, I'm listening. You listen with your ears." In their own mode, interacting with each other, ethnic blacks who know each other don't feel they have to look at each other while talking. They don't nod their heads or make little noises to show that they're listening the way whites do.

Old-time Pullman porters used to do a lot of head-bobbing and foot-shuffling and yessing, which was a response to their being hassled by whites. In those days, not knowing the nature of the white listening system, they didn't want to take chances and so they produced an exaggerated version of what whites expected, to show their customers that they were paying attention.

*pt:* What about the feeling many blacks have that they're invisible men?

**Hall:** That's another cultural difference. Depending upon the part of the country he's from, a white on the street looks at a person until he's about 12 to 16 feet away. Then, unless they know each other, whites automatically look away to avoid eye contact. This automatic avoidance on our part seems to give blacks the feeling of invisibility, because they use their eyes very differently than whites. As high-context people, they're more involved with each other visually and in every other way.

*pt:* Do blacks and whites handle time differently?

**Hall:** Their time is apt to be more polychronic than ours, which caused problems in Detroit when they first began to work on assembly lines and wouldn't show up. At times blacks jokingly refer to CPT or colored people's time when dealing with whites. Their system seems to run much closer to the way the body operates as well as being more situational in character.

Blacks also pay more attention than we do to nonverbal behavior. I once ran an experiment in which one black filmed another in a job interview. Each time something significant happened, the watching black started the camera. When I looked at those films, I couldn't believe my eyes. Nothing was happening! Or so I thought. It turned out that my camera-operator was catching—and identifying—body signals as minor as the movement of a thumb, which foreshadowed an intention to speak. Whites aren't so finely tuned.

***pt:*** Since many of our ethnic groups come from high-context cultures, I suppose that our low-context approach has caused problems for them as well.

**Hall:** There are many such problems, but particularly when urban renewal enters the picture. Planners and politicians are apt to mark ethnic neighborhoods as slums, and classify them for renewal because they do not see the order behind what appears to be disorder. Live, vital, cohesive ethnic communities are destroyed. To make way for a university in Chicago, planners wiped out a Greek and Italian neighborhood, over strong protests. The scars haven't healed yet. It is important to stress that when you scatter such a community, you're doing more than tear down buildings; you're destroying most of what gives life meaning, particularly for people who are deeply involved with each other. The displaced people grieve for their homes as if they had lost children and parents. To low-context whites, one neighborhood is much like the next. To high-context people, it is something else again.

***pt:*** You once said that urban renewal programs were as destructive as enemy bombing.

**Hall:** That was no mere metaphor. Take a good look at any neighborhood that's been hit by urban renewal. It's like a European city after a bombing raid. Furthermore, wasting communities is the first step in a chain of events that ends in destroying our cities. As a last resort and if absolutely necessary, neighborhoods should be relocated en masse. The whole community should be moved together—local policemen, streetcleaners, shopkeepers, and even postal clerks should be moved as a unit. Of course it will never happen. It would make too much sense.

***pt:*** If I had to sum up our talk, I'd say that your work is a plea for sensing context.

**Hall:** If I have only one point to make, it is that nothing is independent of anything else. Yet in the U.S. we use a special-interest approach for solving political, economic and environmental problems, which disregards the interconnectedness of events. Unfortunately, our schools are no help because they consistently teach us *not* to make connections. I feel strongly that there should be a few people at least whose task is synthesis—pulling things together. And that is impossible without a deep sense of context.

# Primary Groups

## Charles Horton Cooley

*Charles Horton Cooley argues that human nature is a social nature and is clearly expressed in group life. Cooley describes primary groups as "spheres of intimate association and cooperation" that are vital to the process of socialization.*

By primary groups I mean those characterized by intimate face-to-face association and cooperation. They are primary in several senses, but chiefly in that they are fundamental in forming the social nature and ideals of the individual. The result of intimate association, psychologically, is a certain fusion of individualities in a common whole, so that one's very self, for many purposes at least, is the common life and purpose of the group. Perhaps the simplest way of describing this wholeness is by saying that it is a "we"; it involves the sort of sympathy and mutual identification for which "we" is the natural expression. One lives in the feeling of the whole and finds the chief aims of his will in that feeling.

It is not to be supposed that the unity of the primary group is one of mere harmony and love. It is always a differentiated and usually a competitive unity, admitting of self-assertion and various appropriative passions; but these passions are socialized by sympathy, and come, or tend to come, under the discipline of a common spirit. The individual will be ambitious, but the chief object of his ambition will be some desired place in the thought of the others, and he will feel allegiance to common standards of service and fair play. So the boy will dispute with his fellows a place on the team, but above such disputes will place the common glory of his class and school.

The most important spheres of this intimate association and cooperation—though by no means the only ones—are the family, the play group of children, and the neighborhood or community group of elders. These are practically universal, belonging to all times and all stages of development; and are accordingly a chief basis of what is universal in human nature and human ideals. The best comparative studies of the family, such as those of Westermarck[1] or Howard,[2] show it to us as not only a universal institution, but as more alike the world over than the exaggeration of exceptional customs by an earlier school had led us to suppose. Nor can anyone doubt the general prevalence of play-groups among children or of informal assemblies of various kinds among their elders. Such association is clearly the nursery of human nature in the world about us, and there is no apparent reason to suppose that the case has anywhere or at any time been essentially different.

As regards play, I might, were it not a matter of common observation, multiply illustrations of the universality and spontaneity of the group discussion and cooperation to which it gives rise. The general fact is that children, especially boys after about their twelfth year, live in fellowships in which their sympathy, ambition, and honor are engaged even more often than they are in the family. Most of us can recall examples of the endurance by boys of injustice and even cruelty, rather than appeal from their fellows to parents or teachers—as, for instance, in the hazing so prevalent at schools, and so difficult, for this very reason, to suppress. And how elaborate the discussion, how cogent the public opinion, how hot the ambitions in these fellowships.

Nor is this facility of juvenile association, as is sometimes supposed, a trait peculiar to English and American boys; since experience among our immigrant population seems to show that the offspring of the more restrictive civilizations of the continent of Europe form self-governing play groups with almost equal readiness. Thus Miss Jane Addams, after pointing out that the "gang" is almost universal, speaks of the interminable discussion which every detail of the gang's activity receives, remarking that "in these social folk-motes, so to speak, the young citizen learns to act upon his own determination."[3]

Of the neighborhood group it may be said, in general, that from the time men formed permanent settlements upon the land, down, at least, to the rise of modern industrial cities, it has played a main part of the primary, heart-to-heart life of the people. Among our Teutonic forefathers the village community was apparently the chief sphere of sympathy and mutual aid for the commons all through the "Dark" and Middle Ages, and for many purposes it remains so in rural districts at the present day. In some countries we still find it with all its ancient vitality, notably in Russia, where the *mir* or self-governing village group, is the main theatre of life, along with the family, for perhaps 50 million peasants.

In our own life the intimacy of the neighborhood has been broken up by the growth of an intricate mesh of wider contacts which leaves us strangers; to people who live in the same house. And even in the country the same principle is at work, though less obviously, diminishing our economic and spiritual community with our neighbors. How far this change is a healthy development, and how far a disease, is perhaps still uncertain.

Besides these almost universal kinds of primary association, there are many others whose form depends upon the particular state of civilization; the only essential thing, as I have said, being a certain intimacy and fusion of personalities. In our own society, being little bound by place, people easily form clubs, fraternal societies and the like, based on congeniality, which may give rise to real intimacy. Many such relations are formed at school and college, and among men and women brought together in the first instance by their occupations—as workmen in the same trade, or the like. Where there is a little common interest and activity, kindness grows like weeds by the roadside.

But the fact that the family and neighborhood groups are ascendant in the open and plastic time of childhood makes them even now incomparably more influential than all the rest.

Primary groups are primary in the sense that they give the individual his earliest and completest experience of social unity, and also in the sense that they do not change in the same degree as more elaborate relations, but form a comparatively permanent source out of which the latter are ever springing. Of course they are not independent of the larger society, but to some extent reflect its spirit; as the German family and the German school bear somewhat distinctly the print of German militarism. But this, after all, is like the tide setting back into creeks, and does not commonly go very far. Among the German, and still more among the Russian, peasantry are found habits of free cooperation and discussion almost uninfluenced by the character of the state; and it is a familiar and well-supported view that the village commune, self-governing as regards local affairs and habituated to discussion, is a very widespread institution in settled communities, and the continuator of a similar autonomy previously existing in the clan. "It is man who makes monarchies and establishes republics, but the commune seems to come directly from the hand of God."[4]

In our own cities the crowded tenements and the general economic and social confusion have sorely wounded the family and the neighborhood, but it is remarkable, in view of these conditions, what vitality they show; and there is nothing upon which the conscience of the time is more determined than upon restoring them to health.

These groups, then, are springs of life, not only for the individual but for social institutions. They are only in part moulded by special traditions, and, in larger degree, express a universal nature. The religion or government of other civilizations may seem alien to us, but the children or the family group wear the common life, and with them we can always make ourselves at home.

By human nature, I suppose, we may understand those sentiments and impulses that are human in being superior to those of lower animals, and also in the sense that they belong to mankind at large, and not to any particular race or time. It means, particularly, sympathy and the innumerable sentiments into which sympathy enters, such as love, resentment, ambition, vanity, hero-worship, and the feeling of social right and wrong.

Human nature in this sense is justly regarded as a comparatively permanent element in society. Always and everywhere men seek honor and dread ridicule, defer to public opinion, cherish their goods and their children, and admire courage, generosity, and success. It is always safe to assume that people are and have been human. . . .

To return to primary groups: The view here maintained is that human nature is not something existing separately in the individual, but a *group-nature or primary phase of society*, a relatively simple and general condition of the social mind. It is something more, on the one hand, than the mere instinct that is born in us—though that enters into it—and something else, on the other, than the more elaborate development of ideas and sentiments that makes up institutions. It is the nature which is developed and expressed in those simple, face-to face groups that are somewhat alike in all societies; groups of the family, the playground, and the neighborhood. In the essential similarity of these is to be found the basis, in experience, for similar ideas and sentiments in the human mind. In these, everywhere, human nature comes into existence. Man does not have it at birth; he cannot acquire it except through fellowship, and it decays in isolation.

If this view does not recommend itself to common sense I do not know that elaboration will be of much avail. It simply means the application at this point of the idea that society and individuals are inseparable phases of a common whole, so that wherever we find an individual fact we may look for a social fact to go with it. If there is a universal nature in persons there must be something universal in association to correspond to it.

What else can human nature be than a trait of primary groups? Surely not an attribute of the separate individual—supposing there were any such thing—since its typical characteristics, such as affection, ambition, vanity, and resentment, are inconceivable apart from society. If it belongs, then, to man in association, what kind or degree of association is required to develop it? Evidently nothing elaborate, because elaborate phases of society are transient and diverse, while human nature is comparatively stable and universal. In short the family and neighborhood life is essential to its genesis and nothing more is.

Here as everywhere in the study of society we must learn to see mankind in psychical wholes, rather than in artificial separation. We must see and feel the communal life of family and local groups as immediate facts, not as combinations of something else. And perhaps we shall do this best by recalling our own experience and extending it through sympathetic observation. What, in our life, is the family and the fellowship; what do we know of the we-feeling? Thought of this kind may help us to get a concrete perception of that primary group-nature of which everything social is the out growth.

## CRITICAL-THINKING QUESTIONS

1. *Are primary groups necessarily devoid of conflict? How does Cooley address this issue?*
2. *For what reasons does Cooley employ the term primary in his analysis? What are the characteristics of the implied opposite of primary groups: "secondary groups"?*
3. *What is Cooley's view of human nature? Why does he think that society cannot be reduced to the behavior of many distinct individuals?*

## NOTES

1. *The History of Human Marriage.*
2. *A History of Matrimonial Institutions.*
3. *Newer Ideals of Peace, 177.*
4. *De Tocqueville, Democracy in America. vol. 1. chap 5.*

SOURCE: *Social Organization: A Study of the Larger Mind* by Charles Horton Cooley (New York: Schocken Books, a subsidiary of Pantheon Books, 1962; orig. 1909), pp. 23-31. Reprinted with permission.

# Corner Boys: A Study of Clique Behavior

*William Foote Whyte*

This paper presents some of the results of a study of leadership in informal groupings or gangs of corner boys in "Cornerville," a slum area of a large eastern city. The aim of the research was to develop methods whereby the position (rank or status) of the individual in his clique might be empirically determined; to study the bases of group cohesion and of the subordination and superordination of its members; and, finally, to work out means for determining the position of corner gangs in the social structure of the community.

While my subjects called themselves corner boys, they were all grown men, most of them in their twenties, and some in their thirties. . . . While some of the men I observed were engaged in illegal activities, I was not interested in crime as such; instead, I was interested in studying the nature of clique behavior, regardless of whether or not the clique was connected with criminal activity. . . . I made an intensive and detailed study of 5 gangs on the basis of personal observation, intimate acquaintance, and participation in their activities for an extended period of time. Throughout three-and-a-half years of research, I lived in Cornerville, not in a settlement house, but in tenements such as are inhabited by Cornerville people.

The population of the district is almost entirely of Italian extraction. Most of the corner boys belong to the second generation of immigrants. In general, they are men who have had little education beyond grammar school and who are unemployed, irregularly employed, or working steadily for small wages.

Their name arises from the nature of their social life. From them "the corner" is not necessarily at a street intersection. It is any part of the sidewalk which they take for their social headquarters, and it often includes a poolroom, barroom, funeral parlor, barbershop, or clubroom. Here they may be fond almost any afternoon or evening, talking and joking about sex, sports, personal relations, or politics in season. Other social activities either take place "on the corner" or are planned there. The existence of a hierarchy of personal relations in these cliques is seldom explicitly recognized by the corner boys. Asked if they have a leader or boss, they invariably reply, "No, we're all equal." It is only through the observation of actions that the group structure becomes apparent. My problem was to apply methods which would produce an objective and reasonably exact picture of such structures.

In any group containing more than two people there are subdivisions to be observed. No member is equally friendly with all other members. In order to understand the behavior of the individual member it is necessary to place him not only in his group but also in his particular position in the subgroup.

My most complete study of groupings was made from observations in the rooms of the Cornerville Social and Athletic Club. This was a club of corner boys, which had a membership of about fifty and was divided primarily into two cliques, which had been relatively independent of each other before the formation of the club. There were, of course, subdivisions in each clique.

I sought to make a record of the groupings in which I found the members whenever I went into the club. While the men were moving around, I would be unable to retain their movements for my record, but on most occasions they would settle down in certain spatial arrangements. In the accompanying example (Figure 1) two were at a table playing checkers with one watching, four at another table playing whist and three more watching the game, and six talking together toward the back of the room. As I looked around the room, I would count the number of men present so that I should know later how many I should have to account for. Then I would say over to myself the names of the men in each grouping and try to fix in my mind their positions in relation to one another. In the course of an evening there might be a general reshuffling of positions. I would not be able to remember every movement, but I would try to observe with which members the movements began; and, when another spatial arrangement had developed, I would go through the same mental process as I had with the first. As soon as I got home from the club, I would draw a map or maps of the spatial positions I had observed and any movements between positions which I recalled. The map (Figure 1) indicates the sort of data that came out of these observations.

In this case I have the following notes on movements of the members:

> Eleven walked over to One and pinched his cheek hard, went out of the club rooms, returned and pinched cheek again. One pretended to threaten Eleven with an ash tray. Eleven laughed and returned to seat on couch. I [the observer] asked Eleven about the purpose of the club meeting. He asked Ten and Ten explained. Eleven laughed and shrugged his shoulders. Sixteen, the janitor, served beer for the card players.

On the basis of a number of maps such as this it is not difficult to place most of the men in the clique and grouping within the clique to which they belong. I did not attempt to place all the men, because the club had a fluctuating membership and some of the men were available for observation for only a short time. There were, throughout the ten months of my observation, some thirty-odd members who were active most of the time. Events in the club could be explained largely in terms of the actions of these men; and, therefore, when I had placed them in relation to one another, I did not need to press further in this direction.

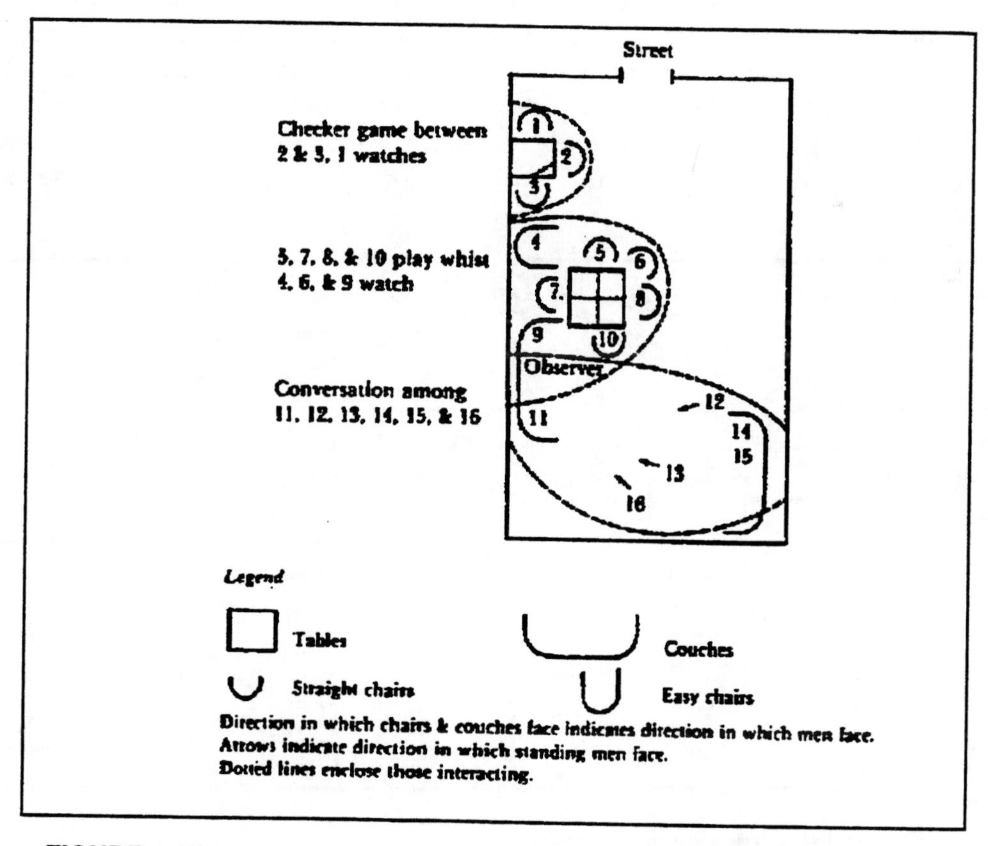


**FIGURE 1 The Cornerville S & A Club, February 29, 1940, 8–8:15 P.M.**

Positional map-making is simply an extension of the techniques of observation and recording which have been used in the past by social anthropologists and sociologists. All these techniques require practice before they can be effectively applied. While my first maps left out a number of men, later I was able to record accurately enough so that on most occasions I could account for every man present at a particular time; and on several occasions I was able to work out two maps giving different positional arrangements during the course of the same period of observation. Beyond two I did not attempt to go, and it was not necessary to do so because there would rarely be more than two positional arrangements in the course of an evening sufficiently different from one another to require additional maps.

While the data from such maps enable one to determine groupings, they do not reveal the position or rank of the men in the groupings. For this purpose other data are needed. In practice they may be gathered at the same time as the positional arrangements are observed.

As I conceive it, position in the informal group means power to influence the actions of the group. I concentrated my attention upon the origination of action, to observe who proposed an action, to whom he made the proposal, and the steps that followed up to the completion of the action. I was dealing with "pair events" and "set events," to use the terminology of Arensberg and Chapple.[1] A "pair event" is an event between two people. A "set event" is an event in which one person originates action for two or more others at the same time. In working out the relations between men in an informal group, this is an important distinction to bear in mind. I found that observations of pair events did not provide a safe guide for the ranking of the members of the pair. At times A would originate action for B, at other times B would originate action for A. In some cases there would be a predominance of originations in one direction; but on the whole the data did not support rankings based upon quantitative comparisons of the rates of origination of action in pair events. Qualitatively one could say that when A originated action for B he used a tone of voice and words which indicated that he held a superior position. To make the extreme case, it is not difficult to tell the difference between an order and a request, although both may originate action. It is not safe, however, to rely upon such qualitative differences. The observer may read into the situation his own impression of the relative positions of the men and thus lose the objective basis for his conclusions.

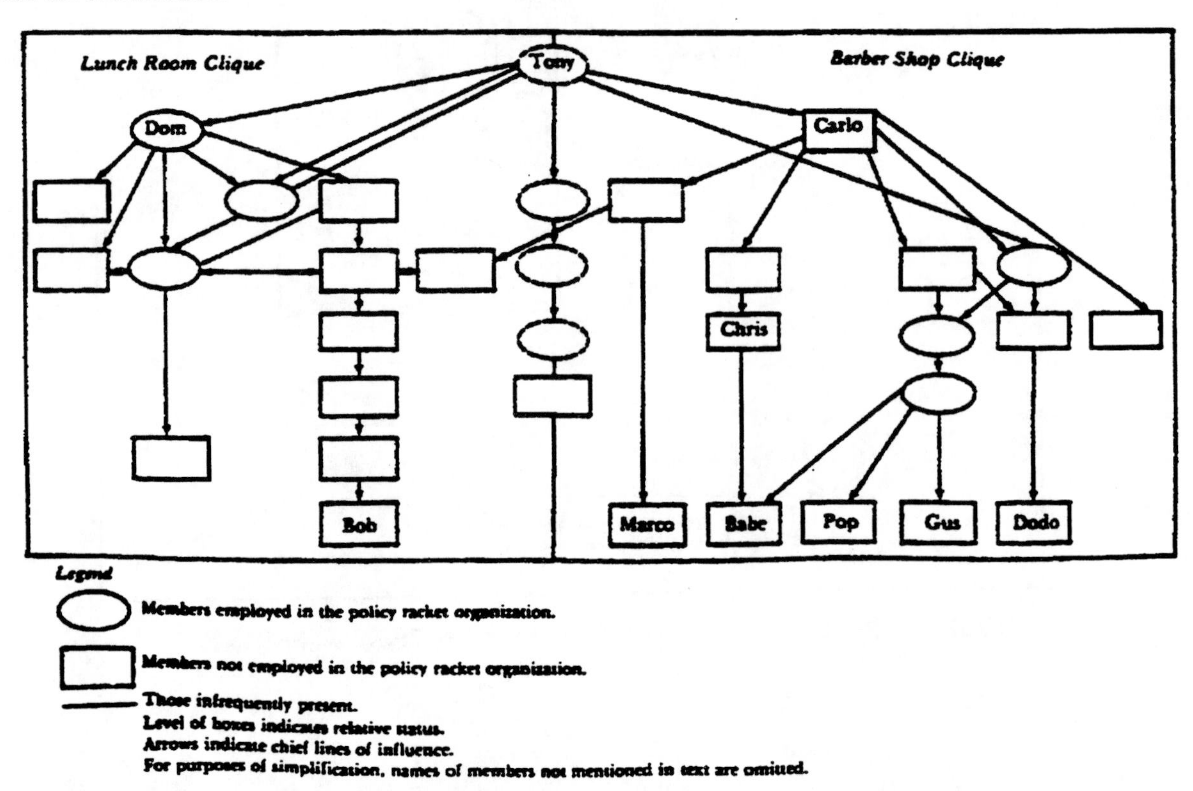


**FIGURE 2 Informal Organization of the Cornerville S & A Club, February 1940**

It is observation of set events which reveals the hierarchical basis of informal group organization. As defined by Arensberg and Chapple,

> a *set* is an aggregate of relations such that every individual related in the set is a member either (a) of a class of individuals who only originate action, or (b) of an intermediate class of individuals who at some time originate action and at another time terminate action, or (c) of a class of individuals who only terminate action.[2]

Study of corner-boy groups reveals that the members may, indeed, be divided and ranked upon this basis. Several examples will illustrate.

At the top of the Cornerville S. and A. Club (see Figure 2), we have Tony, Carlo, and Dom. They were the only ones who could originate action for the entire club. At the bottom were Dodo, Gus, Pop, Babe, Marco, and Bob, who never originated action in a set even involving anyone above their positions. Most of the members fell into the intermediate class. They terminated action on the part of the top men and originated action for the bottom men. Observations of the actions of the men of the intermediate class when neither top nor bottom men were present revealed that there were subdivisions or rankings within that class. This does not mean that the intermediate or bottom men never have any ideas as to what the club should do. It means that their ideas must go through the proper channels if they are to go into effect.

In one meeting of the Cornerville S. and A. Club, Dodo proposed that he be allowed to handle the sale of beer in the clubrooms in return for 75 percent of the profits. Tony spoke in favor of Dodo's suggestion but proposed giving him a somewhat smaller percentage. Dodo agreed. Then Carlo proposed to have Dodo handle the beer in quite a different way, and Tony agreed. Tony made the motion, and it was carried unanimously. In this case Dodo's proposal was carried through, after substantial modifications, upon the actions of Tony and Carlo.

In another meeting Dodo said that he had two motions to make: that the club's funds be deposited in a bank and that no officer be allowed to serve two consecutive terms. Tony was not present at this time. Dom, the president, said that only one motion should be made at a time and that, furthermore, Dodo should not make any motions until there had been opportunity for discussion. Dodo agreed. Dom then commented that it would be foolish to deposit the funds when the club had so little to deposit. Carlo expressed his agreement. The meeting passed on to other things without action upon the first motion and without even a word of discussion on the second one. In the same meeting Chris moved that a member must be in the club for a year before being allowed to hold office. Carlo said that it was a good idea, he seconded the motion, and it carried unanimously.

All my observations indicate that the idea for group action which is carried out must originate with the top man or be accepted by him so that he acts upon the group. A follower may originate action for a leader in a pair event, but he does not originate action for the leader and other followers at the same time—that is, he does not originate action in a set event which includes the leader.

One may also observe that, when the leader originates action for the group, he does not act as if his followers were all of equal rank. Implicitly he takes the structure of the group into account. An example taken from the corner gang known as the "Millers" will illustrate this point. The Millers were a group of twenty corner boys, who were divided into two subgroups. Members of both subgroups frequently acted together; but, when two activities occupied the men at the same time, the division generally fell between the subgroups. Sam was the leader of the Millers. Joe was directly below him in one subgroup. Chichi led the other subgroup. Joe as well as Sam was in a position to originate action for Chichi and his subgroup.

It was customary for the Millers to go bowling every Saturday night. On this particular Saturday night Sam had no money, so he set out to persuade the boys to do something else. They followed his suggestion. Later Sam explained to me how he had been able to change the established social routine of the group. He said:

> I had to show the boys that it would be in their own interests to come with me—that each of them would benefit. But I knew I only had to convince two of the fellows. If they start to do something, the other boys will say to themselves, "If Joe does it—or if Chichi does it—it must be a good thing for us too." I told Joe and Chichi what the idea was, and I got them to come with me. I didn't pay no attention to the others. When Joe and Chichi came, all the other boys came along too.

Another example from the Millers indicates what happens when the leader and the man next to him in rank disagree upon group policy. This is Sam talking again:

> One time we had a raffle to raise money to build a camp on Lake ________ [on property lent them by a local business man]. We had collected $54, and Joe and I were holding the money. . . . That week I knew Joe was playing pool, and he lost three or four dollars gambling. When Saturday came, I says to the boys, "Come on, we go out to Lake ________. We're gonna build that camp on the hill. . . ." Right away Joe said, "If yuz are gonna build the camp on the hill, I don't come. I want it on the other-side. . . ." All the time I knew he had lost the money, and he was only making up excuses so he wouldn't have to let anybody know. . . . Now the hill was really the place to build that camp. On the other side, the ground was swampy. That would have been a stupid place. . . . But I knew that if I tried to make them go through with it now, the group would split up into two cliques. Some would come with me, and some would go with Joe. . . . So I let the whole thing drop for a while. . . . After I got Joe alone, and I says to him, "Joe, I know you lost some of that money, but that's all right. You can pay up when you have it and nobody will say nothin'. But Joe, you know we shouldn't have the camp on the other side of the hill because the land is no good there. We should build it on the hill. . . ." So he said, "All right," and we got all the boys together and went out to build the camp.

Under ordinary circumstances the leader implicitly recognizes and helps to maintain the position of the man or men immediately below him, and the group functions smoothly. In this respect the informal organization is similar to the formal organization. If the executive in a factory attempts to pass over his immediate subordinates and gives orders directly to the men on the assembly line, he creates confusion. The customary channels must be used.

The social structures vary from group to group, but each one may be represented in some form of hierarchy. The members have clearly defined relations of subordination and superordination, and each group has a leader. Since we are concerned with informal organization, the Cornerville S. and A. members must be considered as two groups, with Carlo leading the barbershop boys, and Dom leading the lunchroom boys. Since Tony's position requires special consideration, he will be discussed later.

## BASES OF GROUP STRUCTURE

Observation not only serves to provide a description of the group structure. It also reveals information upon the bases of structure and the factors differentiating between the positions of members. The clique structure arises out of the habitual association of the members over a long period of time. The nuclei of most gangs can be tracked back to early boyhood years when living close together provided the first opportunities for social contacts. School years modified the original pattern somewhat, but I know of no corner gangs which arose through classroom or school-playground association. The gangs grew up "on the corner" and have remained there with remarkable persistence. In the course of years some groups have been broken up by the movement of families away from Cornerville, and the remaining members have merged with gangs on nearby corners; but frequently movement out of the district does not take the corner boy away from his corner. On any evening in Cornerville on almost any corner one finds corner boys who have come in from other parts of the city or from suburbs to be with their old friends. The residence of the corner boy may also change within the district, but nearly always he retains his allegiance to his original corner.

The leader of one group spoke to me in this way about corner boys:

> Fellows around here don't know what to do except within a radius of about 300 yards. That's the truth, Bill. . . . They come home from work, hang on the corner, go up to eat, back on the corner, up (to) a show, and they come back to hang on the corner. If they're not on the corner, it's likely the boys there will know where you can find them. . . . Most of them stick to one corner. It's only rarely that a fellow will change his corner.

The stable composition of the group over a long period and the lack of social assurance felt by most of the members contribute toward producing a very high rate of social interaction within the group. *The structure to be observed is a product of past interactions.*

Out of these interactions there arises a system of mutual obligations which is fundamental to group cohesion. If the men are to carry on their activities as a unit, there are many occasions when they must do favors for one another. Frequently, one member must spend money to help another who does not have the money to participate in some of the group activities. This creates an obligation. If the situation is later reversed, the recipient is expected to help the man who gave him aid. The code of the corner boy requires him to help the man who gave him aid. The code of the corner boy requires him to help his friends when he can and to refrain from doing anything to harm them. When life in the group runs smoothly, the mutual obligations binding members to one another are not explicitly recognized. A corner boy, asked if he helped a fellow-member because of a sense of obligation, will reply, "No, I didn't have to do it. He's my friend. That's all." It is only when the relationship breaks down that the underlying obligations are brought to light. When two members of the group have a falling-out, their actions form a familiar pattern. One tells a story something like this: "What a heel Blank turned out to be. After all I've done for him, the first time I asked him to do something for me, he won't do it." The other may say: "What does he want from me? I've done plenty for him, but he wants you to do everything." In other words, the actions which were performed explicitly for the sake of friendship are now revealed as being part of a system of mutual obligations.

## THE SOCIAL ROLE OF LEADER

Not all the boys live up to their obligation equally well, and this factor partly accounts for the differentiation in status among the men. The man with a low status may violate his obligations without much change in his position. His fellows know that he has failed to discharge certain obligations in the past, and his position reflects his past performance. On the other hand, the leader is depended upon by all the members to meet his personal obligations. He cannot often fail to do so without causing confusion and losing his position. The relationship of status to the system of mutual obligations is most clearly revealed when we consider the use of money. While all the men are expected to be generous, the flow of money between members can be explained only in terms of the group structure.

The Millers provide an illustration of this point. During the time that I knew them, Sam, the leader, was out of work except for an occasional odd job; yet, whenever he had a little money, he spent it on Joe and Chichi, his closest friends, who were next to him in the structure of the group. When Joe or Chichi had money, which was less frequent, they reciprocated. When Joe or Chichi had money, which was less frequent, they reciprocated. Sam frequently paid for two members who stood close to the bottom of the structure and occasionally for others. The two men who held positions immediately below Joe and Chichi in the subgroups were considered very well off according to Cornerville standards. Sam said that he occasionally borrowed money from them, but never more than fifty cents at a time. Such loans he tried to repay at the earliest possible moment. There were four other members, with positions ranging from intermediate to the bottom, who nearly always had more money than Sam. He did not recall ever having borrowed from them. He said that the only time he had obtained a substantial sum from anyone around his corner was when he borrowed eleven dollars from a friend who was the *leader* of another corner-boy group.

The system is substantially the same for all the groups on which I have information. The leader spends more money on his followers than they on him. The farther down in the structure one looks, the fewer are the financial relations which tend to obligate the leader to a follower. This does not mean that the leader has more money than others or even that he necessarily spends more—though he must always be a free spender. It means that the financial relations must be explained in social terms. Unconsciously, and in some cases consciously, the leader refrains from putting himself under obligations to those with low status in the group.

The system is substantially the same for all the groups on which I have information. The leader spends more money on his followers than they on him. The farther down in the structure one looks, the fewer are the financial relations which tend to obligate the leader to a follower. This does not mean that the leader has more money than others or even that he necessarily spends more—though he must always be a free spender. It means that the financial relations must be explained in social terms. Unconsciously, and in some cases consciously, the leader refrains form putting himself under obligations to those with low status in the group.

Relations of rivalry or outright hostility with other groups are an important factor in promoting in-group solidarity, as has been well recognized. . .Present-day corner gangs grew up in an atmosphere of street fighting against gangs of Irish or of fellow-Italians. While actual fights are now infrequent, the spirit of gang loyalty is maintained in part through athletic contests and political rivalries.

As the structures indicate, members have higher rates of interaction with men close to their own positions in their subgroups than with men who rank much higher or much lower or belong to a different subgroup. That is a significant fact for the explanation of group cohesion.

In the case of the Millers, Sam's best friends were Joe and Chichi. As his remarks have indicated, Sam realized that the solidarity of the Millers depended in the first instance upon the existence of friendly and cooperative relations between himself, Joe, and Chichi. A Cornerville friend, who was aware of the nature of my observations, commented in this manner:

> On any corner, you would find not only a leader but probably a couple of lieutenants. They could be leaders themselves, but they let the man lead them. You would say, they let him lead because they like the way he does things. Sure, but he leans upon them for his authority. . . . Many times you find fellows on a corner that stay in the background until some situation comes up, and then they will take over and call the shots. Things like that can change fast sometimes.

Such changes are the result not of an uprising of the bottom men but of a shift in the relations between men at the top of the structure. When a gang breaks into two parts, the explanation is to be found in a conflict between the leader and one who ranked close to him in the structure of the original gang.

The distinctive functions of the top men in promoting social cohesion are readily observable in the field. Frequently, in the absence of their leader the members of a gang are divided into a number of small groups. There is no common activity or general conversation. When the leader appears, the situation changes strikingly. The small units form into one large group. The conversation becomes general, and unified action frequently follows. The leader becomes the focal point in discussion. One observes a follower start to say something, pause when he notices that the leader is not listening, and begin again when he has the leader's attention. When the leader leaves the group, unity gives way to the divisions that existed before his appearance. To a certain extent the lieutenants can perform this unifying function; but their scope is more limited because they are more closely identified with one particular subgroup than is the leader.

The same Cornerville friend summed up the point in this way:

> If we leave the followers, they'll go find some other leader. They won't know what they're doing, but that's what they'll do, because by themselves they won't know what to do. They gather around the leader, and it is the leader that keeps them together.

The leader is the man who knows what to do. He is more resourceful than his followers. Past events have shown that his ideas were right. In this sense "right" simply means satisfactory to the members. He is the most independent in judgment. While his followers are undecided as to a course of action or upon the character of a newcomer, the leader makes up his mind. When he gives his word to one of "his boys," he keeps it. The followers look to him for advice and encouragement, and he receives more of the confidences of the members than any other man. Consequently, he knows more about what is going on in the group than anyone else. Whenever there is a quarrel among the boys, he will hear of it almost as soon as it happens. Each party to the quarrel may appeal to him to work out in a solution; and, even when the men do not want to compose their differences, each one will take his side of the story to the leader at the first opportunity. A man's standing depends partly upon the leader's belief that he has been conducting himself as he should.

The leader is respected for his fair-mindedness. Whereas there may be hard feelings among some of the followers, the leader cannot bear a grudge against any man in the group. He has close friends (men who stand next to him in position), and he is indifferent to some of the members; but if he is to retain his reputation for impartiality, he cannot allow personal animus to override his judgment.

The leader need not be the best baseball player, bowler, or fighter, but he must have some skill in whatever pursuits are of particular interest to the group. It is natural for him to promote activities in which he excels and to discourage those in which he is not skillful; and, insofar as he is thus able to influence the group, his competent performance is a natural consequence of his position. At the same time his performance supports his position.

It is significant to note that the leader is better known and more respected outside of his group than is any of his followers. His social mobility is greater. One of the most important functions he performs is that of relating his group to other groups in the district. His reputation outside the group tends to support his standing within the group, and his position in the group supports his reputation among outsiders.

It should not be assumed from this discussion that corner boys compete with one another for the purpose of gaining leadership. Leadership is a product of social interaction. The men who reach the top in informal groups are those who can perform skillfully the actions required by the situation. Most such skills are performed without long premeditation.

What the leader is has been discussed in terms of what he does. I doubt whether an analysis in terms of personality traits will add anything to such an explanation of behavior. One can find a great variety of personality traits among corner-boy leaders, just as one can among business or political leaders. Some are aggressive in social contacts, and others appear almost retiring. Some are talkative, and other have little to say. Few uniformities of this nature are to be found. On the other hand, they are marked uniformities to be observed in the functions performed by men who hold similar positions in society, and the study of them promises to provide the best clues for the understanding of social behavior.

## THE GANGS AND THE WIDER COMMUNITY

For a community study, data upon five corner gangs are hardly more than a beginning. Two problems were involved in extending the research. First, I had to discover whether I could safely generalize my conclusions to apply them to all corner gangs in Cornerville. Second, I had to fit the corner gangs into the fabric of Cornerville society.

To accomplish the first end I solicited the aid of a number of corner-boy leaders, who made for me more or less systematic observations of their own groups and of groups about them. The generalizations, presented earlier, upon the functions of leaders, indicate why I found them the best sources of information upon their groups. This procedure could not be relied upon as a substitute for observation, for it is only through observation that the student can discover what his informants are talking about and understand their remarks in terms of group structure. Observation suggests a framework of significant behavior patterns and indicates subjects that are relevant for discussion with informants.

The student should realize that this procedure changes the attitude of the corner boy toward himself and his group. The quotations from Cornerville men presented here all show the effects of prior discussion upon me. However, the effort of informants to make explicit statements upon unreflective behavior does not distort the factual picture as long as they are required to tell their stories in terms of observed interactions.

The most thorough study of this kind was made for me by Sam of the millers upon his own group. The structure of the Millers was worked out by Sam over a period of months on the basis of such material as I have quoted. My function was to discuss Sam's observations with him, to point out gaps in his data, and to check them with some independent observations.

All the generalizations presented here have been checked against the experience and observations of four such informants. In this way I have been able to expand my study far beyond what I should have been able to cover alone.

Accomplishment of the second purpose—fitting corner gangs into the fabric of society—required study of the relations which linked group to group and the group to persons who held superior positions in Cornerville—politicians and racketeers, for example.

The observation that the leader is the person to relate his group to other people provides the most important lead for such a study. We see that the social behavior of groups pivots around the actions of certain men who hold strategic positions in them. This does not mean that the leader can make his followers do anything he desires. It does not mean that he customarily leads the group activity and that outsiders, in order to influence the members, must deal with the group through him. This is to be observed particularly at the same time of a political campaign when politicians seek to mobilize group support. Similar observations may be made in order to explain the position and influence of the racketeer in relation to corner-boy groups.

Brief reference to the Cornerville S. and A. study will indicate the nature of the results that may be obtained. Tony, the top man in the chart, was a prominent policy racketeer. The chart indicates that certain members were agents who turned their policy slips in to him. While Tony belonged to the club, his interests were so widespread that he had little time to spend with the members. It was recognized that he held a higher status, that he was not a corner boy.

At the time of the formation of the club, Tony knew Dom, his agent, and recognized Dom's position among the lunchroom boys. He knew Carlo only casually and was not aware of his position as a leader of the barbershop clique. In the course of a political campaign (November 1939) a conflict arose over the endorsement of a candidate for alderman. By playing off one clique against the other, Tony was able to secure the adoption of his policy, but Carlo opposed him vigorously and lost out in a close vote. Carlo's position was strengthened when his candidate defeated the man supported by Tony. Following the election, there was a marked change in Tony's actions. He began to attend every meeting and to spend more time with the members. For his purposes Carlo was the most important man in the club, and he made every effort to cement his social relations with Carlo and to place Carlo under obligations to him. During this period a basis for co-operation between the two men was established. When Tony turned his attention to other activities, he was able to deal with the club through Carlo as well as through Dom.

This story illustrates a method of study, not a set of conclusions. Through observing the interactions between Tony and Dom, Tony and Carlo, Dom and the members of his clique, and Carlo and the members of his clique, one can establish the position and influence of the racketeer in relation to this particular organization of corner boys. Other observations establish Tony's position in the racket organization, which extends throughout the district and far beyond it. They also point out Tony's relations with certain politicians. Only in the study of such specific situations can one arrive at reliable generalizations upon the positions of influence of men in the community.

# CONCLUSION

The methods I have used call for precise and detailed observation of spatial positions and of the origination of action in pair and set events between members of informal groups. Such observations provide data by means of which one may chart structures of social relations and determine the basis of the structures—a system of mutual obligations growing out of the interactions of the members over a long period of time. Observations also point out the distinctive functions of the leader, who serves as chief representative of his group and director and co-ordinator of group activity. A knowledge of the structure and of the social processes carried on through it serves to explain the behavior of individual members in a manner which could not be accomplished if one considered the men as an unstructured aggregation.

Such an understanding of clique behavior seems a necessary first step in the development of knowledge of the nature of the larger social organization into which the cliques fit. Instead of seeking to place each clique member in relation to the total social organization, the investigator may concentrate his attention upon the actions of the leader, who relates his corner boys to other groups and to persons holding superior positions. By discovering these strategic points for social integration and by extending the network of social relations through them, the investigator can place a large number of the inhabitants of his community in their social positions.

SOURCE: William Foote Whyte, "Corner Boys: A Study of Clique Behavior," *American Journal of Sociology* 46 (March 1941): 647-664.

# The Functions of Crime

*Emile Durkheim*

*Common sense lends us to view crime, and all kinds of deviance, as* pathological*—that is, as harmful to social life, despite the obvious social costs of crime, however, Durkheim argues that crime is* normal *because it is part of all societies. Furthermore, he claims that crime makes important contributions to the operation of a social system.*

. . . Crime is present not only in the majority of societies of one particular species but in all societies of all types. There is no society that is not confronted with the problem of criminality. Its form changes; the acts thus characterized are not the same everywhere; but, everywhere and always, there have been men who have behaved in such a way as to draw upon themselves penal repression. . . . There is, then, no phenomenon that presents more indisputably all the symptoms of normality, since it appears closely connected with the conditions of all collective life. To make of crime a form of social morbidity would be to admit that morbidity is not something accidental, but, on the contrary, that in certain cases it grows out of the fundamental constitution of the living organism; it would result in wiping out all distinction between the physiological and the pathological. No doubt it is possible that crime itself will have abnormal forms, as, for example, when its rate is unusually high. This excess is, indeed, undoubtedly morbid in nature. What is normal, simply, is the existence of criminality. . . .

Here we are, then, in the presence of a conclusion in appearance quite paradoxical. Let us make no mistake. To classify crime among the phenomena of normal sociology is not to say merely that it is an inevitable, although regrettable, phenomenon, due to the incorrigible wickedness of men; it is to affirm that it is a factor in public health, an integral part of all healthy societies. This result is, at first glance, surprising enough to have puzzled even ourselves for a long time. Once this first surprise has been overcome, however, it is not difficult to find reasons explaining this normality and at the same time confirming it.

In the first place crime is normal because a society exempt from it is utterly impossible. Crime, we have shown elsewhere, consists of an act that offends certain very strong collective sentiments. In a society in which criminal acts are no longer committed, the sentiments they offend would have to be found without exception in all individual consciousnesses, and they must be found to exist with the same degree as sentiments contrary to them. Assuming that this condition could actually be realized, crime would not thereby disappear; it would only change its form, for the very cause which would thus dry up the sources of criminality would immediately open up new ones.

Indeed, for the collective sentiments which are protected by the penal law of a people at a specified moment of its history to take possession of the public conscience or for them to acquire a stronger hold where they have an insufficient grip, they must acquire an intensity greater than that which they had hitherto had. The community as a whole must experience them more vividly, for it can acquire from no other source the greater force necessary to control these individuals who formerly were the most refractory. For murderers to disappear, the horror of bloodshed must become greater in those social strata from which murderers are recruited; but, first it must become greater through out the entire society. Moreover, the very absence of crime would directly contribute to produce this horror; because any sentiment seems much more respectable when it is always and uniformly respected.

One easily overlooks the consideration that these strong states of the common consciousness cannot be thus reinforced without reinforcing at the same time the more feeble states, whose violation previously gave birth to mere infraction of convention—since the weaker ones are only the prolongation, the attenuated form, of the stronger. Thus robbery and simple bad taste injure the same single altruistic sentiment, the respect for that which is another's. However, this same sentiment is less grievously offended by bad taste than by robbery: and since, in addition, the average consciousness has not sufficient intensity to react keenly to the bad taste, it is treated with greater tolerance. That is why the person guilty of bad taste is merely blamed, whereas the thief is punished. But, if this sentiment grows stronger, to the point of silencing in all consciousnesses the inclination which disposes man to steal, he will become more sensitive to the offenses which, until then, touched him but lightly. He will react against them, then, with more energy; they will be the object of greater opprobrium, which will transform certain of them from the simple moral faults that they were and give them the quality of crimes. For example, improper contracts, or contracts improperly executed, which only incur public blame or civil damages, will become offenses in law.

Imagine a society of saints, a perfect cloister of exemplary individuals. Crimes, properly so called, will there be unknown; but faults which appear venial to the layman will create there the same scandal that the ordinary offense does in ordinary consciousnesses If, then, this society has the power to judge and punish, it will define these acts as criminal and will treat them as such. For the same reason, the perfect and upright man judges his smallest failings with a severity that the majority reserve for acts more truly in the nature of an offense. Formerly, acts of violence against persons were more frequent than they are today, because respect for individual dignity was less strong. As this has increased, these crimes have become more rare; and also, many acts violating this sentiment have been introduced into the penal law which were not included there in primitive times.[1]. . .

Crime is, then, necessary; it is bound up with the fundamental conditions of all social life, and by that very fact it is useful, because these conditions of which it is a part are themselves indispensable to the normal evolution of morality and law.

Indeed, its no longer possible today to dispute the fact that law and morality vary from one social type to the next, nor that they change within the same type if the conditions of life are modified. But, in order that these transformations may be possible, the collective sentiments at the basis of morality must not be hostile to change, and consequently must have but moderate energy. If they were too strong, they would no longer be plastic. Every pattern is an obstacle to new patterns, to the extent that the first pattern is inflexible. The better a structure is articulated, the more it offers a healthy resistance to all modification; and this is equally true of functional, as of anatomical, organization. If there were no crimes, this condition could not have been fulfilled; for such a hypothesis presupposes that collective sentiments have arrived at a degree of intensity unexampled in history. Nothing is good indefinitely and to an unlimited extent. The authority which the moral conscience enjoys must not be excessive; otherwise no one would dare criticize it, and it would too easily congeal into an immutable form. To make progress, individual originality must be able to express itself. In order that the originality of the idealist whose dreams transcend his century may find expression, it is necessary that the originality of the criminal, who is below the level of his time, shall also be possible. One does not occur without the other.

Nor is this all. Aside from this indirect utility, it happens that crime itself plays a useful role in this evolution. Crime implies not only that the way remains open to necessary changes but that in certain cases it directly prepares these changes. Where crime exists, collective sentiments are sufficiently flexible to take on a new form, and crime sometimes helps to determine the form they will take. How many times, indeed, it is only an anticipation of future morality—a step toward what will be! According to Athenian law, Socrates was a criminal, and his condemnation was no more than just. However, his crime, namely, the independence of his thought, rendered a service not only to humanity but to his country. . . .

From this point of view the fundamental facts of criminality present themselves to us in an entirely new light. Contrary to current ideas, the criminal no longer seems a totally unsociable being, a sort of parasitic element, a strange and unassimilable body, introduced into the midst of society. On the contrary, he plays a definite role in social life.

## CRITICAL-THINKING QUESTIONS

1. *On what grounds does Durkheim argue that crime should be considered a "normal" element of society?*
2. *Why is a society devoid of crime an impossibility?*
3. *What are the functional consequences of crime and deviance?*

## NOTE

1. Calumny, insults, slander, fraud, etc.

SOURCE: *The Rules of Sociological Method* by Emile Durkheim, trans. Sarah A. Solovay and John A. Mueller, ed. George E. G. Catlin, renewed 1966 by Sarah A. Solovay, John H. Mueller, and George G. Catlin. Reprinted with permission of The Free Press, Macmillan Publishing Company, a Member of Paramount Publishing.

# Some Principles of Stratification

*Kingsley Davis and Wilbert Moore*
*with a response by Melvin Tumin*

*Why is some degree of social stratification found everywhere? This selection outlines what has become known as the "Davis and Moore thesis": Social stratification is a consequence of the fact that some social positions are more important to the operation of a social system than others. The selection is followed by a critical response by Melvin Tumin, who suggests a number of ways in which social stratification is* dysfunctional *for society.*

Starting from the proposition that no society is "classless," or unstratified, an effort is made to explain, in functional terms, the universal necessity which calls forth stratification in any social system. Next, an attempt is made to explain the roughly uniform distribution of prestige as between the major types of positions in every society. Since, however, there occur between one society and another great differences in the degree and kind of stratification, some attention is also given to the varieties of social inequality and the variable factors that give rise to them. . . .

Throughout, it will be necessary to keep in mind one thing—namely, that the discussion relates to the system of positions, not to the individuals occupying those positions. It is one thing to ask why different positions carry different degrees of prestige, and quite another to ask how certain individuals get into those positions. Although, as the argument will try to show, both questions are related, it is essential to keep them separate in our thinking. Most of the literature on stratification has tried to answer the second question (particularly with regard to the ease or difficulty of mobility between strata) without tackling the first. The first question, however, is logically prior and, in the case of any particular individual or group, factually prior.

## THE FUNCTIONAL NECESSITY OF STRATIFICATION

Curiously, however, the main functional necessity explaining the universal presence of stratification is precisely the requirement faced by any society of placing and motivating individuals in the social structure. As a functioning mechanism a society must somehow distribute its members in social positions and induce them to perform the duties of these positions. It must thus concern itself with motivation at two different levels to instill in the proper individuals the desire to fill certain positions, and, once in these positions, the desire to perform the duties attached to them. Even though the social order may be relatively static in form, there is a continuous process of metabolism as new individuals are born into it, shift with age, and die off. Their absorption into the positional system must somehow be arranged and motivated. This is true whether the system is competitive or noncompetitive. A competitive system gives greater importance to the motivation to achieve positions, whereas a noncompetitive system gives perhaps greater importance to the motivation to perform the duties of the positions; but in any system both types of motivation are required.

If the duties associated with the various positions were all equally pleasant to the human organism, all equally important to societal survival, and all equally in need of the same ability or talent, it would make no difference who got into which positions, and the problem of social placement would be greatly reduced. But actually it does make a great deal of difference who gets into which positions, not only because some positions are inherently more agreeable than others, but also because some require special talents or training and some are functionally more important than others. Also, it is essential that the duties of the positions he performed with the diligence that their importance requires. Inevitably, then, a society must have, first, some kind of rewards that it can use as inducements, and, second, some way of distributing these rewards differentially according to positions. The rewards and their distribution become a part of the social order, and thus give rise to stratification.

One may ask what kind of rewards a society has at its disposal in distributing its personnel and securing essential services. It has, first of all, the things that contribute to sustenance and comfort. It has, second, the things that contribute to humor and diversion. And it has, finally, the things that contribute to self-respect and ego expansion. The last, because of the peculiarly social character of the self, is largely a function of the opinion of others, but it nonetheless ranks in importance with the first two. In any social system all three kinds of rewards must be dispensed differentially according to positions.

In a sense the rewards are "built into" the position. They consist in the "rights" associated with the position, plus what may be called its accompaniments or perquisites. Often the rights, and sometimes the accompaniments, are functionally related to the duties of the position. (Rights as viewed by the incumbent are usually duties as viewed by other members of the community.) However, there may be a host of subsidiary rights and perquisites that are not essential to the function of the position and have only an indirect and symbolic connection with its duties, but which still may be of considerable importance in inducing people to seek the positions and fulfill the essential duties.

If the rights and perquisites of different positions in a society must be unequal, then the society must be stratified, because that is precisely what stratification means. Social inequality is thus an unconsciously evolved device by which societies insure that the most important positions are conscientiously filled by the most qualified persons. Hence every society, no matter how simple or complex, must differentiate persons in terms of both prestige and esteem, and must therefore possess a certain amount of institutionalized inequality.

It does not follow that the amount or type of inequality need be the same in all societies. This is largely a function of factors that will be discussed presently.

## THE TWO DETERMINANTS OF POSITIONAL RANK

Granting the general function that inequality subserves, one can specify the two factors that determine the relative rank of different positions. In general those positions convey the best reward, and hence have the highest rank, which (a) have the greatest importance for the society and (b) require the greatest training or talent. The first factor concerns function and is a matter of relative significance; the second concerns means and is a matter of scarcity.

**Differential Functional Importance** Actually a society does not need to reward positions in proportion to their functional importance. It merely needs to give sufficient reward to them to insure that they will be filled competently. In other words, it must see that less essential positions do not compete successfully with more essential ones. If a position is easily filled, it need not be heavily rewarded, even though important. On the other hand if it is important but hard to fill, the reward must be high enough to get it filled anyway. Functional importance is therefore a necessary but not a sufficient cause of high rank being assigned to a position.[1]

**Differential Scarcity of Personnel** Practically all positions, no matter how acquired, require some form of skill or capacity for performance. This is implicit in the very notion of position, which implies that the incumbent must, by virtue of his incumbency, accomplish certain things.

There are, ultimately, only two ways in which a person's qualifications come about: through inherent capacity or through training. Obviously, in concrete activities both are always necessary, but from a practical standpoint the scarcity may lie primarily in one or the other, as well as in both. Some positions require innate talents of such high degree that the persons who fill them are bound to be rare. In many cases, however, talent is fairly abundant in the population but the training process is so long, costly, and elaborate that relatively few can qualify. Modern medicine, for example, is within the mental capacity of most individuals, but a medical education is so burdensome and expensive that virtually none would undertake it if the position of the M.D. did not carry a reward commensurate with the sacrifice.

If the talents required for a position are abundant and the training easy, the method of acquiring the position may have little to do with its duties. There may be, in fact, a virtually accidental relationship. But if the skills required are scarce by reason of the rarity of talent or the costliness of training, the position, if functionally important, must have an attractive power that will draw the necessary skills in competition with other positions. This means, in effect, that the position must be high in the social scale—must command great prestige, high salary, ample leisure, and the like.

**How Variations Are to Be Understood** Insofar as there is a difference between one system of stratification and another, it is attributable to whatever factors affect the two determinants of differential reward—namely, functional importance and scarcity of personnel. Positions important in one society may not be important in another, because the conditions faced by the societies, or their degree of internal development, may be different. The same conditions, in turn, may affect the question of scarcity; for in some societies the stage of development, or the external situation, may wholly obviate the necessity of certain kinds of skill or talent. Any particular system of stratification, then, can be understood as a product of the special conditions affecting the two aforementioned grounds of differential reward.

## CRITICAL RESPONSE BY MELVIN TUMIN

The fact of social inequality in human society is marked by its ubiquity and its antiquity. Every known society, past and present, distributes its scarce and demanded goods and services unequally. And there are attached to the positions which command unequal amounts of such goods and services certain highly morally-toned evaluations of their importance for the society.

The ubiquity and the antiquity of such inequality has given rise to the assumption that there must be something both inevitable and positively functional about such social arrangements. . . . Clearly, the truth or falsity of such an assumption is a strategic question for any general theory of social organization. It is therefore most curious that the basic premises and implications of the assumption have only been most casually explored by American sociologists. . . .

Let us take [the Davis and Moore] propositions and examine them *seriatim.*

(1) *Certain positions in any society are more functionally important than others and require special skills for their performance.*

The key term here is "functionally important." The functionalist theory of social organization is by no means clear and explicit about this term. The minimum common referent is to something known as the "survival value" of a social structure. This concept immediately involves a number of perplexing questions. Among these are: (a) the issue of minimum vs. maximum survival, and the possible empirical referents which can be given to those terms; (b) whether such a proposition is a useless tautology since any *status quo* at any given moment is nothing more and nothing less than everything present in the *status quo*. In these terms, all acts and structures must be judged positively functional in that they constitute essential portions of the *status quo*; (c) what kind of calculus of functionality exists which will enable us, at this point in our development, to add and subtract long and short range consequences, with their mixed qualities, and arrive at some summative judgment regarding the rating an act or structure should receive on a scale of greater or lesser functionality? At best, we tend to make primarily intuitive judgments. Often enough, these judgments involve the use of value-laden criteria, or, at least, criteria which are chosen in preference to others not for any sociologically systematic reasons but by reason of certain implicit value preferences. . . .

A generalized theory of social stratification must recognize that the prevailing system of inducements and rewards is only one of many variants in the whole range of possible systems of motivation which, at least theoretically, are capable of working in human society. It is quite conceivable, of course, that a system of norms could be institutionalized in which the idea of threatened withdrawal of services, except under the most extreme circumstances, would be considered as absolute moral anathema. In such a case, the whole notion of relative functionality, as advanced by Davis and Moore, would have to be radically revised.

(2) *Only a limited number of individuals in any society have the talents which can be trained into the skills appropriate to these positions (i.e., the more functionally important positions).*

The truth of this proposition depends at least in part on the truth of proposition 1 above. It is, therefore, subject to all the limitations indicated above. But for the moment, let us assume the validity of the first proposition and concentrate on the question of the rarity of appropriate talent.

If all that is meant is that in every society there is a *range* of talent, and that some members of any society are by nature more talented than others. No sensible contradiction can be offered, but a question must be raised here regarding the amount of sound knowledge present in any society concerning the presence of talent in the population.

For, in every society there is some demonstrable ignorance regarding the amount of talent present in the population. *And the more rigidly stratified a society is, the less chance does that society have of discovering any new facts about the talents of its members.* Smoothly working and stable systems of stratification, wherever found, tend to build-in obstacles to the further exploration of the range of available talent. This is especially true in those societies where the opportunity to discover talent in any one generation varies with the differential resources of the parent generation. Where, for instance, access to education depends upon the wealth of one's parents, and where wealth is differentially distributed, large segments of the population are likely to be deprived of the chance even to *discover* what are their talents.

Whether or not differential rewards and opportunities are functional in any one generation, it is clear that if those differentials are allowed to be socially inherited by the next generation, then the stratification system is specifically dysfunctional for the discovery of talents in the next generation. In this fashion, systems of social stratification tend to limit the chances available to maximize the efficiency of discovery, recruitment and training of "functionally important talent."

. . . In this context, it may be asserted that there is some noticeable tendency for elites to restrict further access to their privileged positions, once they have sufficient power to enforce such restrictions. This is especially true in a culture where it is possible for an elite to contrive a high demand and a proportionately higher reward for its work by restricting the numbers of the elite available to do the work. The recruitment and training of doctors in modern United States is at least partly a case in point. . .

(3) *The conversion of talents into skills involves a training period during which sacrifices of one kind or another are made by those undergoing the training.*

Davis and Moore introduce here a concept, "sacrifice," which comes closer than any of the rest of their vocabulary of analysis to being a direct reflection of the rationalizations, offered by the more fortunate members of a society, of the rightness of their occupancy of privileged positions. It is the least critically thought-out concept in the repertoire, and can also be shown to be least supported by the actual facts.

In our present society, for example, what are the sacrifices which talented persons undergo in the training period? The possibly serious losses involve the surrender of earning power and the cost of the training. The latter is generally borne by the parents of the talented youth undergoing training, and not by the trainees themselves. But this cost tends to be paid out of income which the parents were able to earn generally by virtue of *their* privileged positions in the hierarchy of stratification. That is to say, the parents' ability to pay for the training of their children is part of the differential *reward* they, the parents, received for their privileged positions in the society. And to charge this sum up against sacrifices made by the youth is falsely to perpetrate a bill or a debt already paid by the society to the parents. . . .

What tends to be completely overlooked, in addition, are the psychic and spiritual rewards which are available to the elite trainees by comparison with their age peers in the labor force. There is, first, the much higher prestige enjoyed by the college student and the professional-school student as compared with persons in shops and offices. There is, second, the extremely highly valued privilege of having greater opportunity for self-development. There is, third, all the psychic gain involved in being allowed to delay the assumption of adult responsibilities such as earning a living and supporting a family. There is, fourth, the access to leisure and freedom of a kind not likely to be experienced by the persons already at work.

If these are never taken into account as rewards of the training period it is not because they are not concretely present, but because the emphasis in American concepts of reward is almost exclusively placed on the material returns of positions. The emphases on enjoyment, entertainment, ego enhancement, prestige and esteem are introduced only when the differentials in these which accrue to the skilled positions need to be justified. If these other rewards were taken into account, it would be much more difficult to demonstrate that the training period, as presently operative, is really sacrificial. Indeed, it might turn out to be the case that even at this point in their careers, the elite trainees were being differentially rewarded relative to their age peers in the labor force. . . .

(4) *In order to induce the talented persons to undergo these sacrifices and acquire the training, their future positions must carry an inducement value in the form of differential, i.e., privileged and disproportionate access to the scarce and desired rewards which the society has to offer.*

Let us assume, for the purposes of the discussion, that the training period is sacrificial and the talent is rare in every conceivable human society. There is still the basic problem as to whether the allocation of differential rewards in scarce and desired goods and services is the only or the most efficient way of recruiting the appropriate talent to these positions.

For there are a number of alternative motivational schemes whose efficiency and adequacy ought at least to be considered in this context. What can be said, for instance, on behalf of the motivation which De Man called "joy in work," Veblen termed "instinct for workmanship" and which we latterly have come to identify as "intrinsic work satisfaction"? Or, to what extent could the motivation of "social duty" be institutionalized in such a fashion that self-interest and social interest come closely to coincide? Or, how much prospective confidence can be placed in the possibilities of institutionalizing "social service" as a widespread motivation for seeking one's appropriate position and fulfilling it conscientiously?

Are not these types of motivations, we may ask, likely to prove most appropriate for precisely the "most functionally important positions"? Especially in a mass industrial society, where the vast majority of positions become standardized and routinized, it is the skilled jobs which are likely to retain most of the quality of "intrinsic job satisfaction" and be most readily identifiable as socially serviceable. Is it indeed impossible then to build these motivations into the socialization pattern to which we expose our talented youth? . . .

(5) *These scarce and desired goods consist of rights and perquisites attached to, or built into, the positions and can be classified into those things which contribute to (a) sustenance and comfort; (b) humor and diversion; (c) self-respect and ego expansion.*

(6) *This differential access to the basic rewards of the society has as a consequence the differentiation of the prestige and esteem which various strata acquire. This may be said, along with the rights and perquisites, to constitute institutionalized social inequality, i.e., stratification.*

With the classification of the rewards offered by Davis and Moore there need be little argument. Some question must be raised, however, as to whether any reward system, built into a general stratification system, must allocate equal amounts of all three types of reward in order to function effectively, or whether one type of reward may be emphasized to the virtual neglect of others. This raises the further question regarding which type of emphasis is likely to prove most effective as a differential inducer. Nothing in the known facts about human motivation impels us to favor one type of reward over the other, or to insist that all three types of reward must be built into the positions in comparable amounts if the position is to have an inducement value.

It is well known, of course, that societies differ considerably in the kinds of rewards they emphasize in their efforts to maintain a reasonable balance between responsibility and reward. There are, for instance, numerous societies in which the conspicuous display of differential economic advantage is considered extremely bad taste. In short, our present knowledge commends to us the possibility of considerable plasticity in the way in which different types of rewards can be structured into a functioning society. This is to say, it cannot yet be demonstrated that it is *unavoidable* that differential prestige and esteem shall accrue to positions which command differential rewards in power and property.

What does seem to be unavoidable is that differential prestige shall be given to those in any society who conform to the normative order as against those who deviate from that order in a way judged immoral and detrimental. On the assumption that the continuity of a society depends on the continuity and stability of its normative order, some such distinction between conformists and deviants seems inescapable.

It also seems to be unavoidable that in any society, no matter how literate its tradition, the older, wiser and more experienced individuals who are charged with the enculturation and socialization of the young must have more power than the young, on the assumption that the task of effective socialization demands such differential power.

But this differentiation in prestige between the conformist and the deviant is by no means the same distinction as that between strata of individuals each of which operates *within* the normative order, and is composed of adults. . .

(7) *Therefore, social inequality among different strata in the amounts of scarce and desired goods, and the amounts of prestige and esteem which they receive, is both positively functional and inevitable in any society.*

If the objections which have heretofore been raised are taken as reasonable, then it may be stated that the only items which any society *must* distribute unequally are the power and property necessary for the performance of different tasks. If such differential power and property are viewed by all as commensurate with the differential responsibilities, and if they are culturally defined as *resources* and not as rewards, then no differentials in prestige and esteem need follow.

Historically, the evidence seems to be that every time power and property are distributed unequally, no matter what the cultural definition, prestige and esteem differentiations have tended to result as well. Historically, however, no systematic effort has ever been made, under propitious circumstances, to develop the tradition that each man is as socially worthy as all other men so long as he performs his appropriate tasks conscientiously. While such a tradition seems utterly utopian, no known facts in psychological or social science have yet demonstrated its impossibility or its dysfunctionality for the continuity of a society. The achievement of a full institutionalization of such a tradition seems far too remote to contemplate. Some successive approximations at such a tradition, however, are not out of the range of prospective social innovation.

What, then, of the "positive functionality" of social stratification? Are there other, negative, functions of institutionalized social inequality which can be identified, if only tentatively? Some such dysfunctions of stratification have already been suggested in the body of this paper. Along with others they may now be stated, in the form of provisional assertions, as follows:

1. Social stratification systems function to limit the possibility of discovery of the full range of talent available in a society. This results from the fact of unequal access to appropriate motivation, channels of recruitment and centers of training.

2. In foreshortening the range of available talent, social stratification systems function to set limits upon the possibility of expanding the productive resources of the society, at least relative to what might be the case under conditions of greater equality of opportunity.

3. Social stratification systems function to provide the elite with the *political* power necessary to procure acceptance and dominance of an ideology which rationalizes the *status quo*, whatever it may be, as "logical," "natural" and "morally right." In this manner, social stratification systems function as essentially conservative influences in the societies in which they are found.

4. Social stratification systems function to distribute favorable self-images unequally throughout a population. To the extent that such favorable self-images are requisite to the development of the creative potential inherent in men, to that extent stratification systems function to limit the development of this creative potential.

5. To the extent that inequalities in social rewards cannot be made fully acceptable to the less privileged in a society, social stratification systems function to encourage hostility, suspicion and mistrust among the various segments of a society and thus to limit the possibilities of extensive social integration.

6. To the extent that the sense of significant membership in a society depends on one's place on the prestige ladder of the society, social stratification systems function to distribute unequally the sense of significant membership in the population.

7. To the extent that loyalty to a society depends on a sense of significant membership in the society, social stratification systems function to distribute loyalty unequally in the population.

8. To the extent that participation and apathy depend upon the sense of significant membership in the society, social stratification systems function to distribute the motivation to participate unequally in a population.

Each of the eight foregoing propositions contains implicit hypotheses regarding the consequences of unequal distribution of rewards in a society in accordance with some notion of the functional importance of various positions. These are empirical hypotheses, subject to test. They are offered here only as exemplary of the kinds of consequences of social stratification which are not often taken into account in dealing with the problem. They should also serve to reinforce the doubt that social inequality is a device which is uniformly functional for the role of guaranteeing that the most important tasks in a society will be performed conscientiously by the most competent persons.

The obviously mixed character of the functions of social inequality should come as no surprise to anyone. If sociology is sophisticated in any sense, it is certainly with regard to its awareness of the mixed nature of any social arrangement, when the observer takes into account long-as well as short-range consequences and latent as well as manifest dimensions.

## CRITICAL-THINKING QUESTIONS

*1. Why do Davis and Moore argue that all societies attach greater rewards to some positions than to others?*

*2. Does the "Davis and Moore thesis" justify social stratification as it presently exists in the United States (or anywhere else)?*

*3. In what way does Tumin argue that social stratification is* dysfunctional *for a social system?*

## NOTE

1. Unfortunately, functional importance is difficult to establish. To use the position's prestige to establish it, as is often unconsciously done, constitutes circular reasoning from our point of view. There are, however, two independent clues: (a) the degree to which a position is functionally unique, there being no other positions that can perform the same function satisfactorily; and (b) the degree to which other positions are dependent on the one in question. Both clues are best exemplified in organized systems of positions built around one major function. Thus in most complex societies the religious, political, economic and educational functions are handled by distinct structures not easily

interchangeable. In addition each structure possesses many different positions, some clearly dependent on, if not subordinate to, others. In sum, when an institutional nucleus becomes differentiated around one main function, and at the same time organizes a large portion of the population into its relationships, *key* positions in it are of the highest functional importance. The absence of such specialization does not prove functional unimportance, for the whole society may be relatively unspecialized; but it is safe to assume that the more important functions receive the first and clearest structural differentiation.

SOURCES: "Some Principles of Stratification," by Kingsley Davis and Wilbert E. Moore, in *American Sociological Review,* vol. 10, no. 2 (April 1945), pp. 242-44.

"Some Principles of Stratification: A Critical Analysis," by Melvin Tumin in *American Sociological Review,* vol. 18, no. 4 (Aug. 1953), pp. 387-93. Reprinted with permission.

# The Bohemian Grove and Other Retreats

G. William Domhoff

*["Bohemians" of the 1970s and 1980s include such personages as President Ronald Reagan; Vice President George Bush, Attorney General William French Smith; Secretary of State George P. Shultz, former President Richard Nixon; former President Gerald Ford; Supreme Court Justice Potter Stewart; Herbert Hoover, Jr.; Herbert Hoover III; newspaperman William R .Hearst, Jr.; five members of the Dean Witter family of investment bankers; entertainers Art Linkletter and Edgar Bergen; presidents and chairmen of several oil companies such as Marathon Oil and Standard Oil the president of Rockefeller University officers of Anheuser-Busch breweries; the president of Kaiser Industries; bank presidents from California to New York the president and chairman of Hewlett-Packard Co; and many other representatives of American industry, finance, government, and entertainment. When these participants arrive for the annual "campout," an elaborate ritual called the Cremation of Care welcomes them and instructs them to leave all cares behind while they join together for two weeks of lavish entertainment, fellowship, and "communion with nature."]*

The Cremation of Care is the most spectacular event of the midsummer retreat that members and guests of San Francisco's Bohemian Club have taken every year since 1878. However, there are several other entertainments in store. Before the Bohemians return to the everyday world, they will be treated to plays, variety shows, song fests, shooting contests, art exhibits, swimming, boating, and nature rides.

A cast for a typical Grove play easily runs to seventy-five or one hundred people. Add in the orchestra, the stagehands, the carpenters who make the sets, and other supporting personnel, and over three hundred people are involved in creating the High Jinks each year. Preparations begin a year in advance, with rehearsals occurring two or three times a week in the month before the encampment, and nightly in the week before the play.

Costs are on the order of $20,000 to $30,000 per High Jinks, a large amount of money for a one night production which does not have to pay a penny for salaries (the highest cost in any commercial production) "And the costs are talked about, too," reports my . . . informant." "Hey, did you hear the High Jinks will cost $25,000 this year?' one of them will say to another. The expense of the play is one way they can relate to its worth."

Entertainment is not the only activity at the Bohemian Grove. For a little change of pace, there is intellectual stimulation and political enlightenment every day at 12:30 P.M. Since 1932 the meadow from which people view the Cremation of Care also has been the setting for informal talks and briefings by people as varied as Dwight David Eisenhower (before he was President), Herman Wouk (author of *The Caine Mutiny*), Bobby Kennedy (while he was Attorney General), and Neil Armstrong (after he returned from the moon).

Cabinet officers, politicians, generals, and governmental advisers are the rule rather than the exception for Lakeside Talks, especially on weekends. Equally prominent figures from the worlds of art, literature and science are more likely to make their appearance during the weekdays of the encampment, when Grove attendance may drop to four or five hundred (many of the members only come up for one week or for the weekends because they cannot stay away from their corporations and law firms for the full two weeks).

[T]he Grove is an ideal off-the-record atmosphere for sizing, up politicians. "Well, of course when a politician comes here, we all get to see him, and his stock in trade is his personality and his ideas," a prominent Bohemian told a *New York Times* reporter who was trying to cover Nelson Rockefeller's 1963 visit to the Grove for a Lakeside Talk. The journalist went on to note that the midsummer encampments "have long been a major showcase where leaders of business, industry, education, the arts, and politics can come to examine each other."[1]

For 1971, [then-] President Nixon was to be the featured Lakeside speaker. However, when newspaper reporters learned that the President planned to disappear into a redwood grove for an off-the-record speech to some of the most powerful men in America, they objected loudly and vowed to make every effort to cover the event. The flap caused the club considerable embarrassment, and after much hemming and hawing back and forth, the club leaders asked the President to cancel his scheduled appearance. A White House press secretary then announced that the President had decided not to appear at the Grove rather than risk the tradition that speeches there are strictly off the public record.[2]

However, the President was not left without a final word to his fellow Bohemians. In a telegram to the president of the club, which now hangs at the entrance to the reading room in the San Francisco clubhouse, he expressed his regrets at not being able to attend. He asked the club president to continue to lead people into the woods, adding that he in turn would redouble his efforts to lead people out of the woods. He also noted that, while anyone could aspire to be President of the United States, only a few could aspire to be president of the Bohemian Club

Not all the entertainment at the Bohemian Grove takes place under the auspices of the committee in charge of special events. The Bohemians and their guests are divided into camps which evolved slowly over the years as the number of people on the retreat grew into the hundreds and then the thousands. These camps have become a significant center of enjoyment during the encampment.

At first the camps were merely a place in the woods where a half-dozen to a dozen friends would pitch their tents. Soon they added little amenities like their own special stove or a small permanent structure. Then there developed little camp "traditions" and endearing camp names like Cliff Dwellers, Moonshiners, Silverado Squatters, Woof, Zaca, Toyland, Sundodgers, and Land of Happiness. The next steps were special emblems, a handsome little lodge or specially constructed teepees, a permanent bar, and maybe a grand piano.[3] Today there are 129 camps of varying sizes, structures, and statuses. Most have between 10 and 30 members, but there are one or two with about 125 members and several with less than 10. A majority of the camps are strewn along what is called the River Road, but some are huddled in other areas within five or ten minutes of the center of the Grove.

The entertainment at the camps is mostly informal and impromptu. Someone will decide to bring together all the jazz musicians in the Grove for a special session. Or maybe all the artists or writers will be invited to a luncheon or a dinner at a camp. Many camps have their own amateur piano players and informal musical and singing groups which perform for the rest of the members.

But the joys of the camps are not primarily in watching or listening to performances. Other pleasures are created within them. Some camps become known for their gastronomical specialties, such as a particular drink or a particular meal. The Jungle Camp features mint juleps, Halcyon has a three-foot-high martini maker constructed out of chemical glassware. At the Owl's Nest. [President Reagan's club] it's the gin-fizz breakfast—about a hundred people are invited over one morning during the encampment for eggs Benedict, gin fizzes, and all the trimmings.

The men of Bohemia are drawn in large measure from the corporate leadership of the United States. They include in their numbers directors from major corporations in every sector of the American economy. An indication of this fact is that one in every five resident members and one in every three nonresident members is found in *Poor's Register of Corporations, Executives, and Directors*, a huge volume which lists the leadership of tens of thousands of companies from every major business field except investment banking, real estate, and advertising.

Even better evidence for the economic prominence of the men under consideration is that at least one officer or director from 40 of the 50 best industrial corporations in America was present, as a member or a guest, on the lists at our disposal. Only Ford Motor Company and Western Electric were missing among the top 25! Similarly, we found that officers and directors from 20 of the top 25 commercial banks (including all of the 15 largest) were on our lists. Men from 12 of the first 25 life-insurance companies were in attendance (8 of these 12 were from the top 10). Other business sectors were represented somewhat less: 10 of 25 in transportation, 8 of 25 in utilities, 7 of 25 in conglomerates, and only 5 of 25 in retailing. More generally, of the top-level businesses ranked by *Fortune* for 1969 (the top 500 industrial, the top 50 commercial ranks, the top 50 life-insurance companies, the top 50 transportation companies, the top 50 utilities, the top 50 retailers, and the top 47 conglomerates), *29 percent of these 797 corporations were "represented" by at least 1 officer or director.*

## OTHER WATERING HOLES

[Other camps and retreats were founded by wealthy and powerful men, based on the model provides by the Bohemian Grove. One example is the Rancheros Visitadores (Visiting Ranchers) who meet each May for horseback rides through the California ranch land. These are accompanied by feasts, entertainment, and general merrymaking with a Spanish-ranch motif.]

[Among the Rancheros a] common interest in horses and horseplay provides a social setting in which men with different forms of wealth get to know each other better. *Sociologically speaking, the Rancheros Visitadores is an organization which serves the function (whether the organization planned it that way or not) of helping to integrate ranchers and businessmen from different parts of the country into a cohesive social class.*

[T]he Rancheros had to divide into camps because of a postwar increase in membership. There are seventeen camps, sporting such Spanish names as Los Amigos, Los Vigilantes, Los Tontos (bums), Los Bandidos, and Los Flojos (lazy ones). They range in size from fifteen to ninety-three, with the majority of them listing between twenty and sixty members. Most camps have members from a variety of geographical locations, although some are slightly specialized in that regard. Los Gringos, the largest camp, has the greatest number of members from out of state. Los Borrachos, Los Picadores, and Los Chingadores, the next largest camps, have a predominance of people from the Los Angeles area. Los Vigilantes, with twenty members, began as a San Francisco group, but now includes riders from Oregon, Washington, New York and southern California.

In 1928 the Bohemian Grove provided John J. Mitchell with the inspiration for his retreat on horseback, the Rancheros Visitadores. Since 1930 the RVs have grown to the point where they are an impressive second best to the Grove in size, entertainment, and stature. Their combination of businessmen and ranchers is as unique as the Bohemian's amalgamation of businessmen and artists. It is hardly surprising that wealthy men from Los Angeles, San Francisco, Honolulu, Spokane, and Chicago would join Mitchell in wanting to be members of both.

[Another club, the Colorado-based Roundup Riders of the Rockies, imitates the RVs in its emphasis on "roughing it" and socializing.]

The riders do not carry their fine camp with them. Instead, twenty camp hands are employed to move the camp in trucks to the next campsite. Thus, when the Roundup Riders arrive at their destination each evening they find fourteen large sleeping tents complete with cots, air mattresses, portable toilets, and showers. Also up and ready for service are a large green dining tent and an entertainment stage. A diesel-powered generator provides the camp with electricity.

Food service is provided by Martin Jetton of Fort Worth, Texas, a caterer advertised in the southwest as "King of the Barbecue." Breakfasts and dinners are said to be veritable banquets. Lunch is not as elaborate, but it does arrive to the riders on the trail in a rather unusual fashion that only those of the higher circles could afford "lunches in rugged country are often delivered by light plane or helicopter."[4] One year the men almost missed a meal because a wind came up and scattered the lunches which were being parachuted from two Cessna 170s.

In addition to the twenty hired hands who take care of the camp, there are twenty wranglers to look after the horses. The horses on the ride—predominantly such fine breeds as Arabian, Quarter Horse, and Morgan—are estimated to be worth more than $200,000. Horses and riders compete in various contests of skill and horsemanship on a layover day in the middle of the week. Skeet shooting, trap shooting, and horseshoes also are a part of this event.

The Roundup Riders, who hold their trek at the same time the Bohemians hold their encampment, must be reckoned as a more regional organization. Although there are numerous millionaires and executives among them, the members are not of the national stature of most Bohemians and many Rancheros. They can afford to invest thousands of dollars in their horses and their horses and tack, to pay a $300 yearly ride fee, and to have their lunch brought to them by helicopter, but they cannot compete in business connections and prestige with those who assemble at the Bohemian Grove. Building from the Denver branch of the upper class, the Roundup Riders reach out primarily to Nebraska (six), Texas (five), Illinois (five), Nevada (three), California (three), and Arizona (three). There are no members from New York, Boston, Philadelphia, or other large Eastern cities.

Several other regional rides have been inspired by the Rancheros, rides such as the Desert Caballeros in Wickenburg, Arizona, and the Verde Vaqueros in Scottsdale, Arizona. These groups are similar in size and membership to the Roundup Riders of the Rockies. Like the Roundup Riders, they have a few overlapping members with the Rancheros. But none are of the status of the Rancheros Visitadores. They are minor legacies of the Bohemian Grove, unlikely even to be aware of their kinship ties to the retreat in the redwoods.

## DO BOHEMIANS, RANCHEROS, AND ROUNDUP RIDERS RULE AMERICA?

The foregoing material on upper-class retreats, which I have presented in as breezy a manner as possible, is relevant to highly emotional questions concerning the distribution of power in modern America. In this final [section] I will switch styles somewhat and discuss these charged questions in a sober, simple, and straightforward way. . . .

It is my hypothesis that there is a ruling social class in the United States. This class is made up of the owners and managers of large corporations, which means the members have many economic and political interests in common, and many conflicts with ordinary working people. Comprising at most 1 percent of the total population, members of this class own 25 to 30 percent of all privately held wealth in America, own 60 to 70 percent of the privately held corporate wealth, receive 20 to 25 percent of the yearly income, direct the large corporations and foundations, and dominate the federal government in Washington.

Most social scientists disagree with this view. Some dismiss it out of hand, others become quite vehement in disputing it. The overwhelming majority of them believe that the United States has a "pluralistic" power structure, in which a wide variety of "veto groups" (e.g., businessmen, farmers, unions, consumers) and "voluntary associations" (e.g., National Association of Manufacturers, Americans for Democratic Action, Common Cause) form shifting coalitions to influence decisions on different issues. These groups and associations are said to have different amounts of interest and influence on various questions. Contrary to my view, pluralists assert that no one group, not even the owners and managers of large corporations, has the cohesiveness and ability to determine the outcome of a large variety of social, economic, and political issues.

As noted, I believe there is a national upper class in the United States. . . . [T]his means that wealthy families from all over the country, and particularly from major cities like New York, San Francisco, Chicago, and Houston, are part of interlocking social circles which perceive each other as equals, belong to the same clubs, interact frequently, and freely intermarry.

Whether we call it a "social class" or a "status group," many pluralistic social scientists would deny that such a social group exists. They assert that there is no social "cohesiveness" among the various rich in different parts of the country. For them, social registers, blue books, and club membership lists are merely collections of names which imply nothing about group interaction.

There is a wealth of journalistic evidence which suggests the existence of a national upper class. It ranges from Cleveland Armory's *The Proper Bostonians* and *Who Killed Society?* to Lucy Kavaler's *The Private World of High Society* and Stephen Birmingham's *The Right People*. But what is the systematic evidence which I can present for my thesis? There is first of all the evidence that has been developed from the study of attendance at private school. It has been shown that a few dozen prep schools bring together children of the upper class from all over the country. From the evidence it can be argued that young members of the upper class develop lifetime friendship ties with like-status age-mates in every section of the country.[5]

There is second the systematic evidence which comes from studying high status summer resorts. Two such studies show that these resorts bring together upper-class families from several different large cities.[6] Third, there is the evidence of business interconnections. Several . . . studies have demonstrated that interlocking directorships bring wealthy men from all over the country into face-to-face relationships at the board meetings of banks, insurance companies, and other corporations.[7]

And finally, there is the evidence developed from studying exclusive social clubs. Such studies have been made in the past, but the present investigation of the Bohemian Club, the Rancheros Visitadores, and the Roundup Riders of the Rockies is a more comprehensive effort. *In short, I believe the present [study] to be significant evidence for the existence of a cohesive American upper class.*

The Bohemian Grove, as well as other watering holes and social clubs, are relevant to the problem of class cohesiveness in two ways. First, the very fact that rich men from all over the country gather in such close circumstances as the Bohemian Grove is evidence for the existence of a socially cohesive upper class. It demonstrates that many of these men do know each other, that they have face-to-face communications, and that they are a social network. In this sense, we're looking at the Bohemian Grove and other social retreats as a *result* of social processes that lead to class cohesion. But such institutions also can be viewed as *facilitators* of social ties. Once formed, these groups become another avenue by which the cohesiveness of the upper class is maintained.

In claiming that clubs and retreats like the Bohemians and the Rancheros are evidence for my thesis of a national upper class, I am assuming that to cohesion develops within the settings they provide. Perhaps some readers will find that assumption questionable. So let us pause to ask: Are there reasons to believe that the Bohemian Grove and its imitators lead to greater cohesion within the upper class?

For one thing we have the testimony of members themselves. There are several accounts by leading members of these groups, past and present, which attest to the intimacy that develops among members. John J. Mitchell, El Presidente of Los Rancheros Visitadores from 1930 to 1955, wrote as follows on the twenty-fifth anniversary of the group:

> All the pledges and secret oaths in the universe cannot tie men, our kind of men, together like the mutual appreciation of a beautiful horse, the moon behind a cloud, a song around the campfire or a ride down the Santa Ynez Valley. These are experiences common on our ride, but unknown to most of our daily lives. Our organization, to all appearances, is the most informal imaginable. Yet there are men here who see one another once a year, yet feel a bond closer than between those they have known all their lives.[8]

F. Burr Betts, chairman of the board of Security Life of Denver, says the following about the Roundup Riders:

> I think you find out about the Roundup Riders when you go to a Rider's funeral. Because there you'll find, no matter how many organizations the man belonged to, almost every pallbearer is a Roundup Rider. I always think of the Roundup Riders as the first affiliation. We have the closest knit fraternity in the world.[9]

A second reason for stressing the importance of retreats and clubs like the Bohemian Grove is a body of research within social psychology which deals with group cohesion. "Group dynamics" suggests the following about cohesiveness. (1) *Physical proximity is likely to lead to group solidarity.* Thus, the mere fact that these men gather together in such intimate physical settings implies that cohesiveness develops. (The same point can be made, of course, about exclusive neighborhoods, private schools, and expensive summer resorts.) (2) *The more people interact, the more they will like each other.* This is hardly a profound discovery, but we can note that the Bohemian Grove and other watering holes maximize personal interactions. (3) *Groups seen as high in status are more cohesive.* The Bohemian Club fits the category of a high-status group. Further, its stringent membership requirements, long waiting lists, and high dues also serve to heighten its valuation in the eyes of its members. Members are likely to think of themselves as "special" people, which would heighten their attractiveness to each other, and increase the likelihood of interaction and cohesiveness. (4) *The best atmosphere for increasing group cohesiveness is one that is relaxed and cooperative.* Again the Bohemian Grove, the Rancheros, and the Roundup Riders are ideal examples of this kind of climate. From a group-dynamics point of view, then, we could argue that one of the reasons for upper-class cohesiveness is the fact that the class is organized into a wide variety of small groups which encourage face-to-face interaction and ensure status and security for his members.[10]

In summary, if we take these several common settings together—schools, resorts, corporation directorships, and social clubs—and assume on the basis of members' testimony and the evidence of small-group research that interaction in such settings leads to group cohesiveness, then I think we are justified in saying that wealthy families from all over the United States are linked together in a variety of ways into a national upper class.

Even if the evidence and arguments for the existence of a socially cohesive national upper class are accepted, there is still the question of whether or not this class has the means by which its members can reach policy consensus on issues of importance to them.

A five-year study based upon information obtained from confidential informants, interviews, and questionnaires has shown that social clubs such as the Bohemian Club are an important consensus-forming aspect of the upper class and big-business environment. According to sociologist Reed Powell, "the clubs are a repository of the values held by the upper-level prestige groups in the community and are a means by which these values are transferred to the business environment." Moreover, the clubs are places where problems are discussed:

> On the other hand, the clubs are places in which the beliefs, problems, and values of the industrial organization are discussed and related to other elements in the larger community. Clubs, therefore, are not only effective vehicles of informal communication, but also valuable centers where views are presented, ideas are modified, and new ideas emerge. Those in the interview sample were appreciative of this asset; in addition, they considered the club as a valuable place to combine social and business contacts.[11]

The revealing interview work of Floyd Hunter, an outstanding pioneer research on the American power structure, also provides evidence for the importance of social clubs as informal centers of policy making. Particularly striking for our purposes is a conversation he had with one of the several hundred top leaders that he identified in the 1950s. The person in question was a conservative industrialist who was ranked as a top-level leader by his peers:

> Hall [a pseudonym] spoke very favorably of the Bohemian Grove group that met in California every year. He said that although over the entrance to the Bohemian Club there was a quotation, "Weaving spiders come not here," there was a good deal of informal policy made in this association. He said that he got to know Herbert Hoover in this connection and that he started work with Hoover in the food administration of World War I.[12]

Despite the evidence presented by Powell and Hunter that clubs are a setting for the development of policy consensus, I do not believe that such settings are the only, or even the primary, focus for developing policy on class-related issues. For policy questions, other organizations are far more important, organizations like the Council on Foreign Relations, and the Committee for Economic Development, the Business Council, and the National Municipal League. These organizations, along with many others, are the "consensus-seeking" and "policy-planning" organizations of the upper class. Directed by the same men who manage the major corporations, and financed by corporation and foundation monies, these groups sponsor meetings and discussions wherein wealthy men from all over the country gather to iron out differences and formulate policies on pressing problems.

No one discussion group is *the* leadership council within the upper class. While some of the groups tend to specialize in certain issue areas, they overlap and interact to a great extent. Consensus slowly emerges from the interplay of people and ideas within and among the groups.[13] This diversity of groups is made very clear in the following comments by Frazar B. Wilde, chairman emeritus of Connecticut General Life Insurance Company and a member of the Council on Foreign Relations and the Community for Economic Development. Mr. Wilde was responding to a question about the Bilderbergers, a big-business meeting group which includes Western European leaders as well as American corporation and foundation directors:

> Business has had over the years many different seminars and discussion meetings. They run all the way from large public gatherings like NAM [National Association of Manufacturers] to special sessions such as those held frequently at Arden House. Bilderberg is in many respects one of the most important, if not the most important, but this is not to deny that other strictly off-the-record meetings and discussion groups such as those held by the Council on Foreign Relations are not on the front rank.[14]

Generally speaking, then, it is in these organizations that leaders within the upper class discuss the means by which to deal with problems of major concern. Here, in off-the-record settings, these leaders try to reach consensus on general issues that have been talked about more casually in corporate boardrooms and social clubs. These organizations, aided by funds from corporations and foundations, also serve several other functions:

1. They are training ground for new leadership within the class. It is in these organizations, and through the publications of these organizations, that younger lawyers, bankers, and businessmen become acquainted with general issues in the areas of foreign, domestic, and municipal policy.
2. They are the place where leaders within the upper class hear the ideas and findings of their hired experts.
3. They are the setting wherein upper-class leaders "look over" young experts for possible service as corporation or governmental advisers.
4. They provide the framework for expert studies on important issues. Thus, the Council on Foreign Relations undertook a $1 million study of the "China question" in the first half of the 1960s. The Committee for Economic Development created a major study of money and credit about the same time. Most of the money for these studies was provided by the Ford, Rockefeller, and Carnegie foundations.[15]

5. Through such avenues as books, journals, policy statements, discussion groups, press releases, and speakers, the policy-planning organizations greatly influence the "climate of opinion" within which major issues are considered. For example, Foreign Affairs, the journal of the Council on Foreign Relations, is considered the most influential journal in its field, and the periodic policy statements of the Committee for Economic Development are carefully attended to by major newspapers and local opinion leaders.

It is my belief, then, that the policy-planning groups are essential in developing policy positions which are satisfactory to the upper class as a whole. As such, I think they are a good part of the answer to any social scientist who denies that members of the upper class have institutions by which they deal with economic and political challenges.

However, the policy-planning groups could not function if there were not some common interests within the upper class in the first place. The most obvious, and most important, of these common interests have to do with the shared desire of the members to maintain the present monopolized and subsidized business system which so generously overrewards them and makes their jet setting, fox hunting, art collecting, and other extravagances possible. But it is not only shared economic and political concerns which made consensus possible. The Bohemian Grove and other upper-class social institutions also contribute to this process: *Group-dynamics research suggests that members of socially cohesive groups are more open to the opinions of others members, and more likely to change their views of those of fellow members.*[16] Social cohesion is a factor in policy consensus because it creates a desire on the part of group members to reconcile differences with other members of the group. It is not enough to say that members of the upper class are bankers, businessmen, and lawyers with a common interest in profit maximization and tax avoidance who meet together at the Council on Foreign Relations, the Committee for Economic Development, and other policy-planning organizations. We must add that they are Bohemians, Rancheros, and Roundup Riders.

## NOTES

1. Wallace Turner, "Rockefeller Faces Scrutiny of Top Californians: Governor to Spend Weekend at Bohemian Grove among State's Establishment" (*New York Times,* July 26, 1963), p. 30. In 1964 Senator Barry Goldwater appeared at the Grove as a guest of retired General Albert C. Wedemeyer and Herbert Hoover, Jr. For that story see Wallace Turner, "Goldwater Spending Weekend in Camp at Bohemian Grove" (*New York Times,* July 31, 1964), p. 10.
2. James M. Naughton, "Nixon Drops Plans for Coast Speech" (*New York Times,* July 31, 1971), p. 11.
3. There is a special moisture-proof building at the Grove to hold the dozens of expensive Steinway pianos belonging to the club and various camps.
4. Robert Pattridge, "Closer to Heaven on Horseback" (*Empire Magazine, Denver Post,* July 9, 1972), p. 12. I am grateful to sociologist Ford Cleere for bringing this article to my attention.
5. E. Digby Baltzell, *Philadelphia Gentlemen* (New York: Free Press, 1958), chapter 12. G. William Domhoff, *The Higher Circles* (New York: Random House, 1970), p. 78.
6. Baltzell, *Philadelphia Gentlemen,* pp. 248-51. Domhoff, *The Higher Circles,* pp. 79-82. For recent anecdotal evidence on this point, see Stephen Birmingham, *The Right People* (Boston: Little, Brown, 1968), Part 3.

7. *Interlocks in Corporate Management* (Washington: U.S. Government Printing Office, 1965) summarizes much of this information and presents new evidence as well. See also Peter Dooley, "The Interlocking Directorate". *(American Economic Review,* December, 1969).

8. Niell C. Wilson, *Los Rancheros Visitadores: Twenty-Fifth Anniversary* (Rancheros Visitadores, 1955), p. 2.

9. Robert Pattridge, "Closer to Heaven on Horseback," p. 11.

10. Dorwin Cartwright and Alvin Zander, *Group Dynamics* (New York: Harper & Row, 1960), pp. 74-82; Albert J. Lott and Bernice E. Lott, "Group Cohesiveness as Interpersonal Attraction" *(Psychological Bulletin,* 64, 1965), pp. 259-309; Michael Argyle, *Social Interaction* (Chicago: Aldine Publishing Company, 1969), pp. 220-23. I am grateful to sociologist John Sonquist of the University of California, Santa Barbara, for making me aware of how important the small-groups literature might be for studies of the upper class. Findings on the influence process, communication patterns, and the development of informal leadership also might be applicable to problems in the area of upper-class research.